THE ROARING TWENTIES

AN EYEWITNESS HISTORY

THE ROARING TWENTIES

Tom Streissguth

Facts On File, Inc.

The Roaring Twenties

Facts On File, Inc.
11 Penn Plaza
New York NY 10001

Library of Congress Cataloging-in-Publication Data
Streissguth, Thomas, 1958–
　　The roaring twenties: an eyewitness history / Tom Streissguth.
　　　　p. cm.
　　Includes bibliographical references (p.　) and index.
　　ISBN 0-8160-4023-0 (acid-free paper)
　　1. United States—History—1919–1933. 2. United States—History—1919–1933—Sources.
3. United States—History—1919–1933—Chronology. 4. Nineteen twenties. I. Title.

　　E784 .S76 2001
　　973.91—dc21　　　　　　　　　　　　　　　　　　　　00-030919

Facts On File books are available at special discounts when purchased in bulk quantities for businesses, associations, institutions or sales promotions. Please call our Special Sales Department in New York at 212/967-8800 or 800/322-8755.

You can find Facts On File on the World Wide Web at
http://www.factsonfile.com

Text design by Joan M. Toro

Jacket design by Cathy Rincon

Maps and graphs pp. 390, 391, 392, 393, 394, 396, 397 by Sholto Ainslie

Printed in the United States of America.

VB Hermitage 10 9 8 7 6 5 4 3 2 1

This book is printed on acid-free paper.

NOTE ON PHOTOS

Many of the illustrations and photographs used in this book are old, historical images. The quality of the prints is not always up to modern standards, as in many cases the originals are from glass negatives or the originals are damaged. The content of the illustrations, however, made their inclusion important despite problems in reproduction.

CONTENTS

Acknowledgments ix

Introduction xi

1. Postwar Treaties and Turmoil: November 1918–December 1919 1
2. Newfound Freedoms, Old-Fashioned Temperance: 1920 25
3. Depression: 1921 53
4. A Scandalous Administration: January 1922–August 1923 73
5. New Homes and a New Sound: September 1923–February 1924 97
6. Reading, Writing, and Radio: March 1924–December 1924 123
7. A Trial of Science: 1925 153
8. Troubles in the Hemisphere: January 1926–May 1926 181
9. Worldly Explorations: June 1926–May 1927 201
10. National Pastimes: Movies, Sports, Cars: June 1927–January 1928 225
11. Prosperity: 1928 249
12. The End of the Roaring Twenties: 1929 267

Appendix A: Documents 283
Appendix B: Biographies of Major Personalities 362
Appendix C: Maps, Graphs, and Tables 387
Bibliography 403
Index 421

ACKNOWLEDGMENTS

The author thanks the staffs of the Library of Congress, the National Archives, the New York Public Library, the University of South Florida, the Jane Bancroft Cook Library, the Sarasota County Public Library, and the Wilson Library at the University of Minnesota for their help in providing research assistance and background information. For photographic assistance, he thanks Archive Photos, Brown Brothers, Culver Pictures, the Minnesota Historical Society, the State Historical Society of Wisconsin, and the University of South Florida/Tampa. For their help, advice, and encouragement, he thanks Paul Cook, Marie-Christine Rouffiac, Anne Moe, Felipe Cerna, Aude Menard, Pier Gustafson, Marian Streissguth, Patrick Eastman, Harry Lerner, Mark Lerner, George and Kathleen Ghreichi, Michael Hudlow, Karine Hudlow, Chery Hays, Thomas Higgs, Paul Glynn, Serge Leduc, Robert Rosenbluth, Janet Castaldy, Shellie Parkhurst, Patricia Sawyer, and Tom Bodett. For their patience and forbearance he thanks Nicole Bowen and Terence Maikels of Facts On File, Inc.

INTRODUCTION

"I do not choose to run for President in 1928."

A small group of newspaper reporters read the 10 reluctant words, copied onto small slips of paper, around the hour of noon on August 2, 1927, in Rapid City, South Dakota. It was the fourth anniversary of the presidency of Calvin Coolidge, who had assumed office with a similarly unceremonious swearing-in at the home of his father. Silent Cal now handed out his one-sentence expression of disinterest with no further comment or explanation. None seemed necessary.

Coolidge had provided the reporters a small bit of close-mouthed suspense three hours earlier, during his regular morning press conference, when he promised that "If you will return at twelve o'clock, there will be an additional statement." Shortly before the appointed hour, he composed the statement, handed it over to his secretary, Everett Sanders, and instructed Sanders to make up copies—as many copies as might be necessary to supply each expected reporter. None of the reporters would be allowed to leave the room until all had a chance to read the message. This would give them all a more or less even chance at the door, the outside hall, and the long-distance telephone lines to their editors at home.

In its substance and in the careful manner of its presentation, few presidential actions could have provided more contrast to the times in which they took place. Calvin Coolidge presided over the middle of the 1920s, the Roaring Twenties, somewhat like the eye of a hurricane stands in the calm center of a raging Atlantic storm, his words spare and dry against a background of windy radio advertisements, exuberant jazz ensembles, frenetic stock market speculators, garrulous Sunday evangelists, anarchists, flappers, aviators, bootleggers, and the first movies that talked. Yet his philosophy of governance brightly and clearly reflected the opinion of the majority that had elected him: the business of America is business and the primary duty of public government is to get itself out of debt and out of the way of the private corporation.

Coolidge and the two other unremarkable presidents of the decade were landslide-popular, perhaps owing their convincing electoral majorities to their qualities of blandness and predictability. They were comfort leaders, reassuring as kindly old uncles in their appearance, who presided when times were changing fast, too fast for people who had seen their more assured worlds blasted into small fragments by World War I (the Great War). During the 1920s, the sudden acceleration of life, the confounded mobility of women, immigrants, and minority groups out of their customary places on the social ladder, resulted in a counterrevolution that took many forms: Prohibition, the Ku Klux Klan, the Palmer raids, and the arrest and trial of John Scopes on the charge of teaching a nonbiblical scientific theory in a science class. The people struggled to keep up appearances of normalcy, while prosperity and mobility were stirring a cauldron of bad behavior, spiced by the accompaniment of immoral jazz—a slang word for sex.

In the 1920s, new rhythms inspired new dancing, too close for the comfort of parents and moralists. At the St. Paul Auditorium, a dance marathon tests the endurance of Goldilocks Rice and Joe Rock of Chicago, 1929. *(Minnesota Historical Society)*

Heightened communication formed a crucial ingredient in the battle. Presidents were learning about new electronic media, radio, that artfully blended entertainment and news into a package designed for mass consumption. Automobiles and radios were joining the scattered audiences together, and small tales that might normally have been confined to a few column inches in a prewar local newspaper were growing into national epics, broadcast over the radio, discussed in the weeklies and dailies. Heroes were needed and supplied: Charles Lindbergh, Clarence Darrow, William Jennings Bryan, Babe Ruth, and Richard Byrd. Fashions arrived and departed with increasing speed; manias such as dance marathons, crossword puzzles, and flagpole-sitting were inexplicably taken up and then replaced.

A decade of trends and fads meant self-absorption as the members of the new mass audience measured themselves against the images—all designed to sell products—of better hygiene, easier housekeeping, improved salesmanship, and greater wealth. In the meantime, society played fast and loose with its money; wage earners picked up the habits of installment buying and speculation in the stock market. New electronic gadgets shone brightly in the shop windows: vacuum cleaners, washers, dryers, refrigerators, radio sets, irons, and sewing machines were all suddenly available and necessary. In the pages of magazines and novels, the agrarian past slipped into common nostalgia; to be modern and urban meant clean fingernails, education, pressed clothes, convenience, and an office job.

Underneath the tumult was violence—the last frontier combats over territory and self-respect were fought by liquor rustlers, many of them the sons of immigrants, riding shotgun inside bulletproof cars through the urban canyons. One such gangster had made the fortunes of a callow youth named Jay Gatsby, the phony tycoon created by F. Scott Fitzgerald. Gatsby stood as a fictional counterpoint to President Coolidge and lived out a larger-than-life story: rather than retiring through a tedious scribble passed out to reporters in Rapid City, he dies in his elegant Long Island pool, the victim of a crime of passion.

Fitzgerald and perhaps even Coolidge knew that Prohibition was failing, for the most part, and causing a certain cynicism and a loss of respect for the laws and their enforcers. Soon after Coolidge left office, the decade reached its exclamation point in a fusillade of bullets and the cold-blooded mass murder of seven people in a Chicago garage on St. Valentine's Day, 1929, an event that also demonstrated a hopeful truth—the jaded people of the 1920s could still be shocked. Hope and confidence still prevailed, in Chicago and elsewhere, until the fall of that year, when optimism suddenly vanished, evidenced by a long, vertical series of minus signs in the last column of the stock market tables, and when the jazz suddenly went out of the Roaring Twenties.

1

Postwar Treaties and Turmoil
November 1918–December 1919

On July 8, 1919, the steamship *George Washington,* carrying among its passengers President Woodrow Wilson, his wife Edith Wilson, and a small group of White House advisers, arrived in New York harbor after a 10-day journey from Brest, France. The voyage had been uneventful, except for a July 4 celebration held in the middle of the North Atlantic Ocean. During the festivities, President Wilson had delivered a short speech, the first of hundreds he would give to the people of the United States, on the issue that would consume the rest of his presidency: the Treaty of Versailles and the League of Nations.

After more than four years of bloodshed and stalemate, World War I had ended by an armistice signed in the Compiègne forest of northern France on November 11, 1918. In December, the victorious Allies convened a diplomatic conference in Paris to decide on proper rewards for the victors and just punishments for the defeated. President Wilson had arrived, heartily welcomed by Europe's heads of state and joyously acclaimed during enormous parades. An admiring press pronounced President Wilson the savior of Europe and the man who would guarantee that the conflict just ended had been the "war to end all wars."

The United States had suffered more than 50,000 dead in combat but no damages on the home front during the war. It had no interest in acquiring territory or demanding reparations from Germany. Instead, Wilson saw the United States claiming a much loftier reward: a role as the world's peacemaker, a guardian of liberty and democracy. The mechanism to accomplish this goal would be a League of Nations, a group led by the United States and joined by all the nations of the world. On January 8, 1918, while German, French, British, and American soldiers fought in their trenches in northern France, Wilson had described to the U.S. Congress a set of articles known as the Fourteen Points, which outlined, in vague and hopeful phrases, the terms of the future treaty and the new order's principles of self-determination, mutual protection, and democracy.

Through the winter and into the spring of 1919, Wilson and the other leaders of the Allied nations debated the League of Nations and the comprehensive treaty that would put the league in operation. Wilson had high hopes for the agreement, dreaming that it could put an end to the world's long history of

1

military conflict, tyranny, and imperialism. But in a very short time, it became apparent that the demands of more than two dozen nations competing for the spoils of war were creating an unmanageable diplomatic free-for-all. The endless, exhausting debates and conferences in Paris dragged on, and Wilson's dream went terribly wrong. While he spoke of ending war and tyranny, fighting continued in Hungary and Armenia. While he promised self-determination, the French and British seized Germany's overseas colonies. While he promised open negotiations, it was revealed that several secret treaties had been signed during the war among the conference participants. Wilson had insisted on the League of Nations as a condition of the United States signing the Versailles treaty; although the league would be accepted by the Allied powers, his ideals were undermined by the maneuvering of the Allied diplomats and their thirst for land, money, and revenge.

After six months of negotiation and disappointment, Wilson brought home a 268-page peace treaty signed on June 28, 1919, in the Hall of Mirrors at the palace of Versailles. The terms of the treaty were harsh. Germany admitted complete guilt for starting the war and had its navy scrapped and its army nearly disbanded. Alsace-Lorraine, a disputed border province won by Prussia in the Franco-Prussian war of 1870, was returned to France, and the German regions of the Rhineland and the Saarland were occupied and controlled by Allied armies. The treaty also obligated Germany to pay vast sums of money—the figure finally decided upon would be about $40 billion—in reparation for war damages.

Wilson had promised each nation a voice in the peace process, as well as "open negotiations" among the participants. But the four Great Powers—the United States, Italy, France, and Great Britain—found they preferred to negotiate in closed-door sessions, out of the glare of press and public attention. Moreover, the Germans had not been allowed to participate in the negotiations. Instead, they had simply been presented with the treaty's final version and told to sign. The humiliation was total; the seeds of a deep resentment had been planted within the German nation.

LABOR TROUBLES

The entrance of the United States into the war brought about important changes to the nation's economy and to the role of public administration in private business. Seeking rational, centralized control to meet the needs of its commitment in Europe, the federal government set up a War Industries Board to direct production, while the War Food Administration controlled distribution of food. Railroads, as well as telephone and telegraph systems, were nationalized, while public corporations were founded in vital industries such as housing and shipping.

During the war, workers benefited by a scarcity of labor, which brought about full employment and a high demand for their services. At the same time, employers and investors benefited from generous government contracts that guaranteed them a profit over and above the cost of labor and materials. A "no strike" agreement kept the peace between employers and the employed, while union membership rose steadily. By 1920, the United States counted 5 million union members, about 20 percent of the nation's nonfarm labor force.

But the war's end put the national economy through a wrenching peace-time adjustment. Returning veterans flooded the labor market, while jobs were eliminated as a cost-saving measure by employers. When wartime price controls disappeared, inflation soared. Fearing the loss of guaranteed margins on their goods, business owners determined to maintain their wartime profits slashed wages and attempted to eliminate the labor union from the equation. The result was labor trouble, which began soon after Armistice Day and reached a flashpoint in Seattle, Washington, in February 1919.

Seattle had flourished during the war as a shipbuilding port city. The number of unionized Seattle workers increased fourfold between 1914 and 1918, at which point half of the labor force belonged to a union and most unionized workers had organized closed shops, in which union membership was mandatory. The city's Central Labor Council served as the umbrella organization for more than 100 American Federation of Labor (AFL) craft unions. In Seattle, the union concept extended to the establishment of labor-controlled businesses; the Central Labor Council also fielded its own local political candidates. Stirring the pot further were the radical agitators of the Industrial Workers of the World (IWW), a union of nonskilled wage-earners in mining, farming, lumbering, and manufacturing.

Many union leaders, especially those belonging to the IWW, sought to enlarge the union concept from craft to industrial basis, in which national organizations would count all the workers in a single industry among their members. The IWW did not seek to work and cooperate with management over issues of wages and working conditions. Instead, the IWW sought the overthrow of the capitalist system and the establishment of a cooperative economy based on the "one big union" of laborers from all occupations.

The Seattle labor war began in January 1919, when 25,000 members of the Metal Workers Union voted to strike. Through the accidental delivery of a message intended for the Metal Trades Association, a manufacturer's organization, the workers had learned that the U.S. government was urging the association to deny union demands, under the pain of losing government steel contracts. Polled by the Central Labor Council, the members of 110 other unions voted to join the walkout, while the metalworkers' employers refused to negotiate or disappeared from the city altogether.

At 10:00 A.M. on the morning of February 6, 1919, a general strike of 60,000 Seattle workers began. The reaction from those not taking part was fear and suspicion, reinforced by sensational newspaper stories assuring readers that the strike marked the start of a Bolshevik revolution that would sweep the country. Traffic largely disappeared from the streets; vehicles passed only occasionally, bearing signs that read "Exempted by the General Strike Committee." Seattle Mayor Ole Hanson called out the state militia and deputized 2,500 additional policemen. He then released a statement demanding unconditional surrender, blaming Russian Bolsheviks for the action and threatening to shoot on sight anyone judged to be causing disorder.

As shops and factories remained still and silent, police and deputies patrolled the streets. Machine gun positions were raised at key intersections. Seattle residents who had not left the city huddled in their homes, fearing a complete breakdown of law and order that would come as union members began to riot. Much to everyone's surprise, however, the city remained calm. The greatest stir was caused by Mayor Hansen himself, who drove the streets in a flag-draped car, delivering proclamations and threats against the strikers.

Hansen's revolution never came, perhaps to his disappointment. Without the support of the AFL, which condemned the strike, and without a general plan for negotiations, workers slowly returned to their jobs over the next few days. Claiming credit for a total victory, Ole Hanson went on a cross-country speaking tour. A fear of radicals lingered in the public mind, offering a fertile ground for the violence and hyperbole that would later come during the post–World War I Red Scare.

Although the Seattle strike failed, labor trouble was indeed sweeping the country, just as union opponents had promised. Garment workers, harbor workers, cigarmakers, printers, textile workers, telephone workers, and streetcar workers walked off their jobs; by the end of the year, about 4 million members of the labor force had joined at least one strike. The turmoil spread across the border to Canada, where a general strike of about 30,000 workers occurred in Winnipeg, Manitoba. Begun by the metalworkers' and builders' unions, the strike was soon joined by several other unions while Canadian officials accused Seattle's strike leaders and IWW "Wobblies" of coming to Winnipeg to organize it. For two weeks, union members managed the city, until the strike finally collapsed.

The failure of the Seattle and Winnipeg strikes did not discourage organizers and socialists who now planned to make a grand show of May Day (May 1) 1919. In the largest cities, workers paraded banners and flags through the streets while police, National Guardsmen, and ad hoc gangs of veterans and patriots counterattacked with guns, rocks, bottles, and fists. The Boston parade brought about a violent confrontation that left one marcher dead and the city's Socialist Party headquarters in ruins. The police made 116 arrests—all of them of parade participants. In Cleveland, an all-out riot took place that left much of the downtown area in a shambles.

In response to the confrontations, labor leaders made plans for a nationwide general strike to take place on July 4. Rather than higher wages, union recognition, or a redistribution of the means of production, however, the goal of this strike was to be the release of Tom Mooney, a radical union leader convicted of murder. Newspapers across the country denounced the strike as planned chaos, deliberately engineered to bring down the capitalist system. The cities prepared, with Chicago bringing in infantry troops and New York posting police officers at public buildings and at the homes of its wealthiest citizens. When July 4 came and went without incident and without even much of a strike, the nonevent was hailed as a great victory for the forces of law and order.

ILLEGAL OPINIONS

Labor organizers drew much of their vitality from radicals inspired by the doctrines and ideals of socialism, which held that the workers would form the vanguard of a sweeping economic revolution in the industrialized capitalist nations. Despite the patriotic fervor running through the United States, socialism was also reaching a high tide. There were socialist mayors and city council members throughout the East and Midwest; socialist congressman Victor Berger of Milwaukee won election repeatedly despite indictment under the Espionage Act, harassment of his newspaper, the *Milwaukee Leader,* and his expulsion by the House of Representatives in 1919. The Socialist Party of America's best-known leader, Eugene V. Debs, was a four-time presidential candidate who attained political martyrdom by his conviction and imprisonment for an illegal speech delivered during the war.

Debs inspired followers with thunderous speeches and befuddled opponents with his Midwestern earnestness and honesty. A native of Terre Haute, Indiana, he had first made his mark in the labor movement by organizing the American Railway Union, one of the nation's first industrial unions, in 1893. The union flourished after Debs successfully faced down railway magnate James J. Hill, of the Great Northern Railroad, over a wage dispute in the following year. After serving a six-month sentence for defying a court injunction during a strike against the Pullman Palace Car Company of Chicago, Debs came out of prison a socialist, convinced that the police, the courts, and the legislators were writing and enforcing laws to protect business owners from their employees and from organized labor. He ran for president in 1900 as a candidate for the Social Democratic Party, polling 100,000 votes, then organized the Socialist Party of America in 1901. As a perennial Socialist Party presidential candidate, he gradually increased his vote total until, in 1912, 900,000 votes went into his column—the highest socialist vote yet in the country's history.

For Debs and his followers, World War I was nothing more than a contest of international private capital, a fight over colonies and resources ordered by big governments and their bankers, eagerly touted by profiteering defense industries, and fought by their convenient cannon fodder, the workers. In defiance of the Espionage Act of 1917, Debs spoke out publicly against the war and the draft and denounced the government's harassment of socialist organizations and newspapers. Knowing he provided the federal enforcers with their most prominent target, Debs accepted an invitation to speak to a socialist convention at Canton, Ohio, in June 1918. After publicly expressing his antiwar sentiments, he was indicted for inciting resistance to the government in violation of the Espionage Act. His prison term commenced on April 13, 1919, five months after the end of the war.

As the country's best-known political prisoner, Debs organized another presidential run in 1920 from his jail cell in the Atlanta federal penitentiary. As stump speeches and a campaign tour were out of the question, Debs prepared a 500-word weekly article to be distributed to the press and the public by the Socialist Party. As the Red Scare frenzy gradually died down, the public began expressing support, even sympathy, for Debs, which he converted into 920,000 votes in November. One year later, just before Christmas in 1921, Warren Harding granted a presidential pardon after Debs had served two and a half years of his 10-year sentence.

Socialist candidate Victor Berger of Wisconsin calls for taxing the war profiteers, a sentiment that got him a conviction and 20-year jail sentence for giving aid and comfort to the enemy. His conviction overturned in 1921, Berger returned to Congress in 1923 and served until his death in 1929. *(State Historical Society of Wisconsin)*

ADVICE AND DISSENT

While strikes, riots, and trouble continued in the United States, President Wilson's attention remained tightly focused on the ratification of the Treaty of Versailles and the Covenant of the League of Nations by the U.S. Senate (under the Constitution, the Senate must approve all foreign treaties by a two-thirds majority vote). Wilson felt confident of victory. The treaty was the best that could be written under the circumstances, he announced, and the people of the United States supported it, just as they had supported his decision to join World War I and fight with the Allies in 1917. With its guarantees of peace and security, the League of Nations would eventually correct any faults and injustices of the Treaty of Versailles and would bring the world a permanent peace.

On July 10, Wilson officially presented the Versailles treaty to the U.S. Senate. He asked that the senators carry out their traditional duty to "advise and consent" on the treaty's terms and then pass it without further delay or amendments (which would, after several exhausting months in Paris, mean renegotiation with the Allies).

The members of the Senate carefully considered Wilson's request. A majority of them were Republicans elected in opposition to Wilson's Democratic administration. They had won their majority in the off-year elections of 1918, after seeing Democratic victories in 1912, 1914, and 1916. Their most important goals at this point were to hold their hard-won majority and to capture the White House in 1920—goals they believed might be lost if they were seen to simply go along with Wilson and his treaty.

As the summer wore on, opposition to the treaty began to build among the public and in the press. German-Americans denounced it as too harsh; Irish-Americans protested continuing English rule of their land; Italian-Americans opposed the treaty's failure to cede the Adriatic port of Fiume to Italy. Liberals reminded Wilson that during the war he had promised there would be no annexations and no reparations—"peace without victory" as he had called it. Conservatives railed against the League of Nations, claiming that it would establish a tyrannical world government, destroy the sovereignty of the United States, and entangle the country in future European conflicts.

Beyond Washington, D.C., the attention of ordinary citizens began to wane in the face of economic and social turmoil. Strikes in the coal and steel industries slowed manufacturing. The inflation caused by the war undermined the buying power of already low wages, and the arrival of demobilized soldiers glutted the labor market. Race riots exploded in Chicago, Omaha, and other cities, and police and federal agents raided suspected radical and anarchist headquarters. A Bolshevik revolution in Russia—sparked by similar trouble with the workers—threatened to topple the governments of Europe one by one like dominoes, and spread to the United States. In reaction, what would later be known as the Red Scare, largely directed and promoted by Attorney General A. Mitchell Palmer, commenced in the fall of 1919 and resulted in the arrests of thousands and the deportation of wrong-thinking "undesirables" from the port of New York.

RESERVATIONS

Among the Senate Republicans, opposition to the Treaty of Versailles was divided into three camps. The "mild reservationists" agreed to vote for the Treaty of Versailles if some slight amendments were made. "Strong reservationists" were opposed to the treaty in its present form and demanded renegotiation with the Allies. "Irreconcilables" were opposed to the treaty and to the League of Nations in any form. The Irreconcilables were made up of progressives suspicious of the federal government and the eastern business establishments and of nativists adamant that the United States avoid international agreements and entanglements of any kind.

Senator Henry Cabot Lodge of Massachusetts emerged as the opposition's central figure. A crafty and ruthless politician, Lodge used Wilson's own principal weakness—his stubborn refusal to compromise—against the president. As chairman of the Senate Committee on Foreign Affairs, Lodge controlled the debate in Congress. To further wear down public support for the treaty, he decided on a tactic of delay. He first read the entire Treaty of Versailles word for word in the Senate chamber with only a recording clerk for company, an exercise that lasted two weeks. He then called witnesses to testify. Dozens of treaty opponents, whose testimonies filled 1,300 pages, appeared before the committee to give their arguments against ratification and the entire Versailles peace process.

Seeing his treaty stonewalled in the Senate, Wilson invited the members of the committee to the White House to hear his side of the debate. Most conversation turned on Article X of the Covenant of the League of Nations, which became the rallying point of Reservationists and Irreconcilables against the treaty. According to Article X, "The members of the League undertake to respect and preserve as against external aggression the territorial integrity and existing political independence of all Members of the League. In case of any such aggression or in case of any threat or danger of such aggression the Council shall advise upon the means by which this obligations shall be fulfilled."

In other words, the signatories to the covenant would guarantee each other's borders in case of attack—a guarantee, the treaty opponents believed, that the United States and its military forces would be dragged into another foreign imbroglio, its location limited only to the territory of the 40-odd countries in South America, Europe, and Asia that had already signed or would shortly be signing the treaty.

Wilson was asked if Article X presented the United States with a legal obligation to defend the other signers. More than that, Wilson responded, it presented a moral obligation, a matter of conscience far more powerful and binding than any legalistic treaty boilerplate. Wilson's comments left the members of the committee unconvinced of the righteousness and morality of the Covenant of the League of Nations and skeptical of its future benefit to the United States.

By the time the White House meetings had ended, it was plain to Wilson's advisers that the treaty would not be ratified without the 14 reservations Lodge had appended to it (in imitation and mockery of Wilson's own Fourteen Points). They suggested compromise, believing it would surely be better to allow some modifications to the treaty rather than to see it simply defeated. Wilson refused: "Let Lodge compromise!" Any change to the Versailles treaty, he insisted, would betray the Allies and wreck the months of hard negotiating he had already gone through. The United States would sign the Treaty of Versailles and join the League of Nations on the terms he had negotiated, or not at all.

A CAMPAIGN BY TRAIN

Wilson felt certain that if his logic and rhetoric in support of the treaty could be brought directly to the public, he would win. He prepared for a train excursion through the Midwest and the West, regions that were neither strongly opposed to him, as was the Republican Northeast, nor broadly supportive, as in the Democratic South. He would speak at every possible opportunity, in large cities

The stroke suffered by President Wilson during his campaign for the League of Nations and the Treaty of Versailles left him partially paralyzed and too ill to carry out the duties of the presidency. For more than a year, until the inauguration of Warren Harding, an invalid led the United States. *(Library of Congress)*

and small towns, to the gathered citizens. He would appeal to his audiences' sense of justice and convince the people that the Treaty of Versailles and the League of Nations must be ratified. They would apply pressure to their representatives in Washington; the opponents would be swayed by a rising tide of pro-treaty public opinion; the treaty would pass, and he would be vindicated.

On September 3, a seven-car train pulling the presidential car *Mayflower* left Washington. The 27-day trip was to include 26 major public addresses as well as informal speeches made from the train's rear platform. In Columbus, Indianapolis, St. Louis, Omaha, Billings, and points in between, friendly crowds greeted the president and his wife. They waved small flags, struck up bands, held parades, and applauded the president's words. Meanwhile, Senator Lodge sent treaty opponents, including Senators Hiram Johnson of Tennessee and William Borah of Idaho, out on a parallel anti-treaty campaign to denigrate the Versailles agreement, the League of Nations, and President Wilson.

Back in Washington, the Senate hearings were going badly for the president. In a candid moment, William Bullitt, who had been a member of the U.S. delegation to Paris, revealed Secretary of State Robert Lansing's own words to Bullitt on the treaty: "I believe that if the Senate could only understand what this treaty means, it would unquestionably be defeated, but I wonder if they will understand what it lets them in for . . . I believe that the League of Nations at present is entirely useless." Bullitt's attributed remarks, which Lansing did not deny, sparked another round of sharp criticism in the Congress and in the press.

Meanwhile, Wilson's train continued through California, Nevada, Utah, and Wyoming. The long and exhausting journey took a heavy toll on the president's already poor health. By the time the train reached Colorado, Wilson's doctor was insisting on rest. The president was suffering blinding headaches, tremors, and asthma worsened by the constant changes in humidity and altitude. At Pueblo, Colorado, Wilson barely delivered a short and pleading speech to the crowd. That night, he suffered a stroke that paralyzed the left side of his body. Still determined to speak the next day in Wichita, Kansas, Wilson spent several hours arguing with his doctor, his secretary, and his wife on the need to press on and continue the journey. Finally, he agreed to end the trip immediately and to return to Washington.

THE POLICE WALKOUT IN BOSTON

While the president journeyed through the western states in search of public support for the Treaty of Versailles, labor trouble reached a violent crescendo in the east. Sentiment against unions and labor agitators was running ever stronger since the Seattle general strike, and, to many observers, the expected revolution against law and order had finally arrived in the form of a strike by the police officers of Boston, Massachusetts.

The Boston police had many grievances, the worst of which was their miserably low pay—a base salary of $1,100 a year, a little more than half the national average U.S. wage—out of which they had to buy and maintain their uniforms. In 1919, in the interest of having their grievances addressed and resolved, the members of the force organized themselves into the Boston Social Club. In August, the Boston Social Club voted to ask for a charter from the AFL and were duly welcomed by the AFL's Boston Council. Police commissioner Edwin Curtis responded to this action with an order—illegal under Massachusetts law—that the members of the force were not to join any sort of organization or club outside of the police force itself.

On August 26, Curtis put 19 officers on trial, charging them with illegally organizing a union. In hopes of resolving the crisis, Boston mayor Andrew J. Peters then appointed a 34-member advisory committee, under the chairmanship of James J. Storrow, a friend of Commissioner Curtis. On September 3, the day before Curtis was to hand down his decision in the trial of the 19 policemen, the Storrow Committee appealed to Governor Calvin Coolidge to mediate the dispute. Coolidge refused to involve himself; Mayor Peters then persuaded Curtis to postpone his decision until September 8. The Storrow Committee submitted a plan calling for Curtis to acquit the 19, in exchange for the policemen's withdrawal from the AFL.

That weekend, Governor Coolidge remained out of town, having been engaged to deliver an address to the AFL in Northampton. On Monday, Curtis returned to Boston, rejected the Storrow Committee plan, and dismissed the policemen. The Boston police then voted 1,134-2 to strike the next day, a result that meant anarchy to the officials in charge. Peters met with Coolidge and Curtis and asked Coolidge to intervene to prevent the strike. Coolidge again refused to intervene or mediate in any manner and expressed his full support of Curtis in his actions. Curtis felt certain that the police would not dare walk out. Realizing that Curtis was badly misjudging his own employees, Peters then asked Coolidge to call out the state militia to keep order in the streets.

The panicked population of Boston prepared their homes and businesses for the expected riot of revolutionaries and criminals. Students and war veterans formed a volunteer force of deputies to maintain calm in the streets. On Tuesday afternoon, the strike began, with the fireman's union calling a sympathy strike. Several incidents of vandalism against stores occurred that evening, prompting Peters to call out the militia the next morning. Coolidge, meanwhile, did nothing.

On Wednesday evening, clashes between militia and citizens resulted in two deaths. Roaming bands of looters broke into several stores in downtown Boston. The next day, Coolidge issued proclamations calling on all citizens to help restore order, demanding that all police officers follow the orders of the police commissioners, and calling out the National Guard. The strike generated widespread fear; as in Seattle, it was considered a harbinger of the dreaded Bolshevik uprising. Samuel Gompers, president of the AFL, urged the strikers to return to work, even as he sent telegrams protesting the antilabor actions of Peters and Curtis to Governor Coolidge.

With the threat of worsening disorder hanging over the city, the members of the Boston police union voted unanimously to return to work. Coolidge and Curtis responded by announcing that there would be no compromise or arbitration of the grievances that led to the strike. Coolidge responded to Gompers's telegram with a terse message that would make his future political career: "There is no right to strike against the public safety by anybody, anywhere, at any time." The sentiment and his intransigence during the strike made the governor a hero among the large proportion of the population who followed the current business viewpoint—that labor strikes were a form of leftist blackmail to be resisted at all costs.

The Boston police strikers were summarily dismissed from their jobs and then blacklisted. An appeal for reinstatement to the Massachusetts Supreme Court was denied. Meanwhile, the city of Boston granted their replacements a raise in pay.

POSTWAR INFLATION

In the face of angry opposition in the press and among the general population, labor organizers continued their drive for unionization in heavy industry throughout 1919. Many companies in steel, auto, rubber, and other sectors still refused to recognize unions, instead putting forward an "American Plan" that would mandate open shops, in which union membership was not required as a condition of employment, and establish company unions to be run by management. Business leaders also called for the enforcement of "yellow-dog contracts," in which the employee agreed not to join a union, and the use of injunctions by the courts to prevent strikes.

One of the most adamant antiunion men in industry was Judge Elbert Gary, who had been appointed chairman of the U.S. Steel corporation by owner J. P. Morgan. Gary's reputation among employers and capitalists rested on his conduct of the Haymarket trial in 1886, at which he had sentenced seven anarchists to death for inspiring a party or parties unknown to throw a bomb during a clash between police and strikers in Chicago. After Haymarket, when business expansion and a strong export market was raising the demand for their product, Morgan and Gary had built U.S. Steel into the largest corporation in the United States—the country's first $1 billion company.

The success came on the aching backs of U.S. Steel employees, among whom the average work week amounted to 69 hours over seven days. Under the auspices of the National Committee for Organizing Iron and Steel Workers, which was authorized during the war by the War Industries Labor Board, a long-delayed unionizing drive began. Although steelworkers signed up in great numbers, the organizers ran into violence and trouble in Pennsylvania. Anybody caught organizing was liable to be beaten and jailed; those attending union meetings were summarily, and illegally, fired. U.S. Steel and its sister companies also fired anyone caught organizing or joining a labor union. The secretary/treasurer of the organizing committee, William Foster, pressed ahead anyway, signing up thousands of workers.

By the summer of 1919, 100,000 steelworkers had defied Gary and joined the union, seeking some means to protest low wages, long hours, and company ownership of the mills, the towns where the workers lived, and the shops and churches in their communities. On June 20, Samuel Gompers wrote to Gary asking for a meeting and was ignored. In July, the National Committee officially adopted the union's demands for an eight-hour day, a six-day week, and the right to collective bargaining. Three representatives of the National Committee retraced Gompers's footsteps to U.S. Steel headquarters in New York but were not permitted to see the chairman. The committee publicly demanded a conference and threatened a strike.

At Gompers's request, President Wilson sent Wall Street tycoon Bernard Baruch to confer with Gary. Gary refused an audience with the envoy and announced that meeting with labor leaders would be tantamount to recognizing the principle of the closed shop, which he adamantly opposed. Gary's intransigence angered Wilson and alienated the public, but the president had more crucial objectives on hand at this time and decided not to insist. On the same day that the National Committee called for a strike to begin on September 22, Wilson announced that he would call a conference of union and corporate leaders to hold discussions on labor relations. Rather unimpressed with this feeble response to the gathering turmoil in their industry, local union leaders began demanding that the strike go ahead, while Foster announced that the National Committee had voted 12-3 to strike.

On September 22, 250,000 steelworkers walked off their jobs. It was the largest strike in the country's history; within a few days, the number of striking workers reached almost 400,000. The reaction among the public was immediately hostile, with the press giving the general impression that steelworkers were unfairly holding their own companies hostage. As Judge Gary threatened social catastrophe and revolution if the strike succeeded, several congressmen accused William Foster of communist sympathies and revolutionary intentions. As evidence, the press and the congressmen brought out a syndicalist pamphlet Foster had written in 1911.

The strikers were attacked by deputized militiamen, paid by the steel companies, in Pittsburgh, Pennsylvania and other steel towns. Black strikebreakers were employed in Gary, Indiana, a city named for the judge himself and placed under martial law and occupied by army units commanded by General Leonard Wood. The companies employed provocateurs to instigate riots and violence in order to back up their own claims that a revolution was in progress. Twenty people died in the violence.

At the National Industrial Conference called by President Wilson, the steel strike was not permitted to remain on the agenda. A resolution written by Samuel Gompers that would guarantee labor unions the right to organize and the right to bargain collectively with employers was voted down; Gompers then left the conference. Facing the hostility of the public and the indifference of the federal government in its role of mediator, the strikers gradually returned to work. The National Committee formally voted to end the strike in January 1920, and steel remained an open-shop industry in which union membership was strongly discouraged.

For the most part, union representatives called strikes in an attempt to win simple recognition as bargaining agents for better wages, hours, and working conditions. But the people of the United States were not yet ready to see labor unions as equal partners with employers in the conduct of business. Throughout the 1920s, union membership declined from a high point of about 5 million members or 12 percent of the labor force in 1920 to 3.4 million members, or 7 percent of the labor force, in 1929. This decline was one among many symptoms of a drift rightward in the country's political outlook, a general sympathy with business interests that would be encouraged throughout the 1920s by spreading prosperity and the probusiness slant of policies and legislation advanced by the three Republican successors of President Wilson.

The decline of union membership and the decimation of the ranks of labor leaders—hundreds of whom were arrested for their activities or deported from the country altogether as anarchists—had longlasting effects. The low wages of industrial workers depressed the demand for consumer products, which now formed the economy's mainstay. The suppression of union activity also went hand-in-hand with the rise of a powerful criminal underworld. In addition to the income provided from the sale of prohibited alcohol, gangsters would profit from the threat of labor trouble by providing their services as either spies for unions or as strikebreakers in the pay of employers.

CHRONICLE OF EVENTS

1918

November 11: An armistice between the Allies and Germany is signed at Compiègne Forest, France.

November 23: The U.S. War Department reports that 53,169 U.S. soldiers died in battle in World War I.

December 1: The U.S. occupation army enters Germany.

December 13: Woodrow Wilson arrives in Europe to negotiate a peace agreement.

December 22: Wartime food controls are lifted in the United States.

1919

January 1: Edsel Ford is named president of the Ford Motor Company by his father, Henry Ford.

January 1: Author J. D. Salinger is born.

January 3: Herbert Hoover is named to head the postwar relief effort in Europe.

January 6: Theodore Roosevelt, aged 60, dies at his home in Oyster Bay, Long Island.

January 10: The Republican National Committee recommends adoption of women's suffrage.

January 16: The Eighteenth Amendment to the Constitution is ratified when the Nebraska legislature passes Prohibition. The amendment will go into effect one year later.

January 18: The Versailles Peace Conference begins in Paris.

January 25: The 2,200-room Hotel Pennsylvania, largest hotel in the world, opens in New York.

February 8: The first heart electrocardiogram is published in Chicago by James Herrick.

February 12: An international women's suffrage convention opens in Paris, France.

February 14: The United Parcel Service is incorporated in Oakland, California.

February 25: Oregon passes the first state gasoline tax, at one cent per gallon, to help pay for road construction.

March 2: President Wilson announces support for establishment of a Jewish state in Palestine.

March 3: The Boeing company conveys the world's first air mail from Vancouver, British Columbia, to Seattle, Washington.

March 10: The Supreme Court decides in *Schenk v. United States* that, in times of clear and present danger as foreseen in the Constitution, the Espionage Act does not violate the First Amendment.

March 15: The American Legion of World War I veterans is founded in Paris.

March 29: A total eclipse of the sun occurs, giving scientists a chance to verify Albert Einstein's Theory of Relativity by measuring the alteration of the sun's rays.

April 17: Filmmakers and actors D. W. Griffith, Mary Pickford, Charles Chaplin, and Douglas Fairbanks found United Artists to make and distribute their own movies.

April 29: A New York postal worker, Charles Caplan, discovers 16 dynamite bombs packaged for mailing to J. P. Morgan, Oliver Wendell Holmes, Mayor Ole Hanson of Seattle, and other members of the political and business establishment. The bombs spark a fervent nationwide campaign against leftists, union agitators, and immigrants suspected of anarchist and/or communist sympathies.

May 10: Brigadier General Douglas MacArthur is appointed head of West Point.

May 21: By a 304-89 vote, the House of Representatives passes the Nineteenth Amendment. When ratified by the states, the amendment will give women the right to vote.

May 27: The NC-4, a hydroplane belonging to the U.S. Navy, makes the first crossing of the Atlantic Ocean.

June 2: Bombs explode at the homes of seven government officials, including Attorney General A. Mitchell Palmer.

June 4: The Senate passes the Nineteenth Amendment by a 56-25 vote. The amendment is sent to state legislatures for ratification.

June 7: New York State begins the first written tests for drivers' licenses.

June 15: Captain John Alcock of England and Lieutenant Arthur Brown of the United States make the first nonstop flight across the Atlantic in a Vickers-Vimy biplane. The 1,900-mile flight between Newfoundland and Clifton, Ireland, takes 16 hours and 12 minutes.

June 26: Augustus D. Juilliard leaves a $5 million bequest for a music endowment in New York.

June 28: The Versailles Peace Treaty is signed in Paris.

June 29: The War Prohibition Act limiting the sale of alcohol is extended until the military demobilizes.

June 29: Sir Barton becomes the first Thoroughbred horse to win a Triple Crown.

July 1: The nation's first daily mail service by airplane is established between Chicago and New York.

July 4: Jack Dempsey pummels Jess Willard and takes the heavyweight championship in three rounds at the Toledo Arena.

A machine gun battery prepares for action during the race riots that swept through several U.S. cities in 1919. *(Archive Photos)*

July 13: The British dirigible R–34 completes the first round-trip flight across the Atlantic.

July 14: The United States resumes trade with Germany.

July 30: National Guard troops are called out to stop race riots on Chicago's South Side.

August 1: Attorney General A. Mitchell Palmer organizes the General Intelligence Division to combat the threat of anarchist rebellion.

August 2: Railway workers strike for higher wages, public ownership of the railroads, and profit sharing.

August 11: Andrew Carnegie dies of pneumonia.

August 14: The Chicago *Tribune* is found guilty of libel for calling Henry Ford an anarchist. Ford is awarded trial costs and six cents for damages.

August 14: While postwar inflation runs high, the federal government seizes food in Chicago, St. Louis, and Birmingham warehouses in an attempt to stop price gouging.

August 21: A U.S. cavalry force kills four bandits inside Mexico during a mission to rescue two U.S. aviators.

August 31: The Communist Party of the United States is established in Chicago. The party adopts the slogan "Workers of the world, unite!"

September 2: Congress passes a bill banning strikes by railroad workers.

September 9: A police strike in Boston leads to looting and street riots.

September 22: About 300,000 steel workers strike U.S. Steel and other plants in Pennsylvania.

September 25: President Wilson suffers a stroke while campaigning in the West for the League of Nations and the Versailles treaty.

October 9: The Cincinnati Reds defeat the Chicago White Sox to win the World Series; in the next year, eight White Sox players will be accused of conspiring to throw the series.

October 24: The Los Angeles Philharmonic performs its first concert.

October 27: President Wilson vetoes the Volstead Act, the federal statute that enforced Prohibition.

October 28: The Volstead Act is passed over the president's veto.

October 29: Federal troops, under Major General Leonard Wood, mobilize in Gary, Indiana, during a steel strike.

November 1: Coal miners strike in the Midwest and East.

November 10: The House of Representatives expels socialist Victor Berger of Milwaukee by a vote of 390 to 1.

November 11: Members of the American Legion in Centralia, Washington, attack an Industrial Workers of the World (IWW) union hall. Four Legionnaires are killed; an IWW member, Wesley Everest, is tortured and lynched.

November 12: Fearing trouble from miners seeking higher wages and shorter hours, North Dakota places its mines under martial law.

November 19: The Senate refuses to ratify the Versailles peace treaty.

November 23: A supplementary Prohibition Act is passed, limiting the use of medicinal liquor and extending Prohibition to Hawaii and the Virgin Islands.

November 25: Department of Justice agents raid the Union of Russian Workers in New York City and report finding a bomb factory.

December 1: The Prohibition commissioner bans alcohol-based medicine and hair tonic.

December 10: A national coal strike ends after eight weeks; miners accept President Wilson's proposed 14 percent raise.

December 22: The transport ship *Buford* sails to Russia with Alexander Berkman, Emma Goldman, and 247 other deportees accused of sedition and anarchism.

EYEWITNESS TESTIMONY

The Treaty of Versailles and the League of Nations

Our allies, and our enemies, and Woodrow Wilson himself should all understand that Mr. Wilson has no authority whatever to speak for the American people at this time. His leadership and the Fourteen Points and his four supplementary points and his five complementary points and all his utterances every which way have ceased to have any shadow of right to be accepted as expressive of the will of the American people.

Former president Theodore Roosevelt, reacting to the Versailles treaty in the fall of 1918, from Asinof, 1919: America's Loss of Innocence (1990), p. 85.

I glanced at my watch. One minute to 11:00, thirty seconds, fifteen. And then it was 11:00 A.M., the eleventh hour of the eleventh day of the eleventh month. I was the only audience for the greatest show ever presented. On both sides of no-man's land, the trenches erupted. Brown-uniformed men poured out of the American trenches, gray-green uniforms out of the German. From my observer's seat overhead, I watched them throw their helmets in the air, discard their guns, wave their hands. Then all up and down the front, the two groups of men began edging toward each other. Seconds before they had been willing to shoot each other; now they came forward. Hesitantly at first, then more quickly, each group approached the other.

Suddenly gray uniforms mixed with brown. I could see them hugging each other, dancing, jumping. Americans were passing out cigarettes and chocolate. I flew up to the French sector. There it was even more incredible. After four years of slaughter and hatred, they were not only hugging each other but kissing each other on both cheeks as well.

Star shells, rockets and flares began to go up, and I turned my ship toward the field. The war was over.

Eddie Rickenbacker, American air ace, describing the moment of armistice from 500 feet above no-man's land at Conflans, France, on November 11, 1918, in his autobiography Rickenbacker (1967), p. 135.

The armistice between Germany, on the one hand, and the allied governments and the United States, on the other, has been signed.

The State Department announced at 2:45 o'clock this morning that Germany had signed.

The department's announcement simply said, "The armistice has been signed."

The world war will end this morning at 6 o'clock, Washington time, 11 o'clock Paris time.

"Armistice Signed, End of the War! . . .", front-page announcement of the armistice between Germany and the Allied powers, from the New York Times, *November 11, 1918, p. 1.*

. . . there are those among us even who would detract from the splendor of our victory. There are those who attempt by innuendo indirect, and by unshamed criticism to destroy the reputation of our country. Shame on him who points at America the finger of scorn. The sons and daughters of America have pride in their accomplishments and will resent the utterances of those who do not tender her full glory for it. From this point of view it may be easily proclaimed we should have done this or we should not have done that. But I defy the man to raise his voice who would have dared say then, not now, we should not have brought one more gun, nor trained another soldier and to have assumed responsibility for defeat. We sought not responsibility for defeat, we sought victory, and centuries ago Caesar said it for us: "We came, we saw, we conquered." Ah, the living need not sing the praise, for generations yet unborn will contact testimony bear, and the record of America in the great world war will stand the greatest wonder of the world.

Breckinridge Long, audio recording, ca. 1919, from "American Leaders Speak: Recordings from World War I and the 1920 Election, 1918–1920," from the American Memory Collection, Library of Congress.

Your kind note has given me the greatest pleasure. It is a comfort to me to know that you feel just as you do about the League; that the first thing is to consider it thoroughly; that we ought to know, in a matter of such vital importance, just where we are going, and that the American people ought to understand it. The attempt of President Wilson to force it through without consultation with the Senate, equally responsible with him in the making of treaties, is nothing more or less than an attempt to destroy the Constitution.

Henry Cabot Lodge, letter to William Lawrence, on the first publication of the Covenant of the League of Nations in early 1919, from Lawrence, Henry Cabot Lodge *(1925), p. 181.*

What a wretched mess it all is! If the rest of the world will let us alone, I think we had better stay on our own side of the water and keep alive the spark of civilization to relight the torch after it is extinguished over here. If I ever had any illusions, they are all dispelled. The child-nations that we are creating have fangs and claws in their very cradles and before they can walk are screaming for knives to cut the throats of those in the neighboring cradles.

General Tasker H. Bliss, U.S. delegate to the Versailles conference, from letter written to his wife in the spring of 1919, quoted in Hoover, The Ordeal of Woodrow Wilson *(1958), p. 241.*

We have bartered away our principles in a series of compromises with interests of imperialism and revenge, until hardly a shadow of them remains. Instead of assuring the peace of the world by a just reconstitution, this treaty seeks guarantees for a settlement in favor of the victors which reduces the vanquished to a powerless and indefinite servitude. Such a settlement assures neither permanence nor tranquility. My earnest conviction is that our country dishonors itself in adding its signature and guarantee.

Professor Joseph V. Fuller, member of the U.S. delegation to the Versailles conference, in letter to Undersecretary of States Joseph Grew, May 15, 1919, quoted in Hoover, The Ordeal of Woodrow Wilson *(1958), p. 240.*

Our government has consented now to deliver the suffering peoples of the world to new oppressions, subjections and dismemberments.

William C. Bullitt, of the Paris peace delegation, letter of May 17, 1919, to Woodrow Wilson, as quoted in Schlesinger, The Crisis of the Old Order *(1957), p. 14.*

The stage is set, the destiny disclosed. It has come about by no plan of our conceiving, but by the hand of God who led us into this way. We cannot turn back. We can only go forward, with lifted eyes and freshened spirit, to follow the vision. It was of this that we dreamed at our birth. America shall in truth show the way. The light streams upon the path ahead, and nowhere else.

Woodrow Wilson, address to the U.S. Senate, July 10, 1919, quoted in Weinstein, Woodrow Wilson: A Medical and Psychological Biography *(1981), p. 349.*

Why, my fellow citizens, nothing brings a lump to my throat quicker on this journey I am taking than to see the thronging children that are everywhere the first, just out of childish curiosity and glee, no doubt, to crowd up to the train when it stops, because I know that, if by any chance, we should not win this great fight for the League of Nations, it would be their death warrant. They belong to the generation which would then have to fight the final war, and in that final war there would not be merely seven and a half million men slain. The very existence of civilization would be in the balance . . . Stop for a moment to think about the next war, if there should be one. I do not hesitate to say that the war we have just been through, though it was shot through with terror of every kind, is not to be compared with the war we would have to face next time. . . . Ask any soldier if he wants to go through a hell like that again. The soldiers know what the next war would be. They know what the inventions were that were just about to be used for the absolute destruction of mankind. I am for any kind of insurance against a barbaric reversal of civilization.

Woodrow Wilson, speech delivered during the summer 1919 western campaign in support of the League of Nations, quoted in Link, Woodrow Wilson: Revolution, War, and Peace *(1979), p. 118.*

I believe that if the Senate could only understand what this treaty means, it would unquestionably be defeated, but I wonder if they will understand what it lets them in for. . . . I believe that the League of Nations at present is entirely useless.

Secretary of State Robert Lansing, remark made to former Paris Peace Conference delegate William C. Bullitt, who repeated the remark before the Senate Foreign Relations Committee in September 1919, during President Wilson's western campaign for the League of Nations and the Versailles treaty, quoted in Smith, When the Cheering Stopped *(1964), p. 75.*

Read that and tell me what you think of a man who was my associate on the other side and who confidentially expressed himself to an outsider in such a fashion. Think of it! This from a man whom I raised from the level of a subordinate to the great office of Secretary of State of the United States! My God! I did not think it was possible for Lansing to act in this way!

Reaction of President Wilson on reading of Lansing's anti-League remark in the newspapers, September 1919, quoted in Smith, When the Cheering Stopped *(1964), p. 75.*

The deadlock was complete, and on March 19, 1920, when the vote on ratification was taken, the necessary two-thirds were lacking by seven votes. At the last

Representatives of the four major Allied powers break from the formal proceedings at the Versailles Treaty Conference. From left to right, David Lloyd George of Great Britain, Vittorio Orlando of Italy, Georges Clemenceau of France, and U.S. president Woodrow Wilson. *(National Archives)*

moment a number of Democrats joined with the Republican reservationists, making fifty-seven in favor of ratification. It had taken the Peace Conference five months to construct the treaty with Germany in all its complexities, and secure the unanimous approval of the delegates of thirty-one states. The Senate had consumed more than eight months merely in criticizing the treaty and had finally refused to ratify it.

We are, perhaps, too close to the event to attempt any apportionment of responsibility for this failure to cap our military successes by a peace which—when all has been said—was the nearest possible approach to the ideal peace. It is clear that the blame is not entirely on one side. Historians will doubtless level the indictment of ignorance and political obliquity against the Senators who tried, either directly or indirectly, to defeat the treaty. . . . On the other hand, the President cannot escape blame, although the charge will be merely that of tactical incapacity and mistaken judgment. His inability to combine with the moderate Republican Senators first gave a chance to those who wanted to defeat the treaty. His obstinate refusal to accept reservations at the end, when it was clear that the treaty could not be ratified without them, showed a regard for form, at the expense of practical benefit.

Charles Seymour, from Woodrow Wilson and the World War *(1921), pp. 349–350.*

He kept us out of War; kept us out of Peace;
Kept us out of Mexico—mixed us up with Greece,
Kept us out of Sugar, kept us out of Shoes—
He joined the League of Nations and wants us to pay
the dues.
He kept us out of everything and you bet we'll
remember
To do some keeping out ourselves on the second of
November.
Harding in the Home—Coolidge in the Constitution.
America first—November 2nd.

*Anti-Wilson campaign jingle written by Warren Harding's
supporter James J. Davis during the fall of 1920, quoted in
Downes,* The Rise of Warren Gamaliel Harding
1865–1920 (1970), p. 597.

The recorded progress of our Republic, materially and
spiritually, in itself proves the wisdom of our inherited
policy of non-involvement in Old World affairs.
Confident of our ability to work out our own destiny,
and jealously guarding our right to do so, we seek no
part in directing the destinies of the Old World. We do
not mean to be entangled. We will accept no responsibility except as our own conscience and judgment, in
each instance, may determine.

. . . Our supreme task is the resumption of our
onward, normal way. Reconstruction, readjustment,
restoration—all these must follow. I would like to hasten them. If it will lighten the spirit and the resolution
with which we take up the task, let me repeat for our
Nation, we shall give no people just cause to make war
upon us; we hold no national prejudices; we entertain
no spirit of revenge; we do not hate; we do not covet;
we dream of no conquest, nor boast of armed prowess.

*Warren Harding, inaugural address delivered March 4,
1921 on the steps of the Capitol in Washington, D.C.,
as quoted in Lott,* The Inaugural Addresses
of the American Presidents *(1961), pp. 207–209.*

It is evident now, beyond cavil, that no part of Europe
is better off for America's having taken part in the great
war. So also it is evident that the Americans are all the
worse off for it. . . .

. . . the Americans would have been spared certain
untoward experiences that have followed. Most of the
war-debt, much of the increased armament, a good
share of the profiteering incident to the war and the
peace, and all of the income tax would have been
avoided. American statesmen would still have continued
to do the "dirty work" for American bankers in

Nicaragua; they might still have seen their way to man-
handle the Haitians and put the white man's burden on
the black population of Liberia for the profit of
American banks and politicians; it is even conceivable
that they could still have backed the Polish adventures
in Russia and have sent troops and supplies to the
Murmansk and Siberia to annoy the horrid Bolsheviki;
but there is at least a reasonable chance that, in such
event, there would have arisen no "American Legion,"
no Ku Klux Klan, no Knights of Columbus, and no
Lusk Commission. Presumably there would also have
been relatively little of the rant and bounce of Red-
Cross patriotism; no espionage act, no wholesale sentences or deportations for constructive sedition, and no
prosecution of pacifists and conscientious objectors for
excessive sanity.

Thorstein Veblen, "Dementia Praecox," from
The Freeman, *June 21, 1922, quoted in Baritz,*
The Culture of the Twenties *(1970), p. 33.*

Just one word more. I cannot refrain from saying it. I
am not one of those who have the least anxiety about
the triumph of the principles I have stood for. I have
seen fools resist Providence before, and I have seen
their destruction, as will come upon these again, utter
destruction and contempt. That we shall prevail is as
sure as that God reigns.

*Woodrow Wilson, from a speech delivered in Washington,
D.C. on November 12, 1923, in Heckscher,*
Woodrow Wilson *(1991), p. 670.*

Krebs went to the war from a Methodist college in
Kansas. There is a picture which shows him among his
fraternity brothers, all of them wearing exactly the
same height and style collar. He enlisted in the Marines
in 1917 and did not return to the United States until
the second division returned from the Rhine in the
summer of 1919.

. . . By the time Krebs returned to his home town
in Oklahoma, the greeting of heroes was over. He
came back much too late. The men from the town
who had been drafted had all been welcomed elaborately on their return. There had been a great deal of
hysteria. Now the reaction had set in. People seemed
to think it was rather ridiculous for Krebs to be getting
back so late, years after the war was over.

At first Krebs, who had been at Belleau Wood,
Soissons, the Champagne, St. Mihiel, and in the
Argonne did not want to talk about the war at all. Later
he felt the need to talk but no one wanted to hear

about it. His town had heard too many atrocity stories to be thrilled by actualities.

Ernest Hemingway, "Soldier's Home," from In Our Time *(1925), p. 69.*

I had learned from a careful study of the President's acts and utterances during those trying days—and it was as important for me to understand him as it was for his closest friends—that the key to all he did was that he thought of everything in terms of Wilson. In other words, Mr. Wilson in dealing with every great question thought first of himself. He may have thought of the country next, but there was a long interval, and in the competition the Democratic Party, I will do him the justice to say, was a poor third. Mr. Wilson was devoured by the desire for power. If he had been a soldier and a man of fighting temperament, the Government of the United States would have been in grave danger. . . . When it came to actual conflict he lacked nerve and daring, although with his temperament I doubt if he lacked the will. He had as great an opportunity as was ever given in human history to one man. He could have settled the affairs of the world from the White House and taken a position both at the time and in the opinion of posterity which it would have been hard to rival. He would have had the world at his feet, but he could think only of himself, and his own idea was and had been for a long time that the part for him to play was that of the great peacemaker.

Henry Cabot Lodge, explaining President Woodrow Wilson's failure to convince the Senate to ratify the Versailles peace treaty and thus bring the United States into the League of Nations, *from Lodge,* The Senate and the League of Nations *(1925), p. 212–213.*

We even got into War on a Slogan that was supposed to keep us out. After we got in we were going to "Make the world safe for Democracy." And maybe we did—you can't tell, because there is no Nation ever tried Democracy since.

Will Rogers, newspaper column, from Will Rogers; Weekly Articles: The Coolidge Years 1925–1927 *(1981), p. 215.*

Socialists, Anarchists, and Labor Troubles

Fully 90 percent of the Communist and anarchist agitation is traceable to aliens.

A. Mitchell Palmer, in Attorney General's Report, 1918.

I am thinking this morning of the men in the mills and factories; of the men in the mines and on the railroads. I am thinking of the women who for a paltry wage are compelled to work . . . [and children] seized in the remorseless grasp of Mammon and forced into the industrial dungeons, there to feed the monster machines while they themselves are being starved and stunted, body and soul. I see them dwarfed and diseased and their little lives broken and blasted because in this high noon of our twentieth-century Christian civilization money is still so much more important than the flesh and blood of childhood.

Eugene Debs, 1918 courtroom speech delivered at the end of his trial for violating the Espionage Act, reprinted in The American Reader *(1958), 249–250.*

The speedy outcome of the trial which occupied less than five days was a striking testimony to the careful way in which the evidence against Debs had been prepared. Knowing that Debs was scheduled to speak at the socialist convention at Canton on June 16, [1918] Chief Arch C. Klumph, of the Cleveland Division, sent operatives and stenographers to cover the meeting and take down the Debs address verbatim. . . . [This] transcript of the speech was the principal evidence introduced. It showed that Debs had ridiculed the army and navy, had criticized the conduct of the war, had questioned the ideals for which the flag stands and had made further remarks calculated to encourage disloyalty and obstruct the draft.

From "Ten Years in Prison for Eugene V. Debs," article praising the arrest and conviction of Eugene Debs published in the September 21, 1918 edition of The Spy Glass, *publication of the patriotic American Protective League, quoted in Harries,* The Last Days of Innocence *(1997), p. 305.*

Were it not for the universal attempt by the business-owned press of the country to make Socialism stand for pro-Germanism in the public mind, were it not for the astounding campaign by the newspapers aided and abetted by leading business men, and even certain branches of the Federal government, to make Socialism synonymous with Bolshevism and Bolshevism synonymous with murder, pillage, and rape, were it not for this utter pollution of the waters of public judgment and opinion, the first returns from the 1918 would be profoundly discouraging to those Socialists who do not care to blink the facts.

Leftist journalist Evans Clark, "The 1918 Socialist Vote," in The Intercollegiate Socialist, *December–January 1918–1919, p. 17.*

The working class and the employing class have nothing in common. There can be no peace so long as hunger and want are found among millions of working people and the few, who make up the employing class, have all the good things of life.

Between these two classes a struggle must go on until the workers of the world organize as a class, take possession of the earth and the machinery of production and abolish the wage system.

... These conditions can be changed and the interest of the working class upheld only by an organization formed in such a way that all its members in any one industry, or in all industries if necessary, cease work whenever a strike or lockout is on in any department thereof, thus making an injury to one an injury to all.

Instead of the conservative motto, "A fair day's wage for a fair day's work," we must inscribe on our banner the revolutionary watchword, "Abolition of the wage system." It is the historic mission of the working class to do away with capitalism. The army of production must be organized not only for the everyday struggle with capitalists, but also to carry on production when capitalism shall have been overthrown. By organizing industrially we are forming the structure of the new society within the shell of the old.

Manifesto of the Industrial Workers of the World (IWW), 1919, reprinted in Commager, Documents of American History, Vol. II *(1963), p. 158.*

Strikes ... are not industrial economic disputes in their origin, but are the results of a deliberate, organized attempt at a social and political movement to establish soviet government in the United States.

William B. Wilson, secretary of labor, quoted in Asinof, 1919: America's Loss of Innocence, *p. 144.*

Americans who heretofore have either not known what a political prisoner was or have associated him with Russia now have a singular opportunity to study his problem in the United States. There are, at the present time, approximately 500 prisoners in Fort Leavenworth Disciplinary Barracks who have refused military conscription. These are usually called conscientious objectors, and the grounds for their objection are many and various. There are at least 1,000 men and women, perhaps 2,000 (and the number is steadily increasing although the war is really over), in various prisons throughout the country, who were convicted under the Espionage Act or corresponding State laws, not because they were German spies or had any com-munication with Germany or made violent attack of any sort upon our government; but for the expression of opinion which judge and jury decided impaired the national morale or obstructed the course of the war.

Socialist leader Norman Thomas, in "Political Prisoners in the United States," in The Intercollegiate Socialist, *February–March 1919, p. 11.*

There is no right to strike against the public safety by anybody, anytime, anywhere.

Governor Calvin Coolidge, telegram to Samuel Gompers during the Boston police strike in September 1919, quoted in Shannon, America Between the Wars *(1979), p. 33.*

State Guardsmen opened fire with a machine gun on a mob in South Boston late tonight, killing one and wounding several others. The rioting was proceeding, at last reports.

Earlier in the evening, an unidentified man was killed, a woman was shot and severely wounded, and a police officer was beaten by a mob and taken to a hospital in a serious condition, in the rioting in the vicinity of Scollay Square.

Boston was under military rule tonight. After 24 hours of lawlessness such as the city has never before experienced, a sense of security was afforded an outraged public by the appearance in the streets of 5,000 soldiers under orders to restore order and to protect life and property at any cost.

Associated Press dispatch, datelined Boston, September 10, 1919, reprinted in Twentieth-Century America *(1995), p. 106.*

The economic impulses of the revolution today is the demand for a better division of the wealth from this industrialism.

I believe we are now in position to take some stock of and to form some judgment as to the adequacy of these solutions for what I believe every liberal-minded man believes is a necessity—the better division of industrial production.

Herbert Hoover, speech delivered September 16, 1919, to the American Institute of Mining Engineers, quoted in Miller, "A Capitalist's Confession of Faith," The Outlook, *January 1920, p. 15.*

There appears to be a misapprehension as to the position of the police of Boston. In the deliberate intention to intimidate and coerce the government of this Commonwealth a large body of policemen, urging all others to join them, deserted their posts of duty, letting in the enemy. This act of theirs was voluntary, against the advice of their well wishers, long discussed and premeditated, and with the purpose of obstructing the power of the government to protect its citizens or even to maintain its own existence. Its success meant anarchy. . . .

The authority of the Commonwealth cannot be intimidated or coerced. It cannot be compromised. To place the maintenance of the public security in the hands of a body of men who have attempted to destroy it would be to flout the sovereignty of the laws the people have made. It is my duty to resist any such proposal.

Calvin Coolidge, on the Boston police strike, statement of September 24, 1919, quoted in McCoy, Calvin Coolidge: The Quiet President *(1988), pp. 95–96.*

Many causes have been assigned for the three days of race rioting, from July 27 to 30 in Chicago, each touching some particular phase of the general condition that led up to the outbreak. Labor union officials attribute it to the action of the packers, while the packers are equally sure that the unions themselves are directly responsible. The city administration feels that the riots were brought on to discredit the Thompson forces, while leaders of the anti-Thompson forces . . . are sure that the administration is directly responsible. In this manner charges and counter-charges are made, but, as is usually the case, the Negro is made to bear the brunt of it all—to be "the scapegoat." A background of strained relations brought to a head more rapidly through political corruption, economic competition and clashes due to the overflow of the greatly increased colored population into sections outside of the so-called "Black Belt," embracing the Second and Third Wards, all of these contributed, aided by the magnifying of Negro crime by newspapers, to the formation of a situation where only a spark was needed to ignite the flames of racial antagonism.

Walter White, "The Causes of the Chicago Race Riot," from The Crisis, *October 1919, p. 293.*

Eleven companies of Indiana state troops are being rushed to Gary and Indiana Harbor by Governor James P. Goodrich. They are expected to reach the strike zone at 6 o'clock this morning.

They were ordered out last night after Gary had been swept for two hours by rioting strikers and sympathizers. It was the most serious outbreak since the strike was called on Sept. 22.

Scores were arrested and the hospitals were filled with wounded following a pitched battle between 5,000 strikers and several hundred policemen and special deputy sheriffs.

. . . Not a shot was fired by either side during the fighting. Paving stones, bottles, bricks, and clubs were the weapons used by the strikers, and there was hardly a member of the Gary police force who escaped being struck. Missiles were rained down on their heads by strike sympathizers from second story windows.

United States Senate Committee on Labor and Education, Investigation of Strikes in the Steel Industry, *66th Congress, 1st session (1919).*

We were not told that a strike was in progress. We were promised $4.00 a day, with the understanding that we should be boarded at $1.00 a day.

When we took the train a guard locked the doors so that we were unable to get out, and no meals were given us on the way, although we were promised board.

We were unloaded at Lock 4. . . . We were then told to go to work, and when I found out that there was a strike on I got out. They refused to let me out at the gate when I protested about working, and I climbed over the fence, and they caught me and compelled me to go back and sign a paper and told me I would have to go to work. I told them that I would not go to work if they kept me there two years. I was placed on a boat. There were about 200 other people there. The guards informed me that if I made any attempt to again run away that they would shoot me. I got a rope and escaped, as I will not work to break the strike.

Statement of Eugene Steward, African American hired to help break a strike of predominantly white steelworkers at the Pittsburgh Steel Products Company in November 1919, from Foster, The Great Steel Strike and Its Lessons *(1920), pp. 207–208.*

. . . the people, not yet recovered from war hysteria and misled by a corrupt press, cannot perceive the outrage. They even glory in their degradation. Free speech, free press, free assembly, as we once knew these rights, are now things of the past.

Strike leader William Z. Foster, describing conditions during the fall 1919 labor troubles in steel and other industries, in Foster, The Great Steel Strike and Its Lesson *(1920), p. 110.*

C. worked as a laborer in one of the Carnegie Mills, 10 hours on the day shift, 12 hours at night, 6 turns a week, and earned from $53 to $58 in two weeks. He has two children. The family lives in three rooms, which are light, pleasant, and well cared for. Rent is $15 a month. The wife said she wanted to move somewhere where rent was cheaper, but could find no other rooms. I was unable to discover how much food and clothes cost, as she kept no record of them. From $3.25 to $4 a month was paid to the lodge, according to the number of members who were ill. If a member is obliged to omit three monthly payments he is dropped from the lodge. The man was ill with influenza for 12 weeks last year and was obliged to sell the $200 Liberty Bond which he had in order to pay expenses. The bond was sold to the storekeeper, who only gave $180 for it, much to the indignation of Mrs. C. Since the strike began C. has had to sell the only other bond which he had—a $50 one, on which he had only paid $30. The family have no other savings, and the money from the bond is almost gone.

> *Description of an Austrian family of Homestead,*
> *Pennsylvania, during the 1919 strike in the steel industry,*
> *from Commission of Inquiry,* Report on the Steel Strike
> of 1919 *(1920), p. 112.*

In business we must buy as cheaply as our competitor or pay the penalty by insolvency. On this account there seems to the business man to be a certain ethical quality in a good trade. Labor has been looked upon as a commodity to be bought at a price, and one must buy as cheaply as possible or go to the wall. Any man who paid appreciably higher than the going rate of wages in a competitive business was doomed to failure. All these things made it seem right to pay as low wages as could be paid and still get the work done. When Americans would not work for us at the price, we took on the Irish. When the Irish were no longer attracted by what we paid, we turned to the Italians, the Poles, the Lithuanians, the Slavs, and to twenty tribes yet lower in the wage scale, and got them to work for us, and felt that we had done right.

> *Charles A. Miller, general counsel for the Savings Bank*
> *Association of the State of New York, preparing to argue for*
> *a fairer division of income between capital and labor, in "A*
> *Capitalist's Confession of Faith," in* The Outlook,
> *January 1920, p. 16.*

. . . it requires courage in ordinary times to be in a minority, but when the world is mad with the fury of war, the man who has the courage to proclaim a principle which is true for all time is the first victim of the mob. The patriotic fevor during the war was such that it was utterly impossible for any judge or jury to do justice in the ordinary sense of the word . . . I am a pacifist at heart. I detest war, but many a time during the war I found rising within me hatreds such as I thought myself incapable of. I can see how the average juror would find it practically impossible to give a square deal to a man who was charged with having a strong radical statement which appeared to him, the juror, as opposition to the Government and as endangering the country.

> *Socialist Representative Meyer London of New York, during*
> *congressional debate on June 7, 1922, on the subject of*
> *granting amnesty for individuals convicted under the*
> *Espionage Act, from Peterson,* Opponents of War
> 1917–1918, *(1957), p. 281.*

I have heard Republicans who did not speak with the utmost respect for the Eighteenth Amendment, and Democrats who did not admire the Fourteenth and Fifteenth. . . . There are gentlemen in this room famous for their zeal in behalf of constitutional government who never raised their voices to protest when Mussolini quite unconstitutionally captured power in Italy. . . . Mussolini has been blessed by the very men who denounced the Bolsheviki for the self-same crime. . . . No one here can disbelieve in violence more than I . . . but those who justify organized violence in their own cause, who glory in the spies and Secret Service agents of corporations and Government and in political prisoners confined for opinion are in no position to denounce violence.

> *Socialist Party leader Norman Thomas, during a public*
> *debate with state senator Clayton Lusk of New York,*
> *denouncing Lusk's use of spies and informers against sus-*
> *pected subversives, quoted in the* New York Times,
> *February 11, 1923, and in Swanberg,* Norman Thomas:
> The Last Idealist, *(1976), p. 87.*

The police strike was broken by public opinion, led by a business-controlled press, while order was restored by militia in Boston called out by Andrew J. Peters, the mayor. Governor Coolidge sat discreetly on the fence until he saw on which side public opinion was gathering.

> *From "Calvin Coolidge: Made by a Myth,"* The Nation,
> *August 15, 1923, p. 3.*

I had to stand against the current. . . . Most of the aliens had been picked up in raids on labor headquarters; they had been given a drumhead trial by an inspector, with no chance for the defense; they were held incommunicado and often were not permitted to see either friends or attorneys before being shipped to Ellis Island. In these proceedings the inspector who made the arrest was prosecutor, witness, judge, jailer, and executioner. He was a clerk and interpreter as well.

. . . I refused to railroad aliens to boats made ready for their deportation. . . . I faced a continuous barrage from members of Congress, from the press, from business organizations and prosecuting attorneys. Yet day by day aliens, many of whom had been held in prison for months, came before the court; and the judge, after examining the testimony, unwillingly informed the immigration authorities that there was not a scintilla of evidence to support the arrest.

Frederic C. Howe, secretary of labor and frequent opponent of postwar deportations, in Howe, Confessions of a Reformer *(1925), pp. 274–275.*

2

Newfound Freedoms, Old-Fashioned Temperance
1920

On January 16, 1920, the Eighteenth Amendment to the United States Constitution went into effect. At midnight, it became illegal to sell, manufacture, or transport alcoholic beverages anywhere in the United States. The era of Prohibition began.

The fight to ban liquor already had a long history in the United States. Since the middle of the 19th century, church leaders, civic officials, and women's groups had made it their cause. These crusaders saw drink and the saloon as prime suspects in the decline of the nation's moral and physical health. Taking up their cause were city and county lawmakers who passed "dry laws" that banned alcohol—hard liquor, sometimes wine and beer as well—within their jurisdictions. Other states and county governments allowed their municipalities to pass their own "local option" statutes. The first prohibition law had passed in Maine in 1851. By the start of World War I, dry laws and the local option had created a nationwide patchwork of rules and regulations governing the sale, distribution, and consumption of alcohol.

The Prohibition debate represented several long-standing, deep-rooted conflicts within American society, the most basic of which was a clash of stereotypes: the virtuous, independent "yeoman farmers" and small-town citizens versus the unwashed, working-class city dwellers unwilling to abandon the languages and ways of their foreign homelands. Since before the American Revolution, cities had been represented in pamphlets, sermons, and cautionary tales as nests of vice, immorality, corruption, and foreignness, while the village and the farm symbolized hard work, Christian devoutness, thrift, and sobriety. By the turn of the 20th century, many people of the Midwest and South saw the cities of the East, and the largely Catholic (and Jewish) immigrants who lived in these cities, as a threat to their traditional Protestant, small-town values. In the years after Word War I, they also saw their own lives being transformed through the influence of mass communication and commercialism. Chain grocery stores—a symbol of impersonal urban living—were appearing, as were noisy, mass-produced automobiles and factory-made, assembly-line goods: the advance guard of the cultural enemy, the corrupt and immoral urban society arriving via an improved road network, national magazines, and the radio.

Some people believed that Prohibition might be one way to reverse the tide of problems brought ashore by immigrants from strange lands. Studies were done which pointed to liquor as the cause of high crime rates, divorce, child neglect, low productivity, public health problems, and declining church attendance. In Prohibitionist rhetoric, support of dry laws turned into support for an older, better, more virtuous America—the America that had fought for liberty and against tyranny (the widespread use and abuse of liquor in colonial times was ignored). Although the pre-Revolutionary settlers had brought hard-drinking habits across the Atlantic Ocean with them, the notion of temperance had gradually settled in among the Protestant majority in the middle of the 19th century. Beer, whiskey, and rum were moved into dark and violent saloons of ill repute, where they often accompanied gambling and sundry other vices. The post–Civil War waves of Catholic and southern European immigrants suffered from no such religious or cultural stigmas against alcohol, and the freer drinking among them allowed self-styled 100 percent Americans one more example of the unhealthy foreign attributes that, in the opinion of many, were undermining the country's traditions. Knowing that rural and small-town America would provide their largest constituency, Prohibitionists spoke softly concerning the farmer's alcoholic hard cider and loudest against the "urban" forms of alcohol—especially hard liquor and beer.

LOBBYING FOR PROHIBITION

Prohibitionists drew inspiration from the great orators and saloon vandals of the past. John Hawkins of Baltimore preached abstinence after years of intemperate behavior in the 1820s and 1830s. The Woman's Crusade swept across the Midwest in the 1870s, giving birth to the Women's Christian Temperance Union (WCTU), organized by Dr. Diocletian Lewis. Frances E. Willard made a speech a day—for 10 years—against strong drink, stumping for the virtues of sobriety in every state in the Union. The hatchet brought by Carrie Nation into illegal saloons inflicted terrible damages on barroom furniture and marked a new militancy among Prohibitionists in the first years of the 20th century.

The major figure in the modern Prohibition battle, Wayne B. Wheeler of the Anti-Saloon League, proved to be one of the most effective lobbyists and organizers for any cause in the country's history. Using direct mail, church fund-raising, get-out-the-vote drives, and political arm-twisting, Wheeler turned Prohibition into the issue by which all candidates for public office were measured. The pressure mounted during each successive election as Prohibitionists marched and lobbied and alcohol lost its reputation as a healthful tonic in the face of medical reports citing alcohol as a cause of birth defects, cirrhosis of the liver, and other conditions. Wheeler consolidated the movement by merging the Anti-Saloon League with the Women's Christian Temperance Union and the Prohibition Party. In 1913, he organized a march on Washington to demand a constitutional amendment to ban the manufacture and sale of alcoholic beverages.

World War I sharpened the debate and bolstered the cause of Prohibitionists, who noted that German-Americans owned most of the country's breweries and insisted that the nation's scarce wartime resources should be used to supply soldiers, not to intoxicate the public. In the period of 1916–19, per capita consumption of alcohol by adults fell to 1.96 gallons per year, the lowest figure since the 1870s. The elections of 1916 turned into a referendum on Prohibition, with "wet" candidates (those opposing Prohibition) losing ground to the "drys" (those favoring Prohibition). By 1917, the year the United States entered World War I, 27 states were dry. As a dress rehearsal, a Wartime Prohibition Law was proposed and passed, although it would not be signed by President Wilson until July 1, 1919—seven months after the armistice ended World War I.

Wets and drys realized that the U.S. Congress could not successfully prohibit the consumption of alcohol simply by passing federal statutes. The laws would be endlessly challenged in court on constitutional grounds, and so a sweeping amendment to the Constitution itself was necessary. Wheeler had already prepared one. Through his ally, Senator Morris Sheppard of Texas, Wheeler introduced the Eighteenth Amendment of the Constitution, which passed in December 1917, by a vote of 282–128 in the House of Representatives and 65–20 in the Senate. The amendment was then submitted to the states for ratification. The legislatures of three-fourths of the states, or a total of 36 out of 48, would have to ratify the amendment in order for it to go into effect.

Wheeler had worded the amendment to give it sufficient time for passage by the states—in his opinion, a maximum of seven years. In fact, ratification of the Eighteenth Amendment would take a little longer than a year. Prohibition had great usefulness for politicians who, in their endless quest to curry favor and votes from the public, lost nothing by supporting it and who realized that Wheeler's public relations campaign had effectively equated support of Prohibition with honesty, patriotism, upstanding morality, and concern for public welfare.

Mississippi became the first state to ratify the amendment in January 1918. Among the legislators of the 48 states, senates voted 1,310 for and 237 against, a majority of 84.6 percent, and lower houses voted 3,782 for and 1,035 against, a majority of 78.5 percent. After Nebraska became the 36th and deciding vote, on January 29, 1919, 10 more states would ratify, including northeastern states such as New York and New Jersey where the population was largely against Prohibition. Only Rhode Island and Connecticut would fail to ratify the Eighteenth Amendment.

On October 27, 1919, the Volstead Act, the statute that would determine Prohibition's crimes and punishments, was passed by the Senate over President Wilson's veto. As Wayne B. Wheeler sat in the gallery, the senators rose to offer America's leading Prohibitionist a standing ovation. The law he had inspired allowed manufacture of denatured alcohol for use by companies manufacturing certain medical supplies, industrial chemicals, cleaning agents, cosmetics, and food preservatives. The law allowed alcohol to be used for medicinal purposes; it allowed "near beer," or beer with an alcoholic content of .5 percent or lower; it allowed the manufacture and use of alcoholic cider; it allowed the use of alcohol in religious ceremonies. Stocks of intoxicating beverages held before July 1, 1919, could be kept, although the law said such beverages had to be consumed in the home. All other manufacture and sale of alcohol became a federal crime, punishable by a maximum fine of $1,000 and six months in jail on the first offense.

The statute would bring about half a million arrests and nearly 100,000 jail terms over the next 10 years. But Wheeler and the senators did not yet realize that the Volstead Act, with its many exceptions and loopholes, would turn out to be one of the most abject failures in legislative history.

THE RED SCARE

One of the arguments propounded by dry politicians was that alcohol somehow fomented radicalism and socialism. Certainly many members of the working class, especially the urban and northeastern working class, had no intention of obeying the law if they could help it, or afford it. The Wets argued that Prohibition settled an injustice on honest, beer-drinking workers and would bring about the rise of a powerful criminal class of manufacturers and distributors. They gave their own cautionary example of Russia's wartime Prohibition, the subsequent Bolshevik revolution, and the overthrow of the czar.

Certainly the threat of Russian Bolshevism served as a powerful weapon for any politician or interest group that cared to use it. During World War I, legislated patriotism had served the cause of a national war effort; Congress passed the Espionage and Sedition Acts to clamp down on dissent while Liberty Bond drives gave citizens a sense of taking part in a patriotic common cause. The crusade did not end with the Armistice, however. In the minds of many people, anarchism and Bolshevism still posed a threat to the United States, just as they did in postwar Europe. The passions whipped up by the war found a new outlet in a national hunt for the Reds.

Bringing the Red Scare to a boiling point were the actions of the scattered anarchists who really did believe in the violent overthrow of the capitalist system. In April 1919, 29 dynamite bombs were carefully wrapped and mailed to prominent business and political leaders, including J. P. Morgan, John D. Rockefeller, and Justice Oliver Wendell Holmes. All were defused, with one exception that detonated at the home of Senator Thomas Hardwick of Georgia, injuring the senator's wife as well as her maid. On June 2, more bombs went off in New York, Pittsburgh, Washington, D.C., and Boston, the targets being a federal judge, anti-anarchist lawmakers, and a church. One of those bombs was delivered to the front door of Attorney General A. Mitchell Palmer, on R Street in Washington, by an unidentified individual who was blown to pieces by the resulting blast. Scattered among the victim's limbs and clothing were small pamphlets entitled *Plain Words,* signed by a group calling itself The Anarchist Fighters.

Palmer, a native of Pennsylvania and a presidential hopeful, saw an opportunity to place himself into a useful public spotlight. Raised as a pacifist in a Quaker family, he had refused President Wilson's appointment as secretary of war and had instead accepted the post of alien property custodian. In this position he had seen to the redistribution of several hundred million dollars' worth of German and Austrian property to friendly individuals and corporations in the United States. After attaining the office of attorney general, Palmer had resisted calls to persecute radicals and had extended clemency to more than 100 political prisoners jailed under the wartime Espionage Act.

After the explosion on his doorstep, however, Palmer turned into a rabid anti-Bolshevik crusader: the "Fighting Quaker." He secured a congressional appropriation of $500,000 for his crusade and the support of the press and the public, who were convinced by the success of the Bolshevik Revolution in Russia and by postwar social chaos in Europe that an international socialist conspiracy was afoot. The formation of the Communist Party and Communist Labor Party in the United States, the world's capitalist bastion, seemed to underline the threat from the left. Aside from labor secretary William Wilson, Palmer met very little opposition in the presidential cabinet which, with Woodrow Wilson's illness, rarely met anyway. A General Intelligence Division under the leadership of J. Edgar Hoover was founded within the federal Bureau of Investigation. Palmer set Hoover the task of deporting every radical the bureau could find under the Immigration Act of 1917, which ordered deportation—by the Labor Department—of all those advocating violence "against property, public officials, or the government." The sweep began with the rounding up of prominent foreign-born radicals such as Emma Goldman and Alexander Berkman.

The tempo of the raids increased in November, a month that also saw continuing labor unrest and a violent coal strike. In New York and 11 other cities, squads from the Bureau of Investigation invaded leftist headquarters such as the Union of Russian Workers, beating people, destroying furniture, rounding up the usual suspects, and driving panicked crowds into the streets. With no probable cause for making an arrest, the agents carried blank warrants that would be filled in with the appropriate names after the suspects were jailed.

A select group of 249 prominent radicals was assembled on Ellis Island, near the watchful gaze of the Statue of Liberty, and held incommunicado and without charge. On December 22, 1919, the group was shipped out of the country aboard an old troop transport, the *Buford,* with a contingent of 250 soldiers aboard for security. After its Atlantic crossing, the "Soviet Ark" called at Helsinki, Finland, and from there the deportees were sent across the border to Russia.

In the meantime, Palmer sent letters, documents and articles to major newspapers throughout the country, warning them of the threat of radical socialism and a plot to overthrow the U.S. government. The red-baiting rhetoric reached a fever pitch in the media; petitions from state legislatures, citizens' groups, business groups, and other organizations demanding action arrived in Congress. The Senate asked the Department of Justice for an account of the actions it was taking to thwart the threat of Bolshevism. Meanwhile, the weakened, bedridden President Wilson seemed to have disappeared from public view entirely, allowing his wife Edith and the members of the White House staff to assume most of his responsibilities. At one cabinet meeting, however, Wilson did let Palmer know that he had full support with a simple demand: "Palmer, don't let this country see Red!" Thus encouraged, Palmer laid plans for decisive action against those he saw as national enemies. He would use the Alien Law of 1918 as the legal justification for his action.

On January 2, 1920, the Department of Justice began a coordinated nationwide raid on radicals, anarchists, socialists, and bolsheviks. Justice agents, placed within communist organizations, were ordered to arrange gatherings on that night, to see to it that incriminating documents would be made available. In the days before the raids, about 5,000 warrants were sworn and large-scale operations prepared in New York, Boston, Chicago, and Detroit. Several thousand people were then arrested in a sweep of 30 midwestern and eastern cities; federal agents stormed restaurants, homes, storefronts, and other gathering places and carried off the suspects, who found themselves imprisoned without charge.

Palmer proudly announced that the raids had accomplished their purpose— Bolshevism had been beaten, the nation's communist leaders had been rounded up. He then called for even more stringent laws against sedition.

Newspapers were threatened and in some cases closed down for antigovernment sentiments; college professors found themselves expelled for incorrect instruction. In April 1920, five Socialist members of the New York state legislature were expelled from the chamber by a vote of their colleagues for belonging to a "disloyal organization." At the same time, however, Palmer was coming under increasing criticism for the tactics employed by the Department of Justice. Senator Warren Harding, for one, announced his opposition, and Charles Evans Hughes, the Republican candidate for president in 1916, denounced the New York Assembly vote and offered to represent the five Socialist members who had been summarily dismissed for their political views.

In the spring of 1920 came the scheduled trials for those caught in the Palmer Raids. Jurisdiction over deportation cases still rested with the Department of Labor, which at the time was under the direction of acting secretary Louis F. Post. Post and William B. Wilson, the secretary of labor, were legally responsible for deportations. But instead of favoring Palmer's sentiments or actions, Post and Wilson saw to it that the arrested suspects were given fair hearings and representation by counsel. In the end, they released more than half of the suspects. Five hundred ninety-one aliens would be deported.

During congressional hearings that took place after the trials, Post convincingly defended his actions and turned many of the assembled representatives against the attorney general. Palmer's proposed new sedition bills were sharply criticized and defeated. Seeing public opinion turning against him, Palmer tried one last scare, promising the nation that a Bolshevik revolution and a series of assassinations of public officials were in the works for May Day (May 1), 1920. Communists were rounded up and militia called out in fearful preparation, but when May 1 came and went and Palmer's prediction came to nothing, he became a laughingstock, and the Red Scare began to die down. That summer, Palmer won nothing at the Democratic presidential nominating convention, where his nickname was transformed by derisive colleagues from the Fighting Quaker into the Quaking Quitter, or the Faking Fighter.

Nevertheless, the Red Scare had given intellectuals, academics, and left-leaning politicians a deep-seated fear of certain labels: Bolshevik, pro-German, communist, socialist, and Red. It also spelled the end of the Progressive movement within the Republican party, whose members now understood that a government given the power to carry out a sweeping reform of industry and banking could also turn on citizens with the same government's powerful apparatus of repression. Progressives could not overcome the society's desire for stability after the years of wartime turbulence, and the progressive "Bull Moose" Republicans discovered in the summer of 1920 that they had an uphill fight even with such an able leader as Hiram Johnson as their candidate. As it turned out, the party was looking for a figurehead, not a reformer, and in the interest of normalcy selected the comforting image of Warren G. Harding of Ohio.

ENFORCING PROHIBITION

The Eighteenth Amendment had been passed and ratified, but constitutional amendments do not set down the precise nature of criminal acts, organize enforcement or prosecution, or set penalties. The necessary Prohibition enforcement statute was duly passed in September 1919 and was known as the Volstead Act after Andrew J. Volstead, a Minnesota congressman who served as chairman of the House Judiciary Committee and who reported the bill out of committee. The act itself had been authored by Wayne B. Wheeler.

After the original bill was amended by the House Judiciary Committee and passed in the House, it was sent to the Senate Judiciary Committee, while a

Well-publicized raids on breweries, such as this one in Detroit, did little to discourage violations of the Volstead Act and the Eighteenth Amendment. The public was thirsty, and there was too much money at stake. *(National Archives)*

debate grew over the nature of enforcement of the Eighteenth Amendment. The drys wanted stricter enforcement but agreed to compromises so that the law would not spark a negative public reaction. The Senate committee listed places of abode where one could legally possess liquor: homes, apartments, and hotels. Individuals would be allowed to manufacture cider and wine. The Senate struck out a provision against penalties for drunkenness on public vehicles and also allowed the distribution of liquor to patients in hospitals. The statute also gave the government the power to seize and auction off all vehicles—boats, planes, cars, trucks, or horse-drawn carts—used for transporting illegal alcohol.

Congress appropriated $5 million to enforce the Volstead Act. Thirty states, however, allocated nothing, turning the job over to the federal government; the rest only appropriated token amounts for what legislators knew would be an enormous and probably pointless task. Prohibition agents and commissioners were appointed by city, state, and county governments and were given the authority to close and padlock, for one year, any establishment found to be selling liquor. Instead of placing enforcement at the hands of the Department of Justice, Wheeler successfully lobbied for a separate Prohibition Bureau, which became part of the Treasury Department under the direction of the Commissioner of Internal Revenue. Wheeler's own friends and allies—many of them from Ohio—were then appointed to the top jobs.

THE DRY YEARS

On the day before Prohibition began, a federal judge in New York ruled that agents could seize alcohol stored in private warehouses or in safe-deposit boxes. From the seizures, the government consigned 50 million gallons of liquor to its own warehouses for safekeeping (by the end of Prohibition, 20 million gallons of this stock would disappear). At the same time, a frantic, last-minute transfer took place: illegal stocks were moved to private homes, where storage was legal. Mock funerals were held; at Norfolk, Virginia, preacher Billy Sunday ostentatiously laid to rest a 20-foot coffin symbolizing John Barleycorn (the personification of liquor), with 10,000 Prohibitionists in attendance. A very different mourning took place in New York nightspots, where small coffins were distributed to the patrons, who all wore black. In Chicago, gangsters celebrated the start of the Prohibition era by stealing $100,000 worth of whiskey from railroad boxcars.

John F. Kramer, an Ohio lawyer and the first of several commissioners of Prohibition, recruited and prepared his agents to carry out the provisions of the Volstead Act. The number of federal agents during Prohibition would reach a peak of 2,300. But their mediocre salaries of between $1,200 and $2,000 caused many to turn for supplemental income to the bootlegging trade. Prohibition agents sold stocks of liquor which they controlled or knew about to bootleggers; sold permits that allowed people to withdraw alcohol from government warehouses; or simply accepted bribes for looking the other way, upon the discovery of an illegal still, a beer-stocked delivery truck, or an offshore rum-running operation.

The tactics used by the Prohibition Bureau soon made the department widely unpopular. Bribery and wiretapping were used to collect information on suspects. Thousands of businesses were padlocked simply on suspicion, a practice that made it unwise to invest in a wide variety of retail businesses from drugstores to restaurants. Confrontations between bureau agents and bootleggers also resulted in the deaths of innocent bystanders; almost none of these incidents resulted in arrests or indictment of the agents responsible. The public perception that the whole operation was corrupt and ineffective was reinforced by behavior at the highest levels. Andrew Mellon, Secretary of the Treasury and the nominal head of the entire effort, had heavily invested in liquor manufacturing before Prohibition; Senator Sheppard of Texas, Wayne Wheeler's ally, was found to have an illegal still on his property.

Politicians publicly supported Prohibition but privately continued to drink. The most prominent example was President Warren Harding, who was no teetotaler, as was generally known. The members of his inner circle, casually known as the Ohio Gang, made great amounts of money from Prohibition bribery and nonenforcement. They sold pardons and paroles to convicted bootleggers, sold whiskey confiscated by the Justice Department, and accepted bribes from distributors big enough to attract their attention. They had prosecutions dropped and sentences lightened, and sold appointments to the Prohibition Bureau, which in Harding's administration became an all-purpose employment agency for friends of the administration.

During Prohibition, the moonshining art moved down from remote hills and farmyard sheds and into the cities, where concealment from the revenuers proved easy. Normally law-abiding citizens set up stills in their basements, attics, garages, and backyard toolsheds. Corn sugar was bought from manufacturers, then cooked in a still with water and yeast to produce alcohol. Raw alcohol was mixed with glycerin and the juice of juniper berries to create "bathtub gin." Home brewers had simply to buy wort—boiled mash—add yeast and hops to the mixture, brew for the prescribed length of time, bottle, and consume. To make wine, the private vintner bought a legal base known as Vine-Glo that was processed from wine grapes, added water, and waited 60 days for natural fermentation to take its course. Section 29 of the Volstead Act, which permitted the private fermentation of fruit juices, proved a boon to California's wine industry, which prospered from the sale of its grapes and products such as Vine-Glo.

Thousands applied for physicians' and pharmacists' licenses in order to prescribe legal, medicinal alcohol. Drugstores took over storefronts that had previously housed saloons, selling alcohol in the form of home remedies. Bootleggers also bought up entire drugstores for the purpose of ordering alcohol and then arranging its diversion to the illicit market. The major form of Prohibition defiance occurred when bootleggers, after being granted or sold a permit, built plants ostensibly for the purpose of denaturing alcohol. The government permitted the denaturing of alcohol by the addition of soap, iodine, wood alcohol, and other contaminants, some of them fatal. But denatured alcohol could be revived into near-drinkable form with the addition of glycerine, caramel, and other substances, then poured into bottles with fake labels that signified the contents had been "bonded" (inspected by the authorities and passed as authentic). The goods were then diverted into distribution channels and found their way to speakeasies and the public.

The manufacture of .5-percent beer, or near beer, also helped to supply the continuing demand. In this process, the breweries had to first manufacture "normal" beer, then distill out most of its alcohol, which could then be shipped covertly to ready buyers. In many cities, bootleggers never bothered to follow this procedure, instead buying up breweries and simply operating them normally. Brewing companies such as Anheuser-Busch and others that attempted to follow the law saw their sales of near beer suffer from the competition.

A serious aftereffect of all this amateur manufacturing was a sharp rise in illnesses and deaths from contaminated liquor, in addition to a rise in alcoholism. The crisis was worst among low-income consumers, who could not afford the better and safer forms of liquor such as imported, bonded whiskey. Wood alcohol poisonings were common; another disease known as "jake foot" caused painful paralysis and deformities in the toes and instep of its victims.

Meanwhile, speakeasies abounded in New York City, where Club 21, the Three Hundred Club, and the Salon Royale offered music and illicit drinks at all hours of the night. Most speakeasies were owned and operated by gangsters, a phenomenon that added to the newfound allure of criminals expressed in novels, plays, and movies of the 1920s. Speakeasies levied a cover charge, carefully screened customers at the door, and sold watered-down alcoholic drinks at high prices. They represented one sort of advance for women, who had been rarely seen inside the traditional saloon except as entertainers or prostitutes. There were few risks in attending a speakeasy, as alcohol consumption was still entirely legal, and the raids of federal Prohibition agents eventually became so commonplace as to become a form of entertainment for the guests. One famous speakeasy owner, Tex Guinan, had her house band strike up "The Prisoner's Song" whenever a raid commenced.

Prohibition did inflict severe damage on the Broadway entertainment industry. Many Broadway cabarets and nightclubs closed their doors, starting the New York theater district on a long decline from which it would never completely recover. On the opposite coast, in and around the town of Hollywood, California, the new movie industry would flourish by meeting a demand for entertainment suddenly frustrated by the closing of saloons. Former customers began to visit the darkened movie palaces, where bootleggers and gangsters were replacing sheikhs and vamps as the latest cinematic icons.

CROSSING THE BORDERS

Prohibition proved a boon to the economy of Canada, a major source of secreted and smuggled alcohol. The provinces of Canada repealed their own prohibition laws to take advantage of the situation. Tourism from the United States increased sharply, and Canadian hotels, restaurants, and roadhouses did a brisk business. Canadian distillers were hard pressed to meet the demand; the Canadian government, which did nothing to stop or slow the trade, benefited from taxes slapped on distributors who arranged shipment across the U.S. border. The liquor arrived in cars, trucks, boats; U.S. importers knew that customs agents could not possibly patrol a 4,000-mile border. The center of the Prohibition import trade was Detroit, Michigan, where smuggling became an industry second only to automobile manufacturing. The city's policemen and prosecutors were generously paid by criminal entrepreneurs to look the other way.

Smuggling also took place along the East Coast and in the Gulf of Mexico. British liquor was shipped to Canada, Mexico, the Bahamas and other island nations of the Caribbean for transfer to thirsty Americans. In the Caribbean, Rum Row smugglers idled just outside the territorial waters of the United States, off-loading their crates and barrels onto boats fast enough to run past U.S. Coast Guard patrols. The goods provided by Big Bill McCoy, who handled only high-grade whiskey from the Bahamas, earned the appellation of the "Real McCoy." Easing the task of Rum Row smugglers was the rivalry among the Coast Guard, the Customs Service, and the Prohibition Bureau. Among the experienced and capable border guards, the Prohibition Bureau was considered an upstart and was widely looked down on for its corruption and incompetence.

Smuggling by international waters proved easy and profitable for all parties concerned. All the same, the Prohibition laws caused foreign policy problems for the United States. During Prohibition, the United States attempted to extend its three-mile territorial limit at sea in order to prevent Rum Row bootleggers from operating just off the coast. Great Britain objected to this measure and also protested against Prohibition agents seizing vessels flying the British flag outside the territorial limit. Eventually, the United States would sign a treaty with Britain allowing foreign ships to bring liquor into U.S. ports under seal and U.S. agents to seize bootleggers within an hour's distance from shore.

One of the most serious incidents involved the *I'm Alone,* a Canadian ship that was pursued and sunk by a U.S. Coast Guard vessel at a distance of 200 miles from the U.S. coast on suspicion of smuggling activity. After a long round of diplomatic haggling, the United States paid the owners of the *I'm Alone* compensation for the loss of the vessel.

CRIME AND PROHIBITION

The administration of the Prohibition laws was, at best, haphazard and inefficient. The Prohibition commissioners were responsible for issuing search warrants and for holding preliminary hearings of accused bootleggers. In most cases, the commissioner either dismissed the charges outright for inadequate evidence, or sent it to a grand jury, which would return an indictment for prosecution by the appointed district attorney. For the sake of expediency, most people who were charged with Prohibition violations pled guilty and paid a fine. Most judges had little interest in prosecuting Volstead Act cases, in many cases throwing out the indictment for illegally obtained evidence. In some states, the problem of crowded court dockets was solved by simply bringing defendants before the bench in a large group and then either sentencing or dismissing them en masse as quickly as possible.

In many cities, the commissioners simply acted as an arm of the party or politicians that had appointed them to their posts. According to the status of the accused, the commissioner involved might dismiss the case, accept a bribe for dismissing the case, warn the targeted individuals of the impending raid beforehand, or simply throw out the evidence. District attorneys also had a wide range of dubious procedures open to them, one of the most common being to bargain a light fine and no prison time in return for a guilty plea. Even if the case finally reached a jury trial, many jurors, not being teetotalers themselves, felt a strong sympathy for the accused and simply passed on an innocent verdict in the face of compelling evidence to the contrary. This practice was particularly common wherever popular sentiment was set against the Prohibition laws in the first place—areas, as the Prohibitionists believed, most in need of their corrective reforms.

Constitutional questions were raised and never answered by the Volstead Act and its enforcement. The Fourth Amendment prohibits unreasonable search and seizure, and the practice of padlocking speakeasies was commonly challenged on these grounds (in one California case, the padlocked premise was a redwood tree that concealed a still). The Fifth Amendment proscribes the practice of double jeopardy, yet some prominent Prohibition defendants were tried and convicted under state as well as federal laws for the same crime. Prohibition encouraged plea-bargaining by criminals and also had the effect of broadening the state's powers of search and seizure. Private automobiles and boats were seized on suspicion of illegal activity and then sold off. In the Prohibition-related case of *Olmstead v. United States,* the U.S. Supreme Court upheld the practice of wiretapping private homes to obtain evidence of illegal acts.

In some states, such as North Dakota, Virginia, and Kansas, enforcement was effective and backed by dry sentiment; but in larger urban areas, seaports, and the northeastern states, enforcement was usually nonexistent. Connecticut and Rhode Island had not ratified the Eighteenth Amendment at all, and law enforcement agencies in these states felt little compunction to see it obeyed. In Philadelphia, Prohibition severely damaged the justice system as the viruses of graft and patronage spread outward from the state commissioner's office, which dispensed appointments and pardons for a fee and collected political campaign contributions from bootleggers seeking leniency.

In New York, one Prohibition administrator after another quit after just a few months on the job. Prohibition statutes were ignored as local politicians simply used them to dispense favors and protect contributors. State enforcement officers and attorneys, jealously protective of their turf, did not cooperate with federal officials. Although Prohibition commissioners bragged about their successes, most of the time they were simply lying. Most people who wanted to drink continued to do so, refusing to cooperate with the Prohibition agents by informing on their neighbors or on the bootleggers who supplied them. As the realization dawned that the Volstead Act was a failure and that the citizens would continue to drink alcoholic beverages even at the risk of being jailed or fined, the Harding/Coolidge administrations passively accepted the result by not proposing any further enforcement legislation.

By 1923, it was obvious to everyone that enforcement of Prohibition under the circumstances was impossible. In that year, New York Governor Alfred E. Smith would officially repeal Prohibition in his own state; later Nevada, Montana, Wisconsin, Massachusetts, Illinois, and Rhode Island would do the same. The response of the federal government, after nine years of the Volstead Act, was to pass an even more punitive statute known as the Jones Act, which set a fine of $10,000 and a term of five years in jail for first-time offenders. Under the Hoover administration, enforcement would improve; in 1930, seizures of illegal stills jumped tenfold from the first year of enforcement; arrests rose sharply, and agents seized 40 million gallons of illegal alcohol.

By this time, the knowledge of bootlegging had spread throughout the general population, so that by the late 1920s the processes of making bathtub gin, bootleg liquor, home brew and Vine-Glo wine were fairly common knowledge. After the stock market crash of 1929, bootlegging became an attractive method of making money in a shaky, unemployment-ridden economy. The increasing efficiency of enforcement, at the same time, brought the Volstead Act and the Jones Act into even worse repute. The public protested long and loud against the thousands of arrests of otherwise respectable people. Finally, in 1933, the Twenty-first Amendment would repeal the Eighteenth, and the era of Prohibition would end.

SUFFRAGE

Women had led the Prohibitionist vanguard of the late 19th and early 20th centuries, and women played a vital role in the advocacy of progressive causes in the time of President Teddy Roosevelt and muckraking journalists Nellie Bly and Lincoln Steffens. Another cause that gained new regiments of reformers, as well as bitterly opposed traditionalists, was suffrage—one woman, one vote.

In 1915, Carrie Chapman Catt became president of the National American Woman Suffrage Association. A veteran of suffrage movements in New York State, Catt laid down certain conditions for her participation: fellow board members had to work for suffrage full time and state suffrage organizations had to cooperate fully with the national organization. On these terms, she drew up a secret "Winning Plan" and promised that the league would attain its goal of national suffrage within six years.

Suffrage for women had begun in the Territory of Wyoming in 1869. Out west, women played a more equitable role in the economy of what had recently been a frontier, and their presence in politics and business was more generally accepted. By the time of Catt's appointment, every western state except New Mexico had followed Wyoming's example, including Kansas and Illinois. But women still had the right to vote in only 13 states, all of them, save Illinois, with relatively small electoral votes and small clout in presidential elections.

World War I made the crucial difference in the drive for women's suffrage. When the United States entered the war, thousands of women found themselves hired for assembly-line work in busy factories and munitions plants. Women also took unaccustomed jobs as conductors, delivery drivers, traffic cops, and mail carriers. Women led the drive to sell Liberty Bonds, the proceeds of which were used to finance government defense spending. In work judged by society at large to be worthy and patriotic, women emerged from the cloister of the home and appeared on the public podium to take up the cry for victory.

Women also served as prominent leaders of a large peace movement, organized by the Women's Peace Party, that adamantly opposed U.S. involvement in the war. The party's leaders included national chairperson Jane Addams and Jeannette Rankin of Montana, the first woman elected to the U.S. Congress. Rankin worked for universal women's suffrage as well as for the passage of laws granting women citizenship independently of their husbands. She cast one of 50 votes in Congress against U.S. entry into the war. She would repeat her vote against war on December 8, 1941, the sole member of Congress to defy President Roosevelt's declaration against the Axis powers of World War II.

As the war progressed, and as the important role of women in the war effort impressed itself on the public, the suffrage movement began to make progress. Catt and others drove home the point that if the United States would sacrifice its citizens for the sake of democracy in Europe, then it ought to consider extending democracy to the half of its adult population that still did not have the franchise. On January 9, 1918, President Wilson publicly came out for the Anthony Amendment (so named after suffragist Susan B. Anthony), which if passed would grant universal adult female suffrage. On the following day, the amendment passed in the House of Representatives. Claiming to defend states' rights, antisuffrage members of the Senate defeated the amendment on October 1. In May 1919, Wilson again threw his support to the Anthony Amendment, which passed the House once again, by a margin of 304 to 89. On June 4, the Senate finally passed the amendment and sent it to the states for ratification.

The ratification drive began the next month, with Wisconsin, Illinois, Michigan, Kansas, Ohio, New York, Pennsylvania, Massachusetts, and Texas voting to pass. The amendment was blocked in several states by legislators or governors hostile to it. By the time of legislative recesses in the summer of 1920, however, only one additional state was needed for ratification.

In the meantime, on February 18, 1920, the National American Woman Suffrage Association had convened its annual convention in Chicago. At the convention, the organization was renamed the National League of Women Voters. Catt was looking beyond ratification to make this organization into a civic forum that would educate women on their rights as citizens and press for legislation favorable to women and children.

On March 22, 1920, Washington became the 35th state to ratify the Anthony Amendment. One more state was needed. Late that spring, Catt decided that the final battle for ratification of the amendment would take place in Tennessee. Catt sought to take advantage of the state's active suffrage movement to get ratification done before the presidential election that fall. Governor A. H. Roberts cooperated by calling a special session of the legislature to consider the amendment. However, the amendment was opposed by a bloc of business interests, as well as liquor lobbyists who believed women would unanimously vote "dry" on Prohibition legislation. The anti-amendment forces set up convenient and well-stocked bars in hotel rooms and offered their hospitality to lawmakers they believed could be swayed to vote their way.

In the end, the campaign failed. On August 13, after two months of lobbying, the state Senate passed the amendment by a vote of 25 to 4. Five days later, after further delaying actions by antisuffragists, the House finally voted to pass.

A southern court, attended by male attorneys, male police officers, male clerks, and a male judge, swears in a jury. Despite the Nineteenth Amendment, women found slow acceptance into business, politics, and the court system. *(Bergert Brothers Collection, University of South Florida)*

On August 26, Secretary of State Bainbridge Colby (a Tennessean) signed the declaration and universal suffrage was the law of the land.

BIRTH CONTROL

The passage of the Nineteenth Amendment sounded the starting bell for a decade of revolutionary change in the social and economic position of women in the United States. As women found themselves making important crucial contributions to the war effort, their demand for a greater role in the country's economy and government intensified. At the start of the 1920s, these demands were finding their chief spokeswoman and figurehead in the person of Margaret Sanger.

Sanger was born Margaret McKee in Corning, New York. She wanted to be a doctor, but her family was too poor to send her to medical school, and so she had become a nurse. After marrying a successful architect by the name of William Sanger, she settled down in Hastings-on-Hudson, a New York City suburb. After nine years of comfort and boredom, the couple moved to New York City's Greenwich Village. The Sangers began to enjoy an entirely bohemian lifestyle while Margaret Sanger took up the study of revolutionary politics, atheism, and socialism.

Sanger now worked as a nurse among the poor immigrants of the city. The deaths and despair she saw as a consequence of unwanted, uncontrolled pregnancies inspired her to begin, almost single-handedly, the modern birth control movement. She first envisioned a nationwide network of advice centers, which would distribute information on birth control to anyone who asked. But there were laws against disseminating such information, and when Sanger tried to distribute a pamphlet she was indicted for distributing pornography. She fled to Canada and then to England, where she met the psychologist and sex researcher Havelock Ellis. Returning to New York, she opened the nation's first birth control clinic in Brooklyn, was promptly arrested, and served a one-month sentence in prison. In 1921, she organized the American Birth Control Conference and the American Birth Control League. During the conference, she was abruptly arrested again and dragged from the podium while delivering the inaugural speech.

The publicity surrounding the conference and Sanger's arrest gained her invaluable national publicity. The Birth Control League grew steadily; in 1923 the Birth Control Clinical Research Bureau opened in New York City, the first agency to be staffed by doctors. Through the rest of the 1920s, the formerly radical and bohemian notion of birth control gained millions of respectable and middle-class supporters.

FLAPPERS

In the meantime, the dislocation and increased mobility of families and individuals, the more tolerant continental attitudes—an epicurean delight in food, wine, entertainment; generally higher respect for writers and other creative artists; a lower opinion of merchants and the pursuit of commerce, which many Europeans considered a particularly American mania; a more tolerant and relaxed attitude toward sexual relations—brought home by soldiers and nurses from France, and the new roles assumed by women in the wartime workplace all served to weaken the restrictive norms of behavior and dress, especially in the cities, where social mobility was running high. From these liberating circumstances emerged a caricature: the flapper, symbol of the modern woman, evincing new freedom most obviously through her dress—revealing and sometimes sleeveless dresses, skirts raised to the knees, shorter hair ("bobbed" by tolerant barbers), long scarves, flapping galoshes, daring flesh-colored stockings, and all manner of strange hats. Properly brought-up women defied their mothers by daring to wear makeup (especially lipstick), smoke cigarettes, display jewelry rather prominently, and dance closely. Critics saw the accoutrements of prostitutes afflicting respectable society; flappers themselves looked on the elder generation as old-fashioned puritans that now offered the country only hypocrisy and outmoded sentiments.

Attitudes to courtship and marriage changed along with modes of dress. Among some married women, especially in urban society, divorce lost its stigma and became a prerogative, almost a fashion. The divorce rate rose from 8.9 per 100 marriages in 1910 to 13.4 in 1920 and 16.5 in 1928. Single women saw nothing indecent in a series of boyfriends, giving less thought to the proper Victorian ideals of marriage—mating as a social maneuver—than to compatibility and love. Experience gained value over virtue. Kissing, petting, and premarital sex were revealed as more commonplace than had been previously imagined, at least according to fashionable novels such as F. Scott Fitzgerald's *This Side of Paradise,* published in April 1920, and to articles on the subject of sex in popular magazines. By 1923, the year that Holland Rantos invented the rubber diaphragm, Margaret Sanger could offer an alternative in birth control that would be controlled by female partners.

Sex itself would come out in the open as never before, and the central figure taking part in the new regime was Sigmund Freud, an aging Vienna psychologist. Freud had given his first lectures to scientific colleagues in the United States

Bathing suits grew daring; neglect and disdain for prewar moral strictures brought an epidemic of flirtation. *(Minnesota Historical Society/St. Paul Daily News)*

in 1909; his books on dreams and the hidden forces of the psyche circulated widely after the war. Freud taught that sex was a primary motivation behind human actions, and that a healthy libido, its desires acknowledged and met, brought about a healthy mind. He was seconded in libidinal encouragement by the Englishman Havelock Ellis, who had published *Studies in the Psychology of Sex* before the war, and by the Swiss psychologist Carl Jung, who investigated archetypical behavior in modern society. The new books and teachings drew attention and aroused discussion among the better-educated men and women of the 1920s, and as a result sex began to lose its hidden, forbidden qualities. The new mobility and the new privacy offered by the automobile—the perfect vehicle for trysts—were used with enthusiasm by the younger generation, now generally able to escape the supervision of parents and the opprobrium of neighbors.

Popular culture responded: movies featured romance and scantily dressed vamps who did a little more than hint at sex; spicy novels and confessional magazines uncovered the details of thousands of private lives; a new dance music called "jazz" from a slang word for intercourse swayed and thrusted suggestively. Dancing moved from decorous, well-lit ballrooms to new venues—nightclubs, roadhouses, and private parties—that went unchaperoned and unsupervised.

More generally, Freud's psychoanalysis led to the emergence of science as a common currency of ordinary conversation. The topics of biology, psychology, anthropology, and the rest made one look askance at the accepted wisdom of traditional religious teachings on the nature of the world and of human beings. Scientists themselves were made into celebrities; one of the youngest of them was Margaret Mead. She first traveled to the South Pacific in 1925 to study the people of Samoa, New Guinea, and other distant and little-known communities, and published her findings in *Coming of Age in Samoa* in 1928 and *Growing Up in New Guinea* in 1930. There was something vaguely subversive about dissecting Polynesian society for an American audience, and Mead's intentions would come under further public discussion and suspicion with the publication of *Sex and Temperament in Three Primitive Societies* in 1935. Western society was one alternative among many, Mead seemed to say, and the traditional nuclear family of two parents with offspring is only one version of many possible household relationships among kin and acquaintances.

CHRONICLE OF EVENTS

1920

January 1: Harvard defeats Oregon 7-6 in the Rose Bowl collegiate football championship.

January 2: Birth of scientist/author Isaac Asimov.

January 2: Seeking out dangerous radicals and anarchists, Department of Justice agents and local police officers arrest 2,700 people in a sweep of 33 cities.

January 3: The last U.S. troops leave France. On the next day, the French government will officially grant permission for 20,000 bodies of U.S. soldiers to be returned to the United States.

January 5: The Radio Corporation of America (RCA) is founded.

January 5: The Boston Red Sox trade Babe Ruth to the New York Yankees for $125,000.

January 6: Governor Edwin Morrow signs the Nineteenth Amendment to the Constitution, making Kentucky the 24th state to ratify the amendment allowing universal adult suffrage in the United States.

January 10: The Treaty of Versailles goes into effect; the United States is still officially at war with Germany.

January 16: The Eighteenth Amendment goes into effect; Prohibition begins.

February 13: Secretary of State Robert Lansing resigns at the request of President Wilson, under

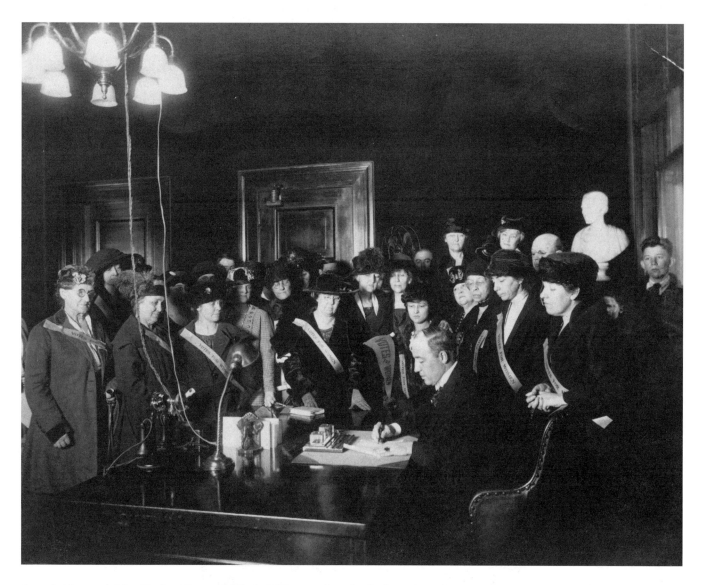

Attended by watchful suffragists, Governor Edwin P. Morrow signs the Anthony Amendment on January 6, 1920, making Kentucky the 24th state to ratify the amendment giving women the right to vote. *(Library of Congress/Gretter Studio, Frankfort, Kentucky)*

charges of holding unauthorized cabinet meetings during the president's illness.

February 28: The Esch-Cummins Transportation Act is passed, creating the Railroad Labor Board. The railroads return to private ownership.

March 1: The Supreme Court, in *United States v. United States Steel,* acquits U.S. Steel of violating the Sherman Anti-Trust Act, establishing the precedent that large corporations are not ipso facto monopolies.

March 1: The U.S. Navy releases all radio stations from the government's control.

March 2: New Jersey legalizes 3.5 percent beer, defying the Volstead Act and the Eighteenth Amendment.

March 11: First Prohibition raid killing takes place in New York City.

March 19: The Versailles treaty is defeated for the last time in the Senate, 49–35.

March 29: Film actors Douglas Fairbanks and Mary Pickford (who was nicknamed "America's Sweetheart") are married in Los Angeles.

April 1: Five members of the state legislature of New York are expelled for membership in the Socialist Party. After being reelected, they will not be allowed to sit in the legislative chamber.

April 5: The New York University Hall of Fame names Frederick Douglass as its first African-American member.

April 7: 50,000 railroad workers strike in Chicago; Attorney General A. Mitchell Palmer accuses the Industrial Workers of the World (IWW) of fomenting the strike as part of its plans for a socialist revolution.

April 9: Military draft for World War I ends.

April 14: Police fire on crowd of IWW strikers in Butte, Montana, injuring 14.

May 3: Future heavyweight boxing champion Sugar Ray Robinson is born.

May 5: Anarchists Nicola Sacco and Bartolomeo Vanzetti are arrested for murder during an armed robbery in Braintree, Massachusetts.

May 5: Labor secretary William Wilson announces that Communist Party membership will not be grounds for deportation from the United States.

May 10: The Socialist Labor Party holds its national convention in New York City, nominating W. W. Cox for president and August Gilhaus for vice president.

May 14: The Socialist Party begins its convention, nominating Eugene Debs for president and Seymour Stedman of Ohio for vice president.

May 19: Twelve people are killed during a firefight between Pinkerton agency detectives and striking coal miners in West Virginia.

May 31: Gaston Chevrolet wins the Indianapolis 500 motor race with an average speed of 88.6 miles per hour.

June 4: Congress passes the Army Reorganization Act, establishing a peacetime army of 300,000.

June 5: The Women's Bureau is established in the Department of Labor; its first director is Mary Anderson, who has responsibility for women's labor issues.

June 5: The Merchant Marine Act reorganizes the United States Shipping Board and prepares for the sale of the wartime merchant fleet to private owners.

June 7: The Supreme Court unanimously votes to uphold the Volstead Act and the Eighteenth Amendment, declaring invalid all state laws defining intoxicating liquors.

June 10: The Water Power Act establishes the Federal Power Commission, which will regulate hydroelectric power plants and issue licenses for the construction and operation of hydropower facilities.

June 10: The Republican Party endorses women's suffrage at its presidential nominating convention.

June 12: The Republican Party nominates Warren Harding for president and Calvin Coolidge for vice president.

June 13: The United States Post Office rules that children may not be sent by parcel post.

July 5: The Democratic Party nominates James M. Cox, governor of Ohio, for president and Franklin Roosevelt for vice president.

July 7: The Department of State lifts an embargo on trade with Russia, noting that the action does not imply recognition of the new Soviet government.

July 16: One month after its founding in Chicago, the Farmer Labor Party nominates Parley P. Christensen of Utah for president and Max S. Hayes of Ohio for vice president.

July 22: The Prohibition Party nominates Aaron S. Watkins of Ohio for president.

August 6: Police and streetcar workers fight in Denver during a strike; three strikers are killed.

August 20: Detroit radio station 8MK begins a daily broadcast of a variety show, "Tonight's Dinner."

August 22: Birth of science fiction author Ray Bradbury.

August 26: The Nineteenth Amendment to the Constitution, allowing national women's suffrage, is proclaimed after Tennessee becomes the 36th state to ratify the amendment.

August 29: Jazz saxophonist Charlie Parker is born.

September 1: Prohibition agents carry out first sweep of New York saloons.

September 5: Film comedian Roscoe "Fatty" Arbuckle is accused of the rape and murder of actress Virginia Rappé.

September 6: In Benton Harbor, Michigan, Jack Dempsey knocks out Billy Miske in the third round to retain his heavyweight boxing crown.

September 8: The first transcontinental mail route is established between New York and San Francisco, moving by air during the day and via train at night.

September 16: A bomb is set off at the intersection of Broad Street and Wall Street in downtown Manhattan, killing 38 people and injuring hundreds. The bombers are never found.

September 28: Eight Chicago White Sox players are indicted on charges of conspiracy to throw the 1919 World Series, earning them the collective nickname "Black Sox."

October 12: The Cleveland Indians defeat the Brooklyn Robins to win the World Series.

October 16: War veterans march in New York in favor of the Bonus Bill, which would compensate veterans for their services during World War I.

October 20: U.S. communist writer John Reed dies of typhus in Moscow.

October 29: Thirteen more people are indicted by a grand jury in Chicago for their role in the Black Sox scandal.

November 2: Radio station KDKA in Pittsburgh begins weekly broadcasts.

November 2: Warren Harding is elected 29th president of the United States, with Calvin Coolidge as vice president.

November 2: California passes the Alien Land Tax by referendum, thus preventing Japanese immigrants from ownership of agricultural land.

November 16: The first postage meter begins operation in Stamford, Connecticut.

November 25: Driver Gaston Chevrolet is killed in an accident on the Los Angeles speedway.

December 10: Woodrow Wilson is awarded the 1919 Nobel Prize in Peace.

December 18: The Detroit Tigers name Ty Cobb as the team manager.

December 21: The 300th anniversary of the landing at Plymouth Rock is celebrated in Massachusetts.

December 28: The United States resumes deportation of Communist Party members.

EYEWITNESS TESTIMONY

Prohibition

REMEMBER

The liquor traffic fought for permission to sell intoxicants to soldiers, knowing full well that drinking would make our boys less fit to win the war.

Breweries went on burning coal to make a harmful product when factories, stores, churches, and schools had to close down.

Millions of bushels of grain were consumed to manufacture intoxicants while patriotic people of America limited their food.

Millions of pounds of sugar were used in making intoxicants, while people were doing without sugar.

Thousands and thousands of cars were used for shipments to and from breweries when absolutely essential war-work was seriously delayed by car shortage.

The brewers financed the traitorous German-American Alliance, whose president received a medal from the Hun kaiser.

The Liquor Traffic has put its selfish interests above America's winning the war. It has resisted the measures to even partially eliminate its evils.

The Liquor Traffic has curtailed only when compelled to—only when Uncle Sam "put the screws to it."

The Liquor Traffic is a menace—from every viewpoint—and ought to be abolished now and forever.

Vote "Yes" for Prohibition Nov. 5th.

Take away the "camouflage" with which the Liquor Traffic tries to disguise itself and the sinister figure pictured here stands revealed.

Take away the smooth phrases and cunning twists of the liquor Traffic's appeal For Permission to continue its career;-get right down to naked truth and you will see that the liquor traffic is asking fathers of Ohio to "give me your boys." . . .

Are you with them? Are YOU for the Booze Huns or for the boys?

Two poster advertisements produced during a fall 1918 referendum on statewide Prohibition in Ohio, from "The Ohio Dry Campaign of 1918," web site of Ohio State University History Department, URL: http://www. cohums.ohio.state.edu/history/ohiodry.

We must turn our energies to other countries until the whole world is brought to understand that alcohol is man's greatest enemy. Thus it is a fortunate thing that the abdication of the Kaiser and the fall of arbitrary power came in the same year as does the fall of the brewery autocracy and that these two evils came down together . . . Now we can go out for the evangelization of the world on the subject of intoxicating liquor.

William Jennings Bryan, at the Worldwide Prohibition Conference of November 1918, from Behr, Prohibition *(1996), pp. 73–74.*

The bibuli [drinkers] are crushed by the sudden triumph of Prohibition. All is lost, including honor. But I have enough good whiskey, fair wine and prime beer secreted to last me two solid years—and by then I hope to be far from these Wesleyan scenes. I sold my motor-car and invested the proceeds in alcohol.

Another great crusade is already under way. It is against copulation. A government bureau has been established to spread the news that the practise is not necessary to health—a heresy hitherto prevalent. Some of the literature is superb—I'll send you specimens. In the Middle West there is also a growing movement against tobacco. In a few years you will see a republic that is chemically pure.

Editor and anti-Prohibition critic H. L. Mencken, from a letter written to Ernest Boyd, January 18, 1919, from Forgue (ed.), Letters of H. L. Mencken, *(1961), p. 136.*

You may drink intoxicating liquor in your own home or in the home of a friend when you are a bona fide guest.

You may buy intoxicating liquor on a bona fide medical prescription of a doctor. A pint can be bought every ten days.

You may consider any place you live permanently as your home. If you have more than one home, you may keep a stock of liquor in each.

You may keep liquor in any storage room or club locker, provided the storage place is for the exclusive use of yourself, family, or bona fide friends.

You may get a permit to move liquor when you change your residence.

You may manufacture, sell, or transport liquor for non-beverage or sacramental purposes provided you obtain a Government permit.

You cannot carry a hip flask.

You cannot give away or receive a bottle of liquor as a gift.

You cannot take liquor to hotels or restaurants and drink it in the public dining rooms.

You cannot buy or sell formulas or recipes for homemade liquors.

You cannot ship liquor for beverage use.

You cannot manufacture anything above one-half of one percent (liquor strength) in your home.

You cannot store liquor in any place except your own home.

You cannot display liquor signs or advertisements on your premises.

You cannot remove reserve stocks from storage.

Description of restrictions on alcohol usage printed on the eve of Prohibition in the New York Daily News, *January 19, 1920, p. 1.*

The slums will soon be only a memory. We will turn our prisons into factories and our jails into storehouses and corncribs. Men will walk upright now, women will smile, and the children will laugh. Hell will be forever for rent.

Reverend Billy Sunday, presiding over a mock funeral for John Barleycorn in Norfolk, Virginia, January 20, 1920.

In State and National Prohibition campaigns, as Young Campaigners for Prohibition, in patriotic regalia, with pennants flying and appealing, significant banners held aloft, the boys and girls prophesied the downfall of the trade that with its cruel heel dated "stifle down the beating of a child's heart." The cry of the children has been heeded by this great nation. Educated by the facts of science, by the precepts of the Bible, and by the joy of temperance service, the children have grown to manhood and womanhood and have helped vote out of existence the traffic in alcoholic beverages.

Anna Gordon, president of the Women's Christian Temperance Union, speaking at the proceedings of the Fifteenth International Congress against Alcohol, 1920.

This law will be obeyed in cities, large and small, and in villages, and where it is not obeyed it will be enforced. The law says that liquor to be used as a beverage must not be manufactured. We shall see that it is not manufactured. Nor sold, nor given away, nor hauled in anything on the surface of the earth or under the earth or in the air.

Prohibition Commissioner John F. Kramer, 1920, as quoted in Stevenson, Babbitts and Bohemians *(1967), p. 89.*

Prohibition is going to last a long time and then one day it'll be abandoned. But it's going to be with us for quite a while, that's for sure. I can see that more and more people are going to ignore the law, and they're going to pay anything you ask to get their hands on

Sending barrels of wine and beer into city gutters was easy for police and Prohibition agents, but the courts, unable to handle the burgeoning case load, customarily lightened sentences or dropped charges altogether on producers and sellers. *(Culver Pictures)*

good-quality liquor. I know what I'm talking about, because as you know I mix with society people who have money. It's going to be the chic thing to have good whiskey when you have guests. The rich will vie with one another to be lavish with the Scotch. That's where our opportunity is—to provide them with all the liquor they can possibly pass on to their guests or guzzle themselves. And we can make a fortune meeting this need.

I want to set up a sound business for importing and distributing Scotch. It is illegal, of course, and will require running risks, but I don't think you mind that. I have the contacts to buy the stuff. I know the Scottish distillers and they know me. I've played poker with them. I've taken a lot of money from them. We're very good friends and there's no problem there. Would you like to discuss this with your Italian friends and let me know? But we have to move quickly. Other people are going to get on the bandwagon.

Professional gambler Arnold Rothstein, making a business proposition to the 18-year-old Meyer Lansky on the commencement of Prohibition in 1920, quoted in Eisenberg, Dan, and Landau, Meyer Lansky: Mogul of the Mob *(1979), pp. 82–83.*

The anti-prohibitionists are fond of making eloquent pleas for the toleration of minorities. One of their recent protagonists has said:

'It is a popular idea that the majority should rule. But this does not mean that the people should vote on every question affecting human life, and that the majority should then pass penal statutes to make the rest conform. No society can hold together that does not have a broad toleration for minorities. To enforce the obedience of minorities by criminal statutes because a mere majority is found to have certain views is tyranny and must result in endless disorder and suffering.'

This, like most generalizations, sounds like something and means nothing. The writer of the above quotation surely cannot mean that *every* minority should be tolerated. A dozen men band themselves together to rob mail-trains. They are a minority. Are they to be tolerated? A group of men form a corporation for the exploitation of oil-wells in Mexico. They go there, bribe the officials, violate the laws, get into trouble, foment strife, evoke international complications and bring nations to the verge of war. They are a minority. Should they be tolerated? A mob breaks into a prison where an accused is waiting trial, overpowers the jailors, takes the accused and hangs him to the nearest tree. The Ku Klux Klan wants to make the world safe for none but native, Protestant whites. "A little house on K Street" harbors a group of individuals who barter official power and place for personal, nefarious ends. A group in Michigan combine to buy one of their number a seat in the United States Senate. Another group engages in the transportation of women for immoral ends. A third smuggles opium. A fourth sells morphine, cocaine, and heroin to drug addicts. These are all minorities in action. Are they all to be tolerated?

Albert Levitt, "Anti-Prohibition Hallucinations," in The South Atlantic Quarterly, *January 1926, pp. 10–11.*

The evil which the old-fashioned preachers ascribe to the Pope, to Babylon, to atheists, and to the devil, is simply the new urban civilization, with its irresistible scientific and economic and mass power. The Pope, the devil, jazz, the bootleggers, are a mythology which expresses symbolically the impact of a vast and dreaded social change. The change is real enough. The language in which it is discussed is preposterous only as all mythology is preposterous if you accept it literally. . . . The overcoming of the Eighteenth Amendment would mean the emergence of the cities as the dominant force in America. . . .

Journalist Walter Lippmann, in Men of Destiny *(1927), pp. 28–31.*

Politicians are ducking, candidates are hedging, the Anti-Saloon League is prospering, people are being poisoned, bootleggers are being enriched, and government officials are being corrupted.

Fiorello La Guardia, congressman from New York, during a House of Representatives debate on Prohibition (1928).

The Eighteenth Amendment to the Constitution of the United States is the most benevolent, the most beneficent, the most far-reaching reform ever inaugurated by any people anywhere in the history of the world and any man who sneers at it is an enemy of God.

Any man who drinks liquor either in public or in private is an anarchist.

Any man who drinks liquor deserves no more respect than the lowest elements, the very dregs of human society.

Any banker who in the privacy of his home has a social dinner for his friends and serves some wine at his table, defying the law, has no right to complain or to ask the protection of society if at the moment he is drinking his wine a burglar breaks into his bank and robs—for he and the burglar are one at heart.

Reverend Arthur James Barton, D.D., general superintendent of the Missouri Baptist General Association and chairman of the executive committee of the Anti-Saloon League of America, speech delivered in support of Prohibition, noted in "Americana," The American Mercury, *January 1928, p. 49.*

According to the W.C.T.U. and Senator Edwards, of New Jersey, the Volstead Act fathers a practically new species of man. The ladies of the former say that he is a defender of youth and the protector of the American Home; Senator Edwards says that he is a grafting thug and double-crosser. Both of these views of the Prohibition agent reveal colored glasses, those of the Senator being Turkey red, and those of the good women cerulean. . . .

So much grotesque nonsense has been written about him by both the wets and the drys that it seems high time that somebody should try to make a more or less unbiased appraisal of him. To be entirely fair is, of course, impossible. All of us see through different lenses, and the particular kind that I wear may not correct astigmatism, but at all events I do not see the agent as either the drys or the wets see him. The Prohibitionists defend him, world without end. They believe that he is, and must be by virtue of his office, a thorough-going Prohibitionist. It is not so. He is not a Prohibitionist, as the term is generally used; nor is he a sopping wet. In this day of extremes, that may sound incredible, but it remains true. The average agent is no more concerned about the merits or demerits of Prohibition than the policeman on the beat is concerned about the propositions of Plato's "Republic."

From a description and analysis of federal Prohibition enforcement by Homer Turner in "Notes of a Prohibition Agent," in The American Mercury, *April 1928, p. 385.*

Formerly these tribunals [federal courts] were of exceptional dignity, and the efficiency and dispatch of their criminal business commanded wholesome fear and respect. . . . The effect of the huge volume of liquor prosecutions, which has come to these courts under prohibition, has injured their dignity, impaired their efficiency, and endangered the wholesome respect for them which once obtained.

Report of the Wickersham Commission on Prohibition, 1929.

The Nineteenth Amendment brought the right to vote and heralded equal opportunity for women in all walks of life—even moonshining. *(Minnesota Historical Society/St. Paul Daily News)*

Jo's was located in the basement of a tenement building. In the low, narrow room, cheap, brightly colored tables, rickety chairs, a few booths and an old piano were crowded as tight as they could be jammed. Liquor was not served, but it was assumed that the patrons would bring it, and order sandwiches and ginger ale. The place was usually crowded and always informal. Girls making a first visit to the place could be sure that the men beside whom they found themselves seated would assume that they were a party for the evening and night. If the girls were first at a table, they were sure to be joined. From time to time someone started to play the piano and people danced in the crowded aisles between the tables with whatever strangers they happened to be sitting besides. The proprietor stood by the door, greeting everybody, eyeing all newcomers and making announcements. . . .

These people had two preoccupations—sex and drink. In the early years of the decade, free love and promiscuity has been a sufficient subject for talk and entertainment in most groups. By 1930, promiscuity was tame and homosexuality had become the expected thing. One girl who came nightly was the joke of the place because she was trying so hard to be a Lesbian,

but when she got drunk she forgot and let the men dance with her.

Recollections of a Prohibition-era speakeasy, from Caroline Ware, Greenwich Village 1920–1930 *(1935), p. 253.*

I never did like to fool with aliens. I sold my boat to Garcia. He rents it out to fishing parties now. Me and Garcia used to run in good loads—Scotch, rye, gin, rum, champagne, wine. Key West was one of the few towns in the country where you could get good stuff that wasn't watered.

Me and Garcia had a good reputation—could practically guarantee delivery. That gave us good business. We always went around and got up orders and collected in advance before we made a trip. It ain't but eighty miles over to Cuba, but that Gulf Stream gets mighty rough for small boats. I've crossed the channel in a storm with only a couple inches freeboard. We moved at night. Sometimes the customs pushed us so close we had to drop the load overboard. Then all they could hold us for was running without lights. When they would get on our trail we'd make a run for shallow water where we could lose 'em, or at least drop the load and pick it up later on. Used to hate to have to throw stuff over in deep water. A good friend of mine got drowned trying to save a few extra bottles.

Captain Antonio, bootlegger, as told to writer Stetson Kennedy in 1938, in Banks, First Person America *(1980), pp. 46–47.*

Listen, plenty goes on in a drug store. In Prohibition they used to peddle booze. I never done it myself. I never went in for that stuff, but I see plenty of it. Well, why not? A shot of good rye is the best medicine yet for whatever ails you. The counter man has the blanks, see, and if he's in cahoots with a doc who wants to pick up a little extra, he'll sell a book of blanks, signed by the doc, to a legger, who fills in for how many cases he wants to take out, and it goes under the prescriptions. On an R.X. you're covered, see, and if any questions asked, it's the doc takes the rap. An R.X. is the prescription blank—comes from "recipe"—that's Latin, "Ray-cee-pay," means "Take of This" so many grams, etc., Latin, you know.

May Swenson, drugstore employee, remembering Prohibition-era business during interview of March 6, 1939, from American Life Histories: Manuscripts from The Federal Writers' Project 1936–1940, *"The American Memory," Library of Congress web site, URL: http://memory.loc.gov.*

Joe Einstein was not what you would call wacky, but he wasn't anything like his famous namesake either. He was just one of the kids in my old gang around Brook Avenue.

. . . This is during Prohibition. I owned a store on Claremont way, renting out tuxedos, and whenever Joe is in the neighborhood he drops in to see me. I wasn't very anxious to have him around, knowing the racket he was in, but it seems he took a grudge against all his old pals except me; he figured he could trust me, I guess, and he used to tell me all his troubles. At that time he went around with a car collecting beer bills; a job for a real tough guy, and Joe had to make out he was a lot tougher than he really was.

He kept flashing a roll and telling me to go around to the speaks with him: Come on, it's all on the house, he would say. The way it worked was like this. When he collected, say, two hundred bucks in one place, he'd leave about ten there. Gimme a beer, he'd tell the owner, or just let him ring it up like that. The Dutchman figured it was a good policy; every businessman gives out a little something to keep goodwill, something like a discount. Naturally, Joe couldn't take it all out in drinks; he needed a little help. Besides, it gave him a chance to prove to me what a bigshot he was, and he always liked to show off.

Sam Goldstein, interview of December 12, 1938, from American Life Histories: Manuscripts from the Federal Writers' Project, 1936–1940, *"The American Memory," Library of Congress web site, URL: http://memory.loc.gov.*

A frequent visitor to the Grand Terrace was the big man himself, Al Capone, who went around town in a seven-ton armored limousine. He liked to come into a club with his henchmen, order all the doors closed, and have the band play his requests. He was free with hundred dollar tips.

"Scarface" got along well with musicians. Only one I ever heard of who had a run-in with the Mr. Big of the syndicates was Mezz Mezzrow, who was working in a night spot in suburban Burnham. It seems Al's youngest brother, Mitzi, went for one of the good-looking entertainers with Mezz's outfit, and Scarface ordered her fired. Mezz argued back while half a dozen of Al's henchmen stood around laughing at the nerve of this musician arguing with Mr. Six-Shooter. Finally Al started laughing too and said, "The kid's got guts."

Another band leader who had considerable contact with the Capone group in those days was Lucky Millinder, who worked for Ralph Capone in a spot controlled by the syndicate in Cicero, headquarters of the Capone gang. Others who held jobs in Capone-controlled clubs were the late Tiny Parham and the late Jimmie Noone, one of the greatest of all jazz clarinetists.

Louis Armstrong once changed managers and was threatened with gangster violence. After that he hired two bodyguards who protected him on and off the job for many months.

Earl Hines, undated interview in Shapiro and Hentoff, Hear Me Talkin' To Ya *(1955), pp. 130–131.*

The Red Scare

You couldn't have asked for anyone more regular than Peters. He was an eminently safe citizen. Although not rich himself, he never chafed under the realization that there were others who possessed great wealth. In fact the thought gave him rather a comfortable feeling.

Furthermore, he was one of the charter members of the war. Long before President Wilson saw the light, Peters was advocating the abolition of German from the public-school curriculum.

...But one night he made a slip. It was ever so tiny a slip, but in comparison with it De Maupassant's famous piece of string was barren of consequences. Shortly before the United States entered the war, Peters made a speech at a meeting of the Civic League in his home town. His subject was: "Interurban Highways: Their Development in the Past and Their Possibilities for the Future." So far, 100 percent American. But, in the course of his talk, he happened to mention the fact that war, as an institution, has almost always had a most injurious effect on public improvements of all kinds....Then he went on to discuss the comparative values of macadam and wood blocks for paving.

Time went by...and Peters bought Liberty Bonds. He didn't join the Army, it is true, but, then, neither did James M. Beck, and it is an open secret that Mr. Beck was for the war.... He did not even know that there was an investigation going on in Washington to determine the uses to which German propaganda money had been put. That is, he didn't know it until he opened his newspaper one morning and, with that uncanny precipitation with which a man's eye lights on his own name, discovered that he had been mentioned in the dispatches. At first he thought it might be an honor list of Liberty Bond holders, but a glance at the headline chilled that young hope in his breast. It read as follows:

PRO-GERMAN LIST BARED
BY ARMY SLEUTH
Prominent Obstructionists
Named at Senate Probe

And then came the list. Peters' eye ran instinctively down to the place where, in what seemed to him to be 24-point Gothic caps, was blazoned the name "Horace W. Peters, Pacifist Lecturer, Matriculated at Germantown (Pa.) Military School." Above his name was that of Emma Goldman, "Anarchist." Below came that of Fritz von Papen, "agent of the Imperial German Government in America," and Jeremiah O'Leary, "Irish and Pro-German Agitator."

Peters was stunned....
Robert Benchley, humorist and drama critic, "The Making of a Red," The Nation, *March 15, 1919, reprinted in* The Nation 1865–1990 *(1990), pp. 24–25.*

A leg lay in the path to the house next to theirs, another leg farther up the street. A head was on the roof of yet another house. As we walked across it was difficult to avoid stepping on bloody hunks of human being. The man had been torn apart, fairly blown to butcher's meat. It was curiously without horror.
Alice Roosevelt Longworth, describing the scene at the Palmer House bombing of June 2, 1919, from Crowded Hours *(1933), pp. 282–283.*

...800 men were imprisoned for 3 to 6 days in a dark, windowless, narrow corridor running around the big central areaway of the city's antiquated Federal Building; they slept on the bare stone floor at night, in the heavy heat that welled sickeningly up to the low roof, just over their heads; they were shoved and jostled about by heavy-handed policemen; they were forbidden the chance to perform a makeshift shave; they were compelled to stand in long lines for access to the solitary drinking fountain and the one toilet, they were denied all food for 20 hours, and after that they were fed on what their families brought in, and they were refused all communication with relatives or attorneys.
Frederick R. Barkley, "Jailing Radicals in Detroit," The Nation *(1920), p. 136.*

Advance information on the activities of the Communist Party revealed that its emissaries were in many cities, boring into labor organizations which hitherto have been noted for their conservatism. Literature obtained by Federal agents made it apparent that the Communist leaders were concentrating on plans to obtain control of well-founded union labor groups. Through this method they were to exert their power politically and put forward candidates which would be regarded by government officials as nothing more than destructive elements within the present government.

The Communist labor group was said to have directed its propaganda more generally among the foreign element of citizenry. From several sources, federal agents gleaned information that the Communist Labor Party was appealing to the foreign workers with the argument that the present government was unfriendly to them and that their rights would never be respected by the appointed authorities. The insertion of the word "labor" in the name of this party was regarded by officials as only a subterfuge, the leaders realizing that it would lend strength to their argument among foreigners.
Associated Press dispatch, datelined Washington, January 2, 1920.

Like a prairie fire, the blaze of revolution was sweeping over every American institution of law and order a year ago. It was eating its way into the homes of the American workman, its sharp tongues of revolutionary heat were licking the altars of the churches, leaping into the belfry of the school bell, crawling into the sacred corners of American homes, seeking to replace marriage vows with libertine laws, burning up the foundations of society.

. . . By stealing, murder, and lies, Bolshevism has looted Russia not only of its material strength, but of its moral force. A small clique of outcasts from the East Side of New York has attempted this, with what success we all know. Because a disreputable alien—Leon Bronstein, the man who now calls himself Trotzky—can inaugurate a reign of terror from his throne room in the Kremlin; because this lowest of all types known to New York can sleep in the Czar's bed, while hundreds of thousands in Russia are without food or shelter, should America be swayed by such doctrines?

Such a question, it would seem, should receive but one answer from America.

Attorney General A. Mitchell Palmer, "The Case Against the Reds," Forum, February 1920, p. 173.

Around in Broad Street the Stock Exchange was running full blast. Trading centered about the Redding post at the center of the pit and William H. Remick, President of the institution, stood nearby chatting with one of the Governors. He heard the terrible detonation, saw the glass raining everywhere, listened a second to cries and groans and excited shouting and running feet, then said quickly:

"I think we had better stop trading for the day."

"Remick Nips Panic on Stock Exchange," account of the September 16, 1920, Wall Street bombing in the New York Times, *September 17, 1920, p. 1.*

The United States has never developed a true proletariat, which often shows fine generosities and chivalries. Instead, it has simply developed two bourgeoisies, an upper and a lower. Both are narrow, selfish, corrupt, timorous, docile, and ignoble; both fear ideas as they fear the plague; both are in favor of "law and order," i.e., of harsh laws, unintelligently administered. The viewpoint of each is precisely that of a corner groceryman. There is, on the one hand, none of the fine fury and frenzy, the romantic daring, the gaudy imagination of the true proletarian, and on the other hand, there is none of the tolerance and serenity of the true aristocrat.

Think of how poltroonishly the upper bourgeoisie reacted to the mere hint of radicalism two years ago! Great captains of industry trembled and blubbered like children; the whole government ran amuck; thousands of innocent persons were pursued like horse thieves. And all to put down a movement that was never clearly organized, and had no efficient leaders and no money, and was without the slightest public support! The boobs, in fact, were against it as violently as the trembling captains. They always are, and for a reason lately plainly stated by Secretary Colby; they hope to rise and believe that they *will* rise—they want the loot protected so that it will be still there when they come to collect their share of it. Until this universal belief in prosperity around the corner dies out in the American people, there can be no serious radical movement in this country.

H. L. Mencken, "Optimistic Note," November 29, 1920, reprinted in On Politics: A Carnival of Buncombe *(1960), pp. 40–41.*

The will-o'-the-wisp of all breeds of socialism is that they contemplate a motivation of human animals by altruism alone. It necessitates a bureaucracy of the entire population, in which, having obliterated the economic stimulation of each member, the fine gradations of character and ability are to be arranged in relative authority by ballot or more likely by a Tammany Hall or a Bolshevist party, or some other form of tyranny. The proof of the futility of these ideas as a stimulation of the development and activity of the individual does not lie alone in the ghastly failure of Russia, but it also lies in our own failure in attempts at nationalized industry.

. . . We in America have had too much experience of life to fool ourselves into pretending that all men are equal in ability, in character, in intelligence, in ambition. That was part of the clap-trap of the French Revolution. We have grown to understand that all we can hope to assure to the individual through government is liberty, justice, intellectual welfare, equality of opportunity, and stimulation to service.

Herbert Hoover, from American Individualism *(1922), p. 38–39.*

If I had my way with these ornery wild-eyed Socialists and IWWs, I would stand them up before a firing squad and save space on our ships.

From an undated sermon by the evangelist Billy Sunday, quoted in Parrish, Anxious Decades *(1992), p. 132.*

The Nineteenth Amendment

The same patriotism which induced women to enter industry during the war should induce them to vacate their positions after war.

Undated, official postwar statement of the AFL Central Federated Union, quoted in Parrish, Anxious Decades *(1992), p. 141.*

Women are too much inclined to follow in the footsteps of men, to try to think as men think, to try to solve the general problems of life as men solve them. If after attaining their freedom, women accept conditions in the spheres of government, industry, art, morals and religion as they find them, they will be but taking a leaf out of man's book. The woman is not needed to do man's work. She is not needed to think men's thoughts. She need not fear that the masculine mind, almost universally dominant, will fail to take care of its own. Her mission is not to enhance the masculine spirit, but to express the feminine; hers is not to preserve a man-made world, but to create a human world by the infusion of the feminine element into all of its activities.

Woman must not accept; she must challenge. . . .

Margaret Sanger, from Woman and the New Race *(1920), reprinted as "The Right to One's Body," in* The American Reader, *(1958) pp. 248–249.*

Hurrah! And vote for suffrage!

Harry Burn, while casting the deciding vote for passage of the Nineteenth Amendment, August 18, 1920.

Those are not Greek gods—they are false and you are as false as these plaster statues. . . . You once were wild here! Don't let them tame you. . . . If my art is symbolic of any one thing, it is symbolic of the freedom of woman. . . .

Isadora Duncan, inflammatory speech delivered at Symphony Hall, Boston, during her tour of the United States in the fall of 1922, from Seroff, The Real Isadora *(1971), p. 327.*

Isadora ain't foolin' me any. She talks about art. Huh! I've seen a lot of these twisters and I know as much about art as any man in America, but I never went to see these dancers for art's sake. No, sir, I'll bet that ninety percent of men who go to see those so-called classical dancers just say they think it's artistic to fool their wives. . . . No, sir, these nude dancers don't get by me. If she goes pulling off her clothes and throwin' them in the air, as she is said to have done in Boston, there's going to be somebody getting a ride in the wagon.

Lew Shanks, mayor of Indianapolis, statement to the press while preparing for the arrival of Isadora Duncan during her 1922 U.S. tour, from Seroff, The Real Isadora, *(1971), p. 329.*

But I do really believe that woman suffrage marks the beginning of some sort of revolution.

. . . I have often talked with Mrs. Emily Newell Blair, the very able and charming resident member of the Democratic National Committee in Washington, about the way men dreaded a change in politics when the women came in, and yet were disappointed when the change didn't come.

. . . "What the men expected, I suppose," she said to me, "was a terrible old-fashioned house cleaning, the kind of a rumpus their mothers used to make in the spring just about the time the first robin came—carpets up, dust in every room, all the family in flight. I clean house with a vacuum cleaner, don't you? My husband hardly knows the cleaning's going on. But it is. That's the way it seems to me women are breaking into politics. A room at a time."

Florence Jaffray Hurst Harriman, From Pinafores to Politics *(1923), p. 351.*

The pioneer feminists were hard-hitting individuals, and the modern young woman admires them for their courage—even while she judges them for their zealotry and their inartistic methods. Furthermore, she pays all honor to them, for they fought her battle. But *she* does not want to wear their mantle (indeed, she thinks they should have been buried in it), and she has to smile at those women who wear it to-day—with the battle cry still on their lips. The worst of the fight is over, yet this second generation of feminists are still throwing hand grenades. They bear a grudge against men, either secretly or openly; of publicity; they rant about equality when they might better prove their ability. Yet it is these women—the ones who do more talking than acting— on whom the average man focuses his microscope when he sits down to dissect the "new woman." For like his less educated brethren, he labors under the delusion that there are only two types of women, the creature of instinct who is content to be a "home-maker" and the "sterile intellectual" who cares solely about "expressing herself"—home and children be damned.

Dorothy Dunbar Bromley, "Feminist—New Style," in Harpers Magazine, *October 1927, p. 552.*

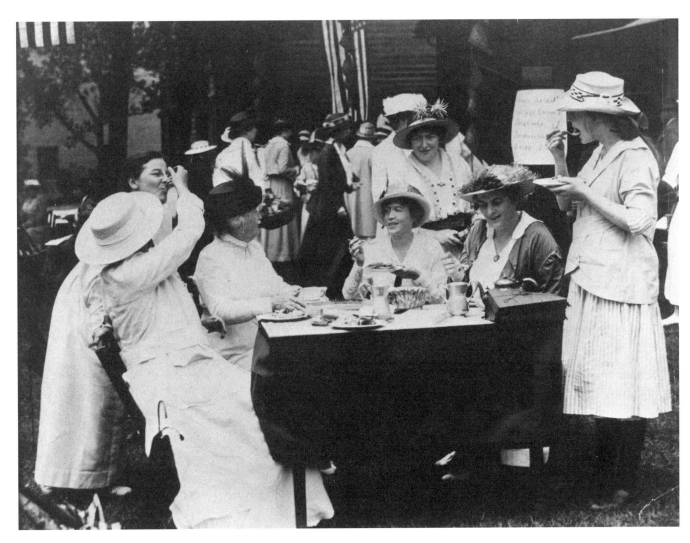

The Minnesota League of Women Voters holds its annual Melting Pot Fete in 1925. *(Minnesota Historical Society)*

At the University of Minnesota, girl students linger after lectures to talk to the instructor. During class they sit near the professor's desk, giggle merrily at his pedagogical jests, smile understandingly at his well-known eccentricities, make their pretty eyes look deep and sympathetic when he comes to the point of his discourse. Thus do the wily co-eds, whose actual intelligence measures but 25 on a scale of 100, compensate for a ten-point deficiency in intellect, and extract grades equal to those attained by charmless male students whose measure of intelligence on the same scale is 35. Authority for this condition is Dr. George Thomas, president of the University of Utah, who lately cautioned his faculty members to guard against such insidious influence, prevalent in most co-educational institutions.

"Coy Co-Eds," item in Time *magazine, October 10, 1927, p. 29.*

3
Depression
1921

World War I and the peace that followed brought about fundamental changes in the economy of the United States. The customary wartime manufacturing boom had resulted from a sharp rise in domestic demand and foreign exports. The labor force enjoyed full employment, and employers benefited from wartime wage controls, which had the effect of increasing their profit margins. Price controls kept the cost of living stable for consumers.

Things changed rapidly after the armistice. With the nations of Europe in a state of economic chaos, demand for exports from the United States fell—a situation worsened by already high tariffs that the federal government placed on imported goods. The overproduction built into the American economy touched off a depression that grew more severe through the winter and spring of 1921. New investment and business activity slowed while high inventories caused a backlog of unsold goods in manufacturing industries. Consumer prices rose sharply with the lifting of price controls, and workers saw their hard-earned dollars losing value. At the same time, the arrival of veterans in the labor market caused a surplus of workers. To compensate, the New York Central Railroad imposed a pay cut of 22.5 percent on its 43,000 workers. In October, the Ford Motor Company closed its plants and forced its dealers to take delivery of 175,000 surplus automobiles. Shoe and textile manufacturers in the Northeast also suffered, and the coal mining industry saw a drop in prices and profits from which it would not recover for the rest of the decade.

The depression of 1921 hit hardest at the country's farmers. During the war, the agricultural sector benefited from stable prices; the government had done its part by supporting the price of staple crops such as wheat until May 1920. Mechanization of plowing, seeding, harvesting, and other chores once carried out by manual labor had increased farm production and efficiency. Income rose even faster than production, and by the end of the war many farmers were speculating on increasingly valuable land. Believing they had nothing to lose, they bought new goods and acreages on the credit confidently extended to them by small-town bankers. Land prices rose steadily until they reached a postwar peak in 1919.

Then a sharp drop in food exports to the bankrupt nations of Europe, and the end of government price supports in early 1920, touched off a devastating farm bust that would last for nearly two decades. Their incomes falling (even as they brought in a bumper crop in 1920), millions of farmers heavily mortgaged for their land and machinery saw it foreclosed and repossessed by the banks. Determined to fight inflation, the Republican administrations of the 1920s would do little to keep commodity prices up or ease interest rates. The war was over, and the farmers were on their own.

Fueling the agricultural depression were changes in dietary habits in the United States, particularly in the cities. The discovery of the vitamin had completely changed society's outlook on health and on diet. Everyday domestic menus grew more varied, as the customary diet of starch and meat was extended with fruits, vegetables, and dairy products. People were also eating less—thin was stylish, Victorian plumpness was out. These food trends did benefit some, as new-fashioned "truck farmers" prospered by supplying fresh vegetables and fruits year-round to city markets and grocery stores. But farmers relying on staples such as wheat and corn saw increased production and stiffer competition in foreign markets depress their prices and their income. At the same time, new fabrics were replacing cotton, the country's basic clothing fabric and the economic cornerstone of the South. The price of cotton sank to 10 cents a pound in 1921—a quarter of its value in the previous year. As prices continued their slide, thousands of farmers in the South and Midwest left their land and moved to the cities.

By 1921, farmers and farm-state representatives were demanding action from Washington, and the agricultural depression was inspiring a protest movement that gave new life to farmers' advocacy groups. A revived Grange (also known as the Patrons of Husbandry), a group of rural radicals that had peaked in the 1870s, now stumped for a system of easy credit and the formation of sales cooperatives through which farmers might attain better, more stable, prices for their produce. Since 1902, the American Society of Equity had been calling for the government to store and hold crops out of the market in times of low prices (a mechanism that would be put into effect later in the decade, without much positive result). Allied to the Society of Equity was the National Non-Partisan League, founded in 1916 for the purpose of socializing American farming. Leaders of the Non-Partisan League called for state ownership of storage elevators, mills, and rural warehouses; state credit banks; public hail insurance; and tax breaks for improvements to the farmer's land, equipment, and buildings.

The Non-Partisan League was advancing a radical program, and despite the hard times it gained only a small following in its home in the Upper Midwest. Far more influential was the federal statute known as the Smith–Lever Act of 1914. This act had appropriated $5 million of the government's money for extension projects, in which scientific advances in the laboratory were practically applied to farming. To carry out the work, farm bureaus in each state were set up to coordinate the work of county extension agents. The program proved so successful that in 1919 a national American Farm Bureau Federation was organized in Chicago. As Warren Harding was settling into the White House, the American Farm Bureau Federation, headed by director Gray Silver, was using its muscle to lobby the new administration and the U.S. Congress for price supports and other forms of public relief.

A Test of the New Administration

The response to the economic slide became the public's first measure of the new administration of President Warren Harding, and Harding would not disappoint those who had supported him. With the friendly cooperation of the 67th Congress, which opened on April 11, 1921, he held faithfully to the probusiness sentiments he had expressed during his 1920 campaign. At the head of the agenda was a reform of the complex, jury-rigged federal budget process. One of the first laws enacted by the 67th Congress, signed by President Harding on June 10, was the Budget and Accounting Act, which provided for a centralized budgeting system, with an appointed director of the budget and comptroller general to prepare and supervise a uniform federal budget. As his first comptroller, Harding named John Raymond McCarl, executive secretary of the Republican Congressional Committee; for budget director he appointed Charles Dawes, a Chicago banker and purchasing agent for the American Expeditionary Force during World War I. In December 1921, with Dawes's advice, Harding would submit a notably small budget of $3.5 billion.

The president next confronted veterans demanding "adjusted compensation" for their underpaid services during the war. In deference to this large, influential lobby, the Senate was giving serious consideration to back pay for veterans at the daily rate of $1 ($1.25 for service overseas) or a paid-up, 20-year life insurance policy to an equivalent face value. Seeking to keep federal spending at a minimum, Harding appeared personally in Congress to argue against this "Bonus Bill" and saw it voted down during that first session in 1921 and in the next year as well.

The approbation earned from the business community for stalling and then defeating the Bonus Bill turned to sincere gratitude on the adoption of tax measures proposed by Treasury Secretary Andrew Mellon. With Mellon's guidance, Congress passed the Revenue Act of 1921, repealed the excess profits tax, and reduced the top marginal tax rate on personal incomes from 65 to 50 percent. To repay corporations for their excess tax payments in the past, the federal treasury began handing out refunds (notably to several of Mellon's own corporations). To make up the consequent budget shortfall, the government raised the tax on net profits from 10 to 12.5 percent, doubled the stamp tax on documents, began taxing bank checks at a rate of two cents each, raised postage for postcards to two cents, and set a new license tax on automobiles.

The administration also responded to the complaints of farmers and to the lobbying of southern and midwestern farm bloc representatives (a generic term for members of Congress from agricultural states) by signing a new "Emergency Tariff" schedule set by Congress in May 1921. The 28 new tariffs and an outright embargo on imported dyestuffs and chemicals were reluctantly supported by conservative Republicans in Congress, who realized that high tariffs they generally favored on manufactured goods were likely to follow.

Soon after the passage of the Emergency Tariff Act, a comprehensive overhaul of the tariff system began winding through the Senate and House. Progress was slow; debate was muted by the exclusion of Democrats from secret meetings of the House Ways and Means Committee, where the bill originated. Finally, in the spring of 1922, under the guidance of Senator Porter McCumber of North Dakota, the bill appeared on the floor of the Senate accompanied by 2,082 amendments, each meeting the demands of an industry or constituency wanting some government-backed market protection for their product. Setting the highest tariff rates in the country's history, the Fordney-McCumber Act passed both houses and was signed by President Harding on September 21, 1922.

The Fordney-McCumber Act opened a new era of protectionism, in large part prompted by manufacturing industries that had met wartime demand with their profits limited and now sought more assured profit margins in peacetime markets. The act also echoed industry's new concepts of "scientific management" in its attempt to create a mechanism that would automatically set and steer tariff rates at maximum efficiency. As part of this effort, a bureaucratic contraption known as the Tariff Commission would set the value of imports on the basis of the cost of production of the same goods in the United States. In this way, it was hoped, Congress would not have to subject tariff schedules to the posturings of politics, the lobbying of business interests, and the fickleness of voters.

For all its careful adjustments, however, the act effectively halted the country's foreign trade. Despite the intensive efforts of the Commerce Department under Secretary Herbert Hoover to promote U.S. goods abroad, American manufacturers as well as farmers found it increasingly difficult to sell overseas, where retaliatory tariffs would be quickly put into effect. By stifling imports, the act also made it difficult for European countries to repay their war debts to the United States.

For the time being, it did not seem to matter. Secretary Mellon's friendly tax reforms and a booming market at home satisfied business owners and shareholders. Free markets remained an attractive theory, generally unpracticed, while the protectionist sentiment smartly reflected the nation's desire to be rid of foreign entanglements, military as well as economic. The sentiment would survive the most disruptive event of the decade, the stock market crash of 1929, and prevail again with the passage of the Smoot-Hawley Act, another high tariff that ensured steep duties on U.S. exports, continued protection for the domestic market, and the Great Depression.

HERBERT HOOVER AND SCIENTIFIC MANAGEMENT

Postwar depression reached its depths in the late summer of 1921. On August 16, the Labor Department released an official estimate of 5,735,000 unemployed, the highest number of unemployed workers since the end of the war. The economic problems turned the spotlight on Herbert Hoover, the new secretary of commerce, who was already known and admired for his success as coordinator of the American Relief Administration, which had saved several European countries from mass starvation during and after the war. In the summer of 1921, Hoover raised almost $100 million for food relief to Russia (with the condition that the new Bolshevik government release all Americans held prisoner as a result of the failed military operations against the Red Army during the Russian Civil War). More than 1 million tons of food were distributed through a chaotic and hostile Bolshevik regime; the agency also carried out a vaccination program against typhoid, cholera, and smallpox.

Now it seemed time for Hoover to design and carry out a relief program at home. In September 1921, the President's Conference on Unemployment was convened, with Hoover acting as chairman. Finally having a chance to apply his organizing skill and energy on a national scale, Hoover advanced his philosophy of self-reliance and individualism coupled with respect for public service. To ease the effects of the depression, he proposed a cut in prices that might subtract from corporate bottom lines while boosting demand on the part of the workers. (Over the next several years, he would organize more conferences on child welfare, labor relations, housing, and foreign trade.) Hoover also proposed, and Congress passed, a system of public works at a time when Republican politicians were resisting such programs as unnecessary and wasteful. Although the business sector distrusted such cooperative public programs, Hoover's independence from standard Republican dogma and his management skills raised the public's esteem for him and for his administration.

Taylorism

Actions taken for the sake of private industry left no doubt among business owners that Hoover and the Commerce Department would be helpful to their interests. The department played an important role in the development of new industries such as aviation and radio broadcasting. Through the Bureau of Standards and the Bureau of Foreign and Domestic Commerce, Hoover sponsored an effort to make the country's business more efficient and productive, a campaign that was largely inspired by the new doctrine of scientific management, as invented and promoted by a remarkable business philosopher named Frederick Winslow Taylor.

Born in 1856 in Germantown, Pennsylvania, Taylor was a graduate of the private Phillips Exeter Academy and, to all expectations, headed for a clean, clerical, and mundane career that would place him somewhere in the comfortable middle class. But instead of following the destiny of his birth, he accepted a position with a small Philadelphia machine shop and then, in 1878, the Midvale Steel Company. While undertaking an engineering course at the Stevens Institute of Technology, he devised very thorough studies of workers and their productivity at Midvale. Analyzing each separate and minute component of their actions, he drew up new standards of productivity in order to maximize the company's efficiency.

Taylor opened a consulting firm in 1893 and then applied the new doctrines of Taylorism at the Bethlehem Steel Company in a position of his own invention—efficiency expert. Taylor measured each process, timed each worker, examined every tool. Cutting tools were tempered at a precise temperature (1,725 degrees Fahrenheit) for longest-lasting sharpness. Coal and ore shovelers had their shovelfuls measured, analyzed, and readjusted (to a rate of 21 pounds each) for maximum productivity. Taylor carried out thousands of minute experiments and devised new methods of "time study" that he claimed could be applied to any industry and any job and bring about increased productivity, lower costs, enhanced benefits for workers and, ultimately, a workers' and consumers' utopia.

Taylor died in 1915, but Taylorism and scientific management survived him. It proved a stunning success in war industries and was credited with playing an important role in winning World War I. Taylorism particularly suited the growing and increasingly mechanized industries that would flourish during the 1920s—autos, rubber, chemicals, and steel. It was applied to the academic professions; it showed up in doctors' offices, libraries, stenography pools, newspaper pressrooms, and the administrations of large cities such as Philadelphia. Taylorism was taught at business schools and college engineering departments across the country, and thousands of companies set up their own efficiency experts and personnel managers to run time studies and apply the theories of scientific management.

THE KU KLUX KLAN REVIVED

As the 1920s began, the remembered nightmare of World War I and the worsening economy turned the United States toward isolationism. The Red Scare of 1919 and early 1920 had provided thousands of convenient scapegoats in the persons of anarchists and labor leaders, but antisocialism among the urban population was only part of the story. Small towns and rural areas were undergoing mechanization, depopulation, and an economic depression, and many rural people were questioning the changes and dealing with difficult adjustments. For several million of them, a hitherto defunct secret society of southern chauvinists provided an answer.

The Ku Klux Klan had been organized just after the Civil War by a small group of former Confederate officers for the purpose of reviving and maintaining the culture of the antebellum South as well as white, Protestant supremacy. Although the Klan of the Old South had died out by the end of the 1800s, it was later revived by the self-designated Imperial Wizard, Colonel William Joseph Simmons of Atlanta.

Simmons was a Spanish-American War veteran, who had never passed the rank of private, and a promoter of fraternal organizations that attracted members with brotherhood, secrecy, and ritual. After reading about the Reconstruction Klan and seeing D. W. Griffith's Civil War epic *The Birth of a Nation,* he was inspired to bring about a revival. On Thanksgiving night, 1915, Simmons collected 34 followers and brought them to the slopes of Stone Mountain, Georgia, for initiation into the patriotic, secret, and benevolent order of the Knights of the Ku Klux Klan.

The stated purpose of the organization was to promote morality, virtue, patriotism, Protestantism, and Klan-defined Americanism—and, incidentally, to make money. According to the Klan's original charter, members were forbidden to profit by it. But by 1920, membership was holding steady at only a few thousand, and the new Klan was operating at a loss out of a bleak, small office in Atlanta. Simmons had hoped to support the effort from initiation fees and from the sale of memorabilia, but he had little success until meeting Edward Y. Clarke and Elizabeth Tyler, skilled promoters and fund-raisers trained in good causes such as the Anti-Saloon League and Near East Relief. The couple accepted Simmons's offer to promote the new Klan, formed the Southern Publicity Association (SPA), and went to work.

Clarke and Tyler hired a small army of kleagles (salespersons) to offer new klecktokens (memberships) at $10. The kleagles earned $4 for each new member, while $2 went to the Klan's treasury and $4 went to Clarke and Tyler. Dues to the local klavern (meeting place) amounted to $1 a month. To attract new dues payers, the kleagles exploited the general social malaise, a postwar feeling of dislocation, the widespread suspicion of foreigners and immigrants, and an appeal to patriotism.

A new wardrobe and vocabulary were created for the campaign. Leaders wore robes of multicolored satin and silk, while followers wore simple white cotton. Simmons invented new terms such as klavern, kludd (chaplain), and konklave (meeting). The Searchlight Publishing Company turned out newspapers and journals; a Gate City Manufacturing Company sold robes, hoods, and other gear. In the year and a half after Simmons hired the Southern Publicity Association, the Klan attracted about 1 million new members, and from their

Ku Klux Klan members in full-sheeted regalia parade in Virginia on the night of March 18, 1922. *(Library of Congress/National Photo Company Collection)*

klecktoken percentage, Tyler and Clarke made as much as $40,000 a month. The SPA and the kleagles brought the Klan to nearly every region of the country, including the Far West (in response to a fear of Mexicans and the IWW) and the Northeast (in response to a fear of Jews, eastern Europeans, French Canadians, and anarchists). Detroit, Chicago, Indianapolis, Columbus, Pittsburgh, and Cincinnati held a burgeoning population of Klansmen and Klanswomen.

The Klan was known for silent parades, midnight meetings on hilltops and in forest groves, and whippings. The Klan stood for white supremacy, as well as opposition to Catholics and Jews, and it chose its targets accordingly. In small towns, Klan members carried out summary justice against blacks suspected of making advances toward white women; divorcees; suspected anarchists; adulterers and loose women. Klan whipping squads set out after midnight to hunt down their targets and carry out beatings, tar-and-featherings, and lynchings. Not all attacks were ideological; many Klan members found the hooded disguise convenient for attacking hated neighbors or business competitors.

The organization took off in the South in late 1921 (at one point, in Birmingham, Alabama, the local Klan included more than 10,000 members). An important reason for the success was the all-encompassing nature of Klan membership. The Klan held marches, meetings, picnics, and debates, as well as cross-burnings and whippings. The Klan was a mutual aid society; its members helped each other to the detriment of people it saw as enemies and outsiders.

The rise of the 1920s Klan brought about opposition; most of it, of course, came from intellectuals and liberals of the cities. A series of investigative reports by the New York *World* in September 1921 revealed that the Klan had carried out killings, mutilations, burnings with acid, kidnappings, and countless beatings. The *World* series prompted an investigation by the U.S. Congress, as well as a windfall in new membership applications for the Southern Publicity Association. After the articles appeared, Colonel Simmons happily consented to Congressional interrogation. On the witness stand, he insisted that the Klan was nothing but a fraternal organization, and held that any violence carried out in its name had to be the work of impostors bent on undermining a peace-loving and patriotic organization. Simmons gave such a convincing, disarming performance that the entire matter was dropped.

The investigation by the *World* did turn out one significant fact: in 1919, Tyler and Clarke had been arrested for improper conduct in an Atlanta brothel. The revelation turned many upstanding Klan members against their leadership and allowed Hiram Evans, Grand Dragon of the realm of Texas, to overthrow Simmons in November 1922. Simmons was named Emperor of the Invisible Empire and, in effect, kicked upstairs with a paltry monthly stipend of $1,000.

As the klavern crowds grew, and the parades of white-robed figures stretched for blocks down hundreds of Middle American Main Streets, it seemed there was no stopping the Klan's spreading influence in small-town government, society, religion, and business. No state boasted a bigger or more powerful Klan than Indiana, where many of the state legislators and officials were Klan-supported and Klan-approved. On July 4, 1923, an immense crowd of 200,000 people assembled in Kokomo, Indiana, where Imperial Wizard Evans assisted in the inauguration of David C. Stephenson as the new Grand Dragon of the Invisible Empire for the Realm of Indiana.

An ambitious fellow, Stephenson bragged about his close friendship with Indiana governor Ed Jackson, his direct telephone lines to the White House, and his plans for a run at a Senate seat and perhaps the Republican presidential nomination in 1928. But his power and ambition drew him into a bitter, though hidden, conflict with Hiram Evans. Seeing Stephenson as a threat to southern domination of the organization, Evans and the national Klan headquarters in Atlanta had flatly opposed Stephenson's plan to buy Valparaiso University in Gary, Indiana, and turn it into a "Klan kollege." Evans and Stephenson also feuded over control of the *Fiery Cross,* the northern Klan publication, and over the representation of northern Klan leaders in the kloncillium, or national Klan council. It became apparent that Indiana was too small for both men, as the divided loyalties of Indiana legislators to either Stephenson or Evans were preventing the passage of Klan-friendly legislation on public education. Finally, in September 1923, Stephenson resigned his Klan posts and began plotting the establishment of a rival Klan in which he would be the undisputed top dragon.

In April 1925, however, a scandal occurred that not even the Klan could survive. Stephenson was accused of the rape and murder of Madge Oberholtzer, an employee in the office of the Indiana State Superintendant of Public Instruction. In a deathbed statement, Oberholtzer had detailed her kidnapping on March 25 by Stephenson and two associates, a forced ride on a midnight train to Chicago, and a violent rape that occurred in a lower berth. Stephenson had escorted Oberholtzer out of the train just before reaching the Illinois line, to avoid violation of the Mann Act, which prohibited transportation of individuals across state lines for the purpose of prostitution. He had registered himself and Oberholtzer in a Hammond, Indiana hotel as Mr. and Mrs. W. B. Morgan; while freed temporarily, Oberholtzer had purchased bichloride of mercury tablets, six of which she later swallowed in a suicide attempt. Stephenson proposed bringing her to a hospital, but she refused; she also turned down his offer of marriage. Oberholtzer was then returned to her home, where she died on April 14.

Stephenson was arrested and held without bond, and a media feeding frenzy began. Newspapers fulminated freely for a full year and a half, giving vent to all manner of rumors and conspiracy theories, before Stephenson's trial began on October 12, 1925 in Noblesville, county seat of Hamilton County, Indiana.

Medical evidence introduced at the trial showed that the poison Oberholtzer had swallowed could have been overcome with swift medical treatment, which Stephenson had prevented, and that in addition, a secondary infection—apparently caused by human bites—had been the ultimate cause or her death. The jury, carefully and exhaustingly screened for Klan members and sympathizers, found Stephenson guilty of second-degree murder; his accomplices were found not guilty. Stephenson was sentenced to life in prison.

Stephenson appealed, and while appealing, he threatened the careers of Governor Jackson and several other elected Indiana officials; there were in his possession several "black boxes," he claimed, that contained damaging information. Jackson demurred from signing the pardon, and the black boxes were opened, revealing proof of several different instances of bribery and graft by Klan-allied Indiana legislators. The state attorney general carried out an investigation; the mayor of Indianapolis and several other high city officials went to jail; and the entire city council resigned. Governor Jackson barely escaped prosecution himself. The Indiana scandals utterly discredited the Klan in the eyes of the general public and alienated most of its own members, who dropped their memberships en masse by not renewing their annual klecktokens. Klan membership in the state of Indiana fell from 350,000 to 15,000 in the space of a year; a promised march of 60,000 Klan members through the streets of Washington, D.C., planned for 1925, attracted less than half that number. The Klan ceased to play its role as guardian of national morals and racial purity, although millions still held to its ideals and the name and the accoutrements would survive to inspire new generations of racists after the next world war.

THE IMMIGRATION PROBLEM

An important reason for the appeal of groups such as the Klan was the growth of the foreign-born population of the United States, which reached 14 million, out of a total population of 105 million, by the census year of 1920. Until World War I, official immigration policy had remained fairly open, with few restrictions either on immigration or on citizenship. Although attempts had been made to impose a literacy test on newcomers, presidents Taft and Wilson had successfully vetoed such legislation until 1917, when a literacy test was passed over Wilson's veto.

For most of the country's history, immigrants had arrived from the northern European lands—the British Isles, Germany, and France—that had also furnished the earliest colonial settlers. To many of their descendants, the new immigrants that began arriving in the 1890s seemed unfamiliar. These newcomers came from eastern and southern Europe; they were Italians, Jews, Slavs, Poles, Russians, and Greeks. They were not Protestants, and instead of moving across the Great Plains and prairies to claim rural homesteads and establish farms, they crowded into the cities of the east to work in the streets and sweatshops. They brought with them suspect doctrines such as socialism and anarchism, and to all appearances they made up a large percentage of the agitators and bomb-throwers who were arrested, indicted for sedition or espionage, and shipped out of the country after the war.

Public suspicion of the foreign-born was heightened by an influx of immigrants in the years immediately following World War I. In 1919, 430,000 refugees arrived from Europe, and in 1920 the number doubled. By the dawn of

A family of immigrants pauses at Ellis Island to take in the Statue of Liberty. *(Library of Congress/Portrait of America Series)*

the 1920s, the Red Scare was portraying eastern Europeans as Bolsheviks, and current stereotypes were turning southern Europeans, and especially Italians, into carriers of indolence, disease, and Mafia crime. The anti-immigration sentiment was abetted by native-born labor leaders who, having made important gains for their members during the war, now saw the flood of immigrants as a dire threat to their hard-fought rises in wages and improvements in working conditions. In 1921, the American Federation of Labor proposed a two-year ban on all immigration.

Forced Americanization became one accepted solution to the problem. An Americanization act provided money for classes in English, which were conducted by the American Legion and other patriotic groups. Immigrants found themselves under increasing pressure to throw off their old customs and language and turn themselves into model citizens. Immigration restrictions were undertaken in 1921, when Congress passed and President Harding signed the Emergency Immigration Act, which limited the number of immigrants from each foreign country to 3 percent of the number of foreign-born from that country already in the United States, as set forth in the census of 1910. The total immigrants to be admitted would be limited to 358,000. Northern Europeans were allowed a quota of 200,000, and southern and eastern Europeans 155,000.

In 1924, in an effort to limit southern and eastern European immigration even more, the stricter Johnson Act would be passed, limiting the number of immigrants to 2 percent of the country's population in the United States as measured by the census of 1890, before many immigrants from less-desirable parts of the world had begun arriving on Ellis Island, in New York harbor. In addition, quotas were reduced over a three-year period, and the act set a deadline of July 1, 1927, for a permanent annual restriction of 150,000 European immigrants. Candidates had to pass a strict test of their loyalty, as rendered in documents attesting to their character, nonaffiliation with left-wing parties, and eligibility under the quota system. The legislation did not apply to immigrants from Mexico or Canada.

The deadline of July 1, 1927, was later extended to 1929, when a final system of quotas was enacted limiting immigration to 132,000 from northern Europe and 20,000 total from southern Europe, eastern Europe, and Asia. The quota system first adopted in the 1920s would remain the model for immigration policy for much of the rest of the 20th century.

DISARMING

On April 12, 1921, President Harding asked Congress to formally declare the country at peace. On July 2, 1921, Congress passed a joint resolution following Harding's instructions, and Secretary of State Charles Evans Hughes concluded peace agreements with Germany and Austria. On November 14, the president made the formal proclamation that hostilities with Germany had ended. It had been three years since the war ended—but the isolationist sentiments of Congress and the president held that since the United States should no longer concern itself so closely with occurrences in Europe, it had no need to rush to officially recognize the state of peace in Europe.

The bloodshed and destruction of World War I had led to widespread opposition to further military adventures and U.S. involvement in foreign conflicts of any kind. Antimilitarism set in, and Congress drastically cut the size of the peacetime army down to 150,000. While the Treaty of Versailles, repudiated by the United States Congress, punished Germany with reparations and the loss of territory, diplomats and bureaucrats within the Harding administration worked for some form of universal disarmament to make the threat of a future world war less likely.

Secretary of State Hughes took the lead in this effort. Soon after the Harding administration took office, he invited the representatives of eight countries—Japan, Great Britain, France, China, Italy, Belgium, Portugal, and the Netherlands—to come to Washington to discuss disarmament in the fall of 1921. The Washington Conference on Disarmament was convened on November 11, three years to the day since the end of World War I. During the opening ceremonies, the representatives assembled at Arlington National Cemetery, where the body of an unknown soldier was laid to rest.

Despite their noble announced goals of peace and disarmament, Harding and Hughes had ulterior motives that the other conference participants probably guessed. They saw the Washington Conference as one way to slow an escalating arms race in the Pacific and to break the Anglo-Japanese Treaty that had prevented U.S. dominance of the Pacific region for the past 20 years. During Hughes's opening speech at the Washington Conference, he took the initiative by immediately asking all participants to begin scuttling a total of 2 million tons' worth of ships either at sea or under construction in port. Hughes then went even further by reeling off the names of the ships he wanted to see scrapped. He was greeted by stunned silence, then by enthusiastic applause, the waving of hats, and the stomping of feet.

With Hughes's leadership, the Washington Conference succeeded in bringing forth several treaties. The Five-Power Treaty, signed by the United States, Japan, Great Britain, France, and Italy, stopped all construction of battleships for 10 years and set a ratio of tonnage for battleships (5 United States: 5 British: 3 Japanese: 1.75 French: 1.75 Italian) that allowed the United States and Great Britain to share dominance over the Pacific in a time of growing suspicion of Japanese intentions. A treaty signed by all nine attending nations asked them to respect an open-door policy toward China, and a Four-Power Treaty among United States, Great Britain, Japan, and France held these nations to respect each other's Pacific possessions.

CHRONICLE OF EVENTS

1921

January 1: In football, California defeats Ohio State 28-0 in the Rose Bowl.

January 3: The U.S. Supreme Court rules that labor unions can be persecuted for restraining interstate trade.

January 4: Congress revives the War Finance Corporation to help U.S. farmers.

January 24: The Allies set wartime reparations owed by Germany at $56 billion, to be paid over the next 42 years.

January 25: The nation's unemployment rate reaches 3.5 million.

February 2: Air mail service between New York and San Francisco begins. On February 23, the service will set a record of 33 hours, 20 minutes for the coast-to-coast flight.

February 17: The government reports that there are 9 million automobiles on the road in the United States.

March 3: President Wilson vetoes the Emergency Tariff Bill, the final official act of his presidency.

March 4: Warren Harding is inaugurated as president in Washington, D.C.

March 6: Sanbury, Pennsylvania, begins enforcing a statute requiring skirts to be at least four inches below the knee.

March 23: Parachutist Arthur Hamilton jumps a record 24,400 feet in Illinois.

March 27: A new schedule of tariffs raises duties on a variety of imports, notably agricultural products.

April 2: Albert Einstein arrives in New York for a lecture series on the theory of relativity.

April 10: The U.S. Reclamation Service announces plans for the Boulder Dam on the Colorado River.

April 11: A boxing match transmitted by radio becomes the nation's first electronically broadcast sporting event.

April 12: Warren Harding announces that the United States will not join the League of Nations.

April 15: At a lecture at Columbia University, visiting German physicist Albert Einstein describes time as the fourth dimension.

April 20: The Senate ratifies a treaty with Colombia that reimburses Colombia $25 million for the loss of Panama.

April 23: Sprinter Charlie Paddock sets a new world record of 10.4 seconds in the 100-meter dash.

April 25: Nebraska outlaws ownership of land by resident aliens.

May 2: The Metropolitan Museum of Art in New York opens an exhibition of impressionist and postimpressionist art that includes the works of Matisse, Manet, Degas, and Millet.

May 10: The Ford Motor Company manufactures a record 4,072 cars in a single day.

May 15: Over Long Island, New York, aviator Laura Bromwell loops 199 times, setting a new record.

May 15: The legislature of New York gives state officials the right to ban certain dances.

May 19: President Harding signs the Emergency Quota Act to restrict immigration. The act limits annual immigration to 3 percent of the nationality counted in the census of 1910. No more than 358,000 immigrants are allowed to enter the country in a year.

May 27: Congress passes the Emergency Tariff Act, raising import duties on agricultural goods and embargoing dyestuffs from Germany.

May 31: German and Austrian immigrants are granted citizenship for the first time since the end of World War I.

May 31: By executive order, the administration of naval oil reserves is transferred from the Navy Department to the Department of the Interior.

June 5: Aviator Laura Bromwell dies after losing control of her plane at a height of 1,000 feet.

June 10: Congress passes the Budget and Accounting Act, establishing the Bureau of the Budget and the General Accounting Office.

June 11: Pennsylvania State University graduates the first woman engineer.

June 20: Representative Alice Robertson of Oklahoma becomes the first woman to preside over the House of Representatives.

June 25: For the 40th year, Samuel Gompers is elected president of the American Federation of Labor.

June 30: President Harding appoints William Howard Taft as chief justice of the Supreme Court.

July 1: The Railroad Labor Board reduces railroad employees' pay by 12 percent.

July 2: Congress passes and President Harding signs a resolution formally ending hostilities with Germany and its allies.

July 14: Nicola Sacco and Bartolomeo Vanzetti are convicted of murder in Dedham, Massachusetts.

July 18: Astronaut John Glenn is born.

July 21: To convince military skeptics and to demonstrate the effectiveness of air power, Brigadier

General William "Billy" Mitchell sinks the surrendered German battleship *Ostfriesland* with six 2,000-pound bombs off the coast of Virginia.

July 27: Canadian scientist Dr. Federick Banting isolates insulin from a dog pancreas.

August 9: The federal Bureau of Veterans Affairs is established, with Charles Forbes as its first director.

August 11: President Harding invites Great Britain, France, Italy, Japan, Belgium, China, the Netherlands, and Portugal to participate in a conference on naval arms limitations and on the Pacific region.

August 15: The Packers and Stockyards Act prohibits price manipulation and regulates operators of stockyards.

August 18: William J. Burns is appointed director of the Bureau of Investigation, a new arm of the Justice Department.

August 22: Connecticut's Barber's Commission rules that women who bob hair for a living must get a barber's license and pay a yearly fee of $5.

August 24: By the Grain Futures Trading Act, speculative trading in commodities is discouraged with high tax assessments for certain transactions.

September 7: Tarzan of the Apes, starring a collection of live wild animals, opens on Broadway.

September 25: The Idle Class, a movie that stars Charlie Chaplin, opens.

September 26–30: Department of Commerce Secretary Herbert Hoover chairs a conference on unemployment, which reached 3.5 million earlier in the year. The conference recommends lower prices to increase demand and employment.

October 13: The New York Giants defeat the New York Yankees to win the World Series.

October 15: General Leonard Wood becomes governor general of the Philippines.

October 31: The Sheik, a movie that stars Rudolph Valentino, opens at the Rivoli Theater in New York.

November 1: Sergeant Emil Chambers sets a new record with a 26,000-foot parachute jump over Kansas City.

November 2: Margaret Sanger and Mary Ware Dennett establish the American Birth Control League.

November 11: The Tomb of the Unknown Soldier is unveiled for the first time in the Rotunda of the U.S. Capitol, marking the first celebration of Armistice Day.

November 12: The major naval powers convene in Washington for the Conference for Limitation of Armament.

November 14: The German expressionist film *The Cabinet of Dr. Caligari* opens in the United States about a year after its debut in Germany.

November 23: President Harding signs the Willis-Campbell Act, which forbids doctors from prescribing beer.

November 23: The Sheppard-Towner Act is signed, extending $1 million annually in federal money to the states for the promotion of infant health.

December 2: The first successful test of a helium-filled dirigible takes place in Portsmouth, Virginia.

December 13: At the close of the Washington Conference, the United States, Great Britain, France, and Japan sign a naval treaty that recognizes each country's possessions in the Pacific Ocean.

December 20: Democrats in the House of Representatives block passage of an antilynching bill.

December 22: The Russian Famine Relief Act authorizes $20 million for seed, corn, and preserved milk for Russia.

December 23: Warren Harding commutes the prison terms of socialist Eugene V. Debs and 23 others convicted under the Espionage Act of 1917. The prisoners are released on Christmas Day.

EYEWITNESS TESTIMONY

Inauguration and Depression

When the inaugural was over I realized that the same thing for which I had worked in Massachusetts had been accomplished in the nation. The radicalism which had tinged our whole political and economic life from soon after 1900 to the World War period was passed. There were still echoes of it, and some of its votaries remained, but its power was gone. The country had little interest in mere destructive criticism. It wanted the progress that alone comes from constructive policies.

> *Calvin Coolidge, reminiscing on the inaugural of Warren G. Harding in 1921, from Sobel,* Coolidge: An American Enigma *(1998), pp. 207–208.*

Men who were wicked and men who were unwise, brought the world to its present conditions, and it is not possible with even the utmost sincerity, humanity, patriotism to apply effective remedies immediately. The whole world is involved, and as a whole the world must find the means of readjusting itself to the new conditions in which we find it. You may be sure that suffering and misfortune have not come to any single class of people. . . . The farmers, in our country and elsewhere, are suffering in a way that has certainly made a very special appeal to me, at least, because such special difficulties seem to surround every effort to ameliorate their situation. People who by thrift and saving have secured modest competence find themselves in danger of losing what they have saved. Even the capitalists, whom I beg you not to believe are altogether bad, have had their trouble everywhere. I beg you to feel very sure that the men entrusted with National leadership and responsibility are not blind to these things. Their task is one without precedent, and it will take time, and patience, and above all, ample confidence among all the people to work it out.

> *Florence Harding, letter of encouragement to Mrs. W. W. Brink of June 24, 1921, during the postwar depression, quoted in Anthony,* Florence Harding, The Jazz Age, and the Death of America's Most Scandalous President *(1998), p. 343.*

The Klan Revival

1. Is the motive prompting your ambition to be a Klansman serious and unselfish?
2. Are you a native born, white, gentile American?
3. Are you absolutely opposed to and free of any allegiance of any nature to any cause, government, people, sect, or ruler that is foreign to the United States of America?
4. Do you believe in the tenets of the Christian religion?
5. Do you esteem the United States of America and its institutions above all other government, civil, political, or ecclesiastical, in the whole world?
6. Will you, without mental reservation, take a solemn oath to defend, preserve, and enforce the same?
7. Do you believe in clannishness, and will you faithfully practice same toward Klansmen?
8. Do you believe in and will you faithfully strive for the eternal maintenance of white supremacy?
9. Will you faithfully obey our constitution and laws, and conform willingly to all our usages, requirements, and regulations?
10. Can you always be depended on?

> *From The Kloran, the book of rules and rituals of the Ku Klux Klan, as quoted by Robert Coughlan in "Konklave in Kokomo" and published in* The Aspirin Age *(1949), pp. 118–119.*

An organizer of the Ku Klux Klan was in Emporia the other day, and the men whom he invited to join his band at $10 per join turned him down. Under the leadership of Dr. J. B. Brickell and following their own judgment after hearing his story, the Emporians told him that they had no time for him. The proposition seems to be:

Anti-foreigners
Anti-Catholics
Anti-Negroes

There are, of course, bad foreigners and good ones, good Catholics and bad ones, and all kinds of Negroes. To make a case against a birthplace, a religion, or a race is wickedly un-American and cowardly. The whole trouble with the Ku Klux Klan is that it is based upon such deep foolishness that it is bound to be a menace to good government in any community. Any man fool enough to be Imperial Wizard would have power without responsibility and both without any sense. That is social dynamite.

. . . It is to the everlasting credit of Emporia that the organizer found no suckers with $10 each to squander here. Whatever Emporia may be otherwise, it believes in law and order, and absolute freedom under the

Constitution for every man, no matter what birth or creed or race, to speak and meet and talk and act as a free, law-abiding citizen. The picayunish cowardice of a man who would substitute Klan rule and mob law for what our American fathers have died to establish and maintain should prove what a cheap screw outfit the Klan is.

Kansas newspaper editor William Allen White, letter to Herbert B. Swope of the New York World, *September 17, 1921, from Johnson (ed.),* Selected Letters of William Allen White *(1947), pp. 220–221.*

Just as I do not wish the South to be politically entirely of one party, just as I believe that it is bad for the South, and for the rest of the country as well, so I do not want the colored people to be entirely of one party. I wish that both the tradition of a solidly Democratic South and the tradition of a solidly Republican black race might be broken up. Neither political sectionalism nor any system of rigid groupings of people will in the long run prosper in our country.

I want to see the time come when black men will regard themselves as full participants in the benfits and duties of American citizenship; when they will vote for Democratic candidates, if they prefer the Democratic policy on tariffs or taxation, or foreign relations, or what-not; and when they will vote the Republican ticket only for like reasons. We cannot go on, as we have gone on for more than half a century, with one great section of our population, numbering as many people as the entire population of some significant countries of Europe, set off from real contribution to solving national issues, because of a division on race lines.

Warren Harding, to a segregated audience at 50th anniversary celebration of the founding of Birmingham, Alabama, on October 26, 1921, as quoted in Russell, President Harding—His Life and Times *(1968), pp. 471–472.*

A few years ago I had the adventure of reading Madison Grant's *The Passing of the Great Race,* an impassioned proclamation of the merits of the blond Nordic race, and a lamentation over its decay. At that time such a book was in the nature of a revelation whether you gave faith to its assertions and proofs or scoffed at them. The thing that struck me was the impossibility (as it seemed to me) of any reader remaining unmoved; I thought him bound to be carried to a high pitch of enthusiastic affirmation or else roused to fierce resentment and furious denial . . . I had not heard of Lothrop Stoddard, unless as a special writer and correspondent for magazines. It was

not until April 1920, that *The Rising Tide of Color Against White World-Supremacy* was published. Even so, attention is not readily attracted to a book of this type. Many who have since read it with excitement knew nothing of the volume until, in a speech at Birmingham, Alabama, on 26 October, 1921, President Harding said: "Whoever will take the time to read and ponder Mr. Lothrop Stoddard's book on *The Rising Tide of Color . . .* must realize that our race problem here in the United States is only a phase of a race issue that the whole world confronts."

Grant Overton, from American Nights Entertainment *(1923), quoted in Berman,* The Great Gatsby and Modern Times *(1994), pp. 24–25.*

My worthy subjects, citizens of the Invisible Empire, Klansmen all, greetings. It grieves me to be late. The President of the United States kept me unduly long counseling upon vital matters of state. Only my plea that this is the time and place of my coronation obtained for me surcease from his prayers for guidance.

D. C. Stephenson, addressing spectators during his July 1923, coronation in Kokomo, Indiana, as Grand Dragon of the Ku Klux Klan, Indiana, quoted in Chalmers, Hooded Americanism: The First Century of the Ku Klux Klan, 1865–1965 *(1956), p. 165.*

The Klan is against Jews, for it claims that Jews seek to control the finances of the world. It feels that American whites who are non-Jews cannot cope with them in this project,—are their inferiors in financial ability, and therefore, force and terrorism must be invoked against them. The Klan is against foreigners, for they say these would change our institutions. This presupposes that our institutions are perfect and they cannot be improved. It also presupposes that they cannot stand the contest with the newer ideas. Again a sense of inferiority. The Klan is against Catholics because with a strange bigotry it imagines that they seek to suborn the government to their religion. The silliness of this needs no comment. The Klan is against Negroes, hereditarily so, because "this is the white man's country," and the Negro is disposed not "to remain in his place." Here again, we see a sense of inferiority and fear, seeking an explanation in empty myths; the myth that this is only the white man's country, and it follows that the Negro or any other American has or can be made to have a static, caste place.

The result of the Klan's teaching is always racial intolerance, religious bigotry, jingoism, obsoletism,

A poster announces the annual Spring Festival of the Knights of the Ku Klux Klan. The Klan equated the Caucasian Protestant with the patriotic American and disseminated its views at picnics, public meetings, and sundry social functions. *(State Historical Society of Wisconsin, John Vetter Collection)*

lawlessness and violence. If these things are good, then the Klan is good; if they are evil, then the Klan is evil.

Robert W. Bagnall, writer and observer, in "The Spirit of the Ku Klux Klan," in Opportunity *magazine, September 1923, p. 265.*

"Civilization's going to pieces," broke out Tom violently. "I've gotten to be a terrible pessimist about things. Have you read 'The Rise of the Coloured Empires' by this man Goddard?"

"Why, no," I answered, rather surprised by his tone.

"Well, it's a fine book and everybody ought to read it. The idea is if we don't look out the white race will be—utterly submerged. It's all scientific stuff; it's been proved."

From F. Scott Fitzgerald, The Great Gatsby *(1925), p. 17.*

The Southern white laborer gets low wages measured in food, clothes, shelter, and the education of his children. But in one respect he gets high pay and that is in the shape of the subtlest form of human flattery—social superiority over masses of other human beings. Georgia bribes its white labor by giving it public badges of superiority. The Jim Crow legislation was not to brand the Negro as inferior and to separate the races, but rather to flatter white labor to accept public testimony of its superiority instead of higher wages and social legislation. This fiction of superiority invaded public affairs: No Negro schoolhouse must approach in beauty and efficiency a white school; no public competition must admit Negroes as competitors; no municipal improvements must invade the Negro quarters until every white quarter approached perfection. . . .

. . . This effort to keep the white group solid led directly to mob law. Every white man became a recognized official to keep Negroes "in their places." Negro baiting and even lynching became a form of amusement which the authorities dared not stop. Blood-lust grew by what it fed on. These outbreaks undoubtedly affected profits, but they could not be suppressed, for they kept certain classes of white labor busy and entertained. Secret government and manipulation ensued. Secret societies guided the State and administration. The Ku Klux Klan was quite naturally reborn in Georgia and in Atlanta.

W. E. B. DuBois: "Georgia: Invisible Empire State," from The Nation, *January 21, 1925, p. 65.*

We are a movement of the plain people, very weak in the matter of culture, intellectual support, and trained leadership. We are demanding, and we expect to win, a return of power into the hands of the everyday, not highly cultured, not overly intellectualized, but entirely unspoiled and not de-Americanized average citizen of the old stock.

This is undoubtedly a weakness. It lays us open to the charge of being "hicks" and "rubes" and "drivers of the second-hand Fords." We admit it . . . The Klan does not believe that the fact that it is emotional and instinctive, rather than coldly intellectual, is a weakness.

Hiram Wesley Evans, Imperial Wizard of the Ku Klux Klan,
in "The Klan's Fight for Americanism," in
The North American Review *(1926), reprinted in Baritz,*
The Culture of the Twenties *(1970), pp. 100–101.*

In the morning he lit out. This was the third of July and the Klan was to have the biggest parade of its history in this town on the Fourth. Three big bands, a full gathering of all the hooded hosts in the county, the Civil War men, the Legion boys, and the boy scouts.

The way things happened, Adam must have been completely out of his mind—but like many maniacs he went about things systematically. First he drove his flivver to Oklahoma City. He belonged to the National Guard and got into the armory without any trouble. He came out the back way with two or three packages and loaded them into his car. He had swiped an old machine-gun, pretty well shot. And one of the packages was a hundred rounds of ammunition. Also, he took his rifle and bayonet out of the company rack. . . .

The Klan was leading the procession and the band ahead of it was playing the "Klexology." All the boys were singing it out loud. The tune is "America" and these are the words:

> God of Eternity,
> Guide, guard our great country,
> Our homes and store.
> Keep our great State to Thee,
> Its people right and free,
> In us Thy glory be
> Forevermore.

Crazy Adam got his gun into action at about a hundred yards. Picked off two at the first crack. The Rev. Narcissus Harper through the forehead, and John Hughes, the butcher, through the stomach. Then something happened that saved the entire klavern of Klansmen from annihilation. The old machine-gun jammed.

From "Ku Klux," a short story by W. A. S. Douglas, in
The American Mercury, *March 1928, pp. 278–279.*

The Immigration Question

Thus, under even the most favorable circumstances, we are in for generations of racial readjustment—an immense travail, essentially needless, since the final product will probably not measure up to the colonial standard. We will probably never (unless we adopt positive eugenic measures) be the race we might have been if America had been reserved for the descendants of the picked Nordics of colonial times.

But that is no reason for folding our hands in despairing inaction. On the contrary, we should be up and doing, for though some of our race-heritage has been lost, more yet remains. We can still be a very great people—if we will it so. Heaven be praised, the colonial stock was immensely prolific before the alien tide wrought its sterilizing havoc. Even to-day nearly one-half of our population is of the old blood, while many millions of the immigrant stock are sound in quality and assimilable in kind. Only—the immigrant tide must at all costs be stopped and America given a chance to stabilize her ethnic being. It is the old story of the sibylline books. Some, to be sure, are ashes of the dead past; all the more should we conserve the precious volumes which remain.

One fact should be clearly understood: If America is not true to her own race-soul, she will inevitably lose it, and the brightest star that has appeared since Hellas will fall like a meteor from the human sky, its brilliant radiance fading into the night.

Lothrop Stoddard, arguing for preservation of superior Nordic
genes in U.S. breeding stock, and a ban on immigration,
in Stoddard, The Rising Tide of Color Against White
World Supremacy *(1920), p. 266.*

. . . [M]odern migration is itself only one aspect of a still more fundamental disgenic trend. The whole course of modern urban and industrial life is disgenic. Over and above immigration, the tendency is toward a replacement of the more valuable by the less valuable elements of the population. All over the civilized world racial values are diminishing, and the logical end of this disgenic process is racial bankruptcy and the collapse of civilization.

Now why is all this? It is primarily because we have not yet adjusted ourselves to the radically new environment into which epochal scientific discoveries led us a century ago. Such adaptation as we have effected has been almost wholly on the material side. The no less sweeping idealistic adaptations which the situation calls for have not been made. Hence, modern civilization has been one-sided, abnormal, unhealthy—and nature is exacting penalties which will increase in severity until we either fully adapt or finally perish.

Lothrop Stoddard, The Rising Tide of Color Against
White World Supremacy *(1920), pp. 302–303.*

I know two languages and speak and read two, and you know only one. I know the ways of two countries and you know the ways of only one. I came across the ocean. You have never left Philadelphia. You tell me I never go to church, or to the lodge, or to vote. Well, I have been to many churches, but only once to any one. I go to the Socialist meeting, but only once. I go to the political meeting, but only once. It is always the same—always, at all the churches and all the meetings. The priest and the minister say, "Give us your money." So does the Socialist. So does the anarchist. They give you heaven in the next world, hell here, nothing else. When the king or any big man has a dinner, I and my brothers are not there. We are fighting for them, dying for them, but they have forgotten us. All these people take from me, they don't give to me. You don't see it. I see it. You are the fool, not me.

Anonymous Italian immigrant, answering a rebuke from a native worker for singing an aria from Verdi's Rigoletto, *quoted by Carol Wright in "The Human Factor,"* The Atlantic Monthly, *January 1920, p. 25.*

In the past, we have welcomed the immigrant. We have made it possible to enlist him in the development of our resources and in the creation of our great industries, in the construction of our railroads and of our vast public works; to bring into our citizenship men and women of admirable qualities, who have known how to live and to die for the country of their adoption. This measure casts an undeserved slur upon our foreign-born citizens. It tells them that they are men and women of inferior race, that they are not assimilable, that they are undesirable, that even though they are citizens and performed the duties of citizenship they are not wanted. This is an unfortunate manifestation of a spirit of arrogance and of racial prejudice that bodes ill for the future if it is to be at all encouraged.

Louis Marshall, on behalf of the American Jewish Committee, urging President Harding to veto the 1921 immigration quota bill, reprinted in Sinclair, The Available Man *(1965), p. 216.*

The intellectual superiority of our Nordic group over the Alpine, Mediterranean and negro groups has been demonstrated.

William C. MacDougall and Carl Brigham, A Study of American Intelligence, *1923, p. 3.*

What are Aliens Doing to Us?

Gino Speranza, himself of Italian parentage, tells you in an amazing series of articles now starting in

The World's Work

While we have been trying to Americanize the aliens, what have they done to us? Gino Speranza has gone from New York to New Mexico to find the answer. If the Melting Pot works, it should have done a perfect job with the French in New Orleans, who have been Americans since 1814, with the Mexicans in New Mexico, who have been Americans since 1845. Has the Melting Pot "melted" them? It has not. Rather, it has left a queer stew inside.

Instead of our making Americans of the foreigners among us, in many cases they have imposed their customs and semi-foreign ways on the native Americans. Most thoughtful readers will be astounded, as well as alarmed, to learn what the oldest foreign elements and some of the new immigration groups have done to American institutions and customs in their communities. Mr. Speranza tells you. This subject transcends the tariff, the budget, the presidential election, the crops, Wall Street—everything. Upon the solution of the problem depends the future racial, mental, and moral make-up of our people. This is a feature you should not miss.

Advertisement for The World's Work magazine in The Outlook, *November 7, 1923, p. 427.*

Is the Negro race to preserve its physical identity or to be bleached white within any calculable time with which we need now concern ourselves? A satisfying answer to this query would not only go a long way towards relieving the American mind of a perplexing anxiety, but would also greatly facilitate practical and acceptable plans of race adjustment. The American white man has been so earnestly engaged in volunteer assistance to Providence to keep the races apart that he has failed notice the plain indications of the outcome under the normal operation of biological and social law. A new Negroid type is gradually emerging which clearly foreshadows the immediate, if not the ultimate, physical destiny of the Negro race on this continent.

. . . The dominant white sentiment in America abominates race admixture so far as the European and the African are concerned. Indeed, this is the general attitude of the white towards the non-white portions of the human race, which is most assertive in the Northern European or Nordic type. This feeling has been greatly accentuated in America since the end of the World War. Rabid propaganda has been stimulated and fostered. The resources of science have been ransacked for proof of the evil effect of race fusion. The discarded argument based upon an exploded theory of divine purpose has been resurrected and made to do service for the new propaganda.

Kelly Miller of Howard University, in "Is the American Negro to Remain Black or Become Bleached?" in The South Atlantic Quarterly, *July 1926, pp. 240–241.*

Obviously, the chase of Reds is still a profitable sport in the United States, despite the great scarcity of the game. One seldom picks up a small-town paper without discovering that some retired cavalry captain, or Ku Klux organizer, or itinerant chautauquan has just been to town, alarming the local Babbitts with tales of a Muscovite plot to seize Washington, burn the Capitol, and heave poor Cal into the Potomac. The theme is a favorite one with the evangelical clergy, who connect it with the sinister enterprises of the Pope and the Rum Fleet.

"Editorial" on 1920s Red-baiting, in The American Mercury, *February 1927, p. 163.*

Anna Putriuniate, 17, native of Lithuania, dressmaker in Montreal, Canada, wanted to become a resident of the U.S. She paid a man $50 to show her how. He took her one Sunday night to the gorge dam at Niagara Falls, lowered her by a rope to the trestle of the Michigan Central Railroad. With little, cautious steps she walked along the cold steel girders, while the Whirlpool Rapids 250 feet below her howled at her. She was shrewd enough to put her legs in trousers instead of flapping, treacherous skirts. She reached U.S. soil. Last week she was arrested with four other young women who had crossed from Canada in rowboats the night after her bridge-walk. All were held as witnesses against a band of five alien smugglers. Commented the *New York World:* "Perhaps, in wattle huts and thatched roofs, in crowded slums and picturesque villages of the old familiar parts of the world, they still think of this as the promised land. Hearing their stories, we can hardly do less than strive to make it that."

"In Dead of Night," item in Time *magazine, March 12, 1928, p. 12.*

4

A Scandalous Administration
January 1922–August 1923

One of the most important privileges that comes with the office of the president is the authority to appoint members of the cabinet. Shortly after his inauguration, Warren Harding declared that he would consider ability, popularity, and Republicanism in his choices. Although Harding did not find all of these qualities in equal measure in a single individual, three of his appointments did bring forth loyal and well-regarded men who rendered a capable term of service: Charles Evans Hughes as secretary of state, Herbert Hoover as secretary of commerce, and Andrew Mellon as treasury secretary.

For other appointments, Harding followed different priorities by rewarding personal friends and supporters of his 1920 campaign. Senator Albert Bacon Fall of New Mexico, Harding's secretary of the interior, was a large, gruff fellow whose western drawl and cowboy hats took many members of official Washington somewhat aback. He had been Harding's friend and associate in the Senate, and Harding wanted at least one of his cabinet appointments to satisfy western senators. But at the time he joined Harding's administration, Albert Fall stood almost $150,000 in debt, owed taxes back to the year 1912, and was desperately searching for some way to extricate himself from pending financial disaster. Harding also appointed his campaign manager, Harry Daugherty, as attorney general and head of the Department of Justice (Daugherty himself had been left nearly bankrupt by his financial support of Harding's candidacy—a situation he fully intended to rectify as a member of the cabinet).

Unfortunately for Harding, the rewards tendered for support of his successful campaign did not cease with the appointment of a few cabinet members. In the early days of his presidency, many acquaintances, lobbyists, and politicians from Ohio moved to Washington to take advantage of the change in administration, knowing that Harding would be only too willing to oblige them. Reverend Heber Herbert Votaw, a Seventh-Day Adventist missionary who had spent 10 years in Burma, was appointed superintendent of federal prisons. Harding appointed his friend Daniel Crissinger as controller of the currency. He brought Dr. Charles Sawyer, a homeopathic doctor from his home town of Marion, Ohio, to Washington to serve as White House physician. E. Mont Reilly, a Harding campaign worker, was named governor of Puerto Rico.

73

THE NATIONS CHOICE

LAW & ORDER

AMERICA FIRST

A composite photograph commemorating the inauguration of Warren Harding on March 4, 1921, quotes the slogans that won the White House and Congress for the Republican Party: Law & Order and America First. (Coolidge is on the right.) *(Library of Congress/Harry Lickner)*

A Daugherty confidante, William J. Burns, found himself head of the Bureau of Investigation. Charles Forbes, another close friend, became head of the Veterans Bureau. Jess Smith would serve as the attorney general's accountant and secretary and occupy an office at the Justice Department very near Daugherty's.

It was Smith and Daugherty who would set the tone for public management in the Harding administration. As Daugherty's right-hand man and fixer, Smith spent many of his office hours distributing official Justice Department pardons in exchange for cash and selling withdrawal permits ("B" permits) to well-connected bootleggers that allowed them to legally raid stocks of alcohol set aside for medicinal purposes. Smith's most famous client, George Remus of Cincinnati, paid him $1.50 to $2.00 each for one-case withdrawal permits. Remus made millions selling the bootleg alcohol for a 400 percent markup on the open market, but Smith's influence could not keep him from eventually being indicted, convicted, and jailed in the Atlanta federal penitentiary.

THE OHIO GANG

Jess Smith and Harry Daugherty roomed together in a house on H Street, a lodging provided by an Ohioan, Ned McLean, owner of the *Washington Post*. Here and at a residence at 1625 K Street, also known as the Little Green House and rented by an Ohio operator named Howard Mannington, the members of the "Ohio Gang," those with official positions as well as an entourage of casual and unofficial friends, met and planned their future success as public servants under the protection of Warren Harding. The parlors and back rooms saw patronage deals, liquor-permit sales, and uproarious, Prohibition-defying parties where the Ohio Gang mixed money and power, business and pleasure.

Not long into Harding's term, however, Daugherty received scathing criticism and the threat of impeachment for his pardons of political allies and personal friends, his shadowing of enemies in Congress by federal investigators, and his failure to prosecute war profiteers. Daugherty was especially notorious for his reaction to labor trouble which, like a long line of federal officials before him, he saw as a leftist plot against the federal government and the administration in power. The Daugherty Justice Department favored company-run labor unions and the open shop, which prohibited union membership as a condition for employment. When a railroad strike inconveniently dragged on in 1922, Daugherty persuaded a Harding-appointed federal judge, James Wilkerson, to issue an injunction against the strikers that prohibited them from picketing or from interfering in any way with strikebreakers. Thus denied their legal rights by a court order, the strikers were quickly defeated; Harding stuck by his friend Daugherty despite the impeachment proceedings against him in Congress and a storm of criticism over the injunction.

TEAPOT DOME

There were scandals large and small during Harding's term, but the Teapot Dome affair, in which Daugherty and Fall played leading roles, did the most to wreck the president's reputation in history. Harding could do little to lessen the damage—although the actions which encompassed Teapot Dome took place in 1922, the scandal did not break until October 1923, two months after the president's death.

Controversy over the use and sale of federal land brought about the scandal. In the first decade of the 20th century, the government had begun surveying tracts of public land, believed to be oil-bearing, as possible future oil reserves for the navy. In these years, naval as well as civilian ships were converting from coal to oil. For several reasons, oil was far superior to coal for use as a fuel in navy ships. Not only was it lighter, cleaner, and more efficient, it was also superior in a tactical sense, as it didn't create heavy black clouds that gave away the position of ships that used it. It also eased the movement of ships in distant waters, as coal had made it necessary for the navy to build and protect vulnerable coal stations in far-off ports.

In the meantime, a policy of conservation of public lands, begun during the administration of Theodore Roosevelt and his secretary of the interior, James R. Garfield, sparked a long-running conflict between conservationists and western landowners—ranchers, mining interests, and private railroad companies—who believed the water, oil, and minerals of the West should be left open to exploitation by private investors and land speculators. This conflict, often painted as a broader struggle between East and West, progressive and traditional, continued through World War I, the 1920s, and the end of the 20th century.

The Taft administration was the first to set aside oil reserves which, in cases of sudden war or emergency, the government would be able to draw on for the use of the military. These tracts included Naval Reserve No. 1 at Elk Hills, California, and Naval Reserve No. 2 at Buena Vista, California, both set aside in 1912. In 1915 the Wilson administration set aside Naval Reserve No. 3 at Teapot Dome, near the town of Salt Creek, Wyoming.

World War I came and went without the naval oil reserves being put to use. But military officials and congressmen still worried about a future war with Japan, when fighting at sea would take precedence and when the U.S. Navy might find itself unprepared to range over the immense distances of the Pacific Ocean. While debate continued on opening the reserves to drilling by private companies, the federal government contended with private claims to reserve land. At the same time, the reserves were threatened by siphoning from neighboring properties by oil prospectors, who had side-drilling techniques at their

Rollin Kirby's newspaper cartoon illustrates Albert Fall's discomfort at the public disclosure of his questionable working methods while in office. The "Teapot Dome" oil-leasing scandals provided the country's editorial cartoonists with plentiful visual metaphors. *(Library of Congress)*

disposal. In 1920, Congress gave the secretary of the navy, Josephus Daniels, a mandate to devise a solution to these problems. In response, Daniels authorized the drilling of 21 offset wells to stop the drainage from the naval reserves.

That November, before the drilling could commence, Warren Harding won election. At the Republican convention in Chicago, he had been strongly supported by various oil company executives, who well appreciated that any lease granted by the government for the privilege of drilling on federal reserve land would be worth a fortune. After taking office, Harding rewarded this oil-industry support with his nomination of Albert Fall, who would turn out to be a close and very useful ally of the oil industry, as secretary of the interior.

Fall was an adamant anticonservationist who had once called for the dismantling of the Interior Department altogether. Now, as secretary of the interior, he quickly went to work on the problem of the naval oil reserves. His first obstacle was jurisdiction: the navy, and not the Department of the Interior, operated the oil reserves. To the new secretary of the navy, Edwin Denby, Fall privately suggested transferring control of the reserves to the Department of the Interior. Denby was agreeable, but unfortunately for both men and for the proposed transaction, word of the transfer was getting around.

Hearing the rumors, several high-placed officers in Denby's department, including the navy's chief of engineering, Admiral R. L. Griffin, protested. Undaunted, Fall drafted an executive order and sent it on to Denby. Griffin intercepted the order and, realizing its true purpose, changed the language to require approval of the naval secretary for any proposed leasing out of the reserves to private interests. Fall then changed Griffin's "approval" to "consultation." Denby agreed to sign the order, and sent it to Harding, but attached a letter explaining the opposition to it as well as Griffin's official protest. Fall intercepted this correspondence and sent the order to the president without Denby's letter or Griffin's protest. Thus misled, Harding went along with Fall's wishes and, on May 31, 1921, signed the order.

Fall's next act was to consider the decision taken by Josephus Daniels to drill offset wells. The high bidder for the drilling contract at the Elk Hills, California, reserve was the Pan-American Petroleum and Transport Company, a company belonging to Edward L. Doheny, an old acquaintance of Fall's who had made his fortune prospecting for oil in California and Mexico. Pan-American offered to pay a royalty of 55 percent of the crude oil it drilled. Fall accepted the bid.

Doheny and Fall had been talking about money as well as oil drilling. Fall was in dire need of money for improvement and expansion of his ranch at Three Rivers, New Mexico. He was also in debt for $140,000 to the M.D. Thatcher Estates Land Company of Pueblo, Colorado, and eight years behind in his property taxes. On November 29, 1921, the day after Doheny's proposal was accepted, Doheny's son Edward Doheny Jr. drew $100,000 in cash from the brokerage accounts of Blair Company, placed the money in a black satchel, and brought it to Albert Fall at the Wardman Park Hotel in Washington. Fall made out a promissory note for the cash, then left for El Paso, where he purchased an addition to his property, a neighboring tract known as the Harris Ranch, for the sum of $91,500.

The other beneficiary of Fall's new policy was Harry Sinclair. About the same time as Doheny's satchel was delivered to Fall, Sinclair established the Continental Trading Company in Canada. The four members of the company were Sinclair, of the Mammoth Oil Company, H. M. Blackmer of the Midwest Oil Company, Robert Stewart of Standard Oil, and James O'Neal of the Prairie Oil Company. They were all oil entrepreneurs seeking a guarded location for a certain oil deal that might not stand up under legal or public scrutiny in the United States. Out of sight of stockholders or the press, the men simply arranged to buy several hundred million barrels of Texas crude oil for $1.50 a barrel, then sell it back to their own respective companies for $1.75 a barrel. The small margin added up to a huge windfall that the four men planned to assign to their private bank accounts.

In December of 1921, Sinclair traveled to Three Rivers, New Mexico, to talk with Secretary Fall about Teapot Dome. Sinclair arrived with his attorney, Colonel J. W. Zevely, in his private railroad car, the *Sinco*. Fall showed Sinclair around the ranch and discussed the possibilities of leasing the Teapot Dome reserve. The two men quickly came to an agreement.

On April 7, 1922, Fall leased the entire Reserve No. 3 at Teapot Dome to the Mammoth Oil Company, under the control of Harry Sinclair. As consideration for the lease, Sinclair agreed to pay a royalty of from 12.5 to 50 percent in the form of certificates. The government could redeem the certificates with Mammoth for oil and gasoline at any of 27 storage and transportation points on the United States seacoast, or for the construction of oil storage tanks wherever the Navy Department asked them to be built.

The lease was signed in secret, away from the prying eyes of Fall's government accountants and Mammoth's nosy competitors. Later, Fall would claim that this unorthodox noncompetitive bidding would provide the best deal for the government, and that the terms of a lease involving a strategic commodity such as oil involved national security and thus *should* be kept secret.

In any case, Fall stood to benefit. On May 8, 1922, his son-in-law Mahlon Everhart met Sinclair aboard the *Sinco* in Washington. Sinclair turned over $198,000 in Liberty bonds, sold by the government to finance military purchasing during World War I. Two weeks later, Sinclair turned over an additional $35,000 in bonds in New York. Through Everhart, Fall asked for an additional loan installment, and Sinclair agreed to provide $36,000. Later in the year, he would provide Fall with a payment of $10,000 at Three Rivers; another Wardman Park Hotel transaction involving $25,000 took place in January of 1923.

The bonds had been taken from the treasury of the Continental Trading Company. Most were transferred to the M. D. Thatcher company of Pueblo, Colorado, to pay off Fall's outstanding debts to that company. Fall and Sinclair made no written record of the transactions. But Liberty Bonds bore serial numbers and thus, much to the later embarrassment of both parties, were traceable.

Fall had also opened bids on the construction of oil storage tanks and other construction at Pearl Harbor, Hawaii, which would be the forward military base and storage depot in any Pacific conflict with Japan. Three companies bid, but Doheny's offer to undertake the work in return for 6 million barrels of crude oil proved the most attractive to Fall, and the deal was signed. Later in the year, on November 28, 1921, Doheny proposed building tanks and a refinery in San Pedro California, as well as a pipeline from Elk Hills to the refinery, in return for a 15-year lease on the entire Elk Hills reserve. Fall agreed and the contract was signed on December 11, 1921.

Fall had made an agreement with Admiral Robison of the Navy Department to keep these various leases and arrangements a secret. But word of the leases quickly spread to other members of the Navy Department, to the oil industry, and eventually to the public. A Washington conservationist lawyer, Harry Slattery, heard about the leases from members of the Navy Department, then leaked the information to the *Wall Street Journal*. The *Journal* then ran the news of the Teapot Dome leases on its front page.

Meanwhile, rumors were also circulating in Wyoming. Having received many queries from his constituents on the subject of Teapot Dome, Senator John Kendrick of Wyoming began demanding explanations, as did conservationist senator Robert M. LaFollette of Wisconsin. Fall had already made enemies with conservationists such as LaFollette and Gifford Pinchot, who as members of the progressive wing of the Republican party took strong exception to the exploitation of public lands on the part of private business and mining interests.

The Republican-majority Congress, however, was falling in line with President Harding in an effort to demonstrate party solidarity, effectiveness, and, of course, efficiency. The legislature took little interest until the Department of the Interior finally admitted to the leases and also revealed ongoing negotiations with E. L. Doheny, failing to mention that the department's lease with Doheny had been concluded nearly a year earlier.

THE MARINES CALL AT TEAPOT DOME

The Teapot Dome affair grew even more complicated with the involvement of Colonel James Darden. An important contributor to the Harding campaign, Darden had offered $5,000 to the Harding war chest, which was gratefully accepted and then used to set up the unofficial Ohio Gang Entertainment Committee, which had spent freely on prohibited alcohol during the presidential campaign. By coincidence, Darden also possessed a lease on 160 acres of oil-bearing property within the Teapot Dome reserve. When word got out that Albert Fall had extended a lease on the Teapot Dome reserve, Darden asked Attorney General Daugherty to take some kind of action to help him protect his interests.

Daugherty suggested to Darden that he take his case to court, the usual procedure for disputes over mineral rights on federally owned land. When Secretary Fall heard of the problem, however, he quickly wrote to President Harding, asking that the government take action against Darden in order to protect *his* interests. Harding went along with Fall, promising that if Darden did not stop his drilling and clear out completely, the government would immediately take the steps necessary to throw him out.

Fall wanted above all to avoid a legal battle which would bring his Teapot Dome leases to light in a federal court. He sent out a call for the U.S. Marines, claiming that he could not find Darden to serve him with the proper papers. (At the time, Darden was living in Washington, D.C., at the Lafayette Hotel, in close proximity to Albert Fall as well as to the White House.) Fall put in his request to Assistant Secretary of the Navy Theodore Roosevelt Jr., claiming that both he and Harding wanted Darden's trespassing, oil-drilling squatters forcibly ejected. Roosevelt called on General J. A. LeJeune, the Marine Corps commandant, who then selected Captain George Shuler to carry out the operation.

Fall met with Shuler and apprised him of the delicate situation. Darden was an important political supporter of the president, Fall reported, and Harding did not want to completely alienate his ally. Shuler proceeded to Casper, Wyoming, gathered arms and four enlisted men, and then marched his detachment to Teapot Dome, where the startled drillers were promptly chased off their own property. Captain Shuler put up prominent No Trespassing signs and then went to lunch with the drillers he had just defeated.

THE PRESS AND A PESKY CONGRESS

The Teapot Dome leases ran afoul of much more powerful enemies in Frederick Bonfils and Albert Tammen, joint owners of the *Denver Post*. Bonfils and Tammen had signed an agreement with an oil operator named Leo Stack to share in the proceeds of any money paid out to Stack by the Pioneer Oil Company, which had bought up most of the scattered claims on Teapot Dome that had to be settled by Harry Sinclair before he could begin drilling. To earn their share, Bonfils and Tammen sent out a *Post* reporter, D. F. Stackelback, to Fall's New Mexico ranch to investigate. The *Post* then ran a series of scathing, red-letter, front page stories on the Sinclair deal, characterizing it as a blatant and fraudulent land grab.

The *Post* articles were sent to members of Congress. After this occurred, Sinclair's lawyer, Colonel Zevely, arranged a meeting with Bonfils and Tammen. When the meeting ended without any agreements or arrangements, Bonfils and Tammen resumed printing articles critical of Fall's actions at Teapot Dome. Sinclair reopened negotiations, offering a quarter of a million dollars outright as well as a percentage of profits Sinclair Oil earned at Teapot Dome. The critical articles in the *Post* promptly ceased, but would later have a way of reappearing whenever Sinclair's money was slow to appear.

In the meantime, the querying by members of Congress, administration officials, and the press was finally forcing Albert Fall to admit to some of his actions in public. An investigation was underway, led by Democratic Senator Thomas J. Walsh of Montana. Fall's leases came under strong criticism from conservationists, who noted that for a public official drawing a moderate salary of $12,000 a year, he was doing suspiciously well. The Three Rivers Ranch boasted new wire fencing, paved driveways, and expensive, pedigreed livestock; Fall had also managed to pay off all of his back taxes. He was upgrading local roads; he was building a hydroelectric plant.

The public criticism and the looming shadow of congressional investigation finally prompted Albert Fall to resign his post on January 2, 1923. Harding, who almost always stood by his friends, then offered Fall a seat on the Supreme Court. Fall turned down the appointment, accepting instead a job offer from Harry Sinclair. Admiral Robison also resigned, and also accepted a job with Sinclair's company.

After the death of Warren Harding, in August 1923, the Fall investigation continued, with Senator Thomas Walsh finally calling Fall himself to account with a congressional subpoena. Fall did not appear but did send a letter proclaiming his innocence in the whole affair and denying that he had received any money from either Doheny or Sinclair. The improvements at Three Rivers, he insisted, were the fruit of a $100,000 loan he had received from Ned McLean, the *Washington Post* owner. McLean, like Fall, proved reluctant to testify in Washington, instead taking up residence in Palm Beach, Florida, and hiring A. Mitchell Palmer, the former attorney general, as his attorney to fend off the repeated requests and congressional subpoenas.

In October 1923, a committee under Senator Walsh convened hearings on the disposal of government oil bearing lands in Wyoming and California. In February of the following year, Senator Burton K. Wheeler of Montana passed a resolution to form another investigating committee, this one to investigate the actions of Attorney General Daugherty. As the Walsh committee droned through its hearings over the following months and years, the scandal slowly unfolded, as memoriums to the late president gave way to a sinking feeling among the public that something had indeed been very rotten in the Harding administration.

GRAFT AND THEFT AT THE VETERANS BUREAU

The scandals of the Harding administration did not start or stop with the Teapot Dome affair. One of Harding's worst appointments was that of his friend Charles Forbes, a Democrat from Washington who had hit it off well with Mr. and Mrs. Harding during a senatorial junket the Hardings had taken to Hawaii in 1915. After taking office, Harding had considered several different awards for Forbes, including a membership on the Board of Shipping, the governorship of Alaska Territory, and the ambassadorship to Peru, all of which Forbes declined. Finally, Harding suggested an appointment to the War Risk Insurance Board. Forbes accepted, and when this agency was rolled into the new United States Veterans Bureau, Forbes was named the bureau's first director.

The Veterans Bureau, which the Harding administration established out of several separate bureaus, drew a larger appropriation than any other agency in the federal government—about $500 million a year. It was responsible for the care of injured and sick veterans of World War I, many of whom were permanently disabled and completely dependent on the bureau for care and for housing. It built hospitals, hired staffs of doctors and nurses, and consumed vast amounts of food, medical supplies, clothing, bedding, and other goods from private suppliers.

Forbes made several appointments of his own to important positions in the Veterans Bureau. Carolyn Votaw, sister of President Harding, became a personnel director. Votaw in turn introduced Forbes to Elias Mortimer, a representative of the St. Louis contracting firm of Thompson & Black. Mortimer and his wife Kathryn, as well as Carolyn Votaw and Charles Forbes, formed an intimate circle of friends who spent much of their time entertaining themselves at the expense of the Veterans Bureau.

His friends appointed to high places, Forbes proceeded to run the bureau as if it were a private, for-profit corporation. He managed to have hospital construction contracts transferred from the Department of the Army to the Veterans Bureau, after simply asking Harding for an executive order. As a result, more than $30 million worth of construction contracts came under his personal control. To do a little field investigation for the rewarding of these contracts, he set off in the spring of 1922 with Mr. and Mrs. Mortimer to undertake a survey of 12 future construction sites. In Chicago, Forbes met John W. Thompson, a Thompson & Black partner, after receiving a personal cash gift, sent through Mortimer, of $5,000. The donation had its intended result. Not only did contracts go to Thompson's firm, but Forbes also had Thompson & Black tack $150,000 onto the construction costs of each new hospital, of which Forbes would receive one-third, as well as a 35 percent share of Thompson & Black's profits in the venture, as a kickback.

The investigative journey continued across the Great Plains and the Rocky Mountains, with the Forbeses and the Mortimers enjoying riotous parties while negotiating for large private gains in the awarding of future construction contracts and in the purchase of land for the hospitals at inflated prices by the Veterans Bureau.

After returning to Washington, the industrious Forbes began a second profitable operation at the government warehouses at Perryville, Maryland, which he had also convinced Harding to transfer to his control by executive order. Forbes presented the new federal Bureau of the Budget with a list of supplies at Perryville, including gauze, bandages, sheets, pajamas, soap, medicine, and other goods, that were now "surplus" in Forbes's opinion and that could just as well be sold off to the highest bidder. Forbes had prevailed on Harding to transfer control of these stocks from the Quartermaster of the Army to him, then privately arranged the sale of the goods from the Perryville warehouse to the Thompson & Kelley Company of Boston, which ordered 100,000 pairs of pajamas at 30 cents a pair; 12,000 sheets for six cents each; 45,000 rolls of gauze at 27 cents each; 75,000 towels for 19 cents each, and many other supplies at about 20 percent of their market value, all at a time when veterans' hospitals in the rest of the country were experiencing shortages of the same essential goods.

Forbes kept the transactions strictly private and noncompetitive, ignoring bids from all other companies. Thompson & Kelley also took possession of trucks, tools, and hardware, while Forbes diverted drugs and alcohol to ready buyers on the black market. In all, $3 million worth of supplies were sold to Thompson & Kelley for about $600,000.

Forbes, like Fall, grew careless. Rumors of corruption were beginning to reach President Harding, while Surgeon General Charles E. Sawyer began an investigation of his own into the workings of the Forbes Veterans Bureau. Sawyer brought the sales to the attention of Harding, who issued an order on November 24, 1922, to have the transfers temporarily stopped. Under fire from within the administration, Forbes asked the War Department to look into the situation at Perryville. Major John Carmody was assigned to the duty and gave the Perryville operation a clean bill of health. Harding then dismissed the accusations against Forbes, and issued another order on December 12 allowing the sales to continue.

President Harding turned over the Veterans Bureau to Colonel Charles Forbes, an appointment that would turn out badly for both men. *(Library of Congress/National Photo Company Collection)*

Dr. Sawyer then traveled out to Perryville to see for himself. In the company of Hugh Cumming, he watched as trains loaded with surplus goods left Perryville for their destination in Boston. Sawyer returned to Washington and confronted Attorney General Daugherty, who was no friend of Charles Forbes, with the evidence of his own eyes. Daugherty went directly to Harding. At first unwilling to believe the stories, Harding reluctantly came to the conclusion that his old friend Charles Forbes was a crook. The president ordered the operations stopped permanently and ordered a reorganization of the Veterans Bureau. Harding took it all personally—a reporter happening upon an open door in the White House found the president at Forbes's throat, screaming threats and imprecations. In January 1923, Forbes was sent to Europe, reportedly to look after the U.S. veterans who remained there. Safely out of reach of congressional subpoenas, he soon tendered his resignation to the president.

LAST DAYS OF THE PRESIDENT

In the summer of 1923, exhausted and frightened by the ever-growing scandals and the heavy responsibilities of a job that was beyond his abilities, Warren Harding prepared for a speaking tour of the West. Harding dubbed the journey the Voyage of Understanding; it would provide him with a change of scene and a chance to return to the campaigning mode that he had found so congenial, back in the fall of 1920.

The journey was also intended as a crusade in the manner of the Woodrow Wilson train campaign of 1919. Instead of the League of Nations, however, Harding would be stumping for a Permanent Court of International Justice, or World Court, to be established in The Hague, the Netherlands, under the auspices of the League of Nations. In early 1923, a resolution had been introduced to the Senate by Democrat William King of Utah sanctioning U.S. participation; Senator Henry Cabot Lodge again played spoiler by not allowing the resolution to clear the Committee on Foreign Affairs, which he still headed. Harding's own party voted, nearly unanimously, against the World Court, but Harding fully supported U.S. participation, feeling perhaps that a policy of total isolation world work against U.S. interests in a world that had generally accepted the League of Nations. Still determined to run for reelection in 1924, he believed a cross-country journey would be just the thing to bolster the public's declining opinion of his ability.

Harding realized that his popularity was ebbing, even as the country slowly recovered from the postwar economic depression. The public that had supported him so fervently in early 1921 now saw him as a weak and indecisive leader, one around whom a strong whiff of scandal was beginning to accumulate. On May 29, the gloom surrounding the White House intensified when Harding and Daugherty learned that Jess Smith, Daugherty's assistant, had shot himself. This was not the first suicide within the Harding administration; attorney C. F. Cramer had also done himself in as scandal grew at the Veterans Bureau around the actions of Charles Forbes.

On June 20, Harding's 10-car train set off from Union Station in Washington. At each stop, the president put in an appearance, posing for photographs and speaking to the gathered crowds. In St. Louis, Harding made a speech at the St. Louis Coliseum supporting the World Court—the first public address to be broadcast coast-to-coast live by radio. Afterward, the train made its way to Kansas City and across the plains to Denver. In Utah, Harding took a horseback excursion through Zion National Park; the train then left for Idaho, passed through southern Montana, and stopped for the party to tour Yellowstone Park. At Centralia, Washington, Harding placed wreaths on the graves of the Legionnaires killed during the attack on IWW headquarters on Armistice Day, November 11, 1919.

On July 4, to the sound of a 21-gun salute, the Harding party left Tacoma aboard the *Henderson,* an old Army transport ship. The ship made its way north to Alaska, while the president relaxed in a well-appointed colonel's cabin. At one point, Secretary Hoover, who was accompanying the Hardings, sat down with the president and brought up the subject of scandals in the Justice Department. Hoover advised Harding to admit the scandals and gain credit for honesty; but when he pressed Harding for details, asking after Daugherty's role in the troubles, the president grew quiet. Neither Harding nor Hoover ever brought up the subject again.

In Alaska, the *Henderson* called at the Native American village of Metlakatla, the town of Ketchikan, and Juneau, the territorial capital. The ship sailed past immense cliffs, endless forests, and glaciers, which were pelted with five-inch shells to offer the president a spectacle worthy of his office: an immense avalanche of ice plunging into the ocean depths. From the town of Seward the party made its way by Pullman train to Anchorage and Fairbanks, then returned to Sitka on the Gulf of Valdez. On July 22, as the *Henderson* pulled away from Sitka and Alaska, Harding sat down to share a dinner of boiled crabs with his aide Reddy Baldinger. Meanwhile, the bad omens were continuing for Harding and the Republicans. Criticism of the World Court continued, and in a bellweather special election, the Populist candidate Magnus Johnson defeated the Republican candidate for senator in Minnesota by a wide margin.

The *Henderson* next reached Vancouver, where Harding was given a warm and friendly reception. Feeling ill and uneasy, the president gave a speech to one of the largest crowds of the entire journey in Vancouver's Stanley Park. After the boat left Vancouver, it made for Puget Sound, where in a thick fog it suffered a minor collision with the destroyer *Zeilen.* In Seattle, Harding delivered a speech, written by Hoover, to 60,000 people at Seattle Stadium, in which the president called for strict conservation in Alaska Territory. During the speech, Harding at one moment gripped the lectern, dropped the speech and nearly collapsed. That night, he suffered a violent attack of indigestion, which Dr. Sawyer blamed on tainted crabmeat.

A stop in Portland, Oregon, was canceled and the party left directly for San Francisco, where Harding arrived on July 29. The president quickly checked into Room 8064 at the Palace Hotel. After an attack of pneumonia, the president's remaining speeches and appearances in California were canceled. In the evening of August 3, after listening to his wife read a *Saturday Evening Post* article about him entitled "A Calm View of a Calm Man," Harding quietly passed away. Florence Harding would not allow an autopsy, and a committee of five doctors swiftly agreed to "apoplexy" as the cause of death.

THE PURITAN PRESIDENT

That night, in his hometown of Plymouth Notch, Vermont, Vice President Calvin Coolidge was sworn in as Warren Harding's successor. His father, local magistrate John Calvin Coolidge, administered the presidential oath of office in the dining room of the family's home. Coolidge was the sixth president in the country's history to take office on the death of his predecessor.

Coolidge's most notable achievement as vice president had been to avoid associating himself with Warren Harding's cronies in the Ohio Gang. The Senate hearings on Teapot Dome and on the Veterans Department made no mention of the vice president's role, as there had been none. He was clean, as far as the press and the public were concerned, and his strict bearing and his reasonable words—as few as they were—conveyed an image of a man with common sense and scrupulous honesty.

Coolidge's Puritan upbringing had taught him thrift and the inclination to keep his mouth shut. After graduating from Amherst, he followed an uneventful law career and then followed a conventional ambition into state politics. He won a seat in the Massachusetts legislature, then was elected to lieutenant governor and later, governor. His upbringing did not allow for any lavishness, even on attaining high office, and as the state's highest elected official he lived in a practical, two-room, dollar-a-day Boston apartment. In June 1920, he was considered by the Republican party for vice president, not in recognition of his achievements in office but rather for his actions during the Boston police strike and for a popular statement he had made via telegram to Samuel Gompers of the American Federation of Labor: "There is no right to strike against the public safety by anybody, anywhere, at any time." This simple, straightforward and principled stand, in a time of widely feared labor chaos and Bolshevik revolution, was all it took to win the appointment as Warren Harding's running mate in 1920.

Coolidge's principle goals as president were to balance the federal budget and to avoid problems. After the presidency of Warren Harding, he represented a much-needed return to the "normalcy" that Harding himself had promised but never quite achieved. In an age of spreading political corruption, a loosening of traditional Victorian morals, daring music and outrageous dancing, he stood for rectitude, reticence, and the country's worthy ancestors: the yeoman farmers, minutemen, and republican patriots of the Yankee past. The vote for Coolidge was a nostalgia vote, enthusiastically cast by voters determined to enjoy the 20th century, Prohibition or no Prohibition.

CONVENTIONS OF 1924

Coolidge held and acted on the belief that "the business of America is business," and that private corporations and employers should be let alone to do what they did best—turn over inventory, earn profits, create employment, and reward investors. Coolidge saw free enterprise as integral to a democratic society and modern big business as something miraculous. He left well enough alone by reducing as much as possible the restrictive ties of government regulation, supervision, and taxation. While they enjoyed an economic boom that had begun in the later months of Harding's administration, the public and its elected lawmakers were only too happy to go along.

Coolidge's popularity was such that by the time of the convention season of 1924, the Democratic party appeared divided, slightly obsolete, even endangered. William Gibbs McAdoo and Alfred E. Smith represented the party's two opposed factions. McAdoo, a Georgia-born Wall Street lawyer and the son-in-law of President Wilson, stood for the South and the Midwest, the small town, Prohibition, Anglo-Saxon, and traditional Protestant majority that, in the face of immigration and urbanization, seemed to be turning into a historical memory.

Smith was a New Yorker, raised in sight of the Brooklyn Bridge, a former New York assemblyman and a Prohibition opponent, whom his opponents accused of close association with Tammany Hall and thus big-city machine politics, backroom deals, vote-buying, and other forms of urban corruption. Smith's support came from the younger generation of immigrants' descendants, "hyphenated Americans" whose parents had arrived by steamer from the Old World and who now demanded the equal opportunity their parents had been anticipating upon arrival at Ellis Island.

No Democratic party member, no matter how implacably opposed to Smith and to his city slicker wisecracks, his derby hat, and his checked suit, could deny that as a governor he had been a success. Starting in 1918, and usually in the face of hostile Republican majorities in the New York statehouse, Smith had reformed the state government and instituted new social welfare policies that foreshadowed the New Deal of Franklin Roosevelt. Smith had fought against the expulsion of socialists during the Red Scare of 1919 and had vetoed a bill requiring the state's teachers to prove a satisfactory allegiance to the United States. At the same time, Smith had shown enough fiscal sense and responsibility to earn the respect even of conservative Republicans, who in 1924 watched in reluctant admiration as Smith cut $17 million from the state budget and cut state income taxes by 25 percent, even while advancing new laws for workers' compensation, the 48-hour work week for women and children, and the creation of the Bureau of Housing, which designed new low-cost apartment buildings to replace New York's crowded and unhealthy tenements.

Into his administration Smith brought social reformers and activists, many of them women who were entering politics for the first time thanks to the gender revolution that was beginning to erode the male dominance over business as well as politics. Among the most prominent of these was Frances Perkins, a "radical reformer" according to her enemies, who had worked at Hull House in Chicago before serving as head of the New York Consumer's League. Under Al Smith's sponsorship, Perkins would chair the New York Industrial Commission, and later, under President Franklin Roosevelt, she would serve as Secretary of Labor: the first woman in history to serve in the presidential cabinet.

Smith had been planning his presidential run for some time, and he knew that he would have to sort out for the public his position on Prohibition. When the New York state legislature passed a measure favoring repeal of the Mullan-Gage Act, the New York Prohibition enforcement law, Smith agonized for a long time, then under pressure from his old sponsors in Tammany Hall, decided to sign the repeal, knowing that it would probably contribute to his defeat. Smith knew that Prohibition still had its staunch supporters, and that as much as they enjoyed the flaunting of the Volstead Act, those less staunch still wanted the chief executive to put on a law-abiding appearance.

DENOUNCING THE KLAN

The central issue and dispute of the Democratic convention, the issue that would touch off a bitter war for delegate votes between McAdoo and Smith, was a proposed motion to denounce the Ku Klux Klan. In 1924 the Klan was at the height of its power and popularity, strong in the Midwest as well as the South, striving for national acceptance of its program of race purity and a return to small-town traditions. The anti-Klan resolution, proposed by a group of delegates from the Northeast, was supported by Al Smith and the easterners, while it was opposed by delegates from the South and West as well as by William McAdoo. (Knowing that much of his support came from voters who either belonged to or sympathized with the Klan, McAdoo would not denounce the organization.) While Smith delegates stomped and hooted their disapproval, William Jennings Bryan delivered a fiery speech against the motion. The first ballot, including fractional votes, came out 546.15 to 542.85 against the resolution. Claimed as a victory by McAdoo and his forces, the debate on the anti-Klan resolution set the tone of bitter division that would continue into the nominating contest.

In order to win the nomination as the Democratic presidential candidate, the candidates had to gain two-thirds, or 732, of the 1,098 votes. The first delegate poll went 431.5 for McAdoo, 241 for Smith: the balloting then went on for several days. Smith reached his highest total on the 76th ballot with 368 votes. When a group of western delegates offered a deal in which Smith would support Senator Thomas Walsh of Montana in exchange for their support at the 1928 nomination, Smith turned it down. Neither McAdoo nor Smith were ever able to gain the needed two-thirds; finally, on July 8, after 10 days and 100 ballots, McAdoo and Smith agreed to meet in a room at the Ritz-Carlton hotel to work something out. Smith suggested that both candidates withdraw; McAdoo then suggested a compromise candidate, Edwin Meredith of Iowa; Smith and McAdoo cordially shook hands, having agreed on nothing, and the meeting ended. Soon afterward, the name of John W. Davis of West Virginia was put forward by campaign managers on both sides. Davis, former solicitor general, ambassador to Great Britain, and attorney for banker J. P. Morgan, represented a lukewarm combination of Wall Street money and the Woodrow Wilson administration. On the 103rd ballot, he was nominated, while Governor Charles W. Bryan of Nebraska, the brother of William Jennings Bryan, was chosen as the vice presidential nominee.

In the November presidential election, Davis and Bryan would have to face Calvin Coolidge, the unopposed nominee of the Republican Party, as well as the Progressive Party, which in its July convention had nominated Robert La Follette for president and Burton Wheeler for vice president. (The Progressives would nominate no other candidates for local offices.) La Follette sought public control of railroads, an end to business monopolies, tax reform, and direct election of candidates through primaries rather than through political nominating. Many of these were still popular causes, but La Follette's abilities as a public speaker were in decline, and he could not adapt to the new medium of radio. While delivering a speech on Labor Day, he roamed the platform as always, while his face remained invisible and his voice inaudible for the mass radio audience. The spreading Prohibition-era prosperity for city dwellers also made his reform program less appealing to a largely contented and cynical electorate, while rising farm prices also blunted his appeal to farmers, his bedrock constituency.

That fall, the Progressives put up a total of $221,000 for the presidential campaign, while the Democrats spent $800,000 and the Republicans $4 million. The election results demonstrated that the Republican tide was full while also underlining a strengthening phenomenon of nationwide voter apathy: only 52 percent of registered voters bothered to turn out. Coolidge, with his confident, unruffled manner, won convincingly with 15,725,016 popular and 382 electoral votes. Yet the Progressives managed the best third-party performance in U.S. history: a total of 4,822,856 votes (more than half the Democratic total of 8,385,586), runner-up in 12 western states, and victory in Wisconsin.

CHRONICLE OF EVENTS

1922

January 28: Heavy snow collapses the roof of the Knickerbocker Theater in Washington, D.C., killing 100 people.

January 30: The World Court holds its first session in The Hague, Netherlands.

February 5: The first edition of the *Reader's Digest* is published.

February 6: Treaties are signed at the Conference for Limitation of Armament. The United States, Great Britain, and Japan agree to maintain the number of their capital ships at a ratio of 5-5-3. New capital ships under construction are to be scrapped. The use of submarines in warfare is restricted, and the use of poison gas is outlawed. The United States, Great Britain, and Japan agree to respect each other's Pacific possessions, and the territorial integrity of China is also to be respected.

February 7: A Chippewa said to be the oldest living human dies at the age of 137 in Cass Lake, Minnesota.

February 9: The World War Foreign Debt Commission is established to manage the repayment of more than $10 billion in wartime loans. Over the next few years, the commission will reschedule payments, reduce principal balances, and cancel loans outright.

February 18: The Capper-Volstead Act allows farmers to form cooperatives without violating antitrust laws.

February 21: The dirigible *Roma* explodes at Norfolk, Virginia, killing 34 people.

February 27: The Supreme Court upholds the 19th Amendment granting universal women's suffrage.

March 5: Annie Oakley sets a new trapshooting record, hitting 98 of 100 targets during a competition at the Pinehurst Gun Club in North Carolina.

March 20: President Harding orders the withdrawal of U.S. troops from the Rhineland region of Germany.

March 28: New York bans immigrants and resident aliens from teaching in the public schools.

April 1: A strike of 500,000 coal miners in anthracite and bituminous fields begins in protest of cuts in pay. The miners will return with small concessions in September.

April 7: Secretary of the Interior Albert B. Fall leases the Teapot Dome oil reserve in Wyoming to the Mammoth Oil Company of Harry Sinclair. Later charged with bribery and conspiracy to defraud the government, Fall will be sentenced to a year in prison.

April 15: Senator John Kendrick of Wyoming, responding to questioning by his constituents, asks Albert Fall to explain the leasing of federal oil reserves, including Reserve No. 3 at Teapot Dome, Wyoming.

April 29: On the urging of Senator Robert M. La Follette, Senator Thomas Walsh establishes a senate committee to investigate the leasing of government-owned oil-bearing lands in Wyoming and California.

May 15: In *Bailey v. Drexel Furniture,* the Supreme Court declares the child labor clause of the War Revenue Act of 1919 unconstitutional.

May 26: The Narcotics Control Board is established by an act of Congress.

May 30: Jimmy Murphy wins the Indianapolis 500 auto race with an average speed of 94.5 miles per hour.

May 30: The Lincoln Memorial is dedicated in Washington, D.C.

June 10: Birth of actress Judy Garland.

June 21: Coal miners riot in Herrin, Illinois, killing several strikebreakers.

July 20: Chile and Peru present the Tacna-Arica border dispute to the president of the United States for mediation. The dispute will be settled in 1929.

September 19: President Harding vetoes the Soldiers' Bonus Bill. The veto will be overridden in the House but upheld in the Senate on September 20.

September 21: The Fordney-McCumber Tariff Act is passed, establishing protectionist import duties that will severely affect European nations' ability to repay war debts.

September 22: The Cable Act allows a woman to marry an alien (i.e., a foreigner) without losing U.S. citizenship. Foreign women marrying U.S. citizens are not automatically granted citizenship.

October 3: Rebecca L. Felton is appointed senator from Georgia on the death of Thomas Watson. She is the first woman to serve as a senator, and her term lasts one day.

October 6: Attorney General Harry Daugherty bans the sale of liquor on U.S. ships anywhere in the world, or on foreign ships lying within 3 miles of the coast.

December 4: The Second Central American Conference meets in Washington, principally to foster negotiation between Honduras and Nicaragua. The conference will reestablish the Central American Court of Justice.

Calvin Coolidge poses with his sons on a White House porch, June 30, 1924. Coolidge represented a straitlaced Republican antidote for citizens alarmed by the decade's new liberties. *(Library of Congress/National Photo Company Collection)*

December 10: Niels Bohr wins a Nobel prize for work on the quantum theory.

1923

January 7: The Baltimore *Sun* runs an exposé of Ku Klux Klan atrocities in Morehouse Parish, Louisiana.

January 10: Harding withdraws the American Army of the Rhine, the last of the U.S. troops stationed in Germany.

January 31: After Charles Forbes comes under scrutiny for irregularities in the Veterans Bureau, the Harding administration announces a reorganization of the Bureau.

February 24: In an address to the Senate, President Harding urges that the United States adhere to the decisions of the World Court.

February 28: By the British Debt Refunding Act, Great Britain's $4.6 billion debt is rescheduled for payment over a period of 62 years, at interest of 3.3 percent.

March 2: The Senate begins its investigation of the Veterans Bureau under Charles Forbes.

March 4: The Intermediate Credit Act establishes 12 regional credit banks to extend loans to farm cooperatives and marketing associations.

March 4: Interior Secretary Albert Fall resigns his position to look after private interests in his home state of New Mexico.

March 11: Charles R. Cramer, assistant to Charles Forbes at the Veterans Bureau, commits suicide.

March 15: Dot King, a glamorous *Ziegfeld Follies* chorus girl also known as the Broadway Butterfly, is found dead in her Manhattan apartment. Robbery is suspected; $30,000 of jewelry is missing. The investigation turns up J. Kearsley Mitchell, a Philadelphia tycoon, but police believe his alibi and the case goes unsolved.

April 9: In *Adkins v. Children's Hospital,* the Supreme Court rules that a minimum wage for women workers in the District of Columbia is unconstitutional.

May 4: The state of New York repeals its own Prohibition enforcement act.

May 23: Florida abolishes flogging at prison labor camps.

May 27: The Ku Klux Klan refuses to publish a list of its members.

June 4: In *Robert T. Meyer v. State of Nebraska,* the Supreme Court rules that state laws prohibiting the teaching of foreign languages are unconstitutional.

June 20: Warren Harding sets out on a tour of the western states.

July 8: Louis Armstrong arrives in Chicago.

August 2: Warren Harding dies in a San Francisco hotel.

August 3: Vice President Calvin Coolidge is sworn in by his father in Plymouth Notch, Vermont, as the 30th president.

August 6: U.S. swimmer Henry Sullivan traverses the English Channel in 28 hours.

August 13: U.S. Steel institutes the eight-hour working day, cutting the average working day of a steelworker from 12 to 14 hours. As other industries follow suit, the drop in production will bolster prices.

August 31: President Alvaró Obregón of Mexico is formally recognized by the United States.

EYEWITNESS TESTIMONY

Warren Harding and Teapot Dome

I expect it is very possible that I would make as good a President as a great many men who are talked of for that position and I would almost be willing to make a bet that I would be a more "commonsensible" President than the man who now occupies the White House. At the same time I have such a sure understanding of my own insufficiency that I should really be ashamed to presume myself fitted to reach out for a place of such responsibility. More than that, I would not think of involving my many good friends in the tremendous tasks of making a Presidential campaign.

There are some people who discuss the availability of my name and I am frank to say I am human enough to rejoice that there are people who think well enough of me to mention me in that connection. More than that, it is a mighty gratifying thing to know that one has friends who are willing to give up their time and their means to back a candidacy, but I should be unhappy every hour from the time I entered the race until the thing were settled, and I am sure I should never have any more fun or any real enjoyment in life if I should be so politically fortunate to win a nomination and election. I had much rather retain my place in the Senate and enjoy the association of friends and some of the joys of living—not the least of these is an occasional trip to Texas.

Warren Harding, replying in a letter to the urging of political allies that he run for president in 1919, quoted in Russell, President Harding: His Life and Times *(1968), p. 314.*

Well, there will be no nomination on the early ballots. After the other candidates have failed, after they have gone their limit, their leaders, worn out and wishing to do the very best thing, will get together in some hotel room about 2:11 in the morning. Some fifteen men, bleary eyed with lack of sleep, and perspiring profusely with excessive heat, will sit around a big table. I will be with them and present the name of Senator Harding. When that time comes, Harding will be selected, because he fits in perfectly with every need of the party and nation. He is the logical choice, and the leaders will determine to throw their support to him.

Harry Daugherty, predicting the "smoke-filled room" nomination of Warren Harding at the 1920 Republican convention, as quoted by Mark Sullivan in Our Times Vol. VI *(1935), p. 37.*

We think you may be nominated tomorrow. Before acting finally we think you should tell us, on your conscience and before God, whether there is anything that might be brought against you that would embarass the party, any impediment that might disqualify you or make you inexpedient, either as candidate or President.

Question put to Warren Harding by Colonel George Harvey during Chicago Republican convention, June 1920, as quoted in Samuel Hopkins Adams, "The Timely Death of President Harding," and printed in Leighton (ed.), The Aspirin Age *(1949), p. 87.*

On Friday morning, June 9, while the nomination speeches were [being made] at the Convention Hall, I sat alone with Warren Harding in his rooms at the Auditorium Hotel. The weather was very hot and he had taken off his coat and waistcoat and was fanning himself vigorously. In the course of our conversation he said: "I cannot afford to keep these rooms any longer and I have sent word downstairs to say that I am giving them up this evening. This convention will never nominate me. I do not propose to go back to the Senate. I am going to quit politics and devote myself to my newspaper." These words were spoken between eleven and twelve o'clock on Friday morning. At about six-fifteen on the following afternoon Warren Harding had been nominated for President of the United States. At the moment when his nomination was made, Frank Lowden and I were sitting with Harding in one of the small rooms back of the platform of the Convention Hall. We three were alone. The roll was being called on the tenth ballot. Suddenly, there was a tremendous roar from the Convention Hall. In an instant, the door of the room in which we three were sitting burst open and Charles B. Warren, of Michigan, leapt into the room, shouting: "Pennsylvania has voted for you, Harding, and you are nominated!" Harding rose, and with one hand in Lowden's and one in mine, he said with choking voice: "If the great honor of the Presidency is to come to me, I shall need all the help that you two friends can give me." In another instant Harry Daugherty arrived, seized Harding, and took him back to the Auditorium Hotel before a crowd could assemble.

Nicholas Murray Butler, reminiscence of the June 1920 Republican convention from his 1936 memoir "Across the Busy Years," reprinted in White, A Puritan in Babylon *(1958), p. 211.*

President Harding attends the World Series with Secretary of Commerce Herbert Hoover and other cabinet members. *(Library of Congress)*

... he tried to imagine himself in Congress rooting around in the litter of that incredible pigsty with the narrow and porcine brows he saw pictured sometimes in the rotogravure sections of the Sunday newspapers, those glorified proletarians babbling blandly to the nation the ideas of high school seniors! Little men with copy-book ambitions who by mediocrity had thought to emerge from mediocrity into the lustreless and unromantic heaven of a government by the people—and the best, the dozen shrewd men at the top, egotistic and cynical, were content to lead the choir of white ties and wire collar-buttons in a discordant and amazing hymn, compounded of a vague confusion between wealth as a reward of virtue and wealth as a proof of vice, and continued cheers for God, the Constitution, and the Rocky Mountains!

F. Scott Fitzgerald, from his novel The Beautiful and Damned, *(1922), p. 3.*

With Wood, Johnson and Lowden out of the way, I knew I could count on friends in every one of their delegations, because I had followed in my pre-convention campaigning the rule that has guided me throughout my political career, which is not to hurt anyone's feelings or to step on anybody's toes if I could find foot room elsewhere. I figured that if politeness and an honest desire not to humiliate any rival just for the sake of winning a few votes were ever going to produce anything, this was the time. Other fellows, just as competent as I, or more so, had made enemies, and it looked to me that there was no one in sight that the convention could unite on except myself.

Warren Harding, commenting on his 1920 nomination and quoted in Sinclair, The Available Man *(1965), p. 136.*

If an optimist is a man who makes lemonade out of all the lemons that are handed to him, then Senator Harding is the greatest of all optimists. He has been told by his friends and his critics that he is colorless and without sap, commonplace and dull, weak and servile. Right you are, says the Senator. You have described exactly the kind of man this country needs. It has tried [Theodore] Roosevelt and Wilson, and look. It can't stand the gaff. I am nothing that they were. I am no superman like Roosevelt and no superthinker like Wilson. Therefore, I am just the man you are looking for. How do I know that? I am distinguished by the fact that nothing distinguishes me. I am marked for leadership because I have no marks upon me. I am just the man because no one can think of a single reason why I am the man. If any one happens to think of a reason then I shall cease to be that normal man which these abnormal times demand.

Editorial by Walter Lippman on the candidacy of Senator Warren Harding for president, 1920, from Lippman, Public Persons *(1976), p. 49.*

After being with Harding for two days, he made me the direct tender of appointment as Secretary of the Interior and urged my acceptance, stating that, among other things, he knew he could count on my advice and assistance should I remain in the Senate, but that he would feel much freer to have me as one of his official advisors associated with him direct. I finally told him I would accept the appointment.

Secretary of the Interior Albert Fall in letter of February 4, 1921, to his wife Emma Fall, quoted in The Shadow of Blooming Grove *(1968), p. 431.*

On the question of the logical content of Dr. Harding's harangue of last Friday I do not presume to have views. But when it comes to the style of a great man's discourse, I can speak with a great deal less prejudice, and maybe with somewhat more competence, for I have earned most of my livelihood for twenty years past by translating the bad English of a multitude of authors into measurably better English. Thus qualified professionally, I rise to pay my small

tribute to Dr. Harding. Setting aside a college professor or two and half a dozen dipsomaniacal newspaper reporters, he takes the first place in my Valhalla of literati. That is to say, he writes the worst English that I have ever encountered. It reminds me of a string of wet sponges; it reminds me of tattered washing on the line; it reminds me of stale bean-soup, of college yells, of dogs barking idiotically through endless nights. It drags itself out of the dark abysm (I was about to write abscess!) of pish, and crawls insanely up the topmost pinnacle of posh. It is rumble and bumble. It is flap and doodle. It is balder and dash.

H. L. Mencken, comment on "Gamalielese," March 7, 1921, reprinted in On Politics: A Carnival of Buncombe *(1960), pp. 41–42.*

It can be said for the present Secretary of the Interior that he has always frankly declared his position on public questions. As a Member of the Senate, his attitude toward the public domain generally, and the naval oil reserves in particular, was well understood . . . Upon every measure that involved the conservation of resources upon the public lands Senator Fall, from New Mexico, was the aggressive opponent of the policy of conservation.

Senator Robert La Follette of Wisconsin, during Senate hearings on leases for Teapot Dome oil reserves, April 28, 1922, from Congressional Record, *1st Session, 68th Congress (1922).*

You yellow dog! You double-crossing bastard!

Warren Harding, in private to Colonel Charles R. Forbes in the spring of 1923, after learning of Forbes's activities at the Veterans Bureau, as witnessed by a reporter for the New York Times, *and quoted in Adams,* The Incredible Era *(1939), p. 297.*

I found Harding exceedingly nervous and distraught. As soon as we were aboard ship he insisted on playing bridge, beginning every day immediately after breakfast and continuing except for mealtime often until after midnight. One day after lunch when we were a few days out, Harding asked me to come to his cabin. He plumped at me the question: "If you knew of a great scandal in our administration, would you for the good of the country and the party expose it publicly or would you bury it?" My natural reply was, "Publish it, and at least get credit for integrity on your side." He remarked that this method might be politically dangerous. I asked for more particulars. He said that he had received some rumors of irregularities, centering around Smith, in connection with cases in the Department of Justice. Harding gave me no information about what Smith had been up to. I asked what Daugherty's relation to the affair were. He abruptly dried up and never raised the question again.

Herbert Hoover, recalling a brief conversation with President Harding on his final voyage to Alaska in July 1923, quoted in Anthony, Florence Harding: The First Lady, The Jazz Age, and the Death of America's Most Scandalous President *(1998), p. 436.*

We went to the Salt Creek district, about forty miles. . . . There was a rig up there, a drilling rig, and they had built a barbed wire fence around it. I went up to the fence and yelled out and asked where the boss was, and a man came over and said he was Harry McDonnell or O'Donnell. I said, "Do you represent the Mutual Oil people?" He said he did. I said, "I am the commandant of this Navy district." I assumed that title, being the only representative of the Navy Department around there, and somebody had to be commandant, so I took the title. I said, "I have orders to stop the work in this part of the reservation." He says, "Well, I have orders to keep everybody outside of this fence." I said, "Well, I have orders here from the Secretary of the Navy that I think will supersede any orders you have." I said, "Do you realize that I am absolutely serious about this thing and I am going to back up what I say?" He looked at the Marines; they had pistols and rifles and everything that goes with it. He said he thought we meant business. I said, "You have got to stop drilling." He said, "I can't give the order." I said, "Who is your boss driller?" So he called over a fellow named Harry Martin, and I said, "Are you in charge of the operation?" He said he was. I said, "How long will it take you to stop this work?" He said "Five minutes." I said, "I will give you ten."

So he went right in and stopped the rig from working. . . . About that time the field superintendant of the Mutual Oil Company came along, and I told him what I had done. He was rather peeved, but wanted to know if he could take the small tools and things that might be stolen if they shut down. I told him he could take anything he wanted, just so he left the ground.

Captain George Shuler, describing action of the U.S. Marines at Teapot Dome to the Senate Committee on Public Lands and Surveys; Hearings on Leases upon Naval Oil Reserves, 1924.

Four years of nullification of the Eighteenth Amendment by the Democratic and Republican officials have demonstrated the soundness of the philosophy of the Prohibition party that a law conferring a right will enforce itself, but a law prohibiting a wrong, financially and politically entrenched, requires a party thoroughly committed to its maintenance and enforcement. Little or no improvement can be expected so long as the friends of the prohibitory law divide themselves among political parties seeking the votes of the law violators and the nullificationists, which votes are regarded to be as necessary to the success of those political parties as are the votes of the law-abiders.

The astounding revelation of corruption and maladministration in government, extending to the Cabinet itself, are but the inevitable consequences of the moral bankruptcy of a political party which, perpetuating the old liquor regime, is dependent upon the wet vote for its margin of plurality.

Platform of the Prohibition Party, announced at its national convention at Columbus, Ohio, on June 6, 1924, from Porter and Johnson, National Party Platforms 1840–1964 *(1966), pp. 288–289.*

So-called "good society" winks at indiscretions, and the libertine mingles freely with the chaste and wins the plaudits of the bold adventurer, whose exploits give piquancy and zest to the otherwise colorless inanities of the drawing room. The youth, reared in such an atmosphere, comes to regard chastity as a cheap and worthless virtue, and gives unbridled rein to his passions. A scandal thus becomes a matter that relieves the tedium of a dull and prosaic existence and lends freshened interest to the news items of the day.

Bishop James E. Freeman, deploring the decline of morals in public as well as private life, in "When 'Good Society' Winks," The Literary Digest, *March 6, 1926, p. 31.*

If two men have three coats, both owning one and sharing the third equally, they may take money from their pockets and put it into their other pockets in such ways that wise men will not know whether to call them fools, thieves, or gamblers.

Of like sort is the problem that has confronted the Federal courts and square-jawed Thomas James Walsh, chief inquisitor of the Senate Committee on Public Lands, in the strange transactions of three oil companies remotely connected with the Oil Scandals. The ultimate object of reviewing these transactions is to expose the suppose source of the Liberty Bonds which Oilman Harry Ford Sinclair is known to have given Albert Bacon Fall, the defamed Secretary of the Interior who leased Teapot Dome to Sinclair. But the immediate motive, when Inquisitor Walsh renewed his inquiries last week, seems compounded as much of professional pique as of public conscience.

From a report on the ongoing Teapot Dome inquiry, "Corruption—Old Oil," in Time, *February 13, 1928, p. 16.*

Though violation of the Eighteenth Amendment was a matter of course in Washington, it was rather shocking to see the way Harding disregarded the Constitution he was sworn to uphold. Though nothing to drink was served downstairs, there were always cocktails in the upstairs hall outside the President's room. While the big official receptions were going on, I don't think the people had any idea what was taking place in the rooms above. One evening . . . a friend of the Hardings asked me if I would like to go up to the study. I had heard rumors and was curious to see for myself what truth was in them. No rumor could have exceeded the reality; the study was filled with cronies, Daugherty, Jess Smith, Alec Moore, and others; the air heavy with tobacco smoke, trays with bottles containing every imaginable brand of whiskey stood about, cards and poker chips ready at hand—a general atmosphere of waistcoat unbuttoned, feet on the desk, and the spittoon alongside.

Alice Roosevelt Longworth, describing the activities of the Ohio Gang in Longworth, Crowded Hours *(1933), p. 324.*

Calvin Coolidge

In looking ahead in the next four or eight years, I think what America needs more than anything else is a man who will in himself be a demonstration of character. I think Coolidge comes more nearly being that man than any other man in either party.

Dwight Morrow, letter of 1920 written to Thomas W. Lamont, as quoted in Schlesinger, The Crisis of the Old Order *(1957), p. 56.*

This country has come to a considerable degree of "normalcy." What it needs now is a stabilization of its favorable situation and confidence that this will continue. Wages are very high and unemployment is negli-

gible. Labor is, indeed, very well off. Business is good and industry is humming. The farm hysteria is hardly as vocal now as it was thirty days ago. Outside the wheat states, the farmer is going along very well. He had ample credit—too much in fact, according to his best friends. The all-around condition of the country is sound and warrants much optimism. Far-reaching changes, such as are constantly sought by the political dare-devil doctors, are the last thing this country needs.

Editorial from the Philadelphia Public Ledger *in the fall of 1923, reprinted in Sobel,* Coolidge: An American Enigma *(1998), p. 245.*

This is a business country . . . and it wants a business government.

Calvin Coolidge, statement of October 24, 1924, quoted in Schlesinger, The Crisis of the Old Order *(1957), p. 61.*

Jim did not care at present to have the Democrats elect the next President because he could not think of any likely candidate who wanted what he wanted. He admired the remarkable ability of our present President to suit the country in its present mood, but thought he would make a very nice king. As a President he seemed to Jim not to do enough, but as a constitutional monarch to keep hold of the ends of the reins and let his ministers drive, he thought he might do handsomely.

. . . His feeling was that Mr. Coolidge's immense success in acquiring the approbation of the people of the United States was due to the fact that he represents the disposition of lovers of the old order to hold on to conditions of existence which are passing. The jig was up with the old order, so Jim thought. It died in the war; but a considerable proportion of mankind was all for embalming it and keeping it in the show window. Mr. Coolidge—so Jim thought—had an instinctive and hereditary affection for the departed and though, as said, Jim felt he would have made a better king than president, he did not mind his being President in this interval while the remains of the old order are awaiting interment.

Edward S. Martin, describing the political opinions of his friend Jim Lines, in "Our Satisfaction with Mr. Coolidge," from Harper's, *November 1925, pp. 765–766.*

Yes sir, Cal is the President for real honest-to-God Americans like us.

There's a lot of folks that pan him, but what are they? You can bet your sweet life he isn't popular with the bums, or yeggs, or anarchists, or highbrows, or cynics—

Calvin Coolidge is depicted fishing along the Brule River in Douglas County, northern Wisconsin. Coolidge had himself photographed in a variety of outdoorsy settings in order to satisfy the public appetite for active and vigorous presidents, an aspect first inspired by Teddy Roosevelt. *(State Historical Society of Wisconsin)*

I remember our pastor saying one time, "A cynic is a man who sneers, and a man who sneers is setting himself up to tell God that he doesn't approve of God's handiwork!" No sir! You can bet Coolidge ain't popular with the Bolsheviks, or the lazy boob of a workman that wants fifteen bucks a day for doing nothing! No sir, nor with the cocaine fiends, or the drunkards, or the fellows that don't want the Prohibition law enforced—

Not that I never take a drink. What I say about Prohibition is: Once a law has been passed by the duly elected and qualified representatives of the people of these United States, in fact, once it's on the statute books, it's *there,* and it's there to be enforced. There hadn't ought to be any blind pigs or illegal stills. But same time, that don't mean you got to be a fanatic.

Sinclair Lewis, in "The Man Who Knew Coolidge,"
The American Mercury, *January 1928, p. 3.*

The Convention of 1924

While the results of the futile ballots were droned from the platform in the Garden yesterday, there sat in the exact center of the great hall the one man whose name would stampede the convention were he put in nomination. He is the only man to whom the contending factions could turn and at the same time save their faces and keep square with the folks at home. And that man does not want the nomination and actually would be alarmed if he knew what people were saying about him in the delegations and in the lower labyrinths of the building. . . . From the time Roosevelt made his speech in nomination of Smith, which was the one great speech of the convention, he has been easily the foremost figure on floor or platform. That is not because of his name. There are many Roosevelts. It is because, without the slightest intention or desire to do anything of the sort, he has done for himself what he could not do for his candidate.

Believing Roosevelt to be out of reach, the delegates cast a lingering look at him over their shoulders and renewed the search for somebody who could be nominated. . . . But always back to Roosevelt their gaze would go, and more than once it was found expedient to hush a little delegation which was talking about sending up his name, lest unforeseen results might happen. . . .

"Looker On," anonymous column, from the New York Herald Tribune, *July 1, 1924, quoted in Roosevelt,* F.D.R.: His Personal Letters, 1905–1928 *(1948), p. 562.*

Well, I saw something yesterday that for stupidity, lack of judgment, nonsensicality, unexcitement, uselessness and childishness has anything I've ever seen beaten. It was the Democratic National Convention. . . .

It does seem that out of all this barrage of everlasting talk, that maybe just accidentally some one would have made an original remark, or perhaps coined some epigram that could be remembered. But no. . . .

Now, I never propose a thing unless I have a solution to it. Make every speaker, as soon as he tells all he knows, sit down. That will shorten your speeches so much you will be out by lunch time every day.

Or make them be censored and not allow one man to repeat what some other man has said. That would cut it down to just one speech at each convention.

Will Rogers, article written during the 1924 Democratic convention, from Yagoda, Will Rogers: A Biography, *(1993), p. 211.*

The gang rule first came into the Republican Party last May when a flock of dragons, kleagles, cyclopes, and fuzzy furies came to Wichita from Oklahoma and held a meeting with some Kansas terrors and whambedoo-dles. They selected Ben Paulen to run as Republican candidate of the Ku Klux Klan . . . later the Cyclopes, Kleagles, Wizards, and willopus-wallopuses began parading in the Kansas cow pastures, passing the word down to the shirttailed rangers that they were to go into the Kansas primaries and nominate Ben Paulen.

William Allen White, speaking during his 1924 independent challenge to Republican candidate Ben Paulen for governor of Kansas, and quoted in Chalmers, Hooded Americanism: The First Century of the Ku Klux Klan, 1865–1965 *(1965), p. 147.*

In this country it is not necessary to protect any church. I have such confidence in the Catholic Church, which was for fifteen hundred years my mother church as well as yours, that I deny it needs political aid. . . .

The Jews do not need this resolution. They have Moses, they have Elijah, and they have also Elisha, who drew back the curtain and revealed upon the mountain top an invisible host greater than a thousand Ku Klux Klans.

. . . Jew and Gentile, Catholic and Protestant stand for God, on whom all religion rests, and Protestant and Catholic stand for the Christ. Is it possible that . . . at this time, in this great land, we are to have religious warfare? . . . I cannot believe it. God forbid! I call you back in the name of our party. I call you back in the name of the Son of God and Savior of the world. Christians, stop fighting. Banish the Hymn of Hate; our song must be "Blest be the tie that binds our hearts in Christian love."

William Jennings Bryan, speech denouncing anti-Klan resolution at the 1924 Democratic convention, quoted in Hibben, The Peerless Leader: William Jennings Bryan *(1929), p. 383.*

5

New Homes and a New Sound
September 1923– February 1924

The corollary of President Coolidge's faith in the free movement of capital was the free movement of individuals, and during the 1920s the people of the United States pursued their freedom of movement with a vengeance. For farmers who could not make farming pay in the agricultural depression, a move to the city and steady-paying factory work was in order. At the same time, the affordable Model T Ford made personal transportation feasible for the urban middle class, and the growing road network, which had been brought about in large part by the passage of the Federal Highways Act of 1916, linked cities and towns with hardtop roads that made long-distance driving tolerable, even enjoyable. Cities began their transformation into metropolitan areas as families that could afford to do so began moving to the suburbs that lay just beyond the city limits.

The busiest migration of the era took place among the African-American population, which had been on the move from South to North since just before World War I. A crucial spur to this migration was a 1910 Supreme Court decision that ended debt peonage for blacks in the South. The segregation imposed by Jim Crow laws, a wave of lynchings, and the denial by southern state governments of the constitutionally guaranteed right to vote put more black families on the northbound trains and highways; another root cause was the destruction of cotton, the South's staple agricultural product, by the boll weevil, a pest that had first arrived in Texas from Mexico in the 1890s. Moving at 40 to 60 miles a year, hordes of boll weevils made their way northeast through the cotton-producing states, in some years destroying as much as 50 percent of the crop. When World War I began, the overseas market for cotton was disrupted, further damaging the South's cotton-based economy. Available work for laborers dried up, while black tenant farmers found their credit with merchants cut off and many landowners unwilling to provide the supplies needed for cultivating and harvesting their crops.

Black migrants knew they would have much less trouble finding better-paid work in the northern states, especially after the beginning of World War I in the summer of 1914. The war abruptly ended emigration of unskilled laborers from Europe; and after the United States entered the war in 1917, recruitment into the U.S. Army separated thousands of American workers from their factory jobs.

Near Tampa, Florida, African Americans attend an auction of home lots reserved as "A City for Colored People." *(Bergert Brothers Collection, University of South Florida)*

The labor shortage raised the demand for unskilled workers from the South who had once seen their way blocked by exclusionary practices of northern trade unions and by the prejudice of employers who favored European immigrants. In the meantime, northern black newspapers encouraged the move with articles and employment advertisements; the *Chicago Defender,* the nation's leading black-owned-and-operated newspaper, designated May 15, 1917, as the start of what it called the Great Northern Drive. Within the South itself, another migration was taking place from rural to urban areas, helped along by white tenant farmers and smallholders who believed they would benefit by the disappearance of their black competitors. The result of the movement away from the southern countryside was the establishment of a predominantly urban black population throughout the country.

After the war, the Great Migration to the North continued in full force as southern blacks sought better job opportunities, schooling for their children, and freedom from the everyday racism that still took place in the South. Labor recruiters arrived in southern cities offering free passage to Detroit, Chicago, Indianapolis, and Cleveland, and the depopulation grew into a serious threat to southern factory bosses and large-scale farmers. In response, recruiters were forced back on northbound trains and would-be migrants were arrested on false charges, refused train tickets, and prohibited from entering train stations.

As the most important rail junction in the country, and the industrial hub of the Midwest, Chicago became the capital of the postwar northern migration. (The city's African-American population rose from 40,000 in 1910 to more than 100,000 in 1920, doubling its black percentage.) Traveling northward along the Mississippi River Valley, migrants came to Chicago from Louisiana, Mississippi, Alabama, Arkansas, and Texas. The new arrivals gathered in growing black districts such as the South Side of Chicago, where southern dialect could be heard from one end to the other of certain blocks and entire neighborhoods. Hundreds of new black-owned stores, banks, and real estate firms were founded on the South Side. As some black entrepreneurs found themselves still barred from business and government, they went into the business of cabarets, sports, and entertainment and catered to the growing black audience that was not welcome at many white-owned nightclubs or amusement parks.

The migration north was accompanied by growth in African-American policy and advocacy organizations, such as the National Urban League, formed in 1911 to create a network of local chapters in the cities to expand economic opportunity for blacks. Urban League offices were usually the first stop for southern migrants searching for the new jobs and better opportunities they expected to find. By 1920, more than 400 chapters of the National Association for the Advancement of Colored People (NAACP), founded in 1909, were also in existence to fight for desegregation, an end to lynching, equal opportunity, and the right to vote. In education, activism and advocacy also grew as black students formed their own student associations and denied the accommodative ideas of Booker T. Washington, the African-American educator who had urged blacks of an earlier time to make their peace with white social institutions and economic power. In the South, on the campuses of Fisk, Howard, Morehouse, Tuskegee, and other black colleges founded after the Civil War, students organized strikes to protest their second-class status among white colleges and the paternalistic attitudes of their predominantly white professors and college administrators. The unrest eventually reached a crisis at Fisk University, in Nashville, where a student demonstration turned violent on the night of February 4, 1925, prompting President Fayette McKenzie to call out the police. A strike at Howard University later that spring eventually brought the resignation of another white college president, J. Stanley Durkee. As the 1920s continued, students demanded that these institutions be placed under the administration and management of African Americans.

REACTION

The black migration north, the rapid transformation of the cities, and the growth of the new African-American urban community also touched off a postwar reaction that developed into the worst series of race riots yet seen in the United States. The prelude occurred as black veterans returned home to hostile small towns and cities in the South, where the sight of an African American in uniform was often enough to touch off a beating and, on some occasions, a lynching. White-dominated police departments, militias, and local governments did little to maintain order, but black soldiers, having experienced trench warfare in northern France, did not provide such easy targets in Knoxville; Charleston; Washington, D.C.; and Longview, Texas, where all-out race riots resulted.

The determination on the part of African Americans to organize and demand their equal rights also brought violence. In Phillips County, Arkansas, a group of black sharecroppers indebted to white landowners for their homes and equipment organized the Progressive Farmers and Householders Union to demand a market price for their crops and a better accounting of their debts. In October 1919, the group was attacked during a meeting at Hoop Spur, Arkansas, and in the troubles that followed as many as 100 blacks were murdered. Trials that took place after the violence led to the sentencing of 12 blacks to death for instigating the violence, a due-process lynching that was only stopped through the efforts of the antilynching crusader Ida B. Wells and the NAACP.

In the migratory center of Chicago, which had attracted more than 50,000 new black residents during the war, racial tensions were boiling in the midsummer of 1919. The limited housing available to black families, poor representation by labor leaders for black workers in the steel and meatpacking industries, and segregation in schools and public facilities all worsened the sense of injustice among those who had come north to escape just such treatment. The Chicago riot was ignited on a Lake Michigan beach in late July, when a small raft piloted by a black teenager drifted into an area designated "whites only." From the beach, a crowd of whites stoned the boy, who then drowned; fighting broke out and lasted a full two weeks as mobs burned, looted, and battled in neighborhoods throughout the city. Illinois governor Frank Lowden called in state National Guard units, which restored order after more than 40 deaths, thousands of injuries, and the burning of houses, apartment buildings, shops, and businesses. Governor Lowden then appointed a Chicago Commission on Race Relations, composed of white and black members, which produced a thick report and served as a sounding board for grievances, but accomplished little else over the next few years.

GARVEYISM

In an era that considered itself scientific and increasingly practical and efficient, the conflict between whites and blacks gave rise to meticulously argued solutions to the racial problem from both sides of the color line. From among the majority came Madison Grant, chairman of the New York Zoological Society, who wrote *The Passing of the Great Race* to argue for the superiority of Anglo-Saxon culture and the impossibility of assimilating the non-northern European peoples into the mainstream. The title of Lothrop Stoddard's best-selling book, *The Rising Tide of Color Against White World Supremacy,* neatly summed up his argument as well as his prognosis for a peaceful multiracial future. While Grant stumped for sterilization of the "mongrel races" to prevent their further proliferation as well as miscegenation, Stoddard sounded the alarm against Mediterraneans as well as Asians, Africans, and Bolsheviks. Both men supported closing the national gates through federal legislation and, if possible, sending the immigrants home.

Among blacks, the movement for separatism gained strength through the machinations of the Jamaican immigrant Marcus Garvey. Educated in London, where he adopted the black nationalist doctrine of Pan-Africanism, Garvey had returned to Jamaica in 1914 and founded the Universal Negro Improvement Association (UNIA). In 1916 he arrived in the United States during an immigration wave originating in the West Indies, by way of the more generous immigration quotas assigned by U.S. law to the colonial territories of Great Britain and France. Garvey quickly perceived that West Indian blacks had a culture and style of their own and did not always get along with African Americans. Nevertheless, he emerged in the early 1920s as the most prominent leader of a growing "Back to Africa" movement that was causing raucous controversy among all classes of black writers and workers.

Garvey set up his UNIA headquarters in the center of Harlem which, with the tide of southern migration and the uptown movement of city residents of color, had become a national locus of dissent against white-dominated culture and institutions. Mounting a soapbox at the corner of 135th Street and Lenox Avenue, he drew large crowds with his booming oratory and his radical solutions, which helped the UNIA to attract thousands of new dues-paying members. After the war's end, the UNIA grew into a nationwide organization, hosting meetings, parties, weddings, funerals, and all manner of social events in Liberty Halls, established in each city that was home to more than 10,000 of his UNIA members.

Garvey stood for the total independence of African America. Through his speeches and his editorials in the UNIA paper *Negro World,* he spoke against mixing of the races, condemned those who argued for assimilation, and praised the accomplishments of past African civilizations. A Negro Factories Corporation was set up; UNIA-supported groceries, laundries, and restaurants did business; and a shipping operation called the Black Star Line was planned. Garvey founded UNIA courts, manufactured UNIA passports, and established the African Orthodox Church. He attracted 20,000 supporters to the first International Convention of the Negro Peoples of the World in Madison Square Garden, in August 1920, where he was named the provisional president of Africa. He was intentionally building a nation-within-a-nation—a separate black republic that in his plans and dreams would one day ride Black Star Line vessels to a permanent new homeland on the continent of Africa.

The Black Star Line itself became the corporate embodiment of Garvey's philosophy. The company would supplant white-owned steamship companies among the rising black race; it would hire black seamen and black officers only, and it would provide transportation for the black masses booking passage to the new black republic on the west coast of Africa. Five-dollar shares were sold to thousands of investors, with the money going toward purchase and operation of three steamships that would commence freight-carrying operations between the east coast of the United States and the Caribbean.

Garvey had his share of enemies, however, and his stagy costumes and relentless self-promotion turned many of the most influential black writers, including W. E. B. DuBois, against him. In 1922, the downfall of the UNIA began with Garvey's strange decision to meet in Atlanta with Edward Young Clarke, a leader of the Ku Klux Klan. Seeing a mirror-image movement growing as quickly as his own, Garvey may have hoped to further the cause of black separatism by making some kind of arrangement with the leading organization dedicated to the segregation of the races. When it was revealed to the public, however, the meeting turned many of Garvey's aides and followers against him. The UNIA broke into competing, hostile factions: those remaining loyal to Garvey himself, and those now loyal only to the UNIA and Garvey's original ideals.

Financial manipulations and mismanagement brought about the end of the UNIA in late 1923. It was found that stock subscriptions to the Black Star Line had instead lined the pockets of Garvey and his aides, while the three ships of the Black Star Line were, respectively, sunk, seized, and placed in permanent drydock for repairs. Garvey was indicted by the federal government and tried for mail fraud. A five-week trial in New York City resulted in his conviction by an all-white jury on June 18, 1923, and imprisonment in the federal penitentiary in Atlanta. President Coolidge would commute his sentence and deport him from the United States as an undesirable alien in 1927.

THE HARLEM RENAISSANCE

By the time of Marcus Garvey and the Universal Negro Improvement Association, the formerly white, middle-class uptown neighborhood of Harlem had drawn more than 200,000 blacks—two-thirds of the city's black population—into its high-rent, subdivided apartments. The procession of black renters into Harlem began with the efforts of an African-American realtor named Philip Payton, who brought African-American tenants north of Manhattan's Central Park in the early years of the 1900s. Thousands of black renters moved to Harlem from the overcrowded San Juan Hill neighborhood, on the west side of Manhattan; others came from Brooklyn, others from the Caribbean, and still more arrived after World War I from the South. By the 1920s a distinct and self-contained African-American city had coalesced around 135th Street and Seventh Avenue, stretching about 15 blocks north and south. It was well-known in the rest of the city and country as catering to a visiting nighttime population of whites, who arrived after a short taxi ride uptown to enjoy segregated nightclubs and other anti-Prohibition venues such as the Cotton Club.

Harlem became an oasis for black immigrants from more hostile, predominantly white locales. Here the police and many shopowners were black, and here residents discovered a freedom not experienced when living as a minority among the whites. For evening entertainment, there were black movie theaters showing "race films"—films made by and starring African Americans. There were prospering nightclubs and cabarets, and libraries and schools that proved that African Americans could fend for themselves when given their liberty and opportunity. New black churches flourished in the neighborhood; the largest was the 8,000-member Abyssinian Baptist Church, headed by the Rev. Adam Clayton Powell.

Stars of the stage, the bandstand, and the pulpit provided models of success in worlds once dominated by whites. Roland Hayes, Paul Robeson, and Ethel Waters drew admiring audiences to Broadway and uptown theaters. Harlem high society collected around A'Lelia Walker, the daughter of Madame C. J. Walker, an African-American hair care entrepreneur who had died in 1919 and left her daughter a fortune. In 1927 A'Lelia Walker converted her Harlem mansion into a famous and exclusive gathering place, nicknamed The Dark Tower, which vied for worthy guests with other prominent Harlem salons at the homes of author James Weldon Johnson and the Reverend Frederick Cullen, the foster father of writer Countee Cullen. Newly arriving writers and artists also called at 580 St. Nicholas Avenue, in Harlem's prosperous Sugar Hill neighborhood, where Ethel Ray Nance, Ethel Waters, Regina Anderson, and Louella Tucker made the necessary introductions to editors and writers whose works garnered the catchall label of the Harlem Renaissance.

Alain Locke, born in 1885 and educated at Harvard and Oxford, served as a mentor to the new arrivals. A professor at Howard University, Locke was also principal contributor to *Opportunity* magazine, founded by the National Urban League in 1923 and edited by Charles S. Johnson, and he edited *The New Negro,* a leading journal of Harlem Renaissance writing, art, and society. Since his university days, Locke had immersed himself in the questions of race, art, and cultural traditions and had been advancing the idea of cultural pluralism, which demanded acceptance of the contributions of African Americans on a plane equal to, and distinct from, the works of those of European ancestry, who were to Locke's thinking simply another group of hyphenated Americans. Locke also asked that blacks accept and embrace their own folk traditions in their writing, music, and art. In 1927, he edited *Four Negro Poets,* a volume which included works by Claude McKay, Jean Toomer, Countee Cullen, and Langston Hughes, providing a vital introduction to the Harlem Renaissance to readers throughout the country. In 1929, Locke began an annual listing of important African-American writers in the pages of *Opportunity,* an important roll call of black literary talent that continued until 1943.

On May 1, 1925, the Harlem Renaissance reached one of its high points at an awards dinner sponsored by *Opportunity* magazine at the Fifth Avenue Restaurant. Under Johnson's editorship, *Opportunity* had chronicled the Great Migration of blacks from the South to the North and advocated the writing by and about members of the new urban black society. The Opportunity awards symbolized the acceptance of, or at least interest in, this writing by European-American literary elites. Presiding among the 24 judges were editor Alexander Woollcott, a white who was the unofficial leading man of the literary lunches held at the Algonquin Round Table (so named for the literary circle that met at the Algonquin Hotel); white playwright Eugene O'Neill; James Weldon Johnson, the executive secretary of the NAACP; and Jessie Fauset, literary editor of *The Crisis,* the NAACP publication edited by W. E. B. DuBois.

For most whites in New York, Harlem represented a playground, an opportunity to escape the stricter norms of behavior that were still expected in midtown and downtown neighborhoods. Carl Van Vechten, a music critic of the *New York Times,* held an ongoing and mixed-race salon at his home on West 55th Street that made him one of the leading white patrons of the Harlem Renaissance. Here Van Vechten introduced book publishers to the new crop of Harlem writers, and here composer George Gershwin and author Theodore Dreiser mixed with author and anthropologist Zora Neale Hurston, Langston Hughes, actor Paul Robeson, and James Weldon Johnson. It was Van Vechten who had arranged publication of Langston Hughes's internationally renowed book of poetry, *The Weary Blues,* with Alfred A. Knopf. Fascinated by all forms of the modernist movement and by "primitivist" art and music free of classical European form and style, Van Vechten himself was an aspiring writer whose novel *Nigger Heaven* was a study of Harlem society based on the leading figures, as well as leading stereotypes, of the Harlem Renaissance. Published in 1926, the book was a hit among white audiences and encouraged further efforts at primitivist works by African Americans seeking commercial success and acceptance outside of their usual and expected audiences. But *Nigger Heaven* also represented an affront to black writers such as W. E. B. DuBois, Alain Locke, and many others, who took offense at the title as well as the rendering of blacks as one-dimensional exotics presented to a white audience for amusement and entertainment only.

The fascination for "primitive" artists, musicians, and writers made up an important aspect of the avant-garde movements of the 1920s. Seeing a vitality and spontaneity in black expression that was free of the constraints and corruption of more "advanced" white society, writers such as O'Neill and Van Vechten consciously imitated that expression in their novels and plays. For the African

Americans, however, the Harlem Renaissance meant something else entirely—the emergence of a distinct and valued voice, the voice of the New Negro who would replace old stereotypes with assertive new writing, poetry, and painting, which would in turn end African Americans' status as second-class thinkers and artists or as a social problem to be solved by concerned and enlightened members of white society. Those who subscribed to and advanced the concept of the New Negro included Alain Locke and educator William Pickens (who wrote a book entitled *The New Negro* [1916]), as well as W. E. B. DuBois, all of whom hoped that the concept and the works would eventually lead to a wider acceptance of African Americans in American society as a whole.

White patronage, of a traditional and distinctly European cultural bent, still proved crucial to the writers of the Harlem Renaissance. In 1927, Hughes met another white patron, Charlotte Osgood Mason, a woman convinced that the earthier and primitive sensibility of the American Negro represented the salvation of modern art. After sponsoring a tour of the South by Hughes, Mason, also known as "Godmother" to her black proteges, took writer Zora Neale Hurston as well as artist Aaron Douglas in hand. But Mason had more than money to offer—she also gave advice, guidelines, and certain rules. By the end of 1920s, Hughes and Hurston were growing weary of Mason's overbearing patronage and broke with her for good.

Although Harlem would remain an African-American neighborhood, and a beacon for southern migrants, the Harlem Renaissance would not survive the stock market crash of 1929 and the Great Depression that followed. Unemployment ravaged Harlem families; businesses large and small collapsed, nightclubs closed their doors, and banks turned away their own depositors. Patronage on the part of Godmother and other wealthy white sponsors slipped away, while the market in black images, words, and rhythms gave way to new vogues for the white audience. Writers, artists, and musicians began leaving Harlem for the country at large; Hurston returned to her native Florida; Charles Johnson, James Weldon Johnson, and Aaron Douglas moved to professorships at Fisk University, A'Lelia Walker died and The Dark Tower closed down. Along with many other urban neighborhoods, Harlem began a slow slide into poverty and crime that no amount of creative writing or mainstream acceptance could stop.

THE JAZZ AGE

While writers undertook to describe the modern African-American experience in their poetry and novels, a new musical era was underway in New York and Chicago. Many historians mark the start of the "Jazz Age" on November 12, 1917—the day the Department of the Navy closed a 38-square-block neighborhood known as Storyville in the city of New Orleans. Fearing for the health of its sailors, the navy shut the doors of Storyville's brothels and nightclubs, forcing hundreds of New Orleans musicians to search elsewhere for their livelihoods. For more than 10 years, New Orleans musicians had already been traveling north, seasonally, by steamboat up the Mississippi River and by train to Kansas City, Chicago, and a few other places where nightclubs offered patrons entertainment by small bands playing what everyone called "New Orleans jazz." After Storyville was closed down, jazz musicians began moving north to take up permanent residence—several dozen of them landing in the great migratory target of Chicago alone.

The music they played was a combination and rearranging of several different musical forms and performance styles dating to the middle of the 19th century. Some time after the Civil War, field songs and spirituals sung by slaves and former slaves in the South were transformed into the blues, a new form of music in which the performer freely altered the notes of the conventional major scale. The blues method invited spontaneous improvisation, a personal expression of melody and rhythmic accent, and gave rise to a new repertoire of short, 12-bar standards transmitted from town to town, roadhouse to roadhouse throughout the rural South. Blues singers Bessie Smith and Ma Rainey packed in crowds at traveling shows and later became the first African-American performers to release studio recordings to a mass audience.

As blues audiences grew, new compositional styles such as ragtime transformed marches, quadrilles, and the other old forms of music familiar in New Orleans into vehicles for a new generation of bandstand and bawdy-house virtuosos. In New York, ragtime arrived in the 1890s via *Black America* and other minstrel shows that brought black composers and performers to Broadway, newly established as the Main Street of American theater. In Chicago, in 1905, the Pekin Temple of Music opened at 2700 South State Street, under the direction of Robert T. Motts and with the support of John Johnson, the city's leading African-American saloonkeeper and promoter. The Pekin was the city's first all-black theater, a place where blacks performed for other blacks who could sit anywhere they pleased, rather than being relegated to the balcony or back row. The song, dance, and dramatic acts presented at the Pekin, and later at the Lafayette and Lincoln Theaters of New York, introduced audiences to the new crop of African-American talent, including Bill "Bojangles" Robinson, Abbie Mitchell, Nettie Lewis, a superstar comedian named Bert Williams, and Clarence Muse, who later became a Hollywood star. With the Great Migration bringing a new audience to the northern cities, the 1920s would see a full flowering of black musical theater. *Shuffle Along,* written by Noble Sissle and Eubie Blake,

"Who's the Crazy Guy?" "Crazy! Him? That's th' slickest bimbo in the place. Just busts phonograph records t'pieces, glues 'em t'gether again—an' turns ten new jazz hits a day!" *(Library of Congress)*

opened on Broadway in 1921, leading the way to more African-American productions for the rest of the decade.

African Americans had invented jazz, but white Americans began to take it up after the war for listening, for drinking, and for dancing. Jazz signified revolt against sweet-tempered parlor music and polite entertainment, and defiance against Prohibition and Puritanism of all kinds. The young, white middle class adopted black music as a badge of rebellion against the strictures of an earlier time, discredited now by the disastrous war and the corruption of European nations once held up as cultural models. As the party picked up in Harlem and along Chicago's State Street, and whites began showing up at Negro showcases, the sense of jazz as novel and liberating exuberance intensified. New black urbanites held rent parties, at which a small admission fee allowed them to satisfy performers as well as landlords, and which became one of the most common vehicles by which jazz was introduced to its future listeners and devotees. In "black-and-tan" clubs, black musicians provided the entertainment to white and black audiences. Other clubs were owned by blacks and run primarily for blacks; some were owned and operated by whites. The famous Cotton Club in Harlem was for whites only, who paid for entertainment provided by blacks.

New Orleans–style musicians organized themselves into groups of six or seven musicians, playing cornet, trombone, and clarinet as lead melodic instruments and drums, string bass or tuba, and guitar or banjo providing rhythm. Often, when jazz groups moved to permanent engagements on nightclub bandstands or in dance halls, a piano was added. The musicians played by ear, and the tunes were memorized. Generally, the cornet played embellishments on the melody, the clarinet provided middle-register counterpoint, and the trombone filled in the bottom. Skilled musicians wove a hypnotic musical braid, chaotic to some listeners but fascinatingly complex and expressive to others who heard it as an accompaniment to the accelerating tempo of life in the cities. Two white bands, The New Orleans Rhythm Kings and the Original Dixieland Jazz Band, were among the first groups to make jazz recordings and among the first to bring jazz to a white audience. These and other groups like it applied the new jazz idioms—syncopation, improvisation, polyphony—to old New Orleans standards as well as the music of vaudeville and Broadway.

The term jazz itself had been in use for at least 20 years (and may have been coined) by a classically trained pianist named Jelly Roll Morton. A New Orleans creole of flamboyant manners and dress, Morton tamed the raucous improvisatory style of New Orleans jazz and wrote strict note-for-note arrangements for his musicians. He added intriguing introductions to the start, surprising codas to the finish, and carefully composed breaks and riffs in the middle sections that gave many of his pieces the sound of brief symphonic suites. Morton's Creole Jazz Band took Chicago and other cities by storm before breaking up in 1924, leaving hundreds of imitators behind to work out the compositional possibilities of jazz.

Jazz was still music for dancing, and not yet for polite listening. Dancing became the favored activity at music halls, private parties, and nightclubs; to meet a growing demand for good times, new dances were invented. Schools began offering classes in social dancing; square dancing returned to popularity; and ballet was in vogue. Couples took up fox-trots, camel walks, toddles, and tangos, and women abandoned frilly and voluminous clothes in large part to facilitate dancing. In 1924, a black show called "Runnin' Wild" introduced a very tricky new dance called the Charleston, which had nightclubbers moving and gesturing awkwardly across hundreds of dance floors. While new dances such as the Charleston shocked the staid, the General Federation of Women's Clubs, at its 1923 convention, voted for a national crusade to annihilate jazz. For people fighting against the Prohibition tide of loose morals and behavior, jazz did its worst damage in its effect on a proper woman's demeanor.

THE CHICAGO STYLE

Jazz moved into the mainstream via sheet-music publishers and the radio. Most important to those who performed it, however, jazz forms still allowed innovation and improvisation. The creative possibilities of jazz brought the attention of highbrow musical critics, especially in Europe, with the help of "serious" performances given overseas and at home in staid classical concert halls. As the 1920s progressed, jazz emerged from its ghetto of popular, lowbrow entertainment to become a recognized and internationally admired art form, the signature art of the United States.

The practitioners of the "Chicago style" had been working the cafes, cabarets, vaudeville showcases, and dance halls along State Street since just before World War I. In the 1920s, these musicians were creating a wider range of tone, in which the music alternated between loud and soft volume in contrast to New Orleans style, in which they performed at high volume all the time. Generally, trumpets and clarinets carried the melody, while rhythm parts were taken over by piano players. The cornet dropped out in favor of the trumpet, while reedy saxophones replaced the soft-toned clarinets. Drummers using bigger kits of snare, toms, cymbals, and bass became more prominent, giving an offbeat accent that drove the music forward. The New Orleans–style banjo fell into disfavor; the string bass permanently replaced the tuba and its players began improvising more freely around the tonic notes in the lowest register.

The collective improvisation that marked New Orleans style went out of style while collective parts were shortened in favor of the soloists. Instead of "breaks" performed over two or four bars by the soloist, the musical monologue now could go on for several choruses. The spotlight on soloing ability allowed the rise of jazz's early musical superstars. In 1920, Joe "King" Oliver came north to Chicago, where he recruited a young New Orleans horn player, Louis Armstrong. Born in 1900 in New Orleans, Armstrong had an astounding natural technique that allowed him to play in the highest registers of the cornet, and later the trumpet, at full power and expressiveness. His endless improvisatory inventiveness, combined with his supple and often surprising sense of rhythm, contributed a new word and a new feeling to jazz: swing. With Armstrong, the King Oliver Creole Jazz Band went on to record a series of gramophone recordings that defined the Chicago sound. In 1924, Armstrong joined the Fletcher Henderson band in New York, but soon returned to Chicago, where he formed his own small groups, the Hot Five and the Hot Seven. Playing with Armstrong in these groups made stars of his sidemen, including Johnny Dodds on clarinet, Kid Ory on trombone, and Armstrong's wife Lil Hardin on piano. White cornetist Leon "Bix" Beiderbecke arrived in Chicago from Davenport, Iowa, with a careful, precise style that riveted audiences and musicians alike.

The orchestral possibilities of the piano had been suggested by the compositions of Jelly Roll Morton; in the 1920s these possibilities were worked out further by a new crop of pianists appearing as featured soloists. James P. Johnson had earlier pioneered the new "stride" style of ragtime music in which broken chords in the left hand support exotic melodic and rhythmic excursions in the right. Thomas "Fats" Waller and Willie "The Lion" Smith drew largely on Johnson's style for their own compositions and improvisations; also starring in the stride style were Eubie Blake, Earl Hines, Teddy Weatherford, Joe Turner, and Claude Hopkins.

The size of jazz bands changed as well. The first ensembles were small groups that played in small clubs. Larger halls demanded larger bands, which were also needed by radio shows and by arrangers seeking a wider range of tone and color. High schools and neighborhood community houses sponsored their own jazz bands, as did newspapers including the Chicago *Daily News* and the Chicago *Defender.* While Benny, Freddie, and Harry Goodman got their start in the Jane Addams Hull House Band, jazz instruction was added to the curriculum of Chicago's technical schools and high schools.

On the east coast, Harlem became the second capital of the new jazz style. The New York sound smoothed over the rough patches of the Chicago style, making it palatable for the growing and multiracial record-buying audience. Harlem nightclubs, beginning with "Happy" Rhone's Black and White Club and continuing with Connie's Inn, The Nest Club, and others, offered bootleg liquor as well as live entertainment, for the most part to white audiences only. Opening in 1926, the Savoy Ballroom presented Fletcher Henderson and his Rainbow Orchestra, the precursor to the big bands of the 1930s and 1940s. Henderson's complex arrangements took full advantage of contrasting tonal qualities of the competing groups of saxophones, trumpets, and trombones; his technique of call-and-response melodic sections, and his featuring of skilled soloists playing to the accents of a busy ensemble accompaniment, would be imitated among jazz composers for the next two decades.

Harlem's best-known venue was the Cotton Club, with a strictly whites-only audience, where the bill of fare between the years 1927 and 1931 featured the orchestra of Edward "Duke" Ellington. Born in Washington, D.C., Ellington studied piano as a youth and came under the influence of stride pianists from Chicago and Harlem, particularly James P. Johnson and Fats Waller. Ellington's creative vision went far beyond the keyboard, however, and in the early 1920s he began writing ensemble pieces, including the *Black and Tan Fantasy,* for New York's star instrumentalists. Having moved permanently to New York, Ellington organized a band called the Washingtonians, which performed at Club Barron's in Harlem and the Kentucky Club in midtown Manhattan. He was then hired to replace King Oliver's band at the Cotton Club. This engagement, which began in December 1927, allowed Ellington to put together a new pit band of his own and create all kinds of accompaniments for the dramatic skits and chorus routines presented on the big stage, as well as dance music for the patrons. While honing his compositional skills for the best soloists in New York, Ellington created the most respected and admired jazz ensemble in the country, with crucial assistance from the new radio networks NBC and CBS, which began broadcasting daily, half-hour segments direct and live from the Cotton Club.

Jazz in Concert

By the winter of 1924, a large and well-mannered group of white musicians under the leadership of Paul Whiteman were rehearsing for a jazz-tinged yet very serious concert to take place in New York's ornate Aeolian Hall, featuring guest performer/composer George Gershwin. A son of Russian Jewish immigrants, George Gershwin grew up on the Lower East Side of New York. While taking piano lessons, George quickly showed a natural talent for songwriting and arranging. He first made his mark on Tin Pan Alley, the strip of commercial music publishers doing business along West 28th Street between Fifth and Sixth Avenues in Manhattan. Gershwin wrote short commercial tunes intended for publication as sheet music, for use in vaudeville and variety shows, and for sale to the general public. His first published song, "When You Want 'Em You Can't Get 'Em," appeared in 1916. Gershwin later worked on Broadway, where he wrote musical scores for a string of shows. Years after his first success, "Swanee" (popularized by Al Jolson), he would write such popular songs as "Lady Be Good," "The Man I Love," "Summertime," and "Someone to Watch Over Me." Theatergoers memorized the tunes and lyrics, humming them by day and bringing home the sheet music to try out on their own instruments at home.

Gershwin's melodies were adopted by jazz performers and became standards. Gershwin himself had spent much of his youth listening to and imitating the ragtime music he heard uptown in Harlem. He incorporated jazz style into his own piano playing and brought its new concepts of harmony and melody into his show tunes. At the same time, classical training had given Gershwin a taste for the music of contemporary European composers, including Igor Stravinsky, Claude Debussy, and Maurice Ravel. The possibilities of combining American jazz with the works of "serious" composers rooted in the classical tradition intrigued him. In 1923 he wrote a one-act opera, *135th Street;* today, that opera is entirely overshadowed by his later operatic work, *Porgy and Bess* (1935). On November 1, 1923, he accompanied a Canadian-born mezzosoprano, Eva Gauthier, in a concert of American and European songs at Aeolian Hall on West 43rd Street in New York. The "Recital of Ancient and Modern Music for Voice," as Gauthier called it, included works by, among others, Béla Bartók, Paul Hindemith, Arnold Schoenberg, Darius Milhaud—and Irving Berlin, Jerome Kern, and Gershwin. Gauthier's performance was the first to mix classical and jazz music on a concert stage.

On January 7, 1924, Gershwin suddenly discovered, much to his surprise, that a further contribution on his part to the marriage of jazz and classical music was imminent—in fact, it would take place on February 12, at the Aeolian Hall, in a program of music to be conducted by Paul Whiteman. Gershwin and Whiteman had once idly discussed the possibilities of such a concert; now, in the Ambassador Billiard Parlor, his brother Ira, who had written the lyrics for several of his shows and songs, read in the New York *Tribune* that George would be contributing a "jazz concerto" for Whiteman's upcoming concert: "An Experiment in Modern Music."

A successful bandleader who specialized in "sweet" dance music, Whiteman, like Gershwin, yearned for highbrow respectability among the critics and the public. He employed a classically trained arranger, Ferde Grofé, to arrange popular tunes for a large orchestra. In 1923, while on a trip to Europe, he conceived the idea of a grand concert hall appearance in New York to make a formal introduction of jazz music to the concertgoing public. He would not be the first to present jazz in a concert hall setting; that honor belonged to James Reese Europe and his Clef Club Symphony Orchestra, which appeared at Carnegie Hall on May 2, 1912, and again in March 1914. Whiteman had once spoken to Gershwin about a possible collaboration on a serious concert hall work, to be

Lieutenant James Reese Europe returns from France with his 15th New York Regiment Band. A popular bandleader who had teamed up with dancing stars Vernon and Irene Castle just before the war, Europe played a leading role in bringing jazz into the mainstream. *(Library of Congress/Underwood and Underwood)*

premiered by his orchestra. As the 2,800-seat Carnegie Hall had been previously booked, Whiteman had to settle for the 1,300-seat Aeolian Hall.

With a new Broadway show, *Sweet Little Devil,* in the works, Gershwin was hard pressed for time, but he realized that Whiteman's presumptuous announcement represented a golden opportunity. That same afternoon, he began work on a concerto for piano and orchestra in the study of his family's apartment on West 110th Street. Grofé was given the task of arranging the music, which Gershwin originally scored for two pianos.

With the concerto finished in only three weeks, Whiteman immediately began rehearsing the piece in the Palais Royal nightclub. Whiteman extended an open invitation to members of the press to attend, lending valuable advance publicity to the concert as well as to Gershwin. Having advertised the concert as "An Experiment in Modern Music," Whiteman and his publicity agents managed to draw an enthusiastic mob to the Aeolian Hall box office, where the crowd for tickets was likened to the scene at a championship boxing match. Greatly aiding the word of mouth was a jazz concert/lecture, held two days previously, hosted by Harvard music professor Edward Burlingame Hill at the Anderson Art Galleries on Park Avenue, and heavily promoted by Whiteman's press agent, Stella Karns.

Karns made sure that composer Sergei Rachmaninoff, violinist Fritz Kreisler, conductor Leopold Stokowski, and other luminaries of the European concert and opera stage, as well as leading newspaper columnists, were provided with tickets to Aeolian Hall. The concert was indeed a high-concept affair, half entertainment and half instruction. Whiteman intended to take his audience through the entire history of jazz, from its primitive beginnings to its more sophisticated present. As such, the first number on the program was "Livery Stable Blues," an example of "primitive" jazz that had been recorded by the Original Dixieland Jazz Band. The program continued with "So This Is Venice," an arrangement by Ferde Grofé, and arrangements by Victor Herbert of three Irving Berlin songs, a suite entitled "Semi-Symphonic Arrangement of Popular Melodies."

As many jazz historians have argued, Whiteman, instead of popularizing jazz, was robbing it of most of its vitality, and the concert of February 12 nearly died of its own didactic pretentions. However, near the end of the concert, Gershwin appeared on stage to perform as piano soloist in the next-to-last number—*Rhapsody in Blue* (the evening's finale would be Edward Elgar's *Pomp and Circumstance*). As an introduction, Gershwin stretched out semi-improvisationally for several minutes while the Paul Whiteman Orchestra patiently waited. The *Rhapsody* then continued through several mini-movements, in imitation of a classical concerto, but one in which Gershwin rendered all the newfangled harmonies and rhythmic showmanship of jazz. Applause thundered toward the stage as the final chord died away, and Gershwin left the stage much better known and regarded by critics and the public than he had been upon entering it. Although the Aeolian concert was officially "standing room only" that afternoon, Whiteman still managed to lose $7,000 on the venture, although it made him and his orchestra nearly as famous as George Gershwin. Gershwin himself played the success of *Rhapsody in Blue* into a series of additional performances, in Carnegie Hall on April 21 and on tour the next month, in Rochester, Pittsburgh, Cleveland, Indianapolis, and St. Louis. Dressed in a classical suit by the son of Russian immigrants, jazz had reached the heartland.

CHRONICLE OF EVENTS

1923

September 10: A Special Claims Convention is signed in Mexico City, settling claims of U.S. citizens for damages suffered during the Mexican revolution.

September 14: Assisted by ringside correspondents, who push him back into the ring after a nine-count in the first round, boxer Jack Dempsey knocks out Luis Angel Firpo of Argentina, the "Wild Bull of the Pampas," in the second round at the Polo Grounds in New York.

September 15: J. C. Walton, the governor of Oklahoma, puts the state under martial law and calls out 6,000 National Guard troops in reaction to Ku Klux Klan violence. In October, the Oklahoma Supreme Court will uphold a state senate vote suspending Governor Walton from office. Walton will be impeached and ousted by the Oklahoma House in November.

October 4: Actor Charlton Heston is born.

October 6: Lieutenant Al Williams sets a new record average air speed of 243.76 miles per hour in a Curtiss biplane during the Pulitzer Trophy contest in St. Louis.

October 12: Samuel Gompers is reelected president of the American Federation of Labor, at the age of 73.

October 15: The New York Yankees defeat the New York Giants in six games in the World Series.

October 25: The Senate Public Lands Committee, under the chairmanship of Senator Thomas Walsh of Montana, opens hearings on the Teapot Dome transactions under the Harding administration. The first witness at the hearings is Albert Fall, secretary of the Interior under President Harding, who defends his practice of leasing government land without competitive bidding as "Business, purely." Walsh's case, carefully assembled over the last 18 months, will result in the conviction of Fall, the first cabinet member in history to go to jail.

October 26: Death of electrical engineer Charles Steinmetz, who holds more than 200 patents, in Schenectady, New York.

November 1: The Goodyear Tire and Rubber Company of Akron, Ohio, negotiates the right to manufacture dirigibles in the United States.

November 6: Colonel Jacob Schick is issued a patent for the first electric shaver.

November 8: Adolf Hitler attempts a coup in the Buergerbraukeller, a beer hall in Munich.

November 25: The first transatlantic radio broadcast takes place between England and the United States.

November 29: A commission led by banker Charles Dawes convenes to study the German economy. Hyperinflation in Germany is driving the mark to an exchange rate of 1 trillion to the dollar.

December 6: In his first address to Congress, President Coolidge calls for participation in the World Court, nonparticipation in the League of Nations, strict enforcement of the Prohibition laws, and further economy on the part of the federal government. The speech is the first official presidential address to be broadcast on radio.

December 8: The United States signs a treaty of friendship with Germany in Washington. The Senate will ratify the treaty, with reservations, on February 10, 1925.

December 10: Robert Millikan receives the Nobel Prize in physics for his investigation into electric charges and the photoelectric effect.

December 15: Fearing the spread of economic chaos across Europe, President Coolidge appoints Charles G. Dawes chairman of a committee to formulate a reparations and debt-reduction plan for Germany, where hyperinflation has destroyed the value of the mark. The Dawes Commission will come up with the Dawes Plan on April 9, 1924, in which Germany's debt payments are restructured and the total amount of reparations reduced.

December 18: Secretary of State Charles Hughes refuses to extend diplomatic recognition to the Soviet Union.

1924

January 16: The McNary-Haugen Bill is introduced in both houses of Congress. The bill would create a federal farm board to purchase crop surpluses and either keep them off the market or sell them abroad. The bill will not be passed until February 1927; it is then vetoed by President Coolidge on February 25, 1927.

February 3: Former president Woodrow Wilson dies in Washington, D.C.

February 8: Congress passes a joint resolution asking the president to cancel the oil leases in Wyoming and California negotiated by Secretary of the Interior Albert Fall under the Harding administration; the resolution also authorizes President Coolidge to seek indictments against Fall and others involved in the leases.

Paul Whiteman and his soft-pedaled big-band jazz lent themselves to caricature. But Whiteman's sponsorship of George Gershwin at the Aeolian Hall transformed jazz into an art form taken seriously by critics and classically trained composers. *(Library of Congress)*

February 12: Accompanied by the Paul Whiteman Orchestra, pianist/composer George Gershwin gives the premiere performance of his jazz concerto *Rhapsody in Blue* in New York's Aeolian Hall.

February 21: President Coolidge opposes the independence of the Philippines, stating that the people of the Philippines are not ready to govern themselves.

February 27: The United States signs a treaty with the Dominican Republic, canceling the right of the United States to intervene in the affairs of the Caribbean nation to guarantee its stability. In July 1924, U.S. Marines are withdrawn.

February 29: Charles Forbes is indicted for defrauding the government of $250 million. On February 4, 1925, he will be sentenced to two years in prison and a $10,000 fine.

EYEWITNESS TESTIMONY

The Northern Migration

We return from the slavery of uniform which the world's madness demanded we don to the freedom of civil garb. We stand again to look America squarely in the face and call a spade a spade. We sing: This country of ours, despite all its better souls have done and dreamed, is yet a shameful land.

It *lynches*. . . . It *disfranchises* its own citizens. . . . It encourages *ignorance*. . . . It *steals* from us. . . . It *insults* us.

This is the country to which we Soldiers of Democracy return. This is the fatherland for which we fought! But it is *our* fatherland. It was right for us to fight. The faults of *our* country are *our* faults. Under similar circumstances, we would fight again. But by the God of Heaven, we are cowards and jackasses if now that that war is over, we do not marshal every ounce of our brain and brawn to fight a sterner, longer, more unbending battle against the forces of hell in our own land.

> *We return.*
> *We return from fighting.*
> *We return fighting.*

African-American writer and philosopher W. E. B. DuBois in "Returning Soldiers," in The Crisis, *journal of the National Association for the Advancement of Colored People, May 1919, p. 14.*

Much has been written and said concerning the housing situation in Chicago and its effect on the racial situation. The problem is a simple one. Since 1915 the colored population of Chicago has more than doubled, increasing in four years from a little over 50,000 to what is now estimated to be between 125,000 and 150,000. Most of them lived in the area bounded by the railroad on the west, 30th Street on the north, 40th Street on the south and Ellis Avenue on [the] east. Already overcrowded, this so-called "Black Belt" could not possibly hold the doubled colored population. One cannot put ten gallons of water in a five-gallon pail. . . . Various plans were discussed for keeping the Negroes in "their part of the town," such as securing the discharge of colored persons from positions they held when they attempted to move into "white" neighborhoods, purchasing mortgages of Negroes buying homes and ejecting them when mortgage notes fell due and were unpaid, and many more of the same calibre. The language of many speakers was vicious and strongly prejudicial and had the distinct effect of creating race bitterness.

Walter F. White, African-American journalist, in an analysis of the 1919 Chicago riots, "Chicago and its Eight Reasons," from The Crisis, *October 1919, p. 296.*

Four summers ago, a few months after America entered the World War, there arrived in New York from the island of Jamaica a coal-black Negro of the purest African type, whose muscular, chunky, short body was burdened with a negligible load of tangible assets, but whose prognathic-jawed, broad-nosed, kinky-haired head was fairly bursting with an idea that was as great and as heavy as it was intangible.

. . . Unknown to the vast majority of his own race, unwelcomed by the very few who did know him, unheralded by any of them upon his arrival, he took with him to his obscure lodging in that part of Harlem which constitutes the largest and greatest Negro city in the world, his still more obscure idea. He was then just plain Marcus Garvey from Jamaica. To-day he is the Honorable Marcus Garvey, president of the Provisional Republic of Africa, president of the Universal Negro Improvement Association and African Communities League of the World, president of the Black Star Line of oceangoing steamships, president of the Negro Factories Corporation, editor and publisher of the *Negro World,* the most powerful Negro newspaper on earth, and he is acclaimed by millions of his color as the Black Moses, destined, as one fervent biographer says, "to rank in history alongside Nador, Alaric, Attila, Genghis Khan, Cromwell, Napoleon, Bismarck, and Washington."

Truman Hughes Talley, "Marcus Garvey—The Negro Moses?" from The World's Work, *December 1920, p. 153.*

As he came out of the wings on stage, the first thing that hit him was the flashlight. Sharp—Lord knows that man was so sharp he was bleeding (our expression when we mention someone that's well dressed).

. . . It was a long time before Bojangles could open his mouth. That's how popular he was and well-liked by all who understood his greatness as a dancer and showman. He waited after the thunderous applause had finished, and looked up into the booth and said to the man who controlled the lights—Bill said to him, "Give me a light, *my* color." And all the lights all over the house went out. And me sitting there when this happened, with the whole audience just roaring with laughter. When I realized it, I was laughing so loud, until Bill Johnson was on the verge of taking me out of there. . . .

Police search black suspects in Chicago during postwar race turmoil. *(Brown Brothers)*

Then Bojangles went into his act. His every move was a beautiful picture. I am sitting in my seat in ecstasy and delight, even in a trance. He imitated a trombone with his walking cane to his mouth, blowing out of the side of his mouth making the buzzing sound of a trombone, which I enjoyed. He told a lot of funny jokes, which everybody enjoyed immensely. Then he went into his dance and finished by skating off the stage with a silent sound and tempo. *Wow,* what an artist. I was sold on him ever since.

Jazz cornetist Louis Armstrong, reviewing a performance of Bill "Bojangles" Robinson at Chicago's Erlanger Theater in the fall of 1922, quoted in Bergreen, Louis Armstrong: An Extravagant Life *(1997), pp. 208–209.*

The Negro of the States is physically a part of his nation, while the West Indian Negro is a colonial, separated by an ocean from the power which rules over him. And like British colonials of many races he has an idea, tinged with hope, that some time he may become entirely independent. The West Indian blacks whom Garvey found in New York were therefore the first to be moved by the idea of entire racial separateness, even to the absurd extent of having a continent assigned to a color,—a condition which commercial interdependence and scientific intercommunication make impossible.

There are other differences in these group complexes that help to explain Garveyism: the American Negro is used to the theory, and more or less to the actuality, of democracy and equality. If American Negroes had planned the "Republic of Africa," we should have heard nothing of "Knights and Ladies of Ethiopia," "Knights Commander of the Nile" and "Dukes of Uganda." Those are reactions of the British substratum. When Garvey was traveling through the States, advertising "Black Star" stock and "Back to

Africa" schemes, he required the men and women of his retinue to address him as "Your Highness," and what was the amused astonishment of a colored American housewife in Ohio, who had rented rooms to Garvey and his followers, when one of Garvey's female attendants descended the stairway and announced: "His Highness would like ham and eggs, or pork chops and gravy, for his supper."

William Pickens, "The Emperor of Africa," from Forum,
August 1923, p. 1,790.

The housing of Negroes, unfortunately, is bound doubly by the housing for the whites. The former have less capital for building and can borrow less. The homes they get are most often those abandoned by the whites and so long as there is nothing better in sight no one, however strong his antipathy to contact with Negroes as neighbors, actual or potential, is likely to abandon what he has. . . . This is anything but cheerful. . . . In 61 percent of the cities an actual shortage exists; in 53 percent of the cities rents are still on the increase; in 36 percent they are given as stationary. The most interesting feature of the inquiry is the reported tendency of many families to move into the suburbs.

This is after all perhaps the most hopeful sign for the relief of the Negroes. This movement to the suburbs is most noticeable in the larger northern cities, where the greatest problems of Negro housing have been encountered. Once an appreciable outlet is provided, an opening will be made in the iron ring which now with such uncompromising rigor holds the Negroes within prescribed residential areas too crowded for further building, and in buildings too old to keep up.

Unsigned editorial, Opportunity *magazine, October
1923, p. 290.*

Out of the vast host of students at Howard everyone should be a potential leader. You must be preparing to save the world from the present chaotic conditions. Be a factor in the organizations for the advancement of the Negro and humankind: *A leader should come among us to make Marcus Garvey's dream a reality.*

Editorial, The Hilltop, *a Howard University publication,
February 4, 1924.*

In its endeavor to avoid any injustice toward Marcus Garvey and his followers, *The Crisis* has almost leaned backward. Notwithstanding his wanton squandering of hundreds of thousands of dollars we have refused to assume that he was a common thief. In spite of his monumental and persistent lying we have discussed

only the larger and truer aspects of his propaganda. We have refrained from all comment on his trial and conviction for fraud. We have done this too in spite of his personal vituperation of the editor of *The Crisis* and persistent and unremitting repetition of falsehood after falsehood as to the editor's beliefs and acts and as to the program of the N. A. A. C. P.

In the face, however, of the unbelievable depths of debasement and humiliation to which this demagog has descended in order to keep himself out of jail, it is our duty to say openly and clearly:

Marcus Garvey is, without doubt, the most dangerous enemy of the Negro race in America and the world. He is either a lunatic or a traitor. He is sending all over this country tons of letters and pamphlets appealing to Congressmen, businessmen, philanthropists and educators to join him on a platform whose half concealed planks may be interpreted as follows:

That no person of Negro descent can ever hope to become an American citizen.

That forcible separation of the races and the banishment of Negroes to Africa is the only solution of the Negro problem.

That race war is sure to follow any attempt to realize the program of the N. A. A. C. P.

We would have refused to believe that any man of Negro descent could have fathered such propaganda if the evidence did not lie before us in black and white signed by this man.

W. E. B. DuBois, in "A Lunatic or a Traitor," from
The Crisis, *May 1924, p. 8.*

Look around at your cabin. Look at the dirt floor and the windows without glass! Then ask your folks already up north about the bathrooms with hot and cold water, the steam heat and the glistening hardwood floors which down home you see only when you polish them. What chance has the average black to get these things down home? And if he does get them how can he be sure but that some night some poor cracker will get his gang together and come around and drive him out? Step on a train and ride for a day and a night to freedom. Your nickel is worth as much as the other fellow's nickel in the Northern streetcars and you sit wherever you can find a seat. You tip your hat to no man unless you desire to do so.

From The World's Work, *May 1924, quoted in Furnas,*
Great Times *(1974), p. 291.*

We have recently seen a considerable migration of our Negro citizens to other parts of the country, partly due to economic causes and partly to a condition of law-lessness which has led the Negroes to fear for the safety of their homes and lives.

I ask you whether we wish to encourage this migration until the last Negro leaves us, or shall we remove its causes and keep them with us? I unhesitatingly assert that the prosperity of Georgia depends upon our keeping the Negro here. Our only alternative is to let them go and replace them by immigration from Central and Eastern Europe, bringing with it the Bolshevist and the Anarchist into the purest Anglo-Saxon state in the Union, where ninety-seven percent of our white population is American born of unmixed parentage and American bred in American ideas.

. . . The question of social equality long ago settled itself and the false hopes held out in other sections, having been found fallacious, are today not considered by the better class of our Negroes.

Atlanta businessman George J. Baldwin, address to the Atlanta Chamber of Commerce, "The Migration: A Southern View," Opportunity, June 1924, p. 183.

The Negro is dying out, and he is going to die faster and more rapidly in the next fifty years than he has in the past three hundred years. There is only one thing to save the Negro, and that is an immediate realization of his own responsibilities. Unfortunately we are the most careless and indifferent people in the world! We are shiftless and irresponsible, and that is why we find ourselves the wards of an inherited materialism that has lost its soul and its conscience. It is strange to hear a Negro leader speak in this strain, as the usual course is flattery, but I would not flatter you to save my own life and that of my own family. There is no value in flattery. Flattery of the Negro for another quarter of a century will mean hell and damnation to the race. How can any Negro leader flatter us about progress and the rest of it, when the world is preparing more than ever to bury the entire race? Must I flatter you when England, France, Italy, Belgium and Spain are all concentrating on robbing every square inch of African territory, the land of our fathers? Must I flatter you when the cry is being loudly raised for a white America, Canada, Australia, and Europe, and a yellow and brown Asia?

Marcus Garvey, speech of August 1, 1924, before the delegates of the 4th Annual International Convention of Negro Peoples of the World at Carnegie Hall, New York, reprinted in The Marcus Garvey and Universal Negro Improvement Association Papers, Vol. V (1986), pp. 631–632.

The southern industrialist is . . . very much interested in the Negro, for he supplied much of the common labor, some of the semi-skilled labor, and more and more of the skilled labor on which southern industry depends for its operation. Now it is an axiom of business management that by and large, the more intelligent labor becomes, the more valuable it becomes; that the workman who lives in a better home is more contented and therefore a better workman, the home ownership, habits of thrift, ideals of honest and fair dealing are big factors in making more permanent and profitable relations between employer and employee. . . . The effect therefore that industrial welfare work, now so generally carried on by large corporations, is having and will continue to have on the great masses of Negroes, North and South, promises to be a big factor in Negro progress. . . . Negroes in industry are constantly being trained on consistent constructive labor. To a large extent their intelligence is developed to a higher and higher point through their manual work. In addition to this, all through the North and South today the Negro in industry is coming under the influence of a scientific social welfare system that is, in general, working, and in many instances working with great efficiency, toward the same ends as those which Hampton and Tuskegee and the whole system of education they represent are striving for.

From the Southern Workman, the official organ of The Hampton Institute, an institute for Negro improvement, November 1924, pp. 530–536.

The tide of Negro migration, northward and cityward, is not to be fully explained as a blind flood started by the demands of war industry coupled with the shutting off of foreign migrations, or by the pressure of poor crops coupled with increased social terrorism in certain sections of the South and Southwest. Neither labor demand, the boll weevil, nor the Ku Klux Klan is a basic factor, however contradictory any or all of them may have been. The wash and rush of this human tide on the beach line of the northern city centers is to be explained primarily in terms of a new vision of opportunity, of social and economic freedom, of a spirit to seize, even in the face of an extortionate and heavy toll, a chance for the improvement of conditions. With each successive wave of it, the movement toward the larger and the more democratic chance—in the Negro's case a deliberate flight not only from countryside to city, but from medieval America to modern.

From Alain Locke, prominent African-American philosopher and spokesperson for the New Negro Movement, in The New Negro (1925), p. 6.

This restless spirit was encouraged by the conditions under which many rural Negroes were forced to live. The peonage system has been rampant in the South. The Arkansas riots of 1919 developed from the peon existence which Negro farmers were forced to live. When they united their counsels in order to demand an accounting of their landlords, they were accused of conspiracy to murder the white planters. These Negroes, seeking only to protect themselves, were killed by the hundreds. Conditions in Georgia were made known in 1921, when the owner of a plantation in Jasper County had eleven of his workers murdered in order to prevent the facts of peonage from becoming known to investigating federal officers. The case caused Governor Hugh M. Dorsey to publish a pamphlet on *The Negro in Georgia,* in which many cases of peonage and economic exploitation were described. With these conditions in existence and with the apprehension created by the publicity occasioned by these discoveries, the basis was laid for a migration of the Negro population. They moved from the country to the city and from the South to the North.

Charles H. Wesley, describing the reasons for black migration in the early 1920s, in Negro Labour in the United States, 1850–1925 *(1927), pp. 286–287.*

Billy Biasse telephoned to the doctor, a young chocolate-complexioned man. He was graduate of a Negro medical college in Tennessee and Columbia University. He was struggling to overcome the prejudices of the black populace against Negro doctors and wedge himself in among the Jewish doctors that prescribed for the Harlem clientele. A clever man, he was trying, through Democratic influence, to get an appointment in one of the New York hospitals. Such an achievement would put him all over the Negro press and get him all the practice and more than he could handle in the Belt.

Ray had sent Jake to him. . . .

The landlady brought Jake a rum punch. He shook his head. With a premonition of tragedy, she waited for the doctor, standing against the chiffonier, a blue cloth carelessly knotted around her head. . . .

In the corridor she questioned Billy Biasse about Jake's seizure.

"All you younger generation in Harlem don't know no God," she accused Billy and indicted Young Harlem. "All you know is cabarets and movies and the young gals them exposing their legs a theirs in them jumper frocks."

"I wouldn't know 'bout that," said Billy.

"You all ought to know, though, and think of God Almighty before the trumpet sound and it's too late foh black sinners. I nevah seen so many trifling and ungodly niggers as there is in this heah Harlem."

Claude McKay, African-American novelist, from chapter XV of Home to Harlem *(1928), pp. 219–220.*

What Americans call the Negro problem is almost as old as America itself. For three centuries the Negro in this country has been tagged with an interrogation point; the question propounded, however, has not always been the same.

. . . It is not a static condition; rather, it is and always has been a series of shifting interracial situations, never precisely the same in any two generations. As these situations have shifted, the methods and manners of dealing with them have constantly changed. And never has there been such a swift and vital shift as the one which is taking place at the present moment; and never was there a more revolutionary change in attitudes than the one which is now going on.

. . . It is a new thought that the Negro has helped to shape and mold and make America. It is, perhaps, a startling thought that America would not be precisely the America it is today except for the powerful, if silent, influence the Negro has exerted upon it—both positively and negatively.

James Weldon Johnson, "Race Prejudice and the Negro Artist," in Harper's, *November 1928, p. 769.*

Sir:

I have the honor to report, as of possible interest, that the notorious negro agitator, Marcus Garvey, landed in Canada at the city of Quebec, about a fortnight ago and, after a few days at that city, proceeded to Montreal. He gave two or three extensive interviews to the local press here, and announced the arrangement of public meetings at this city and at Toronto with the purpose of influencing American negroes to vote for the Democratic candidate for the presidency. He appeared at this Consulate general, apparently with the intention of applying for permission to visit the United States, but after waiting a few moments, departed prior to an interview.

His presence, however, was observed by Consul Smale and Vice Consul Clark; I and the latter communicated with the United States Commissioner of Immigration Landis. Through Mr. Landis the attention of the Canadian immigration authorities was directed to the fact that Garvey is an ex-convict and as such inadmissible to Canada. The Canadian authorities acted quietly and promptly in the matter and forbade Garvey to give any further interviews or to speak in public. Mr. Garvey was granted eight days to depart from the country; and it is understood that he took ship for the West Indies on the evening of November 7, 1928.

I have the honor to be, Sir, Your obedient servant,
WESLEY FROST
American Consul General

Wesley Frost, U.S. consul to Canada, report to Secretary of State Frank Billings Kellogg on the activities of Marcus Garvey in Canada after his deportation from the United States, November 8, 1928, from Hill (ed.), The Marcus Garvey and Universal Negro Improvement Association Papers, Vol. VII *(1990), pp. 290–291.*

The party was on the fifth floor, but even as we entered the lower hall, we could hear the shouts and laughter. It was a successful party then, for, judging by the volume of voices, the four-room flat was packed. That meant that all invitations had been accepted.

The elevator bore us up and let us out. Our smiling hostess stood in her open door. Behind her was a surge of vari-colored faces, the warm white of fair Negroes, the pale white of whites, through yellows and browns to rusty blacks.

We brushed cheeks with our hostess, and our mutual coos of endearment fell on the already false air. We entered the smoke-thickened room, brushed cheeks with a few more people, shook hands with some others, and followed our hostess into the bedroom.

. . . She was on the city payroll, had graduated from a first-class Negro college, belonged to a good sorority, had married respectably, and was now entrenching herself in New York Negro Society. There had been one or two flamboyant indiscretions in her past, and so every once in a while, to assure herself and her home town that she had lived them down, she entertained at a lavish party. She was not yet sufficiently secure to give a small affair. And of all the people lapping up her liquor, hardly one would have come to an intimate dinner.

. . . Our hostess found places for us on the populated divan. We sat among acquaintances, balancing our drinks. To our left were a public school teacher, two Department of Welfare investigators, two writers, one left and one right, a "Y" worker, a white first-string movie critic, a white artist and his wife. To our right were two Negro government officials, two librarians, a judge's daughter, a student red-cap, a Communist organizer, an artist, an actress.

. . . We listened to line conversation around us. A tall unattractive girl on our right had assumed an affected pose. She languished on the divan and blew puffs of smoke through a cigarette holder. Her large foot pivoted on its ankle. She surveyed it dreamily. Her father was a man of importance, and although she had neither beauty nor charm, she had constituted herself the year's number one Negro debutante.

Dorothy West, author and Harlem Renaissance hostess, January 10, 1939, from American Life Histories: Manuscripts from the Federal Writers' Project, 1936–1940, *"The American Memory," Library of Congress web site, URL: http://www.memory.loc.gov.*

Jazz

We took two quarts of bathtub gin, a package of muggles [marijuana], and headed for the black-and-tan joint where King Oliver's band was playing . . . [Armstrong] slashed into Bugle Call Rag. I dropped my cigarette and gulped my drink. Bix was on his feet, his eyes popping. . . . "Why," I moaned, "why isn't everybody in the world here to hear that?" I meant it. Something as unutterably stirring as that deserved to be heard by the world.

Hoagy Carmichael recalling his first hearing of Louis Armstrong in the summer of 1923, in Carmichael, The Stardust Road *(1946), and reprinted in* Louis Armstrong: A Cultural Legacy *(1994), p. 26.*

This colored band is plenty torrid and includes a trumpet player who never need doff his chapeau to any cornetist in the business. He exacts the eeriest sort of modulations and "singing" notes heard.

The Hollywood, a comparatively new Times Square basement cabaret (it opened Sept. 1 last), is on West 49th Street. The band is the sole feature up to midnight, when Harper's Dixie Revue goes on, repeating again at 2 A.M.

The boys can seemingly satisfy without exerting themselves, but for the benefit of the Clipper reviewer they brought out a variety of instruments upon which each demonstrated his versatility. And how!

Elmer Snowden is the leader and banjoist, also doubling with soprano sax. "Bub" Miley is the "hot" cornetist, doubling with the melophone [sic]. John

Anderson doubles trombone and trumpet; Sonny Greer specializes in the vocal interludes when not at the traps; Otto Hardwick, sax and violin; Roland Smith, sax and bassoon; and Duke Ellington, piano-arranger.

The boys look neat in dress suits and labor hard but not in vain at their music. They are well known in several southern places and were at the Music Box, Atlantic City, the past summer. They also broadcast every Wednesday at 3:45 from WHN (Loews State building) radio station.

Critic Abel Green, from the first full-length review of Duke Ellington's band in a major publication (the New York Clipper*), November 23, 1923, quoted in Tucker,* Ellington: The Early Years *(1991), pp. 99–100.*

Mr. Whiteman intends to point out, with assistance of his orchestra and associates, the tremendous strides which have been made in popular music from the day of discordant Jazz, which sprang into existence about ten years ago from nowhere in particular, to the really melodious music of today, which—for no good reason—is still called Jazz.

From "The Why of this Experiment," program notes for Paul Whiteman's Aeolian Hall concert of February 12, 1924, quoted in Jablonksi, Gershwin *(1987), p. 69.*

How trite and feeble and conventional the tunes are [in the *Rhapsody in Blue*]; how sentimental and vapid the harmonic treatment, under its disguise of fussy and futile counterpoint! ...Weep over the lifelessness of the melody and harmony, so derivative, so stale, so inexpressive!

Lawrence Gilman, review of Aeolian Hall concert, New York Tribune, *February 13, 1924, quoted in Slonimsky,* Lexicon of Musical Invective, *p. 105.*

For Daisy was young and her artificial world was redolent of orchids and pleasant, cheerful snobbery and orchestras which set the rhythm of the year, summing up the sadness and suggestiveness of life in new tunes. All night the saxophones wailed the hopeless comment of the "Beale Street Blues" while a hundred pairs of golden and silver slippers shuffled the shining dust. At the grey tea hour there were always rooms that throbbed incessantly with this low sweet fever, while fresh faces drifted here and there like rose petals blown by the sad horns around the floor.

F. Scott Fitzgerald, The Great Gatsby *(1925), p. 158.*

But jazz to me is one of the inherent expressions of Negro life in America: the eternal tom-tom beating in the Negro soul—the tom-tom of revolt against weariness in a white world, a world of subway trains, and work, work, work; the tom-tom of joy and laughter, and pain swallowed in a smile. Yet the Philadelphia clubwoman is ashamed to say that her race created it and she does not like me to write about it. The old subconscious "white is best" runs through her mind. Years of study under white teachers, a lifetime of white books, pictures, and papers, and white manners, morals, and Puritan standards made her dislike the spirituals. And now she turns up her nose at jazz and all its manifestations—likewise almost everything else distinctly racial. She doesn't care for the Winold Reiss portraits of Negroes because they are "too Negro." She does not want a true picture of herself from anybody. She wants the artist to flatter her, to make the white world believe that all Negroes are as smug and as near white in soul as she wants to be. But, to my mind, it is the duty of the younger Negro artist, if he accepts any duties at all from outsiders, to change through the forces of his art that old whispering "I want to be white," hidden in the aspirations of his people to "Why should I want to be white? I am a Negro—and beautiful!"

Poet and essayist Langston Hughes, "The Negro Artist and the Racial Mountain," The Nation, *June 23, 1926, p. 694.*

...the land of America had fashioned me ...a Puritan, a mystic and a striver after the heroic expression ... I believe that most American artists are of the same mould.

Isadora Duncan, My Life *(1927), p. 78.*

The Cotton Club is the Club Richman of Harlem. It is the foremost black and tan cafe featuring a whale of a colored revue that matches any of the preceding editions, all of which have been noteworthy for their artistry and talent.

As in the past, the undressed thing goes double. The almost Caucasian-hued high yaller girls look swell and uncork the meanest kind of cooching ever exhibited to a conglomerate mixed audience. One coocher, boyish bobbed hoyden, said to be especially imported from Chicago for her Annapolis proclivities who does the Harlem River Quiver like no self-respecting body of water. The teasin'est torso tossing yet, and how!

Abel Green, jazz critic reviewing the entertainment and ambiance of the Cotton Club of Harlem for Daily Variety, *December 7, 1927, p. 54.*

Louis Armstrong, Johnny St. Cyr, Johnny Dodds, Kid Ory, and Lil Hardin (left to right) formed the Hot Five and took Chicago by storm in 1925. *(Archive Photos / Frank Driggs)*

. . . a player standing up with a saxophone to his lips could be dipping and swinging, sudden starts and rigidities and tremors, swoops and swerves, give to the instrument the effect of sentience. . . . As for the sounds, the saxophone could be onomatopoetic as no other instrument could. The yowl of a cat, the moo of a cow, the whinny of a horse, a lunatic asylum in which were segregated victims given especially to maniacal laughter, a yawn, a grunt, a belch. A skillful player with an acrobatic tongue slapping against the reed, his fingers fluttering over the score of keys, could achieve titillating arpeggios, glissandos, he could toot and he could tootle, blare and blast, bleat and blat . . .

Mark Sullivan, "Tunes of the Twenties," in Our Times *(1996), pp. 695–696.*

There was a painted canvas sign about two by four feet square hanging outside the best-looking building that housed the Lincoln Gardens Cafe, a sign that read

KING OLIVER AND HIS CREOLE JAZZ BAND. The thing that hit your eye once you got into the hall was a big crystal ball that was made of small pieces of reflecting glass and hung over the center of the dance floor. A couple of spotlights shone on the big ball as it turned and threw reflected spots of light all over the room and the dancers. Usually they'd dance the Bunny Hug to a slow blues like *London Blues* or some other tune in a like slow blues tempo, and how the dancers would grind away. The ceiling of the place was made lower than it actually was by chicken wire that was stretched out, and over the wire were spread great bunches of artificial maple leaves.

George Wettling, undated interview, describing the Lincoln Gardens cabaret in Chicago, in Shapiro and Hentoff, Hear Me Talkin' To Ya *(1966), pp. 99–100.*

When I sat down to play I asked for the music and were they surprised! They politely told me they didn't have any music and furthermore never used any. I then asked what key would the first number be in. I must have been speaking another language because the leader said, "When you hear two knocks, just start playing."

It all seemed very strange to me, but I got all set, and when I heard those two knocks I hit the piano so loud and hard they all turned around to look at me. It took only a second for me to feel what they were playing and I was off. The New Orleans Creole Jazz Band hired me, and I never got back to the music store—never got back to Fisk University.

Lil Hardin, undated interview, describing her audition with
The New Orleans Creole Jazz Band, in Shapiro and
Hentoff, Hear Me Talkin' To Ya *(1966), p. 93.*

One day I went over to see him . . . at his room at Thirty-Fifth and Grand Boulevard (now South Parkway). There he was—in bed with two women, one sitting on each side of him. I tell you, he was some character! . . . He asked me to come work with him. "You know you will be working with the world's greatest jazz piano player . . . not one of the greatest—I am *the* greatest."

Jelly finally got dressed and we went in his car to see the manager of a big-name ballroom out on the South Side. But he and this man could not come to any agreement on the price Jelly wanted for playing there.

Jelly told the manager, "You bring Paul Whiteman out here and pay any price he wants because he has the name of 'King of Jazz.' But you happen to be talking to the real king of jazz. I invented it and I brought it here."

Jelly was a peculiar man—if he liked you he liked you too much, and it was the same way if he hated you. He was also very prejudiced and liked nothing but Creoles.

Musician Lee Collins, undated interview, quoted in
Williams, Jazz Masters of New Orleans *(1967),*
pp. 56–57.

6

Reading, Writing, and Radio
March 1924–December 1924

Since just before the turn of the 20th century, inventors had been turning out new devices for the transmission and reception of telegraph code through the atmosphere without the benefit of signal-carrying wires. In the early 1890s, a young Italian experimenter, Guglielmo Marconi, built the first wireless transmitter/receiver out of a telegraph key, a spark generator, metal aerials, and a "coherer," which detected and passed an electrical signal by cohering loose metal filings within a glass tube. Finding little interest in manufacturing the device on the part of the Italian government, Marconi patented his "wireless telegraphy" invention in 1896 in Great Britain, where he founded the Marconi Wireless Signal Telegraph company.

Over the years, as receivers grew more sensitive and transmitters more powerful, other inventors perceived that this new form of communication might help predict weather, provide communication across the oceans, and save isolated ships in distress. In 1906, the Canadian professor Reginald Fessenden sent the first wireless sound broadcast—consisting of songs, poems, and Fessenden himself performing "O Holy Night" on the violin—out to sea from his transmitting station at Brant Rock, Massachusetts. In a short time, "wireless" turned to "radio," signifying the "radiating" of sound into the atmosphere for one and all to receive.

The possible military uses of radio technology—aerial spotting for artillery, espionage reporting, and battlefield communication—also made it apparent to many government officials that control of radio would prove crucial in the next war. After the United States declared war on April 6, 1917, the federal government ordered all nonmilitary use of wireless radio to stop, then established a monopoly on radio equipment through the Department of the Navy. The navy took control of all radio patents owned by private corporations, including General Electric, Westinghouse, and the Marconi Wireless Telegraph Company of America, and seized transmitting stations, including two owned and operated by the German government at Tuckerton, New Jersey, and Sayville, Long Island.

Civilian use of radio proceeded experimentally during the war. Under a government contract, engineer Frank Conrad of Westinghouse transmitted news and music from his garage near a company assembly plant in East Pittsburgh,

A *Tampa Tribune* delivery truck prepares to deliver the public's information via newsprint. *(Bergert Brothers Collection, University of South Florida)*

Pennsylvania, an activity that convinced Westinghouse management to sponsor regular public radio broadcasting after the end of the war. Initiating the concentration of radio technology in corporate hands, Westinghouse bought out a firm that controlled all of the patents of Reginald Fessenden and, for $335,000, bought the rights to the regenerative and superheterodyne circuits created by the U.S. inventor Edward Armstrong, whose circuits could magnify radio signals many times their original strength to allow transmission over far greater distances.

Despite the many native advances in radio technology, U.S. lawmakers still worried over foreign control of this mysterious science, noting that the British government and the British Marconi company still had control over most of the world's radio communication systems. Many people, in and out of government, believed that the development of new radio technology was too important and militarily strategic to be left to the whims of free enterprise. Government sanctioning of a national monopoly company was seen as the answer.

In 1919, with the encouragement of the federal government, General Electric counsel Owen Young formed the Radio Corporation of America (RCA) to hold all of the radio patents seized and controlled by the government during the war. To prevent foreign control or influence, RCA bylaws held that only American citizens could serve as its directors or officers and that foreigners could not hold more than 80 percent of its stock. The Marconi company's subsidiary in the United States was pressured to sell its equipment to RCA, where military reserve officers readied the new technology for military use. RCA defended its monopoly status against all critics and competitors by claiming that it was working in the interest of national security.

While Young and partners drew up the charter of the Radio Corporation of America, point-to-point radio transmission was evolving into something new. Frank Conrad continued to "broadcast"—sending his short programs freely to anyone with the equipment to receive. In September 1920, the Joseph Horne department store of Pittsburgh began selling receivers expressly designed to capture Conrad's broadcasts. After reading an advertisement run by the store in the *Pittsburgh Sun,* Conrad's boss, Vice President Harry P. Davis of Westinghouse, asked Conrad to build a more powerful transmitter and have it ready by Election Day.

On October 27, 1920, the Department of Commerce granted Westinghouse the first license to operate a public radio station, its call letters to be KDKA and its wavelength to be 360 meters. On November 4, starting at 8 P.M., KDKA produced one of the first national news broadcasts, giving the results of the presidential election to listeners on the East Coast. The station received the tallies by telephone line from the newsroom of the *Pittsburgh Post.* At midnight, when the broadcast was over, the station had scooped the *Post* and every other newspaper in the nation by several hours in informing the public of Warren Harding's landslide victory.

ROOFTOP RADIO

KDKA continued broadcasting, at first for an hour a day, later with expanded evening hours. Westinghouse built new radio transmitters and studios at its plants in Newark, New Jersey (WJZ); at Springfield, Massachusetts (WBZ); and atop the Commonwealth Edison building in Chicago, Illinois (KYW). Westinghouse also faced its first competition in station WDY, established by the Radio Corporation of America in Aldene, New Jersey.

Many of the first radio stations were established by newspapers seeking a new outlet for the sale of information and entertainment; others were operated by department stores, universities, or churches. Local and national news, weather reports, football and baseball scores, and crop reports arrived in the few radio-equipped living rooms after a wireless journey from these stations and their one-room studios. Radio amateurs could also build their own "crystal" sets, using small pieces of galena crystal that received the carrier signal and then passed it to an amplifier. Crystal sets could be fine-tuned to the appropriate wavelengths in order to pull down radio transmissions from distant cities, but it took a certain amount of specialized knowledge to assemble and operate them, and in the public mind, radio remained a hobby for attic-bound inventors.

In 1921, while in search of a spectacular event that would spark a craze for radio, David Sarnoff of RCA hit on the broadcast of a heavyweight boxing match between Jack Dempsey and Georges Carpentier, an event for which promoters were preparing a 90,000-seat stadium in Jersey City, New Jersey. The event was linked to fund-raising efforts by the Fund for a Devastated France and the Navy Club, an organization led by Franklin Delano Roosevelt. Taking advantage of the spreading public interest, Sarnoff installed loudspeakers in public halls up and down the East Coast. Starting at 3 P.M. on July 2, J. Andrew White, editor of *Boxing Age,* delivered the description of the bout via telephone; his reports were written down and then repeated by J. O. Smith, an engineer working at a nearby transmitting station. After the fourth round, just as the overloaded, overheated transmitter began to break down, Dempsey won the bout, as heard "live" by more than 300,000 listeners.

Sarnoff's RCA was setting up research laboratories and hiring a large staff of technicians and designers to contribute new designs and circuitry to its "patent

U.S. Army Chief of Staff, General John "Black Jack" Pershing (seated, right), commander of the American Expeditionary Forces during World War I, experiences wireless radio with four unidentified companions, 1921. *(Underwood & Underwood/Library of Congress)*

pool," which was shared by companies such as General Electric and Westinghouse that held shares in RCA. In this way, the early radio industry was spared patent and copyright litigation, and outsiders were inhibited from developing rival inventions as the leading technology was subject to RCA and allied companies' exploitation.

Broadcasting itself was not subject to the same monopoly, as there was not yet private control of the airwaves. Under Sarnoff's direction, RCA established a new broadcast studio and radio station, call letters WJZ–WJY, at Aeolian Hall in New York City; American Telephone and Telegraph competed directly with its own station, WEAF. Although the American Telephone and Telegraph Corporation (AT&T) built more durable and advanced equipment, RCA was already on the way to completely monopolizing radio manufacturing as well as the broadcasting industry. The company would not sell its transmitting tubes to radio stations that did not exclusively buy RCA equipment. RCA also forced radio manufacturers to use its own transmitting tubes and received a royalty payment for each receiving set and each cabinet that came out of these competitors' factories. Through their catalogues and on their sales floors, Montgomery Ward and other stores offered several lines of radio receivers, also known as "crystal detectors," all of them using RCA tubes and circuitry, all representing a small royalty payment to the RCA treasury.

In 1922 the pace of radio manufacturing and broadcasting accelerated. At the beginning of the year four licensed stations were in existence; at the end of the year there were 576. Reliable vacuum-tube sets replaced crystal detectors. In 1922, the first commercial advertisement was broadcast over WEAF in New York, and the first regular commercial radio programming began on WBAY, another New York station owned by AT&T and that set a price for the sale of its "air time," thus beginning the age of the brief commercial interruption. As the decade continued, radio programmers grew accustomed to subjecting their audiences to the intermittent promotion of cars, soap, washing machines, vacuum cleaners, refrigerators, electric irons, gas stoves, and other products during regular programming.

Radio also began the age of the shortened attention span, as the expanding broadcast audience found a way to defend itself from electronic advertisement: by twisting knobs and indicators through the letters and numbers on a softly illuminated tuning dial to find music, news, sporting events, or weather on a competing station. The radio dial was the world's first channel "clicker," bringing its user the possibility of change and a certain relief from the forced monotony of full-length movies, theatrical plays, and musical concerts.

In 1924 the decade's fastest increase occurred in total radio set sales, from $136 million in 1923 to $358 million in 1924. It was also in 1924 that radio presented the 1924 Democratic Convention to a national audience. For the Democratic Party, the 1924 convention was a bitter, divisive, and exhausting event, the prelude to failure on a national scale in November. But the convention meant a resounding success for the new medium, radio. It was the first electronic mass media event, carried live by a network of small radio stations across the country and followed intently by thousands of people on their home radio receivers. While the Democrats' balloting deadlock continued for several days, and delegates for William Gibbs McAdoo and delegates for Alfred E. Smith found themselves utterly unwilling to compromise their principles or votes for the sake of party unity and White House chances, radio listeners enjoyed the privilege of following the proceedings from the comfort of their living room chairs, rather than from the hot and sweaty confines of Madison Square Garden. Many thus discovered that passively listening and following on the radio was just as good—better, actually—than being a witness to the event itself. The broadcasting of the

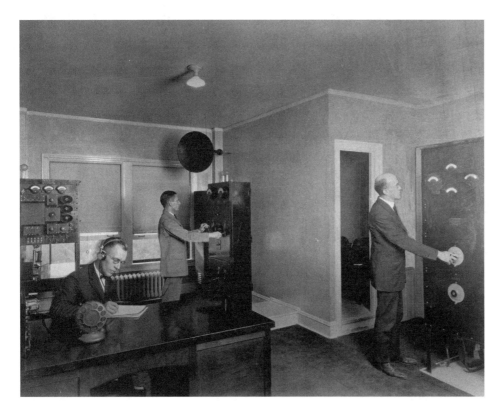

Radio technicians attend to their equipment in the transmitting room of station WLAG, located in the Oak Grove Hotel, downtown Minneapolis. *(Minnesota Historical Society)*

convention placed a revealing spotlight on the workings of politics and would-be presidents; it also had the effect of bringing the vast country together in a common experience. Music, news, and sports had been available on the radio for almost four years, but the ability to escape the artificial world of the studio and bring an important event into the living room, as it occurred, revealed the true potential of the new medium and helped to bring radio into its own.

New Literary Celebrities

Through the 1920s, the disembodied voices and invisible musicians of radio broadcasting remained a novelty, and little more, for citizens operating their living-room receivers. By the end of the decade, when the novelty began wearing off, the medium was developing standard programming formats—the 30-minute dramatic, adventure, or comic serial, the evening concert, the live sports broadcast, the regular news and weather reports. For serious critics in the daily press and monthly journals, however, radio remained an upstart, a bland and utilitarian information medium and nothing more. The nation's best creative talent, in the opinion of these observers, could still be found among its novelists, short story writers, poets, and journalists. Those favoring text and manuscript found support for their outlook in a flowering of literary experimentation and innovation—much of it occurring among a community of postwar expatriates that drew among them young and ambitious writers such as F. Scott Fitzgerald.

Slender, fair, and enamored of the imaginary glitter of the east, F. Scott Fitzgerald left his boyhood home in St. Paul, Minnesota, to attend college in Princeton, New Jersey. In 1917, when the United States entered the war in Europe, Fitzgerald joined the army and was posted to a camp in the vicinity of Montgomery, Alabama. To his great disappointment, the war ended before his ship sailed to Europe. On his discharge in 1919, Fitzgerald left behind a vigorous life with hearty comrades as well as a beautiful Montgomery debutante named Zelda Sayre. He arrived in New York, moved to a furnished apartment in the Bronx, and worked in a poorly paid advertising job. Running out of money, and finding no inspiration in his looming poverty, he returned home to St. Paul to write his first novel, *This Side of Paradise.* Scribner's accepted the book, and life changed for the better.

The novel and its hero, Amory Blaine, struck just the right attitude for the time. Smart and insouciant, adolescent and philosophical, and mirroring Fitzgerald's own escapades and romances, it was a daring novel due to its frank discussions of youth and sexuality; it set a certain tone for literature in the decade to come. Imitators arrived with their novels of youth and dissipation: Percy Marks wrote *The Plastic Age,* which was also set on a college campus; Dorothy Speare wrote *Dancing in the Dark* on the subject of flappers; and Warner Fabian wrote *Flaming Youth,* a book that tested the boundaries of literary legality with its sex, drinking, and more sex.

This Side of Paradise made a slight sensation on its publication in March 1920 but was overshadowed by the publication of Sinclair Lewis's *Main Street* seven months later. Fitzgerald returned to New York, married Zelda, and began to live as outrageously as possible. The couple attended parties, drank excessively, created scenes, and made and lost friends. The new decade brought new liberties; youth was reckless, Prohibition paradoxically inspired alcoholic indulgence, and the Fitzgeralds found themselves admired as well as disliked for a fast life representative of a new era. In 1922, Fitzgerald published *Tales of the Jazz Age,* a collection of stories that had appeared in several magazines, notably *The Saturday Evening Post,* the journal of middlebrow culture and middle-class society. His stories were now earning generous fees and with an income reaching $36,000 in 1923—perhaps 20 times the average income in the United States—Fitzgerald was approaching the life and success he had long been seeking.

Things changed for the worse in early 1924, when Fitzgerald failed with *The Vegetable,* a satirical play inspired by the scandals of the Warren Harding administration. The play's extremely short run of one week brought sober reflection in which Fitzgerald saw himself growing incompetent and lazy. Over the past two years, he had produced one failed play and a few short stories and articles; in sum, about 100 words a day. Feeling doubtful of his talent, he went through a patch of hard work while trying to pay the very large bills he had run up in order to buy and maintain the good life. By selling more stories to popular magazines, he managed to save enough to buy passage on a steamer for Europe, where he intended to settle down, conserve funds, finish a novel in progress, and regain his balance. In early 1924, the Fitzgeralds sailed for France on the steamship *Minnewaska.*

Fitzgerald and Lewis had both believed in the idea that fiction should mirror its times, reflect on the society at large, and comment on its follies. (Previously, Theodore Dreiser had attempted to follow the same ideals with *Sister Carrie,* a novel about a "fallen woman" that was published and banned in 1900 and that had earned him only hectoring condemnation by critics, booksellers, the public, and his own publisher, Doubleday.) But while Fitzgerald celebrated youth and its big-city excitements, Sinclair Lewis created the other enduring literary theme of his decade: disgust and cynicism toward a society gone suddenly and stupidly materialistic. In his novels *Main Street* (1920) and *Babbitt* (1922), Lewis discarded the halcyon prewar spirit of his five earlier novels and delivered biting satires on the new American quest for domestic comfort and expensive furnishings, a quest that he felt betrayed the heroic odysseys of the nation's founders, pioneers, and settlers. *Main Street* was the country's best-selling book in late 1920 and early 1921, eventually selling more than 400,000 copies. Although Lewis disdained materialism and small-town provincialism, he still expected recognition, and when the Pulitzer Prize committee delivered its prestigious award to someone else, he yearned for an appropriate revenge.

Later in the decade, Lewis turned his attentions to the medical profession in *Arrowsmith* (1925) and on hucksering preachers in *Elmer Gantry* (1927). Lewis's commentary on North American society was well received, and for Europeans critical of the United States, these works came to serve as introductions to the envied, prosperous nation that had largely escaped the death and damage of World War I. For his efforts, Lewis was awarded the Nobel Prize in literature in 1930—the first American writer to be so honored. The

After five pedestrian novels and anemic sales, Sinclair Lewis hit his stride with best-selling satiric depictions of middle America, beginning with *Main Street* in 1920. *(Culver Pictures)*

sarcastic and rather embittered acceptance speech he delivered in Stockholm served to avenge his snub by the Pulitzer Prize committee in 1921.

Another small-town writer from the Midwest, Sherwood Anderson, drew public attention a year before Lewis with *Winesburg, Ohio* (1919), a collection of tales that revealed the loneliness of small-town folks like the ones he knew growing up in real-life Camden, Ohio. Anderson had been a manufacturer of paint, and a rather standard-issue American success story, before leaving his family at the age of 40 in 1913 to make a literary name for himself. *Winesburg, Ohio,* his third novel, turned out to be the high mark of his career; the book's psychological tone and themes of desire influenced many other writers throughout the 1920s. His later books, including *Poor White* (1920), *The Triumph of the Egg* (1921), *Horses and Men* (1923), *Dark Laughter* (1925), and *Tar: A Midwest Childhood* (1925), were not as well received by critics or by the public. *Dark Laughter,* in particular, earned the ferocious scorn of Ernest Hemingway, who wrote a parody of the book titled *The Torrents of Spring.* Ironically, the novel proved to be Anderson's only financially successful work.

The arrival of Lewis, Fitzgerald, and Anderson on the literary scene made life easier for popular novelists such as James Branch Cabell and Joseph Hergesheimer. Both authors had succeeded with escapist works that followed the previously accepted emphasis on writing style over inventive plot and exploration of character. As the 1920s arrived, both writers added more explicit realism as well as actual sex to their books, an approach that earned Cabell prosecution over his 1919 novel *Jurgen.* (For all the notoriety earned by *Jurgen* and by Fitzgerald's imitators, literary sex remained largely an imported phenomenon through the 1920s. Discreet wrappers were still required to hide the covers of offending volumes, including James Joyce's *Ulysses* (1922), D. H. Lawrence's *Lady Chatterley's Lover* (1928), and later Henry Miller's *Tropic of Cancer* (1934), following their publication in Europe.)

WAR AND WORDS

In the moment of silence following the bloodbath in Europe, plots and characters relevant to the recently ended war drew critical attention. Poet e. e. cummings used his firsthand experience of wartime imprisonment to write *The Enormous Room* (1922), a prose account of his arrest and jailing for expressing antiwar opinions in his private correspondence. In collaboration with Laurence Stallings, Maxwell Anderson wrote the play *What Price Glory?* in 1924. General disgust with the wastefulness of war and suspicion of its true cause in the interests of international capitalism were the themes vividly expressed by John Dos Passos in *Three Soldiers* (1921), a book turned down by 14 publishers before its acceptance by George H. Doran. Dos Passos saw his mission as patriotic: showing contempt for enshrined institutions and comfortable cultural shibboleths that belied the intentions and philosophies of the founders of the republic. For this crusade, the 1920s would allow him an endless source of material, to be employed in *Manhattan Transfer* (1925), followed by *42nd Parallel* (1930), *1919* (1932), and *The Big Money* (1936), which collectively formed his *U.S.A.* trilogy.

Dos Passos was not the only debunker of the decade; there was also William E. Woodward, who coined the term "debunk" while taking down Washington, Grant, and other American heroes in his novel *Bunk* (1923). Three years earlier, Woodward had left the heart of capitalist darkness—a lucrative position as executive vice president of the Wall Street Industrial Finance Corporation—to write novels. *Bunk* described the adventures of Michael Webb, the author of *The Importance of Being Second-Rate,* a 60,000-page epic of America that is whittled down to 36 pages by editors and becomes a smash hit. Webb is thrown out of the newfound Second-Rate movement for being better than average, and embarks on a career in debunking the country's cherished icons, most of them being the self-made rich.

Cynicism and a revolt against the genteel tradition of prewar novelists bred the satire *Jennifer Lorn* (1923), the first full-length novel written by Elinor Wylie. Well-born and benefiting from a scandalous succession of love affairs, divorces, and marriages, Wylie had been writing poetry since 1912, but her book attracted rapturous praise from well-regarded critics, among them Carl Van Vechten, Maxwell Anderson, and James Branch Cabell.

Of all satirists there was none more cynical than H. L. (Henry Louis) Mencken, the son of a Baltimore cigarmaker who attained the editorship of the Baltimore *Morning Herald* in 1905 at age 25. Mencken later moved to the Baltimore *Sun,* where he remained until 1948 as reporter, editor, and columnist, while moonlighting at *Smart Set,* a literary journal that published early works by F. Scott Fitzgerald, playwright Eugene O'Neill, short story writer and poet Dorothy Parker, Theodore Dreiser, and poet Edna St. Vincent Millay. One day, however, Mencken went too far with an obituary on his favorite target, Warren Harding. The piece was spiked by the publisher, so in October 1923 Mencken and George Jean Nathan left *Smart Set* to begin *The American Mercury,* sponsored by the publisher Alfred A. Knopf. In the pages of the *Mercury,* the most widely read literary magazine of the decade, Mencken joyously exposed and assaulted gaseous politicians, sanctimonious prohibitionists, worthless university professors,

Anti-Prohibition polemicist H. L. Mencken partakes of "Breakfast in a Free State." Mencken's skillful flaying of the moralizing hypocrites and blowhards of the 1920s earned his journal *The American Mercury* valuable controversy and national admiration. *(State Historical Society of Wisconsin)*

humbugging evangelists, the vulgar, the "booboisie" (average American simpletons), and any and all other pundits presumptuous enough to write and publish in the same language, which he also presumed to defend and uphold against all misuse in *The American Language* (1921), his one-volume encyclopedia on the origins and modern usages of English.

Mencken's and Nathan's diverging perspectives of the *Mercury* doomed their partnership. Nathan, preferring art, bought Eugene O'Neill's *All God's Chillun Got Wings* for the second issue of the magazine; Mencken, favoring satire, gleefully skewered the booboisie by reprinting improbably thick-headed and provincial newspaper extracts. Nathan found all the entertainment he needed in the world of books and theater, while Mencken couldn't get enough of politics, religion, the laws of censorship and society at large. Nathan moved in sophisticated circles and attended glamorous parties on the upper stories of Manhattan apartment buildings; Mencken traveled up to Boston to get himself arrested for selling the copy of *The American Mercury* containing the salacious Herbert Asbury story "Hatrack."

The American Mercury swam in a crowded current of newspapers, journals, and popular magazines, all dispensing advice and criticism on the new fiction and drama, helping to foster sales and public interest in the work of emerging writers. Frank Crowninshield presented the writings of Dorothy Parker, Robert Benchley, Edmund Wilson, and Edna St. Vincent Millay in the pages of *Vanity Fair,* while *Harpers, Scribner's, The Atlantic Monthly, The Dial, The Nation, The Freeman, The Bookman,* and *The Century* gave prominent column inches to literary news and notices. Also in the 1920s, Harold Ross, the editor of the *American Legion Magazine,* began assembling *The New Yorker* out of words and images conjured by the era's fashionable irony and urban sophistication.

Newspapers abounded in the larger cities, their publishers unapologetically printing literary opinion at its most controversial. Heywood Broun wrote sports, books, and theater; Franklin Pierce Adams ("F. P. A.") wrote a column for the New York *Tribune* and later the New York *World,* which also sported Robert Benchley. A nontraditional yet standard career path seemed to have begun: journalists made celebrities out of themselves while posing as tough-minded and street-savvy truth seekers; they later graduated to columns and then made the cut to professional novelists and screenwriters. The one-time boy acrobat Ben Hecht had made waves with his newspaper stories in Chicago; popularity egged him on to write *Erik Dorn,* the story of a Chicago journalist who escapes a life of spritual suffocation to take his place in the crowd of expatriates in Europe.

The genteel business of book publishing went through changes, as editors seeking notoriety as well as sales brought out a new wave of younger U.S. authors and their writing, elevating them over previously stylish English imports. Alfred A. Knopf created the artsy Borzoi Books, Horace Liveright quit Wall Street to join Albert and Charles Boni and form Boni and Liveright, and Maxwell Perkins looked after the work of F. Scott Fitzgerald and Ernest Hemingway at Scribner's. In the case of Sinclair Lewis, it was the author that made the publisher, as Lewis cajoled Alfred Harcourt into publishing *Main Street,* one of the smash antiestablishment hits of the decade.

A nonfiction work written by the Englishman H. G. Wells also made a splash, reaching the top of U.S. best-seller lists for more than four years, despite having absolutely no trouble with the law. *The Outline of History,* to modern eyes a somewhat tedious and dated survey of everything that ever happened, created a new interest in history, a subject passed over by the general public until the war brought a new interest in Europe's tangled past. *The Outline of History* became a useful handbook for authors seeking to add some borrowed erudition to their plots and characters and, in a few cases, causing outright imitations, including Clement Wood's *Outline of Man's Knowledge* and Willem Van Loon's *The Story of Mankind*. Other nonfiction categories—psychology, biography, anthropology—also benefited from the reading boom. Debunking biographies of Queen Victoria by Lytton Strachey, of P. T. Barnum and Brigham Young by M. R. Werner, of Ulysses S. Grant by *Bunk* author William Woodward, and of George Washington by Rupert Hughes drew good sales by remeasuring heroes once set atop pedestals by prewar authors.

Doing Lunch

The Midwest and the small town may have provided raw material, but the true seat of modern literature was at the Algonquin Hotel, at 59 West 44th Street, New York City. The hotel was frequented by movie stars and bohemians, with literary accents provided by the brief stays of H. L. Mencken. The lunch dates of Alexander Woollcott, Heywood Broun, and Franklin Pierce Adams (F. P. A.) began attracting guests; when manager Frank Case moved his celebrities to a large round table in the hotel's Rose Room, the Algonquin Round Table, or the Vicious Circle as its regular members styled it, was born.

The Round Table became the scene of a daily contest of wit and mild insult, delivered by its founders Woollcott, Broun, and F. P. A., as well as by playwright George S. Kaufman, Donald Ogden Stewart, Harold Ross, novelist Edna Ferber, Laurence Stallings, actress Tallulah Bankhead, Robert Benchley, the competitively witty Dorothy Parker, and a dozen-odd other aspirants and hangers-on. As it grew increasingly conscious of its own sophistication, the Round Table began to attract tourists and eavesdroppers, who demanded nearby tables, in hopes of catching random witticisms. Competition then arrived in the form of the Little Round Table, in the same hotel, which hosted second-string novelists and critics such as Burton Rascoe, Christopher Morley, and Louis Broomfield. The height of the Algonquin Round Table fame was reached on the evening of April 30, 1922, when its members wrote and starred in *No Sirree!,* a revue performed at the 49th Street Theatre.

By acclamation, Dorothy Parker created the most memorable one-liners at the Algonquin. She had started out, after leaving West End, New Jersey, as a drama critic for *Vanity Fair,* but found herself jobless after directing some insulting poetry at Billie Burke, the wife of Broadway maestro Florenz Ziegfeld. Parker continued as a reviewer for *The New Yorker* from 1927 until 1933, while her dry and world-weary poetry appeared in the collections *Enough Rope* (1927) and *Death and Taxes* (1931).

Parker's former colleague at *Vanity Fair,* Robert Benchley, who himself had started out as editor of the *Harvard Lampoon,* attained his first New York notices with witty short essays and stories in *Vanity Fair.* Benchley led the pack of popular humorists, which included the Canadian writer Stephen Leacock, S. J. Perelman, Will Rogers, Ring Lardner, and P. G. Wodehouse, an English import. George Chappell, writing as Walter E. Traprock, F.R.S.S.E.V., N.L.L.D., brought out *My Northern Exposure: The Kawa at the Pole.* Donald Ogden Stewart answered *The Outline of History* with *Aunt Polly's Story of Mankind.*

Women were well-represented among the nation's popular satirists. Edna Ferber wrote *So Big,* a best-selling novel in 1924. Ferber's subject, and market, was middle America, where her magazine stories featuring heroine Emma McChesney had already been read for many years. Anne Parrish wrote similarly clever books on the subject of disturbed domesticity, including *Pocketful of Poses, Semi-Attached,* and *The Perennial Bachelor.* Anita Loos, a native of the West Coast, had been selling film scripts for years, since she was a teenager, and had succeeded with her first book submission, entitled *The New York Hat.* It was some time in 1925 when, peeved at the attentions paid to a "dumb blonde" by her husband and every other gentleman present on a cross-country train, Loos conceived Lorelei Lee, the bubble-headed heroine of *Gentlemen Prefer Blondes.* The story was first published in installments in *Harper's Bazaar* and was illustrated by Ralph Barton. The sudden high demand for the magazine convinced publisher Boni and Liveright to bring Loos's story out as a Christmas-season novelty late in 1925. Eventually *Gentlemen Prefer Blondes* sold hundreds of thousands of copies, becoming a literary theme song of sorts for the 1920s along with Fitzgerald's novel *The Great Gatsby.*

Uptown Writers

New forms and styles of poetry provided a background chorus to the deluge of innovative novels. Poets were highly respected, and several poetry books attained best-seller status. Archibald MacLeish, Elinor Wylie, Wallace Stevens, William Rose Benét, Stephen Vincent Benét, William Carlos Williams, Hilda Doolittle (writing as H. D.), Edna St. Vincent Millay, and Hart Crane brought out notable verse during the 1920s. Edgar Guest's pop poetry found millions of buyers. e. e. cummings became the darling of the avant-garde critics, especially Carl Van Vechten.

Van Vechten himself had escaped from smothering Cedar Rapids, Iowa, to the University of Chicago, then to New York and the *New York Times* as a music critic. His own novels were affected confections of decadent poses and tawdry characters. Since they were not too well liked even by the most tolerant and liberal of critics, it was as a promoter and socialite that Van Vechten made his major contributions. Van Vechten supported anything avant-garde; he drove the early bandwagons for George Gershwin, stage actress Sarah Bernhardt, James Joyce, cubism, atonality, and the Harlem Renaissance. He played a crucial part in introducing downtown editors to the crop of writers emerging uptown in Harlem, where a good deal of innovation in American writing was taking place. Thanks to Van Vechten and other patrons, Harlem writers were gaining notice and praise from white publishers and editors, who saw the African-American experience as one possible antidote to the spiritual sterility of the industrial age.

The Jamaican-born writer Claude McKay had made stops at Tuskegee University and Kansas State College, where he first read the book that changed his outlook—W. E. B. DuBois's *The Souls of Black Folk*—before arriving in New York in 1914. His first poems were published pseudonymously in *Seven Arts* magazine. McKay also edited *The Liberator* magazine, founded by the radical Max Eastman. McKay did not feel entirely comfortable in Harlem, sensing social stratification there and perceiving his own treatment as an outsider. When he traveled to England in 1919, expecting to find some common bonds with the colonists of his native Jamaica, he was confronted only with a more virulent brand of racism.

McKay returned to the United States in 1920 and in 1922 published *Harlem Shadows,* a poetry collection that presaged the coming Harlem Renaissance in African-American literature. Still feeling like an outcast and humiliated by continuing encounters with racism from both whites and blacks, he decided to bolt for the Soviet Union and take part in the communist utopia foreseen by Marx, as brought about by Lenin. With Max Eastman, he attended the Congress of the Fourth International, was received by the highest officials of the new Soviet regime, and given a place of honor on the reviewing stand on May Day, 1923. Soon disillusioned with Soviet society as well, McKay left in June 1923 for Berlin and Paris, where he joined a community of African-American expatriates.

While McKay lived abroad, the 1925 *Opportunity* prize for the poem "The Weary Blues" launched the career of Langston Hughes. Soon after the landmark *Opportunity* ceremony at the Fifth Avenue Restaurant, Carl Van Vechten arranged for a publication of a volume of Hughes's poetry by Alfred A. Knopf. Hughes was born in Joplin, Missouri, in 1902, attended high school in Cleveland, and was already attracting notice with his poetry by the time he arrived in New York in 1921. He enrolled at Columbia University to study mining but soon was circulating among the patrons and writers of Harlem and forming a friendship with Countee Cullen, who had moved to Harlem as a teenager after his adoption by the Reverend Frederick Cullen, pastor of the Salem Methodist Episcopal Church. Countee was first published at the age of 15; his first collection of poetry, *Color,* appeared in 1925. In 1926 he became assistant editor for *Opportunity* magazine, and in 1927 published two more collections, *Copper Sun* and *The Ballad of the Brown Girl.*

Almost on arrival from rural northern Florida in early 1925, Zora Neale Hurston made one of the biggest splashes of all. Hired as a secretary and chauffeur by novelist Fannie Hurst, she began studying with renowned anthropologist Franz Boas at Barnard College. Hurston achieved a second and more prominent career as a Harlem Salon celebrity with her inventive storytelling skills and tales of Eatonville, Florida, her hometown. After winning an *Opportunity* prize for her short story "Spunk" and her play *Color Struck,* she joined Langston Hughes, Wallace Thurman, Richard Nugent, and Aaron Douglas to establish *Fire!!,* an iconoclastic literary journal, which appeared in November 1926 and promptly folded. With its single issue, *Fire!!* and its editors made their share of important enemies, including W. E. B. DuBois, by addressing subjects forbidden even to African-American writers such as homosexuality and prostitution.

The deep-seated conflicts involved while getting by in a white culture served novelist Nella Larsen as material for her novels *Passing* (1929) and *Quicksand* (1928). Raised in a Danish immigrant family in Chicago as Nellie Walker, Larsen had trained as a nurse, working at Tuskegee Institute and later for the New York Board of Health. After her marriage to a scientist, Dr. Elmer Imes, she retired from nursing and took work at the New York Public Library's 135th Street branch, where she gained a librarian's very thorough knowledge of the books and journals of the Harlem Renaissance. Both of her novels were accepted by Alfred A. Knopf, who by the end of the decade was regarded by many as one of the country's most talented and visionary publishers. Larsen's work earned her a Guggenheim Fellowship in 1930, which allowed her to travel to Europe in order to research a new book. A charge of plagiarism for her short story "Sanctuary" and the breakup of her marriage in 1933, however, eventually stilled her literary voice. She broke ties with the writers and artists she had known and, by the 1940s, had returned to a relatively anonymous life as a nurse.

WRITERS OVERSEAS

There were many writers, black and white, who despaired of ever finding what they needed in the United States and accordingly arranged passage to Europe. Their leading patron was Gertrude Stein, herself a transplant from Allegheny, Pennsylvania and Johns Hopkins University who hosted the best-known literary salon in Paris, a few small rooms on the Rue de Fleurus that would be decorated during the 1920s with the city's top literary and artistic talent, including F. Scott Fitzgerald, Ernest Hemingway, Pablo Picasso, and Henri Matisse. Stein's own work was obscure enough to earn her the modernist label; she became much better known for a passing remark (later published as the epigraph to Hemingway's first novel *The Sun Also Rises*) that characterized her fellow emigrés as the "Lost Generation."

T. S. (Thomas Stearns) Eliot was perhaps the original member of the Lost Generation, having arrived from Harvard for postgraduate study at the Sorbonne in Paris in 1910. Eliot had been converted to the avocation of poetry by *The Symbolist Movement in Literature,* a book by Arthur Symons that he had discovered in a Harvard library. In France, where he felt liberated from the conservative commercialism of his family, he collected groundbreaking verse which was later published as a small, leatherbound volume entitled *Inventions of the March Hare.* In 1914, on the eve of the war, he moved to England, and into Merton College, Oxford. Winning acceptance in the Bloomsbury Group, a literary circle that included Virginia Woolf, Lytton Strachey, and E. M. Forster, Eliot published his first book, *Prufrock and Other Observations* in 1917, and then two volumes in 1920: *Poems* and *Sacred Wood,* a book of criticism. Eliot had also found steady employment at Lloyds Bank, but troubles in his home life, including a chaotic marriage and depression, came to the fore in poetry that cast aside old notions and rules of rhythm and meter and adopted as its principal subject decay—the gradual disintegration of traditional faith and the loss of order and direction in the modern world.

The American writers and artists abroad enthusiastically took up Eliot's disillusionment as expressed in *The Waste Land,* which was edited by Ezra Pound and published in 1922. The poem had been in the works since 1914 and was formed from a long collection of incidents and memories collected from Eliot's personal experiences among the English. The intensity, the dense and playful alliterations, and the rhythmic syncopations of the poem reminded readers of jazz. Symbolism and surrealism, as experienced by Eliot in the study of avant-garde art, also found their way into the work. *The Waste Land* became a kind of poetic anthem for expatriates and for the avant-garde literary fellowship in the United States, but the same audience would never be able to square its opinions with Eliot's adopted Anglican religion nor, later, with his endorsement of the concept of Order in the persons of Benito Mussolini and Adolf Hitler.

Eliot and a number of other expatriate poets and writers often sought counsel with the red-headed, craggy eminence of all expatriates, the Idaho-born poet Ezra Loomis Pound. After reaching the continent in 1907, Pound began a lifelong and exhaustive investigation of poetic art and history. His first book of poetry, *A Lume Spento,* had been published at his own expense in Venice, after which he traveled to London to meet one of his many literary idols, William Butler Yeats. After reading some poems by his friend Hilda Doolittle (who later took the pseudonym H. D.), Pound thrust himself to the head of England's avant-garde literary scene by introducing and defining imagism, an attempt to strip away the old rules of poetry by creating a new style based on concrete images and a precise reflection of the real world. He championed the works of T. S. Eliot, James Joyce, and many other neglected experimental writers and artists, valuing experimental expression over conformity to taste and traditionalism. In 1920, he brought out a lengthy poem, *Hugh Selwyn Mauberley,* that expressed a strong disillusionment with what he saw as cramped and musty British literary traditions. Seeking a more bohemian life, Pound moved to Paris in 1921, where he continued work on a poetic epic known as the *Cantos,* begun in 1915 and not finished until the end of the 1930s. Pound left the bohemian lifestyle of London and Paris, and moved to Italy in 1924. There he sympathized with the politics of Italian fascist dictator Benito Mussolini, formulating opinions that guaranteed an undying controversy around his poetry and criticism.

The Return of the Fitzgeralds

Reading and hearing about the stylish expatriate community then collecting in Stein's salon and other locales in Paris, the Fitzgeralds eagerly decamped from New York harbor. In France, as Scott and Zelda Fitzgerald knew, a large community of writers, artists, and cultural tourists had already arrived from the United States determined to escape, at least for a while, the aspects of U.S. culture they despised: materialism, small-town hucksterism, and low-brow culture. After staying for a brief time in Paris, they moved to the town of St. Raphael, on the French Riviera, and into a house, the Villa Marie. They hired a cook and a maid, as well as an English nanny to look after their daughter, Scottie. As a complete withdrawal from social life still seemed out of the question, they made friends with Gerald and Sara Murphy, a wealthy American couple whom they had met in Paris. The Murphys, who lived in a larger house on the Riviera called the Villa America, played hosts to a fine roster of American expatriates including Cole Porter, John Dos Passos, and Ernest Hemingway, as well as famous French actors, dancers, musicians, and painters.

The Fitzgeralds, for whom the quiet life seemed not worth living, attended parties and had escapades. They spent little time exploring the surrounding culture, took no interest in art, music, museums, or theater, and never learned to speak French. Feeling the greatest admiration for the social graces and the money of the Murphys, Fitzgerald could not change old habits in a new surrounding. He strained the Murphys' patience with his drinking, bad manners, sophomoric antics, and constant attention-seeking, while Zelda, feeling restless, isolated, and jealous of the fame her husband had achieved, took to swimming, sunbathing, and a romance with Edouard Jozan, a handsome French aviator. The affair ended abruptly, but Scott realized that something important had changed: he could no longer count on his wife's fidelity, and he and Zelda were turning into aging and mundanely flawed Americans abroad. The jazz-tinted alcoholic comedy was turning tragic as the Roaring Twenties passed from drunken adolescence to a hangover of sober remorse.

One consolation remained: a fine novel. His exuberance as well as his regrets came through admirably in *The Great Gatsby* (1925), in which an ordinary young man from the Midwest named Jay Gatz meets and falls in love with a rich young woman named Daisy. Before the marriage can take place, Gatz is called away to war; while he is off fighting in Europe, he loses Daisy to a well-moneyed fellow named Tom Buchanan. Desperate to find her again and win her away from her callous husband, Gatz transforms himself into a mysterious, much-gossiped-about aristocrat by the name of Gatsby, who has been to war, attended Oxford, and made money in shadowy activities left unexplained. "Gatsby" buys an ornate mansion on a wealthy Long Island peninsula, just across the bay from the Buchanan estate, and gives lavish all-night parties to attract his lost love by the light of Chinese lanterns and the blaring of jazz ensembles.

Jay Gatsby's plan works, with the help of his neighbor Nick Carraway, who serves Fitzgerald as a distracted and distant narrator. Jay and Daisy meet again, suffering awkwardness, nostalgia, and love. They plan an elopement and a divorce from Tom Buchanan. Just as a happy ending seems to be in sight, tragedy occurs: Gatsby accidentally kills Tom Buchanan's mistress. Buchanan directs his mistress's grieving husband to Gatsby's front door, and Gatsby is murdered while lazily floating in his swimming pool. Gatsby's house empties of guests and servants; death and disillusion have triumphed over youth and hope.

Daisy Buchanan stood for Zelda Sayre; the author modeled Tom Buchanan on Tommy Hitchcock, a champion polo player whom Fitzgerald had known and admired in Great Neck, Long Island, and who had all the things Fitzgerald regretfully lacked: good breeding, money, and courageous military exploits. The fictional gambler Meyer Wolfshein, who plays a suitably mysterious role in Gatsby's business dealings, is based on Arnold Rothstein, a New York gambler who played a key role in the 1919 "Black Sox" scandal. The Polish-born and British-bred author Joseph Conrad provided Fitzgerald with his literary inspiration. Fitzgerald had read and studied Conrad's novels while working on *Gatsby,* and had consciously borrowed Conrad's use of symbolism, his sense of disillusion, the narrative device of skipping backward and forward in time, and the distant narrator in the form of Nick Carraway, a Jazz Age version of Conrad's narrator Charlie Marlow in *Heart of Darkness* and *Lord Jim*.

In late October 1924, after missing several promised delivery dates, Fitzgerald sent the finished typescript to Maxwell Perkins, his editor at Scribner's in New York. Seeking to escape his own disillusionment, he then left the Riviera villa for Italy, where the Fitzgeralds would have a series of disappointments and misadventures that would forever sour them on the expatriate life in Europe.

Scribner's published *The Great Gatsby* in April 1925. To Maxwell Perkins, it seemed a promising time to bring out a short, skillfully written novel that cast bittersweet doubts on the excesses of the times. Book publishers were starting to do a brisk business in the United States; Morrow, Viking, Harcourt Brace, and several other new publishing houses were founded as the rate of literacy climbed and the public began to enjoy expanded leisure hours in which to read magazines, books, and newspapers.

A MAN AMONG WRITERS

In April 1925, the Fitzgeralds moved back to Paris, where they met a self-confident and physically imposing American writer, still generally unknown, named Ernest Hemingway. In many ways, Hemingway appeared the opposite of F. Scott Fitzgerald. He felt no interest in the wealthy and glamorous, and no need to maintain a lifestyle that matched, or at least imitated, theirs. Much to Fitzgerald's envy, Hemingway had seen action in World War I and could claim to be one of the first Americans wounded during the war. He had been living in Paris since 1921, having shifted from journalism to fiction and worked out a spare and direct writing style that dropped the complex syntax and the nuanced descriptions of appearance, action, and emotion so carefully set down by Fitzgerald, Conrad, and others of the old school. In 1923, Hemingway had published his first book, *Three Stories and Ten Poems,* in an edition of 300 copies, and then had completed a collection of vignettes, *in our time,* first published in 1924. An expanded *In Our Time* (1925) that included new short stories would make his reputation among the expatriates in Europe and eventually among the reading public in the United States.

In Our Time sold only a few hundred copies in the year of its publication, but publisher Horace Liveright had faith in Hemingway, granting him a three-book contract in the belief that his future books would sell as his reputation took hold in the United States. By the time Hemingway arrived in New York in February 1926, Liveright was eagerly anticipating a new manuscript dealing with the expatriate community in Europe. Instead, Hemingway shipped him *The Torrents of Spring,* a parody of the work of Sherwood Anderson, one of the best-selling authors on Liveright's own list. Liveright rejected the book and asked after *The Sun Also Rises,* a book about a group of disillusioned American expatriates at their worst, uselessly drinking and fornicating from city to city while nursing scorn for their homeland. Hemingway had placed several of his acquaintances in the book in thinly disguised poison-pen portraits. Both author and prospective publisher knew it would attract attention; both also knew that Hemingway was blazing new ground with his startlingly reticent and direct writing style, free of the pretensions, embellishments, and overarching analysis of the past.

Hemingway had ulterior motives for disappointing Horace Liveright. The author was unhappy with the sales of *In Our Time* and with Liveright's promotion of the book, and he envied Fitzgerald's relationship with a top-drawer editor, Maxwell Perkins. After a meeting that went well enough, considering the circumstances, Liveright agreed to cancel Hemingway's contract, and soon thereafter Hemingway signed with Scribner's, where Perkins promptly accepted *The Torrents of Spring* as well as *The Sun Also Rises.* Critics, writers, and intellectuals acclaimed *In Our Time* as well as *The Sun Also Rises,* knowing that Hemingway was pioneering a groundbreaking new literary style that would soon have its legion of imitators. The promise of his first two books was fulfilled by *A Farewell to Arms,* which appeared in 1929 and brought Hemingway a popularity he would be hard-pressed to equal for the remainder of his life.

CHRONICLE OF EVENTS

1924

March 18: The House of Representatives passes the Soldiers' Bonus Bill, a $2 billion measure that will create "certificates"—amounting to about $1 per day for World War I service in the United States and $1.25 for service overseas. The certificates, which average $1,000 in value, are in the form of 20-year "endowment" policies against which policyholders can borrow and are fully redeemable only in 1945. The bill will be passed by the Senate on April 23. But budget-cutting is foremost on the agenda of President Coolidge, who vetoes the bill on May 15. The House will then override the veto on May 17, and the Senate on May 19. In 1932, at the depths of the Depression, a so-called Bonus Army will march on Washington to demand immediate payment of the certificates.

March 18: The Thief of Baghdad, a film starring Douglas Fairbanks, premieres.

March 24: Pope Pius XI appoints as cardinals Archbishop Patrick Joseph Hayes of New York and Archbishop George W. Mundelein of Chicago.

March 28: President Coolidge asks for the resignation of Attorney General Harry M. Daugherty, who acquiesces.

April 3: Actor Marlon Brando is born.

April 9: Its economy destroyed by postwar inflation, Germany accepts the Dawes Plan for war reparations. The plan was created by a U.S. commission headed by Charles G. Dawes, director of the U.S. Bureau of the Budget. The Dawes Plan allows a loan to Germany, reorganizes Germany's monetary system, and eases the schedule of reparations payments. In 1930, as Germany again experiences economic problems, the Dawes Plan will be replaced by the Young Plan, which reduces reparations payments.

April 14: The Metro and Goldwyn moving picture companies merge to form Metro-Goldwyn-Mayer.

May 19: The Soldiers Bonus Act is passed by the Senate over President Coolidge's veto of May 15.

May 24: By the Rogers Act, the Foreign Service is established to handle diplomatic missions and foreign consulates.

May 26: Congress passes a new Immigration Quota Law, limiting the annual total of immigrants to about 150,000. The number of new immigrants from a single country is limited to 2 percent of that nationality already in the United States, as counted in the 1890 census. Immigrants from Japan will be completely excluded.

May 26: Operetta composer Victor Herbert dies in New York.

May 31: "Thrill killers" Nathan Leopold and Richard Loeb confess to the murder of Bobby Franks in Chicago.

June 2: After failing in 1916 and 1919 to pass federal child labor laws, Congress passes a Child Labor Amendment to the U.S. Constitution. By 1950, only 26 states ratify the amendment, well short of the two-thirds needed for passage, and the amendment is dropped.

June 2: The Snyder Act grants citizenship to all Native Americans living within the United States.

June 2: The Revenue Act reduces surtax on high incomes, as well as estate and income taxes, and provides for publication of tax returns.

June 5: The Prohibition Party meets in Columbus, Ohio, and nominates Herman P. Faris of Missouri for president and Marie C. Brehm of California for vice president.

June 10–12: The Republican party nominates Calvin Coolidge for reelection at its nominating convention in Cleveland. Charles G. Dawes is nominated for vice president.

June 15: The 10 millionth Model T rolls off the assembly line at the River Rouge plant of the Ford Motor Company.

June 30: A federal grand jury indicts Albert Fall, Harry Sinclair, Edward Doheny Sr. and Edward Doheny Jr. for bribery and conspiracy to defraud the United States as a result of the Congressional hearings on Teapot Dome.

June 30: Comedian Will Rogers joins the *Ziegfeld Follies* production on Broadway.

July 1: Day and night air mail service is established between New York and San Francisco.

July: U.S. forces withdraw from the Dominican Republic.

July 4 and 5: Progressives hold the National Convention of the Conference for Progressive Political Action in Cleveland, Ohio. They select Senator Robert La Follette of Wisconsin to run for president and Senator Burton Wheeler of Montana to run for vice president.

July 9: The Democratic Party holds its nominating convention in New York City. A tumultuous 102-ballot contest between Al Smith and William McAdoo results in a compromise nomination, John W. Davis of West Virginia for president and Charles W. Bryan—brother of William Jennings Bryan—of Nebraska for vice president.

July 21: Defended by Clarence Darrow, whose oratory spares them from a death sentence, wealthy "thrill killers" Nathan Leopold and Richard Loeb are sentenced to life in prison for the murder of Bobby Franks.

August 16: The Allies and Germany informally accept the Dawes Plan providing for repayment of war debts and reparations. The plan will be signed August 30.

August 24: The Agricultural Credits Act is passed with the intention of limiting the rising number of farm bankruptcies.

September 18: The U.S. Marines leave Santo Domingo. Their departure ends a 20-year U.S. supervision of the Dominican economy and government, enforced since Theodore Roosevelt's presidency, when the nations of Europe threatened to forcibly collect on the island nation's debts.

November 4: Republican Calvin Coolidge is elected president by 382 electoral votes to 136 for the Democrats, and 13 votes (all from Wisconsin) for Progressive candidate Robert La Follette.

November 6: Senator Henry Cabot Lodge, leading opponent of the League of Nations, dies in Cambridge, Massachusetts.

November 6: The Metropolitan Opera production of *Boris Godunov* opens in New York.

November 11: The New York Stock Exchange breaks trading volume records with 2,226,226 shares bought and sold.

November 17: The U.S. sends a representative to the Opium Conference of the League of Nations in Geneva.

December 13: Samuel Gompers, longtime president of the American Federation of Labor (AFL), dies in San Antonio, Texas. William Green is elected the new head of the AFL on December 19.

December 27: A treaty is signed with Santo Domingo, formally ending U.S. military involvement.

EYEWITNESS TESTIMONY

The Radio Age

I have in mind a plan of development which would make radio a household utility in the same sense as the piano or the phonograph. The idea is to bring music into the house by wireless. . . . The receiver can be designed in the form of a simple "Radio Music Box" and arranged for several different wave lengths. . . . The main revenue to be derived will be from the sale of the "Radio Music Boxes" which if manufactured in lots of one hundred thousand or so could yield a handsome profit. . . . Aside from the profit . . . the possibilities for advertising for the company are tremendous; for its name would ultimately be brought into the household and wireless would receive national and universal attention.

> *David Sarnoff, assistant traffic manager of the American Marconi wireless company, in 1916 memo to his superiors, quoted in Douglas,* The Early Days of Radio Broadcasting *(1987), p. 15.*

I am in a log shack in Canada's northland. . . . Three bosom friends are here in the shack with me—my ax, my dog, and my wireless receiving set. These are vital possessions. If I lose my ax, a frozen death awaits me when the wood fire dies. If I lose my dog—well, you who love your dogs in places where human friends abound just remember where I am. If I lose my wireless set, then I am again cut off from the great outside world which I have so recently regained. . . .

I reach over and touch a switch and the music of an orchestra playing at Newark, N.J., fills the room. . . . A slight turn of the magic knob and I am at Pittsburgh, Pa., listening to a man telling stories to thousands of America's listening children. With that magic knob I can command the musical programs and press news sent out from a dozen radio broadcasting stations. At will I amuse myself or garner the details of a busy world where things are happening. . . .

. . . I may be at "the back of beyond," but the whole world has marched right up to the edge of the little copper switch at my elbow.

> *M. J. Caveney, describing the effect of the new medium of radio on life in the northern wilderness, in "New Voices in the Wilderness,"* Collier's *magazine, April 1920, p. 18.*

The sending of the election returns by the "Detroit News" radiophone Tuesday night was fraught with romance and must go down in the history of man's conquest of the elements as a gigantic step in his progress. In the four hours that the apparatus, set up in an out-of-the-way corner of The News Building, was hissing and whirring its message into space, few realized that a dream and a prediction had come true. The news of the world was being given forth through this invisible trumpet to the waiting crowds in the unseen market place.

> *Story on an early radio transmission in the* Detroit News, *September 1, 1920, quoted in Hilmes,* Radio Voices: American Broadcasting 1922–1952, *p. 69.*

So Bertha and George, in the name of the thousands of listeners in, let me extend congratulations and best wishes. Also let me add, that it was the most impressive wedding ceremony I ever heard, not excepting my own. For you know how it is, if you're doing it yourself, well, you are just not accountable. If your own sis, or big brother, or only daughter are getting married, your are busily engaged in seeing that they look all right, and in shedding a few loose tears, and wondering how it will turn out. Or if it is one those swell church affairs, you are there to see the styles and criticise [sic] your neighbor, so there it goes. But over the Radio you have none of these distracting circumstances. And—"If not, hereafter and forever behold [sic] your peace"—, Well, when I heard that, with tears brimming in my eyes, just like in dear, old Dad's, I says to myself all quiet and still inside, "yes dear Bertha and George, if you'll just do that, if you just obey that injunction, you'll trot double and keep in pretty good step all along the matrimonial road. I know, I've been there and am still traveling double.

> *Letter from an admiring KDKA listener after the broadcast wedding of George Albert Carver and Bertha Annie McMunn, who were married at the Pittsburgh Electrical Show on November 18, 1922, from "Radio Wedding Impressed Listeners,"* Radio Broadcasting News, *December 9, 1922, p. 1.*

MR. SHUGG: What's the radio entertainment for this evening? Oh, we are going to hear Mrs. Wiffin sing "Oogie Woogie Wah Wah" at the Broadcasting Station at Upper Sandusky. Is the antenna out?

MRS. SHUGG: The whole thing is out, as far as I'm concerned. You hear nothing but advertisements, stock market reports, who won the last race—I nearly broke my leg on those wires today. You haven't the things hooked up right. I feel as though I were in a trench with barbed wire entanglements on every side. Sit down and eat your dinner!

W. C. Fields, "Ten Thousand People Killed: A Musical Revue and Vaudeville Sketch, Copyrighted 1922," as quoted in Fields, W. C. Fields By Himself: His Intended Autobiography *(1973), pp. 119–121.*

Look at a map of the United States . . . and try to conjure up a picture of what radio broadcasting will eventually mean to the hundreds of little towns that are set down in type so small that it can hardly be read. How unrelated they seem! Then picture the tens of thousands of homes . . . not noted on the map. These little towns, these unmarked homes in vast countries seem disconnected. It is only an idea that holds them together—the idea that they form part of a territory called "our country" . . . if these little towns and villages so remote from one another, so nationally related and yet so physically unrelated, could be made to acquire a sense of intimacy, if they could be brought into direct contact with one another! This is exactly what radio is bringing about. . . . It is achieving the task of making us feel together, think together, live together.

Stanley Frost, "Radio Dreams That Can Come True," in Collier's *magazine, June 10, 1922, quoted in Douglas,* Listening In: Radio and the American Imagination *(1999), p. 76.*

Driblets of advertising, most of it indirect so far, but still unmistakable, are floating through the ether every day. Concerts are seasoned here and there with a dash of advertising paprika. You can't miss it; every little classic number has a slogan all its own, if it's only the mere mention of the name—*and* the address, *and* the phone number—of the music house which arranged the programme. More of this sort of thing may be expected. And once the avalanche gets a good start, nothing short of an Act of Congress or a repetition of Noah's excitement will suffice to stop it.

Joseph H. Jackson, commenting with trepidation on the future of media advertising in "Should Radio Be Used for Advertising?" in Radio Broadcast *magazine, November 1922, p. 76, and quoted in Hilmes,* Radio Voices *(1997), p. 17.*

Radio gadgetry took the front rank in the windows of electronic and hardware stores after RCA introduced the era of broadcasting. *(Bergert Brothers Collection, University of South Florida)*

3:00	Violet Pearch, pianist
3:20	Elsa Rieffin, soprano
3:30	Things to tell the housewife about cooking meat
3:45	Elsa Rieffin, soprano
4:00	Home—Its Equipment by Ada Swan
4:15	Rinaldo Sidoli, violinist
4:30	Ballad of Reading Gaol, part 1, by Mrs. Marion Leland
4:45	Rinaldo Sidoli, violinist
5:00	Ballad of Reading Gaol, part 2, by Mrs. Marion Leland
5:15	Rinaldo Sidoli, violinist
5:30	Rea Stelle, contralto
6:00	Peter's Adventures by Florence Vincent
7:30	Frederick Taggart, baritone
8:15	Lecture by W. F. Hickernell
8:30	Viola K. Miller, soprano

8:45   Salvation Army band concert
9:15   Viola K. Miller, soprano
9:30   Salvation Army Band, Male Chorus
10:00   Concert

Schedule of first day of regular broadcasting, May 16, 1923, radio station WJZ, Newark, from Lewis, Empire of the Air *(1991), pp. 163–164*

Who is to make speeches? Who is to sing songs? Who tells jokes? Who decides on the kind of speech? Shall it be Senator Lodge or Emma Goldman? Shall it be orthodox Republican or reformed socialists? Shall it be stout conservative or unregenerate bolshevism? . . . There is nothing to prevent the most ardent bolshevist from setting up a station and soliciting the multitudes with Utopian invitations.

From a cautionary article on the future of radio by Robert M. Lee, "Who is to Be All Highest of World Radio?" from the Chicago Tribune, *December 19, 1923, p. 6.*

We can choose the broad road of further research and achievement that will carry the art to its highest destiny, or we can take the primrose path of easy accomplishment and rest upon the facilities that already have been created. . . . The day is not far when technical developments in the arts will enable our country, through superpower stations, to reflect its best thought to other nations of the world, and at that time the United States will take the same position of leadership in worldwide broadcasting that it occupies today in worldwide telegraphic communications.

David Sarnoff, expounding on the future of radio communications before a congressional subcommittee on October 9, 1924, quoted in Lyons, David Sarnoff *(1966), p. 120.*

Radiola 30—eight-tube Super-Heterodyne with power speaker: uses no batteries, $575. All the new discoveries have been combined in this beautiful instrument. Its

An early radio studio prepares for broadcast with singers and pianist, while a technician stands at the controls. *(Library of Congress)*

hidden loudspeaker is the new RCA cone type power speaker. And it operates entirely from your lighting socket (A.C.)—with *no batteries.* It is unsurpassed in tone and in performance. The prices includes everything. Just plug in—and tune in—with a single control!

From a full-page advertisement of the Radio Corporation of America, in The Literary Digest, *March 6, 1926, p. 1.*

The "Mike" is found in many pulpits, but Portland, Maine, has founded and is beginning the maintenance of a radio church, whose congregation is limited neither by space nor creed. The Rev. Howard O. Hough had had some successful experience with broadcasting, and was encouraged to resign from the Advent Christian Church, we read, to devote himself to the new possibilities presented by an unseen congregation. The First Radio Parish of Portland resulted, and it was recently established with a dedicatory service, with clergymen and others representing nine denominations present in the broadcasting studio. Financial support of the church is said to have been pledged by business men of the city. A violin, a pianist, and a mixed quartet assist at the services.

"A Radio Church," *description of early religious programming from* The Literary Digest, *May 15, 1926, p. 30.*

Amos: Trusting, simple, unsophisticated. High and hesitating in voice. It's "Ain't dat sumpin?" when he's happy or surprised and "Awa, awa, awa," in the frequent moments when he is frightened or embarassed. . . . Andy gives him credit for no brains but he's a hard earnest worker and has a way of coming across with a real idea when ideas are most needed. He looks up to and depends on—

Andy: Domineering, a bit lazy, inclined to take credit for all of Amos's ideas and efforts. He's always "workin on the books," or "testin his brain," upon which, according to Andy all of the boys' joint enterprises depend. He'll browbeat Amos, pick on him, but let anyone else pick on the little one—then look out.

Description of Amos and Andy, early African-American radio characters, in Correll and Gosden, All About Amos and Andy *(1929), p. 43.*

Though less widely diffused as yet than automobile owning or movie attendance, the radio nevertheless is crowding its way in among the necessities in the family standard of living. Not the least remarkable feature of this new invention is its accessibility. Here skill and ingenuity can in part offset money as an open sesame to swift sharing of the enjoyments of the wealthy. With but little equipment one can call the life of the rest of the world from the air, and this equipment can be purchased piecemeal at the ten-cent store.

As this new tool is rolling back the horizons of Middletown for the bank clerk or the mechanic . . . and as it is wedging its way with the movie, the automobile, and other new tools into the twisted mass of habits that are living for the 38,000 people of Middletown, readjustments necessarily occur. Such comments as the following suggest their nature:

"I don't use my car so much any more. The heavy traffic makes it less fun. But I spend seven nights a week on my radio. We hear fine music from Boston." (From a shabby man of fifty.)

From Robert S. and Helen Merrill Lynd, Middletown: A Study in Modern American Culture *(1929), pp. 269–270.*

Writers and Expatriates

The author has made no attempt to discriminate. He is a realist. Not as Samuel Butler was a realist. Not as Oliver Optic was a realist. Not as Arnold Bennett is a realist. (There are lots of other names that could be used to show that the present reviewer is well read. Maugham would be a good one, too.) Not as Maugham is a realist. . . .

Perhaps we should stand by the character who opens this book and introduces us into the Kingdom of Make-Believe—Mr. V. Aagard, the old "Impt. & Expt." How one seems to see him, impting and expting all the hot summer days through, year in and year out, always heading the list, but always modest and unassuming, always with a kindly word and a smile for passers by on Broadway. . . .

. . . It is the opinion of the reviewer that the weakness of the plot is due to the great number of characters which clutter up the pages. The Russian school is responsible for this. . . .

Humorist Robert Benchley, reviewing the telephone book in "The Most Popular Book of the Month," in Vanity Fair, *February 1920, quoted in Altman,* Laughter's Gentle Soul: The Life of Robert Benchley *(1997), p. 153.*

Why is it, I wonder, that not one other critic has given me credit for a deliberate departure in form in search of a greater flexibility? They have all accused me of bungling through ignorance—whereas, if I had wanted to, I could have laid the whole play in the farm interior, and made it tight as a drum a la Pinero. Then, too, I should imagine the symbolism I intended to convey by the alternating scenes would be apparent even from a glance at the program. It rather irks my professional pride, you see, to be accused of ignorance of conventional, everyday technique. . . . I've been longing to protest about this to someone ever since I read the criticisms by really good critics who blamed my youthful inexperience—even for poor scenery and the interminable waits between the scenes!

Eugene O'Neill, reacting to hesitantly favorable reviews of Beyond the Horizon, *his first Broadway play, by Alexander Woollcott, in letter to Barrett Clark, February 1920, as quoted in Gelb and Gelb,* O'Neill *(1973), p. 411.*

So you guys are critics, are you? Well, let me tell you something. I'm the best writer in this here gottdamn country and if you, Georgie, and you, Hank, don't know it now, you'll know it gottdamn soon. Say, I've just finished a book that'll be published in a week or two and it's the gottdamn best book of its kind that this here gottdamn country has had and don't you guys forget it! I worked a year on the gottdamn thing and it's the goods, I'm a-telling you! Listen, when it comes to writing a novel, I'm so far ahead of most of the men you two think are good that I'll be gottdamned if it doesn't make me sick to think of it! Just wait till you read the gottdamn thing. You've got a treat coming, Georgie and Hank, and don't you boys make no mistake about *that!*

Sinclair Lewis, to H. L. Mencken and George Jean Nathan, vigorously promoting his forthcoming book Main Street *at a gathering in the home of editor T. R. Smith on October 20, 1920, from Churchill,* The Literary Decade *(1971), pp. 30–31.*

In January, Sinclair Lewis will be hailed as
   the greatest living writer
In February, he will be supplanted by Joseph
   Hergesheimer
In March, D. H. Lawrence
In April, F. Scott Fitzgerald
In May, Robert Charles Benchley
In June, George Santayana
In July, James Joyce

In August, Marcel Proust
September 1–15, Sherwood Anderson
September 15–30, James Branch Cabell
October 1–10, Heywood Broun
October 10–31, Thomas Mann
November 1–15, T. S. Eliot
November 15–17, Ben Hecht
November 17–30, Harry Kemp
December 1–4, Ellen Glasgow
December 4–13, Stuart P. Sherman
December 18–23, Willa Cather
December 23–31, Will Rogers

Christopher Morley, providing tongue-in-cheek New Year's predictions on the national literary scene in his column "Bowling Green" in the New York Post, *January 1921, from Churchill,* The Literary Decade, *pp. 47–48.*

The dramatic critic's function is somewhat akin to that of the attendant at some Florentine Court whose uneasy business was to taste each dish before it was fed to any one that mattered. He is an ink-stained wretch invited to each new play and expected, in the little hour that is left him after the fall of the curtain, to transmit something of that play's flavor, to write with whatever of fond tribute, sharp invective or amiable badinage will best express it, a description of the play as performed, in terms of the impression it made upon himself. If he likes it or dislikes it, he may even have time for a brow-furrowing attempt to say why, from which attempts spring all the foolish charges that he brings some silly little foot-rule of his own into the theatre with which to measure severely all the plays exhibited to him.

Alexander Woollcott, explaining his pose and function as a drama critic in his "Second Thoughts" column in the New York Times *of December 11, 1921, quoted in Chatteron,* Alexander Woollcott *(1978), p. 87.*

Mr. Benchley and his companions amount to something like an antidote to the patent medicines administered by the popular magazines. The great function which they perform is making Business look ridiculous. It is not enough that people should laugh at Mr. Addison Sims of Seattle; they must also learn to laugh, as Mr. Benchley teaches them to, at Window Card Psychology, and the Woonsocket Wrought Iron Pipe—nor must they forget Mr. Joseph I. Gonnick and his Cantilever Bridges. . . .

But why does Mr. Benchley stop here? Why isn't he more savage? Why does he cling so long to the pleasant nonsense of the Harvard Lampoon? We know that he can write first-rate satire from his sketch The Making of a Red. . . . Why does he never let his private indignations get into his humorous work?

The truth is, I suppose, that if Mr. Benchley and his friends do not set out to *ecraser l'infame*, it is because they are not sufficiently detached from it. In spite of the fact that they make fun of it, they still identify themselves with it. In order to attack it effectively, they would have to tear themselves up by the roots.

Edmund Wilson, commenting on Robert Benchley and other writers associated with the Algonquin Round Table, in The New Republic *in 1922, quoted in Gaines,* Wit's End: Days and Nights of the Algonquin Round Table *(1977), pp. 117–118.*

The scum of Greenwich Village, New York, has been skimmed off and deposited in large ladleful on that section of Paris adjacent to the Cafe Rotonde. New scum, of course, has risen to take the place of the old, but the oldest scum, the thickest scum and the scummiest scum has come across the ocean, somehow, and with its afternoon and evening levees has made the Rotonde the leading Latin Quarter show place for tourists in search of atmosphere.

Ernest Hemingway, "American Bohemians in Paris," The Toronto Star Weekly, *March 25, 1922, from White (ed.),* By-Line: Ernest Hemingway *(1967), p. 23.*

An American came over to London and was very anxious to be taken for an Englishman. So he ordered a lot of English clothes from a Savile Row tailor, also spats and an eyeglass and stayed in his room at the hotel till they were ready. Then he put them all on, spats and eyeglasses and everything, and got a cane and went out for a stroll. A loafer sort of chap sheltered there, too. "Wet day," said the loafer. The American, not wanting to give himself away by speaking, smiled and nodded. "Nasty weather," said the loafer. The American smiled and nodded again. There was a pause. "*I've* got a cousin in New York," said the loafer. "Wonder if you ever met him?"

Joke told by P. G. Wodehouse to his stepdaughter, Leonora, in letter of December 23, 1923, and quoted in Donaldson (ed.), Yours, Plum *(1990), p. 31.*

Things seem to have been brought to a head by the epidemic of suicides, which have broken out since spring. A well-known New York lawyer, who came over to open up a business here, got into the vortex. After drinking and drugging for weeks, he took an overdose and died. Last week it was a young New Yorker of twenty-three in a Champs Elysees hotel after all his friends had failed to sober him during the course of his existence in the drinking spots around Montparnasse and Raspail.

Despite the apparent Bohemian idleness, which is all an average visitor to the quarter sees, there is plenty of hard work being done around the quieter spots near the two big boulevards.

"Terror Sweeps Latin-Quarter at Reform Bid: Montparnasse Sector Called Big 'Sink of Iniquity.'" Story on troubles among U.S. expatriates in Paris, from The Chicago Tribune, *Paris edition, August 9, 1924, quoted in Reynolds,* Hemingway: The Paris Years *(1989), p. 229.*

Dear Max:

The royalty was better than I expected. This is to tell you about a young man named Ernest Hemmingway, who lives in Paris, (an American), who writes for the transatlantic Review & has a brilliant future. Ezra Pound published a collection of his short pieces in Paris, at some place like the Egotist Press. I havn't it hear now but its remarkable & I'd look him up right away. He's the real thing.

F. Scott Fitzgerald, letter to Maxwell Perkins, October 10, 1924, from Dear Scott/Dear Max *(1971), p. 78.*

Dear Max:

Under separate cover I'm sending you my third novel:

The Great Gatsby

. . . The book is only a little over fifty thousand words long but I believe, as you know, that Whitney Darrow has the wrong psychology about prices (and about what class constitute the bookbuying public now that the lowbrows go to the movies) and I'm anxious to charge two dollars for it and have it a full size book.

Of course I want the binding to be absolutely uniform with my other books—the stamping too— and the jacket we discussed before. This time I don't want any signed blurbs on the jacket—not Mencken's or Lewis' or Howard's anyone's. I'm tired of being the author of *This Side of Paradise* and I want to start over.

F. Scott Fitzgerald, letter to Maxwell Perkins, October 27, 1924, from Dear Scott/Dear Max *(1971), p. 80.*

I think you have every right to be proud of this book. It is an extraordinary book, suggestive of all sorts of thoughts and moods. You adopted exactly the right method of telling it, that of employing a narrator who is more of a spectator than an actor. . . .

. . . You once told me you were not a *natural* writer—my God! You have plainly mastered the craft, of course; but you needed far more than craftsmanship for this.

Maxwell Perkins, letter to F. Scott Fitzgerald on receiving the manuscript of The Great Gatsby *in November 1924, from Meyers,* F. Scott Fitzgerald *(1994), pp. 121–22.*

"Don't confuse reading with culture or art," she said, when her face cleared. There was laughter in her blue eyes. "Not in this country, at any rate. So many books are sold today because of the economic condition of this country, not the cultural. We have a great prosperous middle class, in cities, in suburbs, in small towns, on farms, to whom the expenditure of $2 for a book imposes no suffering. What's more, they have to read it. . . . they want a book to read mornings after breakfast when the maid takes care of the apartment housework; they want a book to keep in the automobile while they're waiting for tardy friends or relatives; they want fillers-in, in a word, something to take off the edge of boredom and empty leisure. Publishers, who are, after all, business men, recognize the demand and pour forth their supply. It's good sense, it's good psychology. It's the same thing that is responsible for the success of the cinema. It is, as a matter of fact, the cinema public for whom this reading material is published. But it has no more to do with culture than with anarchy or philosophy. You might with equal reason ask whether we are becoming a more cultured people because so many more of us are buying chiffoniers and bureaus and mirrors and toilet sets."

Willa Cather to Rose C. Feld, from "Interview," New York Times, *December 21, 1924, p. 11.*

. . . So then we rode around and we saw Paris and we saw how devine it really is. I mean the Eyefull Tower is devine and it is much more educational than the London Tower, because you can not even see the London Tower if you happen to be two blocks away. But when a girl looks at the Eyefull Tower she really knows she is looking at something. So I suppose that is the real historical reason why they call it the Eyefull Tower.

. . . So then we went to dinner and then we went to Momart and it really was devine because we saw them all over again. I mean in Momart they have genuine American jazz bands and quite a lot of New York people

which we knew and you really would think you were in New York and it was devine. So we came back to the Ritz quite late. So Dorothy and I had quite a little quarrel because Dorothy said that when we were looking at Paris I asked the French veecount what was the name of the unknown soldier who is buried under quite a large monument. So I said I really did not mean to ask him, if I did, because what I did mean to ask him was, what was the name of his mother because it is always the mother of a dead soldier that I always seem to think about more than the dead soldier that has died.

Anita Loos, from Gentlemen Prefer Blondes *(1925), p. 98–100.*

I believe that on the first night I went to Gatsby's house I was one of the few guests who had actually been invited. People were not invited—they went there. They got into automobiles which bore them out to Long Island and somehow they ended up at Gatsby's door. Once there they were introduced by somebody who knew Gatsby and after that they conducted themselves according to the rules of behavior associated with amusement parks. Sometimes they came and went without having met Gatsby at all, came for the party with a simplicity of heart that was its own ticket of admission.

F. Scott Fitzgerald, from The Great Gatsby *(1925), p. 44.*

I thought of Gatsby's wonder when he first picked out the green light at the end of Daisy's dock. He had come a long way to this blue lawn and his dream must have seemed so close that he could hardly fail to grasp it. He did not know that it was already behind him, somewhere back in that vast obscurity beyond the city, where the dark fields of the republic rolled on under the night.

F. Scott Fitzgerald, from The Great Gatsby *(1925), p. 189.*

Whatever else this vasty double-header may reveal about its author, it at least shows brilliantly that he is wholly devoid of what may be called literary tact. . . . It was ten years since he had published his last novel, and so all his old customers . . . were hungry for another. . . . The time was thus plainly at hand to make a ten strike. What was needed was a book full of all the sound and solid Dreiser merits, and agreeably free from the familiar Dreiser defects. . . . Well, how did Dreiser meet the challenge? He met it, characteristically, by throwing out the present shapeless and forbidding monster—a heaping cartload of raw materials for a novel, with rubbish of all

sorts intermixed—a vast, sloppy, chaotic thing of 385,000 words—at least 250,000 of them unnecessary!
H. L. Mencken, commenting on Theodore Dreiser's An American Tragedy, *in* The American Mercury, *March 1925, quoted in Swanberg,* Dreiser *(1965), p. 303.*

Of the many new writers that sprang into notice with the advent of the post-war period, Scott Fitzgerald has remained the steadiest performer and the most entertaining. Short stories, novels, and a play have followed with consistent regularity since he became the philosopher of the flapper with *This Side of Paradise.* With shrewd observation and humor he reflected the Jazz Age. Now he has said farewell to his flappers—perhaps because they have grown up—and is writing of the other sisters that have married. But marriage has not changed their world, only the locale of their parties. To use a phrase of Burton Rascoe's—his hurt romantics are still seeking that other side of paradise. And it might almost be said that *The Great Gatsby* is the last stage of illusion in this absurd chase. For middle age is certainly creeping up on Mr. Fitzgerald's flappers.
Edwin Clark, "A Farewell to Flappers," New York Times, *April 19, 1925, p. 9.*

Reading "The Great Gatsby," one has an impression that the author entertained in his urbane and ever more polished imagination ideas for a melodrama, a detective story, and a fantastic satire, with his usual jazz-age extravaganza adding its voice to the mental conversation. And the result is not confusion, but a graceful, finished tale, as if each of the four had contributed a keen, well-timed remark to a good-mannered and highly efficient committee meeting.
Review of The Great Gatsby *in the* International Book Review, *May 1925, p. 426.*

The novel is one that refuses to be ignored. I finished it in an evening, and had to. Its spirited tempo, the motley of its figures, the suppressed, under-surface tension of its dramatic moments, held me to the page. It is not a book which might, under any interpretation, fall into the category of those doomed to investigation by a vice commission, and yet it is a shocking book—one that reveals incredible grossness, thoughtlessness, polite corruption, without leaving the reader with a sense of depression, without being insidiously provocative.
Review of The Great Gatsby, *Walter Yust,* Literary Review, *May 2, 1925, p. 3.*

At this moment . . . the world-slinging classes, radical and fundamentalist, are further from reality than they have ever been. . . . As mechanical power grows in America general ideas tend to restrict themselves more and more to Karl Marx, the first chapter of Genesis and the hazy scientific mysticism of the Sunday supplements. I don't think it's any time for a group of spellbinders to lay down the law on any subject whatsoever. Particularly I don't think there should be any more phrases, badges, opinions, banners, imported from Russia or anywhere else. . . . Why not develop our own brand?
Novelist John Dos Passos, from "The New Masses I'd Like," in the radical journal New Masses, *June 1925, quoted in Wrenn,* John Dos Passos *(1961), p. 52.*

I wonder what your idea of heaven would be—A beautiful vacuum filled with wealthy monogamists all powerful and members of the best families all drinking themselves to death. And hell would probably be an ugly vacuum full of poor polygamists unable to obtain booze or with chronic stomach disorders that they called secret sorrows.

To me heaven would be a big bull ring with me holding two barrera seats and a trout stream outside that no one else was allowed to fish in and two lovely houses in the town; one where I have my wife and children and be monogamous and love them truly and well and the other where I would have my nine beautiful mistresses. . . . I would write out at the Hacienda and send my son in to lock the chastity belts onto my mistresses because someone had just galloped up with the news that a notorious monogamist named Fitzgerald had been seen riding toward the town at the head of a company of strolling drinkers.
Ernest Hemingway, letter to F. Scott Fitzgerald written en route to Pamplona, July 1, 1925, as quoted in Bruccoli, Some Sort of Epic Grandeur *(1981), p. 229.*

The plot works out not like a puzzle with odd bits falling into place, but like a tragedy, with every part functioning in the completed organism. I cannot find in the earlier Fitzgerald the artistic integrity and the passionate feeling which this book possesses.
Gilbert Seldes, review of The Great Gatsby, The Dial, *August 1925, p. 162.*

Ernest Hemingway has a lean, pleasing, tough resilience. His language is fibrous and athletic, colloquial and fresh, hard and clean; his very prose seems to have an organic being of its own. Every syllable counts towards a stimu-

To late-1920s critics, Ernest Hemingway's straightforward novels and stories, stripped of surface emotion as well as adjectives, served as a welcome antidote to the turgid style and European pretensions of turn-of-the-century literature. *(Brown Brothers)*

lating, entrancing experience of magic. He looks out upon the world without prejudice or preconception and records with precision and economy, and an almost terrifying immediacy, exactly what he sees.

From a review of Ernest Hemingway's In Our Time, New York Times, *October 18, 1925, p. 8.*

These plotless sketches and stabbing bits of interwoven prose which achieve in their ensemble a clarified unity are written in what might be called a sort of fundamental language. The sentences drive to the crux of the matter with a merciless bareness and yet at the same time they fairly quiver with a packed quality of meaning.

From a review of Ernest Hemingway's In Our Time, New York World, *October 18, 1925, p. 7.*

Le Grand Gertrude Stein warned me when I presented her with a copy [of *In Our Time*] not to expect a review as she thought it would be wiser to wait for my novel. What a lot of safe playing kikes. Why not write a review of one book at a time? She is afraid that I might fall on my nose in a novel and if so how terrible it would have been to have said anything about this book no matter how good it may be.

. . . You might, if you liked the goddam book, and I think you will because it is pretty good and hard and solid and they are all damning it for being hard-boiled and cold and lacking in verbal beauty and felicity, whatever the hell that is, do something for Eliot's thing. . . . Eliot doesn't know whether I am any good or not. He came over and asked Gertrude if I were serious and worth publishing and Gertrude said it were best to wait and see—that I am just starting and there wasn't any way of knowing yet.

Ernest Hemingway, letter to Ezra Pound, November 8, 1925, quoted in Mellow, Hemingway, A Life Without Consequences *(1992), p. 316.*

Things are queer in Paris, and I have written mama not to come back here on her way home unless I write her that there is no danger of unpleasantness to Americans. The situation is fantastic beyond anything you can imagine. Envy and jealousy and spite against the Americans, because our currency is stable, and because we can't see why we should present France with her war debt, has turned into actual hate against us, so that we are the most unpopular nation on earth today. When I left Baden-Baden there was, in my train compartment at Strasbourg . . . a lovely American woman. . . . She heard me speak German to the porter. We were the only Americans on the long train. It was packed jammed with fat Germans speeding merrily on their way to Paris to spend their marks. The American woman, hearing me, said "Oh, how fortunate you are to speak German. I wish I could."

I said that German wasn't much use in Europe, and that if she could speak enough French to get around, she was much better off. But she said no, that wasn't it. She meant that if she could speak German she would feel so much more comfortable in Paris.

Novelist and playwright Edna Ferber, describing travel conditions in Europe in a letter to her daughter, Julia Ferber, in the summer of 1926, quoted in Goldsmith, Ferber: A Biography *(1978), pp. 383–384.*

Ben was a robustly tall man in his early thirties, with a huge, half-bald head, and dark brown hair inclined to be frizzly. His long, pointed nose, severely arched eyebrows, and widely thin lips gave him the look of a complacent, pettily cruel Devil—a street urchin who had donned the mask of Mephistopheles but could not quite conceal the leer of a boy intent upon practical jokes and small tormentings. He was a master in the arts of dramatic exaggeration and belittling, never quite telling the truth and never quite lying, and his immeasurable vanity made him always determined to dominate any conversation. He had an Oriental volubility and people would often sit beside him for an hour or more and vainly try to insert a beginning remark or express an uninterrupted opinion. . . .

. . . For years he had followed the luring dream of amassing a large fortune through the creation of dexterously dishonest stories, plays, and press-agent campaigns, and while he had accumulated thousands of dollars in these ways, the dream of wealth persistently refused to be captured. He lacked the grimly plodding, blind instinct necessary for such a goal, and his financial harvests were always quickly gathered and dissipated. This babbling immersion in the garnering of money, however, gave him the paradoxical air of an esthetic Babbitt.

Novelist Maxwell Bodenheim, describing Ben Hecht in the person of Ben Helgin in his novel Ninth Avenue, *published in November 1926, and quoted in MacAdams,* Ben Hecht: The Man Behind the Legend *(1990), pp. 97–98.*

[The book] is written abominably by a man who evidently despises style, elegance, clarity, even grammar. Dreiser simply does not know how to write, never did know, never wanted to know. . . .

Indeed, to read Dreiser with profit you must take your coat off to it, you must go down on your knees to it, you must up hands and say, "I surrender." And Dreiser will spit on you for a start.

But once you have fairly yielded to him he will reward you—yes, though his unrelenting grip should squeeze the life out of you. "An American Tragedy" is prodigious.

English reviewer Arnold Bennett, opining on Theodore Dreiser's An American Tragedy, *in the* London Evening Standard, *December 30, 1926, quoted in Swanberg,* Dreiser *(1965), p. 302.*

Ben is in Atlantic City now and I have read every book in the house and am writing this just because there doesn't seem to be anything else to do. And also because we have a friend, Joe Frazier, who is a magazine editor and the other day I told him I would like to try my hand at a short story, but I was terrible at plots, and he said plots weren't essential; look at Ernest Hemingway; most of his stories have hardly any plot; it's his style that counts.

Mrs. Ben Drake, in Ring Lardner, "Liberty Hall," in Round-Up *(1929), p. 55.*

The single apéritif before lunch was very good and we had several more. That night there was a party to welcome us at the Casino, just a small party, the MacLeishes, the Murphys, the Fitzgeralds and we who were living at the villa. No one drank anything stronger than champagne and it was very gay and obviously a splendid place to write. There was going to be everything that a man needed to write except to be alone.

Zelda was very beautiful and was tanned a lovely gold colour and her hair was a beautiful dark gold and she was very friendly. Her hawk's eyes were clear and calm. I knew everything was all right and was going to turn out well in the end when she leaned forward and said to me, telling me her great secret, "Ernest, don't you think Al Jolson is greater than Jesus?"

Nobody thought anything of it at the time. It was only Zelda's secret that she shared with me, as a hawk might share something with a man. But hawks do not share. Scott did not write anything any more that was good until after he knew that she was insane.

Ernest Hemingway, from A Moveable Feast *(1964), pp. 185–186.*

7

A Trial of Science
1925

Important changes had come over the United States since the turn of the 20th century. Assembly lines developed by Henry Ford and others transformed manufacturing from a craft practiced by skilled workers into a science valued for its precision and efficiency. New discoveries and theories—especially the theory of evolution propounded by the British naturalist Charles Darwin—were turning many people skeptical of the eternal truths set out by the Bible and the Christian church. The country was changing from a rural to an urban society, as proven by the census of 1920, which described the United States, for the first time, as a country where a majority of the people lived in cities. By the 1920s, American society had also begun atomizing into distinct social and ethnic groups—immigrant, native, Protestant, non-Protestant, urban, rural, progressive, fundamentalist—each with its own outlook and its own agenda, each rivaling the others in political and economic arenas, and each with its selected representatives in the media, the pulpit, and in the chambers of state and federal legislatures.

The transformations inspired fear. Many people believed that the moral foundations of the country were coming apart under the strains of urbanization, immigration, and the new science. "Patriotic fundamentalism" arose, its believers dead set against anything they perceived as foreign and progressive. The defeat of President Wilson's objectives at the Versailles conference led to further self-doubt and questioning on the part of internationalists and idealists; the noble cause of 1917 had turned into a disillusioned withdrawal from European affairs. A search for remedies took the form of new laws and crusades: Prohibition legislation, the Espionage Act, the Red Scare, and the anti-immigration bills of 1917, 1921, and 1924.

FUNDAMENTALISM VERSUS MODERNISM

Under the pressure of these conflicts and changes, a profound divide opened within the Christian church itself. The modernists of the church allowed science its place, admitted that the Bible was written by humans, and believed that holy Scripture was open to varying interpretations. Modernism swayed the members of many mainline Protestant denominations, who saw the Christian religion declining into ritualistic irrelevancy if it could not accept proven scientific theories and discoveries. On the other side, fundamentalists resisted change of any kind and criticized all aspects of science and religious "modernism." In 1895, at the Niagara Bible Conference, the fundamentalists had summarized their doctrine in five basic points: (1) The infallibility of the Bible; (2) The divinity of Jesus Christ; (3) The virgin birth of Jesus Christ; (4) The atonement of Jesus Christ for the sins of man; and (5) The resurrection of Christ. On these points they would not yield or compromise. Nor would they tolerate Darwinism, evolution, or natural selection: these, they felt, were dark, pitiless, cynical notions that allowed only for the victory of the strong over the weak and provided a convenient tool for tyrants and wealthy capitalists who worshipped only free markets and the dollar. "Social Darwinism," to a fundamentalist, also signified the terrifying possibilities of eugenics, in which scientists would attempt to improve the human species through genetic manipulation. Although eugenics was still a subject for academics and theorizers, its sinister possibilities began filtering down to the general public through the writings and speeches of fundamentalist believers.

In the 1920s, the fundamentalists found their rallying point in a nationwide drive to ban the teaching of Darwinism and evolution, which argued for the development of new species over vast spans of time and thus denied the creation story in the Bible. During this time, William Bell Riley founded the Anti-Evolution League of Minnesota, later the Anti-Evolution League of America. In 1923, a national Baptist convention decreed that its member scientists must concede the fundamental truths taught in the Bible, including the Virgin Birth, the Genesis account of divine creation, and the Second Coming of Christ. This crusade found its most fertile ground in the South, the Baptist home field that combined strong religious sentiment with antimodernist and antinorthern feeling. College professors teaching evolution found themselves out of their jobs at Baylor University and Southern Methodist University, private Texas institutions led by fundamentalist believers.

The modernists, in turn, took comfort in the expanding scope of public education. By 1920, 2 million students were attending high school, a tenfold rise since 1890. New high schools were being built where only primary education had been available, and school attendance laws in many states now required attendance through high school. Since public schools were supported by public tax dollars, however, they were susceptible to the whims of elected legislatures. Anti-evolution lawmakers made the case that the people had the right to determine, through state law, how their education dollars were spent and how they would have teachers instruct their children. Those opposed to such laws saw themselves as fighting for the basic constitutional right of free speech, against the unconstitutional establishment of a state religion, and for the advancement of a practical scientific curriculum in the schools. The times grew ripe for a test case, a showdown in court.

The drive against Darwin in the public schools gathered force in 1921, when a state law banning the teaching of evolution was proposed by the Kentucky Baptist State Board of Missions. In 1922, the Kentucky legislator G. W. Ellis sponsored the bill, which would punish the teaching of evolution by a fine of at least $50 or a jail sentence of up to one year. The Ellis bill was defeated by a single vote. Similar bills lost in Georgia, West Virginia, Alabama, and Texas in 1923, but in that year the Oklahoma legislature passed an anti-evolution restriction on school textbooks. The Florida state house passed a resolution warning teachers not to teach Darwinism "as true." In 1924, the North Carolina state

Church members gather for a group portrait following Sunday services. Despite the controversies surrounding evolution, and a growing skepticism of organized religion expressed in many books and highbrow journals, churches still offered citizens a worthwhile and valued sense of community. *(Bergert Brothers Collection/University of South Florida)*

Board of Education dropped two biology texts that covered the subject of evolution. An anti-evolution bill passed in Florida in 1924 but carried no penalties.

Meanwhile, the evolution debate raged in the press and on the speaking platforms. Celebrities emerged, and there was no fundamentalist celebrity more comfortable before a large audience than William Jennings Bryan. A former Democratic congressman from Nebraska, Bryan had first taken the national spotlight with a rousing speech delivered at the 1896 Democratic national convention in Chicago. Bryan's cause at Chicago had been relief for indebted farmers and "free silver." The Democrats had nominated him three times for president, and three times, as a populist, anti-imperialist, pacifist candidate, he had lost. In 1915, he had resigned the highest post he had ever achieved—secretary of state—over President Woodrow Wilson's drift toward intervention in World War I.

Now Bryan had a new cause: the fight against evolution. To a man who professed to believe in the Bible as literally true, evolution was only an unproved theory, a product of earthly and fallible intellectuals, while religious faith was historic and time tested. Bryan worked hard for the passage of anti-evolution laws by state legislatures, advising lawmakers and sometimes assisting in the writing of the statutes. In early 1925, he turned his attention to the state of Tennessee, where evolution had been a key issue during the 1924 political campaigns and where Bryan and William Bell Riley had already delivered major speeches.

That spring, fundamentalism and modernism were approaching a showdown in the small Tennessee town of Dayton. On March 13, the state legislature of Tennessee passed a statute known formally as the Tennessee Anti-Evolution Act. The statute had been written by representative John Washington Butler of Macon County. Butler had been inspired by an itinerant preacher who told the story of a young schoolteacher who had returned from her university believing in evolution and no longer in God. Butler converted to the cause of the anti-evolutionists and, after his election as a state legislator in 1924, set out to write a law to stop the teaching of evolution. The result was House Bill 185, Public Acts of Tennessee for 1925:

AN ACT prohibiting the teaching of the Evolution Theory in all the Universities, Normals and all other public schools of Tennessee, which are supported in whole or in part by the public school funds of the State, and to provide penalties for the violations thereof.

SECTION 1. BE IT ENACTED BY THE GENERAL ASSEMBLY OF THE STATE OF TENNESSEE, That it shall be unlawful for any teacher in any of the Universities, Normals, and all other public schools of the State which are supported in whole or in part by the public school funds of the State, to teach any theory that denies the story of the Divine Creation of man as taught in the Bible, and to teach instead that man has descended from a lower order of animals.

SECTION 2. BE IT FURTHER ENACTED, That any teacher found guilty of the violation of this Act, shall be guilty of a misdemeanor and upon conviction, shall be fined not less than One Hundred ($100.00) Dollars nor more than Five Hundred ($500.00) Dollars for each offense.

After introducing the bill, Butler saw it gain strong support from fundamentalist preachers in Nashville and, unexpectedly, little opposition from universities, from newspapers, or from the Tennessee Department of Education. Many people who opposed the law saw it as a popular measure, but purely symbolic, and believed that much like Prohibition, it would be honored only in the breach. Many lawmakers agreed. Believing that the senators would vote it down, the members of the Tennessee lower house passed the Butler Act on January 28, 1925, by a 71-5 vote. The senators then favored it 24-6, believing it would be vetoed by the governor. The governor signed it on March 21, certain that it would not be enforced.

TESTING THE CASE

Soon after the passage of the Butler Act, Lucille Milner, secretary of the American Civil Liberties Union (ACLU), clipped a newspaper story reporting the event. She brought the article to the attention of Roger Nash Baldwin, the director of the ACLU's national headquarters in New York. Soon afterward, the board of the ACLU announced it would finance a test case to challenge the law in Tennessee. Founded in New York during the war to protect antiwar demonstrators and pacifist draft evaders, the ACLU had recently been occupied in representing immigrants, suspected communists, and anarchists in trouble with the federal authorities. Still a small and little-known organization, the ACLU saw the Butler Act as fruitful ground for promotion of its most current issues: academic liberty and First Amendment–protected free speech.

In Dayton, Tennessee, mining engineer George Rappelyea read about the ACLU's offer in the May 4 issue of the Chattanooga *Times* and decided to take up the challenge. Rappelyea had come to Tennessee from New York. He belonged to a Methodist church, where he had been convinced by the church's minister—certainly a liberal man by Tennessee standards—that evolution was compatible with the teachings of the Bible. At F. E. Robinson's Drug Store, Rappelyea chanced to meet John T. Scopes, the local high school science teacher and football coach. The two men began a discussion, during which Scopes admitted to Rappelyea that, as a science teacher, he could not avoid informing his students of Darwin's theory of evolution. Indeed, the textbook that he used—*Civic Biology,* written by George Hunter of the DeWitt Clinton High School in New York City—was sold right out of the drugstore where their conversation was taking place. *Civic Biology* not only explained evolution, it also illustrated the theory with a "tree of evolution" on page 194. Evolution and all, *Civic Biology* had been approved for use by the state board of education and by the local school board.

Rappelyea asked Scopes to allow himself to be caught teaching evolution, arrested, and charged. Scopes agreed, believing that a test case was a worthy matter and that the whole matter would be kept quiet. A friendly local attorney, Mr. Sue Hicks, agreed to prosecute. Rappelyea swore out a warrant for Scopes's arrest before the justice of the peace, which was promptly served by a policeman. The Scopes case had begun.

Although he was an admitted evolutionist, Scopes may not have realized that the society he was living in was evolving as well. As the country turned urban, and as communication via newsprint and electronic media improved and accelerated, local events that would once have been little noticed were being turned into national media spectacles. Such had been the case in January 1925 with Floyd Collins, a small-town Kentuckian trapped while wandering in a cave. Collins had been interviewed and written up in newspapers across the country and then was nationally mourned on the occasion of his tragic death. Collins and a series of other short-term celebrities now made national headlines, engaging the nation in stories, sometimes insignificant ones, that carried a bit of "human interest" for the masses.

The first defender hired for John Scopes, John Randolph Neal, had run and lost against Austin Peay for the Democratic primary nomination for Tennessee governor. After being fired during a faculty debate over the teaching of evolution at the University of Tennessee, Neal had founded his own law school in Knoxville. He now came directly to Dayton to offer his services to Scopes and was accepted. Inspired by his own experience of academic intolerance, Neal saw the issue as the sanctity of the classroom: the right to teach as one saw fit without the interference of public sentiment and arbitrary laws.

When the news coverage intensified, anti-evolutionists began to fear that Sue Hicks and other local Dayton attorneys were not up to the task of prosecuting the Butler Act in front of an entire nation. Bigger guns were needed, and on May 13, William Bell Riley's World's Christian Fundamentals Association (WCFA) sent William Jennings Bryan a telegram asking him to appear for the prosecution. Seeing an opportunity to promote the trial even further, Sue Hicks also sent Bryan an invitation, which was soon accepted.

Darrow, Leopold, and Loeb

Word of the upcoming Scopes trial also reached Clarence Seward Darrow, a nationally known defense attorney from Chicago. Darrow was a freethinking, skeptical, agnostic, political liberal—in most ways the opposite of William Jennings Bryan—who saw religion as increasingly irrelevant to the dominant concern of the society he lived in: making money. Darrow had first made his name defending socialist Eugene V. Debs during the Pullman Strike of 1894. Although he had retired from practice, he was persuaded to take the Scopes case by the journalist H. L. Mencken, and by the prospect of battling his fundamentalist nemesis William Jennings Bryan.

Darrow was best known for an impassioned closing argument by which he had saved the "thrill killers" Nathan Leopold and Richard Loeb from execution. The case had begun on May 22, 1924, when the body of 14-year-old Bobby Franks was discovered in a drainage culvert by a railroad worker in Hammond, Indiana. Soon after the discovery, police searching in the nearby trees and vacant lots found a pair of horn-rimmed glasses with peculiar hinges. After checking the sales records of distributor Almer Coe & Co., it was determined that only three individuals in the Chicago area had bought such glasses. One was an elderly lady, another an attorney who had been in Europe for the last six weeks. The third customer had been a young and promising college student by the name of Nathan F. Leopold Jr.

To avoid the distraction of journalists and publicity, Leopold was brought to a hotel suite for questioning. He readily admitted that the glasses resembled a pair that he had left at home. When the glasses were not found in a search of the home, his brother provided a plausible explanation: Nathan, a teacher of ornithology at Chicago's University High School, often went bird-watching in the area, and probably had absent-mindedly dropped his glasses in the high weeds.

The police accepted the explanation and continued the questioning. When asked for his whereabouts on the day of the murder, Leopold provided his alibi. He and a friend, Richard Loeb, had driven a couple of girls, by the names of Mae and Edna, out to Lincoln Park that night. Loeb was promptly brought in and interrogated on the subject of his whereabouts, but failed to mention the double date. Instead, he claimed, he had left Leopold after having dinner at Leopold's house.

Although Leopold and Loeb had carefully arranged their mutual alibi, their coordination had broken down. Both agreed that the Mae-and-Edna story would be offered to the police if either of them were arrested less than a week after the murder. But Leopold had calculated his week from the last efforts made to destroy evidence after the crime had taken place. When he was picked up, Loeb had figured more than seven days since the murder and claimed not to remember his whereabouts. When the police pointed out the discrepancy in the two stories, Loeb confessed to the killing of Bobby Franks.

Murders were nothing new in Chicago, but these murderers were unique. If the public envisioned murder as an act committed by the degenerate, the criminal, or the desperate, the public now would have to make a revision. Nathan Leopold was a prodigy who had entered the University of Chicago at 14 and graduated four years later as a member of Phi Beta Kappa, the national honor society. At 18, Loeb, the son of a well-known attorney for Sears, Roebuck, had graduated from the University of Michigan. Both grew up in wealthy households, both were cared for by nurses and governesses, both were apparently of sound mind and body.

But after their first meeting at the University of Chicago, Leopold and Loeb discovered they had something else in common: a chronic superiority complex that they believed placed them above the laws and morals governing the ordinary. Leopold was a follower of Friedrich Nietzsche and had adopted Nietzsche's concept of the superman—an individual that rises above the masses by virtue of superior intellectual gifts. Loeb simply liked to get away with things, including vandalism, theft, and arson. By the spring of 1924, the two were prepared to carry out a project of long planning, a perfect crime: kidnapping a random victim, collecting a ransom, and murdering the victim to eliminate the witness.

On May 21, 1924, Nathan Leopold rented a Willys-Knight touring car, then drove it to his home. The pair left Leopold's own car with a chauffeur, instructed the chauffeur to inspect the squeaking brakes, and left in the rented car. Late that afternoon, they encountered Bobby Franks, who knew them, and invited Franks into the front seat of the car for a ride home. After climbing into the car, Franks was clubbed to death with a chisel by Loeb, who was sitting in the back seat. The body was wrapped in a robe, driven to the Pennsylvania Railroad's lonely right-of-way in Hammond, stripped, disfigured with acid, and jammed into a culvert.

Leopold then contacted Jacob Franks, the victim's father, and demanded $10,000 in small bills, to be delivered in a cigar box at a prearranged spot. But when the body was discovered the day after the crime and was identified despite the acid poured on it to deter identification, the ransom went unpaid and the police were soon collecting evidence that would bring about the arrests.

The trial of Leopold and Loeb began on July 23, 1924. Loeb's family had engaged the services of Clarence Darrow, knowing of Darrow's successful opposition to the death penalty in the 102 capital murder charges he had defended during his career. Darrow assented to courtroom help from Benjamin and Walter Bachrach, brothers related to the Loeb family. The prosecution attorneys included Illinois state attorney Robert E. Crowe, Joseph Savage, Joseph Sbarbaro, Thomas Marshall, and Milton Smith.

Darrow's first line of defense was modern psychology. A team of leading psychologists was hired to examine the accused and to write up a comprehensive psychological profile to explain the murder. Under Crowe's direction, the prosecution had the straightforward tasks of introducing the confessions of Leopold and Loeb into evidence and explaining in detail the thorough planning of the murder, thus proving the premeditation that under Illinois law would merit the death penalty.

On the eve of the trial, Darrow unexpectedly switched the plea from not guilty to guilty. Knowing that the two crimes for which Leopold and Loeb were indicted—murder and kidnapping for ransom—were both punishable by death, Darrow wanted to lessen the state's chances of winning an execution on one of the charges if the other failed. Nevertheless, Crowe and his team called a total of 102 witnesses to the stand to lay out all the grisly details and facts, confessions, and evidence, to which Darrow readily agreed.

Darrow then led the parade of his defense witnesses, doctors and psychologists who would support the idea that Leopold and Loeb were sane but unable to determine right and wrong, suffering from a condition of the mind that would mitigate the plea of guilty and legally excuse them from death in the electric chair. Presiding Judge John Caverly allowed the evidence, and the packed courtroom was offered X rays, medical tests, blood pressure charts, and the summations of doctors who found that overactive pituitary glands and other premature developments led to an abnormal state of mind. The prosecution pointed out that the evidence had been given entirely by the accused, that the accused were known liars, and that medical experts for the state had derided premature development as a mitigating factor in premeditated murder.

Beginning on August 22, 1924, Darrow began a three-day summation that would go down in history as one of the most eloquent criminal defenses ever delivered in a courtroom. He pointed out that the wealth and background of the accused had drawn media attention, packed the courtroom, and resulted in insistence on the death penalty rather than the usual life sentence. He announced that nobody under the age of 23 had ever been put to death in Illinois and claimed that Leopold and Loeb needed the $10,000 ransom money to meet gambling debts. He also showed that Leopold and Loeb were mentally unbalanced, their powerful intelligences unhinged by Nietzschean philosophy and overactive adolescent imaginations. Darrow concluded with an attack on capital punishment, insisting that legally sanctioned murder begets only more crime and violence.

After a two-day riposte by Robert Crowe, the final decision was placed in the hands of Judge Caverly, who spent more than a week deliberating before delivering his decision on September 10. Caverly explained that neither the guilty plea nor an abnormal psychological profile mitigated the circumstances calling for a death sentence. But he added that in the interest of "enlightened humanity," he would not condemn the accused to death but rather sentence them to life in prison for the murder and 99 years for the kidnapping, recommending against parole. Leopold and Loeb were sent to the state penitentiary at Joliet, and then to Stateville, where Loeb was murdered by a fellow inmate in 1936. On March 13, 1958, Leopold was paroled from Stateville. He left the following day for Puerto Rico, where he worked as an X-ray technician, earned a master's degree in social service, and became a researcher for the Puerto Rico Department of Health. He remained a model citizen until his death in 1971.

Nothing in the Leopold-Loeb case or in his career as a criminal defense attorney had quite prepared Clarence Darrow for an argument over Darwinism and high school science. His private interests ran to scientific discovery and clear-thinking and modern rationalism, however, and so he enthusiastically took up the cause of evolution and John T. Scopes.

In the meantime, on May 25, 1925, Judge John T. Raulston, whose circuit included Rhea County and Dayton, Tennessee, summoned a special session of the Rhea County grand jury. Attorney General A. Thomas Stewart of Winchester introduced *Civic Biology* into evidence and then called three of Scopes's students to testify. The 13-member Dayton grand jury returned an indictment in one hour. Judge Raulston then announced a special trial term commencing July 10.

Dayton had six weeks to prepare. Civic boosters formed a Scopes Trial Entertainment Committee to arrange for visitor accommodations. The downtown Aqua Hotel was repainted; shops were tidied up; telephone booths were installed for the use of visitors and for the press, who would set up headquarters in a makeshift pressroom above a Main Street hardware store. Loudspeakers, a bandstand, and a barbecue pit appeared on the courthouse lawn. A small airstrip was constructed outside of town. A central card file of rooms to let in private homes was made available to the visitors. George Rappelyea prepared an abandoned, 18-room house for the use of defense lawyers and scientific experts who, according to the strategy prepared by Clarence Darrow, would defeat the Butler Act and the case against John Scopes by testifying for the theory of evolution.

In the meantime, Arthur Garfield Hays, representing the ACLU, joined Clarence Darrow and New York divorce lawyer John Randolph Neal for the defense.

Antievolution books, many of them authored by the creationist celebrity William Jennings Bryan, are sold in Dayton, Tennessee, during the trial of John T. Scopes for teaching evolution. *(Brown Brothers)*

The Scopes team planned to show that the law was too vague to be enforced. They would show that the Bible was open to various interpretations. Using the testimony of 11 scientists who had volunteered to appear, they would also suggest that the Bible and evolutionary theory were not irreconcilable and maintain that many honest and sincere scientists believed in both.

Darrow also intended to get the trial of John Scopes played on a bigger stage. On July 3, the defense asked for removal of the case to the federal district court in Nashville. By this motion, Darrow sought a ruling from the district court on the constitutionality of the law, rather than a decision on the minor matter of Scopes's guilt or innocence. Much to the relief of the people of Dayton, however, Judge John Gore denied the motion, and the case remained in Judge Raulston's court.

On July 7, William Jennings Bryan arrived in Dayton. For the largely fundamentalist people of Dayton, Bryan arrived as a hero; he spent much of his first day greeting crowds of supportive locals in the streets and shops. Although he was aging and his thundering voice had weakened, Bryan could still speak with great conviction of the duty of public schools to follow the beliefs of those who paid for them: the people. Governments that funded the schools had the right to direct their curricula, and if elected representatives sought to bar evolution—a theory, after all, and not a proven fact—they had the right to do so. Bryan had prepared a lengthy, rousing speech to be delivered as the closing argument for the prosecution. The victory he expected at Dayton would be the springboard for a fervent nationwide campaign against subversive modernism. It would turn the tide against the immorality of the Jazz Age and return the United States to the pious traditions of the common, God-fearing people.

More than 100 reporters arrived to cover what became known as the Monkey Trial. Camera crews sent daily newsreel footage to movie theaters around the country. Telegraph operators set up around the courthouse to transmit the trial word for word via Western Union. Radio engineers from WGN in Chicago broadcast the trial live, for the first time in history. H. L. Mencken wrote scathing columns for the Baltimore *Sun*. John Washington Butler himself, author of the statute Scopes had violated, would contribute his observations and opinions as a wire service reporter.

A platform was set up on the courthouse lawn. Fundamentalists and modernists immediately began using the platform to fight a battle of speeches, in support of or against evolution. Preachers delivered their sermons, while six extra policemen, hired for the event from Chattanooga, patrolled the streets. A showman named Harry Backenstahl brought a circus ape, named Joe Mendl, to appear in suit, tie, and hat. The fundamentalists had the better of it as police banned all speakers taking Scopes's side from the stand. Evolutionists protested; by the opening of the trial both sides were gagged. Only the local high school band would be permitted use of the platform during the trial.

THE MONKEY TRIAL

The Scopes trial began on Friday, July 10, 1925. The day was hot; the spectators sweltered in the standing-room-only courtroom. Outside, vendors offered soft drinks, hot dogs, sandwiches. Banners favoring Bryan and the Bible against evolution and Charles Darwin hung from windowsills in plain view of the crowds milling on the courthouse lawn.

Inside, warm applause greeted William Jennings Bryan as he entered the court. After Judge Raulston brought the proceedings to order, Reverend L. M. Cartwright delivered a prayer. To ensure that the indictment of John Scopes was legal, Raulston read it out to an entirely new grand jury, which returned a second indictment by the end of the morning. A trial jury was impaneled consisting of 12 men, most of whom had never heard of the theory of evolution. This encouraged Darrow, who prided himself on his ability to select juries and sway them to his cause.

The trial resumed on Monday, July 13. After a prayer was offered by Reverend M. H. Moffitt, Darrow raised an objection to the opening prayers, and was overruled. After Attorney General A. T. Stewart read out the indictment, the defense offered a motion to quash it. On 13 separate grounds, counsel Arthur Hays reasoned, the Butler Act violated the Tennessee constitution as well as the Fourteenth Amendment of the U.S. Constitution, which, in theory, protected citizens from unreasonable laws and the unchecked power of the police and the courts:

> No state shall make or enforce any law which shall abridge the privileges or immunities of citizens of the United States; nor shall any state deprive any person of life, liberty, or property, without due process of law; nor deny to any person within its jurisdiction the equal protection of the laws.

The defense also argued that the Butler Act established a certain religious doctrine in the public schools, thus violating the doctrine of the separation of church and state. To further make the point that the Butler Act violated constitutional principles, Hays read out a fundamentalist statute of his own, which punished the teaching of the heliocentric orientation of the solar system with death.

Prosecution attorney Sue Hicks replied with the case of *Leeper v. State of Tennessee,* which allowed the state to require uniform textbooks and uniform administration of the schools. The employer of a schoolteacher, Hicks pointed out, had the right to instruct that teacher in the obligations of his job, including the methods and content of classroom teaching. Hicks's colleague A. T. Stewart added that the doctrine of "freedom of religion" applied only to church worship, not to state-sponsored education.

After hearing the arguments, Raulston announced that he would need time to consider the motion to quash. His decision came on Wednesday in the form of a 6,000-word opinion denying the motion. The Butler Act did not establish a religion in violation of the constitutions of either Tennessee or the United States, and the indictment of John Scopes had properly followed the law. The trial would go forward.

The defense then entered John Scopes's plea: not guilty. Darrow's purpose was to try the Butler Act, not to acquit his client. He did not seek a verdict of innocent but rather a public debate, which he was sure he would win, on the merits of evolution and the proper place of religion: in the church. In case of a guilty verdict, the debate could be brought to a higher court on appeal, providing an even larger forum for Darwin's contested theory.

Both sides gave their opening arguments. The jury was sworn, and the prosecution called Walter White as its first witness. White revealed that, on May 4, Scopes had admitted teaching from *Civic Biology.* On further testimony, it was revealed that the book had been adopted by the Tennessee Textbook Commission in 1919 for a period of five years. After the contract to use the book had expired, the commission had selected no other book to replace it.

The prosecution then called Howard Morgan as a witness. He was a boy of 14 and a student of John Scopes. Morgan testified that on or about April 2, 1925, Scopes had taught him that humans had descended from a one-cell organism. Darrow questioned Morgan and read out passages from the textbook. Had the lessons harmed him? Morgan answered no and was soon excused. His classmate Harry Shelton took the stand, testifying that he had not left the church after being exposed to the theory of evolution.

A. E. Robinson was then questioned. Robinson admitted that he had been selling *Civic Biology* for six or seven years out of his drugstore and that he was a member of the local school board. Darrow read out the book's passages on evolution; after Robinson was excused, Stewart then had the first two chapters of Genesis read into the record. The prosecution called two more students, whose testimonies were taken down without cross-examination. The prosecution rested its case.

The defense now called its expert witnesses. First to take the stand was Maynard M. Metcalf, a distinguished zoologist, a professor at Johns Hopkins, and a member of the Congregationalist church. When Darrow asked Metcalf if he was an evolutionist, Metcalf replied, "Under certain circumstances, that question would be an insult. Under these circumstances, I do not regard it as such." When Darrow asked if there were any scientists who were *not* evolutionists, another legal wrangle began. When the prosecution moved to prohibit the testimony of any outsiders as hearsay, a last, crucial decision was imminent: whether Judge Raulston would permit scientific testimony of any kind. On Thursday, July 16, the two sides made their arguments. The defense would bring witnesses who would demonstrate that science and religion did not necessarily conflict. The prosecution wanted to exclude the testimony as irrelevant. If Raulston chose for the defense, the trial would continue. If he did not, it would quickly end.

William Jennings Bryan stood to speak. He insisted that the state of Tennessee was within its rights and that no self-styled experts had the right to tell the state what to do. He attacked the theory of evolution itself, arguing that, according to simple logic, humans could not descend from monkeys if both species still existed. There was no proof for such a theory, thus it had no place in a science class. Bryan also protested that evolutionists were making man insignificant: a single species, a mere animal among a million others. Bringing evolution to its logical conclusion created beings without a conscience, such as Leopold and Loeb, whom Darrow himself had so well defended the previous year.

Bryan rested to friendly but not enthusiastic applause from the spectators. Dudley Field Malone replied. In a 25-minute exhortation, he reminded the court of the trial of Galileo and the burning of the library of Alexandria. He asked the spectators to "keep your Bible. Keep it as your consolation, keep it as your guide. But keep it where it belongs, in the world of your own conscience, in the world of your individual judgment. . . . Keep your Bible in the world of theology, where it belongs. . . ." He asked the people to preserve their classrooms for the pursuit of truth, wherever it might lead. The speech was so well-reasoned and beautifully delivered that the courtroom spectators, as well as attorneys for the prosecution, gave it an enthusiastic ovation. Fearing that Malone's ringing words might somehow get his client acquitted of the charge—the last result he wanted—Darrow warned his colleague to cease and desist.

After further argument, Raulston adjourned the court. Malone's speech had left the prosecution reeling. But Darrow realized that Raulston, after thinking the issue over, would probably rule against the defense and bar scientific experts from testifying. That night, Darrow instructed the expert witnesses to prepare their statements for the press instead of for the courtroom. He then asked Charles Potter to begin a thorough study of his Bible, and to draw up a list of Biblical contradictions and impossibilities. Nobody knew it yet, and nobody must know it, but Darrow was preparing to call his last, best witness: William Jennings Bryan.

DARROW V. BRYAN

On Friday the 17th, the scientific witnesses dictated their testimony to stenographers in the courthouse. Darrow watched over the group like a professor monitoring final exams, intending to see that the testimony was released, if not through the trial itself, then directly to the press and thus to the spectators in Dayton and beyond.

After the trial resumed, Raulston delivered his opinion: the Butler Act was clear enough, and the opinions of experts would shed no further light on it. Their testimony would be excluded. After the trial was adjourned, both sides issued statements to the press. Bryan felt confident of final victory. Not only would Scopes be convicted, but the theory of evolution would be disgraced and the Bible would triumph. Darrow accused Bryan of hiding behind legal technicalities and not even permitting the defense to present its own case. After writing his last scathing account of the people of Dayton, H. L. Mencken left town, and the radio crews took down their equipment. The people of Dayton felt somewhat disappointed at the imminent end of the Scopes trial, which had seemed to hold such promise.

On Sunday, Darrow gave a lecture on Tolstoy at the Tivoli Theater in Chattanooga, while Bryan addressed a gathering of 500 at the town of Pikeville. When Darrow returned to Dayton, he and the defense team adjourned a strategy meeting. They sat down Dr. Kirtley Mather, a Harvard geology professor, and instructed him to assume the role of William Jennings Bryan. For two hours, the attorneys directed pointed questions about the Bible and the Christian religion, the book of Genesis, and the story of Creation. Darrow was warming up for the coming confrontation.

The Scopes trial resumed on Monday, July 20. Arthur Hays read out the words of Governor Peay on his signing the Butler Act into law. The quotation ended with the words "Probably the law will never be applied." The prosecution objected; Hays replied that he sought to demonstrate the intention behind the bill—it was a symbolic measure, never to be enforced. Judge Raulston ordered the governor's words excluded from the record, then allowed the defense to spend one hour reading the statements of five scientists into the record.

That afternoon, the judge ordered everyone out of the courtroom. The floor was supporting a heavy load; the ceiling plaster downstairs was cracking and there was danger of a collapse. Outside, on the courthouse lawn, the judge and attorneys took their places on the platform that had been constructed for the use of music bands and speakers before the trial. As the spectators found their places on benches and boxes, Arthur Hays called William Jennings Bryan to the witness stand. The prosecution immediately objected on the ground that calling an attorney involved in the case to the stand threatened to make a spectacle and a farce out of the proceedings. The startled Bryan replied by asking to call Darrow, Malone, and Hays to the stand. Darrow readily agreed.

Refusing to testify, Bryan realized, would cause him a serious loss of face just as the prosecution was about to win its expected victory. He was confident he could handle the situation and eager to finally match wits with Darrow. When Judge Raulston asked Bryan for his consent, it was willingly given. As it had during much of the trial, the jury sat far enough away so that it could not hear the questioning, as the judge assumed it would not become part of the trial record.

Darrow began. "You have given considerable study to the Bible, haven't you, Mr. Bryan?" Bryan replied, "Yes, sir, I have tried to." Darrow asked if everything in the Bible should be held to be literally true. Bryan replied that everything in the Bible should be accepted as it is given. Darrow asked: Did a whale literally swallow Jonah? Did miracles happen? Did Joshua make the sun stand still? The earth? What would happen if the earth were to suddenly stand still? What was the date of the Flood? What was the date of Creation? As Bishop Usher of Ireland and many Bibles stated, was it 4004 B.C.? Did not civilizations exist that were much older than that?

Growing uncomfortable, Bryan parried the questions. The Bible said "big fish," not "whale," and God could make big fish, whales, and man do whatever He pleased. Miracles were simply things beyond the power of man to perform. The man who wrote the book of Joshua was divinely inspired to tell his tale, and did not necessarily understand what he was writing. God used language that was understood by the people of that time. On many subjects and questions Darrow raised, Bryan confessed ignorance. Some people may claim that civilizations existed before 4004 B.C.—he had no evidence and did not claim to know himself. The defense sought to try the Christian religion, and he was defending it.

Darrow continued his questioning.

> "Would you say the earth was only four thousand years old?"
> "Oh, no, I think it is much older than that."
> "How much?"
> "I couldn't say."
> "Do you say whether the Bible itself says it is older than that."
> "I don't think the Bible says itself whether it is older or not."
> "Do you think the earth was made in six days?"
> "Not six days of twenty-four hours."
> "Doesn't it say so?"
> "No."

CLOSING ARGUMENTS

With that reply, the trial seemed to come to a sudden stop. The creation story was a parable, a metaphorical tale, not literal truth: on the witness stand, William Jennings Bryan himself had said so. Shocked Bryan partisans stared in amazement and confusion, while an angry Bryan stood up to proclaim that Darrow was attempting to cast ridicule on those who believed in the Bible. "I am simply trying to protect the word of God against the greatest atheist or agnostic in the United States" he said, shaking his fist at Darrow.

Eager for the counterattack, Bryan hoped to have Darrow on the stand the next day; but lead prosecutor Stewart would not allow it. Bryan had been shown up, Stewart realized, and the literal interpretation of the Bible shown to be so absurd that even the national champion of the fundamentalist cause could not

manage to defend it. Darrow's relentless questioning had revealed that his opponent knew little or nothing about geology, biology, linguistics, ancient civilizations, Buddhism, Zoroastrianism, or any other subject that might shed light on
the question of evolution versus creation.

On Tuesday, Raulston opened the session by officially expunging Bryan's
testimony. Darrow asked to continue his questioning, as Bryan had never been
dismissed from the stand. Raulston denied the request. Darrow then announced
that the defense would rest its case and asked that the jury be brought in and
instructed to deliver a guilty verdict. This would save the trial for an appeal.

Stewart accepted the suggestion for the prosecution. Raulston ordered in the
jury, which had been allowed to hear only three hours of argument and testimony
during the entire trial; the rest of the time; jury members had been sequestered
out of earshot. The judge gave them instructions to find Scopes guilty if they
found, as was testified to, that he had taught that man descended from a lower
order of animals. They must also decide what fine should be levied. If more than
$100, they must decide on the amount. If $100 would be sufficient, they had only
to pronounce the verdict and leave punishment to the judge's discretion.

To this instruction, Stewart raised an objection. According to Tennessee law,
juries had to impose any fine exceeding $50. Raulston believed that judges
could always fix minimum fines—in this case, $100; however, the judge erred.

The jury left the courtroom at 11:15 A.M. and returned nine minutes later
with its verdict: guilty. The fine was left up to the court. Scopes was allowed to
say a few words in his own defense, and Raulston proceeded to impose the fine
of $100. Bail was set at $500, which was provided to Scopes by the Baltimore
Sun, H. L. Mencken's paper. Raulston granted the defense permission to appeal
the verdict and then invited final words from everyone involved. The Scopes
trial was over.

The next few days were filled with contentious statements from Bryan and
Darrow. Bryan defiantly promised to carry on the fight against evolution.
Darrow gave his philosophy of agnosticism, explained his trial practice, and
defended his interrogation of Bryan. Meanwhile, John Scopes considered his
future. He decided not to return to Dayton to teach that fall, although the
school board had invited him back.

Scopes had something else on his mind and during an aimless drive in the
nearby countryside, he made a confession to a reporter, William Hutchinson. He
had skipped the lesson dealing with evolution; he had been occupied with
something else. His students, thankfully, did not remember and had been carefully coached by the lawyers on what to say in a mutual effort to get the verdict
that everyone sought. John Scopes was not guilty; in fact, he had an alibi, but
had revealed it to nobody until this moment. Scopes asked Hutchinson to tell
nobody, and write nothing, until the Supreme Court had returned its verdict in
the expected future appeal.

Bryan had copies printed of the concluding speech he had prepared for the
close of the trial—which, through Raulston's haste and Darrow's maneuvering,
was never actually delivered. He laid plans for a tour of Palestine and the founding
of a fundamentalist school in Dayton, to be named the William Jennings Bryan
University. On Friday, July 24, he had lunch with Judge Raulston in Raulston's
home town of Winchester. He returned to Dayton on Sunday, July 26. He went
to church, ate lunch with his wife, and then died quietly in his sleep.

The scientists on the defense team asked John Scopes what he would do.
Scopes answered that he would like to study geology at the University of

Chicago. The scientists agreed to form a committee, and the tuition for Scopes's study was raised. Meanwhile, George Rappelyea left Dayton for employment with the Gulf Coast Investment Company in Mobile, Alabama. A new, expurgated version of Hunter's science textbook, entitled *New Civic Biology*, was ordered by the Tennessee Textbook Commission. The book made no mention of evolution. Other states ordered and stocked evolution-free textbooks. In the next year, the Mississippi state legislature passed an anti-evolution law similar to the Butler Act. In the Mississippi town of Meridian, ripped-out textbook pages mentioning evolution were burned in public.

In January 1926, the Scopes defense team filed its appeal, signed by Darrow, Neal, Malone, and several other attorneys, in the Tennessee Supreme Court. The prosecution fought the appeal by placing the Butler Act in a category of laws that should not be vulnerable to review by the courts. The case was argued in late May and June of that year; the decision was handed down on January 15, 1927. The court upheld the law as constitutional, but also held that Judge Raulston had committed judicial error by setting the fine instead of allowing the jury to do so, per Tennessee law. The judgment was reversed, and the case was sent back to the circuit court with a recommendation of *nolle prosequi,* or "Proceed no further." Attorney General Stewart accordingly dropped the matter, and the case of *Tennessee v. Scopes* came to a quiet end. Much to the frustration of the ACLU, there would be no appeal of the matter in the United States Supreme Court.

The Tennessee Anti-Evolution Act was repealed in 1967.

A Trial of Anarchy

Both Darrow and Bryan may have considered the Scopes trial a success; Judge Raulston might opine that he had carried himself well, and John T. Scopes himself could look forward to a lifetime of notoriety for his few days in the national media spotlight. But one other national trial did not turn out so well; in fact, it would go down as a defeat and a disgrace for nearly all concerned after August 23, 1927, when Nicola Sacco and Bartolomeo Vanzetti were led to the electric chair in the Massachusetts State Prison in Charleston and put to death.

The two men were electrocuted for the murders of Frederick Parmenter and Alessandro Berardelli, employees of the Slater and Morrill Shoe Company of South Braintree, Massachusetts. The victims had been shot to death on April 15, 1920, during an armed robbery in the company's yard that also resulted in the theft of $16,000 in payroll money. Three weeks after the robbery, on May 5, Sacco and Vanzetti were arrested while traveling together on a streetcar. The arresting officers relieved the two men of concealed revolvers—Sacco's .32-caliber Colt and Vanzetti's .38-caliber Harrington and Richardson—and took them to the station house for questioning. In the next few days, Sacco and Vanzetti were paraded before several eyewitnesses to the South Braintree robbery. On September 14, they were indicted for murder.

The trial, appeal, and review in the case of Sacco and Vanzetti began on May 31, 1921, in Dedham, Massachusetts, and was presided over by Judge Webster Thayer, a man strongly inclined to condemn and convict defendants found guilty of having left-leaning political opinions. George Vahey served as the first defense counsel, but Sacco and Vanzetti were suspicious of Vahey's motives and sympathies, a suspicion that grew more intense soon after the trial began, when Vahey formed a law partnership with District Attorney Frederick Katzmann,

Nicola Sacco (right) and Bartolomeo Vanzetti (center) are led in handcuffs from the courtroom. Charged with armed robbery and murder, Sacco and Vanzetti were also found guilty of anarchist sympathies and sent to the electric chair. *(Brown Brothers)*

the prosecutor in the case. Vahey was fired by his clients, and Fred Moore, a well-known defender of radicals and no friend of the judge or of the courts of Massachusetts—where he did not even belong to the state bar—was hired.

During a trial lasting 35 days, the prosecution brought forward several dozen eyewitnesses to place Sacco and Vanzetti at the scene of the crime. Sacco was accused of the shooting; Vanzetti was said to have taken part as a lookout and driver and to have stolen the gun later found in his possession from Berardelli. Several defense eyewitnesses, however, provided strong alibis. Some of these witnesses placed Sacco in Boston at the Italian consulate on the day of the robbery; others testified that Vanzetti was following one of his normal occupations as a fish peddler in the city of Plymouth. Counsel for the defense also pointed out that neither Sacco nor Vanzetti could be tied to any of the robbery money and that before their arrest they had made no effort whatsoever to conceal their movements, change their names, or to elude the police. They had no prior association with criminals, no criminal records, and no history of violent acts in any form.

Ballistics evidence was introduced to prove that a bullet from Sacco's gun had killed Berardelli, but the fatal bullet also turned out to be a very weak link in the prosecution's case. Two expert witnesses could not identify the bullet as having been fired from Sacco's particular gun—one of more than 300,000 Colt .32s in existence. In addition, according to eyewitnesses, Berardelli was shot four times by the same man with the same gun. As the prosecution freely admitted, three of the bullets in Berardelli's body came from a .32-caliber Savage automatic. A bullet claimed by the prosecution to have been the fourth was fired from a .32-caliber Colt and was assumed to have been fired from Sacco's gun. It was strongly insinuated by the defense, however, that it had actually been fired by a police officer in an unknown location shortly after Sacco's arrest on May 5.

Despite the defendants' strong alibis and a serious lack of evidence, Sacco and Vanzetti were finally convicted of the crime on the theory of "consciousness of guilt." Their conduct during and immediately after their arrest was said to be that of guilty men attempting to escape arrest, therefore they were guilty. The fact that the men possessed concealed weapons and that they lied about their movements on the day of their arrest, and about the source of their weapons, also persuaded the judge and jury against them. The verdict came in on July 14, 1921.

Sacco and Vanzetti suffered serious disadvantages in this contest: they were foreign radicals, Italian immigrants, and closely associated with a circle of anarchists headed by another immigrant, Luigi Galleani. During World War I, the *Cronaca Suvversiva* (the Subversive Chronicle), Galleani's publication, had come out strongly against the war and had encouraged resistance, violent resistance if necessary, to the war effort and to all forms of authority. While Galleani and his subscribers were being targeted by the Justice Department as a dangerous anarchist group, Sacco and Vanzetti had followed Galleani's advice and dodged the draft by not registering for it, as required by law, and, in 1917, by fleeing to Mexico. Since that time, the great fear of leftists, immigrants, and other troublemakers had taken hold in the United States. Several years of peace and prosperity had not lessened these sentiments, which were made even stronger in

Massachusetts by a long history of industrial labor trouble, the dominant Anglo-Saxon, Puritan culture of New England, and the presence of a large, foreign-born population that was not welcomed by the native-born.

By the time of the South Braintree robbery, Sacco and Vanzetti were well known to the federal Department of Justice, yet they had never committed any acts the federal authorities could use as an excuse to deport them from the country. After the arrests, agents of the Justice Department in Boston cooperated with prosecutors by placing spies in contact with Sacco and Vanzetti in prison, infiltrating Sacco and Vanzetti defense committees, and supplying information about the pair's radical activities to the district attorney. For the Justice Department, the murder of Parmenter and Berardelli turned out to be a convenient justification for ridding the nation of two undesirables in the most permanent manner possible.

APPEALS

By late 1925, William G. Thompson, a well-regarded Boston lawyer, had taken over the defense of Sacco and Vanzetti from their previous attorney, Fred Moore. Thompson led the defense case through a series of eight appeals, claiming that eyewitnesses and evidence had been tampered with, that Judge Thayer had been guilty of misconduct during the trial, and that a witness named Roy Gould could have provided testimony tending to exculpate the accused. Thompson also claimed that Proctor, one of the state's expert witnesses, was prepared to impeach his own testimony and swear there was no ballistics evidence against Sacco.

The defense also had new evidence to introduce to the case. On November 18, 1925, while on death row at the Charleston jail, a prisoner named Celestino Medeiros passed a note to Nicola Sacco, confessing that he had been part of the gang that had carried out the South Braintree robbery and claiming that Sacco and Vanzetti were innocent of the crime. Shortly after this incident, Medeiros signed a series of affidavits further describing his activities, while a member of Thompson's staff began investigating a gang in Providence, Rhode Island, headed by a Frank Morelli, to which Medeiros belonged.

The Morelli gang was a group of professional criminals well known to authorities in southern New England. Morelli held a close resemblance to Nicola Sacco; several witnesses who were shown his photograph mistakenly identified him as Sacco. In the spring of 1920, members of the gang were under indictment for thefts from railroad cars at the South Braintree railroad station; five of the thefts were of shipments of shoes from the factory allegedly robbed by Sacco and Vanzetti. To pay defense lawyers needed in the upcoming trial, the Morelli gang had been in immediate need of funds—easily obtainable, so they believed, from the Slater and Morrill paymaster. In 1923, Frank Morelli himself had been overheard describing the South Braintree robbery to his cellmate, Emil Moller, in the Atlanta federal penitentiary. Although this had been brought to the attention of Fred Moore, then serving as Sacco and Vanzetti's defense attorney, Moore did nothing about it, believing he would not be allowed to introduce Moller's hearsay testimony at any appeal of Sacco and Vanzetti's conviction.

Based on the evidence of Medeiros's note and the activities of the Morelli gang, Thompson delivered a motion for a new trial. Judge Thayer presided over the hearing and summarily denied the motion. In his decision, Thayer chose to simply disregard new eyewitness testimony tending to acquit Sacco and to ignore the confession of Medeiros—who was himself awaiting execution—and declare that the original conviction did not, and would not if upheld, rest on the testimony of eyewitnesses but rather on the theory of "consciousness of guilt." On April 9, 1927, the sentence of death was upheld.

Execution was set for the week of July 10, but official hesitation continued. Governor Alvan Fuller of Massachusetts, after personally interviewing many of the witnesses involved in the trial, granted a reprieve and formed a committee for review of the trial to be headed by Abbott Lawrence Lowell, the president of Harvard University. The commission heard more testimony from witnesses that seemed to absolve Sacco and Vanzetti of the crime, yet took no action besides criticizing Judge Thayer for remarks he uttered while off the bench during the trial. On August 10, the governor granted a reprieve of 12 days.

The conviction of Sacco and Vanzetti brought protests around the country and the world. It brought the attention of many prominent writers, including Edna St. Vincent Millay, Dorothy Parker, and Robert Benchley, all of whom condemned it as a bigoted and incompetent miscarriage of justice. The journalist Heywood Broun argued so passionately for Sacco and Vanzetti in the pages of the New York *World* that his columns on the subject were finally cut by his editor. From their desks overseas, Albert Einstein, H. G. Wells, and George Bernard Shaw also condemned the trial. It brought a trenchant protest from Felix Frankfurter, a well-regarded attorney and Harvard law professor, in the pages of *The Atlantic* magazine. Violent demonstrations, many of them in front of U.S. embassies and consulates, took place in London, Paris, Tokyo, Warsaw, and Buenos Aires.

The many written and spoken defenses of Sacco and Vanzetti did not deter the Massachusetts Supreme Court, which upheld the verdict in 1926. Nor did they have any effect on Supreme Court justice Oliver Wendell Holmes, who turned down an appeal as well as a stay of execution on August 10, 1927.

Just after midnight on August 22, in preparation for an unpopular execution, police and guards were stationed in the vicinity of Charleston State Prison. Streets leading to the prison, where the state had its death row, were blocked off. Marchers organized and began making their way to the prison, only to be headed off by mounted police. Just before dawn, Celestino Medeiros, who had enjoyed a stay of execution in case his testimony was needed at a retrial, went to the electric chair, followed by Sacco and Vanzetti. Their funeral took place on August 27 and was attended by a march of 50,000 people, who were stopped at the cemetery gates and scattered into the streets by the police before trouble could begin.

CHRONICLE OF EVENTS

1925

January 5: Nellie Taylor Ross of Wyoming succeeds her late husband and becomes the first woman governor in U.S. history.

January 20: Miriam "Ma" Ferguson is sworn in as governor of Texas.

January 26: Actor Paul Newman is born.

February 2: Gunnar Kasson and his dogsleds reach Nome, Alaska, with serum to fight an epidemic of diphtheria.

February 4: Charles R. Forbes, head of the Veterans Department under President Harding, is sentenced to a jail term of two years for fraud and bribery.

February 13: The "Judge's Bill" provides that appeals from federal district courts will be heard in appeals courts instead of going to the Supreme Court. The bill will considerably lessen the number of cases allowed to reach the Supreme Court.

February 21: The *New Yorker* begins publication with an issue of 32 pages.

February 24: The Purnell Act authorizes federal funding of agricultural research.

March 4: President Calvin Coolidge and Vice President Charles Dawes are inaugurated.

March 9: Governor "Ma" Ferguson of Texas bans the wearing of masks in public.

March 9: President Coolidge calls for plebiscites to be held in Chile and Peru to ratify the decision of the United States in the Tacna-Arica border dispute.

March 13: By the Butler Act, the state of Tennessee legislature outlaws the teaching of evolution.

March 18: The worst tornado storm in the nation's history hits Missouri, Illinois, and Indiana, killing 689 people.

March 19: African-American civil rights leader Malcolm Little, later known as Malcolm X, is born.

March 23: After 21 years, the Senate ratifies the pending Isle of Pines treaty, allowing Cuba possession of the Isle of Pines.

April 13: Henry Ford sponsors the first commercial air service between Detroit and Chicago.

April 15: Lucille Atcherson of Ohio arrives in Switzerland and becomes the first woman to hold a foreign diplomatic post in U.S. history.

April 19: The United States sends troops to Honduras to protect foreigners during the La Ceiba revolt.

April 20: Charles Mellor of Chicago wins the Boston Marathon with a time of 2 hours, 33 minutes, 35 seconds.

April 25: U.S.–born painter John Singer Sargent dies in London at the age of 69.

April 26: Edna Ferber wins the Pulitzer Prize for her novel *So Big.* Other novels published in 1925 include *Manhattan Transfer,* by John Dos Passos, *Arrowsmith,* by Sinclair Lewis, *An American Tragedy,* by Theodore Dreiser, and *The Great Gatsby,* by F. Scott Fitzgerald.

May 13: A new statute passed by the Florida legislature requires daily Bible readings in public schools.

May 24: Governor Al Smith of New York signs an anti-Prohibition law allowing "2.75" beer, which is five and a half times stronger than the .5 percent "near beer" allowed under the Volstead Act.

May 25: High school teacher John T. Scopes is indicted under Tenessee's Anti-Evolution Bill.

June 5: In golf, Willie Macfarlane defeats Bobby Jones by one stroke at the U.S. Open.

June 10: The United Church of Canada is officially established.

June 17: The United States signs the Geneva Convention, controlling international arms traffic, and a protocol banning the use of chemical and bacteriological weapons.

June 18: Progressive senator and governor Robert M. La Follette of Wisconsin dies in Washington, D.C., at the age of 70.

July 10: Tennessee v. John T. Scopes, the first criminal trial of a teacher of evolution under Tennessee's Butler Act, opens in Dayton, Tennessee.

July 13: Standard Oil adopts the eight-hour workday.

July 26: William Jennings Bryan dies just after the close of the Scopes trial in Dayton, Tennessee.

August 1: The banking firm of Dillon, Read buys the Dodge Brothers automobile company for $146 million, the largest such transaction in the nation's history.

August 3: The U.S. Marines leave Nicaragua after occupying the country for 13 years. The marines will return in 1926.

August 8: The Ku Klux Klan holds a massive rally of 40,000 white-robed adherents in Washington, D.C. A local ordinance prohibits the marchers from wearing hoods or masks.

August 16: The Gold Rush, starring Charlie Chaplin as a hard-luck Klondike miner, debuts in movie theaters across the country.

Jurors discuss the case of *Tennessee v. Scopes,* in which they found the defendant guilty of teaching evolution after being permitted to hear only brief testimony from the teacher and his students. *(Brown Brothers)*

August 18: Belgium signs a debt funding agreement, rescheduling the country's outstanding debt of $417 million.

August 24: Hellen Wills win the U.S. Lawn Tennis Association women's singles championship for the third time in a row.

August 29: Babe Ruth is fined $5,000 for poor play and professional misconduct in St. Louis.

August 31: 150,000 coal miners begin a strike in Pennsylvania.

September 1: A personal tax return made public under the Revenue Act of 1924 shows that John D. Rockefeller Jr. paid the highest rate of personal income tax in the United States, in the amount of $6,277,699.

September 3: The Navy dirigible *Shenandoah* is destroyed in a storm over Ava, Ohio; 14 crew members are killed.

September 12: The president appoints Dwight Morrow chairman of the National Aircraft Board.

September 16: The musical *No, No, Nanette,* by Otto Harbach, Frank Mandell, Irving Caesar, and Vincent Youmans, premieres at the Globe Theater in New York.

September 16: Blues guitarist and singer B. B. King is born.

October 16: The Locarno Pact treaties are initialed in London by Germany, France, Belgium, Great Britain, and Italy. The pact guarantees the borders of Belgium, France, and Germany.

October 16: The Texas State Text Book Board prohibits the teaching of evolution in all Texas schoolbooks.

October 28: The court-martial of Colonel William Mitchell of the U.S. Army Air Service begins. Mitchell is accused of "conduct prejudicial to good order and military discipline, insubordination, and utterances contemptuous of the War and Navy departments." Mitchell had accused the departments of "criminal negligence" of the development of air power. On December 17, he is found guilty and suspended for five years without pay.

November 14: The United States agrees to a reduction in principal and interest on debts contracted during World War I.

November 21: David Stephenson, Indiana grand dragon of the Ku Klux Klan, is convicted of second-degree murder in Indiana.

November 28: The Grand Ole Opry begins Saturday night radio broadcasts from Nashville.

December 6: The German-American Claims commission sets the outstanding claims of the United States against Germany for the sinking of the *Lusitania* in 1915 at $2.5 million.

December 6: The John Simon Guggenheim Foundation is established to award fellowships to worthy artists and scholars. The first Guggenheim fellowships will be awarded in April 1926.

December 10: Vice President Charles Dawes is awarded the Nobel Prize in Peace for the Dawes Plan, which restructured Germany's economy and reparations debt.

December 25: Rear Admiral Julian Latimer of the U.S. Navy disarms Nicaraguan rebels to shore up the regime of President Adolfo Diaz.

December 29: The board of Trinity College of Durham, North Carolina, agrees to rename the school Duke University after tobacco magnate James Buchanan Duke, who made a $40 million trust fund conditional on the change.

EYEWITNESS TESTIMONY

Leopold and Loeb

Dear Sir:

As you no doubt know by this time your son has been kidnapped. Allow us to assure you that he is at present well and safe. You need fear no physical harm for him provided you live up carefully to the following instructions and such others as you will receive by further communications. Should you, however, disobey any of our instructions, even slightly, his death will be the penalty.

1. For obvious reasons make absolutely no attempt to communicate with the police authorities or any private agencies. . . .

2. Secure before noon today $10,000. This amount must be composed entirely of old bills of the following denominations:
$2,000 in $20 bills
$8,000 in $50 bills
The money must be old. Any attempt to include new or marked bills will render the entire venture futile.

3. The money should be placed in a small cigar box or if this is impossible in a heavy cardboard box, securely closed and wrapped in a white paper. The wrapping paper should be sealed at all openings with sealing wax.

4. Have this money with you prepared as directed above and remain home after one o'clock P.M. See that the telephone is not in use. You will receive further instructions then instructing you as to your final course.

. . . should you carefully follow our instructions, we can assure you that your son will be safely returned to you within six hours of receipt of the money.

Ransom note written by Nathan Leopold and Richard Loeb and delivered to Jacob Franks, the father of murder victim Bobby Franks, in May 1924, as quoted in Busch, Prisoners at the Bar *(1952), pp. 147–149.*

"That'll be a snap, Nate. Nothing to it. You saw how smooth this all went off. Just like I told you over and over it would. Are you convinced now that it was easy as falling off a log? And the rest will be even easier. We don't have to get within a hundred yards of anybody. Just sit safe and snug in that alley and wait for them to toss us the dough. Those rubes have about as much chance of catching up with us as a snowball in hell. What do you say, Butch, let's go out and have a few drinks after we make the phone call and mail the letter?"

"Wish I could, Dick. I could use a drink. But you know I have to go home and drive Aunt Birdie and Uncle Al home. And then I have to stay home, at least until after Dad goes to bed. It's my night to be home. Tell you what, though. I can probably sneak out later, when I'm sure Dad's asleep. Say about midnight or twelve-thirty."

"Naw, that's too late. Skip it. What would I do with myself till then? Those coppers will be getting a good night's sleep. We better too, so's to be in top form tomorrow to stay ahead of 'em. About two miles ahead!"

Conversation between Nathan Leopold and Richard Loeb in preparation for collecting the ransom from the family of Bobby Franks, May 1924, as recalled in Leopold, Life Plus 99 Years *(1957), p. 23.*

Dearest Mompsie and Popsie: This thing is all too terrible. I have thought and thought about it, and even now I do not seem to be able to understand it. I just cannot seem to figure out how it all came about. Of one thing I am certain, tho—and that is that I have no one to blame but myself. I am afraid that you two may try and put the blame upon your own shoulders, and I know that I alone am to blame. I never was frank with you—Mompsie and Popsie dear—and had you suspected anything and came and talked to me I would undoubtedly have denied everything and gone on just the same.

. . . I realize that there is always a chance of the death penalty. However, I am not worried and I assure you that although I know I never lived the part—I do know that should I have to pay the penalty, that I at least will die as becomes the son of such a wonderful father and mother as I know now more than ever that I have.

What I wanted to tell you is that I am not really so hardhearted as I am appearing. Of course, dearest ones, I am afraid that my heart is not what it should be, else how could I have done what I did?

Letter from accused murderer Richard Loeb to his parents a few days after his arrest in May 1924, from Stone, Clarence Darrow: For the Defense *(1941), p. 393.*

. . . if I could ever bring my mind to ask for the death penalty, I would not do it boastfully and exultantly or in anger or in hate, but I would do it with the deepest regret that it must be done, and I would do it with sympathy even for the ones whose lives must be taken. That has not been done in this case. I have never seen a more deliberate effort to turn the human beings of a community into ravening wolves and take advantage of everything that was offered to create an unreasoning hatred against these two boys.

> *Clarence Darrow, arguing against the death penalty for defendants Leopold and Loeb in a Chicago courtroom in August 1924, quoted in Tierney,* Darrow: A Biography *(1979), p. 339.*

[Those who wanted the death penalty] have been obliged to resign themselves to the more humane penalty of life sentence. Today, when passion has subsided and the spirit of revenge has gone back to slumber, how few there are who are not as well satisfied as if the murderers had been hanged? This ultimate resignation to life imprisonment in a case where there was an unprecedented cry for hanging, shows that we can be as well satisfied with justice which appeals to our reason as with that which appeals to our passions. This, indeed, is the one hopeful lesson of the whole case. Nothing could so surely prove to us that when we are revengeful we are brutal and that when we are reasonable we are humane. In other words, the one inspiring lesson we have all learned is that in the bottom of our hearts we are, all of us, more humane than we suspected.

> *Commentary on the life sentence passed on Leopold and Loeb in 1924 in* The Prison World, *the journal of the Massachusetts Prison Association, and quoted in Haynes,* Criminology *(1935), p. 459.*

The Scopes Trial

. . . of course like every other man of intelligence and education I do believe in Organic Evolution. It surprises me that at this late date such questions should be raised.

> *Woodrow Wilson, August 29, 1922, letter to Dr. Winterton Curtis, quoted in De Camp,* The Great Monkey Trial *(1968), p. 50.*

The day is not distant when you will be in the grip of the Red Terror and your children will be taught free love by the damnable theory of evolution.

> *Rev. Mordecai Ham, quoted by Rollin Hartt in "Down with Evolution!"* The World's Work, *October 1923, p. 605.*

The hand that writes the paycheck rules the school.

> *William Jennings Bryan, in* Orthodox Christianity vs. Modernism, *(1923), p. 46.*

After a careful examination I can find nothing of consequence in the books now being taught in our schools with which this bill will interfere in the slightest manner. Therefore it will not put our teachers in any jeopardy. Probably the law will never be applied. It may not be sufficiently definite to admit of any specific application or enforcement. Nobody believes it is going to be an active statute.

> *Governor Austin Peay of Tennessee, on the Butler Anti-Evolution Bill, as quoted in Ginger,* Six Days or Forever *(1958), p. 7.*

The Christian parents of the state owe you a debt of gratitude for saving their children from the poisonous influence of an unproven hypothesis.

> *William Jennings Bryan, telegram to Governor Austin Peay, quoted in Larson,* Summer for the Gods, *(1997), p. 59.*

Let your scientific consolation enter a room where the mother has lost her child. Try your doctrine of the survival of the fittest. And when you have gotten through . . . if she is not crazed with it, I will go to her and after one-half hour of prayer and the reading of the Scripture promises, the tears will be wiped away.

> *Billy Sunday, "Historical Fabric of Christ's Life Nothing Without Miracles,"* Memphis Commercial Appeal, *February 7, 1925.*

The constitutional guarantee of separation of church and state, it is believed, offers a ground for contesting the laws requiring Bible reading.

The chief source of inspiration for this new and unprecedented crop of gag laws on teaching are the Ku Klux Klan, the fundamentalists, and the professional patriotic societies. The Klan is back of compulsory Bible reading and antiparochial school laws, the fundamentalists back of the antievolution bills and the professional patriots back of the antiradical and antipacifist measures.

> *Editorial in the* Chattanooga Times, *April 4, 1925, p. 5.*

PROFESSOR J.T. SCOPES, TEACHER OF SCIENCE RHEA COUNTY HIGH SCHOOL, DAYTON, TENNESSEE, WILL BE ARRESTED CHARGED WITH TEACHING EVOLUTION. CONSENT OF SUPERINTENDENT OF EDUCATION FOR TEST CASE TO BE DEFENDED

BY YOU. WIRE ME COLLECT IF YOU WISH TO CO-OPERATE AND ARREST WILL FOLLOW.
Telegram, George Rappelyea to American Civil Liberties Union, April 5, 1925, quoted in De Camp, The Great Monkey Trial (1968), p. 14.

Mr. Robinson, you and John Godsey are always looking for something that will get Dayton a little publicity. I wonder if you have seen the morning paper?
George Rappelyea to F. E. Robinson, May 4, 1925, preparing to suggest the town of Dayton provide a test case of Tennessee's Butler Act, as quoted in Larson, Summer for the Gods, (1997), p. 89.

When I think . . . how petty, mean and contemptible Bryan was and is . . . and that Bryan was popularized almost to idolatry and glorified by press and pulpit as an apostle of truth and an evangel of religion, this shallow-minded mouther of empty phrases, this pious, canting mountebank, this prophet of the stone-age, my blood runs hot in my veins with indignation and resentment at the utterly cruel and perverse ways of the world in which we live and the age-old rule of crowning frauds, hypocrites, time-servers and scoundrels, and murdering prophets, pathfinders and all other true leaders of the people and saviors of the race.
Socialist leader Eugene V. Debs, correspondence on the subject of William Jennings Bryan to Clarence Darrow of June 4, 1925, quoted in Tierney, Darrow: A Biography (1979), p. 371.

When the prosecution of John T. Scopes, teacher of Biology in the Dayton high school, is begun on July 10 it ought to be cried out by the court clerk as the State of Tennessee *vs.* Truth. For the trial brings to a head the attempt of a great commonwealth to determine science by popular vote, to establish truth by fiat instead of study, research, and experiment.

Not that Tennessee stands alone. Unfortunately, it has plenty of company. Tennessee just happened to be the first State to pass a law designed to prevent the teaching of the doctrine of evolution in its publicly supported schools. Kentucky missed passing a similar law by one vote, while only the upper house of the Texas Legislature prevented such legislation going on the statute books. There are restrictions upon teaching evolution in Oklahoma and North Carolina, and a campaign to that end is under way in California. All over the South and West there is agitation with a similar purpose.

Why the South and West? Merely because those sections are primarily rural and the anti-evolution movement has its springs in the small towns and the back blocks. Its champions are mostly among our much-praised native-American stock. They are the people who are generally held up as the safe-deposit vault of our ancient national virtues, but actually—all too often—a people bled white by the migration of their best individuals to the great cities. They distrust schools which are better than their own. They have been deprived of the vigor they brought into the world and left without leadership, a fine soil for fundamentalism, the Ku Klux Klan, and other manifestations of superstition and ignorance.
unsigned editorial, "Tennessee vs. Truth," in The Nation, July 8, 1925, p. 58.

This hypothesis makes every living thing known in animal life a blood relative of every other living thing in animal life, and makes man a blood relative of them all—either an ancestor or a cousin. If this hypothesis were true, we would all be murderers if we swatted a fly or killed a bedbug, for we would be killing our kin, and we would be cannibals whenever we ate any of the mammals that, according to Mr. Scopes' teaching, are included with man in the little circle of the diagram of the *Biology* taught by Scopes.
William Jennings Bryan, statement to the press, July 18, 1925, quoted in De Camp, The Great Monkey Trial (1968), p. 362.

Clarence Darrow (left) and William Jennings Bryan pose before the opening of the trial of John Scopes. Darrow's client was convicted, but Darrow's relentless and skeptical interrogation of Bryan made the evolutionists' case. *(Brown Brothers)*

It is perfectly plain that the scientist is as kind and humane and tolerant as the Fundamentalist. In fact, no one ever heard of a scientific man who ever sought to call the aid of the law to enforce belief in his theories.

Clarence Darrow, statement to the press, July 18, 1925, quoted in De Camp, The Great Monkey Trial *(1968), p. 362.*

There was something peculiarly fitting in the fact that his [William Jennings Bryan's] last days were spent in a one-horse Tennessee village, and that death found him there. The man felt at home in such scenes. He liked people who sweated freely, and were not debauched by the refinements of the toilet. Making his progress up and down the Main Street of little Dayton, surrounded by gaping primates from the upland valleys of the Cumberland range, his coat laid aside, his bare arms and hairy chest shining damply, his bald head sprinkled with dust—so accoutered and on display he was obviously happy. He liked getting up early in the morning, to the tune of cocks crowing on the dunghill. He liked the heavy, greasy victuals of the farmhouse kitchen. He liked country lawyers, country pastors, all country people. I believe that this liking was sincere—perhaps the only sincere thing in the man. His nose showed no uneasiness when a hillman in faded overalls and hickory shirt accosted him on the street, and besought him for light upon some mystery of Holy Writ. The simian gabble of a country town was not gabble to him, but wisdom of an occult and superior sort. In the presence of city folks he was palpably uneasy. Their clothes, I suspect, annoyed him, and he was suspicious of their too delicate manners. He knew all the while that they were laughing at him—if not at his baroque theology, then at least at his alpaca pantaloons. But the yokels never laughed at him. To them he was not the huntsman but the prophet, and toward the end, as he gradually forsook mundane politics for purely ghostly concerns, they began to elevate him in their hierarchy. When he died he was the peer of Abraham. Another curious detail: his old enemy, Wilson, aspiring to the same white and shining robe, came down with a thump. But Bryan made the grade. His place in the Tennesse hagiography is secure. If the village barber saved any of his hair, then it is curing gall-stones down there today.

H. L. Mencken, untitled obituary of William Jennings Bryan, in The American Mercury, *October 1925, pp. 158–159.*

It was in these factional quarrels that Bryan aroused such passionate and sincere devotion to what seemed exalted causes. But always the basis of his appeal was distrust of some other group of men. He would preach idealism not as loyalty to a program but as fear of some alleged enemy. With skill and daring and a certain lack of scruple he appealed to the fears which set men violently against one another.

. . . Even in religion he could not refrain from factionalism, and the last years of his life were devoted to a crusade which set one group of Christians against another. He professed himself a Democrat and a Christian, but at bottom he was always a man looking for a point of conflict where his talent for factionalism could find free play. Thus as a Democrat he spent his chief energies quarreling with Democrats, and as a Christian he ended his life quarreling angrily with other Christians.

Walter Lippman, 1925 editorial written on the death of William Jennings Bryan, from Lippmann, Public Persons *(1976), p. 75.*

If I lose faith in Genesis, I'm afraid I'll lose faith in the rest of the Bible; and if I want to commit larceny I'll say I don't believe in the part of the Bible that says "Thou shalt not steal." Then I'll go out and steal. The same thing applies to murder.

Circuit Judge John T. Raulston, after presiding over the trial of John Scopes, in a speech delivered November 8, 1925, in New York City, quoted in Ginger, Six Days or Forever, *(1958), p. 111.*

The learned judge in the monkey trial says scientific experts must not be heard—a wise decision. If a great state has decided by law that twice two are five it would be foolish to allow mathematicians to testify.

Arthur Brisbane, quoted in Shipley, The War on Modern Science *(1927), p. 211.*

The Court is informed that the plaintiff-in-error is no longer in the service of the State. We see nothing to be gained by prolonging the life of this bizarre case. On the contrary we think the peace and dignity of the State, which all criminal prosecutions are brought to redress, will be better conserved by the entry of a *nolle prosequi* herein.

Tennessee Supreme Court, opinion, Scopes v. Tennessee, *January 15, 1927.*

There is not one specimen to be found in it save the chimpanzee and *Homo sapiens* (or the complete monkey and the complete man) that can be historically defended. . . . They have dug out of the earth a little animal about the size of a fox with (*a*) five toes, which has some similarity to the horse, and they have called him (b) old horse—eohippus; and they have brought up another with three toes, as big as a timber wolf, and because of certain similarities they have called him a horse; and then they have imagined that horse finally developing into the present beautiful beast of domestic service with one toe elongated from the knee to the hoof; and in certain (c) splints on the side of his leg they find the aborted toes. The intervening horses, bridging the gap between these ancient animals and our black beauty, (d) they have sought in vain! Yet they will stand before you with all the assurance of men who had found the last missing link, concerning the evolution of the horse! Why do they begin with that fox-like animal? In the ocean there is (e) a shrimp [said "shrimp," however, being a vertebrate!] that has the head of a horse and his motions in water are much like a plunging charger. (f) Why not begin with him? . . . The present race of men began at their best when between 6,000 and 7,000 years ago God formed their fore-parents in His own image. . . . Man was not only made in the image of God, but in fellowship with his Creator commenced his existence on earth in the highest state of civilization, from which he has descended to every single degradation that has characterized and cursed the race.

Dr. William Bell Riley, founder of the Anti-Evolution League of Minnesota, explaining the contradictions and ambiguities of scientific evolution, and quoted by Maynard Shipley in "The Fundamentalists' Case," in The American Mercury, *February 1928, p. 228.*

Sacco and Vanzetti

Of late a new propaganda has come into our midst. It is the propaganda of force, of might and revolution, and it is prescribed as a remedy for what? For order, for obedience to law and the protection of human life. Think what that means. Oh, how unfortunate that any such a doctrine, so destructive in its character and so revolutionary in all its tendencies should ever have reached the sacred shores of these United States where the spirit of liberty and opportunity and where the freedom of person, of property and of contract are unequalled anywhere in the world.

Judge Webster Thayer, who would later preside over the trial of Sacco and Vanzetti, in a speech delivered at a naturalization ceremony in Dedham, Massachusetts, quoted in The Dedham Transcript, *April 10, 1920 and reprinted in Young and Kaiser,* Postmortem: New Evidence in the Case of Sacco and Vanzetti *(1985), p. 22.*

I hear by confess to being in the South Braintree Shoe company crime and Sacco and Vanzetti was not in said crime. Celestino F. Medeiros.

Note passed to Nicola Sacco by Celestine Medeiros on November 18, 1925, from Grant and Katz, The Great Trials of the Twenties *(1998), p. 45.*

These men were tried at a time when Mitchell Palmer had stirred up the whole country with fear and hatred of the so-called "Reds". . . . It is my belief, based upon a long study of the case, that they had nothing whatever to do with the crime with which they are charged; but that they are victims of the agitation engineered by Mitchell Palmer.

. . . Millions of people in this country and all over the world have come to believe that these men are the victims of capitalistic persecution. There is just enough truth in the charge to make it dangerous. Their adherents can never be convinced that it is not true, and if the men are executed, violent and permanent antagonisms will be created which will certainly not be conducive to social peace and good order, and may lead to serious consequences.

William G. Thompson, Sacco and Vanzetti defense attorney, in letter to Charles B. Rogers of November 19, 1926, quoted in Young and Kaiser, Postmortem: New Evidence in the Case of Sacco and Vanzetti *(1985), p. 76.*

Speaking from a considerable experience as a prosecuting officer . . . I assert with deep regret, but without the slightest fear of disproof, that certainly in modern times Judge Thayer's opinion stands unmatched for discrepancies between what the record discloses and what the opinion conveys. His 25,000-word document cannot accurately be described otherwise than as a farrago of misquotations, misrepresentations, suppressions, and mutilations. The disinterested inquirer could not possibly derive from it a true knowledge of the new evidence that was submitted to him as the basis for a new trial. The opinion is literally honeycombed with demonstrable errors, and a spirit alien to judicial utterance permeates the whole.

Felix Frankfurter, describing Judge Webster Thayer's denial of defense motion for a new trial for Sacco and Vanzetti, from "The Case of Sacco and Vanzetti," in The Atlantic Monthly, *March 1927, pp. 431–432.*

I never knew, never heard, ever read in history anything so cruel as this Court. After seven years' prosecuting they still consider us guilty. And these gentle people here are arrayed with us in this court today.

I know the sentence will be between two classes, the oppressed class and the rich class, and there will be always collision between one and the other. We fraternize the people with the books, with the literature. You persecute the people, tyrannize them and kill them. We try the education of people always. You try to put a path between us and some other nationality that hates each other. That is why I am here today on this bench, for having been of the oppressed class. Well, you are the oppressor.

You know it, Judge Thayer—you know all my life, you know why I have been here, and after seven years that you have been persecuting me and my poor wife, and you still today sentence us to death. I would like to tell all my life, but what is the use?

Nicola Sacco, last words to the court delivered April 9, 1927, as quoted in Sann, The Lawless Decade *(1957), p. 178.*

I am not only innocent of these two crimes but I never commit a crime in my life. I have never steal and I have never kill and I have never spilt blood and I have fought against the crime and I have fought and I have sacrificed myself even to eliminate the crimes that the law and the church legitimate and sanctify.

This is what I say: I would not wish to a dog or to a snake, to the most low and misfortunate creature of the earth—I would not wish to any of them what I have had to suffer for things that I am not guilty of. But my conviction is that I have suffered for things that I am guilty of. I am suffering because I am a radical; I have suffered because I was an Italian and indeed I am an Italian; I have suffered more for my family and for my beloved than for myself; but I am so convinced to be right that if you could execute me two times and if I could be reborn two other times I would live again to do what I have done already. I have finished—thank you.

Bartolomeo Vanzetti, last words to the court delivered April 9, 1927, as quoted in Sann, The Lawless Decade *(1957), p. 179.*

Is Massachusetts subject to dictates of international terrorists? Where has the like ever been known in modern history? The thugs of India, the Camorra of Naples, the Black Hand of Sicily, the anarchists of czardom—when did their attempts to impose their will by violence ever equal in range of operations and vicious directness, the organized effi- ciency of this cabal to which Sacco and Vanzetti belong?

Dean Jon Wigmore of the Northwestern University Law School, replying to Felix Frankfurter's defense of Sacco and Vanzetti on the front page of the April 25, 1927, Boston Evening Transcript, *quoted in Russell,* Tragedy in Dedham: The Story of the Sacco-Vanzetti Case *(1962), p. 371.*

Trial Judge Webster Thayer, cast by Sacco-Vanzetti adherents as the villain of the plot, said last week: "I have made my position clear enough. I did what I had to do. What more can I say? I can only maintain a judicial silence."

"Radicals—Dynamite," unsigned item from Time *magazine, May 23, 1927, p. 9.*

I have understood from the beginning that Judge Thayer wanted to kill us because we were hated and feared by the ragged and golden rabbles so that he will be recompensed by them by being appointed judge of the Massachusetts Supreme Court—this vanity has been the obsession of his live [sic]. . . . Were not the first Christians believed to be blood-drinkers? Yes, they were believed so and insulted, tortured, martyrized by the ragged and golden mobs of their time. Even the so sage Marcus Aurelius feared, hated, insulted, and killed them. Of course the first Christians were outlaws [because] they were against the laws who legalize slavery; against the powerful Roman Empire oppressing mankind and masters of the Courts and laws; they were gods-destroyers but destroyers of false gods. In this was their right, greatness, sanctity; for this they were put to death. What chance of fair deal and acquital [sic] those not only innocent first Christians could have had in being tried by pagans to whom the face of one being Christian was all the crimes and all the guilts at once and in one?

Bartolomeo Vanzetti, letter to Sarah Root Adams of May 25, 1927, and quoted in Frankfurter and Jackson (eds.), The Letters of Sacco and Vanzetti *(1928), pp. 273–274.*

The agitation of the elements of the left throughout the world is increasing in intensity, in these last days, as is shown by the bombs thrown in Buenos Aires against the Ford establishment and the statue of Washington.

Now if the act of clemency is held back still longer it may give the impression that the American authority may have yielded to the pressure of this world-wide subversive activity and this impression can injure the prestige of the United States.

I hope that His Excellency Governor Fuller may give an example of humanity. The example will brilliantly demonstrate the difference between the methods of Bolshevism and those of the great American republic as well as strike from the hands of the subversive elements an instrument of agitation.

Benito Mussolini, message written in July 1927, to the American ambassador to Italy, asking for the commutation of the death sentence passed on Sacco and Vanzetti, quoted in Russell, Tragedy in Dedham: The Story of the Sacco-Vanzetti Case *(1962), p. 381.*

. . . For the things of beauty and of good in this life, mother nature gave to us all, for the conquest and the joy of liberty. The men of this dying old society, they brutally have pulled me away from the embrace of your brother and your poor mother. But, in spite of all, the free spirit of your father's faith still survives, and I have lived for it and for the dream that some day I would have come back to life, to the embrace of your dear mother, among our friends and comrades again, but woe is me!

Nicola Sacco from Charlestown State Prison to his daughter Ines, July 19, 1927, from Letters of a Nation *(1997), p. 194.*

The men in Charlestown Prison are shining spirits, and Vanzetti has spoken with an eloquence not known elsewhere within our time. They are too bright, we shield our eyes and kill them. We are the dead, and in us there is not feeling nor imagination nor the terrible torment of lust for justice. And in the city where we sleep, smug gardeners walk to keep the grass above our little houses sleek and cut whatever blade thrusts a head above its fellows.

"The decision is unbelievably brutal," said the Chairman of the Defense Committee, and he was wrong. The thing is worthy to be believed. It has happened. It will happen again, and the shame is wider than that which must rest upon Massachusetts. I have never believed that the trial of Sacco and Vanzetti was one set apart from many by reason of the passion and prejudice which encrusted all the benches. Scratch through the varnish of any judgment seat and what will you strike but hate thick-clotted from centuries of angry verdicts? Did any man ever find power within his hand except to use it as a whip?

Gov. Alvan T. Fuller never had any intention in all his investigation but to put a new and higher polish upon the proceedings. The justice of the business was not his concern. He hoped to make it respectable. He called old men from high places to stand behind his chair so that he might seem to speak with all the authority of a high priest or a Pilate.

What more can these immigrants from Italy expect? It is not every person who has a president of Harvard University throw the switch for him. . . . If this is lynching, at least the fish-peddler and his friend the factory hand may take unction to their souls that they will die at the hands of men in dinner coats or academic gowns, according to the conventionalities required by the hour of execution.

Heywood Broun, criticizing the actions of the Lowell Commission in upholding the conviction of Sacco and Vanzetti, in the New York World, *August 5, 1927, from Broun,* Collected Edition of Heywood Broun *(1969), pp. 197–198.*

Heartiest congratulations for your decision. Hope to cast my presidential vote for you.

You have redeemed a waning faith in our institutions by a single outstanding act of this century in our history.

Congratulations to our future President, the 100 percent American, who has the courage of his convictions.

You and Calvin Coolidge have shifted the training ground of our Presidents from Ohio to Massachusetts. I am for Calvin Coolidge as long as he lives, after Calvin Coolidge I am for you. You have courage; since the introduction of the direct primary, most politicians lack courage.

Telegrams of support sent to Massachusetts governor Alvan Fuller for his refusal to grant clemency to Sacco and Vanzetti, published in the August 14, 1927, edition of the Boston Herald *and quoted in Joughin and Morgan,* The Legacy of Sacco and Vanzetti *(1948), p. 294.*

Probably not in all the annals of criminal history has any convicted person evaded the carrying out of sentence for as long a time as the now world-famous Sacco and Vanzetti. Found guilty of murder in a scrupulously fair trial and this guilt confirmed by an utterly impartial and thoroughly exhaustive investigation by the Governor and a committee of three other distinguished persons of the highest repute. . . . The whole affair is in imminent danger of approaching a disgraceful fiasco with the sorry spectacle held up to the world of the sovereign state of Massachusetts powerless to enforce her own laws in the face of an impudent gang of alien anarchists and reds carrying out a world-wide campaign of sabotage, terrorism and intimidation on behalf of two condemned men.

G. W. Wardner, letter to the Boston Herald *of August 16, 1927, quoted in Joughin and Morgan,* The Legacy of Sacco and Vanzetti, *(1948), p. 294–295.*

During my interview with you this afternoon I called to your attention a distressing instance of the miscarriage of justice in a neighboring state. I suggested that, for all your careful weighing of the evidence, for all your courage in the face of threats and violent words, for all your honest conviction that these men are guilty, you, no less than the governor of Maine in my story, who was so tragically mistaken, are but human flesh and spirit, and that it is human to err.

Tonight, with the world in doubt, with this Commonwealth drawing into its lungs with every breath the difficult air of doubt, with the eyes of Europe turned westward upon Massachusetts and upon the whole United States in distress and harrowing doubt—are you still so sure? Does no faintest shadow of question gnaw at your mind? For, indeed, your spirit, however strong, is but the frail spirit of a man. Have you no need, in this hour, of a spirit greater than your own?

. . . I cry to you with a million voices: answer our doubt. Exert the clemency which your high office affords.

There is need in Massachusetts of a great man tonight. It is not yet too late for you to be that man.

Edna St. Vincent Millay, letter to Massachusetts governor Alvan T. Fuller on August 22, 1927, the eve of the execution of Sacco and Vanzetti, from Letters of Edna St. Vincent Millay *(1952), p. 222.*

In the moral economy of our still savage world, there is no possible and, consequently, no fitting compensation for the execution of the innocent but some kind of retaliation and punishment. . . . Of course, we do not mean that there is the slightest justification for visiting this punishment on the bodies of the individuals who were responsible for the execution. It would be deplorable and outrageous from every point of view for any comrade of Sacco and Vanzetti to penalize by violence the assumed innocence of their dead comrades. Nevertheless, retaliation of some kind there is bound to be. Messrs. Thayer, Fuller, Grant, Lowell and their followers have started something the consequences of which they will live to regret. A highly

organized society which depends for its health upon a moral balance cannot perpetrate and endorse such a gross miscarriage of justice without paying for the betrayal of its own ideals.

From "Penalties of the Sacco-Vanzetti Execution," unsigned editorial in The New Republic, *September 7, 1927, p. 57.*

The new evidence emerging in the case of Sacco and Vanzetti should make every person in the United States—from radical to reactionary—pause a moment and consider the death penalty as an instrument of justice.

Year after year men are hanged or burned to death in the electric chair, put beyond recall of judge or governor, and every year dead men are found to be innocent of the crime for which they died. It seems difficult to believe that any society—even one which clung to the pound-of-flesh theory of punishment—would continue to use a method of social reprisal which eliminates even the smallest chance of righting a wrong. Who is to claim the pound of flesh for the man who is executed and later found innocent?

"The Death Penalty," unsigned editorial in The Nation, *November 7, 1928, p. 472.*

I asked him, "What the hell are you suing them for? You can't beat a newspaper." He said: "They're implicating me in this Sacco-Vanzetti thing. What they said was true, but it's going to hurt my kid. I don't give a damn about myself. I'm ready to die anyway. But look what they're doing to my boy. He's a legitimate kid. He never knew what was going on before."

I looked at Butsey. I didn't know much about the case except what I'd heard. But he was upset because of what was happening to his boy, not what happened to Sacco and Vanzetti. "We whacked them out, we killed those guys in the robbery," Butsey said. "These two greaseballs [Sacco and Vanzetti] took it on the chin. They got in our way so we just ran over them. Now after all these years some punch-drunk writer has got to start up the whole thing over again—ruin my reputation. . . ." I said: "Did you really do this?" He looked at me, right into my eyes, and said: "Absolutely, Vinnie. Those two suckers took it on the chin for us. That shows you how much justice there really is."

Vincent Teresa, reporting a 1950s-era conversation with Frank "Butsey" Morelli, in Teresa and Renner, My Life in the Mafia *(1974), p. 57.*

8

Troubles in
the Hemisphere
January 1926–May 1926

The Dominion of Canada had been an important partner in the Allied effort during World War I. Canada contributed four infantry divisions as well as wartime loans to Great Britain in the amount of $700 million; Canadian units had played a crucial role in the Allied victory at Vimy Ridge in 1917 and at the breakthroughs at Cambrai and Mons that finally brought the German surrender in the fall of 1918. At the end of the war, Canadians celebrated their own war hero in air ace William A. Bishop, whom the British monarch presented with the Victoria Cross for his 72 kills. During these operations in northern France and Belgium, more than 50,000 members of the Canadian Expeditionary Force had lost their lives.

After the armistice, Canada took a seat of its own at the Versailles peace conference, and although Canadian diplomats endorsed the final treaty as well as the Covenant of the League of Nations (an organization that promised to supplant the now-eclipsed British Empire), the League of Nations met opposition at home. Article X of the League Covenant, in which each country guaranteed the sovereignty of all other members, had set off warnings and hesitations among Canadian politicians, just as it had among Henry Cabot Lodge and his allies in the United States. Having won autonomy from British governance when they were declared citizens of a colonial dominion in 1867, Canadians were not willing to sacrifice that independence to a League of Nations. Yet they realized that their emerging industries remained dependent on foreign markets and that their nation could not imitate the United States by rejecting the new international alliances, no matter how entangling they were. After the Liberals and the Conservatives of the Dominion legislature concluded a long debate, Canada voted to join the League—which was the creation of U.S. president Woodrow Wilson—while the United States did not.

Within Canada, the end of World War I brought about dislocation and unrest. Wartime industry had rapidly accelerated the country's manufacturing economy and its urbanization; the war also caused steep inflation and brought heavy taxes on consumer goods that resulted in a lower standard of living for workers. High demand for workers had strengthened labor unions, however, and during World War I union membership stood higher than at any previous moment in the country's history. The most militant labor leaders, for the most part members of farmers' and laborers' parties in the western provinces, gained popularity through opposition to the more conservative Trades and Labour Congress, the Canadian equivalent of the American Federation of Labor (AFL), whose members came from the more prosperous central provinces. The radical labor movement was also fueled by resentment of wartime profiteering and of the system of honors and titles, both hereditary and nonhereditary, that had come to symbolize the deepening social and economic divisions within the country. Angered and spurred to action by Canada's intervention after the war in the Bolshevik revolution in Russia, the leftists advanced a Soviet-inspired revolutionary structure for the country's workers: One Big Union, a nationwide community of workers organized by their industries rather than by their trades, their employers, or their locations.

THE WINNIPEG GENERAL STRIKE

Following the armistice, western labor leaders had withdrawn from the Trades and Labour Congress, an action that signaled a new era of labor defiance. At a meeting in Calgary in 1919, radical union leaders called for mass action in imitation of the early days of the Russian revolution. On May 15, 1919, during a walkout of metalworkers in Winnipeg, the General Labour Council, the city's central union organization, proclaimed a general strike. About 30,000 people in Winnipeg walked off their jobs, while smaller sympathy strikes began in other cities and provinces throughout the country.

The Winnipeg general strike, and the general fear of radical laborers caused by the successful Russian revolution, inspired employers and politicians to action. On the initiative of Arthur Meighen, a Conservative cabinet representative from Manitoba, the Canadian Parliament amended the laws to allow deportation of undesirable anarchists, socialists, and Bolshevik sympathizers. In Winnipeg, police arrested several of the strike leaders, an action which prompted a rally in support of the strike and the detainees on June 21. During the rally, the police charged the crowd, killing one man, wounding 30 others, and providing a rallying cry for the workers to remember Canada's own "Bloody Saturday." The strike paralyzed the city, allowing a citizens' committee to take control of government functions. But the lack of support from trade unions and workers from the eastern and central provinces doomed the prospects for a nationwide general strike, and in July the metal workers of Winnipeg agreed to a new collective bargaining agreement. Workers throughout the city returned to their jobs.

In a few years, division among union organizers would bring about the slow death of the radical labor movement in Canada. But strong protest still issued from Canadian farmers, who organized themselves into cooperatives such as the United Grain Growers and who turned to political action after the war. The farmers' principal goal was to reduce protective tariffs that prevented them from reaching a more lucrative international market for their goods. In November 1918, the Canadian Council of Agriculture (a national organization representing farmers' organizations in the provinces) advanced the New National Policy, a program of lowered tariffs, taxes on business profits and personal incomes, public ownership of transportation and utility companies, abolition of the Senate, and initiative and referendum. In the fall of 1919, the United Farmers of Ontario won a provincial election and formed a government that lasted until 1923. In Alberta, the United Farmers of Alberta, led by a U.S. Populist, Henry Wise Wood, governed the province from 1921 until 1935.

The protests of Canadian farmers coincided with the growth of the Progressive movement, which in turn drew much of its strength from workers, farmers, and small businessmen of the maritime and prairie provinces who were opposed to the powerful corporate and political interests of Ontario and Quebec. In January 1920, at a farmers' convention in Winnipeg, the National Progressive Party was founded under the leadership of T. A. Crerar. The Progressive movement challenged the two traditional parties, Liberals and Conservatives, that had long governed the country in a familiar and comfortable counterbalance. The Progressives saw big business corrupting the two traditional parties. In a broader sense their revolt, like the Prohibition movement in the United States, was directed against the disorienting changes Canadian society was undergoing after the war. The Progressives were for taxes on business profits, public ownership of utilities and transportation companies, and for initiative, referendum, and recall—echoes of Progressive issues current in the United States before the war. Unfortunately, Progressive politicians also held a vague and idealistic principle against disciplined party voting. Individual members were free to vote their consciences, but while they did so through the early 1920s, the movement made little actual progress except to provide swing votes for bills sponsored by the major parties in the national legislature.

SCANDAL

The Progressive call to action spurred the Liberal Party to advance its own progressive notions in the quest for public support and election wins. Liberals called for reduced tariffs—farm implements and supplies to be admitted duty-free—new business taxes, and the establishment of workers' pensions and unemployment and health insurance. The strategy succeeded under the leadership of William Lyon Mackenzie King, the former minister of labor, who had been chosen at a national convention in the spring of 1919 (the first time a Canadian party had elected a leader from among a convention of delegates, as in the United States). The national election of December 1921 resulted in 117 seats for the Liberals, 65 for the Progressives, and 50 for the Conservatives.

Canada had ended a decade of Conservative governments, but the new Liberal government failed to carry through on its program. With the national treasury greatly weakened by wartime debt (the Dominion had contracted about $2 billion in loans), the careful finance ministers of the King administration insisted on budget-balancing over Progressivism. Tariffs were only gradually reduced, no social insurance laws were adopted, and public utility ownership remained an unrealized notion. The opposition to such measures on the part of the Senate, the upper house of Canada's legislature, also assured that Progressive-style legislation would fail. While populism, radicalism, and labor activism dissipated as the economy steadily improved, Canada's voters found themselves quite underwhelmed by the King administration's performance and returned the Conservative Party to a majority in the election of 1925 with 117 seats to the Liberals' 101 seats and the Progressives' 24.

In Canada's parliamentary system, a prime minister whose party loses its majority in the legislature ordinarily resigns and calls for new elections. But Mackenzie King—who had lost his own seat in the legislature—sought to remain in office by calling on the support of the Progressive swing voters in Parliament, a strategy that worked for about six months. King's support from the Progressives gradually eroded. When the administration hesitated to allow the province of

Lord Byng, British-appointed governor general, would not carry out the dissolution of Canada's parliament requested by the Canadian prime minister, Mackenzie King. His purposes stymied, King would later argue that the refusal constituted a violation of Canada's sovereignty. *(Brown Brothers)*

Alberta greater control of its natural resources, the western provinces also pulled away from King. Then, in the late spring of 1926, scandal erupted when a Conservative member of parliament, Harry Stevens, uncovered a bribery scandal in the Customs Department, under whose authority, it appeared, bootleggers' bribes were allowing smugglers to move liquor over the Canadian border to the United States. By itself this seemed a relatively benign—even expected—activity, but bribed officials were also allowing contraband cigarettes to pass from the United States into Canada—an action that undermined Canadian interests and that was taken much more seriously. The scandal involved the entire Department of Customs and Excise, as well as the minister of customs, a French Canadian.

The scandal embarrassed King's Liberal administration and resulted in a Conservative motion to censure the Customs Department—a motion likely to be successful if Progressives voted in protest with the Conservative majority in Parliament. The vote on the censure motion was scheduled for June 1926, but before it could be taken, King asked the governor general of Canada, Lord Byng, the official representative of the British crown, for a formal dissolution of Parliament. King gave as his reason the inability of his Conservative opponent, Arthur Meighen, to form a viable opposition government.

The governor general refused to carry out a dissolution, maintaining that the Conservative majority should be allowed to form their opposition government in the legislature. King then asked Byng to check with London. Reluctant to assert British authority at a time like this, Byng refused to take the drastic action demanded by the prime minister, and on June 28, King and his government resigned. Lord Byng then called on Arthur Meighen to form a government and conclude legislative business, which prompted King to oppose the governor general's unconstitutional action. Having been rebuffed in his own request for Byng to take pre-emptive action, King now appealed to national pride and to the Canadians' fear of returning to colonial status.

Meighen formed a temporary government, and six other members of his party became ministers without portfolio; they were officially "acting ministers" without salary. By law, however, these ministers had to vacate their seats in the legislature, which in turn weakened Meighen's ability to act. In the meantime, Meighen's abrasive personality put off many voters, as King knew it would. The Progressive swing voters fell out, and on July 1, after losing a parliamentary vote, Meighen requested that Parliament be dissolve. This time Byng granted the request.

Another election ensued, in which King made Byng's refusal of his request an insult to Canadian sovereignty, portrayed Meighen as a reactionary, and condemned the two-day ad hoc Meighen administration as a harbinger of future Conservative tyranny. The Liberals won the election with 119 seats and were assured of the support of a 24-seat bloc of independent members and 11 members of a new hybrid party, the Liberal-Progressives. King returned to power while Meighen resigned as both prime minister and as head of the Conservative party. As members of the Progressive Party returned to the Liberal Party, Canada gradually returned to its two-party orthodoxy.

Postwar problems and conflicts seemed to disappear in the general prosperity of the late 1920s, and the One Big Union disappeared from view. The nation's economy improved as foreign demand for Canadian natural resources and finished goods returned. The favorable balance of trade in turn helped the government to balance its budget and pay its heavy wartime debts.

Good times in Canada would not last until the next election. In the late 1920s and the early 1930s, the economic slump that was signaled by the crash of the U.S. stock market in October 1929 would depress prices, exports, and the nation's earning power.

LATIN AMERICA

The Monroe Doctrine, as announced by President James Monroe in 1823, established the principle that the United States would not tolerate any effort at colonization or interference in the western hemisphere by the European powers. For the next century, the doctrine provided a justification for U.S. intervention

Conservative leader Arthur Meighen rapidly lost support after appointing an ad hoc cabinet of acting ministers, which his opponent Mackenzie King portrayed as an example of Conservative tyranny. *(Brown Brothers)*

in the affairs of the Caribbean and Central and South America. It also brought rivalry between Spain and the United States to a violent conclusion with the Spanish-American War of 1898. After winning this conflict, the United States exercised virtual hegemony over the Caribbean region, annexing Puerto Rico outright and extending control over Cuba's economy and government with the Platt Amendment of 1902. In 1904, President Theodore Roosevelt took the Monroe Doctrine one step further, claiming the right to intervene should internal conditions—such as political chaos or an inability to pay international debts—within an independent Latin American nation warrant any action.

In effect, the so-called Roosevelt Corollary to the Monroe Doctrine allowed the United States to protect its economic interests in the region and to maintain U.S. sovereignty over the Panama Canal, considered by the government of the United States as the vital lifeline of its own economy. Through the government's support of financial assistance by private banks to Latin American nations, the United States also undermined its economic competitors in the region and helped U.S.-based businesses to maintain their monopolies over Latin American resources. The actions and policies of "dollar diplomacy," as it was known, brought about the occupation of Cuba in 1906; occupation of Haiti in 1914; occupation of the port of Veracruz, Mexico, in 1914; and occupation of the Dominican Republic in 1916. By the 1920s, the United States had established protectorates in Cuba, Panama, Nicaragua, Haiti, and the Dominican Republic.

In the aftermath of World War I, however, the Latin American policy of the United States underwent a shift, partially as a result of Wilson's own anti-imperialist pronouncements, partially under the pressure of labor and liberal groups in the United States that criticized U.S. actions in the western hemisphere as outmoded capitalist colonialism. Global war, it was hoped, had ended with the Great War, and the League of Nations (without the participation of the United

States) would see to it that international disputes were peaceably settled. The threat of European intervention in Latin America had all but disappeared; the European countries had neither the will nor the finances to extend their political influence across the Atlantic Ocean and were quite content to allow the United States to look after their citizens and their interests in the region should they be threatened. In its essence, the Monroe Doctrine had prevailed.

The Washington Conference on Central American Affairs, convened in late 1922, was chaired by Secretary of State Charles Evans Hughes. Out of the conference came 13 treaties signed by the various Central American nations. The treaties promised mutual disarmament, free trade, and the study and implementation of new educational and social welfare programs. In addition, a Central American Tribunal was established for the peaceful resolution of judicial disputes; those disputes not resolved were to be submitted to commissions of inquiry. By signing the Treaty of Peace and Amity on February 7, 1923, the nations of Central America promised not to intervene in the civil wars of neighboring countries, not to support or encourage the overthrow of neighboring governments, and to adhere to the principle of single-term presidencies—a policy generally but naively expected to end dictatorship.

The first test of the Washington treaties came in the spring of 1923, when a revolution occurred in Honduras, carried out by a defeated presidential candidate. The United States broke off relations with the usurping government, sent a small battle fleet to the Honduran coasts, landed the marines, and convened a conference of the other four Central American republics to decide on a provisional government. In March 1924, after the new government was installed, the United States embargoed all arms to the country. Perhaps to the surprise of the negotiators, the agreement held and the provisional government survived.

These new treaties and diplomatic maneuverings blended nicely with the foreign policies of Calvin Coolidge, a president who placed the condition of the federal budget above all other concerns and who felt no enthusiasm whatsoever for the expensive, politically risky policies of foreign intervention and enforcement of the Monroe Doctrine. As an avowed believer in a completely independent private sector, Coolidge also did not support using the military to protect U.S. companies abroad. Building on efforts of the Wilson and Harding administrations, the Coolidge administration carried out new methods of promoting U.S. interests in Latin America by allying with and supporting democratically elected local presidents. In the Dominican Republic, U.S. Marines trained and armed local police and military forces to defend landowners and factory owners against insurgency. After the election of Horacio Vásquez in 1924, the United States finally withdrew its military from the Dominican Republic.

NICARAGUA

The problem of Nicaragua remained. Since 1856, when a Sacramento newspaper editor named William Walker arrived with 58 men, in league with Nicaragua's own Liberal party, to conquer the country and turn it into a U.S. colony, the United States had been more or less directly involved in Nicaraguan affairs. In 1909, the administration of President William H. Taft had managed to force the resignation of the Liberal president José Santos Zelaya, who had antagonized the United States by stirring up trouble in neighboring republics and refusing to allow the U.S. Navy to build a base in the Gulf of Fonseca. (Even worse, in the opinion of the United States, Zelaya had threatened to allow Japan or Great Britain to build a second transoceanic canal across southern Nicaragua—direct competition for the Panama Canal.)

Adolfo Díaz, a Nicaraguan employee of a U.S. mining company, was installed as the country's president. In 1912, when a revolution occurred, the Taft administration came to the aide of President Díaz with eight warships and 2,000 marines; after putting down the revolt Díaz was elected to a second, unconstitutional term. In 1914, in exchange for $3 million to pay off its debt, the Díaz government agreed in the Bryan-Chamorro Treaty to grant the United States exclusive rights to build the Nicaraguan canal, the lease of two strategic islands in the Caribbean, and the right to build the navy base in the Gulf of Fonseca. With the support of a 100-strong legation of guards composed of U.S. Marines, U.S. ministers had turned the country into a virtual colony, writing the budget, arranging loans directly from the treasuries of U.S. banks, and extending U.S. control over the collection of import and export duties that were earmarked for the repayment of the country's debt. Meanwhile, Nicaragua remained a very poor nation with inadequate roads and railroads, few schools, and a weak domestic economy that relied on a single export: coffee.

The stated policy of the U.S. government was to establish a legitimate two-party political system that would end the longstanding civil conflict in Nicaragua and bring about a stable and friendly Central American republic. The unstated policy was to establish a two-party political system, on terms and conditions set by the United States, for the benefit of U.S. strategic and economic interests in the rest of Central America. By the early 1920s, the leaders of Nicaragua were in accord with these goals. Under the pressure of tremendous foreign debts and economic stagnation, they agreed to a treaty in 1923 which called for the establishment of a military force intended to keep the political peace under the training and direction of a U.S. officer. The election of a bipartisan ticket in 1924—Conservative Carlos Solórzano as president and Liberal Juan Bautista Sacasa as vice president—seemed to bring the goal of national peace close to achievement. The new government, recognized by the United States, was inaugurated in February 1925.

In the spring of 1925, the Nicaraguan Assembly passed a law officially creating the Guardia Nacional. The United States then sent Major Calvin Carter, a retired U.S. Army officer, to train the first 200 recruits, while U.S. occupying forces prepared to depart. In August 1925, the legation guard sailed away from Nicaragua. For a very brief time, and after 13 years, the United States had no military presence in the country.

The respite from civil war proved brief; the Nicaraguan government still suffered from mischievous and determined opponents. In October, a Conservative opponent of the regime, Emiliano Chamorro, who had signed the Washington treaties in 1923 for Nicaragua, mustered the support of like-minded Nicaraguan officers as well as Adolfo Díaz and delivered an ultimatum: Solórzano must fire the Liberals from his cabinet and government and appoint him, Chamorro, as the new minister of war. A brief confrontation took place between Chamorro's supporters and the Guardia Nacional, which Major Carter's force lost. Solórzano gave in, and Chamorro was given his post. As minister of war, he then insisted on strengthening the Guardia Nacional, which would serve as a personal police force to ensure that he remained in power.

In January 1926, Chamorro forced both Solórzano and Vice President Sacasa into exile and demanded that the Nicaraguan Congress appoint him president. Citing violation of Article II of the Washington treaties, the United States—as well

U.S. Marines relax during the
Nicaragua intervention of 1926.
(National Archives)

as Costa Rica, Honduras, El Salvador, and Guatemala—refused to extend diplomatic recognition to Chamorro's regime and also announced that it would no longer support the Guardia, still under the direction of Major Carter, if it continued to be used for political ends.

Sacasa fled to Mexico, where he prepared his own revolutionary army after an unsuccessful appeal for direct intervention in the conflict by the United States. The Coolidge administration decreed an embargo on arms to Nicaragua and asked Mexico to do the same, a request that was refused (by this time, Mexico was openly supporting Sacasa and providing a base for his army). In May 1926, a small Liberal force landed at the port of Bluefields but was defeated by a detachment of U.S. Marines and the Guardia Nacional, fighting in the service of Chamorro. Another group of rebels sabotaged railroad lines in Chinandega province, while a force led by Anastasio Somoza García attacked in the north.

Another provisional government was set up, a new Congress convened, and Adolfo Díaz pronounced president of Nicaragua. In the meantime, the United States pulled its available levers—foremost being the stream of taxes and tariffs passing through the Nicaraguan Customs Department under the supervision of U.S. officials. The United States chose not to cut off this crucial revenue from the Nicaraguan regime. Although fighting the Liberal revolt was proving costly to the near-bankrupt Nicaraguan government, the United States did not want to force the Conservatives completely out of power and bring about the return of a Liberal government via revolution. In the meantime, the exiled Nicaraguan vice-president, Sacasa, had enlisted the help of President Plutarco Elías Calles of Mexico, who had greatly angered the United States by applying Article 27 of the 1917 Mexican Constitution, which nationalized underground mineral rights. In December 1926, Sacasa landed in Puerto Cabezas and proclaimed himself the legitimate president of Nicaragua.

In a message to Congress on January 10, 1927, President Coolidge announced that arms were being shipped to support the Nicaraguan rebels from ports in Mexico. In response to this action—and claiming as justification the necessary protection of U.S. citizens and business interests—the president allowed Díaz to purchase U.S. arms. Washington had also granted Díaz's request for a return of the marines to Managua. The United States fought the usurping Sacasa government in Puerto Cabezas with aerial bombardment of Liberal troops in the town of Chinandega and by the occupation of Chinandega, León, Matagalpa, and Puerto Cabezas. Liberal positions were overrun and Liberal troops were disarmed.

The fighting prompted the U.S. government to send Henry L. Stimson as the personal representative of Calvin Coolidge to Nicaragua in April 1927 in order to arrange a truce. Upon arriving, Stimson made it clear to the Liberals that the United States would not allow Díaz to be overthrown and proposed that a truce be observed until the scheduled election of 1928, which would be supervised by the United States. Conditions would include total disarmament of all the factions within the country, the arms to be placed in the custody of the United States; a general amnesty; and the establishment of another U.S. Marines–trained national guard. With the promised support of the United

States, and thus feeling confident of eventual victory, the government of Adolfo Díaz offered to allow a few Liberal members into the presidential cabinet.

On May 4, Stimson met with José María Moncada, the leader of the Liberal forces, in the town of Tipitapa. Moncada accepted the terms laid out by the presidential envoy, in exchange for a U.S. guarantee of a supervised election in 1928. The Tipitapa agreement was concluded, and Nicaraguan fighters began turning over their rifles, ammunition, and machine guns. Moncada ordered his troops to surrender their arms, and Henry Stimson returned to the United States. He had made the United States once again the dominant yet unelected partner in the Nicaraguan government, a partner to be favored and cultivated by all factions within the country.

With the cooperation of all factions within Nicaragua, the Peace of Tipitapa might have begun an era of civil peace and bipartisan government. The United States certainly wanted it so. The Coolidge and Hoover administrations saw the peace as a test of U.S. influence and sovereignty in Central America, which held an economic lifeline in the form of the Panama Canal, and as an important ingredient in keeping the dangerously independent and left-leaning tendencies of the government of Mexico in check.

A TROUBLESOME BANDIT

Not everyone within Nicaragua accepted the Peace of Tipitapa, however. One of the Liberal opposition leaders, Augusto C. Sandino García, a general in Moncado's service, refused to go along with the agreement or surrender his arms and troops. Sandino brought 150 of his followers north and began resistance to the Nicaraguan government as well as to the U.S. Marines from the mountains of Jinotega province. Sandino enjoyed the support of many Nicaraguan peasants as well as distant liberals in the United States, notably Oswald Garrison Villard and the editors of *The Nation,* who enthusiastically hailed his proclaimed goal of uniting all of the Central American republics and defeating once and for all U.S. imperialism.

At first, the government of the United States considered Sandino merely a troublesome bandit who could be easily contained in northern Nicaragua. This opinion held until July 16, 1927, when Sandino launched an all-out assault on the Guardia Nacional station in Ocotal. The next day, U.S. bombers attacked Sandino's troops and the city. After this defeat, Sandino retreated to a base at El Chipote, in the northern mountains, while the Guardia Nacional, commanded by U.S. officers, moved into the region. U.S. Marines and bombers took part in another fight at the town of Telpaneca against Sandino's lieutenant, Carlos Salgado. Soon after this defeat, Sandino abandoned El Chipote and began a guerrilla campaign.

In November 1928, a presidential election brought a peaceful change of government, the first in Nicaragua's history, although civilians as well as U.S. marines were killed during the voting. The winner was Moncada, the Liberal candidate. Sandino, meanwhile, became an anti-imperialist hero in Central America as well as in the United States, where rallies took place in support of his campaign against the U.S. Marines. Senator William Borah of Idaho publicly opposed U.S. military intervention in Latin America as did the journalist Carlton Beals, who relayed an influential interview of Sandino for *The Nation.*

Sandino spent a year recruiting in Mexico, then attacked again in 1930. The Guardia Nacional, under the leadership of Captain Lewis B. "Chesty" Puller, defeated him. In 1931, Secretary of State Stimson announced that the United States would withdraw its forces after the 1932 election, which was won by Sacasa. After the U.S. troops left, Sandino had agreed to stop the revolt. But he was assassinated in February 21, 1934, after a meeting with Sacasa. The murder squad was acting on the orders of Colonel Anastasio Somoza, the leader of President Juan Sacasa's Guardia Nacional, who would have his turn as Nicaragua's president beginning in 1936.

MEXICO

Even closer to the United States lay Mexico, a nation that troubled U.S. politicians with its instability as well as its nationalism. The business of Mexico, in the early 20th century, was revolution, and the chronically unsettled condition of the Mexican state posed a serious threat to U.S. entrepreneurs who had claims on Mexican oil and natural resources. The tradition of military trouble between Mexico and the United States went back to the Mexican-American War and the 1848 Treaty of Guadalupe Hidalgo, in which Mexico surrendered a huge swath of western land that later became Texas, California, Utah, Arizona, New Mexico, and parts of Wyoming and Colorado. Through the late 19th and early 20th centuries, the United States had asserted its right to intervene directly in Mexican affairs, with troops if necessary, whenever it saw its interests, property, or citizens threatened.

Since the outbreak of revolution and civil war in Mexico in 1910, U.S. troops had appeared twice on Mexican soil, once at the port of Veracruz and once in the Rio Grande country in hot pursuit of Pancho Villa, a troublesome revolutionary chief who staged a cross-border raid into New Mexico in 1916. Article 27 of the Mexican constitution, which went into effect in May 1917, gave the state ultimate sovereignty over land and natural resources and thus oil and mineral rights held by foreigners. The Mexican government also gave itself the right to review any contracts made with foreign companies for the surrender of land, water, or mineral rights since 1876. Only Mexican citizens or corporations had the right to exploit natural resources—others must apply for a government concession and obey any decisions handed down by Mexican courts or laws promulgated by Mexico's legislatures. As if to underline Article 27 and the assertion of Mexico's claims to its own property, export taxes on petroleum were raised in the same year the Constitution was passed. As if to express its displeasure, the United States government encouraged a rebellion in the oil country and sent four warships to patrol the Mexican coast in the vicinity of Veracruz and to threaten an invasion, an act that persuaded Mexico's President Venustiano Carranza not to enforce, for the time being, the language of Article 27.

Warren Harding, elected three years later with the support of big business, and more particularly by private oil interests, saw a special duty to support and assist U.S. companies operating in foreign lands. Although he needed little encouragement to side with big oil operators in their conflicts with the Mexican government, Harding received encouragement anyway from the Oil Producer's Association (chaired by Edward Doheny) and other lobbying groups and manufacturers' associations. Perceiving that Mexico remained an unstable and unfriendly state, the lobbyists raised alarms over the enforcement of Article 27 and a nationalistic Mexican government that was prepared, they were sure, to relieve private U.S. corporations of their lands and rights. The issue was important to both countries. For Mexico, oil revenues represented one-third of the country's entire national budget; during World War I, 95 percent of U.S. oil imports, crucial for this first petroleum-fueled war, arrived from Mexican ports.

In the meantime, U.S. oil companies were refusing to exchange their titles to land and minerals for Mexican government concessions. Secretary of the Interior Albert Fall, of future Teapot Dome notoriety, demanded that Mexico nullify Article 27 and in the meantime successfully pressured the Harding administration not to recognize the government of President Alvaro Obregón, who was elected in 1920 after the assassination of President Carranza. Obregón knew that to keep his own presidency, he must satisfy nationalist sentiment by standing up to the United States and defying the demands of its administration and oil businesses. At the same time, he also realized that his nearly bankrupt and debt-laden country depended on oil export revenues for its economic survival.

POSITIVE ACTS

In 1921, the Supreme Court of Mexico allowed both sides an important loophole through which to escape the standoff. Upon hearing a plea by a U.S. company against Article 27, the court declared that the land under control of foreign interests should remain in private hands if the owners could prove they had made "positive acts," such as digging or drilling, that were intended to develop it. Any lands where such a positive act was lacking, and any lands sold or conceded after the passing of Article 27 in 1917, remained subject to seizure in the name of the people of Mexico.

A judicial decision, liable as it was to legislative challenge and legalistic maneuvering, did not yet convince U.S. oil interests that Mexico was subservient to their interests, nor did it persuade the Harding administration to recognize Obregón's government. In June 1922, by the de la Huerta-Lamont Agreement, Mexico arranged repayment of an outstanding $500 million debt; still no recognition came. Fearing U.S. support of a rebellion against it, the Mexican government began new negotiations to settle the question in summer of 1923. By the Bucareli Agreements signed in Mexico City, Mexico agreed to abide by the "positive acts" decision and the United States agreed to formally recognize the Obregón administration. Mexico recognized claims made against it since 1868, and a commission was established to handle claims of U.S. citizens for damages suffered during the Mexican revolution. Having finally satisfied the U.S. government—now under the fervently probusiness Calvin Coolidge administration—the Bucareli Agreements drew the ire of Mexican nationalists, who staged a revolt late in 1923 that Obregón put down with arms bought from the United States. To reassert his independence from the United States, Obregón then announced a formal diplomatic recognition on Mexico's part—of the Soviet Union.

On succeeding Obregón in 1924, President Plutarco Elías Calles soon antagonized the U.S. ambassador, James Sheffield, by refusing to make promises or assurances regarding American interests beyond what was already written into the Bucareli Agreements. Sheffield then delivered an angry pronouncement that seemed to threaten more problems over the issue of U.S. property in Calles's country. In the meantime, oil production in Mexico was falling, raising suspicions in the Calles administration that U.S. companies were deliberately reducing their output in order to harm the Mexican economy. Calles responded by proposing a law, duly passed by the legislature of Mexico, asking foreign oil companies to formally apply for legal confirmation of their property rights, based on demonstrating the necessary "positive acts." In any case, the concessions would be granted for a term of 50 years and no more.

This action greatly upset U.S. oil companies, which encouraged further hostile statements and action on the part of the Coolidge administration. The State Department threatened an invasion, while Calles made the defiant gesture of supporting the Nicaraguan rebels fighting their own U.S.-sanctioned government. By this time, however, the Teapot Dome scandal had spent about two full years in the headlines and editorial pages of U.S. newspapers, and few voters or lawmakers, Republican or Democrat, felt much enthusiasm for action, especially military action, designed to benefit private oil companies.

The spring of 1926 brought fresh arguments between the two nations over the nationalization of church property, and the expulsion of foreign clergy, by the Mexican government, which represented a revolution against the church-supported landowners and dictators of the past. Problems also arose over the enforcement of terms of the 1917 constitution, which declared that all clergy had to be native-born, that the church was forbidden to own land, and that political activity of any kind on the part of religious officials was illegal. Catholic schools were closed; Spanish and Irish priests were deported. In response, the U.S. Department of State rattled sabers by declaring to church councils that U.S. church property in Mexico should enjoy exactly the same rights and protections as U.S.–owned oil wells and goldbearing mountainsides.

On January 25, 1927, the U.S. Senate resolved unanimously that differences with Mexico be settled by arbitration. President Coolidge recalled the prointerventionist ambassador James R. Sheffield and appointed Dwight Morrow as Sheffield's replacement. Although he was a partner in the J. P. Morgan banking firm, and thus highly suspect among Mexicans as a lackey of U.S. business interests, Morrow showed skillful diplomacy as well as tact. His pronouncements supported a reasonable compromise between the two countries and an outcome to be ultimately decided in the sovereign courts of Mexico. Morrow's popularity in Mexico increased when he brought along entertainer and humorist Will Rogers, as well as aviation hero Charles Lindbergh, who was fresh from his solo flight across the Atlantic and who was Morrow's future son-in-law, for goodwill tours. In 1928, by the Calles-Morrow compromise, U.S. firms were allowed to retain property purchased before the 1917 constitution and required to sign leases for property bought afterwards (the 50-year limit on such leases was ended). The agreement remained in effect for 10 years, until General Lázaro Cárdenas nationalized all foreign oil properties. For a time, the era of big-stick economic diplomacy and military intervention had come to a peaceful end in Mexico.

CHRONICLE OF EVENTS

1926

January 1: A grandstand collapses at the Tournament of Roses parade in Pasadena, California, killing several people.

January 14: The United States signs a treaty of extradition with Cuba.

January 23: Eugene O'Neill's *The Great God Brown,* starring William Harrigan, opens at the Greenwich Village Theater in New York. Actors in the play wear symbolic masks.

January 27: By a vote of 76 to 17, the Senate adopts a resolution allowing the United States to join the Permanent Court of International Justice, a court established by the League of Nations. Fearing that the Court threatens U.S. sovereignty, the United States will not join as a permanent member, but will participate in proceedings; Charles Evans Hughes acts as the first U.S. representative at the Permanent Court of Arbitration at The Hague, in the Netherlands.

February 9: The Atlanta Board of Education bans the teaching of evolution in the city's public schools.

February 26: President Coolidge signs the Revenue Act, which reduces federal income taxes, surtaxes, excise taxes, and inheritance taxes.

March 7: The first two-way radio conversation takes place between London and New York, in a demonstration organized by AT&T, RCA, and the British General Post Office.

April: The Book-of-the-Month Club is organized, starting a new trend in bookselling via mail subscription. The club has more than 40,000 members by the end of the year.

April 11: Horticulturalist Luther Burbank dies in Santa Rosa, California, at the age of 77.

April 19: John C. Miles of Nova Scotia wins the Boston Marathon with a time of 2 hours, 25 minutes, 40.25 seconds.

April 29: The United States and France sign an agreement allowing France to repay $4.025 billion in wartime loans at 1.6 percent interest over the next 62 years.

May 5: Sinclair Lewis refuses to accept the Pulitzer Prize awarded on May 3 for his novel *Arrowsmith.*

A marine officer supervises prisoners in a Nicaraguan prison workshop. *(National Archives/Department of Defense)*

May 9: Flying a three-engine Fokker plane, Rear Admiral Richard Byrd and Floyd Bennett become the first aviators to successfully reach the North Pole. The flight, lasting 15 hours and 30 minutes and covering 1,545 miles, begins and ends in Spitsbergen, Norway.

May 10: The U.S. Marines, under Rear Admiral Julian Latimer, begin landing in Nicaragua to settle civil war between the Nicaraguan government and anti-government rebels led by General Augusto Sandino. The marines will remain in Nicaragua until 1933.

May 18: Evangelist Aimee Semple McPherson, founder of the International Church of the Foursquare Gospel and the Angelus Temple in Los Angeles, disappears from a public beach. She will reappear in Mexico in the next month, having run off with a radio operator.

May 20: President Coolidge signs the Civil Aviation Act, creating a Bureau of Air Commerce to license aircraft and pilots.

May 25: By the Public Buildings Act, the government authorizes a $165 million expenditure on new federal office buildings.

May 31: A Sesquicentennial Exhibition opens in Philadelphia, to run through November 30.

Eyewitness Testimony

Canada

Here was a young man who knew the surly savagery of the trenches. Who was full brother to every man who had worn khaki. He was a sporting Prince, a steeplechase rider, a lover of boxing, and withal as modest as a university freshman. . . . Is it any wonder that men and women alike cheered this gay, blithe Personage without a surname, and cried God bless the Prince of Wales? A thousand years of tradition were behind him, an aeon of aristocracy, yet in his manner he was like those cheery subalterns who had marched away from this city by the hundreds and thousands.

Canadian writer J. E. Middleton, describing a visit by the Prince of Wales to Toronto in 1919, and quoted in West, Toronto *(1967), p. 234.*

The smuggling of silks, jewelry, tobacco, and other luxuries into Canada from the United States, combined with the shipping of bootleg liquor from Canada into the United States has become an "industry" of such huge proportions, with Montreal and New York City as its pivotal points, that a committee of inquiry of nine members of the House of Commons is investigating charges of neglect of duty made against the Canadian Department of Customs and Excise. Two hundred million dollars' worth of merchandise is said to be smuggled into Canada annually and the Canadian Treasury to be defrauded of revenue amounting to about $30,000,000 year in and year out. This charge was made in the Canadian House of Commons by Hon. H. H. Stevens, Conservative member from Vancouver, and we learn from the press that, as a result, the whole tremendous problem of guarding 3,000 miles of international boundary against smugglers is being studied by the committee of inquiry.

From an editorial, "Canada's Colossal Smuggling 'Industry,'" in The Literary Digest, *May 29, 1926, p. 16.*

With thousands of thirsty U.S. citizens poised expectant along the U.S.–Ontario border, the Ontario Liquor Commission last week announced that it might be another fortnight before liquor sales begin in the Province. Legally, however, Ontario last Monday became wet, added [sic] a new aspect to the U.S. liquor question.

The Ontario Law. Alcoholic liquors of all kinds may be purchased in any amount. They may be purchased at government stores, in government packages. They cannot be re-sold (under a jail-sentence penalty). Liquor can be bought only with permits; consumed only in the consumer's residence or in hotels.

Permits. Citizens' permits cost $2, require 30 days' residence. Tourists' and sojourners' permits also cost $2, require no residence, must be renewed monthly at $2 per renewal. Ontario has printed a million blank permits, in twelve months plans to sell them all. Income: $2,000,000.

Residence. The word "residence" is liberally interpreted. Ontario hotels, boarding-houses, stores, now advertise: "Welcome, visitors. Your room is your residence." Tents are believed to class as residences; tent-cities are planned in which tourists, residing, may legally drink.

Bootleggers. Many a Canadian 'legger is expected to move south to the U.S. The new law makes him superfluous, and even first offenses carry six months' sentence, no fine option, repeated offenses carry long sentences. U.S. 'leggers will thus increase.

Prices. The Government Liquor Commission will establish prices. Forecast: Scotch $7; Canadian whiskey $5; beer (case) $2. Beer will be sold at cost; wines and whiskeys at a profit.

From "Prohibition—Over the Lake," unsigned item in Time *magazine, May 23, 1927, p. 10.*

. . . a new sectionalism had arisen in Dominion affairs, and the class consciousness of the western farmer became a vital factor in Canadian politics.

This seething among the discontented farmers was accompanied by a similar wave of discontent and class consciousness in the ranks of the industrial workers of the Dominion. The war had stimulated a great development in the iron and steel industry and in the production of chemicals, textiles, flour, paper and other products, and the industrial worker had benefited greatly by the steady rise in wages and by the general war prosperity. In the years of reconstruction, however, he began to complain of the rising cost of living and the steady cutting of wages; stimulated somewhat by the revolutionary ideas liberated everywhere by the war, the producer began to demand a new social order and a larger share of the wealth which his labor created.

Review of postwar labor relations in Canadian industry, in Wittke, A History of Canada *(1928), p. 329.*

The transfer of control over Canadian foreign policy from London to Ottawa had not been completed when I arrived in the department in September 1928, but it was well under way. The substance of independence for Canada within the Commonwealth had been won, but some colonial forms and legalities remained; indeed, one or two remain by our own choice to this day. While public opinion generally approved national control over foreign relations—which was, in fact, inevitable with the transformation of empire to commonwealth—there remained an "imperial" minority which watched the change with indignant reluctance and opposed some of its manifestations and implications . . . we achieved our political independence, our sovereignty, precisely at a time when, demonstrably, sovereignty and independence gave no assurance of security or of progress. We had to learn that the aspirations of independence often had to be reconciled with the necessities of interdependence.

Canadian prime minister Lester B. Pearson, recalling Canada's break from the British Commonwealth as he was entering the country's foreign service in the late 1920s, in Pearson, Mike: The Memoirs of The Right Honourable Lester B. Pearson (1972), pp. 64–65.

Latin America and the Caribbean

To Belgium's Congo, to Germany's Belgium, to England's India and Egypt, the United States has added a perfect miniature in Haiti. Five years of violence in that Negro republic of the Caribbean, without sanction of international law or any law other than force, is now succeeded by an era in which the military authorities are attempting to hush up what has been done. The history of the American invasion of Haiti is only additional evidence that the United States is among those Powers in whose international dealings democracy and freedom are mere words, and human lives negligible in face of racial snobbery, political chicanery, and money.

Herbert J. Seligmann, "The Conquest of Haiti," in The Nation, July 10, 1920, p. 35.

We are not, we do not want to be any longer, we could not be Pan Americanists. The United States is to be feared because it is great, rich, and enterprising. What concerns us is to find out whether there is a possibility of balancing its power to the extent necessary to save our political independence and the sovereignty of our countries.

Argentinian sociologist José Ingenieros, from a speech delivered in Buenos Aires in 1922, quoted in Whitaker, The Western Hemisphere Idea: Its Rise and Decline (1954), p. 129.

You, my fellow countrymen of the United States, know full well how sincerely we desire the independence, the unimpaired sovereignty and political integrity and the constantly increasing prosperity of the peoples of Latin America. We have our domestic problems incident to the expanding life of a free people, but there is no imperialistic sentiment among us to cast even a shadow across the pathway of our progress. We covet no territory; we seek no conquest; the liberty we cherish for ourselves we desire for others; and we assert no rights for ourselves that we do not accord to others. We sincerely desire to see throughout this hemisphere an abiding peace, the reign of justice and the diffusion of the blessings of a beneficent cooperation.

Secretary of States Charles Evans Hughes, speech to U.S. citizens in Rio de Janeiro in September 1922, as quoted in Bemis, The Latin American Policy of the United States (1943), p. 203.

. . . the Governments of the Contracting Parties will not recognize any other Government which may come into power in any of the five Republics through a *coup d'etat* or a revolution against a recognized Government, so long as the freely elected representatives of the people thereof have not constitutionally reorganized the country. And even in such a case they obligate themselves not to acknowledge the recognition if any of the persons elected as President, Vice-President or Chief of State designate should fall under any of the following heads:

(1) If he should be the leader or one of the leaders of a *coup d'etat* or revolution, or through blood relationship of marriage, be an ascendant or descendant or brother of such leader or leaders.

(2) If he should have been a Secretary of State or should have held some high military command during the accomplishment of the *coup d'etat,* the revolution, or while the election was being carried on, or if he should have held this office or command within the six months preceding the *coup d'etat,* revolution, or the election.

Clauses written in an attempt to discourage violent revolution in Central America, and agreed to by the five Central American nations and the United States, in the General Treaty of Peace and Amity of October 1922, quoted in Munro, The U.S. and the Caribbean Area (1934), pp. 211–212.

. . . the Monroe Doctrine is not a policy of aggression; it is a policy of self-defense. . . . *Second,* as the policy embodied in the Monroe Doctrine is distinctively the policy of the United States, the Government of the United States reserves to itself its definition, interpretation and application.... *Third,* the policy of the Monroe Doctrine does not infringe upon the independence and sovereignty of other American states.... *Fourth,* so far as the region of the Caribbean Sea is concerned it may be said that if we had no Monroe Doctrine we should have to create one.... Our interest does not lie in controlling foreign peoples; that would be a policy of mischief and disaster. Our interest is in having prosperous, peaceful and law abiding neighbors with whom we can cooperate to mutual advantage.

Secretary of State Charles Evans Hughes, describing the Harding administration's policies toward Latin America in a speech to the American Bar Association in Minneapolis on August 30, 1923, quoted in Stuart, Latin America and the United States *(1938), pp. 66–67.*

Nicaragua seems to be making progress in the art of staging its revolutions. One was brought to a successful conclusion last October so expeditiously that there was not even time to call in the marines, and now the Department of State has been advised that "while the Nicaraguan Congress refused to accept the resignation of President Solorzano, who won a clear-cut victory last fall in the first free election in Nicaragua in thirty-five years, he has been granted a leave of absence, and General Emiliano Chamorro has assumed the duties of the Presidency." No bloodshed; no revolution in the ordinary sense of the term; no fuss.

From "Our Warning to Nicaragua," in The Literary Digest, *February 13, 1926, p. 12.*

Under international law Washington has no more right to say that it will break relations with Nicaragua if a certain man is made President than Nicaragua would have to declare that should President Coolidge not resign, she will have nothing to do with the United States.

From an editorial on Nicaraguan affairs in The Brooklyn Eagle, *quoted in "Our Warning to Nicaragua," in* The Literary Digest, *February 13, 1926, p. 12.*

For many years numerous Americans have been living in Nicaragua, developing its industries and carrying on business. At the present time there are large investments in lumbering, mining, coffee growing, banana culture, shipping, and also in general mercantile and other collateral business.

In addition to these industries now in existence, the Government of Nicaragua, by a treaty entered into

on the 5th day of August, 1914, granted in perpetuity to the United States the exclusive proprietary rights necessary and convenient for the construction, operation, and maintenance of an oceanic canal....

There is no question that if the revolution continues American investments and business interests in Nicaragua will be very seriously affected, if not destroyed.

Manifestly the relation of this Government to the Nicaraguan situation and its policy in the existing emergency, are determined by the facts which I have described. The proprietary rights of the United States in the Nicaraguan canal route, with the necessary implications growing out of it affecting the Panama Canal, together with the obligations flowing from the investments of all classes of our citizens in Nicaragua, place us in a position of peculiar responsibility. I am sure it is not the desire of the United States to intervene in the internal affairs of Nicaragua or of any other Central American republic. Nevertheless it must be said that we have a very definite and special interest in the maintenance of order and good government in Nicaragua at the present time, and that the stability, prosperity, and independence of all Central American countries can never be a matter of indifference to us. The United States can not, therefore, fail to view with deep concern any serious threat to stability and constitutional government in Nicaragua tending toward anarchy and jeopardizing American interests, especially if such state of affairs is contributed to or brought about by outside influences or by any foreign power.

Calvin Coolidge, message to the U.S. Congress concerning the ongoing revolution in Nicaragua, January 10, 1927, from Documents of American History *(1958), p. 389.*

Dispatches from Washington represent Mr. Coolidge as being profoundly impressed by a talk he has had with Senator Edge of New Jersey, who has just returned from the Panama Canal. Senator Edge reports that in the short space of from eight to ten years the Panama Canal will be crowded to capacity if traffic continues to increase as it has in the past few years, and that in order to handle traffic it will be necessary either to enlarge this canal or to undertake the construction of a new one on the Nicaragua route. The eagerness with which Mr. Coolidge is reported to have listened to this is suspicious. He is not given to sudden or passionate enthusiasm, and it is also to be remembered that one of the fifty-seven varieties of excuses he gave for our utterly mistaken intervention in Nicaragua was that we had to protect the concession for a canal which we obtained through the Bryan-Chamorro Treaty of 1916, for which concession we paid $3,000,000 in cash.

"The Nicaragua Canal Bobs Up Once More," unsigned editorial in The Nation, *April 13, 1927, p. 386.*

I am authorized to say that the President of the United States intends to accept the request of the Nicaraguan Government to supervise the election of 1928; that the retention of President Díaz during the remainder of his term is regarded as essential to that plan and will be insisted upon; that a general disarmament of the country is also regarded as necessary for the proper and successful conduct of such election; and that the forces of the United States will be authorized to accept the custody of the arms of those willing to lay them down including the government, and to disarm forcibly those who will not do so.

Letter delivered by Henry Stimson to General José Maria Moncada at the Tipitapa meeting, May 1927, and quoted in Ferrell, The Presidency of Calvin Coolidge *(1998), p. 135.*

Nicaraguans in smart khaki uniforms and armed with rifles, machine guns and dynamite bombs, lay in ambush on the heights commanding a narrow defile in the Nicaraguan mountains. Soon Captain Richard Livingston, U.S.M.C., commenced to lead through the defile an expeditionary force of 200 U.S. Marines, 200 Nicaraguan National Guardsmen, and 200 pack mules. Purpose: To capture Quilali, the remote war base of the recalcitrant General Augusto Sandino whose men were ambushing the defile. Reason: the Sandino troops have been declared outlaws and bandits. Cause: Sandino and his men were the only Nicaraguan faction which refused to lay down and sell their arms under the terms of national peace enforced in Nicaragua by U.S. Marines.

"Marines Trapped," description of a military operation in Nicaragua, from Time *magazine, January 9, 1928, p. 16.*

General Augusto Sandino (center) and his staff pause en route to Mexico in June 1929, during Sandino's ongoing fight against the U.S.-backed Nicaraguan government. *(National Archives/Department of Defense)*

President Hoover prepares to step ashore during a trip to Latin America, 1928. *(Library of Congress)*

If President Coolidge wants to use the Army and the Navy and the marines and the sailors to purify elections, why does he not go into Philadelphia? [Nicaraguans] are moved by the same things that move us. They love their little children. They love their homes. We would call them hovels, but they are the best they have. We have burned them and destroyed them and killed some of their little children, killed some of their wives, killed some of their women, every one of whom was unarmed and not a single one of whom had ever raised a finger against us.

Senator George Norris, objecting to the use of U.S. military in putting down revolution in Nicaragua in a congressional debate of April 23, 1928, quoted in Beneath the United States *(1998), p. 268.*

The very locality where the progress of these republics has been most slow, where the difficulties of race and climate have been greatest; where the recurrence of domestic violence has most frequently resulted in the failure of duty on the part of the republics themselves and the violation of the rights of life and property accorded by international law to foreigners within their territory, has been in Central America, the narrow isthmus which joins the two Americas, and among the islands which intersperse the Caribbean Sea adjacent to that isthmus. That locality has been the one spot external to our shores which nature has decreed to be most vital to our national safety, not to mention our prosperity.

. . . In the five republics of Central America—Guatemala, Honduras, Salvador, Nicaragua, and Costa Rica—however, we have found an entirely different situation existing from that normally presented under international law and practice. . . . Those countries geographically have for a century been the focus of the greatest difficulties and the most frequent disturbances in their earnest course toward competent maturity in the discharge of their international obligations.

Henry L. Stimson, "The United States and the Other Republics," speech delivered to the Council of Foreign Relations in New York on February 6, 1931.

Three days later we reached Corinto, Nicaragua . . . I had already ascertained that the port was in charge of a National Guard corps under the command of Colonel Bleasdale. I had heard about Bleasdale over the Bluefields—from one if his buddies, he was reputed to be the bravest man in the entire marine corps; he literally ate cold steel and fire, and enjoyed it. Now, when I got back on board boat, the steward told me: "Colonel Bleasdale was on board to ask whether you were among the passengers."

. . . I immediately walked down the gangplank and strolled over beside him, striking up a casual conversation. How long had he been in Nicaragua? . . . Did he like it? . . . Our conversation branched out. Soon he became aware that I was not a casual tourist, but well acquainted with Nicaraguan affairs.

. . . "This is a pretty nasty job we have here," said Bleasdale that night. "We're going to get it in the neck from the American public whether we succeed or fail." And he went into a long argument to justify marine intervention. He dilated upon the trials and tribulations of the Nicaraguans. "We are only trying to help them out," was his clinching argument.

"It seems to me the only ones you are helping out are a bunch of lickspittle politicians," was my retort.

Correspondent Carleton Beals describing an encounter in the Nicaraguan port of Corinto during the U.S. Marines' intervention of 1927, in Banana Gold *(1932), pp. 344–346.*

Mexico

It should be made clear that this Government will continue to support the Government in Mexico only so long as it protects American lives and American rights and complies with its international obligations.

The Government of Mexico is now on trial before the world.

James Sheffield, U.S. ambassador to Mexico, responding to enforcement of Article 17 of the Mexican constitution in the 1920s, quoted in Bryn-Jones, Frank B. Kellogg: A Biography *(1937), p. 176.*

So long as I have anything to do with the Mexican question, no government of Mexico will be recognized, with my consent, which does not first enter into a written agreement promising to protect American citizens and their property rights in Mexico.

Albert B. Fall, Harding administration Secretary of the Interior, around spring 1921, quoted in Meyer and Sherman, The Course of Mexican History *(1979), p. 578.*

I utterly disclaim, as unwarranted . . . a claim on our part to superintend the affairs of our sister republics, to assert an overlordship, to consider the spread of our authority beyond our own domain as the aim of our policy, and to make our power the test of right in this hemisphere.

Secretary of State Charles Evans Hughes, criticizing past U.S. government policy of intervention in Central America, in a 1923 speech entitled "Observations on the Monroe Doctrine," quoted in Beneath the United States *(1998), p. 258.*

. . . Few spectacles could be more demoralizing than that of the ruin of a Republic that half a dozen years ago was eagerly pressing forward in the van of progress—a Republic that was rich and powerful, whose credit stood high in the world's finances. . . .

Certainly there could scarcely be a Central American President who, surveying Mexico as it was under the great Porfirio Diaz and as it is now under the motley collection of bandits who abuse its government, could be blamed if he determined never again to lend countenance to those liberal measures under the guise of which was brought about the ruin of Mexico! The tragedy has been extraordinarily impressive. That so stately a structure could have been brought to earth in so short a time would have been believed possible by no one either to the north or south of Mexico.

There is no denying, moreover, that from the hard-and-fast practical point of view the moral that the fate of Mexico holds out is startling. A premature attempt at moral and intellectual reform in an uneasy-blooded country, peopled mostly by unedu-

cated Indians, is as dangerous as flinging a lighted match into a magazine.

Lament over the state of post-revolutionary Mexico in Koebel, Central American *(1925), p. 164.*

The men in Mexican official life are with few exceptions ignorant of government, of economics, and of finance. . . . International obligations rest very lightly upon them. The courts are notoriously corrupt and government by Presidential decree, from which there is no appeal, is frequently resorted to. . . . In my talks with the President, I have emphasized our desire to help and have offered any assistance he would be willing to accept, particularly along educational and economic lines. The unpopularity of Americans, especially since the Veracruz incident, probably deters him from making use of our help because of its possible political effect except when it concerns the question of borrowing money. Back of it all lies the peculiar psychology of the Latin-Americans, or more properly, Latin-American mind.

Ambassador James Sheffield, April 13, 1925 description of Mexican officialdom in private correspondence, from The Presidency of Calvin Coolidge *(1998), pp. 126–127.*

It should be made clear that this Government will continue to support the Government in Mexico only so long as it protects American lives and American rights and complies with its international obligations.

The Government of Mexico is now on trial before the world. We have the greatest interest in the stability, prosperity, and independence of Mexico. . . . But we cannot countenance violation of her obligations and failure to protect American citizens.

Secretary of State Frank B. Kellogg, summer 1925, quoted in Meyer and Sherman, The Course of Mexican History *(1979), p. 585.*

We are quite sure that the domination of radicalism at Mexico City, crystallized in the persecution of priests and seizures of Church vessels and vestments, will weaken Mexico in the high court of world sentiment. A feeling of respect for her autonomy has been more apparent in the American press and among the people than in the actions of the Government in Washington. That feeling was growing. It can not continue to grow in the face of an adverse psychology created by news of what Christendom is bound to regard as outrages on worship and worshipers. President Calles is on the wrong track. Orderly government needs the Church as much as the Church needs orderly government.

Editorial on the growing anticlericalism and radicalism of the Mexican government in the Brooklyn Eagle, *and quoted in "Mexico Outlawing the Church," in* The Literary Digest, *March 6, 1926, p. 31.*

The protection of the rights of present foreign property holders in Mexico serves only to soften and not to block the blow that Mexico has aimed against foreign exploitation of its resources. The new laws provide for the abandonment, if its courts hold it legal, of majority controls in Mexican companies by foreign interests and for the sale of all properties held by foreign individuals within five years after the death of the present titleholder.

President Calles has made a long step forward in his "Mexico for Mexicans" movement, and barring accidents—they do happen in Mexican politics— within a generation the hold which foreigners, many of them Americans, had gained in Mexican resources will be materially weakened, if not entirely wiped out.

From an article describing the 1926 accords between Mexico and the United States over foreign-held property, in the Jersey City Journal, *quoted in "Our Tiff with Mexico Settled,"* The Literary Digest, *May 1, 1926, p. 16.*

The Mexican government therefore does not deny that the American government is at liberty to intervene for its nationals; but that does not stand in the way of carrying out an agreement under which the alien agrees not to be the party asking for the diplomatic protection of his government. In case of infringement of any international duty such as denial of justice would be, the right of the American government to take with the Mexican government appropriate action to seek atonement for injustice or injury which may have been done to its nationals would stand unimpaired. Under these conditions neither would the American government have failed to protect its nationals nor the Mexican government to comply with its laws.

Mexican foreign minister Saenz, note of October 7, 1926, during dispute over jurisdiction of U.S. nationals in Mexican courts, quoted in Latin America and the United States *(1943), pp. 176–177.*

Is the hand of the Third International clutching at the throat of Mexico? For weeks and months the propaganda has been put out that Mexico and Central America have come under the domination of communistic teachings and that this is the cause of trouble in that part of the world. I venture to assert that the Third International, that Russia, has not one thing to do with Mexico or with Mexican policies. No country on this Western Continent has been more outspoken or vigilant against communism than Mexico. Her labor organization and her President have not left the world in doubt. Mexico has her troubles and her own idea of dealing with them, and her policies, wise or unwise, are of her own making. She alone is responsible for those policies and for their execution. Communism and Russian influence have no more to do with either the origin or execution of those policies than they have to do with the policies of our own Government. The only Communists who ever made any trouble with Mexico went there from the United States and were sent back by the Mexican Government.

William E. Borah, in "Neighbors and Friends: A Plea for Justice to Mexico," in The Nation, *April 13, 1927, p. 393.*

Dwight and Capt. Winslow went over to the plane and brought him back to the grandstand in our open car. Dwight brought him to the President, who welcomed him and gave him the keys of the city. Lindbergh only said, "Thank you" very simply. The throng on the field shouting and screaming with joy was indescribable. As we went to the car our clothes were almost torn off. Dwight, Constance, Lindbergh, General Alvarez, and I were in the car, Burke driving. Ceto and two officers on the running board. Oh! The crowds in the streets on the way to the Embassy! On trees, on telegraph poles, tops of cars, roofs, even the towers of the Cathedral. Flowers and confetti were flung every moment. We took him to the Chancery and to the balcony to wave to the crowd. He had soup and a bath while the Staff had a buffet lunch. We all drank to him in champagne. Then he came out and met all the Staff, telegraphed to his mother, and saw the reporters. We left him sleeping tonight as we went to the University Club dinner for Will Rogers.

Mrs. Dwight Morrow, diary entry describing the arrival of Charles Lindbergh in Mexico City on December 14, 1927, quoted in Ross, The Last Hero *(1964), p. 165.*

9
Worldly Explorations
June 1926–May 1927

World War I having finished, and a new era of radio communication and air transportation having begun, the United States and several other nations undertook new voyages to the unmapped corners of the globe.

For the past century in the United States, exploration signified westward expansion, land, and business. In 1805, after returning from a westward voyage across the full extent of North America, Meriwether Lewis and William Clark reported to President Thomas Jefferson that the hoped-for Northwest Passage, an all-water trading route linking the Atlantic and Pacific Oceans, probably did not exist, at least along the Missouri River route that Jefferson had ordered them to follow. In the next decades, the passage was forgotten in the exploration of western North America, the conquest of the Native Americans, and the acquisition and settlement of territories west of the Mississippi River.

In 1890, with the final defeat of the Lakota Indians of Dakota Territory, the western frontier of the United States was unofficially closed. Yet there was still plenty of dangerous occupation available for explorers seeking out regions as yet unknown to the human race. Most of the territory north of an imaginary line at 66.6 degrees north latitude—the Arctic Circle—had not yet been seen or mapped. What exactly the Arctic contained could only be guessed at, although the Yukon Gold Rush of 1896, and the ongoing prospecting for Alaskan oil, vigorously exercised the imaginations of government officials and the heads of private mining and petroleum corporations. There might be vast undersea oil deposits, or mountain valleys containing gold, silver, or coal. There might be schools of whales, which were still valued for their meat and oil, as well as seal, fox, and marten, all of which bore valuable pelts. Besides simple scientific curiosity, Arctic exploration might satisfy economic and strategic needs. Supported by governments and private scientific societies, British, Scandinavian, Canadian, and American expeditions through the ice-strewn passages north of Canada, Greenland, and Russia became almost commonplace.

The purchase of Alaska in 1867, an act commonly known as "Seward's Folly," gave the United States an important gateway into the Arctic. Justification for the purchase was strategic as well as economic. With the ice-capped island of Greenland, which Secretary of State William Henry Seward also proposed to buy, the United States could control the two oversea approaches into the Arctic—from the North Atlantic and the North Pacific—and easily reach the Arctic's resources through the exploration, charting, occupation, and administration of lands already claimed by British Canada and Russia. Although Greenland would remain under the sovereignty of Denmark, Seward's ideas promoted further government-sponsored exploration of the Arctic until the ill-fated 1884 expedition of Major Adolphus Greely, in which 19 men died of starvation. The government ended its financing, and for 40 years after this disaster, Arctic exploration was underwritten by private interests, carried out by individuals backed by scientific societies and wealthy industrialists.

CANADA AND THE ARCTIC

In the years following Seward's Folly, explorers from the United States pressed into the Alaskan Yukon and north of the Arctic Circle while ignoring the inconvenient geography of the Dominion of Canada. After Great Britain formally ceded its claims to the Arctic to Canada in 1880, the Canadian government also authorized nautical surveys and established new Arctic outposts for the Royal Canadian Mounted Police. Eager to exploit Arctic resources for themselves, Canadians worried about countries claiming sovereignty by virtue of occupation and administration, rather than via discovery. Canada sent its own sea-and-land expeditions northward, including one voyage in 1902 under the command of Captain Joseph Bernier that disputed the possession of a large Arctic territory previously explored by Norwegians.

Realizing that its sovereignty was being challenged by foreign nations, Canada announced a claim to all of the lands lying between its eastern and western coasts, northward as far as the North Pole. In 1903, Canada and the United States made a final attempt to resolve an old dispute over the boundary between Canada's Yukon Territory and Alaska, a dispute that dated to a treaty between Russia and Great Britain in 1825 that vaguely described the unseen Arctic frontier of the Yukon. The disputed region offered strategically located ports and river outposts as well as mining districts suspected of holding deposits of gold, silver, coal, and oil. Instead of negotiating directly with Canada, President Theodore Roosevelt submitted the dispute to an international arbitration commission, which included British representatives friendly to the U.S. The result was a substantial award of territory to the United States.

By the early 1900s, the race for the North Pole was on. Expeditions from European nations—Italy, Norway, Denmark, Germany, and Russia—used as base camps Spitsbergen and Franz Joseph Land, as they were the northernmost points with a dependable supply of food. In 1906, an expedition under the command of Roald Amundsen of Norway crossed the Arctic in the icebreaker *Gjoa*—the first such traverse of the northern passages made entirely by ship. (The use of icebreakers shortened the expensive and dangerous periods in which explorers were forced to use heavy dogsleds to travel on the shifting icepack.) After making eight preliminary expeditions dating back to 1886, Robert Peary of the United States set out in 1908 for the North Pole from Sydney, Nova Scotia, in the steamer *Roosevelt*. Peary was particularly proud that the expedition used only U.S. ships, supplies, and crew (the captain and the crew of the *Roosevelt* were, however, Newfoundlanders).

On April 6, 1909, Peary reached the North Pole with his crew. He returned home safely and eventually overcame Dr. Frederick Cook's claim that he had accomplished the same feat a full year earlier. His lifelong goal reached, Peary left future Arctic voyages to the new breed of explorers—the aviators.

DIRIGIBLES AND AIRPLANES

The airplane and the helium-filled dirigible promised greater range, speed, and mobility for Arctic explorers. Air travel also seemed to lessen the danger of starvation and the trouble of navigating through the Arctic's treacherous pack ice. The first attempt to reach the North Pole through the air took place in 1896, when the Swedish scientist Salomon August Andrée and a crew of two set out from Spitsbergen in the helium-filled balloon *Eagle*. Over the course of a fog-shrouded, 65-hour flight, the *Eagle* reached 82 degrees north latitude before being abandoned by its crew, which wandered over the ice for more than two months before dying of starvation or, as some conjectured, by asphyxiation from the gas of their cook stoves.

By the 1920s, the era of insurmountable dangers had come to an end, and Arctic exploration took on more commercial motivations. A casual measurement of distances across the top of a globe revealed that air routes between many points in North America, Europe, and Asia were shorter across the North Pole than across the oceans. Several private U.S. aviation companies began considering regular flights northward and began planning a network of supply stations for future transarctic routes. The government once again sponsored exploratory flights into the Arctic, and permanent air bases were established at Spitsbergen, Franz Joseph Land, and the coasts of Greenland.

A leading proponent of arctic exploration in the postwar years was General William (Billy) Mitchell, assistant chief of the U.S. Army Air Service. The leader of the U.S. expeditionary air forces in World War I, Mitchell insisted that future air power would make battleships obsolete and that an entirely independent branch of the military was needed for the air service. Mitchell saw control of airspace as the most crucial ingredient in future military conflicts; foreseeing a conflict with Japan, he also sought to establish a Pacific defense perimeter, made up of air bases and supply points, to run from Alaska, along the western coast of the United States and as far south as the Panama Canal. As a start, he asked for government sponsorship of flights to map and establish defensive posts in Alaska, even though poor flying conditions still prevented regular flights there.

In 1920, to demonstrate the capability of aircraft in the Arctic and to study the problems of weather and supply in any future Arctic conflict, Mitchell mapped out a 6,000-mile flight from Long Island, New York, to Nome, Alaska, across both U.S. and Canadian airspace. The expedition was planned with all the precision and thoroughness the Army Air Service could muster. Supplies of food, gasoline, and spare parts were transported to a series of landing points along the route, which crossed the international border at Portal, North Dakota, and proceeded to Edmonton, Alberta; Juneau, Dawson, Fairbanks, and Nome, Alaska. It would be the first peacetime U.S. air expedition in history to cross a foreign country. To avoid any disputes over sovereignty and airspace, the U.S. government made an official application, which was approved by the government of Canada.

Commanded by Captain St. Clair Streett, the flight began on July 15, 1920, and reached Nome 56 hours later. Along the way, the crew photographed previously unknown regions of the Canadian Arctic and proved that a permanent air route to Nome from the eastern United States was feasible.

THE *SHENANDOAH* AND RICHARD BYRD

The success of General Mitchell's New York-to-Nome flight encouraged the U.S. military to plan further expeditions to map the Arctic and to set up new outposts in the still-unexplored regions between northern Alaska and the North Pole. In the early months of the Coolidge administration, the U.S. Navy prepared for the flight of the *Shenandoah,* a dirigible built by the navy in Philadelphia. The expedition was promoted by Secretary of the Navy William Denby, who proposed that the United States claim any new land discovered between Point Barrow (at the northern edge of Alaska) and the North Pole in order to forestall any claim to the same territory by Canada. The *Shenandoah* was to be accompanied by six supply airplanes, a heavy demand on the resources of the navy of that time. As a result of the great costs and risks of the flight, however, the *Shenandoah* expedition was bogged down in the United States Congress after hearings were convened on the mission in December 1923. Considering the projected $180,000 cost of the expedition too high a price to pay, Congress declined to appropriate the necessary funds, and the project had to be shelved. Two years later, in September 1925, the *Shenandoah* was deliberately sent into heavy weather and was lost, an event that provoked General Mitchell into a scathing attack on army and navy commanders, for which he was subsequently court-martialed.

There would be more Arctic exploration, a subject that still drew the close attention of the press, which was in search of peacetime heroes and newsworthy exploits. It also drew generous funding from private sources, flush from "Coolidge prosperity" and the steady rise of the stock market. After the *Shenandoah* mission was scrapped, a former naval reserve officer, Donald MacMillan, announced plans to sail the steamship *Bowdoin* into the Arctic in the summer of 1925 with the backing of the National Geographic Society. At the same time, U.S. Navy Commander Richard Byrd was proposing his own flight over the North Pole in an airplane.

Byrd, who had applied for a place on the *Shenandoah* mission, was one of the most qualified individuals in the military for such a mission. He had served as commander of U.S. naval air forces in Canada during World War I and had made a successful transatlantic dirigible flight in 1921. Byrd wanted to test high-altitude and extreme-cold airplane flight; he wanted to show the feasibility of commercial aviation in the Arctic; and he wanted the fame and the promotion that would come with achieving the first successful flight over the North Pole. Byrd was also convinced that planes would perform better than dirigibles in the Arctic because they could fly higher, giving pilots a wider range of view, and were not as vulnerable to sudden shifts in Arctic winds. To prove it, he asked the navy for equipment: four air-cooled airplane motors to be acquired from a private source, and a two-member crew.

When Secretary of the Navy Curtis Wilbur learned of MacMillan's plans, he proposed that the navy take part by supplying MacMillan with aircraft from the Bureau of Aeronautics. Wilbur also suggested that Byrd and MacMillan combine their expeditions. Inspired by the impertinent General Mitchell, the U.S. government now was anxious to claim undiscovered land on the route to the North Pole and forestall the use of the Arctic by rival nations during any future war. The planned expedition would explore Ellesmere Island, Baffin Island, Labrador, and northern Greenland—a territory inconveniently under the sovereignty of Denmark. Byrd would fly a series of missions from base camps toward the Pole, setting up fuel depots for a final short run. MacMillan was officially placed in command, with Byrd second-in-command and responsible for the expedition's aircraft. The *Bowdoin,* with the trawler *Peary* alongside, set out from the coast of Maine on June 17, 1925.

A Rendezvous in Greenland

MacMillan, Byrd, and the navy had not taken into account the reaction of Canadian officials to the voyage. After learning of MacMillan's plans, and worried over the inclusion of U.S. military equipment, aircraft, and personnel, Canada insisted that the explorer apply for formal permission before leaving the United States. For his part, MacMillan was well aware that U.S. explorers had already been to Ellesmere Island and Axel Heiberg Island, and he fully intended to claim these regions for the United States should he reach them.

MacMillan made no contact with Canadian officials before starting out; the National Geographic Society decided not to apply for a permit on its own as the expedition was not to cross land internationally recognized as Canadian. Whether or not MacMillan would cross territory claimed by Canada, the U.S. State Department announced that it would not respond to Canada's request until MacMillan reported his position. In response to the polite impassivity of the U.S. government and the expedition's leader, the Canadian legislature hurriedly passed the Northwest Territories Act in the same month that the *Bowdoin* and the *Peary* left port. The act required that all explorers seeking to cross territory claimed by Canada file detailed plans and request formal permission to enter Canadian territory, and present a manifest of all aircraft to be used and pilots to be employed. To enforce the new law, Canada sent a ship of its own, the *Arctic* under Commander George Mackenzie, to find MacMillan's ships.

MacMillan arrived at Etah, Greenland, on August 1. In a short time, survey flights over northern Greenland began, as did bad weather, thick fog, and aircraft engine trouble. As the weather worsened in the middle of the month, MacMillan made the decision not to attempt flights over Baffin Island or Labrador. Meanwhile, the State Department, having changed its mind and now desiring to avoid any diplomatic or military confrontation, relayed orders to MacMillan to comply with Canada's requests and make an informal application for the expedition from Commander Mackenzie, who was approaching Etah in the *Arctic.* When Mackenzie reached Etah on August 19, Byrd presented himself to Mackenzie on board the *Arctic,* described flights already made by his pilots, and was informed by the Canadian that a permit would have to be issued. Unaware of the diplomatic maneuvering that had already taken place, Byrd replied with a lie: that a permit had been issued before the expedition had set out. Mackenzie diplomatically stated that he may not have heard of the permit being issued because of radio trouble on his own ship. The *Arctic* then sailed away from Etah and the MacMillan party prepared to return home.

The MacMillan expedition had frustrated Commander Byrd in several ways. He preferred to be in command, not second in command, and he did not agree with MacMillan's decision to scrap the scheduled air exploration from Etah. He did not care for delicate negotiation or diplomatic niceties. He saw himself as an adventurer, standing above the petty concerns of small men in meeting rooms and legislative chambers. After returning to the United States, Byrd immediately began planning a transpolar air expedition of his own.

UNEVENTFUL FLIGHT

The navy granted leave to Byrd and Floyd Bennett, a machinist, while Byrd arranged funding from the National Geographic Society; he also gathered contributions from Edsel Ford and John D. Rockefeller. The Federal War Shipping Board loaned a steamer, the *Chantier,* to bring him north. In their Fokker trimotor airplane, Byrd and Bennett planned to fly north from Spitsbergen to the Pole in May 1926. They would then establish a base at Cape Bridgeman in Greenland, sail to Etah in the *Chantier,* allow the ship to be iced in, and spend the winter there.

In the meantime, Byrd learned that Roald Amundsen was planning a dirigible flight over the pole. In the airship *Norge,* Amundsen crossed the entire Arctic, reaching a remote spot known to explorers as the Pole of Inacessibility, which lies between the North Pole and Alaska at the very center of the Polar ice cap. On learning of Amundsen's flight, Byrd canceled the exploratory phases of his flight and concentrated on the flight over the North Pole. The risky flight attracted great attention in the press, always searching for a good story, a hero to praise or an upstart to knock back down to size. The risks of Byrd's flight were obvious: the cold, fog, and unpredictable storms of the Arctic; the unreliability of magnetic compasses near the Pole; the risks of getting lost and confused over uncharted territory; and the chance of a crash and subsequent slow starvation on the ice.

The flight began May 9, 1926, from King's Bay on Spitsbergen, with Bennett in the pilot's seat and Byrd working as the navigator. The weather was calm; relying solely on his compass and on his sense of direction in this land without landmarks, Byrd headed directly for the Pole. After reaching it, the aviators circled the Pole once and immediately headed back to Spitsbergen. The entire flight took 16 hours and proceeded without incident. Byrd had proved that the airplane was feasible for long-range Arctic flights. In early 1927, Byrd and Bennett were awarded the Congressional Medal of Honor. Byrd was not yet satisfied, and immediately began plans for a transatlantic flight between New York and Paris. Although Byrd would also complete that flight successfully in July 1927, the place of honor in daring long-distance aeronautics that year would go to a civilian, and a very different kind of flier.

Richard Byrd poses with a group of souvenir penguins brought aboard ship during an expedition to the South Pole. An intrepid pioneer of air navigation into the earth's still-uncharted polar ice caps, Byrd actually spent most of his time aboard naval and merchant ships steaming though the North and South Atlantic. *(Archive Photos)*

For barnstormers and stunt fliers such as Lillian Boyer, airplanes were most useful and profitable as a means of entertainment. *(Minnesota Historical Society)*

THE BIRTH OF AIR MAIL

The airplane had changed warfare and expanded scientific exploration, but still did not provide much everyday use to the general public except as a crop duster, an amusement park ride, and a circus spectacle of wing-walkers and stunt fliers. At the close of World War I, 24 aircraft factories were operating in the United States. Nearly all of them were fulfilling military contracts, and most would abruptly close down at the end of the war. The nation's military leaders still did not see the value of planes, as opposed to ships, troops, and artillery, and the government would spend no money supporting the development of the aircraft industry.

Yet as the 1920s progressed and fragile biplanes gave way to sturdier, heavier, and slightly safer and more reliable monoplanes, the aviation industry began to consider the possibilities of regular freight and passenger service. In the spring of 1926, the United States government awarded two Contract Air Mail (CAM) routes to small, private companies. The first such route, designated CAM-1, linked New York and Boston. At four o'clock on the afternoon of April 15, 1926, at Lambert Field in St. Louis, Missouri, the town's leading citizens held a formal inauguration ceremony for CAM-2, the route granted to the firm of Robertson Aircraft to carry the mail between St. Louis and Chicago.

On hand at the ceremony were prominent citizens of St. Louis as well as the three pilots hired to fly the route: Thomas P. Nelson, Philip R. Love, and Charles A. Lindbergh. Thirteen-year-old Myrtle Lambert, the daughter of Major Albert Lambert, who had built Lambert Field, christened the DeHavilland-4 airplane *St. Louis.* Soon afterward, three large sacks of mail were loaded into Love's DH-4, which lifted into the sky to follow its 300-mile northeasterly course.

SKILLED PILOTS

Robertson Aircraft had high hopes for the new service and high expectations of its pilots. Lindbergh, in particular, did not disappoint the company as he proved to be a skilled and tireless promoter of Robertson's prospects and services. Financial backers showed patience, while the pilots endured hard weather and dangerous

A passenger/mail plane prepares for takeoff. *(Bergert Brothers Collection, University of South Florida)*

night flying. Yet the officers of Robertson Aircraft soon found their company carrying half of the amount of mail necessary to allow them a profit. Many people did not see the advantages of a slightly quicker delivery time (one day faster than train service) in exchange for the added risk of their mail crashing and burning in Robertson's fragile and extremely flammable airplanes, which had already seen several years of service as military reconaissance aircraft in France.

Not very mindful of profits and losses, Lindbergh quickly grew bored with the daily routine of picking up and delivering mail to small Midwestern airfields. At the time of the inauguration of the CAM-2 service at Lambert Field, he was 24 years old, a native of Little Falls, Minnesota, and a dropout in his sophomore year from the University of Wisconsin. Before landing the mail-service job with Robertson, he had worked as a barnstorming pilot, flying from one small town to another to give exhibitions of stunt flying, to provide paying customers with their first experience of flight, and to offer an eclectic menu of aerial services, from flying weddings to mock dogfights to "deaf flights," in which the hard-of-hearing were brought several thousand feet above the ground and subjected to sharp rolls and steep dives that, according to aeronautic hucksters, world cure or at least improve their condition. In 1925, when Commander Richard Byrd announced plans for a flight over the North Pole, Lindbergh applied to join Byrd's team as a pilot but was turned down. He had then moved into a spare room in a building near Lambert Field and joined the 35th Division Air Service of the Missouri National Guard, for which he worked as a flight instructor.

When storms and darkness were not occupying him (twice on the CAM-2 run he had to use his parachute), Lindbergh had many hours in which to meditate on his future. One evening in the fall of 1926, while flying at several thousand feet over Illinois, he was struck with the idea of attempting endurance and distance records as a solo pilot. He had heard of a new, heavier airplane, the Wright-Bellanca, which could cruise at more than 100 miles an hour and would be the most fuel-efficient plane yet built. Calculating the speed and amount of fuel the

Bellanca could carry, Lindbergh figured that it might carry him alone, nonstop, between New York and Paris—a feat that no pilot had yet dared to attempt.

THE ORTEIG PRIZE

Lindbergh knew that accomplishing the New York–Paris run would win him more than mere notice among his fellow aviators. The Atlantic Ocean route was still the grand prix of European and American aviation. In May 1919, the U.S. Navy had staged an expensive transatlantic expedition comprising four "NC" biplanes, crewed by five aviators and designed to take off and land on water, if necessary. A single plane from among the five had managed to struggle from Newfoundland to the Azores and then on to Lisbon, becoming the first aircraft to complete a transatlantic flight.

Transatlantic crossings became media events, symbolizing a new, more peaceful interdependence between Europe and North America. After the navy's expedition, the London *Daily Mail* announced a prize of $50,000 for the first nonstop flight between the continents. In June 1919, Captain John Alcock and Lieutenant Arthur Brown of Great Britain completed the trip from St. John's, Newfoundland, to Clifden, Ireland, in 16 hours, 12 minutes, a total distance of 1,936 miles. In the same year, during a moment of delirious postwar enthusiasm, and perhaps simply for the sake of competing with the prize offered by the *Daily Mail,* a French-American hotel owner named Raymond Orteig offered a prize of $25,000 to the first aviator, or aviators, to make a nonstop flight between New York and Paris.

Orteig was sincere but also knew it would be a long time before any pilot would claim his money—the airplane had not yet been built that carried sufficient fuel for the 3,315-mile flight, and the route followed a long, empty stretch of the North Atlantic Ocean that meant probable death for any pilot who experienced engine trouble, a storm, or navigation problems. There were no attempts to claim the Orteig Prize for more than seven years, until September 15, 1926, when René Fonck, a French World War I ace, took off from Roosevelt Field in Long Island, New York, with a crew of three in a plane specially designed by Igor Sikorsky, a Russian aircraft inventor who had arrived in the United States in 1919. The overloaded plane immediately crashed into a ditch at the end of the runway, killing Fonck's radio operator and mechanic.

Lindbergh was no military ace; in fact, he had only been flying for a few years. He had grown up a loner, a boy who spent his time exploring the northern Minnesota woods, the banks of the Mississippi River, and his own backyard with only his dog for company. Fonck's disaster convinced Lindburgh to attempt the New York-to-Paris route alone and to do it in a single-engine plane. In this way, he would avoid the problems of selecting and rejecting members of a crew; with a single-engine plane he would also run a lesser risk of engine problems. He could carry minimal weight—only food rations, water, a flashlight, and a life raft. He would depend on himself to chart the necessary course and fly the plane; he would personally see to the mechanical preparations, fund-raising, and the application for the Orteig Prize.

In the late fall of 1926, Lindbergh set out to raise the necessary money—about $10,000, by his estimate, to buy a Wright-Bellanca. He knew there was competition—experienced pilots were backed by syndicates determined to turn a dollar on Orteig's offer. After his successful flight to the North Pole,

Commander Byrd had announced his intention to capture the prize the following summer. The French team of Charles Nungesser and François Coli were preparing for the flight in France, and a pair of American military pilots, Noel Davis and Stanton Wooster, won sponsorship by the American Legion.

Lindbergh was young, but experienced in the matter of promoting, and in these boom years nearly every business in the country was looking for some stunt, association, or public event that would bring notice from newspaper journalists and the public. Asking for the purchase of $1,000 shares, he first met with Earl Thompson, a St. Louis insurance executive. Thompson agreed to put up a share, as did Major Lambert and Major Lambert's brother Wooster. Lindbergh also got the backing of his employers at Robertson Aircraft; the State National Bank of St. Louis; the St. Louis *Post-Dispatch;* and Knight, Dysart & Gamble, a St. Louis brokerage firm.

In late November, Lindbergh traveled to New York to meet with officials of the Wright Aeronautical Corporation and Giuseppe Bellanca, the designer of the Wright-Bellanca. The reply to his proposition was tentative, as Bellanca told him the plane was intended solely as a demonstration aircraft for the purposes of exhibiting the new Wright Whirlwind engine. Lindbergh returned home, waited for a decision from New York, and began collecting maps, weather reports, and information about his planned route. As the uncertainty continued into early 1927, he contacted the Ryan Aircraft Company of San Diego about the possibility of obtaining a custom-built, single-engine monoplane. Ryan replied that it could deliver such a plane in two months and that it would cost about $6,000 without a motor. The plane's specifications included a 380-gallon fuel capacity and a cruising speed of 100 miles an hour, which would allow Lindbergh to complete a New York-to-Paris run in about 36 hours.

Soon after this communication, Lindbergh received a message from Bellanca, who offered to build a plane capable of transatlantic flight for $15,000. Since their last meeting, Bellanca had gone into business with a new firm, the Columbia Aircraft Company. Lindbergh met with his St. Louis backers, who agreed to the deal, and set off for New York with a check for $15,000. Upon meeting Columbia's executives, however, he discovered that they expected Lindbergh to have a crew—and to allow them to select its members. Lindbergh would have to agree to this condition, they believed, as the Bellanca they now owned was the only plane that could possibly make the flight. Realizing that a serious misunderstanding had taken place, and unable to convince the executives that he would be making the flight alone, Lindbergh left New York with his check.

On the urging of his backers, he then traveled to San Diego, where he clearly explained to the Ryan Aircraft Company that the plane was to be built from scratch and to his specifications. After considering the project, Ryan agreed to build the plane and fit it with an engine for a price of $10,580, delivery to be made within 60 days. The cockpit would be placed behind a series of five gas tanks; to save weight, there would be no parachute, no radio, no sextant for estimating position, and no night-flying equipment. The contract was signed on February 25, 1927. Harold Bixby of the State National Bank of St. Louis suggested the name for the plane, which Lindbergh accepted—*The Spirit of St. Louis.*

A GOOD STORY

The first attempt of what would prove to be a busy and tragic transatlantic season took place at Roosevelt Field on April 16, 1927. Commander Richard

Byrd, his spectacular run over the North Pole with Floyd Bennett still fresh in the public memory, piloted a Fokker three-engine plane to the western end of the runway, then crashed the overburdened plane on takeoff, injuring three members of his crew. On April 24, Clarence Chamberlain, flying the Bellanca built by the Columbia Aircraft Company, damaged the *Columbia*'s landing gear and had to abort his flight. On the 26th, during a test flight, Noel Davis and Stanton Wooster died in a crash of the *American Legion*. On May 8, the French pilots Charles Nungesser and François Coli successfully took off from Le Bourget airfield near Paris, navigated westward past the coast of France, and disappeared somewhere in the North Atlantic Ocean, never to be found.

In San Diego, meanwhile, Charles Lindbergh was making practice runs with his Ryan monoplane, which had been carried out of its construction hangar in pieces and reassembled on April 25. Through more than 30 trial runs designed to test the plane's flying characteristics under certain wind conditions and payloads, he found only minor adjustments necessary. Under optimum conditions, Lindbergh estimated that *The Spirit of St. Louis* could fly a distance of 4,200 miles, well past the distance he had charted from New York to Paris.

On May 10, Lindbergh brought the plane from San Diego to St. Louis, taking off in the late afternoon in order to practice flying *The Spirit of St. Louis* in the dark. He arrived in St. Louis at 8:20 A.M., having set a new speed record for the 1,500-mile flight. Not wanting to delay, he left the next day, realizing that Byrd as well as the Columbia team might have their planes repaired and ready to take off before he could get as far as New York. After leaving St. Louis, Lindbergh reached Long Island in 7 hours, 22 minutes, setting a new overall speed record for the flight between the coasts. The Columbia team, however, was experiencing problems choosing its crew, and its flight was grounded by legal action until the dispute could be resolved.

By this time, Lindbergh was attracting attention from the press. Without calculation on his part, the flight of *The Spirit of St. Louis* had become a good story,

Charles Lindbergh (second from right) and colleagues make ready at Springfield, Illinois, for the inaugural mail run of Robertson Aircraft. *(Minnesota Historical Society/Swenson Studio)*

and he was being transformed from a fly-by-night mail-carrier into a national icon. Lindbergh was the dark-horse candidate, the newcomer, the Lone Eagle, the barnstorming underdog who had arrived from small-town boyhood to defy fate and hard weather over a lonely stretch of cold, dangerous ocean. Daring to claim the Orteig Prize alone and precariously flying on a single engine became the hallmarks of a fresh national myth, created and retold by a society experiencing a somewhat disappointing new age of commercialism, materialism, and narrow-mindedness. While *The Spirit of St. Louis* crossed over Manhattan Island and approached Roosevelt Field, agents were already preparing offers for Lindbergh to carry out speaking tours and appear in Hollywood movies. Company vice presidents wanted the Lone Eagle to pitch their products; photographers barged into hotel rooms for photographs; the newspapers all wanted exclusive stories.

Meanwhile, Commander Byrd had graciously offered Lindbergh the use of a specially constructed runway at Roosevelt Field. While waiting for bad weather to clear over the North Atlantic, Lindbergh tried out the runway and found it better and longer than he had expected. On the morning of May 20, 1927, with reports that the weather was clearing to the northeast, he made the decision to go. Final preparations were made, 450 gallons of gasoline were loaded into the plane's five fuel tanks, and at about 7:40 A.M. Lindbergh took his place in the wicker porch chair that served as his pilot's seat. *The Spirit of St. Louis* taxied into position, struggled down the runway, briefly went airborne, twice bumped back onto the ground, and finally cleared, by about 20 feet, a set of telephone wires at the eastern edge of Roosevelt Field.

LANDING IN PARIS

While waiting for the completion of work on his plane in San Diego, Lindbergh had charted his flight by dividing it into 36 one-hour, 100-mile segments and calculating a change of magnetic course at the end of each segment. Now, as the burdened plane made its sluggish way over the northern coast of Long Island, its pilot checked for landmarks: railroad tracks, radio masts, smokestacks, highways. Each hour, he switched the engine's fuel supply from one tank to the next, marking these changes in a small logbook. The plane and the weather were cooperating; the pilot, having been unable to sleep the night before while under siege by curious journalists, began to realize that his greatest challenge would be to stay awake through a 36-hour flight.

After leaving Massachusetts behind, *The Spirit of St. Louis* flew over open water of Nova Scotia, then Newfoundland. The plane was still low enough to be spotted by people on the ground, who waved, pointed, and chased after *The Spirit of St. Louis* in their automobiles. By the time the plane left the Canadian seacoast, it was already growing dark, with a moonless night offering Lindbergh no visual clues about where *The Spirit of St. Louis* was heading or how high above the water it was. The air grew colder; shining his flashlight out at the wings, he spotted ice forming on the struts. A storm began to rock the plane with turbulence; to get out of the weather he changed course, to the south as he approximated by his malfunctioning compasses, and quickly lost his bearings.

Dawn broke, but with only the monotonous ocean waves to look at, Lindbergh began drifting off to sleep. Halfway through the flight, his mind numbed and his body aching and stiff, he began to see shapeless, white phantoms inside the plane, moving around the cockpit, giving him messages. Looking out the window, he spotted rugged, mountainous islands where none were supposed to be, then realized he was watching the mirages created by thick banks of drifting fog. To wake himself, he occasionally dropped the plane to just a few feet of altitude to allow the breaking whitecaps to spray into the cockpit. Unable to concentrate, he left off making entries in his log.

Meanwhile, people on the ground were following Lindbergh's flight with rapt attention through newspaper and radio dispatches. At public occasions and sporting events, speakers delivered short messages of hope and pride, and the public respectfully observed long moments of silence. After the last sighting of *The Spirit of St. Louis* over Newfoundland, there had been media silence: no word of Lindbergh's progress would be heard until he reached Europe. The public had to wait, expecting the worst, with the radio and newspapers playing up the suspense.

After passing a small group of fishing boats, Lindbergh finally spotted the coast of Ireland, where the people of a small village came out of their houses to wave at him. He passed over southwestern England and the English Channel, as special newspaper editions appeared in France. As night fell again the French government ordered all airfields between Cherbourg and Paris to be illuminated. Just as he crossed over the coast of Normandy, Lindbergh took his first food of the flight and drained his canteen of water. Spotting the bright glow of boulevard lights that marked Paris, he circled once around the Eiffel Tower and headed for Le Bourget airfield on the northern edge of the city.

The landing took place at 10:24 P.M. at Le Bourget, on May 21, after a flight of 33.5 hours and 3,600 miles. The safe and routine ending on the Le Bourget runway turned out to be one of the most famous single events of the 1920s. News of Lindbergh's landing in Paris reached New York by telegraph six minutes after the event, while the aviator was mobbed at Le Bourget by the crowd of more than 150,000 people that had come to the airport to witness the landing. The crowd swept over lines of police and soldiers, trampled over a fence, took Lindbergh out of the plane and passed him over their heads. Ambassador Myron Herrick took charge of the pilot and escorted him to his official residence at the American Embassy, where journalists besieged the building. At 3:00 A.M. Lindbergh gave an impromptu press conference in his pajamas—The *New York Times* had been granted an exclusive on the story, but the *Times* representative Carlyle MacDonald had agreed to waive the exclusivity, temporarily.

Heiress Louise Boyd made Arctic exploration her life's work, carrying out seven expeditions and, in 1928, leading a three-month search for Norwegian explorer Roald Amundsen. Amundsen, as it turned out, had died in a 1925 plane crash while searching for the lost Italian explorer Umberto Nobile. *(Library of Congress)*

THE HERO

Downstairs at the embassy, a pack of journalists as well as cameramen and newsreel photographers waited for Lindbergh to wake up. Upon hearing that he was safe, the United States broke into a spontaneous, nationwide celebration, and Lindbergh became the most famous individual in the world. Fire engines sounded their sirens, automobiles blasted their horns, churches rang their bells.

Impromptu parades were carried out all over, and newspapers devoted their front pages and radio stations their programming to nothing but news of Lindbergh's flight. The pilot and the plane were brought home on a ship, the *Memphis*. In Washington, Lindbergh and the plane were honored with a 21-gun salute. President Coolidge officially welcomed him home, and an enormous ticker-tape parade through New York was held in his honor.

Lindbergh's record did not stand for long. On his way home aboard the navy transport *Memphis*, he was notified of the flight of the *Columbia*, with Clarence Chamberlain at the controls, on its way to Europe. Chamberlain would set a new distance record of 3,900 miles on this flight to Germany, while Charles Levine, the plane's owner, would become the world's first transatlantic aerial passenger. The successful flights signaled a new era in transportation, one that would draw the two continents closer and open minds to the possibilities of the airplane.

AMELIA EARHART

Lindbergh's and Chamberlain's flights would be followed by three more Atlantic crossings in the summer of 1927, one of which, a flight from New York to France, was piloted by Commander Byrd. Seeing an opportunity for publicity, the publisher G. P. Putnam had urged Lindbergh to write an account of his flight for the firm of G. P. Putnam's Sons. That summer, Putnam also learned that Commander Byrd had sold his Fokker trimotor, the *Friendship*, which was equipped with pontoons for takeoff and landings at sea, to Amy Phipps Guest, heiress to a fortune in steel and the wife of Frederick Guest, the former British Air Minister. Amy Guest wanted to make an Atlantic crossing of her own as a passenger, but when Putnam learned that her family was prohibiting her from making the flight, he persuaded Captain Hilton Railey to telephone a woman pilot and inquire after her interest in taking part in the first Atlantic crossing by a woman.

Railey then spoke with Amelia Earhart, a native of Atchison, Kansas, who had moved with her family from city to city while her father, Edwin Earhart, struggled to meet debts and overcome alcoholism. She had left home in 1916 for Ogontz School in Rydal, Pennsylvania, where the redoubtable school owner and principal, Dr. Abby Sutherland, impressed her with a strong-willed and imperious independence. Earhart moved to New York to attend Columbia University in the fall of 1919, but in the spring of 1920 moved to Los Angeles, where at the occasion of a Winter Air Tournament she was captivated by the new aeronautic novelties of stunt flying, airplane racing, and wing walking. Her first flying lessons followed quickly at Kinner Field.

The studious and independent Earhart paid little attention to what friends, family, and society expected of her. She most admired those women who had defied social conventions to follow careers and establish themselves as lawyers, mayors, bankers, athletes, or aviators. Soon after mastering flying, she bought her first plane, which was built by Bert Kinner; she had it painted yellow and named it the *Canary*. On October 22, 1922, she established an altitude record of 14,000 feet over Rogers Field, Los Angeles, and on May 15, 1923, received a pilot's license from the Fédération Aéronautique Internationale (FAI), the 16th woman in the world to do so. Finding little remuneration for her ability as a high-altitude pilot, she moved back east soon thereafter, accepting employment as a social worker at Denison House in Boston.

The Flight of the Friendship

It was while working at Denison House, and moonlighting as a demonstrator and salesperson for Bert Kinner's aircraft at Dennison Field in Squantum, Massachusetts, that Amelia Earhart first heard from Captain Hilton Railey of the flight of the *Friendship*. With Putnam's encouragement, Commander Byrd had already helped to select the crew for the flight: Wilmer Stultz, a 28-year-old veteran military pilot, was selected to fly the plane, and Louis Gordon of the Army Air Service was chosen as mechanic and copilot. The ground team included Commander E. P. Elmer as technical adviser, Captain William Rodgers as navigator, and Dr. James Kimball as weatherman. Stultz would be paid $20,000 for his work; Gordon would earn $5,000; Earhart would carry the honorary title of captain of the flight and earn only the publicity and the chance for further opportunities if the flight were successful. She would also own the distinction of being the first woman to cross the Atlantic Ocean in an airplane.

Earhart accepted the offer, intending to return to Denison House if she survived. A bit aghast at the international mobbing of Charles Lindbergh, she wanted to keep the flight a secret, avoid publicity, and keep the planning and preparation as simple as possible. To prepare for the worst, she wrote up a will and brief letters of farewell to her family, all to be opened in the event of her death.

On Sunday, July 3, 1928, the party boarded the *Friendship* and took off, after several tries, from Boston Harbor and headed north to Canada. Stultz landed the plane in foggy Halifax harbor later that morning, then the crew checked into a hotel. The next day the *Friendship* reached Trepassey, Newfoundland, where Earhart avoided reporters by ducking into a small convent. In a short time, minor glitches turned into serious problems. Unable to get the *Friendship* airborne because of high winds, Stultz took to drinking. On June 16, worried over the events, Earhart pulled rank as captain and ordered Gordon and Stultz to prepare for a takeoff the next morning. Stultz was coaxed from bed, plied with coffee, and ordered to take the pilot's seat. After three tries and after dumping all excess fuel, a drowsy, hungover, and angry Stultz finally got the *Friendship* airborne at 11:40 A.M.

Three hundred miles from Trepassey, the *Friendship* entered a thick snowstorm. Stultz took the plane down; after another 100 miles he allowed Gordon to take the controls and promptly fell asleep. The *Friendship*'s radio went dead a few hours later. At 6:30 the next morning, the crew switched to emergency fuel. Twenty hours and 40 minutes after taking off, Stultz sighted a coast, then a town; he circled the town and then brought the plane down into the water at Burry Port, Wales, 140 miles from their destination at Southampton.

The *Friendship* was officially greeted by Norman Fisher, sheriff of Carmanthenshire, who had arrived alongside the aircraft in a small dinghy. Although she had not once touched the controls during the voyage, the flight of the *Friendship* made Amelia Earhart the best-known female pilot in the world. The Lindberghian hoopla and publicity surrounding the flight was put to good use as she set a series of new aeronautic records over the next 10 years, including a solo nonstop flight across the Atlantic in 1932 and the first nonstop flight from Hawaii to California in 1935. Her disappearance over the Pacific Ocean in 1937, during an attempt at a round-the-world voyage with navigator Fred Noonan, gained her tremendous international regard but also marked a tragic end to aviation's glamorous pioneer era.

CHRONICLE OF EVENTS

1926

June 1: Actress and popular icon Norma Jean Mortenson, later Norma Jean Baker and finally Marilyn Monroe, is born.

June 1: World's Fair opens in Philadelphia, Pennsylvania.

July 2: Congress authorizes the establishment of the U.S. Army Air Corps.

July 3: Veterans of the Civil War and the Spanish-American War see their pensions and benefits increased by the Pension Act.

July 5: A subway strike begins in New York City. After four weeks, subway workers will return to work without any wage gains.

July 10: Lightning strikes an ammunition depot at Lake Denmark, New Jersey, starting a series of explosions that will continue for several days and kill 31 people.

July 10: Bobby Jones wins the U.S. Open golf tournament.

July 16: The Son of the Sheik, a film starring Rudolph Valentino, premieres.

July 26: The Sanctuary of Our Lady of Victory in Lackawanna, New York, becomes the first Roman Catholic church to be consecrated as a basilica by the Vatican.

July 26: Robert Todd Lincoln, son of Abraham Lincoln, dies in Manchester, Vermont, at the age of 83.

August 5: Don Juan, a film starring John Barrymore, premieres at the Warner Theater in New York City. The picture is the first to have a synchronized musical score, produced by a phonograph.

August 6: With a time of 14 hours, 31 minutes, 19-year-old Gertrude Ederle of New York becomes the first woman to swim the English Channel.

August 23: Film actor Rudolph Valentino dies, touching off rioting by bereft fans around the world.

September 18: A violent storm sweeps across Florida and the Gulf Coast states, killing 372 people and injuring more than 6,000. Thousands of homes are damaged or destroyed, putting a sudden end to a speculative real estate boom that had driven property values in Florida to enormous heights.

September 20: Members of the Dion O'Bannion gang attack headquarters of Chicago bootlegger and gangster Al Capone, who escapes injury.

September 23: In Philadelphia, Gene Tunney defeats Jack Dempsey in 10 rounds to win the world heavyweight boxing crown.

September 29: To deal with declining sales of the Model T automobile, the Ford Motor Company slows production by instituting the eight-hour work day and the five-day work week.

October 25: In Myers v. United States, the Supreme Court rules that the Tenure of Office Act of 1876 is unconstitutional, and that presidents have the authority to remove executive officers, such as cabinet members, from their posts. The decision reverses a Senate act of 1876 which led to the impeachment and trial of President Andrew Johnson over the removal of military officers from their posts.

October 31: Magician Harry Houdini dies from peritonitis caused by a blow to the abdomen.

November 2: In Congressional elections, the Democrats gain seats in both the Senate and the House of Representatives. The Republican majority is narrowed to 49-46 in the Senate and to 237-195 in the House.

1927

January 1: Massachusetts becomes the first state to require drivers to carry automobile insurance.

January 5: The Fox movie studio introduces Movietone technology, allowing synchronization of sound and motion on movie film.

January 7: The first commercial telephone line opens between New York and London. Walter Gifford, president of American Telephone and Telegraph (AT&T) initiates the line with the phrase "Hello, London."

January 27: The Senate resolves that differences between the United States and Mexico over land and mineral rights of private U.S. companies be arbitrated.

January 28: The Concerto for Piano and Orchestra by Aaron Copland is performed for the first time by the Boston Symphony, with the composer appearing as soloist.

February 11: The Senate passes the McNary-Haugen bill, introduced in Congress in 1924 to allow the government to purchase crop surpluses. The bill will pass the House on February 17 but will be vetoed by President Coolidge, on the grounds that it illegally fixes prices, on February 25.

February 18: The United States and Canada establish formal diplomatic relations. The first U.S. ambassador to Canada is William Phillips; the first Canadian ambassador to the United States is Charles Vincent Massey.

February 23: President Coolidge signs the Radio Control Act, establishing a five-member Federal Radio

Commission. Public ownership of radio frequencies is established and the Radio Commission is established to issue licenses.

March 3: The Prohibition Reorganization Act creates the Prohibition Bureau, an arm of the Treasury Department.

March 4: A direct cable link with Germany is established for the first time since World War I.

March 7: In the *Nixon v. Herndon* decision, the Supreme Court rules that a Texas law prohibiting blacks from voting in a primary election is unconstitutional.

March 17: The Supreme Court finds that the Teapot Dome and Elk Hills oil reserves were leased to the Mammoth Oil Company fraudulently. The reserves are returned from the Interior Department to the oversight of the Department of the Navy by an executive order.

March 29: Major H. O. D. Seagrave sets a new speed record for automobiles at Daytona Beach, Florida, reaching 203.79 miles per hour in a Sunbeam.

April: The Mississippi River begins to overrun its banks, rising more than 50 feet above normal in some places, and to flood 20,000 square miles in several southern states. Hundreds of people drown and 675,000 are left homeless.

April 6: Aristide Briand, foreign minister of France, suggests a treaty to outlaw war. Negotiations will later bring about the Kellogg-Briand Pact, signed by 15 nations on August 27, 1928.

April 7: The first public television image, in which Walter Gifford in New York sees and converses with Secretary of Commerce Herbert Hoover in Washington, is broadcast.

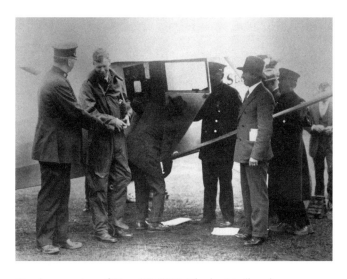

On the morning of May 20, 1927, Charles Lindbergh prepares for takeoff at Roosevelt Field, 36 hours, as he had calculated it, from Paris. *(Brown Brothers)*

April 10: George Antheil's *Ballet Mechanique,* scored for 10 pianos, auto horns, buzz saws, cowbells, and other instruments not commonly seen on the concert stage, debuts at Carnegie Hall in New York.

May 20: Captain Charles Lindbergh takes off in his monoplane, the *Spirit of St. Louis,* from Roosevelt Field on Long Island, New York. He will fly 33 hours and 39 minutes nonstop from New York to Paris, becoming the first pilot to achieve the transatlantic crossing solo.

May 26: The Treasury Department authorizes new paper currency. The new bills are smaller than the existing ones by one-third. They will begin circulating July 10, 1929.

EYEWITNESS TESTIMONY

Commander Byrd and the North Pole

What are we going to do with the *Shenandoah* if we don't fly to the Pole? I want to see the Stars and Stripes carried to the North. Don't read American history! Make it!

> *Captain Bob Bartlett, quoted in "Shenandoah, Torn From Her Mast By Gale. . . " the New York Times, January 17, 1924, p. 2.*

Here we are! as the sun's image started to cover his sextant bubble. We were over the North Pole! With motors throttled and heads uncovered we descended to within 300 feet of the ice and dropped the three flags [American, Norwegian, and Italian]. As we circled I hung over the side of the fuselage of our floating wings, lost in wonder at the sight of the goal, the attainment of which had acted as the motive force to produce some of the most wonderful journeys, in the face of terrible conditions, in the history of our race.

> *Lincoln Ellsworth, navigator of Roald Amundson's flight, on attaining the Pole on May 11, 1926, two days after Commander Byrd, from Mirsky,* To the North *(1934), p. 345.*

I suddenly saw what I thought was a bad oil leak in the right-hand motor. I took the wheel and asked Bennett to give me his opinion of the seriousness of the leak. He jotted down that it was very bad and that he was afraid the motor would not last long. What should we do? It was one of the big moments. We decided to keep on for the Pole and decide what to do after reaching it. We would fly with that motor as long as it would run. We were about an hour from the coveted goal and every minute of the time we were taking unexplored regions off the map. It was tough to have motor trouble here so near the Pole and so far from land, but we would go on. . . .

At the end of the hour I took my calculations and found that we were at the Pole! We reached it at 9:04 A.M. Greenwich time, just about the hour we had hoped to get there.

Bennett and I shook hands simply and I went back into the cabin, stood at attention, and saluted for Admiral Peary.

> *Commander Richard Byrd, recalling his flight to the North Pole in May 1926, quoted in Williams,* Conquering the Air *(1926), p. 221.*

At Spitzbergen, Roald Amundsen greets Commander Byrd (center) on the deck of the *Chantier,* just after Byrd's flight over the North Pole. *(Library of Congress)*

We continued on until we had been out eight hours and thirty-five minutes. . . . At the end of this period Byrd came forward and shook hands with me in a matter-of-fact way. I knew that we had reached the Pole . . . it was impossible to speak for the roar of the engines. We saluted the memory of Peary. . . . We dropped nothing upon the snow below us, for Peary had dropped a flag there.

> *Navigator Floyd Bennett, diary entry describing Richard Byrd's successful air voyage to the North Pole on May 9, 1926, from Simmons,* Target: Arctic *(1965), p. 91.*

The height on which I stand, and the pure air which surrounds me, gives me a wide outlook, and I see our sledge tracks in the white snow out over the edge of the earth's circumference, through the uttermost lands of men to the North. I see, as in a mirage, the thousand little Native villages which gave substance to the journey. And I am filled with a great joy; we have met the great adventure which always awaits him who knows how to grasp it, and that adventure was made up of all our manifold experiences among the most remarkable people in the world!

. . . In my joy at having been permitted to take this long sledge journey, my thoughts turn involuntarily to a contrasting enterprise ending also in Alaska, where last Spring, people were awaiting the visit of daring aviators from the other side of the globe. And from my heart I bless the fate the allowed me to be born at a time when Arctic exploration by dog sledge was not yet a thing of the past. In this sudden retrospect, kindled by the great backward view from East Cape, indeed, I bless the whole journey, forgetting hardship and chance misfortune by the way, in the exultation I feel in the successful conclusion of a high adventure!

Explorer Knud Rasmussen, describing the 1921–24 Thule expedition from Hudson Bay to Point Barrow and contrasting land and air Polar exploration of the 1920s, in the introduction to his book Across Arctic America *(1927), pp. iv–v.*

. . . Byrd and Bennett took that chance. All they knew was that the weather looked good around Spitsbergen and that the best long-distance guess of the meteorologists was that it was good also on the sea to the north. The season was the late Arctic winter. The sky was clear, the wind light, and no fog or clouds interfered with navigation. They flew to the North Pole (almost the same distance as if they had flown from Newfoundland half way to Ireland), circled it, and flew back faultlessly—without any landmark to guide them and therefore wholly dependent on the arts of navigation—struck the right headland of Spitsbergen as accurately as a Southampton liner making Sandy Hook, and landed without accident. The coldest weather of the trip was ten degrees warmer than the coldest temperature recorded for New York City. None of the other bogeys materialized—which might all have been luck, though extraordinary luck if the Arctic were as bad as supposed. We shall come back to that point later.

The thrill seekers were disappointed at Byrd's North Pole story; where nothing goes wrong, there is nothing hair-raising to tell.

Vilhjalmur Stefansson, "The Airplane and the Arctic: New Pioneers Dispel an Old Myth," in Harpers Magazine, *October 1927, p. 599.*

I realized that an adventure like our polar flight aroused great public interest. I knew before I left that there would be a certain amount of risk in crossing the polar ice, just as there is in any flight over unknown terrain. I had gumption enough to see that such a stunt is great stuff for the publicity hounds. But my idea of a national hero was somebody like George Washington or John J. Pershing. They had held the safety of our country in their hands. They had suffered the agony of long campaigns. They had led armies of victory against a public enemy.

I hadn't done anything so valiant. Nor did Bobby Jones, or Gertrude Ederle, who came after me.

Commander Richard Byrd poses with the plane that carried him across the Antarctic, 1930. *(Minnesota Historical Society)*

"Yes, they are national heroes, too," admitted a newspaperman whom I queried about this curiously American phenomenon.

"But what is a national hero, and why?" I persisted.

"Oh, someone who's worth two columns and a front-page streamer, fireboats and a basket of medals," came the cynical reply.

Richard E. Byrd, "This Hero Business," in The Ladies Home Journal, *January 1927, reprinted in* The Journal of the Century *(1976), p. 133.*

During the fall of 1923 I had several talks with Colonel E. Lester Jones re my Polar drift proposition. One day in Washington I saw the *Shenandoah* flying over the city. It then occurred to me, why not have her fly over the Polar Sea and decide if land is or is not there? The more I thought about it the more I was convinced that it could be done and it should be done by the Navy.

. . . Things began to move rapidly. Before I knew it I was up in a closed room with a lot of captains and admirals. We gathered around a table covered with charts and records of ships that had been in the Arctic. It was very impressive, but I cannot say that I liked it. I had been too much in the North to be willing to plan for an expedition by studying out of books. The trouble is the Arctic isn't anything like the books after you get there.

. . . It seemed that the people who thought the Navy should have dirigibles wanted to prove their usefulness. Also a good deal of stress was laid on the fact that one million square miles north of Alaska were still unexplored. If land were discovered in that big space it might prove a sort of half-way station between Europe and Asia after the transpolar air route came in.

Explorer Captain Robert A. Bartlett, recalling U.S. Navy planning for Arctic exploration in Bartlett, The Log of Bob Bartlett *(1928), pp. 304–305.*

Charles Lindbergh

We specialize in Fair and Carnival Exhibition Work, Offering Plane Change in Midair, Wing Walking, Parachute Jumping, Breakaways, Night Fireworks, Smoke Trails, and Deaf Flights.

Business card, Charles Lindbergh, from Berg, Lindbergh *(1998), p. 84.*

Lindbergh did it. Twenty minutes after 10 o'clock tonight suddenly and softly there slipped out of the darkness a gray-white airplane as 25,000 pairs of eyes strained toward it. At 10:24 the *Spirit of St. Louis* landed and lines of soldiers, ranks of policemen and stout steel fences went down before a mad rush as irresistible as the tides of the ocean.

"Well, I made it," smiled Lindbergh, as the white monoplane came to a halt in the middle of the field and the first vanguard reached the plane. Lindbergh made a move to jump out. Twenty hands headed for him and lifted him out as if he were a baby. Several thousands in a minute were around the plane. Thousands more broke the barriers of iron rails round the field, cheering wildly.

. . . It was two French aviators—Major Pierre Weiss and Sergeant de Troyer who rescued Captain Lindbergh from the frenzied mob. When it seemed the excited French men and women would overwhelm the frail figure which was being carried on the shoulders of a half dozen men, the two aviators rushed up with a Renault car and hastily snatching Lindy from the crowd, sped across the field to the commandant's office.

. . . Not since the armistice of 1918 had Paris witnessed a downright demonstration of popular enthusiasm and excitement equal to that displayed by the throngs flocking to the boulevards for news of the American flier, whose personality has captured the hearts of the Parisian multitude.

Edwin L. James, "Lindbergh Does It! . . ." New York Times, *May 22, 1927, page 1.*

. . . that reception I got was the most dangerous part of the whole flight. If wind and storm had handled me as vigorously as that Reception Committee of Fifty Thousand, I would never have reached Paris and I would be eating a 3-o'clock-in-the-afternoon breakfast here in Uncle Sam's Embassy.

There's one thing I wish to get straight about this flight. They call me "lucky Lindy," but luck isn't enough. As a matter of fact, I had what I regarded and still regard as the best existing plane to make the flight from New York to Paris. I had what I regard as the best engine, and I was equipped with what were in the circumstances the best possible instruments to making such efforts. I hope I made good use of what I had.

"Lindbergh's Own Story of Epochal Flight . . ." Charles Lindbergh, the day after his nonstop flight from New York to Paris, in the New York Times, *May 23, 1927, p. 1.*

We noted that the *Spirit of St. Louis* had not left the ground ten minutes before it was joined by the Spirit of Me Too. A certain oil was lubricating the engine, a certain brand of tires was the cause of the safe take-off. When the flyer landed in Paris every newspaper was "first to have a correspondent at the plane." This was a heartening manifestation of that kinship that is among man's greatest exaltations. It was beautifully and tenderly expressed in the cable Ambassador Herrick sent the boy's patient mother: "Your incomparable son has done me the honor to be my guest." We liked that; and for twenty-four hours the world seemed pretty human. At the end of that time we were made uneasy by the volume of vaudeville contracts, testimonial writing and other offers, made by the alchemists who transmute glory into gold. We settled down to the hope that the youthful hero will capitalize himself for only as much money as he reasonably needs.

Editorialist E. B. White, commenting on the Lindbergh hoopla in The New Yorker *of May 28, 1927, and quoted in Kunkel,* Genius in Disguise: Harold Ross of The New Yorker *(1995), pp. 147–148.*

I do not believe that any human being has ever received a more spontaneous or overwhelming reception. It has been estimated that there were 200,000 people present at the aerodrome waiting for Lindbergh's appearance although there had been no organized publicity beforehand. The anticipations of the authorities are indicated by the fact that there were some seventy policemen distributed round the aerodrome to keep order. This little force was, of course, utterly inadequate to deal with the situation, and it was almost inevitable that order should break down.

It has often been said that the behavior of that vast crowd was a deplorable exhibition of mob law, but I have never thought so myself. The English crowd is usually a well-behaved crowd; indeed it is often rather too well-behaved. It takes a very special occasion to stir up even a decent show of enthusiasm, and there generally is little need for the authorities to worry about the crowd getting out of hand.

…As Lindbergh approached the aerodrome escorted by a number of other planes, the vast crowd surrounding the aerodrome began to surge forward, breaking down such barriers as there were in a cumulative effort to get a better view of this hero of the Atlantic….

Major Mayo, British representative of the Guggenheim Fund for the Promotion of Aeronautics, describing Lindbergh's reception in Croydon, England on May 29, 1927, quoted in Cleveland, America Fledges Wings *(1942), pp. 90–91.*

Lindbergh himself is coming home as the guest of the United States navy. But the best part of his achievement is that it was a purely civilian undertaking. Though he ranks as a captain in the Missouri National Guard, he flew not in uniform but in the clothes of the air pilot he had been, and he stuck to his civilian clothes in Paris and London. This befitted the son of the man who denounced the World War as set forth elsewhere in this issue; it certainly was in keeping with the American spirit. Yet already plans are made to exploit the hero for military purposes. Army, navy, and marine-corps contingents are to escort him from the station in Washington to the Washington Monument; the Governor of Misouri is to make him a colonel, and some of the militarists are already citing his deed, not as a wonderfully fortunate exploit which has brought America nearer to the English and French than at any time since the armistice but as proving that now we are open to attack from Europe and therefore must at once vote many millions more for fliers and aeroplanes.

Unsigned editorial in The Nation, *June 15, 1927, p. 655.*

Hark, a Homer winds our way to write the yet unwritten epic of the West. Shine on, O Sunspots of our Genius. . . . The World's Sunspot today is Capt. Lindbergh, that intrepid and dauntless American youth, who as a Mercury of Love and vast Simplicity of Heart has given the Old World a valid introduction to great America. Young Lindbergh rode the waves of air to glory, and he flew the cross currents of rule and curriculum,—stumbling blocks in the path of the Inspired. More power to him, as he vibrantly interprets Democracy. Capt. Lindbergh believed in his inspiration—monoplaning across the Atlantic with but a single motor, and at last, the Old and the New World have met in a kiss of living understanding, fanned into being by his "Spirit of St. Louis." Captain Lindbergh on the wings of a like Inspiration, thus ever to burnish our Golden Gate with the gleams of our Genius. . . .

Tribute to Charles Lindbergh after his transatlantic solo flight, written by Mrs. Vernille De Witt-Warr in the Marin County Review, quoted in The American Mercury, *January 1928, p. 49.*

I want so intensely to get this across to people, some people—those who will get "it"—what Colonel L. is. I feel that they should know. I want terribly to enlighten people about him—from the newspaper prejudice.

Lindbergh's success captured the imagination of a nation searching for new heroes. The result was a storm of newspaper and radio coverage and the biggest ticker-tape parade Broadway had ever seen. *(Brown Brothers)*

How can I best tell them, best reach them—how explain? What points can I give?

He is great not because he crossed the ocean alone. He might have shown his genius in some other way. This explains the mad devotion of him. The flight gave him to the world. He is not a *type* of anything, as the newspapers have made him. Keen, intelligent, burning, thinking on all lines—The intensity of life, burning like a bright fire in his eyes. Life focused in him— When he in turn focuses his life, power, force on *anything,* amazing things happen.

. . . Nothing "grates": never a false note, a hint of smallness—never a tinny sound, as one might expect in a vulgar phrase, or badly kept fingernails—

His cool "knowing what he is about" *all* the time—utter lack of recklessness, an amazing, impersonal kind of courage—

Most of his modesty is not modesty—more selfless than that: impersonality.

Anne Morrow Lindbergh, diary entry of January 1928, from Lindbergh, Bring Me A Unicorn *(1971), p. 113.*

Whatever may be the fate of the United States of America in years to come, whether enemies abroad or at home finally encompass the destruction of this great republic—a possibility that seems impossible now— still the judgment of history must everlastingly record that the United States of America produced

Lindbergh. That, in many ways, will be compensation for whatever national sins we may commit.

Editorial comment from the Muscatine (Iowa) Journal and News-Tribune, *as quoted in* The American Mercury, *March 1928, p. 308.*

I opened the door, and started to put my foot down onto ground. But dozens of hands took hold of me—my legs, my arms, my body. No one heard the sentences I spoke. I found myself lying in a prostrate position, up on top of the crowd, in the center of an ocean of heads that extended as far out into the darkness as I could see. Then I started to sink down into that ocean, and was buoyed up again. Thousands of voices mingled in a roar. Men were shouting, stumbling. My head and shoulders went down, and up, and down again, and up once more. It was like drowning in a human sea. I lost sight of the *Spirit of St. Louis.* I heard several screams. I was afraid that I would be dropped under the feet of those milling, cheering people; and that after sitting in a cockpit-fixed position for close to thirty-four hours, my muscles would be too stiff to struggle up again.

Charles Lindbergh, description of arrival at Le Bourget airfield in Paris, from The Spirit of St. Louis *(1953), p. 496.*

There comes a point when the body's demand for sleep is harder to endure than any other pain I have encountered, when it results in a state of semiconsciousness in which an awareness exists that is less acute but apparently more universal than that of the normal mind. Before my flight was halfway finished, I found that I could not force myself to stay awake through will power. The rational mind I had previously known and relied upon had less and less effect on my body's responses. There were lengthening periods when it even lost the knowledge of its own existence, when an intelligence without the need for reason had replaced it.

. . . It was the only occasion in my life when I saw and conversed with ghosts.

They appeared suddenly in the tail of the fuselage while I was flying through fog. I saw them clearly although my eyes were staring straight ahead. Transparent, mistlike, with semihuman form, they moved in and out through the fabric walls at will. One or two of them would come forward to converse with me and then rejoin the group behind. I can still see these phantoms clearly in memory, but

after I landed at Paris I could not remember a single word they said.

Charles Lindbergh, recalling the May 1927 flight of The Spirit of St. Louis *in Lindbergh,* Autobiography of Values *(1978) pp. 11–12.*

Amelia Earhart

Dear Snappy,

I have tried to play for a large stake and if I succeed all will be well.

If I don't, I shall be happy to pop off in the midst of such an adventure. My only regret would be leaving you and mother stranded for a while.

I haven't told you about the affair as I didn't want to worry mother, and she would suspect (she may now) if I told you. The whole thing came so unexpectedly that few knew about it. Sam will tell you the whole story. Please explain to mother. I couldn't stand the added strain of telling mother and you personally.

If reporters talk to you, say you knew, if you like.

Yours respectfully,
Sister

Letter, Amelia Earhart to sister Muriel Earhart, written on the eve of her 1928 transatlantic flight aboard the Friendship, *from Rich,* Amelia Earhart: A Biography, *(1989), p. 56.*

Well, the first lady passenger has crossed the Atlantic by air, although what special merit there is in that is not altogether easy to see. In these days of sex-equality, such a feat should not arouse any particular comment. Compared with the solo flights of lady *pilots* as Lady Bailey and Lady Heath, the crossing of the Atlantic *as a passenger* does not seem to us to prove anything in particular. If it were intended to demonstrate that a machine can now cross the Atlantic carrying a full crew and even a passenger, then that was proved by Commander Byrd's flight last year and very much more convincingly. . . .

Commentary on Amelia Earhart's flight aboard the Friendship *in* Flight, *a British aviation magazine, dated June 21, 1928 and quoted in Lowell,* The Sound of Wings *(1989), p. 127.*

Ever since landing in England I have been learning about what it means to be a public person. . . . Today I have been receiving offers to go on the stage, appear in movies, and to accept numerous gifts ranging from an automobile to a husband. The usual letters of criticism and threats which I have always read celebrities receive have also arrived. And I am caught in a situation where very little of me is free. I am being moved instead of moving. . . . But having undertaken to go through with this trip I have to go through with it. That is the drawback of being a public person—you cannot fall down. People's eyes are on you.

Amelia Earhart, statement quoted in the New York Times, *June 21, 1928, and quoted in Ware,* Still Missing *(1993), p. 45.*

Just now with aviation in its most fluid state, there is every chance for women; perhaps almost as many chances as there are for men. The woman who can create her own job is the woman who will win fame and fortune . . . there are many possible openings in aviation for women; some of these are as saleswomen, as founders of flying schools for women, as developers of flying fields, as pilots, as organizers of "air taxi" companies, as designers, perfecting or inventing in the field of many needs of a profession still in its infancy. . . . The field is clear for the pioneer and if the pioneer has good ideas nobody will ask whether the pioneer is a man or woman.

Amelia Earhart, in address to the Women's Committee of the British Empire after her transatlantic flight in June 1928, quoted in Lowell, The Sound of Wings *(1989), pp. 128–129.*

10 National Pastimes: Movies, Sports, Cars
June 1927–January 1928

The world war had helped the young movie industry in the United States overcome its chief competition in Europe and begin collecting a worldwide audience. In Europe, the needs of a war industry took precedence over those of entertainment; the film industries of France, England, Germany, and Russia had shut down for the duration, while U.S. studios continued producing 20-minute "two-reelers" and full-length films. Having moved to southern California, the film business was able to produce movies throughout the year; it was also vitalized by talented immigrants and refugees—notably Charles Chaplin and Erich von Stroheim. During the 1920s, Hollywood began to consolidate itself into a studio system that would transform movie making from a helter-skelter art form into an industry comparable in income and net profit to the smokestack enterprises located on the opposite coast.

Just before the war, director D. W. Griffith had made important innovations in movie production. Disdaining the spontaneous plots and action of earlier films, he employed carefully constructed shooting scripts. He replaced the typical light comedy with epic drama, decorated with elaborate sets and populated by gigantic casts. He also developed new camera and editing techniques to illustrate his scripts' underlying themes and metaphors. His films, such as *The Birth of a Nation* (1914), *Intolerance* (1916), and *Broken Blossoms* (1919), demonstrated that serious film, in the hands of certain directors, could stand as an artistic equal to theater and opera.

During the 1920s, the newfangled movie star system, developed just before the war, combined with the trailblazing techniques of D. W. Griffith to create a galaxy of nationally recognized screen icons. Writers, producers, and publicity departments associated with the major movie production houses created all the attendant personalities and appropriate imagery for the new stars, which included Theda Bara as "The Vamp," Charles Chaplin as "The Tramp," Rudolph Valentino as "The Sheik," Mary Pickford as a young innocent, Douglas Fairbanks as a swashbuckling hero, William S. Hart as a cowboy, Adolphe Menjou and Erich von Stroheim as decadent Europeans, Gloria Swanson and Joan Crawford as elegant sophisticates and Clara Bow as the "It" Girl.

The cast and crew of *Free Air,* a film based on the novel by Sinclair Lewis, work on location in the small Midwestern town of Rosemont (renamed Schoenstrom), Minnesota. *(Minnesota Historical Society)*

Wallace Ford watches intently as Virginia Bruce drops a short putt somewhere in southern California. As contract players for MGM, Ford and Bruce were expected by studio heads to entertain themselves with upper-class diversions such as golf, still considered an aristocratic pursuit by the moviegoing public. *(Culver Pictures)*

While the screen stars were emerging, a small group of wealthy corporations emerged from the chaotic competition of the small and often poorly financed production companies of the pioneering days. Many of the studio heads were operators of nickelodeons and amusement parks who built new theaters for the purpose of exhibiting two-reelers. They then began producing films for exhibition and later created distribution networks for these films to bring them to a national audience. In this way Adolph Zukor founded the Famous Players company, bought out several rival companies including Jesse Lasky's Feature Play Company and Lewis J. Selznick's Picture Company, absorbed a distributing firm, Paramount, and created a vertically integrated amalgamation of film production and sale known as Paramount Pictures. In 1924, theater owner Marcus Loew purchased the Metro Picture Company and the Goldwyn Picture company, hired Louis B. Mayer as a head producer, and established Metro-Goldwyn-Mayer, or MGM. The "block-booking" of the era, in which independent theater owners were forced to show all the films a certain studio shipped in order to show any of them, guaranteed a reliable profit and cash flow for the studio; even more profitable was the establishment of theater chains that were wholly owned and operated by the studios.

Zukor, Mayer, and comparable movie moguls came to exercise close control over their directors, writers, and actors. Studio heads determined what films were to be made; they wrote the contracts, paid the salaries, and held final approval over casting, scripts, and editing. They manipulated the screen and public images of their stars for maximum profit and exercised a strong influence over the public's developing cinematic taste. In the 1920s, the lowbrow "B" movie—the type of movie that drew the largest and most reliable audiences—became Hollywood's dominant product, replacing the comic two-reeler as well as the large-scale epics and arty dramas of D. W. Griffith and other ambitious directors. One exception to the studio system occurred in 1919, when Charlie Chaplin, Mary Pickford, D. W. Griffith, and Douglas Fairbanks combined to form their own independent production company, United Artists, that simply made films and then sold them for release to distributors, a mode of operation that foreshadowed Hollywood business methods of the 1960s and later. United Artists only survived through the public name recognition of its four star partners and spawned no imitators for many years.

SCANDAL

The scandals attending the directors and stars of moving pictures made the industry all the more fascinating to the public, all the more dangerous to those who feared the changing fashions in music, clothing, and entertainment. Nickelodeons and darkened movie houses had been alarming moralists since before the turn of the century; the film industry, even as it matured into a big business of the 1920s, remained ripe for scandal, as it combined theatrical players—the subject of salacious public attention since Shakespeare's day and earlier—with a milieu of low-rent public entertainment.

To those who most strongly objected to them, the movies were projecting lust, materialism, and lackadaisical morality to a gullible and impressionable public. Several well-publicized scandals did nothing to placate guardians of public sensibilities and encouraged further morbid attention on the part of the press. Mary Pickford's quick divorce from Owen Moore and remarriage to Douglas Fairbanks in 1920 secretly titillated the audiences that had wondered half-skeptically at her screen image as "America's Sweetheart." In 1922 the clean-living, all-American matinee idol Wallace Reid was committed to a sanatorium, where he soon died, for drug addiction. In the same year director William Desmond Taylor was murdered, his assailant unknown, in his Hollywood apartment.

The spectacular scandals and trials of Roscoe Conkling "Fatty" Arbuckle may have been the final impetus for the systematic moral self-regulation that the Hollywood film industry would undertake in the 1920s. Beginning in 1916, Arbuckle played a congenial, overweight slapstick comic for director Mack Sennett's Keystone Film Company and then for Paramount. His rising popularity prompted producer Joseph Schenck to give him a lucrative long-term contract and creative control over a series of two-reelers and feature films. He was instantly recognized by millions of fans, especially in his straitlaced home state of Kansas, but Arbuckle also frequently got himself in trouble. In Boston, during the final engagement of a press tour, the events at a post-dinner celebration, which Arbuckle did not attend, led to the payment of $100,000 to the district attorney, presumably for legal action not taken against moral offenses not publicized. Then, in September 1921, another private party that took place within several lavish suites at the St. Francis Hotel, in downtown San Francisco, culminated in the death of a young actress named Virginia Rappé. Arbuckle was there, and so, unfortunately for him, was a scandal-mongering hanger-on by the name of Maude Delmont, who had a notorious criminal record that included counts of fraud, extortion, and racketeering. Seeing the tragic occurrences as a financial opportunity, Delmont began spreading the rumor that Virginia Rappé was the victim of a brutal sexual assault. With the story picked up by the sensationalist Hearst newspapers, ever the guardians of patriotism and public morality, Arbuckle found himself charged with murder, and his films were withdrawn from circulation.

The case of California v. Roscoe Arbuckle began in November 1921, and ended two months later with a hung jury. A second trial began in January 1922, and ended with the same result. Arbuckle's lawyers had shown that statements imputed to Rappé by the prosecution had been manufactured by the eyewitnesses; that she had died as a result of chronic cystitis brought on by venereal disease, a condition that had finally resulted in a ruptured bladder; and that the prosecution had not allowed attending doctors to attest to Rappé's own dying statements: that Arbuckle had had nothing to do with her injuries. Nevertheless, a third trial began on March 13, 1922, and this time the accused was acquitted after a deliberation of five minutes by the jury. The damage to Arbuckle's career was done, however, and in this era of carefully molded public images he was damaged goods in the eyes of the public and the movie studios.

The Motion Pictures Producers and Distributors Association (MPPDA) had been formed March 11, 1922, with Will Hays—a church elder, former chairman of the Republican National Committee, postmaster general, and confidante of President Harding—invited to act as its head. The MPPDA was the instrument by which Hollywood reviewed its own product and set guidelines for writers and directors in the matter of sex, violence, drug and alcohol use, and depictions of the church and clergy. Six days after Arbuckle's acquittal, Hays slapped a lifetime ban on Fatty from the movie industry. Later that year, the Hays Office drew up a list of 200 movie undesirables who also suffered from bad public reputations. Those blacklisted found themselves unemployable in the movie industry, most for the rest of their lives.

Hays would lift the ban on Fatty Arbuckle later that year, an action that only brought renewed outrage from church groups, civic associations, and the press. In October 1927, concurrent with the release of *The Jazz Singer,* starring Al Jolson in the first sound movie, the "Hays Office" promulgated a code of "Don'ts"— themes and subjects to be avoided, which included drug trafficking, profanity, white slavery, and ridicule of the clergy—and "Be Carefuls"—themes and subjects to be approached with caution, which included rape, surgery, seduction, crime, brutality, lustful kissing, and sedition. By the mid-1930s, the Production Code Administration of the Hays Office was reviewing all scripts and completed films in advance of their release for their adherence to the Hays Code.

After his acquittal, Arbuckle acted in one more film, James Cruze's *Hollywood,* in 1923, and continued to direct under the name of William Goodrich. Will Hays remained in his position for another 25 years. In the front offices, the reaction to the trials and acquittal of Fatty Arbuckle had reminded studio heads that sacrificing one overweight scapegoat, and a regimen of voluntary self-censorship, was far preferable to seeing local and federal governments exercise control over their scripts and productions.

Stars of Tennis and Golf

The trials of Fatty Arbuckle, the founding of United Artists, and the innovation of movie sound were headlining events in a decade when the attention of the population was focused more sharply than before on diversion and entertainment. Also benefiting from an enhancement in leisure time were professional and collegiate sports, which by the end of the 1920s could boast image-laden star systems of their own. Their deeds and praises sung by equally legendary sportswriters such as Grantland Rice, Ring Lardner, Westbrook Pegler, and Damon Runyon, the athletic heroes of the 1920s shone brightly in a celebrity-worshipping era, an era when some of the greatest athletes in the country's history reached their prime.

Tennis emerged from its origins as an upper-class diversion to become a widely popular competitive sport. Born in 1905 in California, Helen Wills was given a new racket and a membership at the Berkeley Tennis Club for her 14th birthday. After three years of lessons with William "Pop" Fuller, she won her first national tennis championship in 1923 at the age of 17. At the Summer Olympics of the following year, she won gold medals in both singles and doubles competition. In 1927 she became the first American woman to win the Wimbledon tennis championship in England in 20 years, and in the following two years ran down opponents for singles titles in France and the United States. Altogether, she won seven U.S. and eight Wimbledon titles before abruptly retiring from tournament play in 1938.

Wills's dominance in women's tennis was matched by the play of the tall and taciturn, full-court perfectionist William Tatem "Big Bill" Tilden. An artist who worked in backhands, forehands, lobs, slices, and befuddling changes of pace, Tilden won his first Wimbledon championship in 1920, the first American male to do so, and proceeded to win two more in short order while racking up seven U.S. national titles during the 1920s. Tilden was also successful in Davis Cup competition, winning 17 singles matches and losing only five, and took the National Clay Court championship six times in a row.

Tilden had once been a Shakespearean actor, and unsubtle histrionics became a hallmark of his playing style. He would respond to catcalls from the audience by simply abandoning the match; he would sleepwalk through the first two sets against a weaker opponent just to draw a crowd to the inevitable comeback and victory; when favored by a linesman's bad call, he would quite purposefully lose the following point. While winning U.S. and Wimbledon victories he also appeared on the stage and wrote plays, novels, and books of tennis instruction.

Golf emerged during the 1920s with its superstar in the person of Robert Tyre "Bobby" Jones, whose mastery of the game and string of national championships seemed all the more heroic coming after a long and frustrating period as an also-ran and sudden-death loser. Born in 1902 in Atlanta, Jones was the son of a college baseball player good enough to be offered a contract by the Brooklyn Dodgers immediately after his graduation. Robert P. Jones had been admonished by his own father to pursue a career in law, however, and took to golf, as did many up-and-coming men in business, to establish and extend his professional contacts.

Bobby Jones developed his sweet swing in adolescence by imitating a Scottish professional named Stewart Maiden. Jones had begun by winning junior championships at the age of nine and club championships at 12; he took a state open tournament in 1916, at 14. That same year, he competed in his first national amateur championship, at the Merion Cricket Club in Philadelphia, and led at the end of the first round. Although he eventually lost to Bob Gardner, Jones was already a national figure in amateur competition, at that time the leading golf tournament circuit.

His early promise perhaps dogged by high expectations, Jones then experienced long years of frustration. He lost the national amateur tournament again in 1920, and in 1921 lost at the British Amateur. In every major competition, he seemed to fall apart in the final round after holding solid leads. His habit of finishing in second place raised suspicions among golf writers and observers that he could not handle the enormous pressures of competitive golf. In 1922 Jones did nothing to quiet the critics—he lost to Gene Sarazen at the U.S. Open and to Jess Sweetser in the U.S. Amateur. After competing in 11 major tournaments in seven years, he had yet to win a title.

The break in his fortunes finally came in the summer of 1923, when the U.S. Open was held at the Inwood Country Club on Long Island. Jones entered the final round leading by three strokes, then blew the lead with a bogey, bogey, double-bogey finish to wind up in a tie with Bobby Cruikshank. The play-off took place the next day; while a huge gallery of spectators followed the two men around the course, Jones and Cruikshank fought to an even score as far as the final hole. Then, with a tremendous midiron second shot from 200 yards out, Jones landed his ball six feet from the hole and wound up with a two-stroke victory.

Jones won the U.S. Amateur a total of five times and the U.S. Open four times. In 1926, he shot what he considered to be his finest round of competitive golf at the British Open, a six-under-par 66 in a qualifying round that made the final rounds something of an anticlimax. The win at the British Open earned Jones a ticker-tape parade down Broadway when he returned home. In the next year, while studying law at Emory University, he won the U.S. Amateur as well as the British Open. Three years later, Jones achieved a Grand Slam, winning all four major tournaments—the British Amateur, the British Open, the U.S. Open, and the U.S. Amateur—the last of which he won at the same Merion Cricket Club course where he had first burst onto the golf scene in 1916. Two months later, Jones retired from golf, his astounding feat of that year never to be duplicated.

FOOTBALL

Harold Edward "Red" Grange, born in 1903 as the son of a Wheaton, Illinois, police chief, also came from a middle-class background. At Wheaton High School he excelled in track and basketball but starred on the football field, where during his career he scored an astounding 74 touchdowns, an average of five in every game he played. On arrival at the first practice led by Coach Bob Zuppke at the University of Illinois, Grange was assigned to the seventh team but within a week rose to first-string running back, going on to place on the All-America team his freshman year. His artful running style completely defeated opposing defenders, who in pursuit often found themselves grasping at an elongating shadow headed for the goal line.

During his first college game against Nebraska in 1923, Grange, nicknamed the "Galloping Ghost," scored three touchdowns. (The next summer, to further strengthen himself in preparation for his sophomore year, Grange signed on as an

Commenting "I don't love football enough to play it for free," Harold "Red" Grange (left, with unidentified fan) signed big contracts after his college career and played a large part in attracting spectators to the professional game. *(Bergert Brothers Collection/University of South Carolina)*

ice hauler.) On October 18, 1924, he put on an amazing display of skill and speed that would go down as the "Most Famous 12 Minutes of Football in History." Starting off the game with a 95-yard kickoff return for a touchdown, Grange followed up with three more touchdown runs—67, 56, and 44 yards—before the end of the first quarter. The crowd's cheering for Grange's spectacular broken-field running delayed the start of the second quarter for five minutes.

During three seasons at the University of Illinois, Grange had 31 touchdowns and ran 3,637 yards. He made the All-America team as a halfback in 1923 and 1924 and as a quarterback in 1925. Grange's whirling, ghostlike runs brought football the measure of glamor and spectacle that eventually boosted it into the front rank of American spectator sports. Old football stadiums could not handle the crowds arriving to watch his Illinois team; while tens of thousands packed the stands, millions listened to Grange's exploits described on the radio. After his third year at Illinois, the Galloping Ghost considered offers in politics, real estate, and the movies. He settled on a career as a one-man traveling football exhibition, playing on Sundays for enormous fees with new professional teams in Chicago and New York. Grange's exploits on the football field gave the professional game a tremendous boost in the public's estimation.

BOXING

College football was an amateur sport, a spectacle still unhindered by promoters and salaries. At this time, sports promoters turned to the professional boxing ring for the greatest returns on their investment. The decade was marked by a series of spectacular boxing events, grave national gladiatorial contests that were described as epics by a fascinated press. In 1923, Jack Dempsey defended his title as heavyweight champion against Luis Angel Firpo, the "Wild Bull of the Pampas." The fight began with a swift knockdown by Firpo, but Dempsey recovered to knock down his opponent seven times. Fifty-eight seconds into the second round, Dempsey sent Firpo to the canvas for good.

With the victory over Firpo, Dempsey reached the peak of his career. He had come from the hardscrabble mining country around Manassa, Colorado, where he was born in 1895. After a brief career as a copper miner, he worked as a dance hall bouncer and lumberjack. As a teenager he began training as a boxer, winning his first bout for a purse of $2.50 in 1915 and then fighting in dozens of small-time bouts all over the western United States. Uncertain of the advantages of a professional career, he reluctantly agreed to be managed by Jack "Doc" Kearns of San Francisco, who matched Dempsey against leading heavyweights, 21 of whom Dempsey beat in the year 1918 alone. On July 4, 1919, Dempsey beat 245-pound Jess Willard, the Pottawatomie Giant, in three rounds to win the heavyweight title. His reputation damaged by avoiding the draft

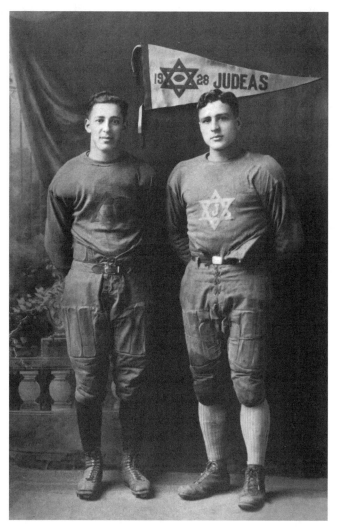

Morris Hillman (left) and Ernie Kaplan, members of the Judeas, an amateur football team sponsored by the Emanuel Cohen Center, Minneapolis. *(Minnesota Historical Society)*

during World War I, Dempsey was not yet the public's favorite when his manager arranged a defense of the title against the French war hero Georges Carpentier in the summer of 1921. The fight, which Dempsey won in four rounds, was the first sporting event to be nationally broadcast and rewarded its promoters with the first $1 million dollar gate in history.

The sporting public always favored a winner, and after his victory over Carpentier, Dempsey toured the country giving exhibitions to enthusiastically partisan spectators. In the meantime, with his boxing skills unchallenged by worthy opponents, he grew rusty and lost the lightning-quick jabs and crosses that had floored nearly all previous opponents. At the same time, a challenge by Harry Wills, an African American and former New Orleans stevedore who went by the names the Brown Panther and the Dark Prince, went unanswered. Dempsey later explained that the promoter Tex Rickard had instructions from Washington not to put on a fight between the races, fearing another outbreak of Klan marches and public riots.

In 1926, the ex-marine Gene Tunney outboxed Dempsey to a 10-round victory and the heavyweight title. In the summer of 1927, Dempsey was given a rematch, which took place before 100,000 spectators at Soldier Field in Chicago. In the seventh round, the eager Dempsey had Tunney on the floor and on the ropes before moving to a neutral corner for the referee's count. The extra seconds gave Tunney time to recover, return to his feet, and bob and weave for the rest of the fight to retain his championship. The "Battle of the Long Count" became the most famous bout of many sensational matches during the 1920s and marked the end of Dempsey's championship career.

THE BLACK SOX AND THE BABE

At the beginning of the decade, professional baseball had barely survived a scandal that nearly destroyed it. In September 1920, during a grand jury investigation into an unrelated gambling matter, it was revealed that eight members of the Chicago White Sox of the American League had tried to deliberately lose games to the Cincinnati Reds of the National League, during the World Series held in October 1919. The accused players were paid as much as $10,000 by a ring of professional gamblers for their non-efforts during the series, and they had succeeded—the Reds won the series by five games to three. The scandal outraged the press and the public, who had looked to baseball as a wholesome relief from the conflicts, violence, and stresses of the War and its aftermath. The guilty players were considered national traitors; the game itself was tainted, no longer free, it seemed, from the tumult that raged outside the peaceful confines of big-city ballparks.

The result of the so-called Black Sox scandal was an entirely new management structure for baseball. Previously, the two professional leagues had been governed by a three-man National Commission made up of representatives drawn from the ranks of team owners. On November 12, 1920, the owners appointed a federal judge, Kenesaw Mountain Landis, as the new baseball commissioner. Landis would serve a term of seven years and have final authority over all disputes involving the teams, the players, and the two leagues.

Judge Landis was best known for his severe treatment of radicals and pacifists during World War I. He was considered honest and uncompromising; he had also acted favorably towards professional baseball in 1915 during an antitrust suit brought against an upstart organization known as the Federal League. Even before the trial of the Black Sox players ended in a verdict of not guilty for lack of evidence, Landis made it clear that none of the accused would be permitted to return to professional baseball.

In the years following the Black Sox scandal, the charismatic Landis and a young player named George Herman "Babe" Ruth helped bring about baseball's gradual recovery. Ruth, a pitcher traded from the Boston Red Sox to the New York Yankees in 1919, was transformed into an outfielder by Yankees general manager Ed Barrow and had responded to the new position by setting new single season baseball records of 59 home runs and 171 runs batted in. With the generous assistance of the management of the Boston Red Sox, the owners of the New York Yankees had acquired several other talented players and, in the autumn of 1921, won their first league championship.

Ruth pioneered a new style of heavy hitting that brought fans back to the ballparks and turned the attention of sportswriters away from player scandals, high salaries, and the general bickering and greedy behavior of the team owners. To further clean up the game, baseball outlawed the spitball and the cuffed ball, forcing pitchers to deliver honest fastballs, curves, and sliders that gave the hitters a fair chance and allowed the sport to feature exciting offense over dull, workaday defense. At the same time, Branch Rickey of the St. Louis Cardinals created a "farm system" of small-town teams that developed skilled players for the big leagues. By the mid-1920s, baseball games were attracting an average of 5 million paying customers to the parks each year, and the game seemed to have fully recovered.

The New York Yankees had the good fortune to become the best team in the American League at a time when spectator sports of all kinds were drawing new fans. Babe Ruth towered over all the other new sport celebrities like "Big Bill" Tilden and Red Grange. Ruth's was a classic American story—a street kid and reform-school troublemaker from a bad neighborhood in Baltimore who had a natural talent for nothing but throwing and hitting a ball. Even though Ruth had a mediocre season in 1926, the Yankees still won another American League championship in that season and were already gathering the aura of a championship dynasty. Fortune turned against them during game seven of the World Series, which was played at the new Yankee Stadium in the Bronx. In the seventh inning, with the bases loaded, and an opportunity to drive in runs that would have won the game and probably the series for the Yankees, shortstop Tony Lazzeri was struck out by Grover Cleveland Alexander, a pitcher working without a single day of rest. The Yankees then lost game seven and the series.

In the spring of 1927, the Yankees management was determined to make amends. Miller Huggins, hired as manager in 1918, laid down rules that he hoped would finally instill a winning attitude in players made too comfortable by success, public acclaim, and high salaries. Huggins allowed no horseplay on the field or in the dugout and no talk about anything other than baseball on the bench. He set down a strict 1 A.M. curfew for his players and discouraged late nights during home stands by having the players come to Yankee Stadium and sign in at 10 o'clock each morning.

In the preseason of 1927 the issue most prominent in the columns of the sports pages was Babe Ruth's salary. Ruth had returned the contract the Yankees owner, Jacob Ruppert, had sent him at the beginning of the year, threatening to leave baseball rather than sign on Ruppert's terms. (Baseball owners benefited from the "reserve clause," upheld by a Supreme Court decision in 1922, which tied each player to a particular team during their entire professional career.) In

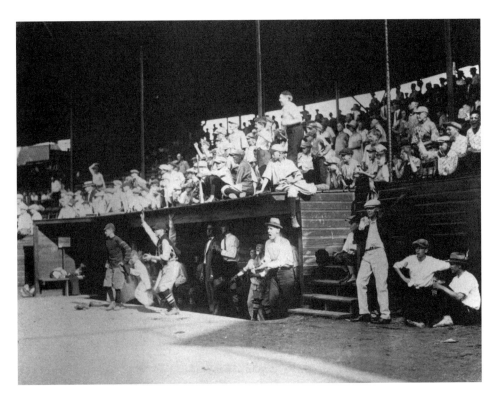

Spectators cheer at a children's baseball game, 1925. *(Minnesota Historical Society)*

response, Ruppert negotiated through the newspapers. Ruth was demanding $100,000 a season, for two seasons, nearly double the $52,000 a year he had been making since 1922. He also wanted a refund of $7,700 in fines that had been levied against him, for various instances of professional and personal misconduct.

Eventually Ruth settled for $70,000. He would earn all of it, hitting 60 home runs—a record that would stand until 1961—and powering a lineup that completely overmatched all opposing pitchers. That season, the Yankees demolished the rest of the American League, winning a total of 110 games and losing only 44, while Yankee Stadium set a single-season attendance record of 2,246,096. In the National League, the Pittsburgh Pirates ran a three-way race for their league championship with the New York Giants and the St. Louis Cardinals, finally taking the pennant with the last games of the season.

The 1927 World Series began on October 5 in Pittsburgh. Game one was broadcast over two radio networks and announced by Graham McNamee to 53 stations and an audience as high as 20 million. Despite the advantage of an enthusiastic home crowd and despite outhitting the Yankees 9-6, the Pirates made a series of defensive mistakes in the third inning that cost them the game, which was decided by a final score of 5-4. Babe Ruth's three singles made up one-half of the total Yankee offense. On October 6, Yankees pitcher George Pipgras dazzled the Pirate batters with his intimidating fastball, which he threw on all but four occasions. Crucial runs were scored on sacrifice flies by Ruth and Tony Lazzeri, and the Yankees won the game by a final score of 6-2.

By this time, it was apparent to restless and discouraged fans in Pittsburgh, and to all those paying attention to the World Series, that the Pirates were overmatched. On October 7, in Yankee Stadium, the Yankees won game three, 8-1. Left-hander Herb Pennock pitched a fine game through seven innings backed up by dazzling defensive play from Joe Dugan, Mark Koenig, and Tony Lazzeri. In the seventh inning, the Yankees scored six runs, highlighted by a home run from Ruth.

On October 8, the Yankees and the Pirates played the closest game yet of the series. The Babe hit his second home run of the series in the fifth inning; Pittsburgh scored on errors by Moore and Lazzeri in the seventh. In the bottom of the ninth inning, the score was tied, 3-3. With Johnny Miljus pitching for the Pirates and Yankee runners on second and third base, Ruth was given an intentional walk, which loaded the bases with nobody out. First baseman Lou Gehrig, now working on a consecutive-game appearance record that would last for almost 70 years, struck out; Bob Meusal struck out. With two men out and the bases still loaded, Tony Lazzeri came up next with a chance to avenge his infamous strikeout in the seventh inning of the seventh game of the 1926 series. But there would be no hitting heroics and only small vengeance for Lazzeri, as the game ended on a wild pitch from Miljus that bounced off the top of the catcher's glove. Earl Combs strolled in from third base, scoring the winning run, and the World Series was over.

THE FORD EMPIRE

Mass entertainment and the immense audience for professional sports represented two symptoms of a growing homogenization of American society. Spectators witnessed identical feats and worshipped the same heroes, coast to coast. This large-scale blending of taste and diversion was reflected further in the nation's mode of transport, which was increasingly being carried out in cars, all manufactured by a single company headquartered in suburban Detroit that was run by the benevolent industrial dictator Henry Ford.

Henry Ford had built his first automobile, a two-cylinder "gasoline buggy," in the autumn of 1892 and had begun testing it in 1893, a year of a serious nationwide economic depression. Fifteen years later, the Ford Motor Company, where about 350 workers were employed, turned out the first Model T, which was sold to the public in a variety of models at prices between $850 and $1,000. The Model T was a basic machine, easy to repair and maintain, and useful for driving on the dirt roads and rough surfaces that still predominated in the

The Model T auto was basic, reliable transportation, ideal for touring as well as more formal occasions such as weddings. *(Minnesota Historical Society/Henry A. Briol)*

United States. More than 10,000 copies of the Model T were sold in the first year of production.

Contrary to the usual economic patterns of the time, Ford's product declined in price as the years went by. By 1911, Ford was employing 4,000 workers, producing more than 30,000 cars a year, and selling them for less than $700. At the same time, he was reinventing manufacturing processes through standardization, a mode of production in which parts for all models were made interchangeable and the actions of workers and machinery within the factory were carefully planned and timed. Efficiency and cost were the prime considerations; when it was found that the resins in black paint dried slightly faster than those in any other color, the Model T was promptly turned a monotonous shade of black that remained the sole option for buyers until the mid-1920s.

At Ford's 60-acre Highland Park, Michigan, auto plant—the largest in the world—Ford "took the work to the workers" by setting up a moving assembly line, along which a series of precisely calculated operations were carried out, from fastening mudguards to the chassis to finally driving the car out onto the street. On the theory that well-paid workers would make the best customers for his goods, Ford also raised his wages to $5 a day—an action that scandalized his competitors and other manufacturing employers throughout the nation—and lowered the price of the basic and unchanged Model T automobile to less than $500. By 1914, the Model T was selling so well that Ford no longer bothered to advertise it.

In 1920, the assembly lines at Highland Park were turning out a new copy of the Model T every 60 seconds, and the wage in a Ford factory had risen to $6 a day. The price of the car had fallen to less than $400, making Ford's automobiles affordable to nearly anyone who had a paying job. The construction of a new, hard-surfaced road network was proceeding at a rapid pace (40,000 miles a year by the middle of the decade), allowing those with automobiles an easy form of travel from one farm, city, and state to the next. The automobile also sparked the growth of suburbia, from which city workers made daily commutes over the roads to their jobs in central business districts. The automobile gave rise to ancillary manufacturing and service businesses: the first motels set out their registers, and the first traffic lights were raised on street corners.

RETHINKING THE MODEL T

Ford sought to create a wholly integrated and self-sufficient operation, from top to bottom, controlling suppliers and distribution himself and discouraging any outside investment. He used lumber grown on his own plantations, setting up his own sawmills to cut the wood and purchasing a fleet of barges to tow it around. He also built glass factories to supply windshields and headlamps. The Ford company owned coal mines in Kentucky, for use in generating electricity at the automobile factories; Ford dug his own iron ore for casting into iron and steel. As much as possible, Ford manufactured his own parts, machinery, and machine tools. He also bought a private railroad for the hauling of coal, iron ore, and other raw materials. Ford's scrap plants recycled used steel, rubber, brick, paper, oil, wood, and sand. In 1928 Ford representatives would stake out the future site of Fordlandia, a huge acreage along the banks of the Tapajos River in South America, in order to produce a new type of rubber.

Ford was perhaps the most practical utopian in history. He turned his corporation into an industrial religion, its central doctrine the achievement of lasting world peace and prosperity through the mass production of standardized goods, which would be made available to increasing numbers of people, who would thereby find limitless opportunities for employment and self-fulfillment. The basic Model T served as the great democratic sacrament—the vehicle that allowed people to travel as far as they wished, whenever they wished, thus speeding up the free enterprise system and bringing a new era, a golden age of democratic transportation.

Despite his professed concern for the general welfare of industrial workers, Ford and his managers controlled and disciplined their employees with dictatorial enthusiasm. Workers were subject to instant dismissal for the use of alcohol or tobacco, even in their own homes. The employees were also strictly forbidden to join unions. Assembly-line work turned laborers into automatons, subject to stress and fatigue brought on by the deadening repetition of their timed, measured, and carefully supervised operations.

In 1923, Ford produced 57 percent of all the cars made in the United States and about one-half of all the cars made in the world. By 1926, there were 88 Ford manufacturing and assembly plants in operation, 60 of them in the United States, and the company's total capacity had reached 2 million cars a year. Slight innovations were made—an electric starter and a foot accelerator were added, new colors became available, and the Model T's ride was improved with balloon tires invented by Henry Firestone. But despite the ongoing success of the Ford company and the growing acceptance all over the world of Ford's ideas and ideals, the Model T was growing out of fashion and was threatening to turn into an industrial relic. It was a bumpy, cranky, hard-starting car that looked like a box. It made a top speed of about 40 miles an hour, ideal for the dirt roads of the past but not for city streets or for smoother concrete roads that were under construction between major cities throughout the country.

In the beginning, more than 20 years earlier, Ford had designed the Model T as a utilitarian machine that could run farm machinery when it was not on the road. Car buyers no longer looked to automobiles as equipment, and most of them had no need to run farm machinery (for that, Ford had developed the Fordson tractor, a power plant on wheels that served to automate the hard labors of the farm). Marketing sense was introduced by rival automobile companies, most notably by Ford's competitor Alfred P. Sloan, who had been the head of General Motors (GM) since 1923. Car buyers were using their old cars as trade-ins to get the newest, latest, and slightly more expensive models. Customers, especially women, wanted new colors and designs, more comfort, ease of use, and a fashion statement.

Competition from General Motors and Chevrolet, as well as Hudson and Packard, was cutting into sales. Ford's market share fell from 54 percent to 45 percent in 1925 and continued to decline. GM offered new features such as hydraulic brakes, which made the ride smoother; automatic wipers; a one-piece windshield; and new models every year. The invention of pyroxylin finishes in 1925 allowed manufacturers to begin painting their cars in a variety of new colors. Also, automobiling had become increasingly convenient, with filling stations and garages opening everywhere, precision parts such as spark plugs making maintenance and repair on the part of the owner largely unnecessary, closed cars protecting passenger and driver from the sun and the weather, and balloon tires making the ride smoother and more comfortable.

During the 1920s, electric streetcars still posed formidable competition for the limited space on city streets. *(Bergert Brothers Collection/University of South Florida)*

GM and Ford's other competitors had also joined the 1920s trend of offering their goods on credit. As the pressure to consume increased, installment buying was gaining acceptance among consumers, whether they purchased clothing, furniture, appliances, radios, or automobiles. Ford resisted this change for many years. The son of a farmer, he had a limited education and a reverent respect for the past, when the virtues of hard work, thrift, and religious faith held sway. Instead of changing company policies, he blamed slothful local dealers for declining sales and punished them with the "crossroads policy," in which rival Model T dealers were licensed right across the street from those falling into disfavor. He did not realize or did not foresee that the mass production and consumption of automobiles would also cause drastic changes in the society and its values. A telling symptom of Ford's nostalgia was the building of Greenfield Village in Dearborn, Michigan, a museum that was actually a reconstructed small town, complete with barns, forges, general stores, and Ford's own little one-room schoolhouse.

In 1926, Ford finally gave in to the trends and made the epochal decision to scrap the Model T. Shortly after driving the 15 millionth Model T off his assembly line on May 26, 1927, he announced the complete redesign of the basic Ford automobile. He shut down the assembly lines, laid off 10,000 workers, and scrapped 40,000 machines. Nearly 10,000 Ford dealers across the country suddenly had no new cars to sell and had to depend for their income on the sale of spare parts and old inventory. Only plants manufacturing spare parts for the Model T remained in operation. At a cost of more than $100 million, the Ford Motor Company was completely retooled. A manufacturing center, the immense River Rouge plant, was prepared to replace the Highland Park factory for production of the new Model A. New and more powerful generators were installed; new presses were designed that would manufacture a car stamped out of steel, not assembled from a complex kit of welded cast iron parts.

As a direct result of these actions, total car sales in the United States—in a time of prosperity and rapid growth—fell by more than 1 million from the previous year, and the Chevrolet became the top-selling brand. Throughout the late spring and summer, the country waited in suspenseful expectation of the new Ford model. As the date of the unveiling approached, to prepare the public and whet the consuming appetite the company ran full-page advertisements in 2,000 newspapers, a campaign that cost a total of $1.3 million. Assembly began in the autumn of 1927; the first Model A rolled off the assembly line on October 20. The cars were driven into showrooms under cover of canvas tarpaulins to guard the secret of their appearance. Finally, the new Model A was unveiled on December 2, 1927. The gears were greatly simplified; hydraulic shock absorbers and balloon tires smoothed the ride; safety glass was installed; and a new four-cylinder engine allowed a top cruising speed of 55 miles an hour. Adapted from the Lincoln by Ford's son Edsel, the Model A design was sleek and stylish and provided respectable competition to the most marketable cars brought out by General Motors. Henry Ford priced the new model at an affordable $495, less than the comparable models of his competition, and even allowed it to be bought on credit.

The Model A was given a front-page illustration in every major newspaper in the country. People crowded into the auto showrooms for a look; in Detroit a mob of 100,000 stormed the Model A exhibit. In New York, Madison Square Garden was rented out for a week as a showroom. Ford sent his top managers on cross-country tours to gather publicity for the new model among the people of small towns and farms that still might not be subject to the avalanche of notice and advertisement in newspapers, magazines, and on the radio. By Christmas, a half million orders were on the books. Production of the Model A reached 6,000 per day in the middle of 1928.

By 1929, 23 million cars were on the road, an increase from 6.8 million in 1919. The modern highway altered the landscape, allowing increased mobility for everyone and slowly but surely putting urban trolleys and the railroads out of business. The automobile industry also accelerated the nation's business. By 1929 it was employing 7 percent of all manufacturing workers and supporting rubber, steel, and glass factories; oil refineries; and construction businesses. With the automobile in the lead, the nation's industry, once tied to the heavy manufacturing, mining, and construction demanded by geographic expansion, was being transformed to meet the needs and tastes of households and consumers.

The use of private automobiles gave rise to new occupations—attendant and mechanic—for Mrs. Fred R. Crosby, employed by the Capitol Curve filling station in St. Paul. *(Minnesota Historical Society)*

CHRONICLE OF EVENTS

1927

June 4: Clarence Chamberlain and Charles Levine set a new nonstop aviation record of 3,905 miles during a 43-hour flight between New York and Germany.

June 20: The Limitation of Naval Armaments Conference, called for by President Coolidge, opens in Geneva, attended by the United States, Japan, and Great Britain.

June 28–29: The first successful flight between Hawaii and California takes place in a Fokker monoplane piloted by Lester Maitland and Albert F. Hegenberger. The flight lasts 25 hours, 50 minutes.

July 2: Helen Wills wins the women's singles title at the Wimbledon tennis championship in England. U.S. players also win mixed doubles, men's doubles, and women's doubles.

July 29: The first electric respirator, or "iron lung," invented by Dr. Philip Drinker and Dr. Louis A. Shaw, is installed at Bellevue Hospital in New York City.

August 2: Before an appearance in Rapid City, South Dakota, President Coolidge hands out small slips of papers to reporters. The slips read, "I do not choose to run for president in 1928."

August 4: The Naval Armaments Conference concludes in Geneva, having produced no agreement.

August 7: In Buffalo, Vice President Charles Dawes and the Prince of Wales officially inaugurate the International Peace Bridge between the United States and Canada.

August 23: More than six years after their conviction for taking part in an armed robbery and murder, Nicola Sacco and Bartolomeo Vanzetti are electrocuted at Charlestown State Prison in Massachusetts. The executions take place despite widespread protests by those

Harmonica champions, St. Louis County Farm Bureau Recreational Institute, Pike Lake Auto Club, 1927 *(Minnesota Historical Society)*

Overshadowed in press coverage by the exploits of Babe Ruth and Lou Gehrig, the 1927 New York Yankees pitching staff still managed to shut down opponents on most days. From left to right, Sam Jones, Joe Bush, Bob Shawkey, Waite Hoyt, Carl Mays, Herb Pennock, Dutch Ruether, and George Pipgras. *(Brown Brothers)*

who believed the two had been railroaded for their anarchist beliefs.

September 10: France defeats the United States by three matches to two to win the international Davis Cup tennis championship.

September 14: Dancer Isadora Duncan is accidentally strangled when her scarf is entangled in an automobile wheel in Nice, France.

September 22: Jack Dempsey loses again in a rematch with Gene Tunney for the heavyweight boxing title.

September 27: Babe Ruth hits his 60th home run of the season at Yankee Stadium.

September 29: St. Louis is hit by a powerful tornado that lasts only 5 minutes but kills 87 and injures 1,500.

October 6: The first movie to have synchronized speech as well as music, *The Jazz Singer,* starring Al Jolson, premieres.

October 5–8: The New York Yankees defeat the Pittsburgh Pirates in four straight games to win the World Series.

October 10: The Supreme Court rules that the Teapot Dome oil lease between the Department of the Interior and the Mammoth Oil Company was fraudulent and therefore invalid.

November 5: Walter Hagen wins the Professional Golfers' Association (PGA) Tournament for the fourth time in a row.

November 12: The 1.8-mile Holland Tunnel, the first underwater automobile tunnel in the United States, opens under the Hudson River between Jersey City, New Jersey, and New York City.

November 22: Funny Face, with music composed by George Gershwin, premieres in New York.

December 2: The Ford Motor Company begins selling the new Model A automobile.

December 4: The Duke Ellington Orchestra opens at the Cotton Club in Harlem.

December 13: Charles Lindbergh leaves for a goodwill tour of Mexico after being invited by Ambassador Dwight Morrow. Lindbergh will make a six-week tour of Central and South America.

December 17: The 40-man crew of the U.S. submarine *S-4* dies after the submarine collides with the U.S. Coast Guard ship *Paulding* and sinks off Provincetown, Massachusetts.

December 25: The legislature of Mexico reverses the "positive acts" stipulation for foreign ownership of oil and mineral rights on Mexican soil, thus granting unlimited concessions to foreign companies and repudiating the 1917 constitution.

December 27: The musical *Show Boat,* with music by Jerome Kern and libretto by Oscar Hammerstein, and produced by Florenz Ziegfeld, opens on Broadway.

EYEWITNESS TESTIMONY

Movies, Morals, and Sound

Acquittal is not enough for Roscoe Arbuckle. We feel that a great injustice has been done him. We feel also that it was only our plain duty to give him his exoneration, under the evidence, for there was not the slightest proof adduced to connect him in any way with the commission of a crime.

He was manly throughout the case, and told a straightforward story on the witness stand, which we all believed. The happening at the hotel was an unfortunate affair for which Arbuckle, as the evidence shows, was in no way responsible.

We wish him success, and hope that the American people will take the judgment of fourteen men and women who have sat listening for thirty-one days to the evidence, that Roscoe Arbuckle is entirely innocent and free from all blame.

Statement of the jury, April 12, 1922, ending the third and final murder trial of Roscoe "Fatty" Arbuckle, from Grant and Katz, The Great Trials of the Twenties *(1998), p. 91.*

EXHIBITORS! Do you realize that on August 6th motion pictures will have been completely revolutionized by "VITAPHONE"? On that day "VITAPHONE" will bring the realization of a new future to the theaters of the world; a future brighter in its aspects, broader in its scope, and greater in its possibilities than any other period in the development of motion pictures.

What the telephone means to modern life; what the railroad means to modern travel; what the world's greatest inventions mean to civilization today—that is what Warner Bros. bring to motion pictures in "VITAPHONE."

Like the rumblings of a coming storm, word-of-mouth comment comes low and slowly, but gathering power as it sweeps onward, it carries like lightning to the far corners of the world. Such will be the praise for "VITAPHONE"! Already you have heard of it. And on August 6th the whole world will thrill to the greatest news the entire motion picture industry has ever heard. The World Premiere of "VITAPHONE"— remember the date, August 6, 1926.

Promotional announcement prepared by Warner Brothers for its new Vitaphone sound system, run in Moving Picture World *of August 7, 1926, quoted in Geduld,* The Birth of the Talkies: From Edison to Jolson *(1975), p. 120.*

The picture was called *Mother Knows Best.* They hadn't really caught on yet how to regulate sound. In the talkie part at the end, there was a scene in which Mother was dying, and her final gasps were so thunderous that it must have been quite easy to hear them right out on Yonge Street.

Canadian bandleader Jack Arthur, recalling the first sound movie performances in Toronto in 1927, in West, Toronto *(1967), p. 247.*

The Academy will take aggressive action in meeting outside attacks that are unjust.

It will promote harmony and solidarity among the membership and among the different branches.

It will reconcile internal differences that may exist or arise.

It will adopt such ways and means as are proper to further the welfare and protect the honor and good repute of the profession.

It will encourage the improvement and advancement of the arts and sciences of the profession by the interchange of constructive ideas and by awards of merit for distinctive achievements.

It will take steps to develop the greater power and influence of the screen.

In a word, the Academy proposes to do for the motion picture profession in all its branches what other great national and international bodies have done for other arts and sciences and industries.

Goals of the newly founded Academy of Motion Picture Arts and Sciences, published on June 20, 1927, and quoted in Holden, Behind the Oscar *(1993), p. 88.*

While I was in New York, a friend told me that he had witnessed the synchronization of sound in films and predicted that it would shortly revolutionize the whole film industry.

I did not think of it again until months later when the Warner Brothers produced their first talking sequence. It was a costume picture, showing a very lovely actress—who shall be nameless—emoting silently over some great sorrow, her big, soulful eyes imparting anguish beyond the eloquence of Shakespeare. Then suddenly a new element entered the film—the noise that one hears when putting a seashell to one's ear. Then the lovely princess spoke as if talking through sand. . . . As the picture progressed the dialogue became funnier, but not as funny as the sound effects. When the handle of the boudoir door turned I thought someone had cranked up a farm tractor, and when the door closed it sounded like the collision of two lumber trucks. At the beginning they knew nothing about controlling sound: a knight-errant in armor clanged like the noise in a steel factory, a simple family dinner sounded like the rush hour in a cheap restaurant, and the pouring of water into a glass made a peculiar tone that ran up the scale to high C. I came away from the theater believing the days of sound were numbered.

Charles Chaplin, recalling his first encounter with movie sound, in Chaplin, My Autobiography *(1964), p. 324.*

Suddenly the anti-Hollywoodites had their moment of victory—the Arbuckle scandal! Fatty Arbuckle was arrested in San Francisco and charged with rape and murder. We all knew him as a big good-natured comedian who would never intentionally have harmed anyone. He was no different from scores of other successful Hollywood actors—drinking too much, spending too freely, and wasting himself on hangers-on unworthy of his generosity. During his sensational trials the clown's face appeared on front pages, unsmiling. San Franciscans were furious because Hollywood had left a garbage can in its doorway, and Fatty got little sympathy in that direction. The trials finally ended with Arbuckle acquitted. When he returned to Hollywood he was met by a chilling reception; both from producers and erstwhile associates. Only a few friends rallied to his support. They, too, soon faded into the background and Fatty Arbuckle realized he could never recapture the success that had been his before that tragic incident in San Francisco.

Silent-era screenwriter Frances Marion, recalling the trials of Fatty Arbuckle, in Off With Their Heads *(1972), p. 86.*

The only evidence, if you can call it evidence, that they had against Roscoe was what the newspapers said about him. And most of that came from Maude Delmont, who was the cause of the whole thing. But they never published in the papers that Maude Delmont had seventy-two affidavits out against her for being a professional correspondent, a woman that's found in bed with a husband when a photographer bursts into a room and takes a picture. That was when they had these setup divorces and the only grounds for divorce was adultery. Maude Delmont had gone to the well too often, she'd made it into a racket, and so the cops were down on her. When the cops found out Maude had been at the party at the St. Francis Hotel, she must have made a deal with the district attorney. They'd forget about the seventy-two affidavits if she'd

frame Roscoe. I'm as certain of that as I'm certain of anything, because in all three trials they never put her on the stand once. She would have made a terrible witness, and her testimony would have been shredded by our lawyers.

Minta Durfee Arbuckle, widow of Fatty Arbuckle, explaining the machinations behind Fatty Arbuckle's trial for rape and murder, in Wagner, You Must Remember This *(1975), pp. 38–39.*

U.S. Sports

It was in the Dempsey-Carpentier show at Jersey City that he first ran receipts for a prize fight above $1,000,000, the total in this contest reaching approximately $1,650,000.

He had startled the pugilistic realm again by offering Dempsey $300,000 for this international spectacle with $200,000 set aside for Carpentier, the Beau Socker of the Fleur-de-lis.

It was a healthy jump from the $30,000 he offered Nelson and Gans at Goldfield to the $500,000 he offered Dempsey and Carpentier at Jersey City. But again the fighters got their cash to the last thin dime and once again Tex Rickard made money on the show. No other promoter has ever put on a million-dollar boxing show. Tex Rickard put on three that netted close to $5,000,000 in receipts.

. . . Rickard's business has been to pick the two men he thought would draw the biggest crowd and the largest gate receipts. He has always been a student of crowd psychology, a great listener who has heard much but said little.

It never occurred to Tex Rickard that Georges Carpentier would give Jack Dempsey much of a battle. But here was every detail of a great international spectacle in reach, with a much greater appeal to the crowd than any mere ring battle could carry that might last ten rounds.

Sportswriter Grantland Rice, describing business methods of boxing promoter Tex Rickard, in "The King Maker," Collier's, *November 13, 1926, p. 36.*

I have a much better club than last year, and if we don't run into misfortunes we ought to stay on top . . . it's possible for us to take a slump at any time, but just now I'm not worrying a great deal. You see my boys are hitting the ball consistently and my pitchers are working very smoothly. The Yankees, as a team, have

Boxing fans surround the ring at a bout on the outskirts of Tampa, Florida. During the 1920s, most small-time matches, and several championship fights, were held in the open air. *(Bergert Brothers Collection/University of South Florida)*

improved in every way. Gehrig, Lazzeri, and Koenig, the young infielders, are showing the result of last year's experience by playing with more confidence and steadiness. Koenig is destined to become one of the finest shortstops in the majors. He is handling balls that he couldn't reach a year ago, and is throwing wonderfully. Gehrig is the hardest hitting first baseman I've seen and that is saying a lot. Lazzeri is the best second baseman in the American League. Joe Dugan isn't hitting but his third base play is excellent. In case of accidents to my regular infielders, I'll be well fortified. Durst can play first base, while Morehart, Gazella and Wera are ready to jump into the other positions.

The pitchers? They've surprised me, particularly Hoyt and Ruether. Pennock hasn't lost a game yet and Shocker is coming along nicely. Moore . . . has done splendid relief work.

Manager Miller Huggins, assessing his New York Yankees baseball team in June 1927, two months into the season, as quoted on "The 1927 Yankees" web site, URL: http://www.angelfire.com/pa/1927/27quotes.html.

Babe had smashed out two home runs the day before to bring his total to 59 for the season, or the exact equal of his 1921 record. He had only this last game to set a new record. Zachary, a left-hander, was by the nature of his delivery a hard man for the Babe to hit. In fact Babe got only two homers in all his life against Tom.

Babe came up in the eighth and it was quite probable that this would be his very last chance to break his own record. My mother and I were at the game and I can still see that lovely, lovely home run. It was a tremendous poke, deep into the stands. There was never any doubt that it was going over the fence. But the question was, would it be fair? It was fair by only six glorious inches!

The Babe later professed himself to be unimpressed and unexcited and certainly not surprised by the blow. "I knew I was going to hit it," he insisted. I didn't, although I was now used to his rising to occasions.

What delighted him as much, more than the homer, was the spectacle of his pal, Charlie O'Leary, jumping and screaming on the coaching lines, his bald head glinting in the failing sun. Charlie had thrown away his cap in jubilation when the umps signalled the ball fair.

Babe knew the extent of Charlie's joy because he knew his little friend was almost psychopathic about his bald dome. They didn't play "The Star-Spangled Banner" before every game then, only on festive occasions. On these occasions Charlie would hide. The baring of Charlie's gleaming head was an appreciated tribute to the popularity of that historic homer.

Helen Woodford (Mrs. Babe Ruth) September 1927 quoted in The Permanent Book of the 20th Century *(1994), pp. 168–169.*

. . . the factor that made the series almost a farce—the factor that enabled the Yankees to run off four consecutive victories (a feat previously performed by only the Boston National League club in 1914) was not so much New York pitching, or New York hitting. It was "errors by—," errors by Pittsburgh.

For making errors each Pittsburgh player received $3,728; for taking advantage of them each Yankee, $5,592.

From "World's Series," a summary of the 1927 World Series in Time *magazine, October 17, 1927, p. 36.*

More profound blah has been scribbled and spoken about the significance of our national vogue for sports than upon almost any topic, including Fundamentalism, Freud, the League of Nations, and the hot weather. Every after-dinner orator, conducting drives for college or Y.M.C.A. gymnasium funds, has pointed with pride and fountain pen to our outdoor enthusiasms as a convincing proof of racial and social vigor.

. . . Contrary to the opinions of professional and amateur sport promoters, the writer contends it is doubtful if the tremendous furor over motors and sports proves anything—except that our civilization has reached a highly artificial state, and that most of our citizens are bored with their jobs.

Certainly the judgment of comparative values has become warped. The head-lines of to-day, recounting, as this is written, Babe Ruth's thirty-third home run of the season, will scarcely be perpetuated by historians. About the time that one and one-half millions of our fellow citizens lined the sidewalks from the Battery to Central Park to cheer for Gertrude Ederle, a modest, unassuming chemist came to town. He was unheralded by the Vienna papers when he left, he was unnoticed by our metropolitan dailies when he arrived.

He came to this country to work in a research laboratory for seventy-five dollars a week. And he had been invited to continue his research here, because his discoveries of the secrets of cell growth and cell change may lead to the conquest of cancer, drug addiction, and tuberculosis. Cheering multitudes have not disturbed

his work, although six surgeons gave him a table-d'hôte dinner at a second-rate club.

John Smith, driving to his golf club in his Whosis Eight sedan, is quite properly more interested in Bobby Jones's putting and the mystery of Detroit—Will Henry put steam heat and bath in his new model?

From "Gas and the Games," by George S. Brooks in Scribner's, August 1928, p. 189.

Henry Ford and the Model A

Dear Henry Ford:

We of the South affectionately acclaim you, instead of Lincoln, as the Great Liberator. Lincoln has freed his thousands, you have freed your ten thousands. The rutted roads on mountain sides and water sogged wheel tracks on low lands have been smoothed, that the wheels of Fords may pass. The sagged barbed wire gates of barren cotton patches and blighted corn fields have been thrown open that brainblinded and soul-blinded recluses might ride joyously into the world with their families in Fords. An army of white clad serfs on small Southern farms in Ford cars and trucks are pushing

The Skinner and Roleff families picnic along the Seward River in 1922. Automobiles made camping and day trips into the countryside feasible for urban families. *(Minnesota Historical Society/William Roleff)*

onward and upward into a conscious heirship in the nations of civilized living. . . .

Letter to Henry Ford from an Alabama correspondent, 1926, quoted in Wik, Henry Ford and Grass-Roots America *(1972), p. 125.*

But Ford does praiseworthy things which neither Rockefeller nor Carnegie attempted, at least on any considerable scale. He regularly takes on hundreds of convicts newly released from prison and treats them exactly the same as other workmen. He also gives employment to more than his share of "the maimed, the halt and the blind." He believes it is the duty of industry to absorb a share of handicapped humans. He reasons that he can better fulfil his obligations to society by doing such things and also by using his profits to expand his business operations and his employment roll than by handing over large sums for philanthropic purposes. He receives, it is said, an average of 10,000 begging letters every week. The writers, however, waste their postage stamps.

. . . Certain labor factions extol him to the skies for his $6-a-day minimum wage; others brand his factory methods as infamous, as forcing men to become mere automatons. He has been called, "the best employer in America," and "absolutely impossible to work with"; those holding the latter view cite the burst-up between Ford and one after another of his leading early associates, including the Dodge brothers, James Couzens and others. His "Peace Ship" escapade, to "get the boys out of the trenches by Christmas," drew both laudation and condemnation; Ford himself, it may be interesting to know, still regards the project as one of the most worthy he ever essayed.

From Forbes and Foster, Automotive Giants of America *(1926), pp. 106–107.*

If the approaching automobile war between Henry Ford and General Motors Corp. were symbolized in armaments, Mr. Ford would be a cannon and General Motors a machine gun. When a Ford product strikes the market squarely, as did Model T when first shot into a world of pedestrians, the battle is over. But when the Ford product misses, as Model T has been missing ever since economic prosperity in the U.S. caused the public to shift from mere transportation to touring with style, it misses by a mile. Though Henry Ford has added to his weapon such potent arms as the Lincoln motors and an airplane manufacturing unit, his big gun has always been the Model T Ford. General

Motors, on the other hand, spreads its shots. It sends out a car to strike every purse—Chevrolet, Oldsmobile, Pontiac, Oakland, Buick, LaSalle, Cadillac. It carefully picks up its dead shells and turns them into electric refrigerators, an effective barrage to cover a retreat.

"Ford v. G. M. C.," from Time *magazine, October 10, 1927, p. 32.*

The old car was too slow. . . . The public was satisfied with it. And that's a sign we ought to change to something better. Since the public does not tell us what it wants, we give it what it ought to have. Once it needed a car that would go through mud and over the worst roads. It didn't know it, but we did, so we gave it the old car. Now the public ought to have speed, since roads are so much better than they were. Therefore we gave it speed. That's the whole story of the new car.

Henry Ford, quoted in Waldemar Kaempffert, "The Mussolini of Highland Park," from the New York Times Magazine, *January 8, 1928, and quoted in Sloat,* America Before the Crash *(1979), p. 43.*

When I first came over, I worked at Fisher Bodies for three months. I took a three-shift job on production at the start rather than be walkin' around. But then I went to Ford's—like everybody else I'd 'eard about Ford's wages. And you do get the wages. I got $5 a day for the first two months and $6 ahfter, for a year or so—then I ahsked for a raise and got forty cents more a day for two and a hahlf years—I never saw this $7 a day. But the wages are the only redeemin' feature. If he cut wages, they'd walk out on 'im. Ye get the wages but ye sell your soul at Ford's—ye're worked like a slave all day, and when ye get out ye're too tired to do anything—ye go to sleep on the car comin' home. Ye get lackadaisical, as they say in Lancashire—ye haven't got the guts to go. There's people who come to Ford's from the country, thinkin' they're goin' to make a little money—that they'll only work there a few years and then go back and be independent. And then they stay there forever—unless they get laid off. Ye've never got any security in your job. Finally they moved us out to the Rouge—we were the first people down there—we pioneered there when the machinery wasn't hardly nailed down. But when they began gettin' ready for Model A, production shut down and we were out of a job.

. . . It's worse than the army, I tell ye—ye're badgered and victimized all the time. You get wise to the

Auto tourists prepare for a cross-country journey to California, 1925. *(Minnesota Historical Society)*

army after a while, but at Ford's ye never know where ye're at. One day ye can go down the aisle and the next day they'll tell ye to get the hell out of it. In one department, they'll ahsk ye why the hell ye haven't got gloves on and in another why the hell ye're wearin' them. If ye're wearing a clean apron, they'll throw oil on it, and if a machinist takes pride in 'is tools, they'll thrown 'em on the floor when he's out. The bosses are thick as treacle and they're always on your neck, because the man above is on their neck and Sorenson's on the neck of the whole lot—he's the man that pours the boiling oil down that old Henry makes. There's a man born a hundred years too late, a regular slave driver—the men tremble when they see Sorenson comin'. He used to be very brutal—he'd come through and slug the men. One day when they were movin' the plant he came through and found a man

sittin' workin' on a box. "Get up!" says Sorenson. "Don't ye know ye can't sit down in here?" The man never moved and Sorenson kicked the box out from under 'im—and the man got up and bashed Sorenson one in the jaw. "Go to hell!" he says. "I don't work here—I'm working for the Edison Company!"

"Bert" to Edwin Wilson, in "Detroit Motors," from The American Earthquake *(1958), pp. 219–220.*

A dedication service of automobiles to the glory of God was advocated by President E. C. Herrick, of the Newton Theological Institution, at the closing of the Rockland, Me., Summer Conference. "The radio, automobile and all new things must be capitalized to the glory of God," he said.

Notice in the Boston Advertiser, *quoted in* The American Mercury, *January 1928, p. 51.*

There are two ways to make money—one at the expense of others, the other in service to others. The first method does not "make" money, does not create anything. It only "gets" money—and does not always succeed in that. In the last analysis, the so-called gainer loses. The second way succeeds twice—to maker and user, to seller and buyer. It receives by creating, and receiving only a just share, because no one is entitled to all.

Henry Ford, from "Youth, Industry, and Progress," in Forum, *October 1928, pp. 582–589.*

Million by million new motor cars came off the assembly lines of a hundred modern factories. A million and a half in 1921. Two million and a half in 1922. Three million and a half in 1923 and 1924. Four million in 1925 and 1926. Last year's pride became this year's trade-in, and the Used Car Market gathered new recruits. The pace of production was remorseless. By 1926 there were twenty-two motor cars in the United States to every twenty-three families, and the advertisements were already proclaiming this A Two-Car Country.

. . . This was an America in which no traveller from East or West could lose his own home town, however far he rambled. For the rubber wheels of the Motor Age had ironed out the traits that once distinguished one community from another. Titusville was only a lap behind Broadway. And the prophecies inherent in the first low-priced motor cars that took to the roads in 1908 had been fulfilled.

From Merz, And Then Came Ford *(1929), pp. 272–273.*

All the men live within a few miles of the plant and come to work by automobile. Many of them own farms or homes. We have not drawn the men from the farms—we have added industry to farming. One worker operates a farm which requires him to have two trucks, a tractor, and a small closed car. Another man, with the aid of his wife, clears more than five hundred dollars a season on flowers. We give any man a leave of absence to work on his farm, but with the aid of machinery these farmers are out of the shops a surprisingly short while—they spend no time at all sitting around waiting for crops to come up. They have the industrial idea and are not content to be setting hens.

Henry Ford, describing a project of the 1920s to bring small industry to a rural area, quoted in Graves, The Triumph of an Idea *(1934), p. 84.*

The car advanced on you the instant the first explosion occurred and you would hold it back by leaning your weight against it. I can still feel my old Ford nuzzling me at the curb, as though looking for an apple in my pocket. In zero weather, ordinary cranking became impossible, except for giants. The oil thickened and it became necessary to jack up the rear wheel, which for planetary reasons, eased the throw. The lore and legend that governed the Ford were boundless. Owners discussed mutual problems in that wise, infinitely resourceful way old women discuss rheumatism. Exact knowledge was pretty scarce, and often proved less effective than superstition.

Max Cooper, correspondent of the Aberdeen Daily News, *describing Model T ownership, October 13, 1965, in Wik,* Henry Ford and Grass-Roots America *(1972), p. 69.*

11

Prosperity
1928

As the year 1928 dawned over the United States, the Republican Party and the public had good reasons for optimism and complacency. The economy of the United States had quickly righted itself after the postwar recession of 1920–21 and had been expanding without pause or retreat for a full seven years. Production increased steadily throughout the Coolidge years; inflation remained moderate and interest rates low. Gross national income reached $89 billion in 1928, a figure representing $745 per capita, from a grand total of $60 billion, or $651 per capita, in 1918. Bank deposits were up; the value of life insurance contracts was rising; after the belt-tightening required by the war and the depression, public authorities were making greater expenditures for new libraries, schools, and hospitals.

Compared to a 1919 baseline of $100 per day, five-and-dime stores were doing $260 of business per day in 1927, and grocery chains $387. The real purchasing power of wages rose 2 percent every year between 1922 and 1927. In 1925, 75 people in the United States reported incomes of $1 million; in 1927 there were 283. A key to the economic growth and prosperity in the United States and Canada was the one great advantage the two countries enjoyed over their competitors in Europe: they had emerged undamaged from the war, with their manufacturing industries, cities, agricultural land, and transportation systems intact. In both countries, the labor strife of 1919 and 1920 gradually calmed, and the violent controversies over radical politics began to dim in the collective memory.

Natural resources were readily available and cheap. Standardization and the techniques of mass production pioneered by Henry Ford allowed large companies to lower manufacturing costs and to sell their goods to a much larger market. The success of Ford and the automotive industry in general had a domino effect on other industries; many other companies took up Ford's policy of high wages and low prices, with work compartmentalized for increased efficiency. Business also had the advantage of Republican presidencies, which in general disfavored business regulation and trust busting and looked kindly on higher import tariffs that discouraged foreign competition. The business-friendly attitude of Presidents Harding and Coolidge, and the impression of competence and solidity given off by President Herbert Hoover, who would take office early in 1929, contributed to the general confidence felt by investors and consumers.

Public authorities were spending a great deal more on libraries, hospitals, and schools and budgeting a steadily rising amount of money on health, education, and social welfare services. The rise in income and the growing acceptance of the eight-hour working day on the part of employers gave workers more time to spend at their leisure. Car camping came into vogue in the 1920s; spectator sports found a mass audience, and middle-class amateurs took to formerly upper-crust sports such as golf and tennis.

A crucial ingredient of the economic expansion of the 1920s was the changed behavior of retail customers, who began adopting the habits of modern consumers. Millions of buyers sought out electronic gadgets that made home life easier or more entertaining: washers, refrigerators, electric irons, vacuum cleaners, toasters, electric sewing machines, and radios. By the same token, the complex designs of these items and their dependence on the unpredictable, mysterious powers of electricity made them fragile and expendable—to be thrown away for the next model and a new purchase.

Household income did not necessarily keep up with the available venues in which to spend it, and so the modern concept of installment buying on credit was born. Low, easy monthly payments were contracted for the purchase of furniture, appliances, clothing, and luxury items such as carpets and pianos. The product whose sales benefited most from the new concept of paying month-by-month was the automobile. The last holdout against installment buying in the automotive industry fell in 1927, when Henry Ford unveiled the Model A and reluctantly joined competitors such as General Motors in allowing his customers to pay in the future.

Cigar makers select wrappers at Cuesta Ray and Company in Tampa. Cigar making was one of the few industries to resist the tide of mechanization, time-motion studies, and scientific management. *(Bergert Brothers Collection/University of South Florida)*

To increase their productivity, the manufacturing industries of the United States adopted new principles of scientific management that were intended to turn the standard factory into an entirely logical and efficient producer of finished goods. (An official government oversight bureau was inaugurated: the Division of Simplified Practice, which lay within the Department of Commerce led by Secretary Herbert Hoover.) New machinery was invented and installed with the goal of speeding up assembly and reducing the amount of manual labor involved. For many workers, scientific management meant the disappearance of skilled jobs, which were supplanted by repetitious, automated tasks, in which skill was unnecessary. For the national economy, the overall result of this streamlining was an increase in per-capita production, a steady rise in national income, and better returns for the holders of company shares in the public stock markets.

Scientific management was applied most ferociously in the new auto industry. Although Henry Ford had pioneered the conveyor belt and the assembly-line worker's rigidly defined task, Alfred Sloan of General Motors applied scientific management to every facet of his organization—from top management down to nuts-and-bolts assembly. While auto production per man-hour increased sharply through the 1920s, related industries such as tires and petroleum refining also grew with the new transportation. Autos became affordable to the workers who built them; the benefits of personal transportation trickled down to the middle class, then the working class.

The map of the United States grew more complex, with a network of roads now accompanying the steady black lines that indicated railways and canals. Gravel and dirt roads, which rutted and crumbled underneath the balloon tires of heavier Fords, Chevrolets, and Buicks, began to be replaced by concrete and hard asphalt, which allowed the United States to build the most extensive and up-to-date system of roads in the world by the 1920s. New road building brought an increase in land values away from the cities, as suburbs sprang up to accommodate middle-class workers just beginning their escape from changing conditions in the inner cities. Public spending played an important role, as the federal government granted one-half of the total cost of new interstate highways and trunk highways to local authorities.

UNCERTAIN GOOD TIMES

Despite the impressive statistics, the benefits of the economic good times were spread unevenly among the regions and social strata of the country. The Middle Atlantic and industrial regions of the Midwest prospered from the rapid growth in manufacturing industries, especially in industries directly related to the making of motor vehicles. At the same time, in New England, older manufacturing industries such as textile milling and shoe manufacturing waned. Companies in the mining industry suffered from competition and low returns, with miners suffering the most with stagnant and in some cases falling wages, a situation unresolved by their weakening labor unions. In the agricultural states of the Midwest, in the South, and in the Rocky Mountain states, low prices for agricultural staples such as corn and wheat brought long-lasting economic stagnation that found no relief in the growth of cities or improvements in transportation. Heavily in debt for the purchase of their land or machinery, farmers went bankrupt by the thousands and saw their homes and acreages foreclosed on by small-town banks, a condition that foreshadowed economic disaster in the Midwest during the 1930s. The problems in farming and mining regions intensified the general migration of the population into the nation's cities.

In addition, unemployment in the United States did not disappear with the well-advertised prosperity of the Roaring Twenties. The unemployment rate's low point was reached in 1926, when 1.8 percent of the civilian labor force was out of work. From that point, unemployment again began to rise, reaching 4.2 percent in 1928, falling to 3.2 percent in 1929, and jumping to 8.7 percent in 1930, at the start of the Great Depression.

DEMOCRATIC CONVENTIONS

With all the prosperity and newfound comforts, the leaders of the Democratic Party knew they would find themselves hard-pressed to mount effective opposition to the Republicans in the presidential election year of 1928. Yet compared to the rancorous nominating contest held at Madison Square Garden in 1924, the Democratic convention of 1928, held in Houston, was trouble-free.

Delegates and managers took care to avoid controversy and division. There were no roll call votes, no floor fights, no debates over the party platform or over politically charged resolutions. The easy winner, apparent to all from the first day, would be New York governor Al Smith. Democratic delegates favored Smith, an Irish Catholic born to immigrant parents, for his successful and energetic governorship of New York and found in him a perfect representative of the country's accelerating urbanization and the wider acceptance of immigrants and their descendants into the mainstream. Smith, on his side, carefully avoided the question of Prohibition repeal; although all knew him as a "wet" candidate, Smith pledged to uphold the Eighteenth Amendment as the law of the land.

This time around, Smith nearly won on the nominating convention's first ballot, and finally did win with new votes from the Ohio delegation on the second. His running mate, Senator Joseph Robinson of Arkansas, provided balance as a rural-state Protestant and a supporter of Prohibition.

Smith went with the tenor of the times for his campaign by appointing as a campaign manager his cultural opposite: John J. Raskob, a wealthy Republican and former executive with General Motors. Smith knew he could count on a loyal Democratic vote in the South; by appointing Raskob, he also intended to capture some of the business vote, especially those who felt out of touch with Prohibition. Raskob was best known among the voters for his opinion that good stocks should sell at 15 times their earnings, rather than the traditional 10 times, a sentiment that was giving an additional boost to the already overheated stock market. He was also known for supporting Calvin Coolidge in 1924.

Although Smith came out for high tariffs to please Republican business interests, who wanted foreign competition lessened and their profits protected, his statements pleased neither Republican nor Democratic constituencies. The choice of Raskob also left many in the Democratic party distinctly unenthusiastic. They saw the choice as a sellout by Smith and believed that the appointment of the conservative industrialist signaled an end to any faint chance the country had for Progressive-style social and business reforms. Although Smith did manage to win some business support, many liberal Democratic voters turned from their party's nominee to Norman Thomas, the Socialist candidate.

In the Midwest and South, where New York and other big cities signified crime and corruption, Smith was also under suspicion for his New York accent and for his parents—working-class Irish immigrants who lived on the big city's Lower East Side. Despite his promise to enforce the Eighteenth Amendment, his anti-Prohibition sentiments gave dry opponents a clear line of attack. Above all, Smith's Catholicism proved to be a problem in a land where many still held to the myth of the nation's agrarian, small-town, Protestant origins. Before the 1928 candidacy of Al Smith, no Catholic had appeared on the presidential ballot, and the country had a long memory of anti-Catholic violence that flared up with the arrival of Catholic immigrants from Ireland and then southern Europe. Smith's opponents did not hesitate to raise pointed questions on the subject of his religion: Would a Catholic president hold some kind of secret allegiance to the pope and the Vatican? Would he oppose the fundamental principal of separation of church and state?

HOOVER'S RUGGED INDIVIDUALISM

Before the Democrats met in Houston, Secretary of Commerce Herbert Hoover had won the Republican nomination for president in Kansas City by beating back

At his 1929 inauguration, President Herbert Hoover (left, with Vice President Charles Curtis) declared, "In no other nation are the fruits of accomplishment more secure." *(Library of Congress)*

a challenge from Frank Lowden of Illinois, who ran on a plank supporting protection and price support for the country's struggling farmers. Hoover himself seemed to supply something that the 1920s lacked: a spirit of public service, instilled by his Quaker upbringing and carried out most famously with his term as War Food Administrator and his relief work in Europe during and after the war. Hoover praised rugged individualism but also community service and sacrifice that went beyond the virtues of self-interested capitalism.

Hoover's turned out to be the much simpler campaign. The candidate voiced the easy opinion that the prosperity was due to Republican laissez-faire policies and promised the voters that the day was not far distant when poverty would disappear. To discourage the undecided against the Democrats, he warned against the dangers of government ownership and management, threatened by the more socialistic members of his rival party. The result was a victory in November by a margin of 444 electoral votes to 87, while the Republican party carried majorities in the Senate and the House of Representatives.

Democratic partisans could take some comfort after a close examination of the results. The Democratic South had been broken up—Smith lost five Deep

South states to Hoover as well as his home state of New York. Nevertheless, Smith had won more votes than any Democratic presidential candidate in history. Raskob had actively campaigned in the northern farm belt, and there Smith cut down the Republican majorities of the previous two elections and also captured the progressive voters who had supported Robert La Follette. The election of 1928 also began the trend of bringing laborers and recent immigrants onto the Democratic side of the ballot. Also, for the first time, the Democrats won a majority in the nation's 12 largest cities. The union vote, the working classes, and the immigrant vote, especially among Catholic immigrants from Canada, Italy, and Ireland, went into the Democratic column and would stay there for another 50 years.

WALL STREET ENTHUSIASM

Politics and the election of 1928 proved of much less interest to the country at large than the more straightforward affairs of business and the stock market. The market was attracting crowds of speculators and torrents of new money that sparked a wave of buying fever during the year. In addition to the traditional wealthy buyers and sellers, the members of the growing middle class bought in, many of them considering a plunge (buying stocks) on the shares of RCA or Standard Oil as a hallmark of arrival into the ranks of the leisure class. Branch offices of big-city brokerages opened in small-town storefronts, while price quotations ran in the daily newspapers and on brokers' tote boards and chattering telegraphic stock tickers spun out Wall Street's ups and downs in corporate offices. As always, word-of-mouth news and information proved most convincing, and the hottest rumors of the 1920s concerned instant riches earned on Wall Street by butlers, gardeners, chauffeurs, maids, clerks, and barbers—ordinary people providing themselves with an early retirement courtesy of Wall Street.

The stock market boom reached its peak in the early spring of 1928, when people all over the country withdrew their savings to play the market. In March and April, trading volume exceeded 3 million shares on 33 separate days; between 1925 and 1928, the same volume had only been attained six times. On one day in May, volume reached the staggering figure of 4,800,000 shares. Several times, the feverish trading prompted the officers of the exchange to suspend business so that brokers could bring their books and records current; in May trading hours were cut from five to four in order to provide relief for exhausted members of the exchange.

A large percentage of the brokerage accounts were trading on margin, or money borrowed from the brokers by the investors. This practice imitated the new method of installment buying that the public had adopted for purchases of automobiles and household goods (by the end of the 1920s about 15 percent of all purchases were made on credit). On Wall Street, margin buying contributed to the speculative fever; as stock prices rose, so did the value of one's collateral—shares of stock—thus encouraging more borrowing and more buying. The danger of falling prices and margin calls (the demand for repayment of loaned money by the brokers) was disregarded. In general, stock prices did not fall, and when they did, they usually recovered and subsequently reached new highs. Margin calls were rare, and the paper profits of individuals as well as banks and corporations—many of which had nothing better to do with their money than to throw it at the market as well—formed an immense financial pyramid that, as the decade wore on, gradually uncoupled itself from the actual performance of individual companies and the national economy.

At the same time, the government's laissez-faire economic policies encouraged the formation of new corporations whose dubious operations included little in the way of actual production or sales. In certain states such as Delaware newly formed companies could issue stock with no obligation whatsoever to make a regular financial accounting or an annual report to shareholders. A common practice was the establishment of "holding companies" from the assets of a network of local utility companies. The organization of these companies was purposefully made as complex and opaque as possible. Investors could discover very little about their assets, liabilities, income, or profit, and in many cases did not care. In fact, the true purpose of organizations such as Electric Bond and Share, Standard Gas and Electric, and Cities Service was to enrich their founders and directors through issuance of new stock certificates and through inflated rises in the price of their shares.

The traditional benchmark of paying 10 times earnings for a share of stock was forgotten during the stock market run-up. Stocks traded for 20, 30, even 100 times their earnings simply on the expectation that share prices would always, sooner or later, continue to rise. The hot rumors and stock tips and the good business the country was doing made it easy to gamble one's savings on the market, which seemed to be holding to a single direction: up. New technology—placing orders by telephone and getting quotations by the radio—made trading on stocks in the market easier than ever and, for the first time, accessible to the nonwealthy. Many ordinary working people took great interest in price movements as detailed in the financial pages of the daily newspaper; many also trained themselves to read historical price charts, summoning the future by examining the pattern of rising and falling lines on a graph.

Stock investors study the ticker at a broker's office. For the first time, the general public was taking up the once-arcane and aristocratic practice of investing in company stocks and bonds. *(Minnesota Historical Society)*

Waiters, delivery boys, actresses, and others traded on tips they garnered through the vast, national investment grapevine. For the first time, bankers and brokers actively solicited new clients, instead of passively waiting for customers to appear in their lobbies. (In some cases, stock market investing was rather involuntary: employees of holding-company president Samuel Insull were expected to buy shares in his firm; these investors in turn sold Insull's shares to customers, friends, and acquaintances.) Brokers' offices in Manhattan moved uptown; new offices opened in small towns and big cities while the brokerages increased staff and raised new buildings. Bustling trade rooms were kept open to the general public, who were welcome to take a seat and enjoy the spectacle of clerks running about the room collecting order slips, clerks standing by the quote board to erase and rescribble the numbers indicating prices and volume, and clerks standing by to open accounts, accept checks, fill out paperwork, deliver messages, and open doors.

Underneath it all were ominous signs of economic trouble, if investors cared to look and analyze. The profit motive contributed to a rise in earnings for corporations, but the profits were distributed to shareholders rather than workers. The result was a disparity between the earnings of workers and their bosses that grew wider as the decade progressed. Industrial plants were overbuilt, and manufacturing capacity expanded beyond the ability of the society or of foreign markets to absorb the products being produced at such a frenetic, albeit scientifically managed, rate, even if workers were being paid enough to purchase cars or houses. The construction boom peaked in 1925 and immediately began a long slide. Car sales were sluggish; several important sectors—textiles, coal mining, agriculture—were going through semipermanent recession.

Unemployment nagged at the economy and at society; the growing efficiency at manufacturing plants brought a surplus of manual laborers. There was yet no system of unemployment insurance, so the loss of a job often meant loss of a home. Holding companies in electric power, railroads, and banks encouraged concentration of profits and income in the hands of the few. The banking system had serious weaknesses; most banks were still small and independently run, and a failure (common enough in the agricultural areas of the Midwest and South) could bring a chain reaction, unmitigated by any form of corporate bailout or federal deposit insurance. In the boom times of 1921 to 1928, a total of 5,000 banks closed down. The unregulated banking system was riddled with irresponsible speculation on the part of bankers, many of whom played with their depositors' money on Wall Street with disastrous effects.

By the time of Herbert Hoover's presidency some bankers and federal officials were growing uneasy over the rise in risky margin trading. They debated raising the discount rate (the interest rate charged to banks by the Federal Reserve Board) in order to slow down speculation and margin lending. Higher interest rates, it was assumed, would make borrowing more costly for stock speculators and thus reduce the returns they expected on their investments. During the first two Republican administrations of the 1920s, the Federal Reserve Board appointees had emulated the laissez-faire policies of their presidents, believing that the best policy was to do nothing, allow the free market to run its course and if necessary apply its self-corrective functions. President Coolidge had set the tone. A frugal saver who never invested a dollar in the stock market, Coolidge did not believe in interfering with the market or with the laws of supply and demand, to which he gave most of the credit for "Coolidge prosperity."

In July 1928, the government finally took action to cool the fervid stock trading and margin buying by raising the "rediscount" rate of interest, to which margin rates were pegged, to 5 percent. The slight credit tightening did nothing to break the speculative fever. Just after the election of Herbert Hoover, on November 30, 1928, shares of Montgomery Ward rose to 439 $\frac{7}{8}$. Most spectacular and most prominent in the financial pages were the rocketing shares of RCA. First listed on October 1, 1924, at about $26 a share, RCA gyrated through the 60s and 70s in 1925 and 1926, reached $101 in 1927, dipped to 85 in February 1928, and by the end of that year was peaking at $420, just before a stock split that made five new shares for every single old share and paved the way for the expected easier buying, more speculation, and higher market capitalization to benefit the company.

But in that cold month of December, a sudden and unexpected drop occurred at the New York Stock Exchange. In a single day, shares of RCA lost more than $70. Fearing a crash, the Federal Reserve governors chose not to raise interest rates again. Doing so, it was believed, would cut off new business investment and make borrowing money more expensive for the federal government. The crisis soon resolved itself in early 1929 as the market regained its balance and continued its inexorable, inevitable rise.

In the meantime, harbingers of economic depression first began appearing on the prairies of western Canada. While wheat prices remained low but fairly constant through the 1920s, farmers in the U.S. Midwest as well as Canada were able to survive. But a drop in wheat prices in the late 1920s, caused by a market softened by imports from Argentina, and by the recovery of European agriculture from the damages inflicted by World War I, began causing severe hardships in North America. Farmers, who always seemed to be in some sort of difficulty, attracted little concern outside the states and provinces of the two countries where they still formed an important economic sector. Few suspected that equally damaging imbalances were growing in manufacturing and retail industries, and that the rising stock market disguised fundamental problems that would contribute to economic disaster in the following year.

CHRONICLE OF EVENTS

1928

January 16: The Sixth International Conference of American States, also known as the Pan-American Conference, is convened in Havana, Cuba. Latin American representatives introduce a resolution stating that no member has the right to intervene in the internal affairs of any other member. The resolution is a repudiation of the Roosevelt Corollary to the Monroe Doctrine, in which the United States claimed the right to intervene in Latin America as well as block European meddling in the Western Hemisphere. In Havana, U.S. representative Charles Evans Hughes manages to block passage of the resolution.

February 10: The New York Bar Association declares itself opposed to Prohibition and the Volstead Act.

February 11–19: The United States wins two gold medals at the second Winter Olympics, held in St. Moritz, Switzerland.

February 21: During his trial for conspiracy in the Teapot Dome affair, Harry Sinclair is found guilty of contempt of court and sentenced to six months in prison.

March 9: By a vote of 209–157, the House defeats a "lame duck" amendment to the Constitution which would move the presidential inauguration up from March to January.

March 10: The Alien Property Act is signed by President Coolidge, allowing repayment to German nationals in the amount of $300 million for property seized during World War I.

March 13: A dam break causes a flash flood in the Santa Clara Valley in California, killing 450 people.

April 13–18: The Socialist Party convenes and will nominate Norman Thomas of New York for president and James H. Maurer of Pennsylvania for vice president.

May 3: The House again passes the McNary-Haugen bill, but President Coolidge vetoes it for the last time. Farm relief will become an important issue in the 1928 presidential campaign.

May 15: Congress passes the Flood Control Act, providing $325 million for a 10-year program of levee improvement and flood control on the Mississippi River.

May 17: Congress establishes a new air mail postage rate of 5 cents per ounce.

May 22: The Jones-White Act, also known as the Merchant Marine Act, is passed, providing for a loan fund of $250 million for ship construction, allowing

Knights Templar pose with musicians at a Minneapolis convention in 1928. *(Minnesota Historical Society)*

the sale of surplus government ships, and providing for mail freight contracts to help the private shipping business.

May 25: Congress passes the Muscle Shoals Bill, which sanctions government ownership of a hydroelectric plant at Muscle Shoals, Tennessee. President Coolidge will pocket-veto the bill.

May 27: The Workers Party nominates William Z. Foster of Illinois for president and Benjamin Gitlow of New York for vice president.

May 30: Louis Meyer wins the Indianapolis 500 auto race with an average speed of 99.48 miles per hour.

June 12–15: The Republican Party nominates Herbert Hoover for president and Charles Curtis of Kansas for vice president.

June 17–18: Amelia Earhart becomes the first woman to fly across the Atlantic Ocean. With pilot Wilmer Stultz and mechanic Lou Gordon, Earhart takes off from Newfoundland in a Fokker trimotor plane, the *Friendship,* and arrives in Burry Port, Wales, after a flight of 20 hours, 40 minutes.

June 19–20: The United States signs treaties of cooperation with Austria and Denmark.

June 26–29: The Democratic Party convenes in Houston, Texas, and nominates Alfred E. Smith, governor of New York, for president and Joseph T. Robinson of Arkansas for vice president. Smith, a Roman Catholic, will run on an anti-Prohibition platform.

July 25: The United States signs a tariff agreement with the nationalist government of China.

July 29–August 12: The United States wins 24 gold medals at the ninth Summer Olympic Games in the Netherlands.

July 30: George Eastman demonstrates the first color motion pictures in Rochester, New York. The film shows flowers, butterflies, fashion models, and goldfish.

August 25: Richard E. Byrd leaves New York on an ice ship, *The City of New York,* beginning his attempt to reach the South Pole.

August 27: The Kellogg-Briand Pact, a multinational treaty that formally outlaws war as a means of settling disputes, is signed by 15 nations in Paris. Eventually a total of 62 nations will sign the pact.

September 8: Charles Evans Hughes, former secretary of state, is elected by the League of Nations to the Permanent Court of International Justice.

September 19: The Singing Fool, a film starring Al Jolson, premieres.

September 27: The United States formally recognizes the Chinese nationalist government of Chiang Kai-shek.

October 9: The New York Yankees defeat the St. Louis Cardinals in game four to win the World Series.

October 15: The dirigible *Graf Zeppelin* docks at Lakehurst, New Jersey, after its first commercial flight from Friedrichshafen, Germany.

November 6: Herbert Hoover wins the presidential election by 444 electoral votes to 87 for Democratic candidate Al Smith, and Franklin Delano Roosevelt is elected governor of New York.

November 19: President-elect Hoover sets out on a seven-week tour of South America aboard the U.S.S. *Maryland.*

November 23: The New York Stock Exchange sees a record trading day, with a volume of 6,954,020 shares bought and sold.

New media and new transportation allowed campaigning politicians to draw further public attention. On November 3, 1928, Neil Bradley congratulates L. W. Lamb (right) on making the first political speech ever broadcast from an airplane. *(Minnesota Historical Society / C. J. Hibbard)*

November 28: Flying with a crew of three, Richard Byrd reaches the South Pole, returning to camp after a journey of 19 hours.

December 8: The New York Stock Exchange suffers a steep 22-point decline.

December 17: In a memorandum drawn up by Undersecretary of State J. Reuben Clark, the State Department repudiates the Roosevelt Corollary to the Monroe Doctrine with the statement "The Doctrine does not concern itself with purely inter-American relations."

EYEWITNESS TESTIMONY

Business and Prosperity

Even if Government conducts of business could give us more efficiency instead of less efficiency, the fundamental objection to it would remain unaltered and unabated. It would destroy political equality. It would increase rather than decrease abuse and corruption. It would stifle initiative and invention. It would undermine the development of leadership. It would cramp and cripple the mental and spiritual energies of our people. It would extinguish equality and opportunity. It would dry up the spirit of liberty and progress.

> *Herbert Hoover, 1920s-era speech favoring laissez-faire economic policies, quoted in* Twentieth-Century America *(1945), p. 269.*

Now it is the Augustan age and America the modern Rome in full flower. Poor men have risen to Pro-consul. Strong men from the provinces have become Caesars at the capital.

. . . It is our Augustan age. We are all wealthy or those of us who are not wealthy hope to be. That is America today.

> *From Anonymous, "The Great American Ass" (1926), p. 303.*

The academic essayist may tell you that the material things of life are negligible; "money isn't everything," etc. His essays, however, are written with advertised pens on advertised paper, the author resting his feet on an advertised rug and looking forward to an evening of surcease with his books, motor-car, radio outfit, phonograph or player piano—all advertised, all material. He will tell you, perhaps, that his years of poverty were happiest. What he means is that the successful struggle against poverty was enjoyable. Straight poverty is pleasant only to persons like St. Francis of Assisi; and the census taker could not find many of these today.

> *Essay of 1926 from* The New York Sun, *quoted in* Carter, Another Part of the Twenties *(1977), p. 127.*

So popular has installment buying become, with purchasers as well as with manufacturers and merchants, that it is possible today to buy almost everything from candy to private yachts on the deferred payment plan. Within the last twenty years, and particularly within the last six, installment buying has grown like a mushroom, and now there are few things besides carfare, meals at restaurants, and theater tickets that cannot be paid for at so much down and so much periodically.

Installment buying is useful, is often advisable, and is very convenient. No doubt, it is carried too far in some cases. But customers can often get what they want only by this method of buying; and, since the country really has more money than it needs, the additional cost to the purchase has not yet caused any vital difficulties.

> *Hawthorne Daniel, "Living and Dying on the Installment Plan," from* World's Work, *January 1926, p. 329.*

As a business man, Christ stands at the head of the class. Business defined simply means employment, trade, profession, or dealing by way of sale or exchange. Christ seemed to have understood His business relation with His Father from childhood. A close student of the life of Christ will reveal a business-like genius in His mind. He talked much of profit and loss, and counting the cost of things. Jesus was not all emotion by any means. He possessed consecration, but it was intelligent. He put religion in His business and business in His religion. No business man can fail who takes Christ for his example. The fact is, He was born in a racial family that is noted for business the world over, so He naturally had a business run of mind. He believed in money and organized His church on a business basis, equipped with a secretary and treasurer.

> *The Rev. E. W. Perry, explaining the religious foundations of contemporary capitalism in* The Oklahoma Informer, *a "Magazine of Negro Business," and quoted in* The American Mercury, *March 1928, p. 310.*

Back in the days when machinery had to be run by steam or waterpower, cables and belts were the only means of power transmission. This meant that factories had to be located in the immediate neighborhood of the plant or on the bank of the steam from which power was derived. The natural tendency was for industry to group itself around large sources of power.

. . . Then within our knowledge—within our century—electricity was discovered. Electricity possessed this great advantage over all other kinds of power previously produced—it could be instantaneously transmitted over great distances by wire. Power could be generated in one spot and sent out to any number of factories all over the country. The necessity for centralization had been eliminated, and manufacturing went ahead on a larger scale than ever.

Light, heat, and power—think what has been accomplished by this one idea put into action! And the power age has barely begun. In our own shops we are constantly improving our method of manufacture with an eye to efficiency, economy, and the safety and comfort of our employees. Belt transmission has been entirely supplanted by electrically driven machines, which frees us from the danger and annoyance of wheels and belts whirling overhead. Our furnaces, most of which are electrically heated, are so constructed and insulated that the men work in front of them without discomfort. There is no smoke or gas except in a few processes, and, in these, electric ventilators carry off all disagreeable odors and unhealthful fumes.

Henry Ford, "Youth, Industry, and Progress," from Forum, *October 1928, pp. 582–589.*

Styles changed. New gadgets made their way along the country roads. One year it was ethyl gasoline that set the filling stations talking. Next year it was hydraulic brakes

or chromium as a material for radiator caps that kept their polish. New fashions in headlights, new fashions in windshield wipers, new fashions in rumble seats, new fashions in high frequency horns, low frequency horns and thermal heat controls followed one another into favour as rapidly as new fashions in entertainment, food, and clothes. It was more accurate to say of the Motor Age not that it spread the same successful culture across the nation but that it spread successive layers.

For the Motor Age was itself the product of forces working tirelessly for new fashions and for constant change. Modern industrialism had increased the income of millions of Americans and given them more leeway to experiment with luxuries and fads. It had shortened the average workday and given more people leisure time.

From Merz, And Then Came Henry Ford *(1929), p. 279.*

A family enjoys weekend car camping under live oaks and Spanish moss, somewhere in Florida. *(Bergert Brothers Collection/University of South Florida)*

Participants in a Tampa seaside festival prepare at dockside for a costumed production. *(Bergert Brothers Collection, University of South Florida)*

Since 1921, Americans have applied intelligence to the day's work more effectively than ever before. Thus the prime factor in producing the extraordinary changes in the economic fortunes of the European people during the nineteenth century is the prime factor in producing the prosperity of the United States in recent years. The whole process of putting science into industry has been followed more intensively than before; it has been supplemented by tentative efforts to put science into business management, trade-union policy, and Government administration.

From Mitchell, Recent Economic Changes *(1929), a study of the Committee on Recent Economic Changes of the President's Conference on Unemployment (1929), p. 862.*

As a matter of fact, the congregating impulse in human nature isn't what it once was, and for readily discernible reasons. In what we call our modern "community life," most of us are forced to congregate whether we like it or not. People must, of necessity, spend so much time in crowds—in streets, stores, trains, and highways—that they are naturally anxious to escape from the turmoil in their leisure hours.

The theatre is an impractical institution in this age of transportation and communication. Its chief purpose has been to provide refuge and diversion and distraction for those dwellers in cities and towns who were stifled by the narrowness of their own homes. The automobile has made it easy for such people to break away, not only from their homes but from the cities and towns which

are apt to be stiflingly narrow themselves. The airplane will make the escape still easier.

The home is becoming a pleasanter place in which to live. Thanks to mechanical dish-washers, vacuum cleaners and similar boons, the home need no longer be associated with the anguish of drudgery and the horror of boredom. Television will add to its charms, by bringing into it everything that the theatre can offer, and much that the theatre has never been able to offer in the past. Color photography and stereoscopic photography are coming, and will make of the television screen a window through which one can see the exciting semblance of reality.

From "Beyond the Talkies—Television," by R. E. Sherwood in Scribner's, *July 1929, pp. 7–8.*

The Election of 1928

The distinguished Governor of the great State of New York has taken three days laboriously to prepare a vulgar tirade that any resident of Billingsgate or any occupant of the alcoholic ward in Bellevue could have written in fifteen minutes in quite the same style, but with more evidence of education and intelligence. The Wall Street friends of Governor Smith have enabled him to remove his domicile and his refined person from the neighborhood of the Bowery, but he still reverts in manner of thought to the familiar localities of Five Points and Hell's Kitchen, if this may be said without undue offense to these historic localities. . . .

. . . This political epistle is not issued from my ranch house, which Mr. Smith calls with his usual cheap demagogy "the splendor and grandeur of my palatial estate," but from the fair city of Los Angeles. And let me in this connection recall the pleasing fact that this fair city promptly arrests its crooked politicians and speeds them on their way to jail. New York papers please copy, and Tammany Hall politicians please take notice.

. . . The chief difference between my house and the English or Long Island estates of some Tammany leaders is that my house was paid for out of my own funds and not out of subsidies blackmailed from corrupt traction corporations willing to pay high for the priceless privilege of plundering the people of New York City.

William Randolph Hearst, responding to Al Smith's criticism of the Hearst-supported Republican New York mayoral candidate John F. Hylan, who was running against Smith's Democratic ally Jimmy Walker, in the September 3, 1925 edition of the New York American, *reprinted in Swanberg,* Citizen Hearst *(1961), p. 330.*

There will be many, if this man runs for the presidency, who will bristle at the thought of his Catholicism. Spellbinders of the Republican Party will view with alarm for hours on end the perils of Rum and Romanism. It may be that the ludicrous hobgoblins of the Ku Klux Klan will dust off their robes and hold solemn rallies under the banner of intolerance. But vast throngs will crowd into the halls where he speaks, to laugh at his jokes and be won by the first real personality in politics since Roosevelt. And the melody of a city song will sweep the prairies.

From Pringle, Alfred E. Smith, A Critical Study *(1927), p. 100.*

The fact that Alfred E. Smith is a devout and sincere communicant of the Roman Catholic Church is still, it is greatly to be feared, the greatest obstacle to the realization of hopes that he may be elected to the highest office in the land. That this can be so, despite the frankness, courage and completeness of his now famous letter to Charles C. Marshall, is indicative of the degree to which a Christian nation, dedicated to freedom of thought and of worship, can deviate from the teachings of Christ.

. . . American politics is capable of swinish depths. This was demonstrated when Warren G. Harding was running for the presidency and the rumor was circulated, utterly without foundation, that he had a faint strain of Negro blood in his veins. In the corridors of a New York hotel, during the campaign, small white cards bearing a picture of the White House were passed out by mysterious strangers. Under the photographs were the words, "Uncle Tom's Cabin?" The attacks upon Smith's religion will be similarly underhand and cowardly. They will not naturally, be sponsored openly by Democrats opposing his nomination or, in the event that he is chosen as his party's candidate, by the Republicans. They will be anonymous and as hard to trace as they will be slimy. They will take the form, perhaps, of circulars reprinting imaginary cable despatches setting forth that the Vatican is favorable to the candidacy and election of Smith. Intolerance will fight from behind a hood. It will not show its face.

From Henry F. Pringle, Alfred E. Smith: A Critical Study *(1927), pp. 336–337.*

Under the Coolidge administration the rich have declared war on the poor. Let them beware of the retaliation of those that they despise today.

Herbert Claiborne Pell, comment made in January 1928, and quoted in Schlesinger, The Crisis of the Old Order *(1957), p. 125.*

I make no claim here that Smith is a Tammany plug-ugly. I honor him for having risen from the debasing subserviency of those who in the days of his youth sweated dimes from the poor through those who prey on the poor—the saloon-keeper, the tout and the prostitute. This record is, of course, an old record of a young man. But the young man rose on this record. And to-day the issue is formed upon the elements that made this old record—the return of the saloon which Governor Smith as a young man defended so ably, so consistently, so loyally. But the Tammany system goes on to-day, as it went on 100 years ago, and, indeed, as it will go on in our American cities unless Governor Smith and the sinister forces behind him are overthrown. Tammany is indeed Tammany, and Smith is its Major Prophet.

William Allen White, in The New York Herald Tribune, *July 29, 1928, quoted in* A Catholic Runs for President *(1956), p. 133.*

This unbroken series of events all indicates clearly to me that the Smith decision is the most brazen [*sic*] and frantic attempt possible to win the east; to do so with an appeal so wet that whiskey is dry by comparison. Such an appeal would have collateral aspects. It would be primarily to appetite, and secondarily to every sort of group complex, inferiority attitude, and resentment to American standards and ideals which could be contrived. To the aliens, who feel that the older America, the America of the Anglo-Saxon stock, is a hateful thing which must be overturned and humiliated; to the northern negroes, who lust for social equality and racial dominance; to the Catholics who have been made to believe that they are entitled to the White House, and to the Jews who likewise are to be instilled with the feeling that this is the time for God's chosen people to chastise America. . . .

Letter from George Fort Milton to William McAdoo, July 31, 1928, quoted in A Catholic Runs for President *(1956), p. 114.*

I think we would all naturally prefer a man of high culture and character, such as Woodrow Wilson, for president, to a product of the slums of New York with only a Tammany training, and whose highest ambition is to see the time come when he can put his foot on the brass rail and blow the foam off again. This is no "bologny talk" either, are we not told daily that he is honest and means what he says. Just compare this high ambition with that of Woodrow Wilson to establish a League of Nations to prevent war.

Letter, F. O. Ticknor to the Monroe, North Carolina,
Journal, *August 2, 1928, quoted in* A Catholic Runs
for President *(1956), p. 160.*

We in America today are nearer the final triumph over
poverty than ever before in the history of the land.
Herbert Hoover, excerpt from acceptance speech, Republican
convention, August 11, 1928, reprinted in Hoover, The
New Day: Campaign Speeches of Herbert Hoover,
1928, p. 16.

The strategy that brought about the nomination of
Governor Smith was sound in conception, shrewd in
planning, and expert in execution. Not that the nomination of Smith, as an act standing alone, called for
great skill. That was predestined from the day last
September when McAdoo retired from the race, and
the drys could find no other leader to rally behind.
Under the conditions, as respects the nomination, the
Tammany and other managers needed only to walk
into the promised land and take possession.
From "The Paramount Issues: Prohibition Leaps to the
Front," by Mark Sullivan, in World's Work, *September*
1928, p. 493.

The Prohibition Law should reflect and not make
the standard of conduct in each State of this Union.
The attempt to dragoon the body of the voters in
states which do not believe in this law results in
revolt in those states and has brought about conditions of lawlessness and disrespect for law which I
believe the people of this country should face and
should cure.

. . . You can expect nothing from the Republican
Party. The long record of eight years indicates that they
have used the law for patronage purposes and for political expediency. They tried to be wet when they were
with the wets, and dry when they were with the drys.
They have silently stood by and permitted the paralysis
of the whole machinery of government when it comes
to carrying out the mandate of the Constitution and
the statute law. It is because of that that after eight years
they are compelled to promise again that they will do
something about it if given a new lease of life by the
American people.
Al Smith, campaign speech of September 29, 1928, in
Milwaukee, from Campaign Addresses of Governor
Alfred E. Smith *(1929), pp. 118–119.*

The Republican Party isn't a "poor man's party."
Republican prosperity has erased that degrading phrase
from our political vocabulary. Republican efficiency has
filled the workingman's dinner pail—and his gas tank
besides—made the telephone, radio, and sanitary plumbing *standard* household equipment. And placed a whole
nation in the *silk stocking* class. Republican prosperity
has *reduced* hours and *increased* earning capacity, silenced
discontent, put the proverbial "chicken in every pot" and
a car in every backyard to boot.
Republican campaign advertisement, 1928, quoted in Abels,
In the Time of Silent Cal *(1969), pp. 274–275.*

The campaign now draws near a close. The platforms of
the two parties defining principles and offering solutions
of various national problems have been presented and are
being earnestly considered by our people.

After four months' debate it is not the Republican
Party which finds reason for abandonment of any of the
principles it has laid down or of the views it has
expressed for solution of the problems before the country. The principles to which it adheres are rooted deeply
in the foundations of our national life. The solutions
which it proposes are based on experience with government and on a consciousness that it may have the
responsibility for placing those solutions in action.
Herbert Hoover, campaign speech of October 22, 1928, in
New York, quoted in The New Day: Campaign Speeches
of Herbert Hoover *(1928), p. 149.*

I have never known any conflict between my official
duties and my religious belief. No such conflict could
exist. Certainly the people of this state recognize no
such conflict. They have testified to my devotion to
public duty by electing me to the highest office within
their gift four times.

. . . During the years I have discharged these trusts
I have been a communicant of the Roman Catholic
Church. If there were conflict, I, like all men, could not
have escaped it, because I have not been a silent man,
but a battler for social and political reform. These battles would in their very nature disclose this conflict if
there were any.
Al Smith, defending himself against a charge of divided loy-
alties, in Progressive Democracy *(1928), pp. 255–256.*

The issues of the campaign, as usual, have become tangled and obscured. There have been pointless, murky
debates about the tariff, farm relief, government ownership, and other such inanimate and meaningless
things. The true realities lie in the characters of the two
candidates. Which is the more enlightened and courageous, the more likely to formulate rational and effec-

Al Smith campaigns with his trademark derby hat and two Democratic companions in New York, 1928. *(Brown Brothers)*

tive policies, the least likely to yield to privilege and power, the more trustworthy? The question almost answers itself. Al is for the free man because he is a free man himself. If his head failed him, his heart would carry him irresistibly that way. But Hoover will hedge. He will find excuses to hesitate. He knows who his masters are, and he will serve them.

. . . Certainly it would be hard to imagine a more devious fellow. He has all the limber knavishness of the low-down American politician without any of the compensatory picturesqueness. He is like a lady of joy who lacks the saving grace of being beautiful.

H. L. Mencken, editorial of October 29, 1928 in The Baltimore Evening Sun, *quoted in* The Impossible H. L. Mencken *(1991), pp. 304–305.*

The Democratic Party is smashed—of that there is no doubt. It chose to run a Wet and Catholic and it has paid the price. As things look today, no living man above thirty years need expect to see a Catholic nomi-

nated again for the highest office in the land. Moreover, the completeness of Governor Smith's defeat makes impossible his renomination four years hence, as might have been the case had the election been close. If, as now appears, to our great satisfaction, Franklin D. Roosevelt has been chosen Governor of New York, there has risen another star upon the political horizon in Governor Smith's own State to play a great part in the complete party reorganization which must come unless it is simply to fade out.

Unsigned and untitled editorial, The Nation, *November 14, 1928, p. 507.*

. . . In the election of 1928 many Democrats assisted in retiring to private life the only potential miracle-man of high visibility in the party. Obviously the curse of politics is the politician. The Democratic Party seems to suffer a little more in that direction than others of record. Quadrenially its leaders behave as though the first Tuesday after the first Monday in November were to be a Lupercal, and as though each of them were ready to cast the chief candidate in the rôle of Gaius Julius Caesar. Principles may go hang.

Perhaps it is hardly to be expected that a party will show homogeneity when it is composed of Protestant Southern planters and industrialists, Western farmers, Eastern unionized laborers, Catholic Tammany, a Catholic machine in Boston, and other odds and ends. Consider, if you will, the origin of the Whigs from anti-Masons, John Quincy Adams followers, henchmen of Henry Clay, advocates of a national bank, nullifiers, states' rights men, and tariff men, with nothing in common save a hatred of Andrew Jackson and all he stood for. The Democrats have in common only the wistfulness of the "outs."

From "Will the Democrats Follow the Whigs?" by Silas Bent in Scribner's, *November 1929, p. 473.*

My God, just think of it, the great Democratic Party of Jefferson and of Jackson and of Wilson going to Tammany for leadership, with its alien program and interests and its social equality plan and practice, and its foreign secret understanding and practice of slipping in hundreds of thousands of foreigners in violation of the laws of our country to swell the vote of Tammany and help make America Catholic. Take that and thrust it in the face of the great Democratic Party of the South and tell us that we must bow down and worship this new hideous and hateful image which is set up in front of us by the John J. Raskob régime. He is a Republican and an officer in a foreign government. He holds an official position in the kingdom of the Roman Catholic Pope. . . . Shades of Jefferson!

Senator James Heflin, speech of June 12, 1930, quoted in Warren, Herbert Hoover and the Great Depression (1959), p. 50.

The issues which defeated the Governor were general prosperity, prohibition, the farm tariffs, Tammany, and the "snuggling" up of the Socialists. Had he been a Protestant, he would certainly have lost and might even have had a smaller vote. An indication of the small importance of the religious issue in final results was the vote in New York State. Here Governor Smith, a Catholic, had been twice elected Governor, and therefore no great amount of religious bigotry could have existed. It was for other reasons than this Catholicism that his own state rejected him for President.

Herbert Hoover, Memoirs (1952), p. 207.

Stock Market Mania

Indeed, to monkey with the stock market at all is perhaps illogical, in view of all the stories one has heard since childhood about the foolhardiness of attempting to beat an unbeatable game. More, speculation is generally regarded as not only dangerous, but also as downright wicked. Profits derived from it are ill gotten gains, because they were not won by the sweat of one's brow. . . .

Maybe the very difficulty of speculation is what has brought it into disrepute. Most men who enter business eventually fail because of their inability to be successful buyers and sellers. Likewise most men who speculate in stocks lose all the money they risk. Naturally, men who have failed in such an enterprise—and they are in the majority—do not speak any too highly of it. But neither do those who have been unable to master golf mention the game in terms of the highest praise. The fact remains that an occasional man speculates in the stock market as his sole means of livelihood, and contrives to do it year after year. He may not become a millionaire; if he did, he would no longer have to bother with speculation. But neither does he go broke, for in that event he couldn't speculate.

Fred C. Kelly, explaining "Logic and the Stock Market," in The American Mercury, February 1927, p. 148.

Half a dozen weeks ago it grew evident, throughout the country, discussion of the business situation was being superseded by discussion of the extraordinary stock market. . . . But the scene changed in April with great suddenness, when the excitement of speculation spread from Wall Street to the general public. By May, it appeared to have become nation-wide. Buying orders, telegraphed to New York from practically every section of the United States, reached in the aggregate a magnitude never previously witnessed in the history of any market. Habitual dabblers in stocks, who had been following for a series of months the persistent rise in prices, remarked with a kind of bewilderment that "the public had taken the bit in its teeth."

. . . Tangible evidence appeared, in striking form, that the craze for speculation was pervading even the humbler part of the community, evidently because of the knowledge of large speculative profits gained by acquaintances wholly ignorant of finance. The president of a New York savings bank testified that, in April, withdrawals by depositors from all New York City institutions of the kind had been $8,300,000 greater than a year before and that, instead of showing the normal yearly increase, the total savings-deposit fund had actually been reduced since 1927. Personal inquiry, he testified, proved that "depositors who, until a few weeks ago, knew Wall Street only as a name, are withdrawing the savings of years to buy securities 'on margin.'"

From "The Course of a Great Stock-Exchange Speculation," an analysis of the stock market mania of 1928, by Alexander Dana Noyes in Scribner's, July 1928, pp. 133–134.

12

The End of the Roaring Twenties
1929

Alfonse Capone had been a resident of Chicago since 1920. In that year, he arrived from his hometown of New York City at the invitation of Johnny Torrio, the leader of one of Chicago's largest and wealthiest criminal syndicates. Torrio employed Capone as a personal bodyguard before promoting him to manager of the Four Deuces Cafe on South Wabash. The profit realized by the various illegal enterprises carried on at this establishment—gambling, prostitution, and the sale of alcohol—enabled Torrio to expand business into the neighboring city of Cicero, a community just small enough to allow a complete takeover by anyone with the needed ambition and organization. To reward Al Capone, who proved himself adept at business and ready for any sort of murderous violence to discourage rivals, Torrio placed him in charge of the Cicero operations.

Despite his rapid rise in the Torrio organization, Capone managed to keep himself out of the headlines and relatively invisible to the public eye until September 20, 1926. On that day, members of a rival gang riding eight touring cars passed slowly in front of Capone's headquarters at the Hawthorne Hotel, raking the doors and windows with several hundred rounds from their Thompson submachine guns. The hotel suffered considerable damage, but Capone survived the attack without a scratch. From that point on, he was both famous and untouchable, the undisputed criminal king of the city.

Chicago's gangland warfare and crime syndicates did not begin with Prohibition. The Eighteenth Amendment and the Volstead Act, however, offered the city's underworld a tremendous new source of earnings in the manufacture, transport, and sale of alcohol, mainly beer manufactured within the city and whiskey smuggled on speedboats and trucks from Canada. Capone oversaw a large network of warehouses, distilleries, and retail outlets, and he overcame the lightly enforced legal barriers with generous bribes to city officials and police officers. In 1927, to ensure the continued smooth operation of this network, Capone also provided enough money and votes to guarantee the election of mayoral candidate William "Big Bill" Thompson, a man concerned more with the pernicious threat of the British monarchy on American government and society than with violations of the Volstead Act. Thompson's victory brought an even more tolerant attitude to the activities of organized crime in Chicago.

267

Big Bill Thompson enjoys a musical tribute to himself during his mayoral term in late-1920s Chicago. Obsessed with the threat of British influence on American life, Thompson turned a blind eye to corruption and gangsterism in his own city. *(Library of Congress)*

Capone saw his operations not as crime but as strictly business, the satisfaction of a public demand carried out according to time-honored methods of the nation's vaunted tycoons and industrialists. In its best year, his organization took in more than $100 million from gambling, prostitution, and vertically integrated whiskey and beer operations. Few seemed to really mind. While shuddering, pleasantly, at the sensational reports of murder and corruption in Chicago, the wealth-conscious public also felt a certain envy toward Capone's position and influence.

The public did not realize that Capone lived almost every moment in fear for his life. Even as he attempted to portray himself as a legitimate businessman, his ambitious rivals were forming alliances and agreements to take over his operations, and Capone realized they would have no second thoughts about replacing him, through any means possible, as Chicago's most prominent syndicate leader. He moved about the city behind an intimidating screen of armed guards, a miniature army that rode before and behind a specially built, steel-plated, seven-ton, bulletproof limousine.

By 1929, Capone's strongest rival, "Bugs" Moran, had established control over gambling, vice, and bootlegging operations on Chicago's North Side. Moran had also joined forces with a pair of renowned gangsters, the Aiello brothers, in an attempt to take over the Unione Siciliano, another criminal syndicate. In the eyes of local police and federal authorities, Moran and his allies were the prime suspect in the murder of two former presidents of the Unione, Anthony Lombardo and Pasqualino Lolardo. To Al Capone, Moran was the one rival in Chicago to take seriously and, if possible, eliminate.

THE ST. VALENTINE'S DAY MASSACRE

During the 1920s, gangster shootouts and assassinations became commonplace in Chicago, yet for most law-abiding citizens the bloody events provided as much entertainment as fear for public order and personal safety. For the most part, the victims came from the ranks of criminals, for whom sudden violent death was seen as an ordinary occupational hazard. Newsreel films replayed the events as cinematic thrillers, and the newspapers followed the gangland rivalries in lurid and exciting detail. Rather than figures of contempt, shadowy characters such as Meyer Wolfsheim in *The Great Gatsby* (based on Arnold Rothstein, the reputed fixer of the 1919 World Series), and the gangsters played by movie actor George Raft represented glamorous mystery for readers and audiences slumming through fictional underworlds. In general, tolerance for syndicates such as Capone's and the general contempt for Prohibition laws grew stronger as the 1920s wore on. Among the inhabitants of big cities such as Chicago, government efforts to enforce the Volstead Act met with indifference, derision, and—whenever a shootout resulted in the death of an innocent bystander—outright opposition.

The public attitude abruptly changed with events that took place on the North Side of Chicago on St. Valentine's Day, February 14, 1929. At about 10:30 A.M., a car disguised as an official police vehicle, complete with alarm bell and gun rack, pulled up to a garage at 2122 North Clark Street. Waiting inside the garage were five members of the Moran gang as well as two outsiders, all expecting to receive and inspect an entirely routine consignment of liquor from Canada.

Four men, two dressed as policemen, stepped out of the disguised vehicle and entered the garage, while a fifth stayed at the wheel. The visitors entered the garage, brought out sawed-off shotguns and machine guns, ordered the seven others to line up facing a brick wall, and then opened fire at close range. The seven victims slumped to the floor and tumbled into a blood-soaked heap against the garage wall. Immediately leaving the garage, the four assassins took prearranged positions for the benefit of eyewitnesses: the two in civilian clothes walked toward the car with their hands held over their heads, while the two in uniform followed them with guns drawn in the attitude of police carrying out an arrest.

The St. Valentine's Day Massacre became the most notorious single event in U.S. criminal history, the culmination of Chicago-style violence and Prohibition-era lawlessness. Complete with detailed photographs of the crime scene, sensational newspaper accounts speculated on the circumstances surrounding the event. Among the public, rumors had it that the Chicago police were guilty of the crime, or that Moran's rivals among the "Purple Gang" in Detroit had arrived in Chicago to carry out the massacre. However, the majority of suspicions had it that Al Capone was responsible and that Bugs Moran was the true target, as it was Capone's organization that would benefit most from Moran's death. These suspicions led to an official investigation of Vincenzo Damora and John Scalise, associates in Capone's organization. Damora provided an alibi, but Scalise was brought up on charges. Before he could be tried, however, Scalise was murdered by Capone personally at a banquet.

The massacre churned up public opinion against gangsters in Chicago and gave a strong impetus to the Federal Bureau of Investigation to bring a charge, any charge, against Al Capone. Although Capone had been at his winter residence in Palm Beach, Florida, at the time of the St. Valentine's Day Massacre and had thus provided himself with an alibi, he was widely believed to have ordered the murders. He soon found himself pursued on a charge of tax evasion, which resulted in a conviction and a lengthy jail term in 1931. With the repeal of Prohibition in 1933, bootlegging operations disappeared from the cities. Criminal gangs returned to their former lines of business such as prostitution and gambling and took up new ones, such as trade-union racketeering. The criminal organizations in Chicago and elsewhere missed only the reflected glamor of Al Capone and his rivals that had brought the underworld a small and misplaced measure of public respect.

A FATAL CRASH ON WALL STREET

The St. Valentine's Day Massacre struck a climactic accent in the counterpoint of lawlessness accompanying the consumerism, prosperity, and stock market fever of the 1920s. The desire to imitate the "easy money" of Al Capone overcame the investing millions, who sought their own success and respect with a minimum of bloodshed. Although a few observers and experts warned, beginning with the boom of 1928, that stock prices were rising illogically, decoupling

Two stockbrokers have an easy time of it in the spring and summer of 1929. The fever for ever-rising shares brought about a frenzy of buying and selling, but mostly buying. *(Brown Brothers)*

from the underlying rate of earnings that provided the traditional benchmarks, most investors did not care.

Stocks of successful corporations rose with the optimism. Start-up airline companies, automobile manufacturers and their related industries, electric power utilities, and communications companies were especially well regarded, replacing the railroad, steel, and natural-resource companies of the past. Of all the public companies traded at the New York Stock Exchange, RCA was riding the crest of this wave. RCA, whose price climbed above $500 a share in 1929, represented the electronic, mass-media future, profiting as it would from its control of radio technology patents, a network of broadcasting stations, and a system of intercontinental telegraph lines. A monopoly company fully sanctioned by the federal government, RCA produced radio programs as well as transmitters and receivers—controlling content as well as hardware, manufacturing an entire delivery system of information and entertainment that was beginning to link the country in a vast electronic web.

To the people of the 1920s, the letters RCA represented a must-have stock. They also came to stand for the most flagrant and underhanded forms of stock manipulation. Shares of the company provided the basis for the decade's most highly organized "stock pool," a shrewd creation meant to benefit a private circle of investors by removing all chance and risk from investing. The members of the stock pool committed their funds to the common purpose and appointed a pool manager to direct operations and clear transactions among the various members. Members of the pool then simply traded the shares of a single company back and forth, bidding incrementally higher in order to gradually force the price upward. The general public saw that the stock was being actively traded on rising prices, and outsiders bought shares as well.

The stock pool operation was neither illegal nor, in some cases, even secret. Many were publicly announced in the course of detailed, presumably disinterested reports in the financial papers. Although outsiders reading the latest news of the stock pool attempted to time their buys and sells in order to take their own advantage, few of them managed to make a profit, as nonmembers were never privy to the prearranged price at which bona fide members of the pool "pulled the plug." The stock having reached its target, the pool manager organized the wholesale sale of the stock back on the market. Members took their profits and prepared for the next opportunity, while outsiders were left counting their losses.

HERBERT HOOVER TAKES ACTION

Despite the general prosperity and confidence, the new president did not wish to emulate Calvin Coolidge by standing pat and saying as little as possible. Herbert Hoover was above all an engineer: a busy man who created and carried out complex plans, whether they were meant to exploit an underground mine or to feed the starving millions in a war-ravaged nation. With the general support of the public, who saw him as one of the most competent presidents they had ever elected, Hoover pressed ahead with his program: reduction of government control over public lands and utilities, benign indifference to the increasing concentration of capital in monopoly companies, and support for high tariffs that eased competition for domestic producers.

In the spring of 1929, when farm prices and the plight of the farmer were still considered more pressing issues than the ongoing feverish speculation in the stock market, Hoover called for a special session of Congress to deal with the problems. Following Hoover's recommendations, Congress set up the Farm Board under the chairmanship of Alexander Legge. The Farm Board would control the market for farm commodities and set up "stabilization corporations" to deal with temporary surpluses. The board was meant to stop the sharp swings in commodity prices that caused trouble and bankruptcy for farmers unable to accurately forecast a return on their investments of land, seed, and equipment.

While the Farm Board began its corrective actions, which would ultimately prove a failure in its task of stabilizing commodity prices, members of the Federal Reserve board, charged with control and oversight of the nation's money supply through a system of regional banks, came to the conclusion that they had to do something as well. They had already met on February 2, 1929, and set a policy of not offering money at the rediscount rate to member banks for the purpose of making speculative loans. Instead, the banks were to use the money only for legitimate business purposes and, not coincidentally, to reduce their holdings of securities. From then on, the Federal Reserve refused all requests to raise rediscount rates at its member banks, notably that of New York City, the principal source of money borrowed and then invested on the New York Stock Exchange.

In March, just after this decision, another break in stock prices occurred. "Call money" interest rates, loaned for speculation, rose as high as 20 percent. To head off the ballooning interest rates, the National City Bank of New York announced it was making $20 million in money available at 15–20 percent, an action that helped the stock market to recover. Public corporations began lending their own money at 8 or 9 percent, undercutting the rates charged by the

Federal Reserve. Brokers' loans rose to $6 billion, nearly double the outstanding amount in 1927. At this point, about one million people were buying on margin and about 300 million shares were being held on margin.

In the meantime and in the background, the economy of the United States was slowing, for a variety of reasons. Business inventories climbed from $500 million in 1928 to $1.8 billion in 1929, creating an expensive backlog of unsold goods in company warehouses. Construction spending fell off, while the rate of annual growth in consumer spending fell from 7.4 percent in 1927–28 to 1.5 percent in 1928–29. During the past several years, U.S. businesses had overbuilt production capacity as a high rate of business investment, encouraged by low interest rates, was pouring an ever greater amount of goods onto an increasingly reluctant consumer market. While corporate heads strived for rising earnings, profits, and dividends for their shareholders, they denied wage increases to their workers as a return for the increased production. Demand for consumer goods gradually lessened; by the summer of 1929 commodity prices and industrial production were falling in tandem.

THE CRASH

The debate over interest rates continued, with the president himself unsure of the wisest policy. In August 1929, with signs of the economic downturn growing more visible, the federal government raised the discount rate to 6 percent. On September 3, 1929, stock prices reached their peak. Brokers' loans to investors reached a record of $6.8 billion in October, indicating higher-than-ever margin buying. In the year preceding October, new issues of common stock had also reached a record amount: $5.1 billion.

The market slipped again, to general unconcern. Many people felt the drop in prices represented just another temporary readjustment, or that the high volume of new stock issues was dragging down prices, which would gradually recover as the shares were bought and held. The confidence began a rapid and tumultuous decline starting on the morning of Monday, October 21, when ticker tapes began running late due to heavy trading at the exchange. The delayed quotes prevented brokers from knowing the most current stock prices; the uncertainty fueled doubts, and then panic. A wave of selling took place, and by noon the ticker tapes were running a full hour late. On that day, price quotations did not catch up with trading until nearly two hours after the market's close.

A slight recovery took place on Tuesday, October 22, that did very little to restore general confidence. Buyers disappeared, sellers grew more adamant, and as the middle of the week was reached, the awareness grew that the market was going through something much worse than a temporary drop in prices. On Wednesday, when a steep drop took place in the last hour of trading, a full-scale stock market crash was underway. Sellers flooded the market with orders to unload shares at the market price, whatever it may be. At the end of trading at 3:00 P.M., the ticker tape was running 104 minutes late. To cover the losses in stocks bought on margin, brokers sent out calls for money. When investors realized that a large number of "margin calls" were going out, and a wholesale liquidation of stocks was in progress in order to raise the demanded cash, panic set in.

October 24, 1929, would go down in financial history as "Black Thursday." At the start of the day, selling took place in huge trading blocks. The system of brokers' loans and easy credit began tumbling, the selling and the falling prices

The plummeting stock market brought doleful crowds to the front doors of the New York Stock Exchange in October 1929. *(Brown Brothers)*

multiplying the margin calls and turning the paper profits into losses and then bankruptcies. In the course of the day, a record volume of 12,894,650 shares would be traded as the lack of information, frightening rumors, and lagging tickers increased the panic. Traders and clerks at the stock exchange were unable to cope with the volume; brokers across the country were unable to get their orders to the exchange floor. While brokers' offices were mobbed, crowds began gathering in the vicinity of Wall Street, staring at the windows lining the concrete canyons in a futile search for information.

Around midday, at the offices of J. P. Morgan and Company, a group of six bankers gathered for an emergency meeting: Charles Mitchell of the National City Bank, Albert Wiggin of Chase National Bank, Thomas Lamont of the Morgan Bank, William Potter of the Guaranty Trust Company, Seward Prosser of the Bankers Trust, and George F. Baker of the First National Bank. In an attempt to prop up the crashing market, they agreed to commit as much as $40 million each to a buying pool on behalf of the banks they represented. Richard Whitney, vice president of the New York Stock Exchange, then proceeded from the meeting to the exchange floor in order to relay the news to traders and the public in the most dramatic fashion possible. He made buying bids on 15 or 20 prominent stocks, in large blocks of 10,000 shares, at the last price.

On Friday, government officials issued reassuring statements, insisting that the country's economy and the stock market were still on a sound footing. Tycoons such as John D. Rockefeller, their personal savings presumably safe, demonstrated their own confidence by publicly announcing new investments. Prices held fairly steady on Friday and on Saturday. But on Sunday, when the market was closed, panic again set in as brokers sent out more margin calls. For many investors, new to the market during the Roaring Twenties, stock market investing was still a mysterious process. The steady and delirious rise in prices over the 1920s turned into a very sudden fall, equally difficult to explain, that was setting off a desperate rush to sell at any price, a mirror-image hysteria that resumed early during the session of Monday, October 28, during which there were at some moments no bids to buy certain stocks at any price. The market was caught in a downward spiral, impossible for the most powerful and resourceful banks or investors to stem.

On Tuesday, October 29, 16 million shares changed hands. Billions of dollars had been lost, and thousands of investors as well as brokers were going bankrupt. The stock exchange closed at noon on Thursday, and all day Friday and Saturday. Stock prices continued to fall until the middle of November; on November 13, the *New York Times* average of 50 leading stocks hit 164.43, compared to 311.90 in September. In the space of a few weeks, stocks had lost approximately 40 percent of their value. Late in the fall of 1929, prices stabilized slightly, then fell again for another two and a half years until hitting bottom in the middle of 1932. Commodity prices continued their slide, and in an example of the increasing international linkage of financial systems, several foreign exchanges crashed in imitation of the New York exchange. Banks and corporations that had lent money for speculation began calling in their loans; those firms that could not recover enough of their money began closing their doors for good.

The expansion of credit that had taken place in the 1920s came to a sudden end; the economy and consumers struggled to adjust. The high debts created by installment buying now brought about bankruptcies. When banks found they could not recover loans they had made to consumers and brokers, they spread panic among those who had deposited their life savings and presumed their money to be safe. The public began withdrawing its money from the now-suspect banking system, which was suddenly in dire need of some form of the government interference that Harding, Coolidge, and Hoover had warned the country about over the last decade. The millions of defaults, large and small, began a drop in consumer demand that would last for years. While production fell sharply, unemployment increased. Cities, small towns, and farms were all affected, prompting a backlash against Herbert Hoover, a victory for Franklin Roosevelt in 1932, and a new order of business for the federal government. The Great Depression was under way.

CHRONICLE OF EVENTS

1929

January 2: The United States and Canada sign an agreement for the preservation of Niagara Falls and for the development of hydropower along the U.S.-Canada border.

January 7: Major Carl Spaatz lands at Los Angeles after a flight of 150 hours and 40 minutes in *The Question Mark,* the longest flight to date.

January 14: Strike Up the Band, with music by George Gershwin, opens in New York.

January 15: The Senate ratifies the Kellogg-Briand Pact by a vote of 85 to 1.

January 15: Civil rights leader Martin Luther King Jr. is born.

January 22: The federal government drops charges against 30 nightclub operators for Prohibition violations, stating that no jury will vote to convict.

February 2: In an attempt to dampen speculation in the stock market, the Federal Reserve Bank forbids its members banks to make loans for the purpose of buying stocks on margin.

February 11: The Dawes Plan is restructured by Owen D. Young and the Committee on German Reparations. The Young Plan reduces Germany's debt, extends the time for repayment, and creates the Bank for International Settlements.

February 11: At a gala 82nd birthday party, to which President Hoover and Henry Ford have been invited, inventor Thomas Edison announces the development of a new, fast-growing and easily harvested rubber plant.

February 13: For the navy, Congress authorizes the construction of 19 new cruisers and 1 aircraft carrier by the Cruiser Act.

February 14: Six members of the Bugs Moran gang and one bystander are murdered in a Chicago garage. Members of Al Capone's criminal organization are suspected.

February 17: The first in-flight movie is exhibited, sponsored by Universal Air Live.

March 4: Herbert Hoover is inaugurated as the 31st president.

March 8: The United States supplies aircraft and weaponry to the government of Mexico to assist in putting down a revolt in the Mexican provinces.

April 4: New York Police Commissioner Grover Whalen declares that the city has 32,000 speakeasies and sharply criticizes the Prohibition law.

Five members of the Bugs Moran gang, as well as two outsiders, were rubbed out in a Chicago garage on St. Valentine's Day, 1929, ending for a time the public's blasé attitude toward organized crime. *(Brown Brothers)*

April 9: Suspected of liquor smuggling, the Canadian ship *I'm Alone* is sunk by a U.S. Coast Guard cutter 200 miles offshore in the Gulf of Mexico. The British and Canadian governments make a strong protest that the ship was in international waters.

April 16: Secretary of State Henry Stimson announces that the United States will not recognize the Soviet Union.

May 7: U.S. troops stationed along the border of Mexico are withdrawn as an armed rebellion abates.

May 15: A hospital fire in Cleveland, Ohio, kills 124 people.

May 16: The first Academy Awards show, honoring the year's achievements in motion pictures, is produced by the Academy of Motion Picture Arts and Sciences in Hollywood. *Wings* wins the first award for best picture; Janet Gaynor wins best actress, and Emil Jannings wins best actor.

May 17: President Hoover announces the resolution of the Tacna-Arica boundary dispute between Chile and Peru.

May 17: Al Capone is sentenced to a year in prison for carrying a concealed weapon.

May 20: President Hoover appoints a National Commission on Law Observance and Enforcement to study Prohibition lawlessness. George W. Wickersham chairs the commission.

May 27: In *United States v. Schwimmer,* the Supreme Court upholds the denial of citizenship to Rosika Schwimmer, a Hungarian immigrant who is also a pacifist. Justice Oliver Wendell Holmes dissents. The Supreme Court also upholds the constitutionality of the presidential pocket veto, which allows the president to veto a bill by neither signing nor returning it within 10 days of the adjournment of Congress.

May 27: Colonel Charles Lindbergh marries Anne Spencer Morrow, the daughter of Dwight Morrow, in Englewood, New Jersey.

June 7: In Paris, the Young Plan is announced as a replacement for the Dawes Plan with a new schedule of lower reparations payments to be made by Germany. The Young Plan agreement will be formally signed in January 1930.

June 15: The Agricultural Marketing Act establishes the Federal Farm Relief Board, which in 1930 will set up stabilization corporations to buy surplus produce off the market.

June 27: Bell Labs unveils the first color television prototype.

July 1: The Immigration Act of 1924 formally goes into effect, calling for quotas on immigration based on the 1920 census.

July 10: New U.S. paper currency, smaller by one-third, goes into circulation.

July 24: President Hoover proclaims the Kellogg-Briand Pact to be in force.

July 30: In the *St. Louis Robin,* pilots Forrest O'Brine and Dale Jackson set a new flight endurance record of 420 hours.

September 8: John Dewey forms the League for Independent Political Action to establish a new political party.

September 24: Lieutenant General James Doolittle makes the first instruments-only flight at Mitchell Field, New York.

October 2: Violence breaks out during a strike of textile workers at the Marion Manufacturing Company in Marion, North Carolina, killing three and wounding 20 strikers.

October 24–29: During several days of panic selling, margin calls, and forced liquidation, the stock market plunges. On October 29, a total of 16 million shares trade hands and the market suffers $8 billion in losses. The crash will worsen an economic downturn that is already in progress, lessen capital investment, force layoffs, close down banks, and impoverish investors.

October 29: The steamship *Wisconsin* sinks in Lake Michigan; nine people drown.

November 11: The 1,850-foot-long Ambassador Bridge between Detroit and Windsor, Ontario, is dedicated.

November 21: President Hoover meets with business and union leaders at the White House to discuss the economic crisis and the stock market crash.

November 29: During a 19-hour flight, Lieutenant Commander Richard Byrd and Bernt Blachen become the first to fly an airplane over the South Pole.

December 2: Secretary of State Henry Stimson appeals, in the spirit of the Kellogg-Briand Pact which the Soviet Union and China have both signed, to those two nations to peacefully settle their dispute over Manchuria.

December 3: Edsel Ford announces an increase in the minimum wage from $6 to $7 a day at the Ford Motor Company.

December 16: President Hoover signs an income tax reduction bill that reduces 1929 taxes by a total of $160 million.

Eyewitness Testimony

Late Prohibition and the St. Valentine's Day Massacre

Sure, I got a racket. So's everybody. Name me a guy that ain't got a racket. Most guys hurt people. I don't hurt nobody. Only them that get in my way. I give away a lot of dough. Maybe I don't support no college or build no libraries, but I give it to people that need it, direct.

Al Capone to journalist Robert St. John in 1924, as quoted in Bergreen, Capone: The Man and the Era *(1994), p. 122.*

Under our system of government a political controversy is settled when the several state legislatures ratify a constitutional amendment growing out of that controversy and an enabling statute is passed. Thereafter nothing can honorably be done except obey the law, or repeal the statute, or re-amend the Constitution. That is why Mr. Chief Justice Taft, who was a staunch opponent of Prohibition, now insists upon it that the Eighteenth Amendment and the Volstead Act must be enforced and obeyed. There is nothing else for a decent man to do. For a long time I was an honest foe of Prohibition. I fought as valiantly as I could for the cause in which I believed. That cause is lost. I was legally defeated. I cannot now honestly and decently try to get by illegal means that which I cannot obtain legally. I cannot urge others to disobey the law and hinder its enforcement. If I did I should be like the base-ball player who, having been struck out, throws his bat at the umpire and incites the bleachers to riot.

Albert Levitt, "Anti-Prohibition Hallucinations," in the South Atlantic Quarterly, *January 1926, p. 12.*

Drinking in hotel rooms of America "has increased 95% since the adoption of Prohibition," in the opinion of Richard R. Lane, owner of hotels in Des Moines, Cedar Rapids and Davenport, Iowa, who is attending a convention of the Northwest Hotel Association.

"The maids know—they carry out the bottles. Extra bellboys are required to carry the cracked ice, and hotel room furniture tells the story. In many instances furniture has been all but ruined by guests who scrape the caps from their bottles.

"Only one feature of Prohibition has benefited hotel men," Mr. Lane observed. "It has boomed the sale of ginger ale. But this acts as a boomerang, because guests are wrecking furniture by opening the ginger ale bottles on it."

Associated Press dispatch on the state of the hotel business and the progress of Prohibition, as quoted in The American Mercury, *February 1927, p. 178.*

. . . one man stood out as the greatest gang leader in history—Alphonse Capone, sometimes known as big-hearted Al because of his extravagance in buying floral pieces, but usually called Scarface Al because of a pretentious scar down the left side of his face.

. . . Al travels in a bullet-proof car. He surrounds himself with eight men selected for thickness of torso who form an inner ring about him when he appears in public. They are tall and he is short, a precaution against any attempt to aim at him through the spaces between their necks. For Al's protection, the eight men wear bullet-proof vests. Nothing smaller than a fieldpiece could penetrate his double-walled fortress of meat.

Correspondent Alva Johnston describing Chicago gang leader Al Capone in "Gangs a la Mode," The New Yorker, *August 25, 1928, as quoted in Bergreen,* Capone *(1994), pp. 154–155.*

Nobody knows whether the majority of the American people is wet or dry; but certainly the division is too nearly equal—the minority, on whichever side, is too strong and stubborn—to permit the hope that either wet or dry victory could be final for years to come. The drys failed to end the argument by putting prohibition into the Constitution; the wets could not end it by taking it out. For this is what is known as a moral issue; in other words, an issue which most people approach emotionally, not rationally. So long as people feel intensely about it, there can never be a final settlement of the differences over liquor.

Elmer Davis, from "What Can We Do About It? The Candid Misgivings of a Wet," in Harper's, *December 1928, p. 1.*

The question is frequently asked, "Is the Eighteenth Amendment making us a nation of lawbreakers?" There are two answers, depending upon the meaning of the question. If it is intended to ask whether many people are disobeying the law and whether the Amendment is helping to break down respect for the law itself, the answer is emphatically, yes. If, on the other hand, the question is intended to imply that we were a law-abiding nation before we went dry, the answer is as emphatically, no. Any law that goes counter to the strong feeling of a large part of the population is bound to be disobeyed in America. Any law that is disobeyed inevitably results in lawbreaking and lowering respect for law as law. The Eighteenth Amendment is doing that on a gigantic scale, but it is operating upon a population already the most lawless in spirit of any in the great modern civilized countries. Lawlessness has been and is one of the most distinctive American traits. . . . Americans themselves are, and almost always have been, less law-abiding than the more civilized European nations.

James Truslow Adams, in Our Business Civilization: Some Aspects of the Culture *(1929), pp. 101–102.*

Never in all the history of feuds or gangland has Chicago or the nation seen anything like today's wholesale slaughter. I've seen Chicago's booze and vice rackets for years, but never before have seven men been lined up and shot down in cold blood.

Patrick Roche, federal investigator, reacting to the St. Valentine's Day Massacre of February 14, 1929, quoted in Bergreen, Capone: The Man and the Era, *p. 312.*

I've got more brains on my feet than I have in my head.

Journalist Willis O'Rourke of the Chicago Evening American, after visiting the site of the St. Valentine's Day Massacre, February 14, 1929, as quoted in Bergreen, Capone: The Man and the Era, *p. 312.*

Once in the racket you are always in it, it seems. The parasites will trail you begging for money and favors and you can never get away from them no matter where you go. I have a wife and a boy who is eleven— a lad I idolize—and a beautiful home in Florida. If I could go there and forget it all I would be the happiest man in the world.

Al Capone, as told to Major Lemuel B. Schofield of Philadelphia shortly after the 1929 St. Valentine's Day massacre and Capone's arrest on a gun possession charge, quoted in Sann, The Lawless Decade *(1957), p. 213.*

Authority makes the leader reckless; the need for easy money guides that recklessness, and the result is obvious. His gang takes a name and adopts a specialty— raiding banks, chain stores, filling stations, payroll wagons, or mail trucks. Leader and gang are at last in on the big money. They attract the attention of the racketeer, whose mobs require reinforcements, since the casualties are large, and who finds recruits for his murder mobs in the skilled ranks of the gang. . . . Boys

who started with bunches become what are known in underworld circles as heavies, a title which carries much weight among criminals.

The gambler and the speakeasy proprietor are, by the very nature of their unlawful undertakings, subject to levy from blackmailers and competitors. A beer truck needs guards; a gambling joint must be protected against hold-ups and extortion; an underworld-political machine on election day needs "workers" with guns to protect the interests of the racketeer. The murder mob supplies these services, using whatever weapons are suited to the occasion; machine guns and automatic rifles for the general run of business; hand grenades ("pineapples") for the doorsteps of judges, prosecutors, and public officials who have earned the enmity of the racketeer.

From Howard McLellan, "Boys, Gangs, and Crime," article deploring the recruitment of children into criminal gangs, in The Review of Reviews, *March 1929, p. 57.*

Murders more or less wholesale or retail scarcely cause a ripple of comment. Seven undesirables wiped out with incredible brutality either by bandit policemen or gang opponents—and the newspapers are through with it in forty-eight hours. Flaring headlines one day, casual mention the second, and a submerged paragraph the third. Outside of Chicago, where it happened, the popular judgment seemed to be, "Well, that's Chicago for you. . . ."

This hard-boiled state of mind has become very nearly universal on this continent, and it's a pretty terrible thing to contemplate if you happen to have even a very little bit of sentimentality left in your make-up. It makes you feel rather fearful that the killers, the footpads, the big or little crooks in and out of politics can get away with anything. The entire body politic, embracing both sexes that have the vote, appears to be sensation proof, utterly indifferent to all manner of explosions and cataclysms unless an immediate injury is brought to its own threshold.

From "Hard Boiled," unsigned editorial in World's Work, *April 1929, p. 33.*

Cigar smoke hung in a heavy blue haze over the long polished table. Ash trays piled high betrayed the inner emotions of the little group as it listened to a tall, spare man with a thin-square-jawed face.

They had every right to be tense and at least subconsciously apprehensive, I thought. For they were the "Secret Six," known more formally as the Citizens Committee for the Prevention and punishment of Crime, a special committee of the Chicago Association of Commerce. And only a closely guarded anonymity assured their continual well-being.

There may have been fear under their outer determination, but they were the hope of a frightened city as it struggled feebly in a web of bombs and bullets, alcohol and assassination. That was Chicago in 1929, a city ruled by the knife, pistol, shotgun, tommygun and "pineapple" of the underworld, a jungle of steel and concrete clutched fast in the fat, diamond-studded hand of a scar-faced killer named Al Capone.

From a study of the Prohibition underworld by federal agent Elliot Ness, in Ness, The Untouchables *(1947), pp. 1–2.*

When I was working with Shorty I was living on the North Side of Chicago. I told my folks I was working. Your folks have a tendency to believe the best.

At that time the North Side—at least where I was living—was wide open. Everything went there. All the big speakeasies were going, gambling places were going, the police never bothered anybody; everything was payoff, you know. And you had more of a transient population, people that were living in kitchenettes. And a lot of younger people, girls and fellas that were kicking around. It was something on the order of your old Greenwich Village and your old Rush Street area.

We never had any trouble getting rid of the stuff we stole. Shorty knew a lot of people around the North Side. There were plenty of opportunities there to do business. I gradually picked up connections of my own. There was one hotel, there was nothing but thieves in it. There were burglars over there and cannons and stickup-men and junkies and everything. It was a connection spot for fixes—no matter what you were caught doing you could always get it straightened out through someone in the place. If you had the money.

Description of 1920s-era Chicago, from Martin (ed.), My Life in Crime *(1952), p. 102.*

Panic on Wall Street

Reading the Dow-Jones averages in the manner formulated a quarter of a century ago by the late Charles H. Dow, the indication is plainly bullish. . . . All this is irrespective of the fact that stock prices are relatively very high and have now been advancing for a full four years. Beyond offering the somewhat trite reflection that no tree grows to the sky, there is no need to moralize about it. The stock market is saying, in so many words, that the business outlook is good and likely to continue so for as far ahead as general information can calculate, assuming

that Wall Street is the reservoir of all that everybody knows about everything connected with business.

From The Wall Street Journal, *October 3, 1927, quoted in Patterson,* The Great Boom and Panic *(1965), pp. 29–30.*

In the crowd there's a Chinaman wearing a hat which rests on his ears. He's got a dead cigar in a mouth of dead teeth. He's standing on tip-toe to see over the shoulders of a woman wearing a big fancy hat. She's holding out her wedding ring and shouting "you want more margin—you can't have more margin." He's drunk as a lord. Everybody is shouting. They're all trying to reach the glass booths where the clerks are. Everybody wants to sell out. The boy at the quotation board is running scared. He can't keep up with the speed of the way stocks are dropping. The board's painted green. The guy who runs it is Irish. He's standing at the back of the booth, on the telephone. I can't hear what he's saying. But a guy near me shouts, "the sonofabitch has sold me out!"

Pat Bologna, Wall Street shoeshine boy, describing the action in a Wall Street brokerage house on Thursday, October 24, 1929, in Thomas and Morgan-Witts, The Day the Bubble Burst *(1979), p. 356.*

Gambling in stock has become a national disease. This malady reaches all classes of people, from preachers to stable boys. . . . It was inevitable that a day of reckoning would come and that billions would be lost as the water and hot air were eliminated from hundreds of stock issues. In my opinion there will be further declines as the people begin to learn the facts and to use common sense. There has been not only an inflation in the value of stocks, but in various forms of property. This has resulted in a somewhat fictitious prosperity.

Senator King of Utah, comments made during the October 1929, stock market crash, quoted in Patterson, The Great Boom and Panic *(1965), p. 135.*

WALL STREET LAYS AN EGG

DROP IN STOCKS ROPES SHOWMEN

MANY WEEP AND CALL OFF
CHRISTMAS ORDERS—
LEGIT SHOWS HIT

MERGERS HALTED

The most dramatic event in the financial history of America is the collapse of the New York Stock Market.

The stage was Wall Street, but the onlookers covered the country. Estimates are that 22,000,000 people were in the market at the time.

Tragedy, despair, and ruination spell the story of countless thousands of marginal stock traders. Perhaps Manhattan was worst hit in the number of victims. Many may remain broke for the rest of their lives, because the money that disappeared via the ticker tape was the savings of years.

Front-page headline and article, Variety, *Wednesday, October 30, 1929, p. 1.*

It was a combination of fear and mob psychology that carried the debacle to the absurd lengths it reached; but obviously the market must have been extremely vulnerable to offer so little resistance. For why should this sudden hysteria, this utter lack of confidence, spread like wild-fire into every important financial center at a time when the country as a whole is enjoying at least a normal prosperity? The explanation lies, of course, in the speculative mania that has so long dominated the thinking of the financial community and in that time has jockeyed the prices of certain securities up to extravagant levels. This speculative spirit has long assumed that nothing could ever interrupt the greatest bull market on record.

. . . Undoubtedly this so-called "healthy reaction" will do much toward sobering Wall Street's speculative enthusiasm and establishing more realistic standards of stock values. It is a costly process, however, for the thousands, wise or unwise, who have had their accounts wiped out.

"Wall Street's Crisis," from The Nation, *November 6, 1929, p. 510.*

The worst panic in Wall Street's history—at least in peace times—record-breaking in magnitude and in wide-spread losses, was nevertheless an entirely new kind of panic. Future historians, it is freely predicted, will speak of it as "the prosperity panic of 1929." . . . But this October catastrophe on Wall Street was purely a speculative stock market panic, all authorities agree. The downward moves in other markets were repercussions of the crash in stock values in New York. One writer frankly terms it "a gamblers' and not an investors' panic."

. . . And yet, through it all, the prevailing note of newspaper editorial comment was that of confidence, and reassuring statements about business conditions were given out by economists, bankers, business executives,

and political leaders, from President Hoover down. Nor was this all mere talk, for on the very day of the biggest crash the United States Steel Corporation and the American Can Company made a practical expression of their belief in existing and coming prosperity by each declaring extra dividends of one dollar a share.

From "Wall Street's 'Prosperity Panic'" in The Literary Digest, *November 9, 1929, p. 5.*

In Chicago philanthropist Julius Rosenwald, board chairman of Sears Roebuck Co. guaranteed the margin accounts of all his employees. Two days later Chicago's public utility tycoon and opera promoter Samuel Insull announced that he would do the same thing. And so did Samuel W. Reyburn, president of Manhattan's department store Lord & Taylor. But the climax came when the wizened little man who lives in the fortressed home in Pocantico Hills, N.Y. said: "My son and I have for some days past been purchasing sound common stock." In memory of many a trader in Wall Street, John D. Rockefeller Sr. had never spoken on the market. Nor did he often speak on any subject.

. . . Friday there were no quotations nor Saturday for the Exchange was closed. Clerks who had passed many a sleepless night, slept, then returned to clean up the greatest amount of work which brokerage houses have ever had in so short a time. In the hurly-burly many an error had been made. The clerks had to discover them, rectify them. But in the Stock Exchange Friday and Saturday there was quiet.

From "Faith, Bankers, and Panic," in Time *magazine, November 11, 1929, pp. 45–46.*

Stock market prices had had an immense slaughter. Whether the next move will be up or down, I do not know. But the market has a bottom. There are cushions, and even powerful springs at the bottom, in the buying by investors who are waiting for the turn, and in the covering purchases by short sellers.

Encouraging words of Benjamin M. Anderson of the Chase National Bank, speech of November 21, 1929, quoted in Patterson, The Great Boom and Panic *(1965), pp. 177–178.*

One of the most painful phases of the situation was due to the false belief from day to day that the bottom had been reached. In trying to save something out of the wreck, people were throwing good money after bad. To the extent of uncounted millions of shares, speculators—one can hardly call them investors—had

Unemployed men line up outside a soup kitchen opened by Al Capone in Chicago. The city's top mobster hoped such charity would win him a reprieve from investigations by the FBI. *(National Archives)*

made only partial payment. They had bought on what is known as "margin," through stock-brokers, who completed the purchase for their customers by borrowing from the banks on the security of the stocks themselves. The decline in prices was so rapid that in thousands of cases there was no time to call upon the customer to protect his nominal ownership by paying more money on account.

Albert Shaw, "The Progress of the World," from The Review of Reviews, *December 1929, p. 36.*

I saw them sold out, dozens of them, scores of them. I watched their faces when the customers' men gave them the news. I saw men's hair literally turn white. I saw a woman faint dead away; they carried her out cold. I heard a middle aged doctor say: "There goes my son's college education."

Terrible sights. Terrible sounds. Sitting there hour after hour, watching my own "investments" shrink and shrivel, my heart ached for the poor people around me.

From a description of the Wall Street panic in "Now I've Gone Back to Work" in American Magazine, *February 1930, and quoted in Patterson,* The Great Boom and Panic *(1965), p. 172.*

Accountants, architects, engineers, lawyers; all who served industry directly and indirectly, merchant and manufacturer who supplied its needs, went down in the general debacle. Men of character and standing, who from youth had been pillars of the social structure, found themselves derelict. Their posts of trust and service were gong; their savings of a lifetime were lost; their investments were worthless. Craftsmen whose skilled hands had ever assured them a livelihood, wandered aimlessly in futile quest for work.

Past wealth or past glory meant nothing: men inured to leadership for generations found themselves without means and without prospects. Thousands who had given generously to others in the past became recipients of charity.

Description of aftereffects of the stock market crash from Winkelman, Ten Years of Wall Street *(1932), p. 353.*

In the days of our phantom prosperity, we were sleek and self-satisfied. We were well-fed and wanted nothing so much as to be left alone. We were impatient of those queer persons who were forever raising critical questions about our political, social, and economic policies. As if anything could be wrong with a civilization that was paying such excellent dividends!

. . . Almost the sole exception to this reluctance to reconsider the orthodoxies of our traditional habits was the lush growth of bootleg religions and the rise of an apostolate of fakirs who led thousands of otherwise intelligent Americans to believe that, in their wistful quest for the deeper meanings of existence, they could suck the juices of a living gospel from the dead rinds of ancient superstitions or the green stalks of bogus psychologies. It may be that mankind will always rebel in this irrational manner against an era that becomes so exclusively absorbed in the goods and chattels of a crass prosperity. At any rate, aside from this gullible embracement of improvised religions, and its perfect willingness to scrap machines and methods of production in even early stages of obsolescence, the American mind betrayed a baffling immunity to new ideas as long as the economic skies were bright. And even the new religionists, with fat pay checks in hand and seated at the wheels of fast cars, closed their minds to political and economic reconsiderations.

From Glenn Frank, Crisis Points in National Policy *(1934), pp. 23–24.*

I never did like the idea of living on scallions in a left bank garret. I like writing in comfort. So I went into business, a classmate and I. I thought I'd retire in a year or two. And a thing called Collapse, bango! socked everything out. 1929. All I had left was a pencil.

Luckily, I had a friend named Ira Gershwin, and he said to me, "You've got your pencil. Get your rhyming dictionary and go to work." I did. There was nothing else to do.

. . . I was relieved when the Crash came. I was released. Being in business was something I detested. When I found that I could sell a song or a poem, I became me, I became alive. Other people didn't see it that way. They were throwing themselves out of windows.

Someone who lost money found that his life was gone. When I lost my possessions, I found my creativity. I felt I was being born for the first time. So for me the world became beautiful.

. . . We thought American business was the Rock of Gibraltar. We were the prosperous nation, and nothing could stop us now. A brownstone house was forever. You gave it to your kids and they put marble fronts on it. There was a feeling of continuity. If you made it, it was there forever. Suddenly the big dream exploded. The impact was unbelievable.

E.Y. (Yip) Harburg, interview, in Terkel, Hard Times: An Oral History of the Great Depression *(1970), p. 21.*

These beautiful yachts that cost half a million dollars were sitting around (on the West Coast) with barnacles on them. These are the people who jumped out of windows. Who's gonna buy a yacht? A man came up to me and said, "Hey, any of these yachts for sale?" I said, "Are you kiddin'? They're all for sale." The guy was a bootlegger. So I sold half-million dollars yachts to bootleggers. For five or ten thousand dollars. And took my six percent commission on them. Beautiful.

Sally Rand, describing business opportunities after the stock market crash, as quoted by Studs Terkel and reprinted in Prohibition: Thirteen Years that Changed America *(1996), p. 132.*

APPENDIX A
Documents

1. Woodrow Wilson's Fourteen Points
2. From the Espionage Act of 1918
3. Covenant of the League of Nations
4. From Justice Oliver Wendell Holmes's dissent in the case of *Abrams v. United States*
5. Eighteenth Amendment
6. Nineteenth Amendment
7. From the National Prohibition Act (also known as the Volstead Act)
8. The Declaration of Rights of the Negro Peoples of the World (1920)
9. From Warren G. Harding's inaugural address
10. The Emergency Quota Act of 1921
11. Treaty between the United States of America, the British Empire, France, and Japan
12. The Hays Code (1924)
13. The Progressive Party platform
14. Teapot Dome
15. The Immigration Act of 1924
16. Clarence Darrow, "Mercy for Leopold and Loeb"
17. From Calvin Coolidge's inaugural address
18. Charles Lindbergh's application for the Raymond Orteig Prize
19. Bartolomeo Vanzetti's final statement to the court
20. List of "Don'ts and Be Carefuls," adopted by California Association for Guidance of Producers
21. Kellogg-Briand Pact
22. Herbert Hoover's "Rugged Individualism" speech
23. Herbert Hoover's inaugural address
24. The American Civil Liberties Union creed (1929)
25. Sinclair Lewis, "The American Fear of Literature"
26. From the report of the Wickersham Commission on Prohibition (1931)

1. WOODROW WILSON'S FOURTEEN POINTS, DELIVERED JANUARY 8, 1818

[Speech delivered to Congress, outlining the president's war aims and his program for a postwar peace agreement]

It will be our wish and purpose that the processes of peace, when they are begun, shall be absolutely open and that they shall involve and permit henceforth no secret understandings of any kind. The day of conquest and aggrandizement is gone by; so is also the day of secret covenants entered into in the interest of particular governments and likely at some unlooked-for moment to upset the peace of the world. It is this happy fact, now clear to the view of every public man whose thoughts do not still linger in an age that is dead and gone, which makes it possible for every nation whose purposes are consistent with justice and the peace of the world to avow nor or at any other time the objects it has in view.

We entered this war because violations of right had occurred which touched us to the quick and made the life of our own people impossible unless they were corrected and the world secure once for all against their recurrence. What we demand in this war, therefore, is nothing peculiar to ourselves. It is that the world be made fit and safe to live in; and particularly that it be made safe for every peace-loving nation which, like our own, wishes to live its own life, determine its own institutions, be assured of justice and fair dealing by the other peoples of the world as against force and selfish aggression. All the peoples of the world are in effect partners in this interest, and for our own part we see very clearly that unless justice be done to others it will not be done to us. The programme of the world's peace, therefore, is our programme; and that programme, the only possible programme, as we see it, is this:

I. Open covenants of peace, openly arrived at, after which there shall be no private international understandings of any kind but diplomacy shall proceed always frankly and in the public view.

II. Absolute freedom of navigation upon the seas, outside territorial waters, alike in peace and in war, except as the seas may be closed in whole or in part by international action for the enforcement of international covenants.

III. The removal, so far as possible, of all economic barriers and the establishment of an equality of trade conditions among all the nations consenting to the peace and associating themselves for its maintenance.

IV. Adequate guarantees given and taken that national armaments will be reduced to the lowest point consistent with domestic safety.

V. A free, open-minded, and absolutely impartial adjustment of all colonial claims, based upon a strict observance of the principle that in determining all such questions of sovereignty the interests of the populations concerned must have equal weight with the equitable claims of the government whose title is to be determined.

VI. The evacuation of all Russian territory and such a settlement of all questions affecting Russia as will secure the best and freest cooperation of the other nations of the world in obtaining for her an unhampered and unembarrassed opportunity for the independent determination of her own political development and national policy and assure her of a sincere welcome into the society of free nations under institutions of her own choosing; and, more than a welcome, assistance also of every kind that she may need and may herself desire. The treatment accorded Russia by her sister nations in the months to come will be the acid test of their good will, of their comprehension of her needs as distinguished from their own interests, and of their intelligent and unselfish sympathy.

VII. Belgium, the whole world will agree, must be evacuated and restored, without any attempt to limit the sovereignty which she enjoys in common with all other free nations. No other single act will serve as this will serve to restore confidence among the nations in the laws which they have themselves set and determined for the government of their relations with one another. Without this healing act the whole structure and validity of international law is forever impaired.

VIII. All French territory should be freed and the invaded portions restored, and the wrong done to France by Prussia in 1871 in the matter of Alsace-Lorraine, which has unsettled the peace of the world for nearly fifty years, should be righted, in order that peace may once more be made secure in the interest of all.

IX. A readjustment of the frontiers of Italy should be effected along clearly recognizable lines of nationality.

X. The peoples of Austria-Hungary, whose place among the nations we wish to see safeguarded and assured, should be accorded the freest opportunity to autonomous development.

XI. Rumania, Serbia, and Montenegro should be evacuated; occupied territories restored; Serbia accorded free and secure access to the sea; and the relations of the several Balkan states to one another determined by friendly counsel along historically established lines of allegiance and nationality; and international guarantees of the political and economic independence and territorial integrity of the several Balkan states should be entered into.

XII. The Turkish portion of the present Ottoman Empire should be assured a secure sovereignty, but the other nationalities which are now under Turkish rule should be assured an undoubted security of life and an absolutely unmolested opportunity of autonomous development, and the Dardanelles should be permanently opened as a free passage to the ships and commerce of all nations under international guarantees.

XIII. An independent Polish state should be erected which should include the territories inhabited by indisputably Polish populations, which should be assured a free and secure access to the sea, and whose political and economic independence and territorial integrity should be guaranteed by international covenant.

XIV. A general association of nations must be formed under specific covenants for the purpose of affording mutual guarantees of political independence and territorial integrity to great and small states alike.

In regard to these essential rectifications of wrong and assertions of right we feel ourselves to be intimate partners of all the governments and peoples associated together against the Imperialists. We cannot be separated in interest or divided in purpose. We stand together until the end.

For such arrangements and covenants we are willing to fight and to continue to fight until they are achieved; but only because we wish the right to prevail and desire a just and stable peace such as can be secured only by removing the chief provocations to war, which this programme does remove. We have no jealousy of German greatness, and there is nothing in this programme that impairs it. We grudge her no achievement or distinction of learning or of pacific enterprise such as have made her record very bright and very enviable. We do not wish to injure her or to block in any way her legitimate influence or power. We do not wish to fight her either with arms or with hostile arrangements of trade if she is willing to associate herself with us and the other peace-loving nations of the world in covenants of justice and law and fair dealing. We wish her only to accept a place of equality among the peoples of the world,—the new world in which we now live,—instead of a place of mastery.

2. From the Espionage Act of 1918, May 16, 1918

Be it enacted, That section three of the Act . . . approved June 15, 1917, be . . . amended so as to read as follows:

"Sec. 3. Whoever, when the United States is at war, shall willfully make or convey false reports or false statements with intent to interfere with the operation or success of the military or naval forces of the United States, or to promote the success of its enemies, or shall willfully convey false reports, or false statements, or say or do anything except by way of bona fide and not disloyal advice to an investor . . . with intent to obstruct the sale by the United States of bonds . . . or the making of loans by or to the United States, or whoever when the United States is at war, shall willfully cause . . . or incite . . . insubordination, disloyalty, mutiny, or refusal of duty, in the military or naval forces of the United States, or shall willfully obstruct the recruiting or enlistment service of the United States, and whoever, when the United States is at war, shall willfully utter, print, write, or publish any disloyal, profane, scurrilous, or abusive language about the form of government of the United States, or the Constitution of the United States, or the military or naval forces of the United States, or the flag . . . or the uniform of the Army or Navy of the United States, or any language intended to bring the form of government . . . or the Constitution . . . or the military or naval forces . . . or the flag . . . of the United States into contempt, scorn, contumely, or disrespect . . . or shall willfully display the flag of any foreign enemy, or shall willfully . . . urge, incite, or advocate any curtailment of production in this country of any thing or things . . . necessary or essential to the prosecution of the war . . . and whoever shall willfully advocate, teach, defend, or suggest the doing of any of the acts or things in this section enumerated and whoever shall by word or act support or favor the cause of any country with which the United States is at war or by word or act oppose the cause of the United States therein, shall be punished by a fine of not more than $10,000 or imprisonment for not more than twenty years, or both. . . ."

3. Covenant of the League of Nations, Originally finalized on April 28, 1919 and with amendments adopted up to December 1924

THE HIGH CONTRACTING PARTIES, In order to promote international co-operation and to achieve international peace and security by the acceptance of obligations not to resort to war, by the prescription of open, just and honourable relations between nations, by the firm establishment of the understandings of international law as the actual rule of conduct among

Governments, and by the maintenance of justice and a scrupulous respect for all treaty obligations in the dealings of organised peoples with one another, Agree to this Covenant of the League of Nations.

Article 1

The original Members of the League of Nations shall be those of the Signatories which are named in the Annex to this Covenant and also such of those other States named in the Annex as shall accede without reservation to this Covenant. Such accession shall be effected by a Declaration deposited with the Secretariat within two months of the coming into force of the Covenant. Notice thereof shall be sent to all other Members of the League.

Any fully self-governing State, Dominion or Colony not named in the Annex may become a Member of the League if its admission is agreed to by two-thirds of the Assembly, provided that it shall give effective guarantees of its sincere intention to observe its international obligations, and shall accept such regulations as may be prescribed by the League in regard to its military, naval and air forces and armaments.

Any Member of the League may, after two years' notice of its intention so to do, withdraw from the League, provided that all its international obligations and all its obligations under this Covenant shall have been fulfilled at the time of its withdrawal.

Article 2

The action of the League under this Covenant shall be effected through the instrumentality of an Assembly and of a Council, with a permanent Secretariat.

Article 3

The Assembly shall consist of Representatives of the Members of the League.

The Assembly shall meet at stated intervals and from time to time as occasion may require at the Seat of the League or at such other place as may be decided upon.

The Assembly may deal at its meetings with any matter within the sphere of action of the League or affecting the peace of the world.

At meetings of the Assembly each Member of the League shall have one vote, and may have not more than three Representatives.

Article 4

The Council shall consist of Representatives of the Principal Allied and Associated Powers, together with Representatives of four other Members of the League. These four Members of the League shall be selected by the Assembly from time to time in its discretion. Until the appointment of the Representatives of the four Members of the League first selected by the Assembly, Representatives of Belgium, Brazil, Spain and Greece shall be members of the Council.

With the approval of the majority of the Assembly, the Council may name additional Members of the League whose Representatives shall always be members of the Council; the Council, with like approval may increase the number of Members of the League to be selected by the Assembly for representation on the Council.

The Council shall meet from time to time as occasion may require, and at least once a year, at the Seat of the League, or at such other place as may be decided upon.

The Council may deal at its meetings with any matter within the sphere of action of the League or affecting the peace of the world.

Any Member of the League not represented on the Council shall be invited to send a Representative to sit as a member at any meeting of the Council during the consideration of matters specially affecting the interests of that Member of the League.

At meetings of the Council, each Member of the League represented on the Council shall have one vote, and may have not more than one Representative.

Article 5

Except where otherwise expressly provided in this Covenant or by the terms of the present Treaty, decisions at any meeting of the Assembly or of the Council shall require the agreement of all the Members of the League represented at the meeting.

All matters of procedure at meetings of the Assembly or of the Council, including the appointment of Committees to investigate particular matters, shall be regulated by the Assembly or by the Council and may be decided by a majority of the Members of the League represented at the meeting.

The first meeting of the Assembly and the first meeting of the Council shall be summoned by the President of the United States of America.

Article 6

The permanent Secretariat shall be established at the Seat of the League.

The Secretariat shall comprise a Secretary General and such secretaries and staff as may be required.

The first Secretary General shall be the person named in the Annex; thereafter the Secretary General shall be appointed by the Council with the approval of the majority of the Assembly.

The secretaries and staff of the Secretariat shall be appointed by the Secretary General with the approval of the Council.

The Secretary General shall act in the capacity at all meetings of the Assembly and of the Council.

The expenses of the League shall be borne by the Members of the League in the proportion decided by the Assembly.

Article 7

The Seat of the League is established at Geneva.

The Council may at any time decide that the Seat of the League shall be established elsewhere.

All positions under or in connection with the League, including the Secretariat, shall be open equally to men and women.

Representatives of the Members of the League and officials of the League when engaged on the business of the League shall enjoy diplomatic privileges and immunities.

The buildings and other property occupied by the League or its officials or by Representatives attending its meetings shall be inviolable.

Article 8

The Members of the League recognise that the maintenance of peace requires the reduction of national armaments to the lowest point consistent with national safety and the enforcement by common action of international obligations.

The Council, taking account of the geographical situation and circumstances of each State, shall formulate plans for such reduction for the consideration and action of the several Governments.

Such plans shall be subject to reconsideration and revision at least every ten years.

After these plans shall have been adopted by the several Governments, the limits of armaments therein fixed shall not be exceeded without the concurrence of the Council.

The Members of the League agree that the manufacture by private enterprise of munitions and implements of war is open to grave objections. The Council shall advise how the evil effects attendant upon such manufacture can be prevented, due regard being had to the necessities of those Members of the League which are not able to manufacture the munitions and implements of war necessary for their safety.

The Members of the League undertake to interchange full and frank information as to the scale of their armaments, their military, naval and air programmes and the condition of such of their industries as are adaptable to war-like purposes.

Article 9

A permanent Commission shall be constituted to advise the Council on the execution of the provisions of Articles 1 and 8 and on military, naval and air questions generally.

Article 10

The Members of the League undertake to respect and preserve as against external aggression the territorial integrity and existing political independence of all Members of the League. In case of any such aggression or in case of any threat or danger of such aggression the Council shall advise upon the means by which this obligation shall be fulfilled.

Article 11

Any war or threat of war, whether immediately affecting any of the Members of the League or not, is hereby declared a matter of concern to the whole League, and the League shall take any action that may be deemed wise and effectual to safeguard the peace of nations. In case any such emergency should arise the Secretary General shall on the request of any Member of the League forthwith summon a meeting of the Council.

It is also declared to be the friendly right of each Member of the League to bring to the attention of the Assembly or of the Council any circumstance whatever affecting international relations which threatens to disturb international peace or the good understanding between nations upon which peace depends.

Article 12

The Members of the League agree that, if there should arise between them any dispute likely to lead to a rupture they will submit the matter either to arbitration or judicial settlement or to enquiry by the Council, and they agree in no case to resort to war until three months after the award by the arbitrators or the judicial decision, or the report by the Council. In any case under this Article the award of the arbitrators or the judicial decision shall be made within a reasonable time, and the report of the Council shall be made within six months after the submission of the dispute.

Article 13

The Members of the League agree that whenever any dispute shall arise between them which they recognise to be suitable for submission to arbitration or judicial settlement and which cannot be satisfactorily settled by diplomacy, they will submit the whole subject–matter to arbitration or judicial settlement.

Disputes as to the interpretation of a treaty, as to any question of international law, as to the existence of any fact which if established would constitute a breach of any international obligation, or as to the extent and nature of the reparation to be made for any such breach, are declared to be among those which are generally suitable for submission to arbitration or judicial settlement.

For the consideration of any such dispute, the court to which the case is referred shall be the Permanent Court of International Justice, established in accordance with Article 14, or any tribunal agreed on by the parties to the dispute or stipulated in any convention existing between them.

The Members of the League agree that they will carry out in full good faith any award or decision that may be rendered, and that they will not resort to war against a Member of the League which complies therewith. In the event of any failure to carry out such an award or decision, the Council shall propose what steps should be taken to give effect thereto.

Article 14

The Council shall formulate and submit to the Members of the League for adoption plans for the establishment of a Permanent Court of International Justice. The Court shall be competent to hear and determine any dispute of an international character which the parties thereto submit to it. The Court may also give an advisory opinion upon any dispute or question referred to it by the Council or by the Assembly.

Article 15

If there should arise between Members of the League any dispute likely to lead to a rupture, which is not submitted to arbitration or judicial settlement in accordance with Article 13, the Members of the League agree that they will submit the matter to the Council. Any party to the dispute may effect such submission by giving notice of the existence of the dispute to the Secretary General, who will make all necessary arrangements for a full investigation and consideration thereof.

For this purpose the parties to the dispute will communicate to the Secretary General, as promptly as possible, statements of their case with all the relevant facts and papers, and the Council may forthwith direct the publication thereof.

The Council shall endeavour to effect a settlement of the dispute, and if such efforts are successful, a statement shall be made public giving such facts and explanations regarding the dispute and the terms of settlement thereof as the Council may deem appropriate.

If the dispute is not thus settled, the Council either unanimously or by a majority vote shall make and publish a report containing a statement of the facts of the dispute and the recommendations which are deemed just and proper in regard thereto.

Any Member of the League represented on the Council may make public a statement of the facts of the dispute and of its conclusions regarding the same.

If a report by the Council is unanimously agreed to by the members thereof other than the Representatives of one or more of the parties to the dispute, the Members of the League agree that they will not go to war with any party to the dispute which complies with the recommendations of the report.

If the Council fails to reach a report which is unanimously agreed to by the members thereof, other than the Representatives of one or more of the parties to the dispute, the Members of the League reserve to themselves the right to take such action as they shall consider necessary for the maintenance of right and justice.

If the dispute between the parties is claimed by one of them, and is found by the Council, to arise out of a matter which by international law is solely within the domestic jurisdiction of that party, the Council shall so report, and shall make no recommendation as to its settlement.

The Council may in any case under this Article refer the dispute to the Assembly. The dispute shall be so referred at the request of either party to the dispute, provided that such request be made within fourteen days after the submission of the dispute to the Council.

In any case referred to the Assembly, all the provisions of this Article and of Article 12 relating to the action and powers of the Council shall apply to the action and powers of the Assembly, provided that a report made by the Assembly, if concurred in by the Representatives of those Members of the League represented on the Council and of a majority of the other Members of the League, exclusive in each case of the Representatives of the parties to the dispute, shall have the same force as a report by the Council concurred in by all the members thereof other than the Representatives of one or more of the parties to the dispute.

Article 16

Should any Member of the League resort to war in disregard of its covenants under Articles 12, 13 or 15, it shall ipso facto be deemed to have committed an act of war against all other Members of the League, which hereby undertake immediately to subject it to the severance of all trade or financial relations, the prohibition of all intercourse between their nationals and the nationals of the covenant-breaking State, and the prevention of all financial, commercial or personal intercourse between the nationals of the covenant-breaking State and the nationals of any other State, whether a Member of the League or not.

It shall be the duty of the Council in such case to recommend to the several Governments concerned what effective military, naval or air force the Members of the League shall severally contribute to the armed forces to be used to protect the covenants of the League.

The Members of the League agree, further, that they will mutually support one another in the financial and economic measures which are taken under this Article, in order to minimise the loss and inconvenience resulting from the above measures, and that they will mutually support one another in resisting any special measures aimed at one of their number by the covenant-breaking State, and that they will take the necessary steps to afford passage through their territory to the forces of any of the Members of the League which are co-operating to protect the covenants of the League.

Any Member of the League which has violated any covenant of the League may be declared to be no longer a Member of the League by a vote of the Council concurred in by the Representatives of all the other Members of the League represented thereon.

Article 17

In the event of a dispute between a Member of the League and a State which is not a Member of the League, or between States not Members of the League, the State or States not Members of the League shall be invited to accept the obligations of membership in the League for the purposes of such dispute, upon such conditions as the Council may deem just. If such invitation is accepted, the provisions of Articles 12 to 16 inclusive shall be applied with such modifications as may be deemed necessary by the Council.

Upon such invitation being given the Council shall immediately institute an inquiry into the circumstances of the dispute and recommend such action as may seem best and most effectual in the circumstances.

If a State so invited shall refuse to accept the obligations of membership in the League for the purposes of such dispute, and shall resort to war against a Member of the League, the provisions of Article 16 shall be applicable as against the State taking such action.

If both parties to the dispute when so invited refuse to accept the obligations of membership in the League for the purposes of such dispute, the Council may take such measures and make such recommendations as will prevent hostilities and will result in the settlement of the dispute.

Article 18

Every treaty or international engagement entered into hereafter by any Member of the League shall be forthwith registered with the Secretariat and shall as soon as possible be published by it. No such treaty or international engagement shall be binding until so registered.

Article 19

The Assembly may from time to time advise the reconsideration by Members of the League of treaties which have become inapplicable and the consideration of international conditions whose continuance might endanger the peace of the world.

Article 20

The Members of the League severally agree that this Covenant is accepted as abrogating all obligations or understandings inter se which are inconsistent with the terms thereof, and solemnly undertake that they will not hereafter enter into any engagements inconsistent with the terms thereof.

In case any Member of the League shall, before becoming a Member of the League, have undertaken any obligations inconsistent with the terms of this Covenant, it shall be the duty of such Member to take immediate steps to procure its release from such obligations.

Article 21

Nothing in this Covenant shall be deemed to affect the validity of international engagements, such as treaties of arbitration or regional understandings like the Monroe doctrine, for securing the maintenance of peace.

Article 22

To those colonies and territories which as a consequence of the late war have ceased to be under the sovereignty of the States which formerly governed them and which are inhabited by peoples not yet able to stand by themselves under the strenuous conditions of the modern world, there should be applied the principle that the well-being and development of such peoples form a sacred trust of civilisation and that securities for the performance of this trust should be embodied in this Covenant.

The best method of giving practical effect to this principle is that the tutelage of such peoples should be entrusted to advanced nations who by reason of their resources, their experience or their geographical position can best undertake this responsibility, and who are willing to accept it, and that this tutelage should be exercised by them as Mandatories on behalf of the League.

The character of the mandate must differ according to the stage of the development of the people, the geographical situation of the territory, its economic conditions and other similar circumstances.

Certain communities formerly belonging to the Turkish Empire have reached a stage of development where their existence as independent nations can be provisionally recognized subject to the rendering of administrative advice and assistance by a Mandatory until such time as they are able to stand alone. The wishes of these communities must be a principal consideration in the selection of the Mandatory.

Other peoples, especially those of Central Africa, are at such a stage that the Mandatory must be responsible for the administration of the territory under conditions which will guarantee freedom of conscience and religion, subject only to the maintenance of public order and morals, the prohibition of abuses such as the slave trade, the arms traffic and the liquor traffic, and the prevention of the establishment of fortifications or military and naval bases and of military training of the natives for other than police purposes and the defence of territory, and will also secure equal opportunities for the trade and commerce of other Members of the League.

There are territories, such as South-West Africa and certain of the South Pacific Islands, which, owing to the sparseness of their population, or their small size, or their remoteness from the centres of civilisation, or their geographical contiguity to the territory of the Mandatory, and other circumstances, can be best administered under the laws of the Mandatory as integral portions of its territory, subject to the safeguards above mentioned in the interests of the indigenous population.

In every case of mandate, the Mandatory shall render to the Council an annual report in reference to the territory committed to its charge.

The degree of authority, control, or administration to be exercised by the Mandatory shall, if not previously agreed upon by the Members of the League, be explicitly defined in each case by the Council.

A permanent Commission shall be constituted to receive and examine the annual reports of the Mandatories and to advise the Council on all matters relating to the observance of the mandates.

Article 23

Subject to and in accordance with the provisions of international conventions existing or hereafter to be agreed upon, the Members of the League:

(a) will endeavour to secure and maintain fair and humane conditions of labour for men, women, and children, both in their own countries and in all countries to which their commercial and industrial relations extend, and for that purpose will establish and maintain the necessary international organisations;

(b) undertake to secure just treatment of the native inhabitants of territories under their control;

(c) will entrust the League with the general supervision over the execution of agreements with regard to the traffic in women and children, and the traffic in opium and other dangerous drugs;

(d) will entrust the League with the general supervision of the trade in arms and ammunition with the countries in which the control of this traffic is necessary in the common interest;

(e) will make provision to secure and maintain freedom of communications and of transit and equitable treatment for the commerce of all Members of the League. In this connection, the special necessities of the regions devastated during the war of 1914–1918 shall be borne in mind;

(f) will endeavour to take steps in matters of international concern for the prevention and control of disease.

Article 24

There shall be placed under the direction of the League all international bureaux already established by general treaties if the parties to such treaties consent. All such international bureaux and all commissions for the regulation of matters of international interest hereafter constituted shall be placed under the direction of the League.

In all matters of international interest which are regulated by general convention but which are not placed under the control of international bureaux or commissions, the Secretariat of the League shall, subject to the consent of the Council and if desired by the parties, collect and distribute all relevant information and shall render any other assistance which may be necessary or desirable.

The Council may include as part of the expenses of the Secretariat the expenses of any bureau or commission which is placed under the direction of the League.

Article 25

The Members of the League agree to encourage and promote the establishment and co-operation of duly authorised voluntary national Red Cross organisations having as purposes the improvement of health, the prevention of disease and the mitigation of suffering throughout the world.

Article 26

Amendments to this Covenant will take effect when ratified by the Members of the League whose Representatives compose the Council and by a majority of the Members of the League whose Representatives compose the Assembly.

No such amendments shall bind any Member of the League which signifies its dissent therefrom, but in that case it shall cease to be a Member of the League.

4. FROM JUSTICE HOLMES'S DISSENT IN THE CASE OF *ABRAMS V. UNITED STATES,* NOVEMBER 10, 1919

This indictment is founded wholly upon publication of two leaflets which I shall describe in a moment. The first count charges a conspiracy, pending the war with Germany, to publish abusive language about the form of government of the United States, laying the preparation and publishing of the first leaflet as overt acts. The second count charges a conspiracy, pending the war, to publish language intended to bring the form of government into contempt, laying the preparation and publishing of the two leaflets as overt acts. The third count alleges a conspiracy to encourage resistance to the United States in the same war and to attempt to effectuate the purpose by publishing the same leaflets. The fourth count lays a conspiracy to incite curtailment of production of things necessary to the prosecution of the war and to attempt to accomplish it by publishing the second leaflet to which I have referred.

The first of these leaflets says that the President's cowardly silence about the intervention in Russia reveals the hypocrisy of the plutocratic gang in Washington. It intimates that "German militarism combined with allied capitalism to crush the Russian revolution," goes on that the tyrants of the world fight each other until they see a common enemy—working-class enlightenment, when they combine to crush it; and that now militarism and capitalism combined, though not openly, to crush the Russian revolution. It says that there is only one enemy of the workers of the world and that is capitalism; that it is a crime for workers of America, etc., to fight the workers' republic of Russia, and ends: "Awake! Awake, you Workers of the World! Revolutionists." A note adds: "It is absurd to call us pro-German. We hate and despise German militarism more than do you hypocritical tyrants. We have more reasons for denouncing German militarism than has the coward of the White House."

No argument seems to me necessary to show that these pronunciamentos in no way attack the form of government of the United States, or that they do not support either of the first two counts. What little I have to say about the third count may be postponed until I have considered the fourth. With regard to that it seems too plain to be denied that the suggestion to workers in the ammunition factories that they are producing bullets to murder their dearest, and the further advocacy of a general strike, both in the second leaflet, do urge curtailment of production of things necessary to the prosecution of the war within the meaning of the Act of May 16, 1818, c. 75, 40 Stat. 553, amending part 3 of the earlier Act of 1917. But to make the conduct criminal that statute requires that it should be "with intent by such curtailment to cripple or hinder the United States in the prosecution of the war." It seems to me that no such intent is proved.

I am aware of course that the word intent as vaguely used in ordinary legal discussion means no more than knowledge at the time of the act that the consequences said to be intended will ensue. Even less than that will satisfy the general principle of civil and criminal liability. A man may have to pay damages, may be sent to prison, at common law might be hanged, if at the time of his act he knew facts from which common experience showed that the consequences would follow, whether he individually could foresee them or not. But, when words are used exactly, a deed is not done with intent to produce a consequence unless that consequence is the aim of the deed. It may be obvious, and obvious to the actor, that the consequence will follow, and he may be liable for it even if he regrets it, but he does not do the act with intent to produce it unless the aim to produce it is the proximate motive of the specific act, although there may be some deeper motive behind. . . .

I do not see how anyone can find the intent required by the statute in any of the defendants' words. The second leaflet is the only one that affords even a foundation for the charge, and there, without invoking the hatred of German militarism expressed in the former one, it is evident from the beginning to the end that the only object of the paper is to help Russia and stop American intervention there against the popular government—not to impede the United States in the war that it was carrying on. To say that two phrases taken literally might import a suggestion of conduct that would have interference with the war as an indirect and probably undesired effect seems to me by no means enough to show an attempt to produce that effect. . . .

In this case sentences of twenty years imprisonment have been imposed for the publishing of two leaflets that I believe the defendants had as much right to publish as the Government has to publish the Constitution of the United States now vainly invoked by them. Even if I am technically wrong and enough can be squeezed from these poor and puny anonymities to turn the color of legal litmus paper; I will add, even if what I think the necessary intent were shown; the most nominal punishment seems to me all that possibly could be inflicted, unless the defendants are to be made to suffer not for what the indictment alleges but for the creed they avow—a creed that I believe to be the creed of ignorance and immaturity when honestly held, as I see no reason to doubt that it was held here, but which, although made the subject of examination at the trial, no one has right even to consider in dealing with the charges before the Court.

Persecution for the expression of opinions seems to me perfectly logical. If you have no doubt of your premises or your power and want a certain result with all your heart you naturally express your wishes in law and sweep away all opposition. To allow opposition by speech seems to indicate that you think the speech impotent, as when a man says that he has squared the circle, or that you do not care whole-heartedly for the result, or that you doubt either your power or your premises. But when men have faiths, they may come to believe even more than they believe the very foundations of their own conduct that the ultimate good desired is better reached by free trade in ideas—that the best test of truth is the power of the thought to get itself accepted in the competition of the market, and that truth is the only ground upon which their wishes safely can be carried out. That at any rate is the theory of our Constitution. It is an experiment, as all life is an experiment. Every year is not every day we have to wager our salvation upon some prophecy based upon imperfect knowledge. While that experiment is part of our system I think that we should be eternally vigilant against attempts to check the expression of opinions that we loathe and believe to be fraught with death, unless they so imminently threaten immediate interference with the lawful and pressing purposes of the law that an immediate check is required to save the country. I wholly disagree with the argument of the Government that the First Amendment left the common law as to seditious libel in force. History seems to me against the notion. I had conceived that the United States through many years had shown its repentance for the Sedition Act of 1798, by repaying fines that it imposed. Only the emergency that makes it immediately dangerous to leave the correction of evil counsels to time warrants making any exception to the sweeping command, "Congress shall make no law . . . abridging the freedom of speech." Of course I am speaking only of expressions of opinion and exhortations, which were all that were uttered here, but I regret that I cannot put into more impressive words my belief that in their conviction upon this indictment the defendants were deprived of their rights under the Constitution of the United States.

5. EIGHTEENTH AMENDMENT, RATIFIED JANUARY 29, 1919; EFFECTIVE JANUARY 16, 1920

Section 1. After one year from the ratification of this article the manufacture, sale, or transportation of intoxicating liquors within, the importation thereof into, or the exportation thereof from the United States and all territory subject to the jurisdiction thereof for beverage purposes is hereby prohibited.

Section 2. The Congress and the several states shall have concurrent power to enforce this article by appropriate legislation.

Section 3. This article shall be inoperative unless it shall have been ratified as an amendment to the Constitution by the legislatures of the several states, as provided in the Constitution, within seven years from the date of the submission hereof to the states by the Congress.

6. NINETEENTH AMENDMENT, PROPOSED JUNE 4, 1919; RATIFIED AUGUST 18, 1920

Section 1. The right of citizens of the United States to vote shall not be denied or abridged by the United States or by any state on account of sex.

Section 2. Congress shall have power to enforce this article by appropriate legislation.

7. FROM THE NATIONAL PROHIBITION ACT (ALSO KNOWN AS THE VOLSTEAD ACT), OCTOBER 28, 1919

Be it Enacted . . . That the short title of this Act shall be the "National Prohibition Act."

TITLE II

Prohibition of Intoxicating Beverages

SECTION 3. No person shall on or after the date when the eighteenth amendment to the Constitution of the United States goes into effect, manufacture, sell, barter, transport, import, export, deliver, furnish or possess any intoxicating liquor except as authorized in this Act, and all the provisions of this Act shall be liberally construed to the end that the use of intoxicating liquor as a beverage may be prevented.

Liquor for nonbeverage purposes and wine for sacramental purposes may be manufactured, purchased, sold, bartered, transported, imported, exported, delivered, furnished, and possessed, but only as herein provided, and the commissioner may, upon application, issue permits therefor: Provided, That nothing in this Act shall prohibit the purchase and sale of warehouse receipts covering distilled spirits on deposit in Government bonded warehouses, and no special tax liability shall attach to the business of purchasing and selling such warehouse receipts.

SECTION 6. No one shall manufacture, sell, purchase, transport, or prescribe any liquor without first obtaining a permit from the commissioner so to do, except that a person may, without a permit, purchase and use liquor for medicinal purposes when prescribed by a physician as herein provided, and except that any person who in the opinion of the commissioner is conducting a bona fide hospital or sanatorium engaged in the treatment of persons suffering from alcoholism, may, under such rules, regulations, and conditions as the commissioner shall prescribe, purchase and use, in accordance with the methods in use in such institution, liquor, to be administered under the direction of a duly qualified physician employed by such institution.

All permits to manufacture, prescribe, sell, or transport liquor, may be issued for one year, and shall expire on the 31st day of December next succeeding the issuance thereof . . . Permits to purchase liquor shall specify the quantity and kind to be purchased and the purpose for which it is to be used. No permit shall be issued to any person who within one year prior to the application therefor or issuance thereof shall have violated the terms of any permit issued under this Title or any law of the United States or of any State regulating traffic in liquor. No permit shall be issued to anyone to sell liquor at retail, unless the sale is to be made through a pharmacist designated in the permit and duly licensed under the laws of his State to compound and dispense medicine prescribed by a duly licensed physician. No one shall be given a permit to prescribe liquor unless he is a physician duly licensed to practice medicine and actively engaged in the practice of such profession. . . .

Nothing in this title shall be held to apply to the manufacture, sale, transportation, importation, possession, or distribution of wine for sacramental purposes, or like religious rites. . . . No person to whom a permit may be issued to manufacture, transport, import, or sell wines for sacramental purposes or like religious rites shall sell, barter, exchange, or furnish any such to any person not a rabbi, minister of the gospel, priest, or an officer duly authorized for the purpose by any church or congregation, nor to any such except upon an application duly subscribed by him, which application, authenticated as regulations may prescribe, shall be filed and preserved by the seller. The head of any conference or diocese or other ecclesiastical jurisdiction may designate any rabbi, minister, or priest to supervise the manufacture of wine to be used for the purposes and rites in this section mentioned, and the person so designated may, in the discretion of the commissioner, be granted a permit to supervise such manufacture.

SECTION 7. No one but a physician holding a permit to prescribe liquor shall issue any prescription for liquor. And no physician shall prescribe liquor unless after careful physical examination of the person for whose use such prescription is sought, or if such examination is found impracticable, then upon the best information obtainable, he in good faith believes that the use of such liquor as a medicine by such person is necessary and will afford relief to him from some known ailment. Not more than a pint of spiritous liquor to be taken internally shall be prescribed for use by the same person within any period of ten days and no prescription shall be filled more than once. Any pharmacist filling a prescription shall at the time indorse upon it over his own signature the word "canceled," together with the date when the liquor was delivered, and then make the same a part of the record that he is required to keep as herein provided. . . .

SECTION 18. It shall be unlawful to advertise, manufacture, sell, or possess for sale any utensil, contrivance, machine, preparation, compound, tablet, substance, formula direction, recipe advertised, designed, or intended for use in the unlawful manufacture of intoxicating liquor. . . .

SECTION 21. Any room, house, building, boat, vehicle, structure, or place where intoxicating liquor is manufactured, sold, kept, or bartered in violation of this title, and all intoxicating liquor and property kept and used in maintaining the same, is hereby declared to be a common nuisance, and any person who maintains such a common nuisance shall be guilty of a misdemeanor and upon conviction thereof shall be fined not more than $1,000 or be imprisoned for not more than one year, or both. . . .

SECTION 25. It shall be unlawful to have or possess any liquor or property designed for the manufacture of liquor intended for use in violating this title or which has been so used, and no property rights shall exist in any such liquor or property. . . .

SECTION 29. Any person who manufactures or sells liquor in violation of this title shall for a first offense be fined not more than $1,000, or imprisoned not exceeding six months, and for a second or subsequent offense shall be fined not less than $200 nor more than $2,000 and be imprisoned not less than one month nor more than five years.

Any person violating the provisions of any permit, or who makes any false record, report, or affidavit required by this title, or violates any of the provisions

of this title, for which offense a special penalty is not prescribed, shall be fined for a first offense not more than $500; for a second offense not less than $100 nor more than $1,000, or be imprisoned not more than ninety days; for any subsequent offense he shall be fined not less than $500 and be imprisoned not less than three months nor more than two years. . . .

SECTION 33. After February 1, 1920, the possession of liquors by any person not legally permitted under this title to possess liquor shall be prima facie evidence that such liquor is kept for the purpose of being sold, bartered, exchanged, given away, furnished, or otherwise disposed of in violation of the Provisions of this title . . . But it shall not be unlawful to possess liquors in one's private dwelling while the same is occupied and used by him as his dwelling only and such liquor need not be reported, provided such liquors are for use only for the personal consumption of the owner thereof and his family residing in such dwelling and of his bona fide guests when entertained by him therein; and the burden of proof shall be upon the possessor in any action concerning the same to prove that such liquor was lawfully acquired, and used. . . .

8. THE DECLARATION OF RIGHTS OF THE NEGRO PEOPLES OF THE WORLD, 1920

Statement drawn up in 1920 in New York City by delegates at an international convention of the Universal Negro Improvement Association (founded by U.S. black leader Marcus Garvey in 1914). It declared that blacks have suffered injustices, discrimination, and "inhuman, unchristian, and uncivilized treatment" in most every part of the world and that European nations had taken control of nearly all of Africa, "the Motherland of all Negroes." All blacks were "free citizens of Africa," it stated, and they had the right "to reclaim the treasures and possession of the vast continent of [their] forefathers."

Preamble

Be It Resolved, That the Negro people of the world, through their chosen representatives in convention assembled in Liberty Hall, in the City of New York and United States of America, from August 1 to August 31, in the year of Our Lord one thousand nine hundred and twenty, protest against the wrongs and injustices they are suffering at the hands of their white brethren, and state what they deem their fair and just rights, as well as the treatment they purpose to demand of all men in the future.

We complain:

1. That nowhere in the world, with few exceptions, are black men accorded equal treatment with white men, although in the same situation and circumstances, but, on the contrary, are discriminated against the denied and common rights due to human beings for no other reason than their race and color.

We are not willingly accepted as guests in the public hotels and inns of the world for no other reason than our race and color.

2. In certain parts of the United States of America our race is denied the right of public trial accorded to other races when accused of crime, but are lynched and burned by mobs, and such brutal and inhuman treatment is even practiced upon our women.

3. That European nations have parcelled out among them and taken possession of nearly all of the continent of Africa, and the natives are compelled to surrender their lands to aliens and are treated in most instances like slaves.

4. In the southern portion of the United States of America, although citizens under the Federal Constitution, and in some States almost equal to the whites in population and are qualified land owners and taxpayers, we are, nevertheless, denied all voice in the making and administration of the laws and are taxed without representation by the State governments, and at the same time compelled to do military service in defense of the country.

5. On the public conveyances and common carriers in the southern portion of the United States we are jim-crowed and compelled to accept separate and inferior accommodations and made to pay the same fare charged for first-class accommodations, and our families are often humiliated and insulted by drunken white men who habitually pass through the jim-c[r]ow cars going to the smoking car.

6. The physicians of our race are denied the right to attend their patients while in the public hospitals of the cities and States where they reside in certain parts of the United States.

   Our children are forced to attend inferior separate schools for shorter terms than white children, and the public school funds are unequally divided between the white and colored schools.

7. We are discriminated against and denied an equal chance to earn wages for the support of our families, and in many instances are refused admission into labor unions and nearly everywhere are paid smaller wages than white men.

8. In the Civil Service and departmental offices we are everywhere discriminated against and made to feel that to be a black man in Europe, America and the West Indies is equivalent to being an outcast and a leper among the races of men, no matter what the character attainments of the black men may be.

9. In the British and other West Indian islands and colonies Negroes are secretly and cunningly discriminated against and denied those fuller rights of government to which white citizens are appointed, nominated and elected.

10. That our people in those parts are forced to work for lower wages than the average standard of white men are kept in conditions repugnant to good civilized tastes and customs.

11. That the many acts of injustices against members of our race before the courts of law in the respective islands and colonies are of such nature as to create disgust and disrespect for the white man's sense of justice.

12. Against all such inhuman, unchristian and uncivilized treatment we here and now emphatically protest, and invoke the condemnation of all mankind.

In order to encourage our race all over the world and to stimulate it to overcome the handicaps and difficulties surrounding it, and to push forward to a higher and grander destiny, we demand and insist on the following Declaration of Rights:

1. Be it known to all men that whereas all men are created equal and entitled to the rights of life, liberty and the pursuit of happiness, and because of this we, the duly elected representatives of the Negro peoples of the world, invoking the aid of the just and Almighty God, do declare all men, women and children of our blood throughout the world free denizens, and do claim them as free citizens of Africa, the Motherland of all Negroes.

2. That we believe in the supreme authority of our race in all things racial; that all things are created and given to man as a common possession; that there should be an equitable distribution and

apportionment of all such things, and in consideration of the fact that as a race we are now deprived of those things that are morally and legally ours, we believed it right that all such things should be acquired and held by whatsoever means possible.

3. That we believe the Negro, like any other race, should be governed by the ethics of civilization, and therefore should not be deprived of any of those rights or privileges common to order human beings.

4. We declare that Negroes, wheresoever they form a community among themselves should be given the right to elect their own representatives to represent them in Legislatures, courts of law, or such institutions as may exercise control over that particular community.

5. We assert that the Negro is entitled to even-handed justice before all courts of law and equity in whatever country he may be found, and when this is denied him on account of his race or color such denial is an insult to the race as a whole and should be resented by the entire body of Negroes.

6. We declare it unfair and prejudicial to the rights of Negroes in communities where they exist in considerable numbers to be tried by a judge and jury composed entirely of an alien race, but in all such cases members of our race are entitled to representation on the jury.

7. We believe that any law or practice that tends to deprive any African of his land or the privileges of free citizenship within his country is unjust and immoral, and no native should respect any such law or practice.

8. We declare taxation without representation unjust and tyran[n]ous, and there should be no obligation on the part of the Negro to obey the levy of a tax by any law-making body from which he is excluded and denied representation on account of his race and color.

9. We believe that any law especially directed against the Negro to his detriment and singling him out because of his race or color is unfair and immoral, and should not be respected.

10. We believe all men entitled to common human respect and that our race should in no way tolerate any insults that may be interpreted to mean disrespect to our race or color.

11. We deprecate the use of the term "nigger" as applied to Negroes, and demand that the word "Negro" be written with a capital "N."

12. We believe that the Negro should adopt every means to protect himself against barbarous practices inflicted upon him because of color.

13. We believe in the freedom of Africa for the Negro people of the world, and by the principle of Europe for the Europeans and Asia for the Asiatics, we also demand Africa for the Africans at home and abroad.

14. We believe in the inherent right of the Negro to possess himself of Africa and that his possession of same shall not be regarded as an infringement on any claim or purchase made by any race or nation.

15. We strongly condemn the cupidity of those nations of the world who, by open aggression or secret schemes, have seized the territories and inexhaustible natural wealth of Africa, and we place on record our most solemn determination to reclaim the treasures and possession of the vast continent of our forefathers.

16. We believe all men should live in peace one with the other, but when races and nations provoke the ire of other races and nations by attempting to infringe upon their rights[,] war becomes inevitable, and the attempt in any way to free one's self or protect one's rights or heritage becomes justifiable.

17. Whereas the lynching, by burning, hanging or any other means, of human beings is a barbarous practice and a shame and disgrace to civilization, we therefore declare any country guilty of such atrocities outside the pale of civilization.

18. We protest against the atrocious crime of whipping, flogging and overworking of the native tribes of Africa and Negroes everywhere. These are methods that should be abolished and all means should be taken to prevent a continuance of such brutal practices.

19. We protest against the atrocious practice of shaving the heads of Africans, especially of African women or individuals of Negro blood, when placed in prison as a punishment for crime by an alien race.

20. We protest against segregated districts, separate public conveyances, industrial discrimination, lynchings and limitations of political privileges of any Negro citizen in any part of the world on account of race, color or creed, and will exert our full influence and power against all such.

21. We protest against any punishment inflicted upon a Negro with severity, as against lighter punish-

ment inflicted upon another of an alien race for like offense, as an act of prejudice and injustice, and should be resented by the entire race.

22. We protest against the system of education in any country where Negroes are denied the same privileges and advantages as other races.

23. We declare it inhuman and unfair to boycott Negroes from industries and labor in any part of the world.

24. We believe in the doctrine of the freedom of the press, and we therefore emphatically protest against the suppression of Negro newspapers and periodicals in various parts of the world, and call upon Negroes everywhere to employ all available means to prevent such suppression.

25. We further demand free speech universally for all men.

26. We hereby protest against the publication of scandalous and inflammatory articles by an alien press tending to create racial strife and the exhibition of picture films showing the Negro as a cannibal.

27. We believe in the self-determination of all peoples.

28. We declare for the freedom of religious worship.

29. With the help of Almighty God we declare ourselves the sworn protectors of the honor and virtue of our women and children, and pledge our lives for their protection and defense everywhere and under all circumstances from wrongs and outrages.

30. We demand the right of an unlimited and unprejudiced education for ourselves and our posterity forever[.]

31. We declare that the teaching in any school by alien teachers to our boys and girls, that the alien race is superior to the Negro race, is an insult to the Negro people of the world.

32. Where Negroes form a part of the citizenry of any country, and pass the civil service examination of such country, we declare them entitled to the same consideration as other citizens as to appointments in such civil service.

33. We vigorously protest against the increasingly unfair and unjust treatment accorded Negro travelers on land and sea by the agents and employees of railroad and steamship companies, and insist that for equal fare we receive equal privileges with travelers of other races.

34. We declare it unjust for any country, State or nation to enact laws tending to hinder and obstruct the free immigration of Negroes on account of their race and color.

35. That the right of the Negro to travel unmolested throughout the world be not abridged by any person or persons, and all Negroes are called upon to give aid to a fellow Negro when thus molested.

36. We declare that all Negroes are entitled to the same right to travel over the world as other men.

37. We hereby demand that the governments of the world recognize our leader and his representatives chosen by the race to look after the welfare of our people under such governments.

38. We demand complete control of our social institutions without interference by any alien race or races.

39. That the colors, Red, Black and Green, be the colors of the Negro race.

40. Resolved, That the anthem "Ethiopia, Thou Land of Our Fathers etc.," shall be the anthem of the Negro race. . . .

41. We believe that any limited liberty which deprives one of the complete rights and prerogatives of full citizenship is but a modified form of slavery.

42. We declare it an injustice to our people and a serious impediment to the health of the race to deny to competent licensed Negro physicians the right to practice in the public hospitals of the communities in which they reside, for no other reason than their race and color.

43. We call upon the various government[s] of the world to accept and acknowledge Negro representatives who shall be sent to the said governments to represent the general welfare of the Negro peoples of the world.

44. We deplore and protest against the practice of confining juvenile prisoners in prisons with adults, and we recommend that such youthful prisoners be taught gainful trades under human[e] supervision.

45. Be it further resolved, That we as a race of people declare the League of Nations null and void as far as the Negro is concerned, in that it seeks to deprive Negroes of their liberty.

46. We demand of all men to do unto us as we would do unto them, in the name of justice; and we cheerfully accord to all men all the rights we claim herein for ourselves.

47. We declare that no Negro shall engage himself in battle for an alien race without first obtaining the consent of the leader of the Negro people of the world, except in a matter of national self-defense.

48. We protest against the practice of drafting Negroes and sending them to war with alien forces without

proper training, and demand in all cases that Negro soldiers be given the same training as the aliens.

49. We demand that instructions given Negro children in schools include the subject of "Negro History," to their benefit.
50. We demand a free and unfettered commercial intercourse with all the Negro people of the world.
51. We declare for the absolute freedom of the seas for all peoples.
52. We demand that our duly accredited representatives be given proper recognition in all leagues, conferences, conventions or courts of international arbitration wherever human rights are discussed.
53. We proclaim the 31st day of August of each year to be an international holiday to be observed by all Negroes.
54. We want all men to know that we shall maintain and contend for the freedom and equality of every man, woman and child for our race, with our lives, our fortunes and our sacred honor.

These rights we believe to be justly ours and proper for the protection of the Negro race at large, and because of this belief we, on behalf of the four hundred million Negroes of the world, do pledge herein the sacred blood of the race in defense, and we hereby subscribe our names as a guarantee of the truthfulness and faithfulness hereof, in the presence of Almighty God, on this 13th day of August, in the year of our Lord one thousand nine hundred and twenty.

Signatures:

Marcus Garvey, James D. Brooks, James W. H. Eason, Henrietta Vinton Davis, Lionel Winston Greenidge, A[dr]ian Fitzroy Johnson, Rudolph Ethe[l]bert Brissaac Smith, Charles Augustus Petioni, Rev. Thomas H. N. Simon, Richard Hilton Tobitt, George Alexander McGuire, Rev. Peter Edward Batson, Reynold R. Felix, Harry Walters Kirby, Sarah Branch, Mme. Marie Barrier Houston, Mrs. Georgie L. O'Brien, F. O. Ogilvie, Arden A. Bryan, Benjamin Dyett, Marie Duchaterlier, John Phillip Hodge, Theophilus H. Saunders, Wilford H. Smith, Gabriel E. Stewart, Arnold Josiah Ford, Lee Crawford, William McCartney, Adina Clem. James, William Musgrave LaMotte, John Sydney de Bourg, Arnold S. Cunning, Vernal J. Williams, Francis Wilcem Ellegor, J. Frederick Selkridge, Innis Abel Horsford, Cyril A. Crichlow, Rev. Samuel McIntyre, Rev. John

Thomas Wilkins, Mary Thurston, John G. Befue, William Ware, Rev. J. A. Lewis O. C. Kelly, Venture R. Hamilton, R. H. Hodge, Edward Alfred Taylor, Ellen Wilson, G. W. Wilson, Richard Edward Riley, Miss Nellie Grant Whiting, G. W. Washington, Maldena Miller, Gertrude Davis, James D. Williams, Emily Christmas Kinch, Dr. D. D. Lewis, Nettie Clayton, Partheria Hills, Janie Jenkins, John C. Simons, Alphonso A. Jones, Allen Hobbs, Re[y]nold Fitzgerald Austin, James Benjamin Yearwood, Frank O. Raines, Shedric[k] Williams, John Edward Ivey, Frederick Augustus Toote, Philip Hemmings, Rev. F. F. Smith, D. D., Rev. E. J. Jones, Rev. Dr. Joseph Josiah Cranston, Frederick Samuel Ricketts, Dugald Augustus Wade, E. E. Nelom, Florida Jenkins, Napoleon J. Francis, Joseph D. Gibson, J. P. Jasper, J. W. Montgomery, David Benjamin, J. Gordon, Harry E. Ford, Carrie M. Ashford, Andrew N. Willis, Lucy Sands, Louise Woodson, George D. Creese, W. A. Wallace, Thomas E. Bagley, James Young, Prince Alfred McConney, John E. Hudson, William Ines, Harry R. Watkins, C. L. Halton, J. T. Bailey, Ira Joseph Toussa[i]nt Wright, T. H. Golden, Abraham Benjamin Thomas, Richard C. Noble, Walter Green, C. S. Bourne, G. F. Bennett, B. D. Levy, Mrs. Mary E. Johnson, Lionel Antonio Francis, Carl Roper, E. R. Donawa, Philip Van Putten, I. Brathwaite, Rev. Jesse W. Luck, Oliver Kaye, J. W. Hudspeth, C. B. Lovell, William C. Matthews, A. Williams, Ratford E. M. Jack, H. Vinton Plummer, Randolph Phillips, A. I. Bailey, duly elected representatives of the Negro people of the world.

9. FROM WARREN G. HARDING'S INAUGURAL ADDRESS, MARCH 4, 1921

My Countrymen: When one surveys the world about him after the great storm, noting the marks of destruction and yet rejoicing in the ruggedness of the things which withstood it, if he is an American he breathes the clarified atmosphere with a strange mingling of regret and new hope. We have seen a world passion spend its fury, but we contemplate our Republic unshaken, and hold our civilization secure. Liberty, liberty within the law, and civilization are inseparable, and though both were threatened we find them now secure; and there comes to Americans the profound assurance that our representative government is the highest expression and surest guaranty of both.

Standing in this presence, mindful of the solemnity of this occasion, feeling the emotions which no one may know until he senses the great weight of responsibility for himself, I must utter my belief in the divine inspiration of the founding fathers. Surely there must have been God's intent in the making of this new-world Republic. Ours is an organic law which had but one ambiguity, and we saw that effaced in a baptism of sacrifice and blood, with union maintained, the Nation supreme, and its concord inspiring. We have seen the world rivet its hopeful gaze on the great truths on which the founders wrought. We have seen civil, human, and religious liberty verified and glorified. In the beginning the Old World scoffed at our experiment; today our foundations of political and social belief stand unshaken, a precious inheritance to ourselves, an inspiring example of freedom and civilization to all mankind. Let us express renewed and strengthened devotion, in grateful reverence for the immortal beginning, and utter our confidence in the supreme fulfillment.

The recorded progress of our Republic, materially and spiritually, in itself proves the wisdom of the inherited policy of noninvolvement in Old World affairs. Confident of our ability to work out our own destiny, and jealously guarding our right to do so, we seek no part in directing the destinies of the Old World. We do not mean to be entangled. We will accept no responsibility except as our own conscience and judgment, in each instance, may determine.

Our eyes never will be blind to a developing menace, our ears never deaf to the call of civilization. We recognize the new order in the world, with the closer contacts which progress has wrought. We sense the call of the human heart for fellowship, fraternity, and cooperation. We crave friendship and harbor no hate. But America, our America, the America builded on the foundation laid by the inspired fathers, can be a party to no permanent military alliance. It can enter into no political commitments, nor assume any economic obligations which will subject our decisions to any other than our own authority.

I am sure our own people will not misunderstand, nor will the world misconstrue. We have no thought to impede the paths to closer relationship. We wish to promote understanding. We want to do our part in making offensive warfare so hateful that Governments and peoples who resort to it must prove the righteousness of their cause or stand as outlaws before the bar of civilization.

We are ready to associate ourselves with the nations of the world, great and small, for conference, for counsel; to seek the expressed views of world opinion; to recommend a way to approximate disarmament and relieve the crushing burdens of military and naval establishments. We elect to participate in suggesting plans for mediation, conciliation, and arbitration, and would gladly join in that expressed conscience of progress, which seeks to clarify and write the laws of international relationship, and establish a world court for the disposition of such justiciable questions as nations are agreed to submit thereto. In expressing aspirations, in seeking practical plans, in translating humanity's new concept of righteousness and justice and its hatred of war into recommended action we are ready most heartily to unite, but every commitment must be made in the exercise of our national sovereignty. Since freedom impelled, and independence inspired, and nationality exalted, a world super-government is contrary to everything we cherish and can have no sanction by our Republic. This is not selfishness, it is sanctity. It is not aloofness, it is security. It is not suspicion of others, it is patriotic adherence to the things which made us what we are. . . .

. . . Mankind needs a world-wide benediction of understanding. It is needed among individuals, among peoples, among governments, and it will inaugurate an era of good feeling to make the birth of a new order. In such understanding men will strive confidently for the promotion of their better relationships and nations will promote the comities so essential to peace.

We must understand that ties of trade bind nations in closest intimacy, and none may receive except as he gives. We have not strengthened ours in accordance with our resources or our genius, notably on our own continent, where a galaxy of Republics reflects the glory of new-world democracy, but in the new order of finance and trade we mean to promote enlarged activities and seek expanded confidence.

Perhaps we can make no more helpful contribution by example than prove a Republic's capacity to emerge from the wreckage of war. While the world's embittered travail did not leave us devastated lands nor desolated cities, left no gaping wounds, no breast with hate, it did involve us in the delirium of expenditure, in expanded currency and credits, in unbalanced industry, in unspeakable waste, and disturbed relationships. While it uncovered our portion of hateful selfishness at home, it also revealed the heart of America as sound and fearless, and beating in confidence unfailing. . . .

. . .Our supreme task is the resumption of our onward, normal way. Reconstruction, readjustment, restoration all these must follow. I would like to hasten them. If it will lighten the spirit and add to the resolution with which we take up the task, let me repeat for our Nation, we shall give no people just cause to make war upon us; we hold no national prejudices; we entertain no spirit of revenge; we do not hate; we do not covet; we dream of no conquest, nor boast of armed prowess.

If, despite this attitude, war is again forced upon us, I earnestly hope a way may be found which will unify our individual and collective strength and consecrate all America, materially and spiritually, body and soul, to national defense. I can envision the ideal republic, where every man and woman is called under the flag for assignment to duty for whatever service, military or civic, the individual is best fitted; where we may call to universal service every plant, agency, or facility, all in the sublime sacrifice for country, and not one penny of war profit shall inure to the benefit of private individual, corporation, or combination, but all above the normal shall flow into the defense chest of the Nation. There is something inherently wrong, something out of accord with the ideals of representative democracy, when one portion of our citizenship turns its activities to private gain amid defensive war while another is fighting, sacrificing, or dying for national preservation.

Out of such universal service will come a new unity of spirit and purpose, a new confidence and consecration, which would make our defense impregnable, our triumph assured. Then we should have little or no disorganization of our economic, industrial, and commercial systems at home, no staggering war debts, no swollen fortunes to flout the sacrifices of our soldiers, no excuse for sedition, no pitiable slackerism, no outrage of treason. Envy and jealousy would have no soil for their menacing development, and revolution would be without the passion which engenders it.

A regret for the mistakes of yesterday must not, however, blind us to the tasks of today. War never left such an aftermath. There has been staggering loss of life and measureless wastage of materials. Nations are still groping for return to stable ways. Discouraging indebtedness confronts us like all the war-torn nations, and these obligations must be provided for. No civilization can survive repudiation.

We can reduce the abnormal expenditures, and we will. We can strike at war taxation, and we must. We must face the grim necessity, with full knowledge that the task is to be solved, and we must proceed with a full realization that no statute enacted by man can repeal the inexorable laws of nature. Our most dangerous tendency is to expect too much of government, and at the same time do for it too little. We contemplate the immediate task of putting our public household in order. We need a rigid and yet sane economy, combined with fiscal justice, and it must be attended by individual prudence and thrift, which are so essential to this trying hour and reassuring for the future....

I speak for administrative efficiency, for lightened tax burdens, for sound commercial practices, for adequate credit facilities, for sympathetic concern for all agricultural problems, for the omission of unnecessary interference of Government with business, for an end to Government's experiment in business, and for more efficient business in Government administration. With all of this must attend a mindfulness of the human side of all activities, so that social, industrial, and economic justice will be squared with the purposes of a righteous people.

With the nation-wide induction of womanhood into our political life, we may count upon her intuitions, her refinements, her intelligence, and her influence to exalt the social order. We count upon her exercise of the full privileges and the performance of the duties of citizenship to speed the attainment of the highest state.

I wish for an America no less alert in guarding against dangers from within than it is watchful against enemies from without. Our fundamental law recognizes no class, no group, no section; there must be none in legislation or administration. The supreme inspiration is the common weal. Humanity hungers for international peace, and we crave it with all mankind. My most reverent prayer for America is for industrial peace, with its rewards, widely and generally distributed, amid the inspirations of equal opportunity. No one justly may deny the equality of opportunity which made us what we are. We have mistaken unpreparedness to embrace it to be a challenge of the reality, and due concern for making all citizens fit for participation will give added strength of citizenship and magnify our achievement.

If revolution insists upon overturning established order, let other peoples make the tragic experiment. There is no place for it in America. When World War threatened civilization we pledged our resources and our lives to its preservation, and when revolution threatens we unfurl the flag of law and order and renew our consecration. Ours is a constitutional freedom where the popular will is the law supreme and minorities are sacredly protected. Our revisions, reformations, and evolutions reflect a deliberate judgment and an orderly progress, and we mean to cure our ills, but never destroy or permit destruction by force.

I had rather submit our industrial controversies to the conference table in advance than to a settlement table after conflict and suffering. The earth is thirsting for the cup of good will, understanding is its fountain source. I would like to acclaim an era of good feeling amid dependable prosperity and all the blessings which attend. . . .

. . . We would not have an America living within and for herself alone, but we would have her self-reliant, independent, and ever nobler, stronger, and richer. Believing in our higher standards, reared through constitutional liberty and maintained opportunity, we invite the world to the same heights. But pride in things wrought is no reflex of a completed task. Common welfare is the goal of our national endeavor. Wealth is not inimical to welfare; it ought to be its friendliest agency. There never can be equality of rewards or possessions so long as the human plan contains varied talents and differing degrees of industry and thrift, but ours ought to be a country free from the great blotches of distressed poverty. We ought to find a way to guard against the perils and penalties of unemployment. We want an America of homes, illumined with hope and happiness, where mothers, freed from the necessity for long hours of toil beyond their own doors, may preside as befits the heartstone of American citizenship. We want the cradle of American childhood rocked under conditions so wholesome and so hopeful that no blight may touch it in its development, and we want to provide that no selfish interest, no material necessity, no lack of opportunity shall prevent the gaining of that education so essential to best citizenship.

There is no short cut to the making of these ideals into glad realities. The world has witnessed again and again the futility and the mischief of ill-considered remedies for social and economic disorders. But we are mindful today as never before of the friction of modern industrialism, and we must learn its causes and reduce its evil consequences by sober and tested methods. Where genius has made for great possibilities, justice and happiness must be reflected in a greater common welfare.

Service is the supreme commitment of life. I would rejoice to acclaim the era of the Golden Rule and crown it with the autocracy of service. I pledge an administration wherein all the agencies of Government are called to serve, and ever promote an understanding of Government purely as an expression of the popular will.

One cannot stand in this presence and be unmindful of the tremendous responsibility. The world upheaval has added heavily to our tasks. But with the realization comes the surge of high resolve, and there is reassurance in belief in the God-given destiny of our Republic. If I felt that there is to be sole responsibility in the Executive for the America of tomorrow I should shrink from the burden. But here are a hundred millions, with common concern and shared responsibility, answerable to God and country. The Republic summons them to their duty, and I invite co-operation.

I accept my part with single-mindedness of purpose and humility of spirit, and implore the favor and guidance of God in His Heaven. With these I am unafraid, and confidently face the future.

I have taken the solemn oath of office on that passage of Holy Writ wherein it is asked: "What doth the Lord require of thee but to do justly, and to love mercy, and to walk humbly with thy God?" This I plight to God and country.

10. THE EMERGENCY QUOTA ACT OF 1921, ENACTED ON MAY 19, 1921

[This legislation established the first quota for immigrants to the United States. Sponsored by Senator William P. Dillingham of Vermont, the act set a quota of 357,000 places (aliens); immigrants from a given nation (nationality) were restricted yearly to 3 percent of the population of that nation residing in the United States according to the 1910 census. Immigrants from Asia—already largely excluded by other agreements—and from the Western Hemisphere were exempt from this act. The act also showed evidence of a bias against people from southern and central Europe, while favoring immigrants from the British Isles and northwestern Europe. This national origins quota system set the pattern for American immigration laws for the first half of the twentieth century.]

AN ACT

To limit the immigration of aliens into the United States.

Be it enacted by the Senate and House of Representatives of the United States of America in Congress assembled, That as used in this Act—

The term "United States" means the United States, and any waters, territory, or other place subject to the jurisdiction thereof except the Canal Zone and the Philippine Islands; but if any alien leaves the Canal Zone or any insular possession of the United States and attempts to enter any other place under the jurisdiction of the United States nothing contained in this Act shall be construed as permitting him to enter under any other conditions than those applicable to all aliens.

The word "alien" includes any person not a native-born or naturalized citizen of the United States, but this definition shall not be held to include Indians of the United States not taxed nor citizens of the islands under the jurisdiction of the United States.

The term "Immigration Act" means the Act of February 5, 1917, entitled "An Act to regulate the immigration of aliens to, and the residence of aliens in, the United States"; and the term "immigration laws" includes such Act and all laws, conventions, and treaties of the United States relating to the immigration, exclusion, or expulsion of aliens.

Sec. 2.(a) That the number of aliens of any nationality who may be admitted under the immigration laws to the United States in any fiscal year shall be limited to 3 per centum of the number of foreign born persons of such nationality resident in the United States as determined by the United States census of 1910. This provision shall not apply to the following, and they shall not be counted in reckoning any of the percentage limits provided in this Act: (1) Government officials, their families, attendants, servants, and employees; (2) aliens in continuous transit through the United States; (3) aliens lawfully admitted to the United States who later go in transit from one part of the United States to another through foreign contiguous territory; (4) aliens visiting the United States as tourists or temporarily for business or pleasure; (5) aliens from countries immigration from which is regulated in accordance with treaties or agreements relating solely to immigration; (6) aliens from the so-called Asiatic barred zone, as described in section 3 of the Immigration Act; (7) aliens who have resided continuously for at least one year immediately preceding the time of their admission to the United States in the Dominion of Canada, Newfoundland, the Republic of Cuba, the Republic of Mexico, countries of Central or South America, or adjacent islands; or (8) aliens under the age of eighteen who are children of citizens of the United States.

(b) For the purposes of this Act nationality shall be determined by country of birth, treating as separate countries the colonies or dependencies for which separate enumeration was made in the United States census of 1910.

(c) The Secretary of State, the Secretary of Commerce, and the Secretary of Labor, jointly, shall, as soon as feasible after the enactment of this Act, prepare a statement showing the number of persons of the various nationalities resident in the United States as determined by the United States census of 1910, which statement shall be the population basis for the purposes of this Act. In case of changes in political boundaries in foreign countries occurring subsequent to 1910 and resulting (1) in the creation of new countries, the Governments of which are recognized by the United States, or (2) in the transfer of territory from one country to another, such transfer being recognized by the United States, such officials, jointly, shall estimate the number of persons resident in the United States in 1910 who were born within the area included in such new countries or in such territory so transferred, and revise the population basis as to each country involved in such change of political boundary. For the purpose of such revision and for the purposes of this Act generally aliens born in the area included in any such new country shall be considered as having been born in such country, and aliens born in any territory so transferred shall be considered as having been born in the country to which such territory was transferred.

(d) When the maximum number of aliens of any nationality who may be admitted in any fiscal year under this Act shall have been admitted all other aliens of such nationality, except as otherwise provided in this Act, who may apply for admission during the same fiscal year shall be excluded: Provided, That the number of aliens of any nationality who may be admitted in any month shall not exceed 20 per centum of the total number of aliens of such nationality who are admissible in that fiscal year: Provided further, That aliens returning from a temporary visit abroad, aliens who are professional actors, artists, lecturers, singers, nurses, ministers of any religious denomination, professors for colleges or seminaries, aliens belonging to any recognized learned profession, or aliens employed as domestic servants, may, if otherwise admissible, be admitted notwithstanding the maximum number of aliens of the same nationality admissible in the same month or fiscal year, as the case may be, shall have entered the United States; but aliens of the classes included in this proviso who enter the United States before such maximum number shall have entered shall (unless excluded by subdivision (a) from being counted) be counted in reckoning the percentage limits provided in this Act: Provided further, That in the enforcement of this Act preference shall be given so far as possible to the wives, parents, brothers, sisters, children under eighteen years of age, and fiancees, (1) of citizens of the United States, (2) of aliens now in the United States who have applied for citizenship in the manner provided by law, or (3) of persons eligible to United States citizenship who served in the military or naval forces of the United States at any time between April 6, 1917, and November 11, 1918, both dates inclusive, and have been separated from such forces under honorable conditions.

Sec. 3. That the Commissioner General of Immigration, with the approval of the Secretary of Labor, shall, as soon as feasible after the enactment of this Act, and from time to time thereafter, prescribe rules and regulations necessary to carry the provisions of this Act into effect. He shall, as soon as feasible after the enactment of this Act, publish a statement showing the number of aliens of the various nationalities who may be admitted to the United States between the date this Act becomes effective and the end of the current fiscal year, and on June 30 thereafter he shall publish a statement showing the number of aliens of the various nationalities who may be admitted during the ensuing fiscal year. He shall also publish monthly statements during the time this Act remains in force showing the number of aliens of each nationality already admitted during the then current fiscal year and the number who may be admitted under the provisions of this Act during the remainder of such year, but when 75 per centum of the maximum number of any nationality admissible during the fiscal year shall have been admitted such statements shall be issued weekly thereafter. All statements shall be made available for general publication and shall be mailed to all transportation companies bringing aliens to the United States who shall request the same and shall file with the Department of Labor the address to which such statements shall be sent. The Secretary of Labor shall also submit such statements to the Secretary of State, who shall transmit the information contained therein to the proper diplomatic and consular officials of the United States, which officials shall make the same available to persons intending to emigrate to the United States and to others who may apply.

Sec. 4. That the provisions of this Act are in addition to and not in substitution for the provisions of the immigration laws.

Sec. 5. That this Act shall take effect and be enforced 15 days after its enactment (except sections 1 and 3 and subdivisions (b) and (c) of section 2, which shall take effect immediately upon the enactment of this Act), and shall continue in force until June 30, 1922, and the number of aliens of any nationality who may be admitted during the remaining period of the current fiscal year, from the date when this Act becomes effective to June 30, shall be limited in proportion to the number admissible during the fiscal year 1922.

11. Treaty between the United States of America, the British Empire, France, and Japan, Signed at Washington December 13, 1921

The United States of America, the British Empire, France and Japan,

With a view to the preservation of the general peace and the maintenance of their rights in relation to their insular possessions and insular dominions in the region of the Pacific Ocean,

Have determined to conclude a Treaty to this effect and . . . have agreed as follows:

I

The High Contracting Parties agree as between themselves to respect their rights in relation to their insular possessions and insular dominions in the region of the Pacific Ocean. If there should develop between any of the High Contracting Parties a controversy arising out of any Pacific question and involving their said rights which is not satisfactorily settled by diplomacy and is likely to affect the harmonious accord now happily subsisting between them, they shall invite the other High Contracting Parties to a joint conference to which the whole subject will be referred for consideration and adjustment.

II

If the said rights are threatened by the aggressive action of any other Power, the High Contracting Parties shall communicate with one another fully and frankly in order to arrive at an understanding as to the most efficient measures to be taken, jointly or separately, to meet the exigencies of the particular situation.

III

This Treaty shall remain in force for ten years from the time it shall take effect, and after the expiration of said period it shall continue to be in force subject to the right of any of the High Contracting Parties to terminate it upon twelve months' notice.

IV

This Treaty shall be ratified as soon as possible in accordance with the constitutional methods of the High Contracting Parties and shall take effect on the deposit of ratifications, which shall take place at Washington, and thereupon the agreement between Great Britain and Japan, which was concluded at London on July 13, 1911, shall terminate. The Government of the United States will transmit to all the Signatory Powers a certified copy of the procès-verbal of the deposit of ratifications.

The present Treaty, in French and in English, shall remain deposited in the Archives of the Government of the United States, and duly certified copies thereof will be transmitted by that Government Waco of the Signatory Powers.

IN FAITH WHEREOF the above named Plenipotentiaries have signed the present Treaty. DONE at the City of Washington, the thirteenth day of December, One Thousand Nine Hundred and Twenty-One.

Supplementary Declaration, Signed December 13, 1921

In signing the Treaty this day between The United States of America, The British Empire, France and Japan, it is declared to the understanding and intent of the Signatory Powers:

1. That the Treaty shall apply to the Mandated Islands in the Pacific Ocean, provided; however that the making of the Treaty shall not be deemed to be an assent on the part of The United States of America to the mandates and shall not preclude agreements between The United States of America and the Mandatory Powers respectively in relation to the mandated islands.
2. That the controversies to which the second paragraph of Article 1 refers shall not be taken to embrace questions which according to principles of international law lie exclusively within the domestic jurisdiction of the respective Powers.

12. THE HAYS CODE OF 1924

Whereas, the members of the Motion Picture Producers and Distributors of America, Inc., in their continuing effort "to establish and maintain the highest possible moral and artistic standards of motion picture production" are engaged in a special effort to prevent the prevalent type of book and play from becoming the prevalent type of picture; to exercise every possible care that only books or plays which are of the right type can be produced are used for screen presentation; to avoid the picturization of books or plays which can be produced after such chances as to leave the producer subject to a charge of deception; to avoid using titles which are indicative of a kind of picture which should not be produced, or by their suggestiveness seek to obtain attendance by deception, a thing equally reprehensible; and to prevent misleading, salacious, or dishonest advertising.

Now, therefore, be it resolved by the board of directors of the Motion Picture Producers and Distributors of America, Inc., That said Association does hereby reaffirm its determination to carry out its purposes above set out; and does hereby repledge the best efforts of the members of the Association to that end; and does hereby further declare that they will not produce or promote the production, distribute or promote the distribution, exhibit or promote the exhibition, or aid in any way whatsoever in the production, distribution, or exhibition by the members of this Association or by companies subsidiary to said members or by any other person, firm, or corporation producing, distributing, or exhibiting pictures by whomsoever produced, distributed, or exhibited, which because of the unfit character of title, story, exploitation or picture itself, do not meet the requirements of this preamble and resolution or hinder the fulfillment of the purposes of the Association set out herein.

13. THE PROGRESSIVE PARTY PLATFORM OF 1924, JULY 5, 1924

The great issue before the American people today is the control of government and industry by private monopoly.

For a generation the people have struggled patiently, in the face of repeated betrayals by successive administrations, to free themselves from this intolerable power which has been undermining representative government.

Through control of government, monopoly has steadily extended its absolute dominion to every basic industry.

In violation of law, monopoly has crushed competition, stifled private initiative and independent enterprise, and without fear of punishment now exacts extortionate profits upon every necessity of life consumed by the public.

The quality of opportunity proclaimed by the Declaration of Independence and asserted and defended by Jefferson and Lincoln as the heritage of every American citizen has been displaced by special privilege for the few, wrested from the government of the many.

Fundamental Rights in Danger

That tyrannical power which the American people denied to a king, they will no longer endure from the monopoly system. The people know they cannot yield to any group the control of the economic life of the nation and preserve their political liberties. They know monopoly has its representatives in the halls of Congress, on the Federal bench, and in the executive departments; that these servile agents barter away the nation's natural resources, nullify acts of Congress by judicial veto and administrative favor, invade the people's rights by unlawful arrests and unconstitutional searches and seizures, direct our foreign policy in the interest of predatory wealth, and make wars and conscript the sons of the common people to fight them.

The usurpation in recent years by the federal courts of the power to nullify laws duly enacted by the legislative branch of the government is a plain violation of the Constitution....

Distress of American Farmers

The present condition of American agriculture constitutes an emergency of the gravest character. The Department of Commerce report shows that during 1923 there was a steady and marked increase in dividends paid by the great industrial corporations. The same is true of the steam and electric railways and practically all other large corporations. On the other hand, the Secretary of Agriculture reports that in the fifteen principal wheat growing states more than 108,000 farmers since 1920 have lost their farms through foreclosure or bankruptcy; that more than 122,000 have surrendered their property without legal proceedings, and that nearly 375,000 have retained possession of their property only through the leniency of their creditors, making a total of more than 600,000 or 26 percent of all farmers who have virtually been bankrupted since 1920 in these fifteen states alone.

Almost unlimited prosperity for the great corporations and ruin and bankruptcy for agriculture is the direct and logical result of the policies and legislation which deflated the farmer while extending almost unlimited credit to the great corporations; which protected with exorbitant tariffs the industrial magnates, but depressed the prices of the farmers' products by financial juggling while greatly increasing the cost of what he must buy; which guaranteed excessive freight rates to the railroads and put a premium on wasteful management while saddling an unwarranted burden on the backs of the American farmer; which permitted gambling in the products of the farm by grain speculators to the great detriment of the farmer and to the great profit of the grain gambler.

A Covenant with the People

Awakened by the dangers which menace their freedom and prosperity the American people still retain the right and courage to exercise their sovereign control over their government. In order to destroy the economic and political power of monopoly, which has come between the people and their government, we pledge ourselves to the following principles and policies:

The House Cleaning

1. We pledge a complete housecleaning in the Department of Justice, the Department of the Interior, and the other executive departments. We demand that the power of the Federal Government be used to crush private monopoly, not to foster it.

Natural Resources

2. We pledge recovery of the navy's oil reserves and all other parts of the public domain which have been fraudulently or illegally leased, or otherwise wrongfully transferred, to the control of private interests; vigorous prosecution of all public officials, private citizens and corporations that participated in these transactions; complete revision of the water-power act, the general leasing act, and all other legislation relating to the public domain. We favor public ownership of the nation's water power and the creation and development of a national super-water-power system, including Muscle Shoals, to supply at actual cost light and power for the people and nitrate for the farmers, and strict public control and permanent conservation of all the nation's resources, including coal, iron and other ores, oil and timber lands, in the interest of the people.

Railroads

3. We favor repeal of the Esch-Cummins railroad law and the fixing of railroad rates upon the basis of actual, prudent investment and cost of service. . . .

Tax Reduction

4. We favor reduction of Federal taxes upon individual incomes and legitimate business, limiting tax exactions strictly to the requirements of the government administered with rigid economy, particularly by the curtailment of the eight hundred million dollars now annually expended for the army and navy in preparation for future wars; by the recovery of the hundreds of millions of dollars stolen from the Treasury through fraudulent war contracts and the corrupt leasing of the public resources; and by diligent action to collect the accumulated interest upon the eleven billion dollars owing us by foreign governments.

We denounce the Mellon tax plan as a device to relieve multi-millionaires at the expense of other tax payers, and favor a taxation policy providing for immediate reductions upon moderate incomes, large increases in the inheritance tax rates upon large estates to prevent the indefinite accumulation by inheritance of great fortunes in a few hands; taxes upon excess profits to penalize profiteering, and completely publicity, under proper safeguards, of all Federal tax returns.

The Courts

5. We favor submitting to the people, for their considerate judgment, a constitutional amendment providing that Congress may by enacting a statute make it effective over a judicial veto.

We favor such amendment to the constitution as may be necessary to provide for the election of all Federal Judges, without party designation, for fixed terms not exceeding ten years, by direct vote of the people.

The Farmers

6. We favor drastic reduction of the exorbitant duties on manufactures provided in the Fordney-McCumber tariff legislation, the prohibiting of gambling by speculators and profiteers in agricultural products; the reconstruction of the Federal Reserve and Federal Farm Loan Systems, so as to eliminate control by usurers, speculators and inter-national financiers, and to make the credit of the nation available upon fair terms to all and without discrimination to business men, farmers, and home-builders. We advocate the calling of a special session of Congress to pass legislation as may be needful or helpful in promoting and protecting co-operative enterprises. We demand that the Interstate Commerce Commission proceed forthwith to reduce by an approximation to pre-war levels the present freight rates on agricultural products, including live stock, and upon the materials required upon American farms for agricultural purposes.

Labor

7. We favor abolition of the use of injunctions in labor disputes and declare for complete protection of the right of farmers and industrial workers to organize, bargain collectively through representatives of their own choosing, and conduct without hindrance cooperative enterprises.

We favor prompt ratification of the Child Labor amendment, and subsequent enactment of a Federal law to protect children in industry. . . .

Peace on Earth

12. We denounce the mercenary system of foreign policy under recent administrations in the interests of financial imperialists, oil monopolies and international bankers, which has at times degraded our State Department from its high service as a strong and kindly intermediary of defenseless governments to a trading outpost for those interests and concession-seekers engaged in the exploitation of weaker nations, as contrary to the will of the American people, destructive of domestic development and provocative of war. We favor an active foreign policy to bring about a revision of the Versailles treaty in accordance with the terms of the armistice, and to promote firm treaty agreements with all nations to outlaw wars, abolish conscription, drastically reduce land, air, and naval armaments, and guarantee public referendum on peace and war.

14. TEAPOT DOME, FEBRUARY 8, 1924

A joint resolution directing the President to institute and prosecute suits to cancel certain leases of oil lands and incidental contracts, and for other purposes.

Whereas it appears from evidence taken by the Committee on Public Lands and Surveys of the United States Senate that certain lease of naval reserve No. 3 in the State of Wyoming, bearing date April 7, 1922, made in form by the Government of the United States, through Albert B. Fall, Secretary of the Interior, and Edwin Denby, Secretary of the Navy, as lessor, to the Mammoth Oil Co., as lessee, and that certain contract between the Government of the United States and the Pan American Petroleum & Transport Co., dated April 25, 1922, signed by Edward C. Finney, Acting Secretary of the Interior, and Edwin Denby, Secretary of the Navy, relating among other things to the construction of oil tanks at Pearl Harbor, Territory of Hawaii, and that certain lease of naval reserve No. 1, in the State of California, bearing date December 11, 1922, made in form by the Government of the United States through Albert B. Fall, Secretary of the Interior, and Edwin Denby, Secretary of the Navy, as lessor, to the Pan American Petroleum Co., as lessee, were executed under circumstances indicating fraud and corruption; and

Whereas the said leases and contract were entered into without authority on the part of the officers purporting to act in the execution of the same for the United States and in violation of the laws of Congress; and

Whereas such leases and contract were made in defiance of the settled policy of the Government adhered to through three successive administrations, to maintain in the ground a great reserve supply of oil adequate to the needs of the Navy in any emergency threatening the national security; Therefore be it.

Resolved, etc., That the said leases and contract are against the public interest and that the lands embraced therein should be recovered and held for the purpose to which they were dedicated; and

Resolved further, That the President of the United States be, and he hereby is, authorized and directed immediately to cause suit to be instituted and prosecuted for the annulment and cancellation of the said leases and contract and all contracts incidental or supplemental thereto, to enjoin further extraction of oil from the said reserves under said leases or from the territory covered by the same, to secure any further appropriate incidental relief, and to prosecute such other actions or proceedings, civil and criminal, as may be warranted by the facts in relation to the making of the said leases and contract.

And the President is further authorized and directed to appoint, by and with the advice and consent of the Senate, special counsel who shall have charge and control of the prosecution of such litigation, anything in the statutes touching the powers of the attorney General of the Department of Justice to the contrary notwithstanding.

15. THE IMMIGRATION ACT OF 1924, ENACTED ON MAY 26, 1924

[This legislation amended the U.S. Emergency Quota Act by halving the 1921 quota (placing the number of immigrants at 164,447) and by limiting annual immigration for any group to 2 percent of that group's U.S. population according to the census of 1890. This quota was to apply until 1927, when the limit on immigrants was to be set at 150,000, apportioned by national origin according to the 1920 census. Sponsored by Senator Hiram W. Johnson of California and Senator James A. Reed of Missouri, the act favored immigrants from northern and western Europe. It aroused so much hostility that it was not implemented until 1929.]

AN ACT

To limit the immigration of aliens into the United States, and for other purposes.

Be it enacted by the Senate and House of Representatives of the United States of America in Congress assembled. That this Act may be cited as the "Immigration Act of 1924."

Immigration Visas

Sec. 2. (a) A consular officer upon the application of any immigrant (as defined in section 3) may (under the conditions hereinafter prescribed and subject to the limitations prescribed in this Act or regulations made thereunder as to the number of immigration visas which may be issued by such officer) issue to such immigrant an immigration visa which shall consist of one copy of the application provided for in section 7, visaed by such consular officer. Such visa shall specify (1) the nationality of the immigrant; (2) whether he is a quota immigrant (as defined in section 5) or a non-quota immigrant (as defined in section 4); (3) the date on which the validity of the immigration visa shall expire; and (4) such additional information necessary to the proper enforcement of the immigration laws and the naturalization laws as may be by regulations prescribed.

(b) The immigrant shall furnish two copies of his photograph to the consular officer. One copy shall be permanently attached by the consular officer to the immigration visa and the other copy shall be disposed of as may be by regulations prescribed.

(c) The validity of an immigration visa shall expire at the end of such period, specified in the immigration visa, not exceeding four months, as shall be by regulations prescribed. In the case of an immigrant arriving in the United States by water, or arriving by water in foreign contiguous territory on a continuous voyage to the United States, if the vessel, before the expiration of the validity of his immigration visa, departed from the last port outside the United States and outside foreign contiguous territory at which the immigrant embarked, and if the immigrant proceeds on a continuous voyage to the United States, then, regardless of the time of his arrival in the United States, the validity of his immigration visa shall not be considered to have expired.

(d) If an immigrant is required by any law, or regulations or orders made pursuant to law, to secure the visa of his passport by a consular officer before being permitted to enter the United States, such immigrant shall not be required to secure any other visa of his passport than the immigration visa issued under this Act, but a record of the number and date of his immigration visa shall be noted on his passport without charge therefor. This subdivision shall not apply to an immigrant who is relieved, under subdivision (b) of section 13, from obtaining an immigration visa.

(e) The manifest or list of passengers required by the immigration laws shall contain a place for entering thereon the date, place of issuance, and number of the immigration visa of each immigrant. The immigrant shall surrender his immigration visa to the immigration officer at the port of inspection, who shall at the time of inspection indorse on the immigration visa the date, the port of entry, and the name of the vessel, if any, on which the immigrant arrived. The immigration visa shall be transmitted forthwith by the immigration officer in charge at the port of inspection to the Department of Labor under regulations prescribed by the Secretary of Labor.

(f) No immigration visa shall be issued to an immigrant if it appears to the consular officer, from statements in the application, or in the papers submitted therewith, that the immigrant is inadmissible to the United States under the immigration laws, nor shall such immigration visa be issued if the application fails to comply with the provisions of this Act, nor shall such immigration visa be issued if the consular officer knows or has reason to believe that the immigrant is inadmissible to the United States under the immigration laws.

(g) Nothing in this Act shall be construed to entitle an immigrant, to whom an immigration visa has been issued, to enter the United States, if, upon arrival in the United States, he is found to be inadmissible to the United States under the immigration laws. The substance of this subdivision shall be printed conspicuously upon every immigration visa.

(h) A fee of $9 shall be charged for the issuance of each immigration visa, which shall be covered into the Treasury as miscellaneous receipts.

Definition of "Immigrant"

Sec. 3. When used in this Act the term "immigrant" means any alien departing from any place outside the United States destined for the United States, except (1) a government official, his family, attendants, servants and employees, (2) an alien visiting the United States temporarily as a tourist or temporarily for business or pleasure, (3) an alien in continuous transit through the United States, (4) an alien lawfully admitted to the United States who later goes in transit from one part of the United States to another through foreign contiguous territory, (5) a bona fide alien seaman serving as such on a vessel arriving at a port of the United States and seeking to enter temporarily the United States solely in the pursuit of his calling as a seaman, and (6) an alien entitled to enter the United States solely to carry on trade under and in pursuance of the provisions of a present existing treaty of commerce and navigation.

Non-Quota Immigrants

Sec. 4. When used in this Act the term "non-quota immigrant" means—

(a) An immigrant who is the unmarried child under 18 years of age, or the wife, of a citizen of the United States who resides therein at the time of the filing of a petition under section 9;

(b) An immigrant previously lawfully admitted to the United States, who is returning from a temporary visit abroad;

(c) An immigrant who was born in the Dominion of Canada, Newfoundland, the Republic of Mexico, the Republic of Cuba, the Republic of Haiti, the Dominican Republic, the Canal Zone, or an independent country of Central or South America, and his wife, and his unmarried children under 18 years of age, if accompanying or following to join him;

(d) An immigrant who continuously for at least two years immediately preceding the time of his application for admission to the United States has been, and who seeks to enter the United States solely for the purpose of, carrying on the vocation of minister of any religious denomination, or professor, or a college, academy, seminary, or university; and his wife, and his unmarried children under 18 years of age; if accompanying or following to join him; or

(e) An immigrant who is a bona fide student at least 15 years of age and who seeks to enter the United States solely for the purpose of study at an accredited school, college, academy, seminary, or university, particularly designated by him and approved by the Secretary of Labor, which shall have agreed to report to the Secretary of Labor the termination of attendance of each immigrant student, and if any such institution of learning fails to make such reports promptly the approval shall be withdrawn.

Quota Immigrants

Sec. 5. When used in this Act the term "quota immigrant" means any immigrant who is not a non-quota immigrant. An alien who is not particularly specified in this Act as a non-quota immigrant or a non-immigrant shall not be admitted as a non-quota immigrant or a non-immigrant by reason of relationship to any individual who is so specified or by reason of being excepted from the operation of any other law regulating or forbidding immigration.

Preferences within Quotas

Sec. 6. (a) In the issuance of immigration visas to quota immigrants preference shall be given—

(1) To a quota immigrant who is the unmarried child under 21 years of age, the father, the mother, the husband, or the wife, of a citizen of the United States who is 21 years of age or over; and

(2) To a quota immigrant who is skilled in agriculture, and his wife, and his dependent children under the age of 16 years, if accompanying or following to join him. The preference provided in this paragraph shall not apply to immigrants of any nationality the annual quota for which is less than 300.

(b) The preference provided in subdivision (a) shall not in the case of quota immigrants of any nationality exceed 50 per centum of the annual quota for such nationality. Nothing in this section shall be construed to grant to the class of immigrants specified in paragraph (1) of subdivision (a) a priority in preference over the class specified in paragraph (2).

(c) The preference provided in this section shall, in the case of quota immigrants of any nationality, be given in the calendar month in which the right to preference is established, if the number of immigration visas which may be issued in such month to quota immigrants of such nationality has not already been issued; otherwise in the next calendar month.

Application for Immigration Visa

Sec. 7. (a) Every immigrant applying for an immigration visa shall make application therefor in duplicate in such form as shall be by regulations prescribed.

(b) In the application the immigrant shall state (1) the immigrant's full and true name; age, sex, and race; the date and place of birth; places of residence for the five years immediately preceding his application; whether married or single, and the names and places of residence of wife or husband and minor children, if any; calling or occupation; personal description (including height, complexion, color of hair and eyes, and marks of identification); ability to speak, read, and write; names and addresses of parents, and if neither parent living, then the name and address of his nearest relative in the country from which he comes; port of entry into the United States; final destination, if any, beyond the port of entry; whether he has a ticket through to such final destination; whether going to join a relative or friend, and, if so, what relative or friend and his name and complete address; the purpose for which he is going to the United States; the length of time he intends to remain in the United States; whether or not he intends to abide in the United States permanently; whether ever in prison or almshouse; whether he or either of his parents has ever been in an institution, or hospital for the care and treatment of the insane; (2) if he claims to be a non-quota immigrant, the facts on which he bases such claim; and (3) such additional information necessary to the proper enforcement of the immigration laws and the naturalization laws, as may be by regulations prescribed.

(c) The immigrant shall furnish, if available, to the consular officer, with his application, two copies of his "dossier" and prison record and military record, two certified copies of his birth certificate, and two copies of all other available public records concerning him kept by the Government to which he owes allegiance. One copy of the documents so furnished shall be permanently attached to each copy of the application and become a part thereof. An immigrant having an unexpired permit issued under the provisions of section 10 shall not be subject to this subdivision. In the case of an application made before September 1, 1924, if it appears to the satisfaction of the consular officer that the immigrant has obtained a visa of his passport before the enactment of this Act, and is unable to obtain the documents referred to in this subdivision without undue expense and delay, owing to absence from the country from which such documents should be obtained, the consular officer may relieve such immigrant from the requirements of this subdivision.

(d) In the application the immigrant shall also state (to such extent as shall be by regulations prescribed) whether or not he is a member of each class of individuals excluded from admission to the United States under the immigration laws, and such classes shall be stated on the blank in such form as shall be by regulations prescribed, and the immigrant shall answer separately as to each class.

(e) If the immigrant is unable to state that he does not come within any of the excluded classes, but claims to be for any legal reason exempt from exclusion, he shall state fully in the application the grounds for such alleged exemption.

(f) Each copy of the application shall be signed by the immigrant in the presence of the consular officer and verified by the oath of the immigrant administered by the consular officer. One copy of the application, when visaed by the consular officer, shall become the immigration visa, and the other copy shall be disposed of as may be by regulations prescribed.

(g) In the case of an immigrant under eighteen years of age the application may be made and verified by such individual as shall be by regulations prescribed.

(h) A fee of $1 shall be charged for the furnishing and verification of each application, which shall include the furnishing and verification of the duplicate, and shall be covered into the Treasury as miscellaneous receipts.

Non-Quota Immigration Visas

Sec. 8. A consular officer may, subject to the limitations provided in sections 2 and 9, issue an immigration visa to a non-quota immigrant as such upon satisfactory proof, under regulations prescribed under this Act, that the applicant is entitled to be regarded as a non-quota immigrant.

Issuance of Immigration Visas to Relatives

Sec. 9. (a) In case of any immigrant claiming in his application for an immigration visa to be a non-quota immigrant by reason of relationship under the provisions of subdivision (a) of section 4, or to be entitled to preference by reason of relationship to a citizen of the United States under the provisions of section 6, the consular officer shall not issue such immigration visa or grant such preference until he has been authorized to do so as hereinafter in this section provided.

(b) Any citizen of the United States claiming that any immigrant is his relative, and that such immigrant is properly admissible to the United States as a non-quota immigrant under the provisions of subdivision (a) of section 4 or is entitled to preference as a relative under section 6, may file with the Commissioner General a petition in such form as may be by regulations prescribed stating (1) the petitioner's name and address; (2) if a citizen by birth, the date and place of his birth; (3) if a naturalized citizen, the date and place of his admission to citizenship and the number of his certificate, if any; (4) the name and address of his employer or the address of his place of business or occupation if he is not an employee; (5) the degree of the relationship of the immigrant for whom such petition is made, and the names of all the places where such immigrant has resided prior to and at the time when the petition is filed; (6) that the petitioner is able to and will support the immigrant if necessary to prevent such immigrant from becoming a public charge; and (7) such additional information necessary to the proper enforcement of the immigration laws and the naturalization laws as may be by regulations prescribed.

(c) The petition shall be made under oath administered by any individual having power to administer oaths, if executed in the United States, but, if executed outside the United States, administered by a consular officer. The petition shall be supported by any documentary evidence required by regulations prescribed under this Act. Application may be made in the same petition for admission of more than one individual.

(d) The petition shall be accompanied by the statements of two or more responsible citizens of the United States, to whom the petitioner has been personally known for at least one year, that to the best of their knowledge and belief the statements made in the petition are true and that the petitioner is a responsible individual able to support the immigrant or immigrants for whose admission application is made. These statements shall be attested in the same way as the petition.

(e) If the Commissioner General finds the facts stated in the petition to be true, and that the immigrant in respect of whom the petition is made is entitled to be admitted to the United States as a non-quota immigrant under subdivision (a) of section 4 or is entitled to preference as a relative under section 6, he shall, with the approval of the Secretary of Labor, inform the Secretary of State of his decision, and the Secretary of State shall then authorize the consular officer with whom the application for the immigration visa has been filed to issue the immigration visa or grant the preference.

(f) Nothing in this section shall be construed to entitle an immigrant, in respect of whom a petition under this section is granted, to enter the United States as a non-quota immigrant, if, upon arrival in the United States, he is found not to be a non-quota immigrant.

Permit to Reenter United States after Temporary Absence

Sec. 10. (a) Any alien about to depart temporarily from the United States may make application to the Commissioner General for a permit to reenter the United States, stating the length of his intended absence, and the reasons therefor. Such application shall be made under oath, and shall be in such form and contain such information as may be by regulations prescribed, and shall be accompanied by two copies of the applicant's photograph.

(b) If the Commissioner General finds that the alien has been legally admitted to the United States, and that the application is made in good faith, he shall, with the approval of the Secretary of Labor, issue the permit, specifying therein the length of time, not exceeding one year, during which it shall be valid. The permit shall be in such form as shall be by regulations prescribed and shall have permanently attached thereto the photograph of the alien to whom issued, together with such other matter as may be deemed necessary for the complete identification of the alien.

(c) On good cause shown the validity of the permit may be extended for such period or periods, not exceeding six months each, and under such conditions, as shall be by regulations prescribed.

(d) For the issuance of the permit, and for each extension thereof, there shall be paid a fee of $3, which shall be covered into the Treasury as miscellaneous receipts.

(e) Upon the return of the alien to the United States the permit shall be surrendered to the immigration officer at the port of inspection.

(f) A permit issued under this section shall have no effect under the immigration laws, except to show that the alien to whom it is issued is returning from a temporary visit abroad; but nothing in this section shall be construed as making such permit the exclusive means of establishing that the alien is so returning.

Numerical Limitations

Sec. 11. (a) The annual quota of any nationality shall be 2 per centum of the number of foreign-born individuals of such nationality resident in continental United States as determined by the United States census of 1890, but the minimum quota of any nationality shall be 100.

(b) The annual quota of any nationality for the fiscal year beginning July 1, 1927, and for each fiscal year thereafter, shall be a number which bears the same ratio to 150,000 as the number of inhabitants in continental United States in 1920 having that national origin (ascertained as hereinafter provided in this section) bears to the number of inhabitants in continental United States in 1920, but the minimum quota of any nationality shall be 100.

(c) For the purpose of subdivision (b) national origin shall be ascertained by determining as nearly as may be, in respect of each geographical area which under section 12 is to be treated as a separate country (except the geographical areas specified in subdivision (c) of section 4) the number of inhabitants in continental United States in 1920 whose origin by birth or ancestry is attributable to such geographical area. Such determination shall not be made by tracing the ancestors or descendants of particular individuals, but shall be based upon statistics of immigration and emigration, together with rates of increase of population as shown by successive decennial United States censuses, and such other data as may be found to be reliable.

(d) For the purpose of subdivisions (b) and (c) the term "inhabitants in continental United States in 1920" does not include (1) immigrants from the geographical areas specified in subdivision (c) of section 4 or their descendants, (2) aliens ineligible to citizenship or their descendants, (3) the descendants of slave immigrants, or (4) the descendants of American aborigines.

(e) The determination provided for in subdivision (c) of this section shall be made by the Secretary of State, the Secretary of Commerce, and the Secretary of Labor, jointly. In making such determination such officials may call for information and expert assistance from the Bureau of the Census. Such officials shall, jointly, report to the President the quota of each nationality, determined as provided in subdivision (b), and the President shall proclaim and make known the quotas so reported. Such proclamation shall be made on or before April 1, 1927. If the proclamation is not made on or before such date, quotas proclaimed therein shall not be in effect for any fiscal year beginning before the expiration of 90 days after the date of the proclamation. After the making of a proclamation under this subdivision the quotas proclaimed therein shall continue with the same effect as if specifically stated herein, and shall be final and conclusive for every purpose except (1) in so far as it is made to appear to the satisfaction of such officials and proclaimed by the President, that an error of fact has occurred in such determination or in such proclamation, or (2) in the case provided for in subdivision (c) of section 12. If for any reason quotas proclaimed under this subdivision are not in effect for any fiscal year, quotas for such year shall be determined under subdivision (a) of this section.

(f) There shall be issued to quota immigrants of any nationality (1) no more immigration visas in any fiscal year than the quota for such nationality, and (2) in any calendar month of any fiscal year no more immigration visas than 10 per centum of the quota for such nationality, except that if such quota is less than 300 the number to be issued in any calendar month shall be prescribed by the Commissioner General, with the approval of the Secretary of Labor, but the total number to be issued during the fiscal year shall not be in excess of the quota for such nationality.

(g) Nothing in this Act shall prevent the issuance (without increasing the total number of immigration visas which may be issued) of an immigration visa to an immigrant as a quota immigrant even though he is a non-quota immigrant.

Nationality

Sec. 12. (a) For the purposes of this Act nationality shall be determined by country of birth, treating as separate countries the colonies, dependencies, or self-governing dominions, for which separate enumeration was made in the United States census of 1890; except that (1) the nationality of a child under twenty-one years of age not born in the United States, accompanied by its alien parent not born in the United States, shall be determined by the country of birth of such parent if such parent is entitled to an immigration visa, and the nationality of a child under twenty-one years of age not born in the United States, accompanied by both alien parents not born in the United States, shall be determined by the country of birth of the father if the father is entitled to an immigration visa; and (2) if a wife is of a different nationality from her alien husband and the entire number of immigration visas which may be issued to quota immigrants of her nationality for the calendar month has already been issued, her nationality may be determined by the country of birth of her husband if she is accompanying him and he is entitled to an immigration visa, unless the total number of immigration visas which may be issued to quota immigrants of the nationality of the husband for the calendar month has already been issued. An immigrant born in the United States who has lost his United States citizenship shall be considered as having been born in the country of which he is citizen or subject, or if he is not a citizen or subject of any country, then in the country from which he comes.

(b) The Secretary of State, the Secretary of Commerce, and the Secretary of Labor, jointly, shall, as soon as feasible after the enactment of this Act, prepare a statement showing the number of individuals of the various nationalities resident in continental United States as determined by the United States census of 1890, which statement shall be the population basis for the purposes of subdivision (a) of section 11. In the case of a country recognized by the United States, but for which a separate enumeration was not made in the census of 1890, the number of individuals born in such country and resident in continental United States in 1890, as estimated by such officials jointly, shall be considered for the purposes of subdivision (a) of section 11 as having been determined by the United States census of 1890. In the case of a colony or dependency existing before 1890, but for which a separate enumeration was not made in the census of 1890 and which was not included in the enumeration for the country to which such colony or dependency belonged, or in the case of territory administered under a protectorate, the number of individuals born in such colony, dependency, or territory, and resident in continental United States in 1890, as estimated by such officials jointly, shall be considered for the purposes of subdivision (a) of section 11 as having been determined by the United States census of 1890 to have been born in the country to which such colony or dependency belonged or which administers such protectorate.

(c) In case of changes in political boundaries in foreign countries occurring subsequent to 1890 and resulting in the creation of new countries, the Governments of which are recognized by the United States, or in the establishment of self-governing dominions, or in the transfer of territory from one country to another, such transfer being recognized by the United States, or in the surrender by one country of territory, the transfer of which to another country has not been recognized by the United States, or in the administration of territories under mandates, (1) such officials, jointly, shall estimate the number of individuals resident in continental United States in 1890 who where born within the area included in such new countries or self-governing dominions or in such territory so transferred or surrendered or administered under a mandate, and revise (for the purposes of subdivision (a) of section 11) the population basis as to each country involved in such change of political boundary, and (2) if such changes in political boundaries occur after the determination provided for in subdivision (c) of section 11 has been proclaimed, such officials, jointly, shall revise such determination, but only so far as necessary to allot the quotas among the countries involved in such change of political boundary. For the purpose of such revision and for the purpose of determining the nationality of an immigrant, (A) aliens born in the area included in any such new country or self-governing dominion shall be considered as having been born in such country or dominion, and aliens born in any territory so transferred shall be considered as having been born in the country to which such territory was transferred, and (B) territory so surrendered or administered under mandate shall be treated as a separate country. Such treatment of territory administered under a mandate shall not constitute consent by the United States to the proposed mandate where the United States has not consented in a treaty to the administration of the territory by a mandatory power.

(d) The statements, estimates, and revisions provided in this section shall be made annually, but for any fiscal year for which quotas are in effect as proclaimed under subdivision (e) of section 11, shall be made only (1) for the purpose of determining the nationality of immigrants seeking admission to the United States during such year, or (2) for the purposes of clause (2) of subdivision (c) of this section.

(e) Such officials shall, jointly, report annually to the President the quota of each nationality under subdivision (a) of section 11, together with the statements, estimates, and revisions provided for in this section. The President shall proclaim and make known the quotas so reported and thereafter such quotas shall continue, with the same effect as if specifically stated herein, for all fiscal year except those years for which quotas are in effect as proclaimed under subdivision (e) of section 11, and shall be final and conclusive for every purpose.

Exclusion from United States

Sec. 13. (a) No immigrant shall be admitted to the United States unless he (1) has an unexpired immigra-

tion visa or was born subsequent to the issuance of the immigration visa of the accompanying parent, (2) is of the nationality specified in the visa in the immigration visa, (3) is a non-quota immigrant if specified in the visa in the immigration visa as such, and (4) is otherwise admissible under the immigration laws.

(b) In such classes of cases and under such conditions as may be by regulations prescribed immigrants who have been legally admitted to the United States and who depart therefrom temporarily may be admitted to the United States without being required to obtain an immigration visa.

(c) No alien ineligible to citizenship shall be admitted to the United States unless such alien (1) is admissible as a non-quota immigrant under the provisions of subdivision (b), (d), or (e) of section 4, or (2) is the wife, or the unmarried child under 18 years of age, of an immigrant admissible under such subdivision (d), and is accompanying or following to join him, or (3) is not an immigrant as defined in section 3.

(d) The Secretary of Labor may admit to the United States any otherwise admissible immigrant not admissible under clause (2) or (3) of subdivision (a) of this section, if satisfied that such in admissibility was not known to, and could not have been ascertained by the exercise of reasonable diligence by, such immigrant prior to the departure of the vessel from the last port outside the United States and outside foreign contiguous territory, or, in the case of an immigrant coming from foreign contiguous territory, prior to the application of the immigrant for admission.

(e) No quota immigrant shall be admitted under subdivision (d) if the entire number of immigration visas which may be issued to quota immigrants of the same nationality for the fiscal year has already been issued. If such entire number of immigration visas has not been issued, then the Secretary of State, upon the admission of a quota immigrant under subdivision (d), shall reduce by one the number of immigration visas which may be issued to quota immigrants of the same nationality during the fiscal year in which such immigrant is admitted; but if the Secretary of State finds that it will not be practicable to make such reduction before the end of such fiscal year, then such immigrant shall not be admitted.

(f) Nothing in this section shall authorize the remission or refunding of a fine, liability to which has accrued under section 16.

Deportation

Sec. 14. Any alien who at any time after entering the United States is found to have been at the time of entry not entitled under this Act to enter the United States, or to have remained therein for a longer time than permitted under this Act or regulations made thereunder, shall be taken into custody and deported in the same manner as provided for in sections 19 and 20 of the Immigration Act of 1917: *Provided,* That the Secretary of Labor may, under such conditions and restrictions as to support and care as he may deem necessary, permit permanently to remain in the United States, any alien child who, when under sixteen years of age was heretofore temporarily admitted to the United States and who is now within the United States and either of whose parents is a citizen of the United States.

Maintenance of Exempt Status

Sec. 15. The admission to the United States of an alien excepted from the class of immigrants by clause (2), (3), (4), (5), or (6) of section 3, or declared to be a non-quota immigrant by subdivision (e) of section 4, shall be for such time as may be by regulations prescribed, and under such conditions as may be by regulations prescribed (including, when deemed necessary for the classes mentioned in clauses (2), (3), (4), or (6) of section 3, the giving of bond with sufficient surety, in such sum and containing such conditions as may be by regulations prescribed) to insure that, at the expiration of such time or upon failure to maintain the status under which admitted, he will depart from the United States.

Penalty for Illegal Transportation

Sec. 16. (a) It shall be unlawful for any person, including any transportation company, or the owner, master, agent, charter, or consignee of any vessel, to bring to the United States by water from any place outside thereof (other than foreign contiguous territory) (1) any immigrant who does not have an unexpired immigration visa, or (2) any quota immigrant having an immigration visa the visa in which specifies him as a non-quota immigrant.

(b) If it appears to the satisfaction of the Secretary of Labor that any immigrant has been so brought, such person, or transportation company, or the master, agent, owner, charterer, or consignee of any such vessel, shall pay to the collector of customs of the customs district in which the port of arrival is located the sum of $1,000 for each immigrant so brought, and in addition a sum equal to that paid by such immigrant for his transportation from the initial point of departure, indicated in his ticket, to the port of arrival, such latter sum to be delivered by the collector of customs to the immigrant on whose account assessed. No vessel shall be granted clearance pending the determination of the liability to the payment of such sums, or while such sums remain unpaid, except that clearance may be granted prior to the determination of such question upon the deposit of an amount sufficient to cover such sums, or of a bond with sufficient surety to secure the payment thereof approved by the collector of customs.

(c) Such sums shall not be remitted or refunded, unless it appears to the satisfaction of the Secretary of Labor that such person, and the owner, master, agent, charterer, and consignee of the vessel, prior to the departure of the vessel from the last port outside the United States, did not know, and could not have ascertained by the exercise of reasonable diligence, (1) that the individual transported was an immigrant, if the fine was imposed for bringing an immigrant without an unexpired immigration visa, or (2) that the individual transported was a quota immigrant, if the fine was imposed for bringing a quota immigrant the visa in whose immigration visa specified him as being a non-quota immigrant.

Entry from Foreign Contiguous Territory

Sec. 17. The Commissioner General, with the approval of the Secretary of Labor, shall have power to enter into contracts with transportation lines for the entry and inspection of aliens coming to the United States from or through foreign contiguous territory. In prescribing rules and regulations and making contracts for the entry and inspection of aliens applying for admission from or through foreign contiguous territory due care shall be exercised to avoid any discriminatory action in favor of transportation companies transporting to such territory aliens destined to the United States, and all such transportation companies shall be required, as a condition precedent to the inspection or examination under such rules and contracts at the ports of such contiguous territory of aliens brought thereto by them, to submit to and comply with all the requirements of this Act which would apply were they bringing such aliens directly to ports of the United States. After this section takes effect no alien applying for admission from or through foreign contiguous territory (except an alien previously lawfully admitted to the United States who is returning from a temporary visit to such territory) shall be permitted to enter the United States unless upon proving that he was brought to such territory by a transportation company which had submitted to and complied with all the requirements of this Act, or that he entered, or has resided in, such territory more than two years prior to the time of his application for admission to the United States.

Unused Immigration Visas

Sec. 18. If a quota immigrant of any nationality having an immigration visa is excluded from admission to the United States under the immigration laws and deported, or does not apply for admission to the United States before the expiration of the validity of the immigration visa, or if an alien of any nationality having an immigration visa issued to him as a quota immigrant is found not to be a quota immigrant, no additional immigration visa shall be issued in lieu thereof to any other immigrant.

Alien Seamen

Sec. 19. No alien seaman excluded from admission into the United States under the immigration laws and employed on board any vessel arriving in the United States from any place outside thereof, shall be permitted to land in the United States, except temporarily for medical treatment, or pursuant to such regulations as the Secretary of Labor may prescribe for the ultimate departure, removal, or deportation of such alien from the United States.

Sec. 20. (a) The owner, charterer, agent, consignee, or master of any vessel arriving in the United States from any place outside thereof who fails to detain on board any alien seaman employed on such vessel until the immigration officer in charge at the port of arrival has inspected such seaman (which inspection in all cases shall include a personal physical examination by the medical examiners), or who fails to detain such seaman on board after such inspection or to deport such seaman if required by such immigration officer or the Secretary of Labor to do so, shall pay to the collector of customs of the customs district in which the port of arrival is located the sum of $1,000 for each alien seaman in respect of whom such failure occurs. No vessel shall be granted clearance pending the determination of the liability to the payment of such fine, or while the fine remains unpaid, except that clearance may be granted prior to the determination of such question upon the deposit of a sum sufficient to cover such fine, or of a bond with sufficient surety to secure the payment thereof approved by the collector of customs.

(b) Proof that an alien seaman did not appear upon the outgoing manifest of the vessel on which he arrived in the United States from any place outside

thereof, or that he was reported by the master of such vessel as a deserter, shall be prima facie evidence of a failure to detain or deport after requirement by the immigration officer or the Secretary of Labor.

(c) If the Secretary of Labor finds that deportation of the alien seaman on the vessel on which he arrived would case undue hardship to such seaman he may cause him to be deported on another vessel at the expense of the vessel on which he arrived, and such vessel shall not be granted clearance until such expense has been paid or its payment guaranteed to the satisfaction of the Secretary of Labor.

(d) Section 32 of the Immigration Act of 1917 is repealed, but shall remain in force as to all vessels, their owners, agents, consignees, and masters, and as to all seamen, arriving in the United States prior to the enactment of this Act.

Preparation of Documents

Sec. 21. (a) Permits issued under section 10 shall be printed on distinctive safety paper and shall be prepared and issued under regulations prescribed under this Act.

(b) The Public Printer is authorized to print for sale to the public by the Superintendent of Public Documents, upon prepayment, additional copies of blank forms of manifests and crew lists to be prescribed by the Secretary of Labor pursuant to the provisions of sections 12, 13, 14, and 36 of the Immigration Act of 1917.

Offenses in Connection with Documents

Sec. 22. (a) Any person who knowingly (1) forges, counterfeits, alters, or falsely makes any immigration visa or permit, or (2) utters, uses, attempts to use, possesses, obtains, accepts, or receives any immigration visa or permit, knowing it to be forged, counterfeited, altered, or falsely made, or to have been procured by means of any false claim or statement, or to have been otherwise procured by fraud or unlawfully obtained; or who, except under direction of the Secretary of Labor or other proper officer, knowingly (3) possesses any blank permit, (4) engraves, sells, brings into the United States, or has in his control or possession any plate in the likeness of a plate designed for the printing of permits, (5) makes any print, photograph, or impression in the likeness of any immigration visa or permit, or (6) has in his possession a distinctive paper which has been adopted by the Secretary of Labor for the printing of immigration visas or permits, shall, upon conviction thereof, be fined not more than $10,000, or imprisoned for not more than five years, or both.

(b) Any individual who (1) when applying for an immigration visa or permit, or for admission to the United States, personates another, or falsely appears in the name of a deceased individual, or evades or attempts to evade the immigration laws by appearing under an assumed or fictitious name, or (2) sells or otherwise disposes of, or offers to sell or otherwise dispose of, or utters, an immigration visa or permit, to any person not authorized by law to receive such document, shall, upon conviction thereof, be fined not more than $10,000, or imprisoned for not more than five years, or both.

(c) Whoever knowingly makes under oath any false statement in any application, affidavit, or other document required by the immigration laws or regulations prescribed thereunder, shall, upon conviction thereof, be fined not more than $10,000, or imprisoned for not more than five years, or both.

Burden of Proof

Sec. 23. Whenever any alien attempts to enter the United States the burden of proof shall be upon such alien to establish that he is not subject to exclusion under any provision of the immigration laws; and in any deportation proceeding against any alien the burden of proof shall be upon such alien to show that he entered the United States lawfully, and the time, place, and manner of such entry into the United States, but in presenting such proof he shall be entitled to the production of his immigration visa, if any, or of other documents concerning such entry, in the custody of the Department of Labor.

Rules and Regulations

Sec. 24. The Commissioner General, with the approval of the Secretary of Labor, shall prescribe rules and regulations for the enforcement of the provisions of this Act; but all such rules and regulations, in so far as they relate to the administration of this Act by consular officers, shall be prescribed by the Secretary of State on the recommendation of the Secretary of Labor.

Act to Be in Addition to Immigration Laws

Sec. 25. The provisions of this Act are in addition to and not in substitution for the provisions of the immigration laws, and shall be enforced as a part of such laws, and all the penal or other provisions of such laws, not inapplicable, shall apply to and be enforced in connection with the provisions of this Act. An alien, although admissible under the provisions of this Act, shall not be admitted to the United States if he is excluded by any provision of the immigration laws other than this Act, and an alien, although admissible under the provisions of the immigration laws other than this Act, shall not be admitted to the United States if he is excluded by any provisions of this Act.

Steamship Fines under 1917 Act

Sec. 26. Section 9 of the Immigration Act of 1917 is amended to read as follows:

"Sec. 9. That it shall be unlawful for any person, including any transportation company other than railway lines entering the United States from foreign contiguous territory, or the owner, master, agent, or consignee of any vessel to bring to the United States either from a foreign country or any insular possession of the United States any alien afflicted with idiocy, insanity, imbecility, feeble-mindedness, epilepsy, constitutional psychopathic inferiority, chronic alcoholism, tuberculosis in any form, or a loathsome or dangerous contagious disease, and if it shall appear to the satisfaction of the Secretary of Labor that any alien so brought to the United States was afflicted with any of the said diseases or disabilities at the time of foreign embarkation, and that the existence of such disease of disability might have been detected by means of a competent medical examination at such time, such person or transportation company, or the master, agent, owner, or consignee of any such vessel shall pay to the collector of customs of the customs district in which the port of arrival is located the sum of $1,000, and in addition a sum equal to that paid by such alien for his transportation from the initial point of departure, indicated in his ticket, to the port of arrival for each and every violation of the provisions of this section, such latter sum to be delivered by the collector of customs to the alien on whose account assessed. It shall also be unlawful for any such person to bring to any port of the United States any alien afflicted with any mental defect other than those above specifically named, or physical defect of a nature which may affect his ability to earn a living, as contemplated in section 3 of this Act, and if it shall appear to the satisfaction of the Secretary of Labor that any alien so brought to the United States was so afflicted at the time of foreign embarkation, and that the existence of such mental or physical defect might have been detected by means of a competent medical examination at such time, such person shall pay to the collector of customs of the customs district in which the port of arrival is located the sum of $250, and in addition a sum equal to that paid by such alien for his transportation from the initial point of departure, indicated in his ticket, to the port of arrival, for each and every violation of this provision such latter sum to be delivered by the collector of customs of the alien for whose account assessed. It shall also be unlawful for any such person to bring to any port of the United States any alien who is excluded by the provisions of section 3 of this Act because unable to read, or who is excluded by the terms of section 3 of this Act as a native of that portion of the Continent of Asia and the islands adjacent thereto described in said section, and if it shall appear to the satisfaction of the Secretary of Labor that these disabilities might have been detected by the exercise of reasonable precaution prior to the departure of such aliens from a foreign port, such person shall pay to the collector of customs of the customs district in which the port of arrival is located the sum of $1,000, and in addition a sum equal to that paid by such alien for his transportation from the initial point of departure, indicated in his ticket, to the port of arrival, for each and every violation of this provision, such latter sum to be delivered by the collector of customs to the alien on whose account assessed.

"If a fine is imposed under this section for the bringing of an alien to the United States, and if such alien is accompanied by another alien who is excluded from admission by the last proviso of section 18 of this Act, the person liable for such fine shall pay to the collector of customs, in addition to such fine but as a part thereof, a sum equal to that paid by such accompanying alien for his transportation from his initial point of departure indicated in his ticket, to the point of arrival, such sum to be delivered by the collector of customs to the accompanying alien when deported. And no vessel shall be granted clearance papers pending the determination of the question of the liability to the payment of such fines, or while the fines remain unpaid, nor shall such fines be remitted or refunded: *Provided,* That clearance may be granted prior to the determination of such questions upon the deposit of a sum sufficient to cover such fines or of a bond with sufficient surety to secure the payment thereof, approved by the collector of customs: *Provided further,* That nothing contained in this section shall be construed to subject transportation companies to a fine for bringing to ports of the United States aliens who are by any of the provisos or exceptions to section 3 of this Act exempted from the excluding provisions of said section."

Sec. 27. Section 10 of the Immigration Act of 1917 is amended to read as follows:

"Sec. 10. (a) That it shall be the duty of every person, including owners, masters, officers, and agents of vessels of transportation lines, or international bridges or toll roads, other than railway lines which may enter into a contract as provided in section 23, bringing an alien to, or providing a means for an alien to come to, the United States, to prevent the landing of such alien in the United States at any time or place other than as designated by the immigration officers. Any such person, owner, master, officer, or agent who fails to comply with the foregoing requirements shall be guilty of a misdemeanor and on conviction thereof shall be punished by a fine in each case of not less than $200 nor more than $1,000, or by imprisonment for a term not exceeding one year, or by both such fine and imprisonment; or, if in the opinion of the Secretary of Labor, it is impracticable or inconvenient to prosecute the person, owner, master, officer, or agent of any such vessel, such person, owner, master, officer, or agent shall be liable to a penalty of $1,000, which shall be a lien upon the vessel whose owner, master, officer, or agent violates the provisions of this section, and such vessel shall be libeled therefor in the appropriate United States court.

"(b) Proof that the alien failed to present himself at the time and place designated by the immigration officers shall be prima facie evidence that such alien has landed in the United States at a time or place other than as designated by the immigration officers."

General Definitions

Sec. 28. As used in this Act—

(a) The term "United States," when used in a geographical sense, means the States, the Territories of Alaska and Hawaii, the District of Columbia, Porto Rico, and the Virgin Islands; and the term "continental United States" means the States and the District of Columbia;

(b) The term "alien" includes any individual not a native-born or naturalized citizen of the United States, but this definition shall not be held to include Indians of the United States not taxed, nor citizens of the islands under the jurisdiction of the United States;

(c) The term "ineligible to citizenship," when used in reference to any individual, includes an individual who is debarred from becoming a citizen of the United States under section 2169 of the Revised Statutes, or under section 14 of the Act entitled "An Act to execute certain treaty stipulations relating to Chinese," approved May 6, 1882, or under section 1996, 1997, or 1998 of the Revised Statutes, as amended, or under section 2 of the Act entitled "An Act to authorize the President to increase temporarily the Military Establishment of the United States," approved May 18, 1917, as amended, or under law amendatory of, supplementary to, or in substitution for, any of such sections;

(d) The term "immigration visa" means an immigration visa issued by a consular officer under the provisions of this Act;

(e) The term "consular officer" means any consular or diplomatic officer of the United States designated, under regulations prescribed under this Act, for the purpose of issuing immigration visas under this Act. In case of the Canal Zone and the insular possessions of the United States the term "consular officer" (except as used in section 24) means an officer designated by the President, or by his authority, for the purpose of issuing immigration visas under this Act;

(f) The term "Immigration Act of 1917" means the Act of February 5, 1917, entitled "An Act to regulate the immigration of aliens to, and the residence of aliens in, the United States";

(g) The term "immigration laws" includes such Act, this Act, and all laws, conventions, and treaties of the United States relating to the immigration, exclusion, or expulsion of aliens;

(h) The term "person" includes individuals, partnerships, corporations, and associations;

(i) The term "Commissioner General" means the Commissioner General of Immigration;

(j) The term "application for admission" has reference to the application for admission to the United States and not to the application for the issuance of the immigration visa;

(k) The term "permit" means a permit issued under section 10;

(l) The term "unmarried," when used in reference to any individual as of any time, means an individual who at such time is not married, whether or not previously married;

(m) The terms "child," "father," and "mother," do not include a child or parent by adoption unless the adoption took place before January 1, 1924;

(n) The terms "wife" and "husband" do not include a wife or husband by reason of a proxy or picture marriage.

Authorization of Appropriation

Sec. 29. The appropriation of such sums as may be necessary for the enforcement of this Act is hereby authorized.

Act of May 19, 1921

Sec. 30. The Act entitled "An Act to limit the immigration of aliens into the United States," approved May 19, 1921, as amended and extended, shall, notwithstanding its expiration on June 30, 1924, remain in force thereafter for the imposition, collection, and enforcement of all penalties that may have accrued thereunder, and any alien who prior to July 1, 1924, may have entered the United States in violation of such Act or regulations made thereunder may be deported in the same manner as if such Act had not expired.

Time of Taking Effect

Sec. 31. (a) Sections 2, 8, 13, 14, 15, and 16, and subdivision (f) of section 11, shall take effect on July 1, 1924, except that immigration visas and permits may be issued prior to that date, which shall not be valid for admission to the United States before July 1, 1924. In the case of quota immigrants of any nationality, the number of immigration visas to be issued prior to July 1, 1924, shall not be in excess of 10 per centum of the quota for such nationality, and the number of immigration visas so issued shall be deducted from the number which may be issued during the month of July 1, 1924. In the case of immigration visas issued before July 1, 1924, the four-month period referred to in subdivision (c) of section 2 shall begin to run on July 1, 1924, instead of at the time of the issuance of the immigration visa.

(b) The remainder of this Act shall take effect upon its enactment.

(c) If any alien arrives in the United States before July 1, 1924, his right to admission shall be determined without regard to the provisions of this Act, except section 23.

Saving Clause in Event of Unconstitutionality

Sec. 32. If any provision of this Act, or the application thereof to any person or circumstances, is held invalid, the remainder of the Act, and the application of such provision to other persons or circumstances, shall not be affected thereby.

16. From Clarence Darrow, "Mercy for Leopold and Loeb," August 1924

Conclusion of Clarence Darrow's plea to spare Leopold and Loeb from the death penalty.

. . . Now, your Honor, I have spoken about the war. I believed in it. I don't know whether I was crazy or not. Sometimes I think perhaps I was. I approved of it; I joined in the general cry of madness and despair. I urged men to fight. I was safe because I was too old to go. I was like the rest. What did they do? Right or wrong, justifiable or unjustifiable—which I need not discuss to-day—it changed the world. For four long years the civilized world was engaged in killing men. Christian against Christian, barbarian uniting with Christians to kill Christians; anything to kill. It was taught in every school, aye in the Sunday schools. The little children played at war. The toddling children on the street. Do you suppose this world has ever been the same since then? How long, your Honor, will it take for the world to get back the humane emotions that were slowly growing before the war? How long will it take the calloused hearts of men before the scars of hatred and cruelty shall be removed?

We read of killing one hundred thousand men in a day. We read about it and we rejoiced in it—if it was the other fellows who were killed. We were fed on flesh and drank blood. Even down to the prattling babe. I need not tell your Honor this, because you know; I need not tell you how many upright, honorable young boys have come into this court charged with murder, some saved and some sent to their death, boys who fought in this war and learned to place a cheap value on human life. You know it and I know it. These boys were brought up in it. The tales of death were in their homes, their playgrounds, their schools; they were in the newspapers that they read; it was a part of the common frenzy—what was a life? It was nothing. It was the least sacred thing in existence and these boys were trained to this cruelty.

It will take fifty years to wipe it out of the human heart, if ever. I know this, that after the Civil War in 1865, crimes of this sort increased, marvelously. No one needs to tell me that crime has no cause. It has as definite a cause as any other disease, and I know that out of the hatred and bitterness of the Civil War crime increased as America had never known it before. I know that growing out of the Napoleonic wars there was an era of crime such as Europe had never seen before. I know that Europe is going through the same experience to-day; I know it has followed every war; and I know it has influenced these boys so that life was not the same to them as it would have been if the world had not been made red with blood. I protest

against the crimes and mistakes of society being visited upon them. All of us have a share in it. I have mine. I cannot tell and I shall never know how many words of mine might have given birth to cruelty in place of love and kindness and charity.

Your Honor knows that in this very court crimes of violence have increased growing out of the war. Not necessarily by those who fought but by those that learned that blood was cheap, and human life was cheap, and if the State could take it lightly why not the boy? There are causes for this terrible crime. There are causes, as I have said, for everything that happens in the world. War is a part of it; education is a part of it; birth is a part of it; money is a part of it—all these conspired to compass the destruction of these two poor boys. Has the court any right to consider anything but these two boys? The State says that your Honor has a right to consider the welfare of the community, as you have. If the welfare of the community would be benefited by taking these lives, well and good. I think it would work evil that no one could measure. Has your Honor a right to consider the families of these two defendants? I have been sorry, and I am sorry for the bereavement of Mr. and Mrs. Frank, for those broken ties that cannot be healed. All I can hope and wish is that some good may come from it all. But as compared with the families of Leopold and Loeb, the Franks are to be envied—and everyone knows it.

I do not know how much salvage there is in these two boys. I hate to say it in their presence, but what is there to look forward to? I do not know but what your Honor would be merciful if you tied a rope around their necks and let them die; merciful to them, but not merciful to civilization, and not merciful to those who would be left behind. To spend the balance of their days in prison is mighty little to look forward to, if anything. Is it anything? They may have the hope that as the years roll around they might be released. I do not know. I do not know. I will be honest with this court as I have tried to be from the beginning. I know that these boys are not fit to be at large. I believe they will not be until they pass through the next stage of life, at forty-five or fifty. Whether they will then, I cannot tell. I am sure of this; that I will not be here to help them. So far as I am concerned, it is over.

I would not tell this court that I do not hope that some time, when life and age have changed their bodies, as they do, and have changed their emotions, as they do—that they may once more return to life. I would be the last person on earth to close the door of hope to any human being that lives, and least of all to my clients. But what have they to look forward to? Nothing. . . .

I care not, your Honor, whether the march begins at the gallows or when the gates of Joliet close upon them, there is nothing but the night, and that is little for any human being to expect.

But there are others to consider. Here are these two families, who have led honest lives, who will bear the name that they bear, and future generations must carry it on.

Here is Leopold's father—and this boy was the pride of his life. He watched him, he cared for him, he worked for him; the boy was brilliant and accomplished, he educated him, and he thought that fame and position awaited him, as it should have awaited. It is a hard thing for a father to see his life's hopes crumble into dust.

Should he be considered? Should his brothers be considered? Will it do society any good or make your life safer, or any human being's life safer, if it should be handed down from generation to generation, that this boy, their kin, died upon the scaffold?

And Loeb's, the same. Here are the faithful uncle and brother, who have watched here day by day, while Dickie's father and his mother are too ill to stand this terrific strain, and shall be waiting for a message which means more to them than it can mean to you or me. Shall these be taken into account in this general bereavement?

Have they any rights? Is there any reason, your Honor, why their proud names and all the future generations that bear them shall have this bar sinister written across them? How many boys and girls, how many unborn children will feel it? It is bad enough as it is, God knows. It is bad enough, however it is. But it's not yet death on the scaffold. It's not that. And I ask your Honor, in addition to all that I have said, to save two honorable families from a disgrace that never ends, and which could be of no avail to help any human being that lives.

Now, I must say a word more and then I will leave this with you where I should have left it long ago. None of us are unmindful of the public; courts are not, and juries are not. We placed our fate in the hands of a trained court, thinking that he would be more mindful and considerate than a jury. I cannot say how people feel. I have stood here for three months as one might stand at the ocean trying to sweep back the tide. I hope

the seas are subsiding and the wind is falling, and I believe they are, but I wish to make no false pretense to this court. The easy thing and the popular thing to do is to hang my clients. I know it. Men and women who do not think will applaud. The cruel and thoughtless will approve. It will be easy to-day; but in Chicago, and reaching out over the length and breadth of the land, more and more fathers and mothers, the humane, the kind and the hopeful, who are gaining an understanding and asking questions not only about these poor boys, but about their own—these will join in no acclaim at the death of my clients. These would ask that the shedding of blood be stopped, and that the normal feelings of man resume their sway. And as the days and the months and the years go on, they will ask it more and more. But, your Honor, what they shall ask may not count. I know the easy way. I know your Honor stands between the future and the past. I know the future is with me, and what I stand for here; not merely for the lives of these two unfortunate lads, but for all boys and all girls; for all of the young, and as far as possible, for all of the old. I am pleading for life, understanding, charity, kindness, and the infinite mercy that considers all. I am pleading that we overcome cruelty with kindness and hatred with love. I know the future is on my side. Your Honor stands between the past and the future. You may hang these boys; you may hang them by the neck until they are dead. But in doing it you will turn your face toward the past. In doing it you are making it harder for every other boy who in ignorance and darkness must grope his way through the mazes which only childhood knows. In doing it you will make it harder for unborn children. You may save them and make it easier for every child that sometime may stand where these boys stand. You will make it easier for every human being with an aspiration and a vision and a hope and a fate. I am pleading for the future; I am pleading for a time when hatred and cruelty will not control the hearts of men. When we can learn by reason and judgment and understanding and faith that all life is worth saving, and that mercy is the highest attribute of man.

I feel that I should apologize for the length of time I have taken. This case may not be as important as I think it is, and I am sure I do not need to tell this court, or to tell my friends that I would fight just as hard for the poor as for the rich. If I should succeed in saving these boys' lives and do nothing for the progress of the law, I should feel sad, indeed. If I can succeed, my greatest reward and my greatest hope will be that I have done something for the tens of thousands of other boys, for the countless unfortunates who must tread the same road in blind childhood that these poor boys have trod—that I have done something to help human understanding, to temper justice with mercy, to overcome hate with love.

I was reading last night of the aspiration of the old Persian poet, Omar Khayyam. It appealed to me as the highest that I can vision. I wish it was in my heart, and I wish it was in the hearts of all.

> So I be written in the Book of Love,
> I do not care about that Book above.
> Erase my name or write it as you will,
> So I be written in the Book of Love.

17. FROM CALVIN COOLIDGE'S INAUGURAL ADDRESS, MARCH 4, 1925

My Countrymen: No one can contemplate current conditions without finding much that is satisfying and still more that is encouraging. Our own country is leading the world in the general readjustment to the results of the great conflict. Many of its burdens will bear heavily upon us for years, and the secondary and indirect effects we must expect to experience for some time. But we are beginning to comprehend more definitely what course should be pursued, what remedies ought to be applied, what actions should be taken for our deliverance, and are clearly manifesting a determined will faithfully and conscientiously to adopt these methods of relief. Already we have sufficiently rearranged our domestic affairs so that confidence has returned, business has revived, and we appear to be entering an era of prosperity which is gradually reaching into every part of the Nation. Realizing that we can not live unto ourselves alone, we have contributed of our resources and our counsel to the relief of the suffering and the settlement of the disputes among the European nations. Because of what America is and what America has done, a firmer courage, a higher hope, inspires the heart of all humanity....

...We stand at the opening of the one hundred and fiftieth year since our national consciousness first asserted itself by unmistakable action with an array of force. The old sentiment of detached and dependent colonies disappeared in the new sentiment of a united and independent Nation. Men began to discard the narrow confines of a local charter for the broader opportunities of a national constitution. Under the eternal urge of freedom we became an independent Nation. A little less than 50 years later that freedom and independence were reasserted in the face of all the world, and guarded, supported, and secured by the Monroe doctrine. The narrow fringe of States along the Atlantic seaboard advanced its frontiers across the hills and plains of an intervening continent until it passed down the golden slope to the Pacific. We made freedom a birthright. We extended our domain over distant islands in order to safeguard our own interests and accepted the consequent obligation to bestow justice and liberty upon less favored peoples. In the defense of our own ideals and in the general cause of liberty we entered the Great War. When victory had been fully secured, we withdrew to our own shores unrecompensed save in the consciousness of duty done.

Throughout all these experiences we have enlarged our freedom, we have strengthened our independence. We have been, and propose to be, more and more American. We believe that we can best serve our own country and most successfully discharge our obligations to humanity by continuing to be openly and candidly, intensely and scrupulously, American. If we have any heritage, it has been that. If we have any destiny, we have found it in that direction.

But if we wish to continue to be distinctively American, we must continue to make that term comprehensive enough to embrace the legitimate desires of a civilized and enlightened people determined in all their relations to pursue a conscientious and religious life. We can not permit ourselves to be narrowed and dwarfed by slogans and phrases. It is not the adjective, but the substantive, which is of real importance. It is not the name of the action, but the result of the action, which is the chief concern. It will be well not to be too much disturbed by the thought of either isolation or entanglement of pacifists and militarists. The physical configuration of the earth has separated us from all of the Old World, but the common brotherhood of man, the highest law of all our being, has united us by inseparable bonds with all humanity. Our country represents nothing but peaceful intentions toward all the earth, but it ought not to fail to maintain such a military force as comports with the dignity and security of a great people. It ought to be a balanced force, intensely modern, capable of defense by sea and land, beneath the surface and in the air. But it should be so conducted that all the world may see in it, not a menace, but an instrument of security and peace....

. . . We have never any wish to interfere in the political conditions of any other countries. Especially are we determined not to become implicated in the political controversies of the Old World. With a great deal of hesitation, we have responded to appeals for help to maintain order, protect life and property, and establish responsible government in some of the small countries of the Western Hemisphere. Our private citizens have advanced large sums of money to assist in the necessary financing and relief of the Old World. We have not failed, nor shall we fail to respond, whenever necessary to mitigate human suffering and assist in the rehabilitation of distressed nations. These, too, are requirements which must be met by reason of our vast powers and the place we hold in the world.

Some of the best thought of mankind has long been seeking for a formula for permanent peace. Undoubtedly the clarification of the principles of international law would be helpful, and the efforts of scholars to prepare such a work for adoption by the various nations should have our sympathy and support. Much may be hoped for from the earnest studies of those who advocate the outlawing of aggressive war. But all these plans and preparations, these treaties and covenants, will not of themselves be adequate. One of the greatest dangers to peace lies in the economic pressure to which people find themselves subjected. One of the most practical things to be done in the world is to seek arrangements under which such pressure may be removed, so that opportunity may be renewed and hope may be revived. There must be some assurance that effort and endeavor will be followed by success and prosperity. In the making and financing of such adjustments there is not only an opportunity, but a real duty, for America to respond with her counsel and her resources. Conditions must be provided under which people can make a living and work out of their difficulties. But there is another element, more important than all, without which there can not be the slightest hope of a permanent peace. That element lies in the heart of humanity. Unless the desire for peace be cherished there, unless this fundamental and only natural source of brotherly love be cultivated to its highest degree, all artificial efforts will be in vain. Peace will come when there is realization that only under a reign of law, based on righteousness and supported by the religious conviction of the brotherhood of man, can there be any hope of a complete and satisfying life. Parchment will fail, the sword will fail, it is only the spiritual nature of man that can be triumphant.

It seems altogether probable that we can contribute most to these important objects by maintaining our position of political detachment and independence. We are not identified with any Old World interests. This position should be made more and more clear in our relations with all foreign countries. We are at peace with all of them. Our program is never to oppress, but always to assist. But while we do justice to others, we must require that justice be done to us. With us a treaty of peace means peace, and a treaty of amity means amity. We have made great contributions to the settlement of contentious differences in both Europe and Asia. But there is a very definite point beyond which we can not go. We can only help those who help themselves. Mindful of these limitations, the one great duty that stands out requires us to use our enormous powers to trim the balance of the world. . . .

. . . This Administration has come into power with a very clear and definite mandate from the people. The expression of the popular will in favor of maintaining our constitutional guarantees was overwhelming and decisive. There was a manifestation of such faith in the integrity of the courts that we can consider that issue rejected for some time to come. Likewise, the policy of public ownership of railroads and certain electric utilities met with unmistakable defeat. The people declared that they wanted their rights to have not a political but a judicial determination, and their independence and freedom continued and supported by having the ownership and control of their property, not in the Government, but in their own hands. As they always do when they have a fair chance, the people demonstrated that they are sound and are determined to have a sound government.

When we turn from what was rejected to inquire what was accepted, the policy that stands out with the greatest clearness is that of economy in public expenditure with reduction and reform of taxation. The principle involved in this effort is that of conservation. The resources of this country are almost beyond computation. No mind can comprehend them. But the cost of our combined governments is likewise almost beyond definition. Not only those who are now making their tax returns, but those who meet the enhanced cost of existence in their monthly bills, know by hard experience what this great burden is and what it does. No matter what others may want, these people want a drastic economy. They are opposed to waste. They know that extravagance lengthens the hours and diminishes the rewards of their labor. I favor the policy of economy, not because I wish to save money, but because I wish to save people. The men and women of this country who toil are the ones who bear the cost of the Government. Every dollar that we carelessly waste means that their life will be so much the more meager. Every dollar that we prudently save means that their life will be so much the more abundant. Economy is idealism in its most practical form.

If extravagance were not reflected in taxation, and through taxation both directly and indirectly injuriously affecting the people, it would not be of so much consequence. The wisest and soundest method of solving our tax problem is through economy. Fortunately, of all the great nations this country is best in a position to adopt that simple remedy. We do not any longer need wartime revenues. The collection of any taxes which are not absolutely required, which do not beyond reasonable doubt contribute to the public welfare, is only a species of legalized larceny. Under this republic the rewards of industry belong to those who earn them. The only constitutional tax is the tax which ministers to public necessity. The property of the country belongs to the people of the country. Their title is absolute. They do not support any privileged class; they do not need to maintain great military forces; they ought not to be burdened with a great array of public employees. They are not required to make any contribution to Government expenditures except that which they voluntarily assess upon themselves through the action of their own representatives. Whenever taxes become burdensome a remedy can be applied by the people; but if they do not act for themselves, no one can be very successful in acting for them.

The time is arriving when we can have further tax reduction, when, unless we wish to hamper the people in their right to earn a living, we must have tax reform. The method of raising revenue ought not to impede the transaction of business; it ought to encourage it. I am opposed to extremely high rates, because they produce little or no revenue, because they are bad for the country, and, finally, because they are wrong. We can not finance the country, we can not improve social conditions, through any system of injustice, even if we attempt to inflict it upon the rich. Those who suffer the most harm will be the poor. This country believes in prosperity. It is absurd to suppose that it is envious of those who are already prosperous. The wise and correct course to follow in taxation and all other economic legislation is not to destroy those who have already secured success but to create conditions under which every one will have a better chance to be successful. The verdict of the country has been given on this question. That verdict stands. We shall do well to heed it.

These questions involve moral issues. We need not concern ourselves much about the rights of property if we will faithfully observe the rights of persons. Under our institutions their rights are supreme. It is not property but the right to hold property, both great and small, which our Constitution guarantees. All owners of property are charged with a service. These rights and duties have been revealed, through the conscience of society, to have a divine sanction. The very stability of our society rests upon production and conservation. For individuals or for governments to waste and squander their resources is to deny these rights and disregard these obligations. The result of economic dissipation to a nation is always moral decay.

These policies of better international understandings, greater economy, and lower taxes have contributed largely to peaceful and prosperous industrial relations. Under the helpful influences of restrictive immigration and a protective tariff, employment is plentiful, the rate of pay is high, and wage earners are in a state of contentment seldom before seen. Our transportation systems have been gradually recovering and have been able to meet all the requirements of the service. Agriculture has been very slow in reviving, but the price of cereals at last indicates that the day of its deliverance is at hand. . . .

. . . The encouraging feature of our country is not that it has reached its destination, but that it has overwhelmingly expressed its determination to proceed in the right direction. It is true that we could, with profit, be less sectional and more national in our thought. It would be well if we could replace much that is only a false and ignorant prejudice with a true and enlightened pride of race. But the last election showed that appeals to class and nationality had little effect. We were all found loyal to a common citizenship. The fundamental precept of liberty is toleration. We can not permit any inquisition either within or without the law or apply any religious test to the holding of office. The mind of America must be forever free.

It is in such contemplations, my fellow countrymen, which are not exhaustive but only representative, that I find ample warrant for satisfaction and encouragement. We should not let the much that is to do obscure the much which has been done. The past and present show faith and hope and courage fully justified. Here stands our country, an example of tranquillity at home, a patron of tranquillity abroad. Here stands its Government, aware of its might but obedient to its conscience. Here it will continue to stand, seeking peace and prosperity, solicitous for the welfare of the wage earner, promoting enterprise, developing waterways and natural resources, attentive to the intuitive counsel of womanhood, encouraging education, desiring the advancement of religion, supporting the cause of justice and honor among the nations. America seeks no earthly empire built on blood and force. No ambition, no temptation, lures her to thought of foreign dominions. The legions which she sends forth are armed, not with the sword, but with the cross. The higher state to which she seeks the allegiance of all mankind is not of human, but of divine origin. She cherishes no purpose save to merit the favor of Almighty God.

18. Charles Lindbergh's Application for the Raymond Orteig Prize, February 15, 1927
The Raymond Orteig $25,000 Prize
PARIS—NEW YORK———NEW YORK— PARIS

Trans-Atlantic Flight

(Under the rule of the Fédération Aéronautique Internationale of Paris, France, and National Aeronautic Association of the United States of America of Washington, D.C.)

ENTRY FORM

Name of Aviator Entrant (in full)   Charles A. Lindbergh

Address   c/o Mr. H. H. Knight, 401 Olive Street, St. Louis, Missouri.

Aviator's F. A. I. Certificate No. 6286   Issued by National Aeronautic Ass'n.,

Aviator's Annual License No. 295 (1927)   Issued by National Aeronautic Ass'n.,

PARTICULARS RELATING TO THE AIRCRAFT INTENDED TO BE USED

Type (Monoplane, Biplane, Hydroaeroplane, Flying Boat, etc.)   NYP Ryan Monoplane

Wing area in sq. ft.   290   Load per sq. ft.   15-1/2 lb.

Make and type of engine   Wright J5 Whirlwind Cu. in. Disp.

Approximate capacity of Fuel Tanks   425 gallons

I, the undersigned, Charles A. Lindbergh of c/o Mr. H. H. Knight, 401 Olive St., St. Louis, MO., hereby enter for the Raymond Orteig "New York—Paris" $25,000 Prize upon the following conditions:—

1. I agree to observe and abide by the Rules and Regulations for the time being in force and governing the contest, and to comply in all respects and at all times with the requests or instructions regarding the contest, which may be given to me by any of the Officials of the National Aeronautic Association of the United States of America.

2. In addition to, and not by the way of, limitation of the liabilities assumed by me by this entry under the said Rules and Regulations, I agree also to indemnify the National Aeronautic Association of the United States of America and the Trustees of the Raymond Orteig $25,000 Prize, and Mr. Raymond Orteig, the donor of the New York—Paris Flight Prize, or their representatives or servants, or any fellow competitor, against all claims and damages arising out of, or caused by, any ascent, flight or descent made by me whether or not such claims and demands shall arise directly out of my own actions or out of the acts, actions or proceedings of any persons assembling to witness or be present at such ascent or descent.

3. I enclose my certified check for $250.00 to the order of the Trustees of the Raymond Orteig $25,000 Prize, being Entrance Fee, and request to be entered on the Competitor's Register of the National Aeronautic Association of the United States of America.

Signature (s) Charles A. Lindbergh
Address (s) c/o Mr. Harry H. Knight
(Notary Seal) 401 Olive St.
St. Louis, Mo.

Subscribed and sworn to before me this 15th day of Feb. 1927
Date Feb. 15, 1927

This blank is to be executed and forwarded with certified check to The Contest Committee of the National Aeronautic Association at No. 1623 H. Street, Washington, D.C. and notice thereof immediately communicated to

The Secretary of the Trustees of the Raymond Orteig Twenty-Five Thousand Dollar Prize
c/o Army and Navy Club of America

19. BARTOLOMEO VANZETTI'S FINAL STATEMENT TO THE COURT, APRIL 9, 1927

[Last formal statement made by Bartolomeo Vanzetti, shortly before his execution (along with Nicola Sacco) for the 1920 murder of two shoe-factory employees in the course of a robbery. Maintaining his innocence, Vanzetti restated a belief—widely held by liberals about this cause célèbre—that he and Sacco had been judged guilty at their 1921 trial not because of the evidence against them, but because they were foreign-born and avowed anarchists: "I am suffering because I am a radical and ... because I [am] an Italian." After numerous appeals, a blue-ribbon panel sustained the verdict, and Sacco and Vanzetti were electrocuted on August 23, 1927.]

COMMONWEALTH OF MASSACHUSETTS

Norfolk, ss. Nos. 5545 and 5546

Superior Criminal Court Thayer, J.

COMMONWEALTH V. NICOLA SACCO AND BARTOLOMEO VANZETTI

Present:

Winfield M. Wilbar, District Attorney Wm. P. Kelly, Ass't. District Attorney Dudley P. Ranney, Ass't District Attorney for the Commonwealth.

William G. Thompson, Esq., Herbert B. Ehrmann, Esq., for the Defendants.

Dedham, Massachusetts, Saturday, April 9, 1927. 10 A.M.

Mr. Wilbar. My it please the Court, the matter under consideration at this session is indictments Nos. 5545 and 5546, *Commonwealth vs. Nicola Sacco and Bartolomeo Vanzetti.*

At this time I would like to move the Court to have an interpreter sworn.

[An interpreter is sworn by Clerk of Court Worthington.]

Mr. Wilbar. It appears by the record of this Court, if your Honor please, that on indictment No. 5545, *Commonwealth vs. Nicola Sacco and Bartolomeo Vanzetti* that these defendants stand convicted of murder in the first degree. The records are clear at the present time, and I therefore move the Court for the imposition of sentence. The statute allows the Court some discretion as to the time within which this sentence may be imposed. Having that in mind, and at the request of the defendants' counsel, to which the Commonwealth readily assents, I would suggest that the sentence to be imposed shall be executed some time during the week beginning Sunday, July 10 next.

Clerk Worthington. Nicola Sacco, have you anything to say why sentence of death should not be passed upon you?

Statement by Nicola Sacco

Yes, sir. I am not an orator. It is not very familiar with me the English language, and as I know, as my friend has told me, my comrade Vanzetti will speak more long, so I thought to give him the chance.

I never know, never heard, even read in history anything so cruel as this Court. After seven years prosecuting they still consider us guilty. And these gentle people here are arrayed with us in this court today.

I know the sentence will be between two class, the oppressed class and the rich class, and there will be always collision between one and the other. We fraternize the people with the books, with the literature. You persecute the people, tyrannize over them and kill them. We try the education of people always. You try to put a path between us and some other nationality that hates each other. That is why I am here today on this bench, for having been the oppressed class. Well, you are the oppressor.

You know it, Judge Thayer,—you know all my life, you know why I have been here, and after seven years that you have been persecuting me and my poor wife, and you still today sentence us to death. I would like to tell all my life, but what is the use? You know all about what I say before, and my friend—that is, my comrade—will be talking, because he is more familiar with the language, and I will give him a chance. My comrade, the man kind, the kind man to all the children, you sentence him two times, in the Bridgewater case and the Dedham case, connected with me, and you know he is innocent. You forget all the population that has been with us for seven years, to sympathize and give us all their energy and all their kindness. You do not care for them. Among that peoples and the comrades and the working class there is a big legion of intellectual people which have been with us for seven years, but to not commit the iniquitous sentence, but still the Court goes ahead. And I think I thank you all, you peoples, my comrades who have been with me for seven years, with the Sacco-Vanzetti case, and I will give my friend a chance.

I forget one thing which my comrade remember me. As I said before, Judge Thayer know all my life, and he know that I am never been guilty, never,—not yesterday nor today nor forever.

Clerk Worthington. Bartolomeo Vanzetti, have you anything to say why sentence of death should not be passed upon you?

Statement by Bartolomeo Vanzetti

Yes. What I say is that I am innocent, not only of the Braintree crime, but also of the Bridgewater crime. That I am not only innocent of these two crimes, but in all my life I have never stole and I have never killed and I have never spilled blood. That is what I want to say. And it is not all. Not only am I innocent of these two crimes, not only in all my life I have never stole, never killed, never spilled blood, but I have struggled all my life, since I began to reason, to eliminate crime from the earth.

Everybody that knows these two arms knows very well that I did not need to go in between the street and kill a man to take the money. I can live with my two arms and live well. But besides that, I can live even without work with my arm for other people. I have had plenty of chance to live independently and to live what the world conceives to be a higher life than not to gain our bread with the sweat of our brow.

My father in Italy is in a good condition. I could have come back in Italy and he would have welcomed me every time with open arms. Even if I come back there with not a cent in my pocket, my father could have give me a possession, not to work but to make business, or to oversee upon the land that he owns. He was wrote me many letters in that sense, and other well to do relatives have wrote me many letters in that sense that I can produce.

Well, it may be a boast. My father and my uncle can boast themselves and say things that people may not be compelled to believe. People may say they may be poor when I say that they are to consider to give me a position every time that I want to settle down and form a family and start a settled life. Well, but there are people maybe in this same court that could testify to what I have say and what my father

and my uncle have say to me is not a lie, that really they have the means to give me position every time that I want.

Well, I want to reach a little point farther, and it is this.—that not only have I not been trying to steal in Bridgewater, not only have I not been in Braintree to steal and kill and have never steal or kill or spilt blood in all my life, not only have I struggled hard against crimes, but I have refused myself the commodity or glory of life, the pride of life of a good position, because in my consideration it is not right to exploit man. I have refused to go in business because I understand that business is a speculation on profit upon certain people that must depend upon the business man, and I do not consider that that is right and therefore I refuse to do that.

Now, I should say that I am not only innocent of all these things, not only have I never committed a real crime in my life—though some sins but not crimes—not only have I struggled all my life to eliminate crimes, the crimes that the official law and the official moral condemns, but also the crime that the official moral and the official law sanctions and sanctifies,—the exploitation and the oppression of the man by the man, and if there is a reason why I am here as a guilty man, if there is a reason why you in a few minutes can doom me, it is this reason and none else.

I beg your pardon. [Referring to paper.] There is the more good man I ever cast my eyes upon since I lived, a man that will last and will grow always more near and more dear to the people, as far as into the heart of the people, so long as admiration for goodness and for sacrifice will last. I mean Eugene Debs. I will say that even a dog that killed the chickens would not have found an American jury to convict it with the proof that the Commonwealth produced against us. That man was not with me in Plymouth or with Sacco where he was on the day of the crime. You can say that it is arbitrary, what we are saying, that he is good and he applied to the other his own goodness, that he is incapable of crime, and he believed that everybody is incapable of crime.

Well, it may be like that but it is not, it could be like that but it is not, and that man has a real experience of court, of prison and of jury. Just because he want the world a little better he was persecuted and slandered from his boyhood to his old age, and indeed he was murdered by the prison. He know, and not only he but every man of understanding in the world, not only in this country but also in the other countries, men that we have provided a certain amount of a record of the times, they all still stick with us, the flower of mankind of Europe, the better writers, the greatest thinkers of Europe, have pleaded in our favor. The scientists, the greatest scientists, the greatest statesmen of Europe, have pleaded in our favor. The people of foreign nations have pleaded in our favor.

Is it possible that only a few on the jury, only two or three men, who would condemn their mother for worldly honor and for earthly fortune; is it possible that they are right against what the world, the whole world has say it is wrong and that I know that it is wrong? If there is one that I should know it, if it is right or if it is wrong, it is I and this man. You see it is seven years that we are in jail. What we have suffered during these seven years no human tongue can say, and yet you see me before you, not trembling, you see me looking you in your eyes straight, not blushing, not changing color, not ashamed or in fear.

Eugene Debs say that not even a dog—something like that—not even a dog that kill the chickens would have been found guilty by American jury with the evidence that the Commonwealth have produced against us. I say that not even a leprous dog would have his appeal refused two times by the Supreme Court of Massachusetts—not even a leprous dog.

They have given a new trial to Madeiros for the reason that the Judge had either forgot or omitted to tell the jury that they should consider the man innocent until found guilty in the court, or something of that sort. That man has confessed. The man was tried and has confessed, and the court give him another trial. We have proved that there could not have been another Judge on the face of the earth more prejudiced and more cruel than you have been against us. We have proven that. Still they refuse the new trial. We know, and you know in your heart, that you have been against us from the very beginning, before you see us. Before you see us you already know that we were radicals, that we were underdogs, that we were the enemy of the institution that you can believe in good faith in their goodness—I don't want to condemn that—and that it was easy on the time of the first trial to get a verdict of guiltiness.

We know that you have spoke yourself and have spoke your hostility against us, and you despisement against us with friends of yours on the train, at the University Club of Boston, on the Golf Club of Worcester, Massachusetts. I am sure that if the people who know all what you say against us would have the civil courage to take the stand, maybe your Honor—I am sorry to say this because you are an old man, and I have an old father—but maybe you would be beside us in good justice at this time.

When you sentenced me at the Plymouth trial you say, to the best of my memory, of my good faith, that crimes were in accordance with my principle,—something of that sort,—and you take off one charge, if I remember it exactly, from the jury. The jury was so violent against me that they found me guilty of both charges, because there were only two. But they would have found me guilty of a dozen of charges against your Honor's instructions. Of course I remember that you told them that there was no reason to believe that if I were the bandit I have intention to kill somebody, so that they will take off the indictment of attempt to murder. Well, they found me guilty of what? And if I am right, you take out that and sentence me only for attempt to rob with arms,—something like that. But, Judge Thayer, may give more to me for that attempt of robbery than all the 448 men that were in Charlestown, all of those that attempted to rob, all those that have robbed, they have not such a sentence as you gave me for an attempt at robbery.

I am willing that everybody that does believe me that they can make commission, they can go over there, and I am very willing that the people should go over there and see whether it is true or not. There are people in Charlestown who are professional robbers, who have been in half the prisons of the United States, that they are steal, or hurt the man, shoot him. By chance he got better, he did not die. Well, the most of them guilty without trial, by self-confession, and by asking the aid of their own partner, and they got 8 to 10, 8 to 12, 10 to 15. None of them has 12 to 15, as you gave me for an attempt at robbery. And besides that, you know that I was not guilty. You know that my life, my private and public life in Plymouth, and wherever I have been, was so exemplary that one of the worst fears of our prosecutor Katzmann was to introduce proof of our life and of our conduct. He has taken if off with all his might and he has succeeded.

You know if we would have Mr. Thompson, or even the brother McAnarney, in the first trial in Plymouth, you know that no jury would have found me guilty. My first lawyer has been a partner of Mr. Katzmann, as he is still now. My first lawyer of the defense, Mr. Vahey, has not defended me, has sold me for thirty golden money like Judas sold Jesus Christ. If that man has not told to you or to Mr. Katzmann that he know that I was guilty, it is because he know that I was not guilty. That man has done everything indirectly to hurt us. He has made long speech with the jury about things that do matter nothing, and on the point of essence to the trail he has passed over with few words or with complete silence. This was a premeditation in order to give to the jury the impression that my own defender has nothing good to say, has nothing good to urge in defense of myself, and therefore go around the bush on little things that amount to nothing and let pass the essential points either in silence or with a very weakly resistance.

We were tried during a time that has now passed into history. I mean by that, a time when there was a hysteria of resentment and hate against the people of our principles, against the foreigner, against slackers, and it seems to me—rather, I am positive of it, that both you and Mr. Katzmann has done all what it were in your power in order to work out, in order to agitate still more the passion of the juror, the prejudice of the juror, against us.

I remember that Mr. Katzmann has introduced a witness against us, a certain Ricci. Well, I have heard that witness. It seems that he has nothing to say. It seemed that it was foolishness to produce a witness that has nothing to say. And it seemed if he were called by the Commonwealth to tell to the jury that he was the foremen of that laborer that was near the scene of the crime and who claimed, and it was testified in our behalf, that we were not the men and that this man, the witness Ricci, was his foreman, and he has tried to keep the man on the job instead of going to see what has happening so as to give the impression that it was not true that the man went towards the street to see what happened. But that was not very important. The real importance is that that man say that it was not true. That a certain witness that was the water boy of the gang of the laborers testified that he take a pail and go to a certain spring, a water spring, to take water for the gang—it was not true that he go to that spring, and therefore it was not true that he see the bandit, and therefore it was not true that he can tell that neither I nor Sacco were the men. But it was introduced to show that it was not true that that man go to that spring, because they know that the Germans has poisoned the water in that spring. That is what he say on that stand over there. Now, in the world chronicle of the time there is not a single happening of that nature.

Nobody in American—we have read plenty things bad that the Germans have done in Europe during the war, but nobody can prove and nobody will say that the Germans are bad enough to poison the spring water in this country during the war.

Now, this, it seems, has nothing to do with us directly. It seems to be a thing by incident on the stand between the other thing that is the essence here. But the jury were hating us because we were against the war, and the jury don't know that it makes any difference between a man that is against the war because he believes that the war is unjust, because he hate no country, because he is a cosmopolitan, and a man that is against the war because he is in favor of the other country that fights against the country in which he is, and therefore a spy, and he commits any crime in the country in which he is in behalf of the other country in order to serve the other country. We are not men of that kind. Katzmann know very well that. Katzmann know that we were against the war because we did not believe in the purpose for which they say that the war was done. We believe it that the war is wrong, and we believe this more now after ten years that we understood it day by day,—the consequences and the result of the after war. We believe more now than ever that the war was wrong, and we are against war more now than ever, and I am glad to be on the doomed scaffold if I can say to mankind, "Look out; you are in a catacomb of the flower of mankind. For what? All that they say to you, all that they have promised to you—it was a lie, it was an illusion, it was a cheat, it was a fraud, it was a crime. They promised you liberty. Where is liberty? They promised you prosperity. Where is prosperity? They have promised you elevation. Where is the elevation?

From the day that I went in Charlestown, the misfortune, the population of Charlestown has doubled in number. Where is the moral good that the War has given to the world? Where is the spiritual progress that we have achieved from the War? Where are the security of life, the security of the things that we possess for our necessity? Where are the respect for human life? Where are the respect and the admiration for the good characteristics and the good of the human nature? Never as now before the war there have been so many crimes, so many corruption's, so many degeneration as there is now.

In the best of my recollection and of my good faith, during the trial Katzmann has told to the jury that a certain Coacci has brought in Italy the money that, according to the State theory, I and Sacco have stole in Braintree. We never steal that money. But Katzmann, when he told that to the jury, he know already that that was not true. He know already that that man was deported in Italy with the Federal policeman after our arrest. I remeber well that the Federal policeman with him in their possession—that the Federal policeman has taken away the trunks from the very boarding where he was, and bring the trunks over here and look them over and found not a single money.

Now, I call that murder, to tell to the jury that a friend or comrade or a relative or acquaintance of the charged man, of the indicted man, has carried the money to Italy, when he knows it is not true. I can call that nothing else but a murder, a plain murder.

But Katzmann has told something else also against us that was not true. If I understand well, there have been agreement of counsel during the trial in which the counsel of defense shall not produce any evidence of my good conduct in Plymouth and the counsel of the prosecution would not have let the jury know that I was tried and convicted another time before in Plymouth. Well, I call that a one-sided agreement. In fact, even the telephone poles knew at the time of this trial at Dedham that I was tried and convicted in Plymouth; the jurymen knew that even when they slept. On the other side the jury have never seen I or Sacco and I think they have the right to incline to believe that the jury have never approached before the trial anyone that was sufficiently intimate with me and Sacco to be able to give them a description of our personal conduct. The jury don't know nothing about us. They have never seen us. The only thing that they know is the bad things that the newspaper have say when we were arrested and the bad story that the newspaper have say on the Plymouth trial.

I don't know why the defense counsel have made such an agreement, but I know very well why Katzmann has made such agreement, because he know that half of the population of Plymouth would have been willing to come over here and say that in seven years that I was living amongst them that I was never seen drunk, that I was known as the most strong and steadfast worker of the community. As a matter of fact I was called a mule and the people that know a little better the condition of my father and that I was a single man, much wondered at me and say, "Why you work like a mad man in that way when you have no children and no wife to care about?"

Well, Katzmann should have been satisfied on that agreement. He could have thanked his God and estimate himself a lucky man. But he was not satisfied with that. He broke his word and he tell to the jury that I was tried before in this very court. I don't know if that is right in the record, if that was take off or not, but I hear with my ear. When two or three women from Plymouth come to take the stand, the woman reach that point where this gentleman sit down over there, the jury were sit down in their place, and Katzmann asked this woman if they have not testified before for Vanzetti, and they say, yes, and he tell to them, "You cannot testify." They left the room. After that they testified just the same. But in the meanwhile he tell to the jury that I have been tried before. That I think is not to make justice to the man who is looking after the true, and it is a frame-up with which he has split my life and doomed me.

It was also said that the defense has put every obstacle to the handling of this case in order to delay the case. That sound weak for us, and I think it is injurious because it is not true. If we consider that the prosecution, the State, has employed one entire year to prosecute us, that is, one of the five years that the case has last was taken by the prosecution to begin our trial, our first trial. Then the defense make an appeal to you and you waited, or I think that you were resolute, that you had the resolute in your heart when the trial finished that you will refuse every appeal that we will put up to you. You waited a month or a month and a half and just lay down your decision on the eve of Christmas—just on the evening of Christmas. We do not believe in the fable of the evening of Christmas, neither in the historical way nor in the church way. You know some of our folks still believe in that, and because we do not believe in that, it don't mean that we are not human. We are human, and Christmas is sweet to the heart of every man. I think that you have done that, to hand down your decision on the evening of Christmas, to poison the heart of our family and of our beloved. I am sorry to be compelled to say this, but everything that was said on your side has confirmed my suspicion until that suspicion has changed to certitude. So that you see that one year it has taken before trying us.

Then the defense, in presenting the new appeal, has not taken more time that you have taken in answer to that. Then there came the second appeal, and now I am not sure whether it is the second appeal or the third appeal where you wait eleven months or one year without an answer to us, and I am sure that you have decide to refuse us a new trial before the hearing for the new appeal began. You take one year to answer it, or eleven months,—something like that. So that you see that out of the five years, two were taken by the State from the day of our arrest to the trial, and then one year to wait for your answer on the second or the third appeal.

Then on another occasion that I don't remember exactly now, Mr. Williams was sick and the things were delayed not for fault of the defense but on account of the fault of the prosecution. So that I am positive that if a man take a pencil in his hand and compute the time taken by the prosecution in prosecuting the case, and the time that was taken by the defense to defend this case, the prosecution has taken more time than the defense, and there is a great consideration that must be taken in this point, and it is that my first lawyer betrayed us,—the whole American population were against us. We have the misfortune to take a man from California, and he came here, and he was ostracized by you and by every authority, even by the jury, and is so much so that no part of Massachusetts is immune from what I would call the prejudice,—that is, to believe that each people in each place of the world, they believe to be the better of the world, and they believe that all the other are not so good as they. So of course the man that came from California into Massachusetts to defend two of us, he must be licked if it is possible, and he was licked all right. And we have our part too.

What I want to say is this: Everybody ought to understand that the first of the defense has been terrible. My first lawyer did not stick to defend us. He has made no work to collect witnesses and evidence in our favor. The record in the Plymouth Court is a pity. I am told that they are almost one-half lost. So the defense had a tremendous work to do in order to collect some evidence, to collect some testimony to offset and to learn what the testimony of the State has done. And in this consideration it must be said that even if the defense take double time of the State without delay, double time that they delay the case it would have been reasonable, whereas it took less than the State.

Well, I have already say that I not only am not guilty of these two crimes, but I never commit a crime in my life,—I have never steal and I have never kill and I have never spilt blood, and I have fought against the crime, and I have fought and I have sacrificed myself even to eliminate the crimes that the law and the church legitimate and sanctify.

This is what I say: I would not wish to a dog or to a snake, to the most low and misfortunate creature of the earth—I would not wish to any of them what I have had to suffer for things that I am not guilty of. But my conviction is that I have suffered for things that I am guilty of. I am suffering because I am a radical and indeed I am a radical; I have suffered because I was an Italian, and indeed I am an Italian; I have suffered more for my family and for my beloved than for myself; but I am so convinced to be right that if you could execute me two times, and if I could be reborn two other times, I would live again to do what I have done already.

I have finished. Thank you.

The Court. Under the law of Massachusetts the jury says whether a defendant is guilty or innocent. The Court has absolutely nothing to do with that question. The law of Massachusetts provides that a Judge cannot deal in any way with the facts. As far as he can go under our law is to state the evidence.

During the trial many exceptions were taken. Those exceptions were taken to the Supreme Judicial Court. That Court, after examining the entire record, after examining all the exceptions,—that Court in its final words said, "The verdicts of the jury should stand; exceptions overruled." That being true, there is only one thing that this Court can do. It is not a matter of discretion. It is a matter of statutory requirement, and that being true there is only one duty that now devolves upon this Court, and that is to pronounce the sentences.

First the Court pronounces sentence upon Nicola Sacco. It is considered and ordered by the Court that you, Nicola Sacco, suffer the punishment of death by the passage of a current of electricity through your body within the week beginning on Sunday, the tenth day of July, in the year of our Lord, one thousand, nine hundred and twenty-seven. This is the sentence of the law.

It is considered and ordered by the Court that you, Bartolomeo Vanzetti—

Mr. Vanzetti. Wait a minute, please, your Honor. May I speak for a minute with my lawyer, Mr. Thompson?

Mr. Thompson. I do not know what he wants to say.

The Court. I think I should pronounce the sentence.—Bartolomeo Vanzetti, suffer the punishment of death—

Mr. Sacco. You know I am innocent. That is the same words I pronounced seven years ago. You condemn two innocent men.

The Court.—by the passage of a current of electricity through your body within the week beginning on Sunday, the tenth day of July, in the year of our Lord, one thousand nine hundred and twenty-seven.

This is the sentence of the law.

We will now take a recess.

[At 11.00 A.M., the Court adjourned without day.]

20. List of "Don'ts and Be Carefuls" adopted by California Association for Guidance of Producers, June 8, 1927

Resolved, That those things which are included in the following list shall not appear in pictures produced by the members of this Association, irrespective of the manner in which they are treated:

1. Pointed profanity—by either title or lip—this includes the words "God," "Lord," "Jesus," "Christ" (unless they be used reverently in connection with proper religious ceremonies), "hell," "damn," "Gawd," and every other profane and vulgar expression however it may be spelled;
2. Any licentious or suggestive nudity—in fact or in silhouette; and any lecherous or licentious notice thereof by other characters in the picture;
3. The illegal traffic in drugs;
4. Any inference of sex perversion;
5. White slavery;
6. Miscegenation (sex relationships between the white and black races);
7. Sex hygiene and venereal diseases;
8. Scenes of actual childbirth—in fact or in silhouette;
9. Children's sex organs;
10. Ridicule of the clergy;
11. Willful offense to any nation, race, or creed;

And be it further

Resolved, That special care be exercised in the manner in which the following subjects are treated, to the end that vulgarity and suggestiveness may be eliminated and that good taste may be emphasized:

1. The use of the flag;
2. International relations (avoiding picturizing in an unfavorable light another country's religion, history, institutions, prominent people, and citizenry);
3. Arson;
4. The use of firearms;
5. Theft, robbery, safe-cracking, and dynamiting of trains, mines, buildings, etc. (having in mind the effect which a too-detailed description of these may have upon the moron);
6. Brutality and possible gruesomeness;
7. Technique of committing murder by whatever method;
8. Methods of smuggling;
9. Third-degree methods;
10. Actual hangings or electrocutions as legal punishment for crime;
11. Sympathy for criminals;
12. Attitude toward public characters and institutions;
13. Sedition;
14. Apparent cruelty to children and animals;
15. Branding of people or animals;
16. The sale of women, or of a woman selling her virtue;
17. Rape or attempted rape;
18. First-night scenes;
19. Men and women in bed together;
20. Deliberate seduction of girls;
21. The institution of marriage;
22. Surgical operations;
23. The use of drugs;
24. Titles or scenes having to do with the law enforcement or law-enforcing officers;
25. Excessive or lustful kissing, particularly when one character or the other is a "heavy";

Resolved, That the execution of the purposes of this resolution is a fair trade practice.

21. Kellogg-Briand Pact, Signed at Paris, August 27, 1928; Ratification Advised by the Senate, January 16, 1929; Ratified by the President, January 17, 1929

[Treaty between the United States and other Powers providing for the renunciation of war as an instrument of national policy.]

THE PRESIDENT OF THE GERMAN REICH, THE PRESIDENT OF THE UNITED STATES OF AMERICA, HIS MAJESTY OF THE KING OF THE BELGIANS, THE PRESIDENT OF THE FRENCH REPUBLIC, HIS MAJESTY THE KING OF GREAT BRITAIN IRELAND AND THE BRITISH DOMINIONS BEYOND THE SEAS,

EMPEROR OF INDIA, HIS MAJESTY THE KING OF ITALY, HIS MAJESTY THE EMPEROR OF JAPAN, THE PRESIDENT OF THE REPUBLIC OF POLAND THE PRESIDENT OF THE CZECHOSLOVAK REPUBLIC,

Deeply sensible of their solemn duty to promote the welfare of mankind;

Persuaded that the time has come when a frank renunciation of war as an instrument of national policy should be made to the end that the peaceful and friendly relations now existing between their peoples may be perpetuated;

Convinced that all changes in their relations with one another should be sought only by pacific means and be the result of a peaceful and orderly process, and that any signatory Power which shall hereafter seek to promote its national interests by resort to war should be denied the benefits furnished by this Treaty;

Hopeful that, encouraged by their example, all the other nations of the world will join in this humane endeavor and by adhering to the present Treaty as soon as it comes into force bring their peoples within the scope of its beneficent provisions, thus uniting the civilized nations of the world in a common renunciation of war as an instrument of their national policy;

Have decided to conclude a Treaty and for that purpose . . . and . . . have agreed upon the following articles:

Article I

The High Contracting Parties solemnly declare in the names of their respective peoples that they condemn recourse to war for the solution of international controversies, and renounce it, as an instrument of national policy in their relations with one another.

Article II

The High Contracting Parties agree that the settlement or solution of all disputes or conflicts of whatever nature or of whatever origin they may be, which may arise among them, shall never be sought except by pacific means.

Article III

The present Treaty shall be ratified by the High Contracting Parties named in the Preamble in accordance with their respective constitutional requirements, and shall take effect as between them as soon as all their several instruments of ratification shall have been deposited at Washington.

This Treaty shall, when it has come into effect as prescribed in the preceding paragraph, remain open as long as may be necessary for adherence by all the other Powers of the world. Every instrument evidencing the adherence of a Power shall be deposited at Washington and the Treaty shall immediately upon such deposit become effective as; between the Power thus adhering and the other Powers parties hereto.

It shall be the duty of the Government of the United States to furnish each Government named in the Preamble and every Government subsequently adhering to this Treaty with a certified copy of the Treaty and of every instrument of ratification or adherence. It shall also be the duty of the Government of the United States telegraphically to notify such Governments immediately upon the deposit with it of each instrument of ratification or adherence.

IN FAITH WHEREOF the respective Plenipotentiaries have signed this Treaty in the French and English languages both texts having equal force, and hereunto affix their seals.

DONE at Paris, the twenty-seventh day of August in the year one thousand nine hundred and twenty-eight.

Adhering Countries

When this Treaty became effective on July 24, 1929, the instruments of ratification of all of the signatory powers having been deposited at Washington, the following countries, having deposited instruments of definitive adherence, became parties to it:

Additional adhesions deposited subsequent to July 24, 1929. Persia, July 2, 1929; Greece, August 3, 1929; Honduras, August 6, 1929; Chile, August 12, 1929; Luxemburg, August 14, 1929; Danzig, September 11, 1929; Costa Rica, October 1, 1929; Venezuela, October 24, 1929.

22. FROM HERBERT HOOVER'S "RUGGED INDIVIDUALISM" SPEECH, SPEECH DELIVERED ON OCTOBER 22, 1928

[In this classic example of American conservative philosophy, Hoover condemned the Democratic platform as a misguided attempt to solve the problems of Prohibition, farm relief, and electrical power through state socialism; he extolled free, private enterprise and initiative, or a system of "rugged individualism," as the foundation of America's "unparalleled greatness."

Government entry into commercial business, he argued, would destroy political equality, increase corruption, stifle initiative, undermine the development of leadership, extinguish opportunity, and "dry up the spirit of liberty and progress."]

This campaign now draws near to a close. The platforms of the two parties defining principles and offering solutions of various national problems have been presented and are being earnestly considered by our people.

After four months' debate it is not the Republican Party which finds reason for abandonment of any of the principles it has laid down or of the views it has expressed for solution of the problems before the country. The principles to which it adheres are rooted deeply in the foundations of our national life and the solutions which it proposed are based on experience with government and a consciousness that it may have the responsibility for placing those solutions into action.

In my acceptance speech I endeavored to outline the spirit and ideals with which I would propose to carry that platform into administration. Tonight, I will not deal with the multitude of issues which have been already well canvassed, I propose rather to discuss some of those more fundamental principles and ideals upon which I believe the Government of the United States should be conducted.

Before I enter upon that discussion of principles I wish to lay before you the proof of progress under Republican rule. In doing this I do not need to review its seventy years of constructive history. That history shows that the Republican party has ever been a party of progress. It has reflected the spirit of the American people. We are a progressive people. Our history of 150 years in the greatest epic of human progress. Tonight to demonstrate the constructive character of our Party, I need only briefly picture the advance of fundamental progress during the past seven and a half years since we took over the Government amidst the ruin of war.

First of all, let me deal with the material side. I do this because upon the well-being, comfort and security of the American home do we build up the moral and spiritual virtues as well as the finer flowers of civilization and the wider satisfactions of life.

As a nation we came out of the war with great losses. We made no profits from it. The apparent increases in wages were fictitious. We were poorer as a nation when we emerged from it. Yet during these last eight years we have recovered from these losses and increased our national income by over one-third even if we discount the inflation of the dollar. While some individuals have grown rich, yet that there has been a wide diffusion of our gain in wealth and income is marked by a hundred proofs. I know of no better test of the improved conditions of the average family than the combined increase of life and industrial insurance, building and loan assets, and savings deposits. These are the financial agents of the average man. These alone have in seven years increased by nearly 100 per cent to the gigantic sum of over 50 billions of dollars, or nearly one-six of our whole national wealth. In addition to these evidences of larger savings our people are steadily increasing their spending for higher standards of living. Today there are almost 9 automobiles for each 10 families, where seven and a half years ago only enough automobiles were running to average less than 4 for each 10 families. The slogan of progress is changing from the full dinner pail to the full garage. Our people have more to eat, better things to wear, and better homes. We have even gained in elbow room in our homes, for the increase of residential floor space is over 25 per cent with less than 10 per cent increase in our number of people. We have increased the security of his job to every man and woman. We have decreased the fear of old age, the fear of poverty, the fear of unemployment and these are fears which have always been amongst the greatest calamities of human kind.

All this progress means far more than greater creature comforts. It finds a thousand interpretations into a greater and fuller life. In all this we have steadily reduced the sweat in human labor. A score of new helps save the drudgery of the home. In seven years we have added 25 per cent more electric power to the elbow of every worker, and farther promoted him from a carrier of burdens to a director of machines. Our hours of labor are lessened; our leisure has increased. We have expanded our parks and playgrounds. We have nearly doubled our attendance at games. We pour into outdoor recreation in every direction. The visitors at our national parks have trebled and we have so increased the number of sportsmen fishing in our streams and lakes that the longer time between bites is becoming a political issue. In these seven and one-half years the radio has brought music and laughter, education and political discussion to almost every fireside.

Springing from our prosperity with its greater freedom, its vast endowment of scientific research and the greater resources with which to care for public health, we have according to our insurance actuaries during this short period since the war lengthened the span of life by nearly eight years. We have reduced infant mortality, we have vastly decreased the days of illness and suffering in the life of every man and woman. We have improved the facilities for the care of the crippled and helpless and deranged.

From our increasing resources we have expanded our educational system in eight years from an outlay of 1,200 millions to 2,700 millions of dollars. The education of our youth has become almost the largest and certainly our most important activity. From our ability to free youth from toil we have increased the attendance in our grade schools by 14 per cent, in our high schools by 80 per cent, and in institutions of higher learning by 95 per cent. Today we have more youth in these institutions of higher learning twice over than all the rest of the world put together. We have made progress in literature, art and in public taste.

I do not need to recite more figures and more evidence. There is not a person within the sound of my voice that does not know the profound progress which our country has made in this period. Every man and woman knows that their comfort, their hopes and their confidence for the future are higher this day than they were seven and one-half years ago.

Your city has been an outstanding beneficiary of this great progress. With its suburbs it has, during the last seven and a half years grown by over a million and a half of people, until it has become the largest metropolitan district of all the world. Here you have made abundant opportunity not only for the youth of the land but for the immigrant from foreign shores. This city is the commercial center of the United States. It is the commercial agent of the American people. It is a great organism of specialized skill and leadership in finance, industry and commerce, which reaches every spot in our country. Its progress and its beauty are the pride of the whole American people. It leads our nation in the largest size of its benevolences, in art, in music, literature and drama. It has come to have a greatest voice, than any other city in the United States.

But when all is said and done the very life, progress and prosperity of this city is wholly dependent on the prosperity of the 110,000,000 people who dwell in our mountains and valleys across the 3,000 miles to the Pacific Ocean. Every activity of this city is sensitive to every evil and every favorable tide that sweeps this great nation of ours. Be there a slackening of industry in any part of the country it affects New York far more than the rest of the country. In a time of depression one-quarter of all the unemployed in the United States can be numbered in this city. In a time of prosperity the citizens of the great interior of our country pour into your city for business and entertainment at the rate of 200,000 a day. In fact so much is this city the reflex of the varied interests of our country that the concern of every one of your citizens for national stability, for national prosperity and for national progress is far greater than any other single part of our country.

Contributions to Progress

It detracts nothing from the character and energy of the American people, it minimizes in no degree the quality of their accomplishments to say that the policies of the Republican Party have played a large part in the building of this progress of these last seven and one-half years. I can say with emphasis that without the wise policies which the Republican Party has brought into action in this period, no such progress would have been possible.

The first responsibility of the Republican Administration was to renew the march of progress from its collapse by the war. That task involved the restoration of confidence in the future and the liberation and stimulation of the constructive energies of our people. It is not my purpose to enter upon a detailed recitation of the history of the great constructive measures of the past seven and a half years.

It is sufficient to remind you of the restoration of employment to the millions who walked your streets in idleness to remind you of the creation of the budget system; the reduction of six billions of national debt which gave the impulse of that vast sum returned to industry and commerce; the four sequent reductions of taxes and thereby the lift to the living of every family; the enactment of an adequate protective tariff and immigration laws which have raised and safeguarded our wages from floods of goods or labor from foreign countries; the creation of credit facilities and many aids to agriculture; the building up of foreign trade; the care of veterans, the development of aviation, of radio, of our inland waterways, our highways; the expansion of scientific research, of welfare activities, safer highways, safer mines, outdoor recreation, in better homes, in public health and the care of children. Nor do I need remind you that Government today deals with an economic and social system vastly more intricate and delicately adjusted than ever before. It now must be kept in perfect tune if we would not, through dislocation, have a breakdown in employment and in standards of living of our people. The Government has come to more and more touch this delicate web at a thousands points. Yearly the relations of Government to national prosperity becomes more and more intimate. It has only by keen large vision and cooperation by the Government that stability in business and stability in employment has been maintained during this past seven and a half years. Never has there been a period when the Federal Government has given such aid and impulse to the progress of our people, not alone to economic progress but to development of those agencies which make for moral and spiritual progress.

But in addition to this great record of contributions of the Republican Party to progress, there has been a further fundamental contribution—a contribution perhaps more important than all the others—and that is the resistance of the Republican Party to every attempt to inject the Government into business in competition with its citizens.

After the war, when the Republican Party assumed administration of the country, we were faced with the problem of determination of the very nature of our national life. Over 150 years we have builded up a form of self-government and we had builded up a social system which is peculiarly our own. It differs fundamentally from all others in the world. It is the American system. It is just as definite and positive a political and social system as has ever been developed on earth. It is founded upon the conception that self-government can be preserved only by decentralization of Government in the State and by fixing local responsibility; but further than this, it is founded upon the social conception that only through ordered liberty, freedom and equal opportunity to the individual will his initiative and enterprise drive the march of progress.

During the war we necessarily turned to the Government to solve every difficult economic problem—the Government having absorbed every energy of our people to war there was no other solution. For the preservation of the State the Government became a centralized despotism which undertook responsibilities, assumed powers, exercised rights, and took over the business of citizens. To large degree we regimented our whole people temporarily into a socialistic state.

However justified it was in time of war if continued in peace time it would destroy not only our system but progress and freedom in our own country and throughout the world. When the war closed the most vital of all issues was whether Governments should continue war ownership and operation of many instrumentalities of production and distribution. We were challenged with the choice of the American system of rugged individualism or the choice of a European system of diametrically opposed doctrines—doctrines of paternalism and state socialism. The acceptance of these ideas meant the destruction of self-government through centralization of government; it meant the undermining of initiative and enterprise upon which our people have grown to unparalleled greatness.

The Democratic administration cooperated with the Republican Party to demobilize many of her activities and the Republican Party from the beginning of its period of power resolutely turned its face away from these ideas and these war practices, back to our fundamental conception of the state and the rights and responsibilities of the individual. Thereby it restored confidence and hope in the American people, it freed and stimulated enterprise, it restored the Government to its position as an umpire instead of a player in the economic game. For these reasons the American people have gone forward in progress while the rest of the world is halting and some countries have even gone backwards. If anyone will study the causes which retarded recuperation of Europe, he will find much of it due to the stifling of private initiative on one hand, and overloading of the Government with business on the other.

I regret, however, to say that there has been revived in this campaign a proposal which would be a long step to the abandonment of our American system, to turn to the idea of government in business. Because we are faced with difficulty and doubt over certain national problems which we are faced—that is prohibition, farm relief and electrical power—our opponents propose that we must to some degree thrust government into these businesses and in effect adopt state socialism as a solution.

There is, therefore submitted to the American people the question—Shall we depart from the American system and start upon a new road. And I wish to emphasize this question on this occasion. I wish to make clear my position on the principles involved for they go to the very roots of American life in every act of our Government. I should like to state to you the effect of the extension of government into business upon our system of self government and our economic system. But even more important is the effect upon the average man. That is the effect on the very basis of liberty and freedom not only to those left outside the fold of expanded bureaucracy but to those embraced within it.

When the Federal Government undertakes a business, the state governments are at once deprived of control and taxation of that business; when the state government undertakes a business it at once deprived the municipalities of taxation and control of that business. Business requires centralization; self government requires decentralization. Our government to succeed in business must become in effect a despotism. There is thus at once an insidious destruction of self government.

Moreover there is a limit to human capacity in administration. Particularly is there a limit to the capacity of legislative bodies to supervise governmental activities. Every time the Federal Government goes into business 530 Senators and Congressmen become the Board of Directors of that business. Every time a state government goes into business 100 or 200 state senators and assemblymen become directors of that business. Even if they were supermen, no bodies of such numbers can competently direct that type of human activities which requires instant decision and action. No such body can deal adequately with all sections of the country. And yet if we would preserve government by the people we must preserve the authority of our legislators over the activities of our Government. We have trouble enough with log rolling in legislative bodies today. It originates naturally from desires of citizens to advance their particular section or to secure some necessary service. It would be multiplied a thousand-fold were the Federal and state governments in these businesses.

The effect upon our economic progress would be even worse. Business progressiveness is dependent on competition. New methods and new ideas are the outgrowth of the spirit of adventure of individual initiative and of individual enterprise. Without adventure there is no progress. No government administration can rightly speculate and take risks with taxpayers' money. But even more important than this—leadership in business must be through the sheer rise of ability and character. That rise can take place only in the free atmosphere of competition. Competition is closed by bureaucracy. Certainly political choice is a feeble basis for choice of leaders to conduct a business.

There is no better example of the practical incompetence of government to conduct business than the history of our railways. Our railways in the year before being freed from Government operation were not able to meet the demands for transportation. Eight years later we find them under private enterprise, transporting 15 per cent more goods and meeting every demand for service. Rates have been reduced by 15 per cent and net earnings increased from less than 1 per cent on their valuation to about 5 per cent. Wages of employees have improved by 13 per cent. The wages of railway employees are 2 per cent above pre-war. The wages of Government employees are today . . . will check their figure definitely tomorrow but probably about 70 per cent above pre-war. That should be a sufficient sermon upon the efficiency of Government operation.

But we can examine this question from the point of view of the person who gets a Government job and is admitted into the new bureaucracy. Upon that subject let me quote from a speech of that great leader of labor, Samuel Gompers, delivered in Montreal in 1920, a few years before his death. He said:

"I believe there is no man to whom I would take second position in my loyalty to the Republic of the United States, and yet I would not give it more power over the individual citizenship of our country. . . .

"It is a question of whether it shall be Government ownership or private ownership under control. . . . If I were in the minority of one in this convention, I would want to cast my vote so that the men of labor shall not willingly enslave themselves to Government authority in their industrial effort for freedom. . . .

"Let the future tell the story of who is right or who is wrong; who has stood for freedom and who has been willing to submit their fate industrially to the Government."

I would amplify Mr. Gompers' statement. These great bodies of Government employees would either comprise political machines at the disposal of the party in power, or alternatively to prevent this the Government by stringent civil-service rules must debar its employees from their full rights as free men. If it would keep employees out of politics, its rules must strip them of all right to expression of opinion. It is easy to conceive that they might become so large a body as by their votes to dictate to the Government and their political rights need be further reduced. It must strip them of the liberty to bargain for their own wages, for no Government employee can strike against his Government and thus the whole people. It makes a legislative body with all its political currents their final employer. That bargaining does not rest upon economic need or economic strength but on political potency.

But what of those who are outside the bureaucracy? What is the effect upon their lives of the Government on business and these hundreds of thousands more officials?

At once their opportunities in life are limited because a large area of activities are removed from their participation. Further the Government does not tolerate amongst its customers the freedom of competitive reprisals to which private corporations are subject. Bureaucracy does not spread the spirit of independence; it spreads the spirit of submission into our daily life, penetrates the temper of our people; not with the habit of powerful resistance to wrong, but with the habit of timid acceptance of the irresistible might.

Bureaucracy is ever desirous of spreading its influence and its power. You cannot give to a government the mastery of the daily working life of a people without at the same time giving it mastery of the peoples' souls and thoughts. Every expansion of government means that government in order to protect itself from political consequences of its errors and wrongs is driven onward and onward without peace to greater and greater control of the country's press and platform. Free speech does not live many hours after free industry and free commerce die.

It is false liberalism that interprets itself into the Government operation of business. The bureaucratization of our country would poison the very roots of liberalism that is free speech, free assembly, free press, political equality and equality of opportunity. It is the road, not to more liberty, but to less liberty. Liberalism should be found not striving to spread bureaucracy, but striving to set bounds to it. True liberalism seeks freedom first in the confident belief that without freedom the pursuit of all other blessings and benefits is vain. That belief is the foundation of all American progress, political as well as economic.

Liberalism is a force truly of the spirit, a force proceeding from the deep realization that economic freedom cannot be sacrificed if political freedom is to be preserved. Even if governmental conduct of business could give us more efficiency instead of giving us decreased efficiency, the fundamental objection to it would remain unaltered and unabated. It would destroy political equality. It would cramp and cripple mental and spiritual energies of our people. It would dry up the spirit of liberty and progress. It would extinguish equality of opportunity, and for these reasons fundamentally and primarily it must be resisted. For a hundred and fifty years liberalism has found its true spirit in the American system, not in the European systems.

I do not wish to be misunderstood in this statement. I am defining a general policy! It does not mean that our government is to part with one iota of its national resources without complete protection to the public interest. I have already stated that where the government is engaged in public works for purposes of flood control, of navigation, of irrigation, of scientific research or national defense that, or in pioneering a new art, it will at times necessarily produce power or commodities as a by-product. But they must be by-products, not the major purpose.

Nor do I wish to be misinterpreted as believing that the United States is free-for-all and the devil-take-the-hindmost. The very essence of equality of opportunity is that there shall be no domination by any group or trust or combination in this republic, whether it be business or political. It demands economic justice as well as political and social justice. It is no system to laissez faire.

There is but one consideration in testing these proposals—that is public interest. I do not doubt the sincerity of those who advocate these methods of solving our problems. I believe they will give equal credit to our honesty. If I believed that the adoption of such proposals would decrease taxes, cure abuses or corruption, would produce better service, decrease rates or benefit employees; If I believed they would bring economic equality, would stimulate endeavor, would encourage invention and support individual initiative, would provide equality of opportunity; If I believed that these proposals would not wreck our democracy but would strengthen the foundations of social and spiritual progress in America—or if they would do a few of these things—then I would not hesitate to accept these proposals, stupendous as they are, even though such acceptance would result in the governmental operation of all our power and the buying and selling of the products of our farms or any other product. But it is not true that such benefits would result to the public. The contrary would be true.

I feel deeply on this subject because during the war I had some practical experience with governmental operation and control. I have witnessed not only at home but abroad the many failures of government in business. I have seen its tyrannies, its injustices, its undermining of the very instincts which carry our people forward to progress. I have witnessed the lack of advance, the lowered standards of living, the depressed spirits of people working under such a system. My objection is based not upon theory or upon a failure to recognize wrong or abuse but because I know that the adoption of such methods would strike at the very roots of American life and would destroy the very basis of American progress.

Our people have the right to know whether we can continue to solve our great problems without abandonment of our American system. I know we can. We have demonstrated that our system is responsive enough to meet any new and intricate development in our economic and business life. We have demonstrated that we can maintain our democracy as master in its own house and that we can preserve equality of opportunity and individual freedom.

In the last fifty years we have discovered that mass production will produce articles for us at half the cost that obtained previously. We have seen the resultant growth of large units of production and distribution. This is big business. Business must be bigger for our tools are bigger, our country is bigger. We build a single dynamo of a hundred thousand horsepower. Even fifteen years ago that would have been a big business all by itself. Yet today advance in production requires that we set ten of these units together.

Our great problem is to make certain that while we maintain the fullest use of the large units of business yet that they shall be held subordinate to the public interest. The American people from bitter experience have a rightful fear that these great units might be used to dominate our industrial life and by illegal and unethical practices destroy equality of opportunity. Years ago the Republican Administration established the principle that such evils could be corrected by regulation. It developed methods by which abuses could be prevented and yet the full value of economic advance retained for the public. It insisted that when great public utilities were clothed with the security of part monopoly, whether it be railways, power plants, telephones or what not, then there must be the fullest and most complete control of rates, services, and finances by governmental agencies. These businesses must be conducted with glass pockets. In the development of our great production industry, the Republican Party insisted upon the enactment of a law

that not only would maintain competition but would destroy conspiracies to dominate and limit the equality of opportunity amongst our people.

One of the great problems of government is to determine to what extent the Government itself shall interfere with commerce and industry and how much it shall leave to individual exertion. It is just as important that business keep out of government as that government keep out of business. No system is perfect. We have had abuses in the conduct of business that every good citizen resents. But I insist that the result show our system better than any other and retains the essentials of freedom.

As a result of our distinctly American system our country has become the land of opportunity to those born without inheritance not merely because of the wealth of its resources and industry but because of this freedom of initiative and enterprise. Russia has natural resources equal to ours. Her people are equally industrious but she has not had the blessings of 150 years of our form of government and of our social system. The wisdom of our forefathers in their conception that progress must be the sum of the progress of free individuals has been reenforced by all of the great leaders of the country since that day. Jackson, Lincoln, Cleveland, McKinley, Roosevelt, Wilson, and Coolidge have stood unalterably for these principles. By adherence to the principles of decentralization, self-government, ordered liberty, and opportunity and freedom to the individual our American experiment has yielded a degree of well-being unparalleled in all the world. It has come nearer to the abolition of poverty, to the abolition of fear of want that humanity has ever reached before. Progress of the past seven years is the proof of it. It furnishes an answer to those who would ask us to abandon the system by which this has been accomplished.

There is a still further road to progress which is consonant with our American system—a method that reinforces our individualism by reducing, not increasing, Government interference in business.

In this country we have developed a higher sense of cooperation than has ever been known before. This has come partly as the result of stimulation during the war, partly from the impulses of industry itself. We have ten thousand examples of this cooperative tendency in the enormous growth of the associational activities during recent years. Chambers of commerce, trade associations, professional associations, labor unions, trade councils, civic associations, farm cooperatives— these are all so embracing that there is scarcely an individual in our country who does not belong to one or more of them. They represent every phase of our national life both on the economic and the welfare side. They represent a vast ferment toward conscious cooperation. While some of them are selfish and narrow, the majority of them recognize a responsibility to the public as well as to their own interest.

The government in its obligation to the public can through skilled specialists cooperate with these various associations for the accomplishment of high public purposes. And this cooperation can take two distinct directions. The first is in the promotion of constructive projects of public interest, such as the elimination of waste in industry, the stabilization of business and development of scientific research. It can contribute to reducing unemployment and seasonal employment. It can by organized cooperation assist and promote great movements for better homes, for child welfare and for recreation.

The second form that this cooperation can take is in the cure of abuses and the establishment of a higher code of ethics and a more strict standard in its conduct of business. One test of our economic and social system is its capacity to cure its own abuses. New abuses and new relationships to the public interest will occur as long as we continue to progress. If we are to be wholly dependent upon government to cure every evil we shall by this very method have created an enlarged and deadening abuse through the extension of bureaucracy and the clumsy and incapable handling of delicate economic forces. And much abuse has been and can be cured by inspiration and cooperation, rather than by regulation of the government.

Nor is this any idealistic proposal. For the last seven years the Department of Commerce has carried this into practice in hundreds of directions and every single accomplishment of this character minimizes the necessity for government interference with business.

All this is possible because of the cooperative spirit and ability at team play in the American people. There is here a fundamental relief from the necessity of extension of the government into every avenue of business and welfare and therefore a powerful implement for the promotion of progress.

I wish to say something more on what I believe is the outstanding ideal in our whole political, economic and social system—that is equality of opportunity. We have carried this ideal farther into our life than has any other nation in the world. Equality of opportunity is the right of every American, rich or poor, foreign or native born, without respect to race or faith or color, to attain that position in life to which his ability and character entitle him. We must carry this ideal further than to economic and political fields alone. The first steps to equality of opportunity are that there should be no child in America that has not been born and does not live under sound conditions of health, that does not have full opportunity for education from the beginning to the end of our institutions, that is not free from injurious labor, that does not have stimulation to accomplish to the fullest of its capacities.

It is a matter for concern to our Government that we shall strengthen the safeguards to health, that we shall strengthen the bureaus given to research, that we shall strengthen our educational system at every point, that we shall develop cooperation by our Federal Government with state governments and with the voluntary bodies of the country that we may bring not only better understanding but action in these matters.

Furthermore, equality of opportunity in my vision requires an equal opportunity to the people in every section of our country. In these past few years some groups in our country have lagged behind others in the march of progress. They have not had the same opportunity. I refer more particularly to those engaged in the textile, coal and in the agricultural industries. We can assist in solving these problems by cooperation of our Government. To the agricultural industry we shall need advance initial capital to assist them, to stabilize and conduct their own industry. But this proposal is that they shall conduct it themselves, not by the Government. It is in the interest of our cities that we shall bring agriculture into full stability and prosperity. I know you will cooperate gladly in the faith that in the common prosperity of our country lies its future. . . .

23. HERBERT HOOVER'S INAUGURAL ADDRESS, MARCH 4, 1929

My Countrymen: This occasion is not alone the administration of the most sacred oath which can be assumed by an American citizen. It is a dedication and consecration under God to the highest office in service of our people. I assume this trust in the humility of knowledge that only through the guidance of Almighty Providence can I hope to discharge its ever-increasing burdens.

It is in keeping with tradition throughout our history that I should express simply and directly the opinions which I hold concerning some of the matters of present importance.

Our Progress. If we survey the situation of our Nation both at home and abroad, we find many satisfactions; we find some causes for concern. We have emerged from the losses of the Great War and the reconstruction following it with increased virility and strength. From this strength we have contributed to the recovery and progress of the world. What America has done has given renewed hope and courage to all who have faith in government by the people. In the large view, we have reached a higher degree of comfort and security than ever existed before in the history of the world. Through liberation from widespread poverty we have reached a higher degree of individual freedom than ever before. The devotion to and concern for our institutions are deep and sincere. We are steadily building a new race—a new civilization great in its own attainments. The influence and high purposes of our Nation are respected among the peoples of the world. We aspire to distinction in the world, but to a distinction based upon confidence in our sense of justice as well as our accomplishments within our own borders and in our own lives. For wise guidance in this great period of recovery the Nation is deeply indebted to Calvin Coolidge.

But all this majestic advance should not obscure the constant dangers from which self-government must be safeguarded. The strong man must at all times be alert to the attack of insidious disease.

The Failure of Our System of Criminal Justice. The most malign of all these dangers today is disregard and disobedience of law. Crime is increasing. Confidence in rigid and speedy justice is decreasing. I am not prepared to believe that this indicates any decay in the moral fiber of the American people. I am not prepared to believe that it indicates an impotence of the Federal Government to enforce its laws.

It is only in part due to the additional burdens imposed upon our judicial system by the eighteenth amendment. The problem is much wider than that. Many influences had increasingly complicated and weakened our law enforcement organization long before the adoption of the eighteenth amendment.

To reestablish the vigor and effectiveness of law enforcement we must critically consider the entire Federal machinery of justice, the redistribution of its functions, the simplification of its procedure, the provision of additional special tribunals, the better selection of juries, and the more effective organization of our

agencies of investigation and prosecution that justice may be sure and that it may be swift. While the authority of the Federal Government extends to but part of our vast system of national, State, and local justice, yet the standards which the Federal Government establishes have the most profound influence upon the whole structure.

We are fortunate in the ability and integrity of our Federal judges and attorneys. But the system which these officers are called upon to administer is in many respects ill adapted to present-day conditions. Its intricate and involved rules of procedure have become the refuge of both big and little criminals. There is a belief abroad that by invoking technicalities, subterfuge, and delay, the ends of justice may be thwarted by those who can pay the cost.

Reform, reorganization and strengthening of our whole judicial and enforcement system, both in civil and criminal sides, have been advocated for years by statesmen, judges, and bar associations. First steps toward that end should not longer be delayed. Rigid and expeditious justice is the first safeguard of freedom, the basis of all ordered liberty, the vital force of progress. It must not come to be in our Republic that it can be defeated by the indifference of the citizen, by exploitation of the delays and entanglements of the law, or by combinations of criminals. Justice must not fail because the agencies of enforcement are either delinquent or inefficiently organized. To consider these evils, to find their remedy, is the most sore necessity of our times.

Enforcement of the Eighteenth Amendment. Of the undoubted abuses which have grown up under the eighteenth amendment, part are due to the causes I have just mentioned; but part are due to the failure of some States to accept their share of responsibility for concurrent enforcement and to the failure of many State and local officials to accept the obligation under their oath of office zealously to enforce the laws. With the failures from these many causes has come a dangerous expansion in the criminal elements who have found enlarged opportunities in dealing in illegal liquor.

But a large responsibility rests directly upon our citizens. There would be little traffic in illegal liquor if only criminals patronized it. We must awake to the fact that this patronage from large numbers of law-abiding citizens is supplying the rewards and stimulating crime.

I have been selected by you to execute and enforce the laws of the country. I propose to do so to the extent of my own abilities, but the measure of success that the Government shall attain will depend upon the moral support which you, as citizens, extend. The duty of citizens to support the laws of the land is coequal with the duty of their Government to enforce the laws which exist. No greater national service can be given by men and women of good will—who, I know, are not unmindful of the responsibilities of citizenship—than that they should, by their example, assist in stamping out crime and outlawry by refusing participation in and condemning all transactions with illegal liquor. Our whole system of self-government will crumble either if officials elect what laws they will enforce or citizens elect what laws they will support. The worst evil of disregard for some law is that it destroys respect for all law. For our citizens to patronize the violation of a particular law on the ground that they are opposed to it is destructive of the very basis of all that protection of life, of homes and property which they rightly claim under other laws. If citizens do not like a law, their duty as honest men and women is to discourage its violation; their right is openly to work for its repeal.

To those of criminal mind there can be no appeal but vigorous enforcement of the law. Fortunately they are but a small percentage of our people. Their activities must be stopped.

A National Investigation. I propose to appoint a national commission for a searching investigation of the whole structure of our Federal system of jurisprudence, to include the method of enforcement of the eighteenth amendment and the causes of abuse under it. Its purpose will be to make such recommendations for reorganization of the administration of Federal laws and court procedure as may be found desirable. In the meantime it is essential that a large part of the enforcement activities be transferred from the Treasury Department to the Department of Justice as a beginning of more effective organization. . . .

. . . World Peace. The United States fully accepts the profound truth that our own progress, prosperity, and peace are interlocked with the progress, prosperity, and peace of all humanity. The whole world is at peace. The dangers to a continuation of this peace today are largely the fear and suspicion which still haunt the world. No suspicion or fear can be rightly directed toward our country.

Those who have a true understanding of America know that we have no desire for territorial expansion, for economic or other domination of other peoples. Such purposes are repugnant to our ideals of human freedom. Our form of government is ill adapted to the responsibilities which inevitably follow permanent limitation of the independence of other peoples. Superficial observers seem to find no destiny for our abounding increase in population, in wealth and power except that of imperialism. They fail to see that the American people are engrossed in the building for themselves of a new economic system, a new social system, a new political system all of which are characterized by aspirations of freedom of opportunity and thereby are the negation of imperialism. They fail to realize that because of our abounding prosperity our youth are pressing more and more into our institutions of learning; that our people are seeking a larger vision through art, literature, science, and travel; that they are moving toward stronger moral and spiritual life—that from these things our sympathies are broadening beyond the bounds of our Nation and race toward their true expression in a real brotherhood of man. They fail to see that the idealism of America will lead it to no narrow or selfish channel, but inspire it to do its full share as a nation toward the advancement of civilization. It will do that not by mere declaration but by taking a practical part in supporting all useful international undertakings. We not only desire peace with the world, but to see peace maintained throughout the world. We wish to advance the reign of justice and reason toward the extinction of force.

The recent treaty for the renunciation of war as an instrument of national policy sets an advanced standard in our conception of the relations of nations. Its acceptance should pave the way to greater limitation of armament, the offer of which we sincerely extend to the world. But its full realization also implies a greater and greater perfection in the instrumentalities for pacific settlement of controversies between nations. In the creation and use of these instrumentalities we should support every sound method of conciliation, arbitration, and judicial settlement. American statesmen were among the first to propose and they have constantly urged upon the world, the establishment of a tribunal for the settlement of controversies of a justiciable character. The Permanent Court of International Justice in its major purpose is thus peculiarly identified with American ideals and with American statesmanship. No more potent instrumentality for this purpose has ever been conceived and no other is practicable of establishment. The reservations placed upon our adherence should not be misinterpreted. The United States seeks by these reservations no special privilege or advantage but only to clarify our relation to advisory opinions and other matters which are subsidiary to the major purpose of the court. The way should, and I believe will, be found by which we may take our proper place in a movement so fundamental to the progress of peace.

Our people have determined that we should make no political engagements such as membership in the League of Nations, which may commit us in advance as a nation to become involved in the settlements of controversies between other countries. They adhere to the belief that the independence of America from such obligations increases its ability and availability for service in all fields of human progress.

I have lately returned from a journey among our sister Republics of the Western Hemisphere. I have received unbounded hospitality and courtesy as their expression of friendliness to our country. We are held by particular bonds of sympathy and common interest with them. They are each of them building a racial character and a culture which is an impressive contribution to human progress. We wish only for the maintenance of their independence, the growth of their stability, and their prosperity. While we have had wars in the Western Hemisphere, yet on the whole the record is in encouraging contrast with that of other parts of the world. Fortunately the New World is largely free from the inheritances of fear and distrust which have so troubled the Old World. We should keep it so.

It is impossible, my countrymen, to speak of peace without profound emotion. In thousands of homes in America, in millions of homes around the world, there are vacant chairs. It would be a shameful confession of our unworthiness if it should develop that we have abandoned the hope for which all these men died. Surely civilization is old enough, surely mankind is mature enough so that we ought in our own lifetime to find a way to permanent peace. Abroad, to west and east, are nations whose sons mingled their blood with the blood of our sons on the battlefields. Most of these nations have contributed to our race, to our culture, our knowledge, and our progress. From one of them we derive our very language and from many of them much of the genius of our institutions. Their desire for peace is as deep and sincere as our own.

Peace can be contributed to by respect for our ability in defense. Peace can be promoted by the limitation of arms and by the creation of the instrumental-

ities for peaceful settlement of controversies. But it will become a reality only through self-restraint and active effort in friendliness and helpfulness. I covet for this administration a record of having further contributed to advance the cause of peace. . . .

. . . Other Mandates from the Election. It appears to me that the more important further mandates from the recent election were the maintenance of the integrity of the Constitution; the vigorous enforcement of the laws; the continuance of economy in public expenditure; the continued regulation of business to prevent domination in the community; the denial of ownership or operation of business by the Government in competition with its citizens; the avoidance of policies which would involve us in the controversies of foreign nations; the more effective reorganization of the departments of the Federal Government; the expansion of public works; and the promotion of welfare activities affecting education and the home.

These were the more tangible determinations of the election, but beyond them was the confidence and belief of the people that we would not neglect the support of the embedded ideals and aspirations of America. These ideals and aspirations are the touchstones upon which the day-to-day administration and legislative acts of government must be tested. More than this, the Government must, so far as lies within its proper powers, give leadership to the realization of these ideals and to the fruition of these aspirations. No one can adequately reduce these things of the spirit to phrases or to a catalogue of definitions. We do know what the attainments of these ideals should be: The preservation of self-government and its full foundations in local government; the perfection of justice whether in economic or in social fields; the maintenance of ordered liberty; the denial of domination by any group or class; the building up and preservation of equality of opportunity; the stimulation of initiative and individuality; absolute integrity in public affairs; the choice of officials for fitness to office; the direction of economic progress toward prosperity for the further lessening of poverty; the freedom of public opinion; the sustaining of education and of the advancement of knowledge; the growth of religious spirit and the tolerance of all faiths; the strengthening of the home; the advancement of peace.

There is no short road to the realization of these aspirations. Ours is a progressive people, but with a determination that progress must be based upon the foundation of experience. Ill-considered remedies for our faults bring only penalties after them. But if we hold the faith of the men in our mighty past who created these ideals, we shall leave them heightened and strengthened for our children.

Conclusion. This is not the time and place for extended discussion. The questions before our country are problems of progress to higher standards; they are not the problems of degeneration. They demand thought and they serve to quicken the conscience and enlist our sense of responsibility for their settlement. And that responsibility rests upon you, my countrymen, as much as upon those of us who have been selected for office.

Ours is a land rich in resources; stimulating in its glorious beauty; filled with millions of happy homes; blessed with comfort and opportunity. In no nation are the institutions of progress more advanced. In no nation are the fruits of accomplishment more secure. In no nation is the government more worthy of respect. No country is more loved by its people. I have an abiding faith in their capacity, integrity and high purpose. I have no fears for the future of our country. It is bright with hope.

In the presence of my countrymen, mindful of the solemnity of this occasion, knowing what the task means and the responsibility which it involves, I beg your tolerance, your aid, and your cooperation. I ask the help of Almighty God in this service to my country to which you have called me.

24. THE AMERICAN CIVIL LIBERTIES UNION CREED, 1929

We stand on the general principle that all thought on matters of public concerns should be freely expressed without interference. Orderly social progress is promoted by unrestricted freedom of opinion. The punishment of mere opinion, without overt acts, is never in the interest of orderly progress. Suppression of opinion makes for violence and bloodshed.

The principle of freedom of speech, press and assemblage, embodied in our constitutional law, must be reasserted in its application to American conditions today. That application must deal with various methods now used to repress new ideas and democratic movements. The following paragraphs cover the most significant of the tactics of repression in the United States today.

1. Free Speech.   There should be no control whatever in advance over what any person may say.

The right to meet and to speak freely without permit should be unquestioned.

There should be no prosecutions for the mere expression of opinion on matters of public concern, however radical, however violent. The expression of all opinions, however, radical, should be tolerated. The fullest freedom of speech should be encouraged by setting aside special places in streets or parks and in the use of public buildings, free of charge, for public meetings of any sort.

2. Free Press.   There should be no censorship over the mails by the post-office or any other agency at any time or in any way. Printed matter should never be subjected to a political censorship. The granting or revoking of second class mailing privileges should have nothing whatever to do with a paper's opinions and policies.

If libelous, fraudulent, or other illegal matter is being circulated, it should be seized by proper warrant through the prosecuting authorities, not by the post-office department. The business of the post-office department is to carry the mails, not to investigate crime or to act as censors.

There should be no control over the distribution of literature at meetings or hand to hand in public or in private places. No system of licenses for distribution should be tolerated.

3. Freedom of Assemblage.   Meetings in public places, parades and processions should be freely permitted, the only reasonable regulation being the advance notification to the police of the time and place. No discretion should be given the police to prohibit parades or processions, but merely to alter routes in accordance with the imperative demands of traffic in crowded cities. There should be no laws or regulations prohibiting the display of red flags or other political emblems.

The right of assemblage is involved in the right to picket in time of strike. Peaceful picketing, therefore, should not be prohibited, regulated by injunction, by order of court or by police edict. It is the business of the police in places where picketing is conducted merely to keep traffic free and to handle specific violations of law against persons upon complaint.

4. The Right to Strike.   The right of workers to organize in organizations of their own choosing, and to strike, should never be infringed by law.

Compulsory arbitration is to be condemned not only because it destroys the workers' right to strike, but because it lays emphasis on one set of obligations along those of workers to society.

5. Law Enforcement.   The practice of deputizing privately paid police as general police officers should be opposed. So should the attempts of private company employees to police the streets or property other than that of the company.

The efforts of private associations to take into their own hands the enforcement of law should be opposed at every point. Public officials, employees of private corporations, and leaders of mobs, who interfere with the exercise of the constitutionally established rights of free speech and free assembly, should be vigorously proceeded against.

The sending of troops into areas of industrial conflict to maintain law and order almost inevitably results in the government taking sides in an industrial conflict in behalf of the employer. The presence of troops, whether or not martial law is declared, very rarely affects the employer adversely, but it usually results in the complete denial of civil rights to the workers.

6. Search and Seizure.   It is the custom of certain federal, state, and city officials, particularly in cases involving civil liberty, to make arrests without warrant, to enter upon private property, and to seize papers and literature without legal process. Such practices should be contested. Officials so violating constitutional guarantees should be proceeded against.

7. The Right to a Fair Trial.   Every person charged with an offense should have the fullest opportunity for a fair trial, for securing counsel and bail in a reasonable sum. In the case of a poor person, special aid should be organized to secure a fair trial, and when necessary, an appeal. The legal profession should be alert to defend cases involving civil liberty. The resolutions of various associations of lawyers against taking cases of radicals are wholly against the traditions of American liberty.

8. Immigration, Deportation and Passports. No person should be refused admission to the United States on the ground of holding objectionable opinions. The present restrictions against radicals of various beliefs is wholly opposed to our tradition of political asylum.

No alien should be deported merely for the expression of opinion or for membership in a radical or revolutionary organization. This is as un-American a practice as the prosecution of citizens for expression of opinion.

The attempt to revoke naturalization papers in order to declare a citizen an alien subject to deportation is a perversion of a law which was intended to cover only cases of fraud.

Citizenship papers should not be refused to any alien because of the expression of radical views, or activities in the cause of labor.

The granting of passports to or from the United States should not be dependent merely upon the opinions of citizens or membership in radical or labor organizations.

9. Liberty in Education.   The attempts to maintain a uniform orthodox opinion among teachers should be opposed. The attempts of educational authorities to inject into public school and college instruction propaganda in the interest of any particular theory of society to the exclusion of others should be opposed.

10. Race Equality.   Every attempt to discriminate between races in the application of all principles of civil liberty here set forth should be opposed.

How to Get Civil Liberty

We realize that these standards of civil liberty cannot be attained as abstract principles or as constitutional guarantees. Economic or political power is necessary to assert and maintain "rights." In the midst of any conflict they are not granted by the side holding the economic and political power, except as they may be forced by the strength of the opposition. However, the mere public assertion of the principle of freedom of opinion in the words or deeds of individuals, or weak minorities, helps win it recognition, and in the long run makes for tolerance and against resort to violence.

Today the organized movements of labor and of the farmers are waging the chief fight for civil liberty throughout the United States as part of their effort for increased control of industry. Publicity, demonstrations, political activities and legal aid are organized nationally and locally. Only by such an aggressive policy of insistence can rights be secured and maintained. The union of organized labor, the farmers, radical and liberal movements is the most effective means to this.

It is these forces which the American Civil Liberties Union serves in their efforts for civil liberty. The practical work of free speech demonstrations, publicity and legal defense is done primarily in the struggles of the organized labor and farmers movements.

25. SINCLAIR LEWIS, "THE AMERICAN FEAR OF LITERATURE," DECEMBER 12, 1930

Speech delivered on the acceptance of the Nobel Prize in Literature

Were I to express my feeling of honor and pleasure of having been awarded the Nobel Prize in Literature, I should be fulsome and perhaps tedious, and I present my gratitude with a plain "Thank you."

I wish, in this address, to consider certain trends, certain dangers, and certain high and exciting promises in present-day American literature. To discuss this with complete and unguarded frankness—and I should not insult you by being otherwise than completely honest, however indiscreet—it will be necessary for me to be a little impolite regarding certain institutions and persons of my own greatly beloved land.

But I beg of you to believe that I am in no case gratifying a grudge. Fortune has dealt with me rather too well. I have known little struggle, not much poverty, many generosities. Now and then I have, for my books or myself, been somewhat warmly denounced—there was one good pastor in California who upon reading my *Elmer Gantry* desired to lead a mob and lynch me, while another holy man in the State of Maine wondered if there was no respectable and righteous way of putting me in jail. And, much harder to endure than any raging condemnation, a certain number of old acquaintances among journalists, what in the galloping American slang we call the "I Knew Him When Club," have scribbled that since they know me personally, therefore I must be a rather low sort of fellow and certainly no writer. But if I have now and then received such cheering brickbats, still I, who have heaved a good many bricks myself, would be fatuous not to expect a fair number in return.

No, I have for myself no conceivable complaint to make, and yet for American literature in general, and its standing in a country where industrialism and finance and science flourish and the only arts that are vital and respected are architecture and the film, I have a considerable complaint.

I can illustrate by an incident which chances to concern the Swedish Academy and myself and which happened a few days ago, just before I took ship at New York for Sweden. There is in America a learned and most amiable old gentlemen who has been a pastor, a university professor, and a diplomat. He is a member of the American Academy of Arts and Letters and no few universities have honored him with degrees. As a writer he is chiefly known for his pleasant little essays on the joy of fishing. I do not suppose that professional fishermen, whose lives depend on the run of cod or herring, find it altogether an amusing occupation, but from these essays I learned, as a boy, that there is something very important and spiritual about catching fish, if you have no need of doing so.

This scholar stated, and publicly, that in awarding the Nobel Prize to a person who has scoffed at American institutions as much as I have, the Nobel Committee and the Swedish Academy had insulted America. I don't know whether, as an ex-diplomat, he intends to have an international incident made of it, and perhaps demand of the American Government that they land Marines in Stockholm to protect American literary rights, but I hope not.

I should have supposed that to a man so learned as to have been made a Doctor if Divinity, a Doctor of Letters, and I do not know how many other imposing magnificences, the matter would have seemed different; I should have supposed that he would have reasoned, "Although personally I dislike this man's books, nevertheless the Swedish Academy has in choosing him honored America by assuming that the Americans are no longer a puerile backwoods clan, so inferior that they are afraid of criticism, but instead a nation come of age and able to consider calmly and maturely any dissection of their land, however scoffing."

I should even have supposed that so international a scholar would have believed that Scandinavia, accustomed to the works of Strindberg, Ibsen, and Pontoppidan, would not have been peculiarly shocked by a writer whose most anarchistic assertion has been that America, with all her wealth and power, has not yet produced a civilization good enough to satisfy the deepest wants of human creatures.

I believe that Strindberg rarely sang the "Star-Spangled Banner" or addressed Rotary Clubs, yet Sweden seems to have survived him.

I have at such length discussed this criticism of the learned fisherman not because it has any conceivable importance in itself, but because it does illustrate the fact that in America most of us—not readers alone but even writers—are still afraid of any literature which is not a glorification of everything American, a glorification of our faults as well as our virtues. To be not only a best-seller in America but to be really beloved, a novelist must assert that all American men are tall, handsome, rich, and honest, and powerful at golf; that all country towns are filled with neighbors who do nothing from day to day save go about being kind to one another; that although American girls may be wild, they change always into perfect wives and mothers; and that, geographically, America is composed solely of New York, which is inhabited entirely by millionaires;

of the West, which keeps unchanged all the boisterous heroism of 1870; and of the South, where every one lives on a plantation perpetually glossy with moonlight and scented with magnolias.

It is not today vastly more true than it was twenty years ago that such novelists of ours as you have read in Sweden, novelists like Dreiser and Willa Cather, are authentically popular and influential in America. As it was revealed by the venerable fishing Academician whom I have quoted, we still most revere the writers for the popular magazines who in a hearty and edifying chorus chant that the America of a hundred and twenty million population is still as simple, as pastoral, as it was when it had but forty million; that in an industrial plant with ten thousand employees, the relationship between the worker and the manager is still as neighborly and uncomplex as in a factory of 1840, with five employees; that the relationships between father and son, between husband and wife, are precisely the same in an apartment in a thirty-story palace today, with three motor cars awaiting the family below and five books on the library shelves and a divorce imminent in the family next week, as were those relationships in a rose-veiled five-room cottage in 1880; that, in fine, America has gone through the revolutionary change from rustic colony to world-empire without having in the least altered the bucolic and Puritanic simplicity of Uncle Sam.

I am, actually, extremely grateful to the fishing Academician for having somewhat condemned me. For since he is a leading member of the American Academy of Arts and Letters, he has released me, has given me the right to speak as frankly of that Academy as he has spoken of me. And in any honest study of American intellectualism today, that curious institution must be considered.

Before I consider the Academy, however, let me sketch a fantasy which has pleased me the last few days in the unavoidable idleness of a rough trip on the Atlantic. I am sure that you know, by now, that the award to me of the Nobel Prize has by no means been altogether popular in America. Doubtless the experience is not new to you. I fancy that when you have the award even to Thomas Mann, whose *Zauberberg* seems to me to contain the whole of intellectual Europe, even when you gave it to Kipling, whose social significance is so profound that it has been rather authoritatively said that he created the British Empire, even when you gave it to Bernard Shaw, there were countrymen of those authors who complained because you did not choose another.

And I imagined what would have been said had you chosen some American other than myself. Suppose you had taken Theodore Dreiser.

Now to me, as to many other American writers, Dreiser more than any other man, marching alone, usually unappreciated, often hated, has cleared the trail from Victorian and Howellsian timidity and gentility in American fiction to honesty and boldness and passion of life. Without his pioneering, I doubt if any of us could, unless we liked to be sent to jail, seek to express life and beauty and terror.

My great colleague Sherwood Anderson has proclaimed this leadership of Dreiser. I am delighted to join him. Dreiser's great first novel, *Sister Carrie,* which he dared to publish thirty long years ago and which I read twenty-five years ago, came to housebound and airless America like a great free Western wind, and to our stuffy domesticity gave us the first fresh air since Mark Twain and Whitman.

Yet had you given the Prize to Mr. Dreiser, you would have heard groans from America; you would have heard that his style—I am not exactly sure what this mystic quality "style" may be, but I find the word so often in the writing of minor critics that I suppose it must exist—you would have heard that his style is cumbersome, that his choice of words is insensitive, that his books are interminable. And certainly respectable scholars would complain that in Mr. Dreiser's world, men and women are often sinful and tragic and despairing, instead of being forever sunny and full of song and virtue, as befits authentic Americans.

And had you chosen Mr. Eugene O'Neill, who has done nothing much in American drama save to transform it utterly, in ten or twelve years, from a false world of neat and competent trickery to a world of splendor and fear and greatness, you would have been reminded that he has done something far worse than scoffing—he has seen life as not to be neatly arranged in the study of a scholar, but as a terrifying, magnificent and often quite horrible thing akin to the tornado, the earthquake, and the devastating fire.

And had you given Mr. James Branch Cabell the Prize, you would have been told that he is too fantastically malicious. So would you have been told that Miss Willa Cather, for all the homely virtue of her novels concerning the peasants of Nebraska, has in her novel, *The Lost Lady,* been so untrue to America's patent and perpetual and possibly tedious virtuousness as to picture an abandoned women who remains, nevertheless, uncannily charming even to the virtuous, in a story without any moral; that Mr. Henry Mencken is the worst of all scoffers; that Mr. Sherwood Anderson viciously errs in considering sex as important a force in life as fishing; that Mr. Upton Sinclair, being a Socialist, sins against the perfectness of American capitalistic mass-production; that Mr. Joseph Hergesheimer is un-American in regarding graciousness of manner and beauty of surface as of some importance in the endurance of daily life; and that Mr. Ernest Hemingway is not only too young but, far worse, uses language which should be unknown to gentlemen; that he acknowledges drunkenness as one of man's eternal ways to happiness, and asserts that a soldier may find love more significant than the hearty slaughter of men in battle.

Yes, they are wicked, these colleagues of mine; you would have done almost as evilly to have chosen them as to have chosen me; and as a chauvinistic American—only, mind you, as an American of 1930 and not of 1880—I rejoice that they are my countrymen and countrywomen, and that I may speak of them with pride even in the Europe of Thomas Mann, H. G. Wells, Galsworthy, Knut Hamsun, Arnold Bennett, Feuchtwanger, Selma Lagerlof, Sigrid Unset, Werner von Heidenstam, D'Annunzio, Romain Rolland.

It is my fate in this paper to swing constantly from optimism to pessimism and back, but so is it the fate of any one who writes or speaks of anything in America—the most contradictory, the most depressing, the most stirring, of any land in the world today.

Thus, having with no muted pride called the roll of what seem to me to be great men and women in American literary life today, and having indeed omitted a dozen other names of which I should like to boast were there time, I must turn again and assert that in our contemporary American literature, indeed in all American arts save architecture and the film, we—yes, we who have such pregnant and vigorous standards in commerce and science—have no standards, no healing communication, no heroes to be followed nor villains to be condemned, no certain ways to be pursued and no dangerous paths to be avoided.

The American novelist or poet or dramatist or sculptor or painter must work alone, in confusion, unassisted save by his own integrity.

That, of course, has always been the lot of the artist. The vagabond and criminal François Villon had certainly no smug and comfortable refuge in which elegant ladies would hold his hand and comfort his starveling soul and more starved body. He, veritably a great man, destined to outlive in history all the dukes and puissant cardinals whose robes he was esteemed untrustworthy to touch, had for his lot the gutter and the hardened crust.

Such poverty is not for the artist in America. They pay us, indeed, only too well; that writer is a failure who cannot have his butler and motor and his villa at Palm Beach, where he is permitted to mingle almost in equality with the barons of banking. But he is oppressed ever by something worse than poverty—by the feeling that what he creates does not matter, that he is expected by his readers to be only a decorator or a clown, or that he is good-naturedly accepted as a scoffer whose bark probably is worse than his bite and who probably is a good fellow at heart, who in any case certainly does not count in a land that produces eighty-story buildings, motors by the million, and wheat by the billions of bushels. And he has no institution, no group, to which he can turn for inspiration, whose criticism he can accept and whose praise will be precious to him.

What institution have we?

The American Academy of Arts and Letters does contain along with several excellent painters and architects and statesmen, such a really distinguished university-president as Nicholas Murray Butler, so admirable and courageous a scholar as Wilbur Cross, and several first-rate writers: the poets Edwin Arlington Robinson and Robert Frost, the free-minded publicist James Truslow Adams, and the novelists Edith Wharton, Hamlin Garland, Owen Wister, Brand Whitlock and Booth Tarkington.

But it does not include Theodore Dreiser, Henry Mencken, our most vivid critic, George Jean Nathan who, though still young, is certainly the dean of our dramatic critics, Eugene O'Neill, incomparably our best dramatist, the really original and vital poets, Edna St. Vincent Millay and Carl Sandburg, Robinson Jeffers and Vachel Lindsay and Edgar Lee Masters, whose *Spoon River Anthology* was so utterly different from any other poetry ever published, so fresh, so authoritative, so free from any groupings and timidities that it came like a revelation, and created a new school of native American poetry. It does not include the novelists and short-story writers, Willa Cather, Joseph Hergesheimer, Sherwood Anderson, Ring Lardner, Ernest Hemingway, Louis Bromfield, Wilbur Daniel Steele, Fannie Hurst, Mary Austin, James Branch Cabell, Edna Ferber, nor Upton Sinclair, of whom you must say, whether you admire or detest his aggressive Socialism, that he is internationally better known than any other American artist whosoever, be he novelist, poet, painter, sculptor, musician, architect.

I should not expect any Academy to be so fortunate as to contain all these writers, but one which fails to contain any of them, which thus cuts itself off from so much of what is living and vigorous and original in American letters, can have no relationship whatever to our life and aspirations. It does not represent literary America of today—it represents only Henry Wadsworth Longfellow.

It might be answered that, after all, the Academy is limited to fifty members; that, naturally, it cannot include every one of merit. But the fact is that while most of our few giants are excluded, the Academy does have room to include three extraordinary bad poets, two very melodramatic and insignificant playwrights, two gentlemen who are known only because they are university professors, a man who was thirty years ago known as a rather clever humorous draughtsman, and several gentlemen of whom—I sadly confess my ignorance—I have never heard.

Let me again emphasize the fact—for it is a fact—that I am not attacking the American Academy. It is a hospitable and generous and decidedly dignified institution. And it is not altogether the Academy's fault that it does not contain many of the men who have significance in our letters. Sometimes it is the fault of those writers themselves. I cannot imagine that grizzly-bear Theodore Dreiser being comfortable at the serenely Athenian dinners of the Academy, and were they to invite Mencken, he would infuriate them with his boisterous jeering. No, I am not attacking—I am reluctantly considering the Academy because it is so perfect an example of the divorce in America of intellectual life from all authentic standards of importance and reality.

Our universities and colleges, or gymnasia, most of them, exhibit the same unfortunate divorce. I can think of four of them, Rollins College in Florida, Middlebury College in Vermont, the University of Michigan, and the University of Chicago—which has had on its roll so excellent a novelist as Robert Herrick, so courageous a critic as Robert Morss Lovett—which have shown an authentic interest in contemporary creative literature. Four of them. But universities and colleges and musical emporiums and schools for the teaching of theology and plumbing and signpainting are as thick in America as the motor traffic. Whenever you see a public building with Gothic

Fenestration on a sturdy backing of Indiana concrete, you may be certain that it is another university, with anywhere from two hundred to twenty thousand students equally ardent about avoiding the disadvantage of becoming learned and about gaining the social prestige contained in the possession of a B.A. degree.

Oh, socially our universities are close to the mass of our citizens, and so are they in the matter of athletics. A great college football game is passionately witnessed by eighty thousand people, who have paid five dollars apiece and motored anywhere from ten to a thousand miles for the ecstasy of watching twenty-two men chase one another up and down a curiously marked field. During the football season, a capable player ranks very nearly with our greatest and most admired heroes—even with Henry Ford, President Hoover, and Colonel Lindbergh.

And in one branch of learning, the sciences, the lords of business who rule us are willing to do homage to the devotees of learning. However bleakly one of our trader aristocrats may frown upon poetry or the visions of a painter, he is graciously pleased to endure a Millikan, a Michelson, a Banting, a Theobald Smith.

But the paradox is that in the arts our universities are as cloistered, as far from reality and living creation, as socially and athletically and scientifically they are close to us. To a true-blue professor of literature in an American university, literature is not something that a plain human being, living today, painfully sits down to produce. No; it is something dead; it is something magically produced by superhuman beings who must, if they are to be regarded as artists at all, have died at least one hundred years before the diabolical invention of the typewriter. To any authentic don, there is something slightly repulsive in the thought that literature could be created by any ordinary human being, still to be seen walking the streets, wearing quite commonplace trousers and coat and looking not so unlike a chauffeur or a farmer. Our American professors like their literature clear and cold and pure and very dead.

I do not suppose that American universities are alone in this. I am aware that to the dons of Oxford and Cambridge, it would seem rather indecent to suggest that Wells and Bennett and Galsworthy and George Moore may, while they commit the impropriety of continuing to live, be compared to any one so beautifully and safely dead as Samuel Johnson. I suppose that in the universities of Sweden and France and Germany there exist plenty of professors who prefer dissection to understanding. But in the new and vital and experimental land of America, one would expect the teachers of literature to be less monastic, more human, than in the traditional shadows of old Europe.

They are not.

There has recently appeared in America, out of the universities, as astonishing circus called "the new Humanism." Now of course "humanism" means so many things that it means nothing. It may infer anything from a belief that Greek and Latin are more inspiring than the dialect of contemporary peasants to a belief that any living peasant is more interesting than a dead Greek. But it is a delicate bit of justice that this nebulous word should have been chosen to label this nebulous cult.

Insofar as I have been able to comprehend them—for naturally in a world so exciting and promising as this today, as life brilliant with Zeppelins and Chinese revolutions and the Bolshevik industrialization of farming and ships and the Grand Canyon and young children and terrifying hunger and the lonely quest of scientists after God, no creative writer would have time to follow all the chilly enthusiasm of the New Humanists—this newest of sects reasserts the dualism of man's nature. It would continue literature to the fight between man's soul and God, or man's soul and evil.

But, curiously, neither God nor the devil may wear modern dress, but must retain Grecian vestments. Oedipus is a tragic figure for the New Humanists; man, trying to maintain himself as the image of God under the menace of dynamos, in a world of high-pressure salesmanship, is not. And the poor comfort which they offer is that the object of life is to develop self-discipline—whether or not one ever accomplishes anything with this self-discipline. So this whole movement results in the not particularly novel doctrine that both art and life must be resigned and negative. It is a doctrine of the blackest reaction introduced into a stirringly revolutionary world.

Strangely enough, this doctrine of death, this escape from the complexities and danger of living into the secure blankness of the monastery, has become widely popular among professors in a land where one would have expected only boldness and intellectual adventure, and it has more than ever shut creative writers off from any benign influence which might conceivably have come from the universities.

But it has always been so. America has never had a Brandes, a Taine, a Goethe, a Croce.

With a wealth of creative talent in America, our criticism has most of it been a chill and insignificant activity pursued by jealous spinsters, ex-baseball-reporters, and acid professors. Our Erasmuses have been village schoolmistresses. How should there be any standards when there has been no one capable of setting them up?

The great Cambridge-Concord circle of the middle of the Nineteenth Century—Emerson, Longfellow, Lowell, Holmes, the Alcotts—were sentimental reflections of Europe, and they left no school, no influence. Whitman and Thoreau and Poe and, in some degree, Hawthorne, were outcasts, men alone and despised, berated by the New Humanists of their generation. It was with the emergence of William Dean Howells that we first began to have something like a standard, and a very bad standard it was.

Mr. Howells was one of the gentlest, sweetest, and most honest of men, but he had the code of a pious old maid whose greatest delight was to have tea at the vicarage. He abhorred not only profanity and obscenity but all of what H. G. Wells has called "the jolly coarseness of life." In this fantastic vision of life, which he innocently conceived to be realistic, farmers and seamen and factory-hands might exist, but the farmer must never be covered with muck, the seaman must never roll out bawdy chanteys, the factory-hand must be thankful to his good employer, and all of them must long for the opportunity to visit Florence and smile gently at the quaintness of the beggars.

So strongly did Howells feel this genteel, this New Humanistic philosophy that he was able vastly to influence his contemporaries, down even to 1914 and the turmoil of the Great War.

He was actually able to tame Mark Twain, perhaps the greatest of our writers, and to put that fiery old savage into an intellectual frock coat and top hat. His influence is not altogether gone today. He is still worshipped by Hamlin Garland, an author who should in every way have been greater than Howells but who under Howells' influence was changed from a harsh and magnificent realist into a genial and insignificant lecturer. Mr. Garland is, so far as we have one, the dean of American letters today, and as our dean, he is alarmed by all of the younger writers who are so lacking in taste as to suggest that men and women do not always love in accordance with the prayer-book, and that common people sometimes use language which would be inappropriate at a women's literary club on Main Street. Yet this same Hamlin Garland, as a young man, before he had gone to Boston and become cultured and Howellized, wrote two most valiant and revelatory works of realism, *Main-Travelled Roads* and *Rose of Dutcher's Coolly.*

I read them as a boy in a prairie village in Minnesota—just such an environment as was described in Mr. Garland's tales. They were vastly exciting to me. I had realized in reading Balzac and Dickens that it was possible to describe French and English common people as one actually saw them. But it had never occurred to me that one might without indecency write of the people of Sauk Centre, Minnesota, as one felt about them. Our fictional tradition, you see, was that all of us in Midwestern villages were altogether noble and happy; that not one of us would exchange the neighborly bliss of living on Main Street for the heathen gaudiness of New York or Paris or Stockholm. But in Mr. Garland's *Main-Travelled Roads* I discovered that there was one man who believed that Midwestern peasants were sometimes bewildered and hungry and vile—and heroic. And, given this vision, I was released; I could write of life as living life.

I am afraid that Mr. Garland would not be pleased but acutely annoyed to know that he made it possible for me to write of America as I see it, and not as Mr. William Dean Howells so sunnily saw it. And it is his tragedy, it is a complete revelatory American tragedy, that in our land of freedom, men like Garland, who first blast the roads to freedom, become themselves the most bound.

But, all this time, while men like Howells were so effusively seeking to guide America into becoming a pale edition of an English cathedral town, there were surly and authentic fellows—Whitman and Melville, then Dreiser and James Huneker and Mencken—who insisted that our land had something more than tea-table gentility.

And so, without standards, we have survived. And for the strong young men, it has perhaps been well that we should have no standards. For, after seeming to be pessimistic about my own and much beloved land, I want to close this dirge with a very lively sound of optimism.

I have, for the future of American literature, every hope and every eager belief. We are coming out, I believe, of the stuffiness of safe, sane, and incredibly dull provincialism. There are young Americans today who are doing such passionate and authentic work that it makes me sick to see that I am a little too old to be one of them.

There is Ernest Hemingway, a bitter youth, educated by the most intense experience, disciplined by

his own high standards, an authentic artist whose home is in the whole of life; there is Thomas Wolfe, a child of, I believe, thirty or younger, whose one and only novel, *Look Homeward, Angel,* is worthy to be compared with the best in our literary production, a Gargantuan creature with great gusto of life; there is Thornton Wilder, who in an age of realism dreams the old and lovely dreams of the eternal romantics; there is Stephen Benét who, to American drabness, has restored the epic poem with his glorious memory of old John Brown; and there are a dozen other young poets and fictioneers, most of them living now in Paris, most of them a little insane in the tradition of James Joyce, who, however insane they may be, have refused to be genteel and traditional and dull.

I salute them, with a joy in being not yet too far removed from their determination to give to the America that has mountains and endless prairies, enormous cities and lost farm cabins, billions of money and tons of faith, to an America that is as strange as Russia and as complex as China, a literature worthy of her vastness.

26. FROM THE REPORT OF THE WICKERSHAM COMMISSION ON PROHIBITION, JANUARY 20, 1931
II. THE PRESENT CONDITION AS TO OBSERVANCE AND ENFORCEMENT

Observance

There is a mass of information before us as to a general prevalence of drinking in homes, in clubs, and in hotels; of drinking parties given and attended by persons of high standing and respectability; of drinking by tourists at winter and summer resorts; and of drinking in connection with public dinners and at conventions. In the nature of the case it is not easy to get at the exact facts in such a connection, and conditions differ somewhat in different parts of the country and even to some extent from year to year. This is true likewise with respect to drinking by women and drinking by youth, as to which also there is a great mass of evidence. In weighing this evidence much allowance must be made for the effect of new standards of independence and individual self-assertion, changed ideas as to conduct generally, and the greater emphasis on freedom and the quest for excitement since the war. As to drinking among youth, the evidence is conflicting. Votes in colleges show an attitude of hostility to or contempt for the law on the part of those who are not unlikely to be leaders in the next generation. It is safe to say that a significant change has taken place in the social attitude toward drinking. This may be seen in the views and conduct of social leaders, business and professional men in the average community. It may be seen in the tolerance of conduct at social gatherings which would not have been possible a generation ago. It is reflected in a different way of regarding drunken youth, in a change in the class of excessive drinkers, and in the increased use of distilled liquor in places and connections where formerly it was banned. It is evident that, taking the country as a whole, people of wealth, businessmen and professional men, and their families, and, perhaps, the higher paid workingmen and their families, are drinking in large numbers in quite frank disregard of the declared policy of the National Prohibition Act.

There has been much discussion as to how the consumption of liquor today compares with that before prohibition. It will be necessary to go into that discussion later in considering the amount produced and imported in violation of law. So many purely speculative elements are involved in the making of any figures as to consumption today that in the present connection it is not worth while to make an elaborate review of the statistical material. But it may be remarked that the method of adding to the figures for the period before prohibition, in order to reach a basis of comparison, an annual increase in the proportion shown during the development of organized production and distribution is unsound. That rate of increase could not have gone on indefinitely into the future under any regime. The evidence as to Keely cures, as to arrests for drunkenness and the type of persons found drunk in public, as to deaths from causes attributable to alcohol, as to alcoholic insanity, as to hospital admissions for alcoholism, as to the change in the type of person treated for alcoholism, and as to drunken driving, while in each case subject to much criticism and raising many doubts, yet all seem to point in the same direction.

The Census Bureau figures for the year 1929 indicate a decline in the rate of deaths from alcoholism, and the figures on all the points referred to are still substantially below the pre-prohibition figures. Upon the whole, however, they indicate that after a brief period in the first years of the amendment there has been a steady increase in drinking.

To the serious effects of this attitude of disregard of the declared policy of the National Prohibition Act must be added the bad effect on children and employees of what they see constantly in the conduct of otherwise law abiding persons. Such things and the effect on youth of the making of liquor in homes, in disregard of the policy, if not of the express provisions of the law, the effect on the families of workers of selling in homes, which obtains in many localities, and the effect on working people of the conspicuous newly acquired wealth of their neighbors who have engaged in bootlegging, are disquieting. This widespread and scarcely or not at all concealed contempt for the policy of the National Prohibition Act, and the effects of that contempt, must be weighed against the advantage of diminution (apparently lessening) of the amount in circulation.

These observations are not directed to a comparison between conditions before the Eighteenth Amendment and since, but only to changes taking place during the years since the adoption of the Amendment. The disquieting features above referred to should, of course, be weighed against the recognized fact that very large numbers of people have consistently observed the law.

Enforcement

(a) Enforcement With Respect to Importation and Manufacture

(1) THE SOURCES OF ILLICIT LIQUOR

There are five main sources of illicit liquor: importation, diversion of industrial alcohol, illicit distilling, illicit brewing, and illicit production of wine. In addition, a minor source, namely, diversion of medicinal and sacramental liquor, has at times and in places assumed considerable proportions and must always be borne in mind as a potential mode of supply.

(i) Importation
Importation is chiefly from Canada, both directly and indirectly, since Canada is a large producer and is exceptionally convenient, by proximity and by geographical conditions and conditions of transportation, as a base for smuggling operations. Recently St. Pierre and Miquelon, a group of small islands off Newfoundland, belonging to France, have been growing rapidly in importance as bases for that purpose, both through importations from Canada and as a depot for importations from France. In the Bahamas, Bimini, an island of nine square miles, has become a heavy importer of Canadian whisky, as a depot for Florida, and has been to some extent a depot for supply of rum from the West Indies. The West Indies supply directly a

certain amount. Mexico and Central America have been depots for Canadian whisky. Belize in British Honduras in particular is a depot for supply of the Gulf Coast. Finally, a certain amount, chiefly wines and brandies has been coming from Europe, mostly from France.

Transportation is by land, by water, and by air. Smuggling of liquor by land is by rail or motor, mostly from Canada, and to some small extent by pack animals on the southwestern border. Smuggling by rail takes place chiefly by concealment in or mixing with legitimate freight coming into the United States. It has also been carried on by manipulation of seals and substitution of content or of cars while freight trains were in transit through Canada from one part of the United States to another. Such smugglings of liquor are not easy to prevent because of the importance of not unduly delaying legitimate freight. In order to put a stop to it cooperation of the railroads is needed, and all companies have not always cooperated. Smuggling by motor trucks and automobiles is well organized and is the main factor in land transportation. The conditions of travel today on the main arteries crowd the existing customs facilities beyond the possibility of any adequate control. As to the secondary roads and trails, adequate supervision is substantially impracticable. The organized smugglers are well provided with depots, have excellent equipment, thorough knowledge of the terrain and efficient spies upon the enforcing agencies. Very largely they have neighborhood sympathy behind them. Moreover, there is continual pressure from tourists and travelers to bring in even considerable quantities.

Water transportation is by seagoing vessels, by specially designed or equipped small vessels or boats, by so-called mother boats—with which small craft make connections, or from which they go forth at sea beyond the limits of activity of the Coast Guard, and by river boats. In seagoing vessels liquor comes concealed about the ship for example, mixing cases of or mixed with the legitimate cargo, as, liquor falsely labeled with cases of properly labeled freight. It is difficult for the customs authorities to deal with such things at the more important ports because legitimate freight should not be delayed in transit, because of lack of space in crowded docks for adequate examination, and for lack of enough inspectors. The usual course is to hold for examination one-tenth of all cases, bales, or bundles, taken at random. But substitution by longshoremen or dock

workers and other devices have been used to defeat this method.

Small motor boats may go direct between points on the great lakes, between the Bahamas and the Florida coast, at times from St. Pierre and Miquelon to New England, and on Puget Sound. There has been a high development of special boats for this purpose. Also smuggling through so-called mother boats has been highly developed along all coasts. This form of transportation has been elaborately organized, often with special craft, with radio stations, and with efficient service for soliciting business, directing the movements of boats, ascertaining the movements of enforcement agents, and giving warning of their activities. It has developed all manner of ingenious apparatus, using the newest methods of engineering and of science. The organizations can operate profitably if they can land one boat load of five. The margin of profit is more than enough to take care of all ordinary activities of enforcement agencies. When an organization of this sort is broken up, it is quickly set up again by reorganization of experienced violators knowing exactly what to do and how to do it.

River boats have been active in the past at Detroit and Buffalo, and were especially effective at Detroit. Coordination of the enforcement services at Detroit made a noteworthy change there. But there is evidence that the real effect was to change the locus of smuggling. The figures as to decreased declarations opposite Detroit are impressive until one observes that the deficiencies were more than made up by increases at other points in the long and difficult river boundary between Lake Huron and Lake Erie. It is easy for smugglers to shift the base from one point to another and the shiftings are hard to keep up with . . .

Whisky, either directly or indirectly from Canada, forms the bulk of illicit importation. A considerable quantity of beer also comes from Canada and some wines and brandy. Rum comes in from the West Indies, and occasionally certain amounts of brandy from France and gin from Holland. An unknown amount of wine comes from France, both direct and by way of St. Pierre and Miquelon. That this is by no means inconsiderable is shown by the extent to which these wines are possessed and seem to be procurable not merely along the Atlantic Coast but in cities well in the interior.

It is not easy to estimate with assurance the amount imported. But estimates on the basis of the declarations for export from Canada to the United States prior to the recent action of the Canadian government, are fallacious. In three years ending in 1929, while the reexports of whisky, all of which but a negligible few gallons had gone to the United States, had multiplied by between four and five, the amounts of Canadian whisky declared for export.

(iii) Illicit Distilling

Moonshining had gone on in the region of the Appalachian region from the federal excise law of 1791 down to the National Prohibition Act. The unproductiveness of soil, the lack of occupational opportunities, and the difficulty of utilizing otherwise scanty harvests of corn in that region, made illicit distilling, in defiance of the federal revenue laws, a settled feature of mountain life. After prohibition this practice got a great impetus. For a time illicit distilling went on in the old way . . . But presently it spread to all parts of the land and reached a high degree of development not only in the region where moonshining had always gone on, but also in and about the large cities and in remote districts everywhere. In 1913 the Commissioner of Internal Revenue reported the seizure of 2,375 stills . . . In 1929, in one state alone, the state seized more than this number and the federal government half as many more. For the whole country, the federal seizures of stills were six times as many as in 1913, and the total of state and federal seizures was well over twelve times as many.

Just as the steadily growing market for industrial alcohol led to improved methods and use of new raw materials admitting of greater speed and quantity of production in legitimate distilling, so the growing demand for distilled liquor after the National Prohibition Act led to discovery of new and improved apparatus, new methods and new materials for illicit production. In particular, it has led to discovery of new methods of speedy ageing whereby liquor of good quality may be made in a very short time. The methods of the pre-prohibition moonshiner are as obsolete as those of the pre-prohibition legitimate distiller.

With the discovery and perfection of these new methods, illicit distilling has become for the time being the chief source of supply. In place of the small still operated by the individual moonshiner, there are plants of a capacity fairly comparable to the old-time lawful distillery and all gradations, according to conditions of the locality, between these and the individually operated still turning out but a few gallons.

In consequence of the high development of illicit distilling, a steady volume of whiskey, much of it of good quality, is put in circulation; and the prices at which it is obtainable are a convincing testimony to the ineffectiveness of enforcement as against this source of supply. The improved methods, the perfection of organization, the case of production, the cheapness and easy accessibility of materials, the abundance of localities where such plants can be operated with a minimum risk of discovery, the ease with which they may be concealed, and the huge profits involved have enabled this business to become established—to an extent which makes it very difficult to put to an end.

(iv) Production of Beer

At the time of the National Prohibition Act, brewing was a strong, well-organized industry. It had been originally an industry of local brewers supplying local trade and of vast numbers of small breweries in large cities. But towards the end of the nineteenth century came consolidations and reorganizations on modern lines and elimination to a large degree of local and small breweries. Thus, although the number of breweries in the United States had increased nearly two and one-half times between 1860 and 1880, by 1918 the number had fallen back very nearly to that of fifty-eight years before. This falling off was by no means due wholly to the spread of prohibitory laws. That it was largely due to changed organization of the industry is indicated by the circumstance that in the more populous states where prohibition did not obtain before the Eighteenth Amendment, there had been substantially the same increase in number between 1860 and 1880 and decrease between 1880 and 1918. The weaker enterprises had been for the most part merged with the stronger or abandoned. Moreover, the stronger breweries with modern organization and management had set up a vigorous national organization which is still maintained.

Under the National Prohibition Act the distilleries were enabled to go on as producers of industrial alcohol or of medicinal while the brewers were put out of business, except as they could produce cereal beverage of less than one-half of one per cent of alcohol. They had to devise and work up a new demand or go out of existence. Obviously such a situation was full of possibilities.

After a brief period of making by arrested fermentation, the government allowed cereal beverages to be produced by making beer and dealcoholizing. Beer is made and stored and the alcohol is taken out as cereal beverage. Under such circumstances, control of the production of cereal beverage is clearly necessary. This control is provided for in two ways: (1) permits for production, granted and revoked under provisions of the statute and regulations much as in the case of industrial alcohol, and (2) supervision of production.

. . . Abuses in the production of cereal beverage grow chiefly out of the method whereby large quantities of beer are stored at all times, affording many opportunities for it to get into circulation without having been dealcoholized. Employees, whether, with or without the authority or connivance of the employer, have only to put a hose to a tank, fill cereal beverage kegs with real beer, and send it out as cereal beverage. This practice has been hard to detect and has at times been a prolific source of unlawful beer. Sometimes it has been the real or chief business of the brewery. There are producers above suspicion, and since national prohibition the Brewers' Association has urged action against breweries which engage in unlawful competition with the legitimate cereal beverage. But the system which leaves so much to reliance on the integrity of producers and their employees has unfortunate possibilities. Moreover, when the extracted alcohol is sent from one warehouse to another, or to a denaturing plant, there is opportunity for hijacking and other modes of escape. Also there have been cases of realcoholizing of cereal beverage by insertion of alcohol therein.

Other agencies producing beer are unlawful and socalled wildcat breweries and alley breweries. The former are large-scale breweries operated without permits, either breweries whose permits have been revoked, or brewery plants supposed to have been abandoned or to have been converted to new uses, or unauthorized new plants. The alley breweries are smaller, yet often worthy to be called plants and of considerable capacity. Usually they are in the cellar of what appears to be a dwelling. Sometimes they are fitted up in connection with ostensible filling stations, so as to permit of tanks going back and forth without question, with a well organized system of bottling Plants, covered by an apparently legitimate bottling business, and of so-called "drops" for distribution. These are made possible by the development of production of "wort" or cooled boiled mash. As it contains no alcohol, it is outside of effective control under the National Prohibition Act. In consequence since that Act, permittees and others have produced and sold it in large quantities. Prepared in condensed form for fermentation, requiring nothing more than the addition of yeast, it has made the process of alley brewing simple

and easy. One state has imposed a tax upon wort, and the resulting statistics show a very large production.

In some parts of the country enormous sums of money are derived from the business of illicit beer. The profits from illicit beer are the strength of gangs and corrupt political organizations in many places. In more than one locality beer rings and beer barons have made fortunes out of it. They have been able to go on in defiance of law and despite the efforts of enforcement officers. Moreover, an increased demand has been in evidence recently in several large cities, and the effect is seen in increased activity in illicit production. The making of cereal beverage is a legitimate business and cannot reasonably be eliminated. But so long as it is carried on and there is demand for beer in the large cities, the gross margin of profit in supplying beer, the possibilities of escape from the plants, and the manufacture of wort will give trouble for effective enforcement of prohibition. To limit the production of the materials going into beer, many of them admitting of proper uses, involves serious difficulties, to be considered in another connection.

(v) Production of Wine

Wineries are now operated under basic permits granted by the Bureau of Industrial Alcohol. They are subject to a constant inspection by the Bureau. The wine is stored in bonded warehouses and there are periodical inventories by government inspectors. There has been little trouble here. But there is a potential source of trouble in the manufacture of grape juice, which is not subject to federal control. If enforcement presses heavily on other sources, a leak might well develop here. As in the case of wort and malt syrup, incident to the production of cereal beverage, and as in the case of ethyl acetate, a question is presented how far it is advisable to limit or regulate the production of materials which, on the one hand may have proper uses, and yet, on the other hand, may be or are used toward violations of the National Prohibition Act.

(vi) Production in Homes

Home production of liquor takes three forms; home brewing of beer, home wine-making, and home distilling.

At one time there was an increasing amount of home brewing of beer among the average city dwellers, made possible by the production and sale of malt syrup. The beer had a high alcoholic content, for a light beer can be made only by top fermentation, which is not practicable in homes or in small-quantity production. Today there seems to be less of this than formerly because of the inconvenience, the poor quality of the product, and the low cost of procuring whisky. But the recent increased demand for beer in some sections has led to the development of home brewing by people of lesser means not solely for home use but also for sale. The line between this and alley brewing is easily crossed. One may make for himself and a neighbor or neighbors and another for neighbors and for sale. This type of brewing is hard to get at . . .

Home distilling has gone on from the inception of prohibition and in some localities has at one time or another reached large proportions. Few things are more easily made than alcohol. A homemade apparatus will suffice, and with the variety of materials available and the ease of procuring those materials, any one may carry on home distilling on a small scale. The product is of poor quality, but it is cheap. The line between distilling in the home for home use, distilling for neighbors, distilling in part for neighbors and in part for sale and distilling for bootleggers is not definite and is easily overpassed. Also the fact that much home production of liquor goes on everywhere facilitates use of what appear to be dwellings as cloaks for illicit manufacture.

But there is more to be considered than the difficulties of detection without invasions of homes and violations of constitutional guaranties. The bad effects of such operations, on the verge of or in violation of law, carried on in the home, are self evident. Adults living in such an atmosphere of evasion of law and law breaking and children brought up in it are an obstruction to the present enforcement of the law and a serious threat to law and order in the future.

The difficulties presented by home production differ from those arising in other phases of the general situation in that they involve the arousing of resentment through invasion of the home and interference with home life.

Necessity seems to compel the virtual abandonment of efforts for effective enforcement at this point, but it must be recognized that this is done at the price of nullification to that extent. Law here bows to actualities and the purpose of the law needs must be accomplished by less direct means. An enlightened and vigorous, but now long neglected, campaign of education must constitute those means. Through this there can be brought into the home the knowledge of the moral, physical, financial, economic, and social benefits arising from liquor abstinence, and the thought can be impressed that law observance is one of the prime requirements of good citizenship and of the preservation of public and private security. It is not too much to expect that such knowledge will have a very large effect in supplying what the law itself can not furnish and result in a decided and steady diminution of home violations. If such a situation should be reached, the fact that such violations might never completely cease would present only a condition similar to that obtaining in regard to other laws which are commonly considered as being satisfactorily observed.

Whenever substantial law observance is attained, the need ceases for the power of law enforcement.

(vii) Diversion of Medicinal and Sacramental Liquor and Scientific Alcohol

There is division of opinion in the medical profession as to the therapeutic value of alcohol.

Originally the statute allowed physicians to prescribe any kind of liquor, if duly licensed and in active practice, upon obtaining a permit. It was forbidden to prescribe except after a careful examination or, if that was impracticable, upon the best information obtainable and belief in good faith that use of the liquor as a medicine would afford relief from some known ailment. Not more than a pint of spirituous liquor every ten days might be prescribed. The physician was required to keep a record of prescriptions and the prescriptions were to be upon blanks furnished by the government and under regulations whereby strict supervision was possible. In 1921, the Willis-Campbell Act imposed further stringent limitations. The provision for prescribing malt liquors was eliminated. No vinous liquor containing more than 24 per cent of alcohol by volume was to be prescribed, nor more than a quart of vinous liquor, nor any vinous or spirituous liquor containing separately, or in the aggregate, more than one-half pint of alcohol (equivalent to one pint of spirituous liquor) for use by one person within any period within ten days, nor for more than one hundred prescriptions in ninety days.

For a time there was much resentment at this act on the part of the medical profession. But more recently the profession generally has accepted the situation to the extent of admitting the need of some regulation. Physicians still protest, however, against three features of the act and regulations, namely, the limitation of the amount below what they feel may well be necessary, the limitation on the number of prescriptions a physician may make, and the requirement that the ailment for which liquor is prescribed be set forth on the blank which goes on file in the office of the supervisor of permits and is accessible to the public. This requirement runs counter to fundamental conceptions of professional ethics.

An additional embarrassment exists in the diversity of state laws on the subject and the divergence between the state laws in many jurisdictions and the federal statutes and regulations. There are no less than four well marked types of state law, ranging from states which wholly forbid prescribing of liquor in any form for any disease, through different limitations of kind and quantity, to those which impose no restrictions as to what is prescribed or for what purposes or how. Naturally, the medical profession resents the proposition that a lay legislative body may tell physicians what to prescribe and how much. Yet there have been serious abuses which have led to such legislation. While the bulk of the profession have undoubtedly been scrupulous in adherence to the law, prosecutions have been necessary from time to time and palpable evasions or violations come to light continually. Recently in one city, the federal grand jury called attention to the disproportionate increase in liquor prescriptions with no apparent legitimate reason. Moreover, many physicians feel that however unfortunate it may be on principle to regulate by law what may be prescribed for the sick, it is a protection to the honest practitioner to relieve him from the pressure of those who seek prescriptions for beverage purposes. On the other hand, there is evidence that many general practitioners will not take out permits because of the inconvenience and disagreeable features, but advise patients on occasion that they should take this or that amount or kind of liquor and leave it to them to obtain it as they can.

As in other situations already discussed, a balance between the needs of medical practice and the demands of prohibition is called for and is far from easy to attain. But we are satisfied that in several particulars the causes of resentment on the part of the medical profession operate against a favorable public opinion to such an extent as to outweigh the advantages to enforcement.

We recommend: (1) Abolition of the statutory fixing of the amount which may be prescribed and the number of prescriptions; (2) abolition of the requirement of specifying the ailment for which liquor is prescribed upon a blank to go into the public files of the supervisor of permits, leaving this matter to appear on the physician's own records and accessible to the inspector; (3) leaving as much as possible to regulations rather than fixing details by statutes and reliance upon cooperation of the Bureau of Industrial Alcohol with medical associations, national and state, in the same manner in which the Bureau cooperates with distillers and with trade associations; (4) enactment of uniform state laws on this subject, or, in the alternative, repeal of state laws and leaving the whole matter to federal statutes and regulations.

With respect to the use of alcohol for scientific and educational purposes, the language of the statute is unfortunate and should be revised and amplified to cover all such purposes. In order to meet legitimate uses it invites loose construction and consequent potential evasions. To some extent irritation has resulted. Also some alcohol withdrawn for scientific purposes has escaped through theft, and some leaks have occurred through fraud or conspiracy. But there has been no serious trouble at this point.

(b) Enforcement With Respect to Sale

Bootlegging had gone on for at least a generation before the National Prohibition Act, on reservations where sale of liquor was prohibited, in communities which had taken advantage of local option, and in states which had adopted prohibition. But that bootlegger stands to the bootlegging of today where the pre-prohibition moonshiner stands to the illicit production of today. It is common knowledge, and a general cause of dissatisfaction with enforcement of the National Prohibition Act, that the big operators or head men in the traffic are rarely caught. Agents may discover a still or a speakeasy. They deal mostly with single cases of illicit making and distribution. But these apparently isolated single violations are seldom such in fact. The large still is part of an organized system of production and distribution. Those who are found distilling, or transporting, or selling are merely employees. Behind them are the heads of an organization, supplying the capital, making the plans, and reaping the large profits. It is clear enough that the real problem is to reach these heads of the unlawful business. Experience has taught them to carry on their business with impunity and it is in evidence that they are harder to reach than formerly. To catch them calls for a much higher type of enforcement organization and a higher and more experienced type of agents than have been available in the past. Moreover, the means available for catching the employees, namely, information from neighbors, patrolling roads, watching suspicious places where men loiter, talking with persons occasionally met and learning where liquor may be bought and buying it, are generally not effective to catch the men higher up.

These leaders are often at a long distance from the single act of violation discovered by the prohibition agent. In the investigation made by the grand jury in Philadelphia in 1928–29, it was found that the ramifications of a highly organized system of illicit distribution extended from New York to Minnesota, and the financial operations reached from Philadelphia to Minneapolis.

When conspiracies are discovered from time to time, they disclose combinations of illicit distributors, illicit producers, local politicians, corrupt police and other enforcement agencies, making lavish payments for protection and conducting an elaborate system of individual producers and distributors. How extensive such systems may be is illustrated by some of the conspiracies recently unearthed in which 219 in one case, 156 in another, and 102 in another were indicted and prosecuted. Organized distribution has outstripped organized enforcement.

These things have been particularly evident in the distribution of beer. It must be obvious that increased personnel and equipment are demanded if the enforcement agencies are to cope with this situation, and an increase in the corps of special agents whose function it is to work up the evidence to expose such conspiracies, affords the most hopeful means of substantial accomplishment in the enforcement field. Destruction of alley breweries and padlocking of beer flats and speakeasies has little effect. It gives an appearance of enforcement without the reality.

Speakeasies, blind pigs and blind tigers existed also before national prohibition, wherever local option, or statewide prohibition, or state liquor laws, unacceptable to a local population, gave an opening. But these also were quite different things from the speakeasy in the city of today. At the present time, the term speakeasy covers a wide range from something not much different from the old-time saloon and the speakeasies with a high grade of regular patronage at one pole to the lowest grade of joint selling bad whiskey or bad gin at the other. They are sometimes hardly disguised and obviously operating under official protection. At other times and in other places, they are thinly disguised or thoroughly camouflaged according to local conditions of enforcement as cafes, soft drink stands, pool rooms, clubs, drug stores, or filling stations. The number closed each year by prosecution or injunction is large. But the

number does not decrease on that account. Indeed, it is evident that along with the occasional isolated individual keeper, the type which has come down from the era before prohibition and the type most easily caught, there is a thoroughly organized business which replaces its retail selling agencies as fast as they are discovered and closed up. The number of these places notoriously existing throughout the country, with public tolerance, demonstrates the extent to which experience and organization have carried retail distribution.

Speakeasies, even where they approximate the old-time open saloon, have few of the attractions which were used to bring customers to those drinking places and induce them to stay there and spend their money. Probably a much greater number of those who patronize them can afford to do so than was true in case of the saloon. Thus the closing of the saloon has been a gain even if speakeasies abound. But the saloon was not an unlawful institution. Where it was not carried on in defiance of law its patrons were not assisting in maintaining an unlawful enterprise. Against the gain in eliminating the saloon must be weighed the demoralizing effect of the regime of more or less protected speakeasies upon respect for law and upon law and order generally. Unless the number of speakeasies can be substantially and permanently diminished, enforcement can not be held satisfactory.

In some cities night clubs have notoriously sold to a steady and considerable patronage. At times they have been very bold and some cases, given wide publicity, in which Jury trials have resulted in acquittal of well-known persons in charge of them, have had an unfavorable effect on public opinion. Commonly, they are operated under a system whereby patrons must be identified, to the extent at least of satisfying those in charge that they are not law enforcement agents, before gaining admittance. At times a card identifying the guest as a regular patron is required.

From time to time and in places, drug stores have been found to be engaged in illegal sale. Some have purchased the permit books of physicians with the prescriptions ready signed and have used them as a protection for sale for beverage purposes. Some have split permit liquor with bootleg liquor and thus have been able to dispose of amounts not appearing on the records. More often they have been able to carry on an illicit business by withdrawing pure alcohol for manufacturing purposes, the ultimate use of which is beyond the reach of the checks provided by statutes and regulations. Some have even been found dispensing bootleg liquor as well as filling prescriptions. The drug trade is well organized and no doubt reliance is properly placed upon the organized business and the well-established dealers. But the number of drug stores has increased out of proportion to the increase in population. With the pressure of competition and pressure of enforcement upon other agencies of distribution there will always be a large potential difficulty at this point.

(c) Enforcement With Respect to Transportation

Development of motor transportation had a great impetus during the World War. Unfortunately, that development reached its high point at the time when it became convenient to use motor transportation in violation of the National Prohibition Act. The truck and the automobile are the chief agencies of transportation, although rail, water, and air are used in domestic transportation much as has been seen in connection with smuggling.

In the early years of prohibition, hijacking and banditry also developed. These things had a bad effect on enforcement. Another unfortunate feature, in view of recent conditions of transportation, is the necessity of interference with legitimate use of the roads if enforcement is to be thoroughly effective. The truck driver and motorist of today resent delay. Yet it is obvious that there cannot be absolute assurance that a violation is going on as to every vehicle which have to be stopped and examined. Some state laws give in state enforcement agents very wide powers of searching vehicles, which may be, and have been exercised in a way exasperating to the public. Federal prohibition enforcement and state enforcement are not dissociated in the public mind. They are regarded as parts of one system. The bad features of state enforcement in several jurisdictions are attributed in the public mind to national prohibition.

In view of the general and convenient use of motor transport for carrying illicit liquors, completely effective enforcement of prohibition requires a high degree of potential supervision, power of inspection, and systematizes watching of motor vehicles using the roads.

(d) Evasion in Places Used for Drinking

Not the least demoralizing feature of enforcement of national prohibition is the development of open or hardly disguised drinking winked at by those in charge in respectable places where respectable people gather. People of wealth, professional and business men, public officials and tourists are drinking in hotels, cafes and tourist camps under circumstances where at least knowledge on the part of those in charge that the liquor comes in unlawfully is an inescapable inference. Sometimes this becomes so flagrant that for a time pressure is brought to stop or to limit it. But on the whole it goes on throughout the country in spite of the rulings that furnishing the accessories for drinking with knowledge of how they are to be used is an offense. The pressure from patrons, the state of public opinion, and the difficulty of obtaining proof make it almost impossible to reach these things.

(e) Evidence of Prices

A fair index of the effectiveness of enforcement is furnished by the prices at which liquor may be had in different localities. As to this, there is significant uniform evidence that while certain kinds of imported wines command high prices and now and then the pressure of enforcement raises all prices for a time at some one spot, whisky of good quality is obtainable substantially everywhere at prices not extravagant for persons of means. It is true many cannot afford these prices and for them a large amount of cheap, poor grade, or even poisonous, liquor is constantly produced and is in general circulation. The conclusion is that enforcement is not reaching the sources of production and distribution so as materially to affect the supply.

(f) State Cooperation as Evidenced by the Enforcement Situation in Various Localities.

At the time of the adoption of the Eighteenth Amendment, thirty-three states had adopted prohibition by law or constitution; after the Eighteenth Amendment, twelve other states enacted prohibition laws and eighteen added to or amended their laws generally to correspond with the National Prohibition Act. In many of the first class of states the laws were quite generally enforced before national prohibition. In those states fair cooperation with the federal prohibition forces at first was given, but there has been in recent years a growing tendency, even in states with prohibition laws, to let the federal government carry the burden of enforcement. On May 31, 1923, the New York Legislature repealed its prohibition act. In the same year Nevada repealed its statute and enacted the California prohibition law in its stead. This act was held unconstitutional by the Supreme Court of the State for a defect in its title. No new statute has been enacted and in 1926 the people of the State voted for repeal of the Eighteenth Amendment. Montana repealed its prohibition law in 1926, Wisconsin its law in 1929, and Massachusetts its law by referendum in 1930. In 1930 the people in Illinois and Rhode Island voted for repeal of their state laws. Such action of course seriously affects the attitude of the local authorities in those states respecting the apprehension of violators of the national law.

Conditions are not wholly the same from year to year anywhere. Upheavals in local politics, changes of administration, varying policies in policing, the activities of strong or inactivities of weak personalities in executive positions, contribute to make the course of state enforcement, at least in the average urban local, fluctuating, vacillating, or even spasmodic. Thus the burden upon federal enforcement, is not uniform from year to year in any locality. No precise data are obtainable as to state cooperation. In only a few states does the state maintain a separate department for the enforcement of the prohibition laws. In all of the remaining states with enforcement statutes, enforcement of the prohibition laws is a part of the duties of the general law enforcement officers, and there are not available segregated official figures showing arrests, convictions and seizures under the prohibition laws. Except in the few states maintaining separate prohibition departments, this information could be obtained only by inspection of the records of each county and city in the state, since in no states other than the few maintaining separate prohibition departments are there available printed figures covering the entire state sufficient to permit any accurate figures upon state cooperation or any comparison covering the area of the entire state as to prosecutions for violations of state liquor laws since the adoption of the Eighteenth Amendment as compared with prosecutions before its adoption, or as compared with prosecutions in the federal courts. But the evidence sustains certain general conclusions.

The states may be grouped conveniently in four categories (1) Those where there was prohibition before the National Prohibition Act in which public opinion might have been expected to demand and sustain an active state enforcement and zealous co-operation with the federal government; (2) Those where there was prohibition before the National Prohibition Act in which public opinions either in the state as a whole or in the chief centers, is less vigorous, so that there is on the average perfunctory or spasmodic state enforcement, and at most lukewarm co-operation with the federal government; (3) those which did not have prohibition before the National Prohibition Act, but have state statutes conforming to or in support of it; (4) those in which there was no prohibition before the National Prohibition Act, and there are no state statutes of like effect.

(1) An example of the first type is Virginia, a state as to which happily excellent official statistics are available. Virginia has been a zealous prohibition state since 1914. There is not only a stringent state law reinforcing the federal law, but also a special state enforcing machinery for which considerable appropriations have been made annually. The testimony is uniform that the federal administrator has been more than ordinarily efficient and determined. The state officers likewise have been under exceptional pressure to do their whole duty. They state that the state machinery of enforcement is as efficient as it can be made within the practicable limits of expenditure. It works in entire harmony with the federal agencies. The number of convictions under the state law is impressive, and of seizures thereunder no less so. Yet the number of arrests for drunkenness in Richmond has been growing steadily and has increased by more than one-third in five years. Also the testimony shows that the amount of liquor in circulation has grown steadily. Prices tell the same story. It cannot be said that there is a reasonably effective enforcement in Richmond, and the evidence as to Norfolk and Roanoke is to the same effect.

(2) In the second type of state, which had prohibition before the National Prohibition Act, the conditions are less satisfactory. In too many of these states there has been a tendency to leave enforcement primarily, or as far as possible, to the federal Government, either as a policy of the state, or as a policy in the cities, which often were opposed to prohibition when it was adopted as a regime for the state. By comparison of the prosecutions for violation of the state law before and after national prohibition, and comparison with the constantly rising number of federal prosecutions in these jurisdictions, a growing tendency in states of this type to give over at least a large measure of their former activities is plainly shown. In view of the admission of the federal prohibition authorities that there can be no effective federal enforcement without state co-operation, this tendency is significant.

(3) A like tendency may be seen in the third type of state which did not have prohibition before the National Prohibition Act, but adopted state statutes in furtherance of it. On the whole, in these jurisdictions state enforcement has become distinctly less active than

it was in the beginning, and in some it has substantially broken down for the more important centers. Thus Illinois, which had prohibition prior to the Eighteenth Amendment, adopted in 1923 an act modeled on the National Prohibition Act intended to establish a uniformity of state and federal laws on the subject. But state appropriations for enforcement of prohibition, which were made for a time, have ceased, and the survey made by direction of the United States Commissioner of Prohibition in 1930 says frankly that "a breakdown of state enforcement work is apparent." As a result, this survey shows that enforcement of the federal and state laws is bad in twenty-seven counties and unsatisfactory in sixteen more; is very bad in the chief city of the state, and is bad in every urban community of much importance.

New Jersey, another state which did not have prohibition before the Eighteenth Amendment, enacted in 1922 a statute on the lines of the National Prohibition Act. That state has an effective state police and has always had an enviable record in its handling of crime. But the evidence is clear that state enforcement of prohibition in New Jersey has fallen down.

(4) As to the states of the fourth type which did not have prohibition before the Eighteenth Amendment, and have no state statutes in support thereof, it should be said that both in them and in those which, not having had prohibition originally, have adopted laws to reinforce the federal act, there are localities, which had taken advantage of local option before the National Prohibition Act, in which there is sufficiently strong public opinion to insure not a little co-operation with the federal Government. But for the most part the whole burden is put upon federal enforcement. In this fourth group are some of the most important states of the Union. As to them it is obvious that there is no effective enforcement of prohibition.

(5) In certain localities where there is a large tourist business enforcement fails because of the insistence of business men and property owners that tourists be given a free hand. In such places there is not merely no state enforcement and no state cooperation, but all attempts at enforcement are substantially precluded by public opinion.

It is true that the chief centers of non-enforcement or ineffective enforcement are the cities. But since 1920 the United States has been preponderantly urban. A failure of enforcement in the cities is a failure in the major part of the land in population and influence. Enforcement is at its best in the rural communi-

ties in those states where there was already long established state prohibition before the National Prohibition Act.

X. Conclusions and Reccommendations

1. The Commission is opposed to repeal of the Eighteenth Amendment.
2. The Commission is opposed to the restoration in any manner of the legalized saloon.
3. The Commission is opposed to the federal or state governments, as such, going into the liquor business.
4. The Commission is opposed to the proposal to modify the National Prohibition Act so as to permit manufacture and sale of light wines or beer.
5. The Commission is of opinion that the cooperation of the states is an essential element in the enforcement of the Eighteenth Amendment and the National Prohibition Act throughout the territory of the United States; that the support of public opinion in the several states is necessary in order to insure such cooperation.
6. The Commission is of opinion that prior to the enactment of the Bureau of Prohibition Act, 1927, the agencies for enforcement were badly organized and inadequate; that subsequent to that enactment there has been continued improvement in organization and effort for enforcement.
7. The Commission is of opinion that there is yet no adequate observance or enforcement.
8. The Commission is of opinion that the present organization for enforcement is still inadequate.
9. The Commission is of opinion that the federal appropriations for enforcement of the Eighteenth Amendment should be substantially increased and that the vigorous and better organized efforts which have gone on since the Bureau of Prohibition Act, 1927, should be furthered by certain improvements in the statutes and in the organization, personnel, and equipment of enforcement, so as to give to enforcement the greatest practicable efficiency.
10. Some of the Commission are not convinced that Prohibition under the Eighteenth Amendment is unenforceable and believe that a further trial should be made with the help of the recommended improvements, and that if after such trial effective enforcement is not secured there should be a revision of the Amendment. Others of the Commission are convinced that it has been demonstrated that Prohibition under the Eighteenth Amendment is unenforceable and that the Amendment should be

immediately revised, but recognizing that the process of amendment will require some time, they unite in the recommendations of Conclusion No. 9 for the improvement of the enforcement agencies.

11. All the Commission agree that if the Amendment is revised it should be made to read substantially as follows:

Section 1. The Congress shall have power to regulate or to prohibit the manufacture, traffic in or transportation of intoxicating liquors within, the importation thereof into and the exportation thereof from the United States and all territory subject to the jurisdiction thereof for beverage purposes.

12. The recommendations referred to in conclusion Number 9 are:

1. Removal of the causes of irritation and resentment on the part of the medical profession by:
   (a) Doing away with the statutory fixing of the amount which may be prescribed and the number of prescriptions;
   (b) Abolition of the requirement of specifying the ailment for which liquor is prescribed upon a blank to go into the public files;
   (c) Leaving as much as possible to regulations rather than fixing details by statute.
2. Removal of the anomalous provisions in Section 29, National Prohibition Act, as to cider and fruit juices by making some uniform regulation for a fixed alcoholic content.
3. Increase of the number of agents, storekeeper-gaugers, prohibition investigators, and special agents; increase in the personnel of the Customs Bureau and in the equipment of all enforcement organizations.
4. Enactment of a statute authorizing regulations permitting access to the premises and records of wholesale and retail dealers so as to make it possible to trace products of specially denatured alcohol to the ultimate consumer.
5. Enactment of legislation to prohibit independent denaturing plants.
6. The Commission is opposed to legislation allowing more latitude for federal searches and seizures.
7. The Commission renews the recommendation contained in its previous reports for codification of the National Prohibition Act and the acts supplemental to and in amendment thereof.
8. The Commission renews its recommendation of legislation for making procedure in the so-called padlock injunction cases more effective.
9. The Commission recommends legislation providing a mode of prosecuting petty offenses in the federal courts and modifying the Increased Penalties Act of 1929, as set forth in the Chairman's letter to the Attorney General dated May 23, 1930, H. R. Rep. 1699.

There are differences of view among the members of the Commission as to certain of the conclusions stated and as to some matters included in or omitted from this report. The report is signed subject to individual reservation of the right to express these individual views in separate or supplemental reports to be annexed hereto.

Geo W. Wickersham

Chairman,

HENRY W. ANDERSON,
NEWTON D. BAKER,
ADA L. COMSTOCK,
WILLIAM I. GRUBBI,
WILLIAM S. KENYON,
FRANK J. LOESCH,
PAUL J. MCCORMICK,
KENNETH MACINTOSH,
ROSCOE POUND

APPENDIX B

Biographies of
Major Personalities

Anderson, Marian (1897–1993) *contralto*
Born in Philadelphia, Anderson began her singing career at the age of six in a church choir. After winning a national singing competition in 1925, Anderson gave a debut concert with the New York Philharmonic and then set out on a tour of the United States and Europe. Another European tour in the early 1930s made her international reputation. In 1939, when the Daughters of the American Revolution barred her from performing in Philadelphia's Constitution Hall, Eleanor Roosevelt stepped in to arrange for Anderson to perform on the steps of the Lincoln Memorial. In 1955 she became the first African-American soloist to perform with New York's Metropolitan Opera company, performing as Ulrica in Verdi's *Un Ballo in Maschera*. In the same year, she was named one of the company's permanent members. She was as well-known abroad as in the United States, and after a triumphant European tour in 1958 she was appointed as an alternate U.S. delegate to the United Nations.

Arbuckle, Roscoe Conkling ("Fatty") (1887–1933) *film actor, director*
Born in Smith Center, Kansas, Arbuckle, after a career on the vaudeville stage, moved to California where he found his first movie work as an extra for the Selig Company. He moved on to Mack Sennett's Keystone Film Company, where he performed with Ben Turpin, Charlie Chaplin, and Chester Conklin in dozens of short "two-reelers" as one of the best-known Keystone Kops. Arbuckle also starred in a series of popular "Fatty and Mabel" films with Mabel Normand. In 1917, Paramount rewarded Arbuckle's growing popularity with the generous offer of complete artistic control at the newly founded Comique Film Corporation, established just for him. Over the next few years, Comique made several full-length feature films and launched the

career of comedian Buster Keaton. But on Labor Day, 1921, Arbuckle had the misfortune to be present at a private party at San Francisco's St. Francis Hotel, where the revelries tragically ended with the death of Virginia Rappé, a young, out-of-work actress. Accused of sexually assaulting and murdering Rappé, Arbuckle was tried three times, finally acquitted, and banned from the film industry. The scandal was the worst of several to hit the film industry in the early 1920s, and played an important part in the founding of the Hays Office, which would serve as the film industry's moral watchdog for the next three decades. For the remainder of his shortened career, Arbuckle would direct under the name of William Goodrich.

Armstrong, Louis ("Satchmo") (1900–1971) *jazz cornetist, trumpeter*
Born in New Orleans, Armstrong, nicknamed "Satchmo" for his expansive, satchel-like mouth, first picked up a brass instrument while attending a New Orleans reform school. His natural facility and sharp ear allowed him to follow and imitate the musical innovations then happening in New Orleans, where a new style of improvisatory freedom was being applied to traditional blues and dance forms. After an apprenticeship as a teenager with cornetist Joe "King" Oliver in New Orleans, Armstrong went north to Chicago to join Oliver's band, which became one of the city's leading jazz ensembles. In 1924 he went to New York City to perform with Fletcher Henderson's band, but soon returned to Chicago, where he formed two renowned small groups of his own, the Hot Five and the Hot Seven. Armstrong's virtuosity and incredible range on the trumpet, as well as his innovation in "scat" (wordless) singing, played an important role in transforming jazz from an ensemble style into a showcase for soloists. In the 1930s he began touring Europe, leading big bands, and performing in motion pictures.

His appearances in Europe brought jazz into the musical mainstream abroad.

Baker, Josephine (1906–1975) *singer, dancer, nightclub artist*

Born in St. Louis, Baker appeared as a chorus member in the African-American Broadway revue *Shuffle Along* in 1921 at the age of 15 and later at Harlem's Cotton Club and other popular nightspots in New York City. In 1925, she settled permanently in Paris, where she starred in the African-American production of *La Revue Négre*. With her stage shows at the Folies-Bergére and the Casino de Paris, Baker became one of the most popular entertainers in France, where African-American music and dance became increasingly popular in the postwar years. Baker became a citizen of France in 1937, returning only occasionally to the country of her birth. In the 1950s she retired to an orphanage she operated in the French countryside.

Barrymore, John (1882–1942) *stage and screen actor, member of one of the nation's best-known theatrical families*

Born to Maurice and Georgiana Barrymore in Philadelphia and the brother of Lionel and Ethel Barrymore, both of whom also became distinguished actors, John Barrymore debuted as an understudy in the production of *Captain Jinks* in 1901. His tours in the United States, Europe, and Australia made him one of the world's best-known stage actors of the day, especially notable for superb performances in *Hamlet* and *Richard III* in the early 1920s. He first appeared in motion pictures in 1912 and shared his appearances between film and stage productions until the mid-1920s, when he began working almost exclusively in films. His film credits include *Beau Brummel* (1926), *Don Juan* (1928), *Grand Hotel* (1932), and *Twentieth Century* (1934). He last appeared on the stage in *My Dear Children* in 1939. Barrymore's four marriages and heavy drinking brought him an aura of scandal that made him all the more fascinating to movie audiences taking an immoderate interest in the personal lives of screen actors.

Benchley, Robert (1889–1945) *satirical writer*

Born in Worcester, Massachusetts and educated at Harvard, Benchley, after a short career as advertising copywriter for the Curtis Publishing Company, wrote for *Vanity Fair* from 1919 to 20, and then was hired as a drama critic for *Life* magazine in 1920. He wrote for the *New Yorker* from 1929 until 1940. A member of the literary clique known as the Algonquin Round Table, which met for lunch at New York's Algonquin Hotel, Benchley combined urban sophistication with a witty observance of everyday foibles and absurdities that made him popular among readers living in a fast-changing world. He also had a strong talent for skewering the manias and obsessions of the times, most famously in his story "The Making of a Red," a sarcastic comment on the Red Scare of the 1920s. In addition to magazine columns, he wrote radio and film scripts, and made numerous appearances as a screen actor, including a role in a comic short, *How to Sleep,* which won an Academy Award in 1936. His collections include *Of All Things* (1921), *The Treasurer's Report* (1930), *From Bed to Worse* (1934), *My Ten Years in a Quandary* (1936) and *Benchley Beside Himself* (1943).

Berger, Victor (1860–1929) *socialist leader, congressman*

Born in Austria, Victor Berger emigrated to the United States and, in 1891, settled in Milwaukee. As editor of the Milwaukee *Leader,* he found a ready audience for his socialist program in a city of central European immigrants and workers. In 1910 he became the first socialist elected to the U.S. Congress. During World War I, the federal government suspended the *Leader's* mailing privileges, but the paper survived. Still hoping to thwart Berger's political ambitions, the federal government indicted him under the Espionage Act in 1918, but the indictment made Berger a hero in Milwaukee, and he won reelection. In 1919, after the House of Representatives voted to expel him, a special election was held to fill the empty seat. Berger won the election but was again denied his seat. Berger won three more Congressional elections during the 1920s, but found his politics growing less controversial and less interesting to the public as the 1920s roared on and "Coolidge prosperity" made socialist issues moot among the majority of voters. Berger died in 1929, having served as a martyr to the socialist cause and a reminder of the threat posed by war hysteria to constitutional protections.

Berlin, Irving (Isidore Baline) (1888–1989) *songwriter, composer*

Born in Russia, Berlin immigrated to the United States in 1893. Raised on the Lower East Side of New York City, Berlin began singing on street corners as a boy and later worked as a singing waiter. His first published song, "Marie from Sunny Italy," appeared in 1907. Afterward Berlin worked as a lyricist as well as a composer for small music publishers operating in New York's "Tin Pan Alley" neighborhood. He won a huge audience in 1911 with the song "Alexander's Ragtime Band," a mainstream adaptation of ragtime music imported from the South. He wrote annual revues for the Ziegfeld Follies and in 1921 built his own Music Box Theater in the Broadway district. The Music Box revues became must-see productions of the early 1920s. Berlin's simple yet beautifully catchy tunes, including "Easter Parade," "Blue Skies," "God Bless America," "Always," and "White Christmas," were performed in numerous films, on stage, and in millions of homes on pianos all over the country.

Bethune, Mary McLeod (1875–1955) *leading African-American educator*
Mary McLeod Bethune was born into a family of 17 children on a former slave's farm in Mayesville, South Carolina. Showing promise at a local mission school, she was rewarded a scholarship to attend the Moody Bible Institute in Chicago, from which she graduated in 1895. She dedicated her life to teaching, believing in the power of education to advance equality and economic opportunity for African Americans. With $1.50 in savings, Bethune founded the Daytona Normal and Industrial Institute for Women in Daytona Beach in 1904; her speaking and fund-raising ability allowed her to invest in buildings, supplies, books, and land. In 1923 she merged this institution with the Cookman Institute to create Bethune-Cookman College, the first institution for disadvantaged students to become a four-year college. She led the National Association of Colored Women and in 1935 founded the National Council of Negro Women, which expanded housing and welfare programs during the New Deal. Bethune's close relationship with President Franklin Roosevelt and Eleanor Roosevelt allowed her to advance federal funding for the vocational training of young black students and help many struggling graduates to obtain jobs. During World War II, she worked as an assistant to the Secretary of War and saw to it that black women achieved an equal place in the Women's Army Auxiliary Corps. She helped to found the United Nations in San Francisco in 1945.

Bow, Clara (1905–1965) *actress*
Born in Brooklyn, Bow was popularly known as the "It Girl." Without any theatrical training or experience, she debuted in *Beyond the Rainbow* (1922), and then appeared in *Down to the Sea in Ships* (1922), the film that first made her a national star. She worked under contract for the B. P. Schuilberg studio and was also loaned to First National, where she first played a flapper heroine in *Painted People* (1924). Following were *The Plastic Age* (1925), *Mantrap* (1926), *Wings* (1927), and her first sound effort, *The Wild Party* (1929). Her portrayal of exuberant flappers and independent free spirits reflected a new freedom of the country's urban women, who were working and studying in previously all-male enclaves and finding new venues for self-expression in dress, hair, attitudes, books, and films. But her film career faded in the early 1930s as sound came in and a new crop of Hollywood stars left the former icons of the silent era behind in the public's imagination.

Boyd, Louise (1887–1972) *Arctic explorer*
Born in San Francisco in 1887, Boyd was the daughter of a wealthy mining tycoon, John Franklin Boyd. Fascinated by geography and by the prospect of discovering the unexplored corners of the world, Boyd decided to take up a career as an explorer at the age of 30, after inheriting a fortune. In 1924 she made the first of seven Arctic explorations, sailing to the island of Spitsbergen, between Norway and Greenland. In 1928, she led a three-month hunt for the missing Norwegian explorer Roald Amundsen, who had gone missing while leading a search party of his own; Amundsen was never found. In 1930, Boyd journeyed to the far north of Scandinavia, where she documented Lapp society. Later in the decade she undertook mapping expeditions along the eastern coast of Greenland. In 1938 she was awarded the Cullum Medal by the American Geographic Society and was named to the organization's Society of Fellows, the first woman to achieve the honor. During World War II, she served as a consultant on Greenland and the North Atlantic to U.S. military intelligence.

Brooks, Louise (1906–1985) *movie actress*
Born in Cherryvale, Kansas, Brooks, who grew up in a well-to-do family that prized writing and music, developed a strong sense of straightforward honesty that did not serve her well in Hollywood's sycophantic milieu. Trained in dancing from the age of 10, she moved to New York in 1920 and joined the Denishawn Dancers, where she met and befriended Martha Graham. Brooks closely studied the Ziegfeld Follies as well as the movies of Charlie Chaplin and transformed herself from a small-town girl into a hotly pursued celebrity of New York high society. After a year in London, she

returned to New York and was cast by Florenz Ziegfeld in *Louie the 14th* in 1925, and in the Ziegfeld Follies of 1925–26. Her movie debut took place in the now-vanished film *Street of Forgotten Men.* She appeared in several more films for the Lasky studio, producers of her debut picture, before moving to Hollywood in 1927. By this time she had developed a powerful screen persona, that of a sexy ingenue sporting severely bobbed hair and daringly cut dresses. The German director G. W. Pabst hired her to play the innocent prostitute Lulu in *Pandora's Box,* a poignant and scathing commentary on the upper classes that was released in 1929. When she returned to Hollywood in 1930, much against Pabst's advice, she found herself largely ignored by producers searching for the newest and most willing young actresses. She made her last film, *Overland Stage Raiders,* in 1938, moved back to Kansas in 1940, then returned to New York and fell completely out of the public eye until writing a rich and detailed memoir of her career, *Lulu in Hollywood,* in 1982.

Bryan, William Jennings (1860–1925) *attorney, congressman, secretary of state, presidential candidate*
Born in Salem, Illinois, Bryan moved to Nebraska in 1887. He won election to the House of Representatives in 1890 and 1892, when his leading cause was the free coinage of silver in order to increase the nation's supply of money. In 1896, he delivered the "Cross of Gold" speech at the democratic convention, a dramatic address that landed him the presidential nomination. Bryan lost the presidential elections of 1896, 1900, and 1908, but maintained his popular standing through his weekly newspaper *The Commoner.* In 1912, newly elected President Woodrow Wilson appointed Bryan secretary of state; in this position Bryan argued for neutrality in World War I. In 1915, when the sinking of the *Lusitania* prompted calls for intervention in the war, Bryan resigned his post. In the early 1920s, Bryan became a leading spokesman for fundamentalist Christianity, which opposed the teaching of new scientific doctrines, especially the theory of evolution. In 1925 he was asked to appear for the prosecution in the case of John Scopes, a high school biology teacher accused of violating a Tennessee antievolution law. Bryan won over the jury, the judge, and the courtroom audience, but a cross-examination by Clarence Darrow for the defense brought only a vague, confused, and half-hearted defense of biblical doctrines. Shortly after winning the Scopes trial, Bryan died of a stroke.

Capone, Alphonse (1899–1947) *gangster*
Capone immigrated to Brooklyn from Naples, Italy, the place of his birth. He was still an obscure young thug from Brooklyn when Chicago gangster Johnny Torrio enlisted him in 1920 to help with gang warfare that broke with the coming of Prohibition. Within a few years, Capone had built a powerful criminal organization of his own, using prostitution, gambling, and the sale of illegal beer and whiskey from his own warehouses to a clientele of speakeasy owners in Chicago and surrounding towns. Probably the best-known citizen of Chicago at the height of his career, he had most of the city's government bribed and cooperative through the 1920s. Capone was widely suspected of being the mastermind behind the St. Valentine's Day Massacre in 1929. Although the cold-blooded killing of several members of the rival Moran gang helped Capone extend his control over the Chicago underground, the murders shocked a jaded public and ended the Chicago authorities' easy tolerance for gangster activities. In 1931, Capone was arrested on a charge of tax evasion and convicted. He was released from prison in 1939 and died eight years later in Florida.

Cather, Willa (1873–1947) *novelist*
Born in Winchester, Virginia, Cather and her family moved to the town of Red Cloud in south-central Nebraska when she was 10 years old. The experience of living in the Great Plains, in an era when pioneers from the east were just closing the western frontier, marked much of her later fiction. Cather graduated from the University of Nebraska, worked as a high school English teacher in Pittsburgh, then moved to New York, where she was hired as an editor by *McClure's Magazine* in 1906. She published a volume of poems, *April Twilights,* in 1903, and *The Troll Garden,* a story collection, in 1905. After quitting *McClure's,* she devoted herself to writing novels: *O Pioneers!* (1913), *The Song of the Lark* (1915), and *My Ántonia* (1918). Although she lived the rest of her life in New York City, she never forgot the Midwest; her books celebrate the resilience and imagination of the original pioneers, which Cather set in sharp contrast to the country's restless and rootless urban population. Her novel *One of Ours,* a lament on the psychic consequences of war, won a Pulitzer Prize in 1922. *Death Comes for the Archbishop,* set in the desert southwest, appeared in 1927 to widespread critical and public acclaim.

Catt, Carrie Chapman (Carrie Lane) (1859–1947) *suffrage campaigner*

Catt was born in Ripon, Wisconsin. After graduating from Iowa State College in 1880, Carrie Lane worked as a teacher and as superintendent of schools in Mason City, Iowa. After her marriage to George Catt in 1890, she joined Susan B. Anthony's suffrage campaign in South Dakota. In 1900, she was selected by Anthony as the next president of the National American Woman Suffrage Association (NAWSA). She served until 1904, but again joined the organization as president in 1915; she developed a winning strategy for achieving national woman's suffrage by constitutional amendment. A tireless promoter and lecturer, Catt's ability as an organizer proved key to the passage of state suffrage amendments as well as passage of the Nineteenth Amendment in 1920. In that year, Catt transformed the NAWSA into the National League of Women Voters. After suffrage was attained, she turned her attention to the cause of pacifism. She combined 11 different women's organizations into the National Committee on the Cause and Cure of War in 1925. After the founding of the United Nations, she worked to have women named to important posts in the UN and remained active in UN affairs until her death.

Chaplin, Charlie (1889–1977) *film actor, director, producer, writer*

Born in London in 1889, Chaplin led a hard life in the city's East End slums as an orphan. He found a measure of public respect as a music-hall performer, and caught a big break upon his discovery by Hollywood director Mack Sennett during a U.S. tour in 1913. The Tramp, Charlie Chaplin's most well-known role, became the most recognized movie character in the entire world during the late 1910s and through the end of the silent film era of the 1920s. Chaplin also earned Hollywood's highest salaries; in 1918 he signed with the First National company for an astronomical $1 million per movie. In 1923, he declared his independence from the Hollywood studios by forming the United Artists company with Mary Pickford, Douglas Fairbanks, and D. W. Griffith. As director, producer, writer, and star, he created *The Gold Rush* in 1925, still one of the best-known and most highly regarded of all silent films. The first sound movies, appearing in 1927, ended the careers of many of his contemporaries, but Chaplin survived due to his genius for purely physical comedy. His silent productions included *The Circus* in 1928 and *City Lights* in 1931; his voice was not heard in a movie until *Modern Times* in 1936.

Chrysler, Walter (1881–1948) *industrialist*

The son of a railroad engineer, Walter Chrysler was born in Wamego, Kansas and grew up in Ellis, Kansas. He lived and breathed railroads and machinery at this Union Pacific shop town. After working several years as a highly regarded railroad machinist, Chrysler was hired to run the Buick division of General Motors in Flint, Michigan, in 1912. Building on his experience in the railroad industry, he introduced new production processes and assembly line methods that streamlined auto manufacturing and provided a model for scientific management in U.S. industry that would reach its full flower in the 1920s. In 1920, when the nation was going through its postwar depression, he took over the troubled Willys-Overland company at a salary of $1 million a year. Although the company could not overcome its financial problems and was dissolved in 1921, Chrysler applied his new production methods and design ideas at the Maxwell Motor Corporation. With a design team recruited from Willys-Overland, he created the "Chrysler Six," a moderately priced car that first appeared in 1924. The Chrysler provided direct competition with General Motors' Buick and spurred the complete redesign of the Model T automobile by Henry Ford. To move into the lower-priced car market, in 1928 Chrysler bought the Dodge Motor Company. The automobile industry was ending a decade of technological advancement and consolidation; out of all the failed small- and medium-sized companies a "Big Three" of Ford, General Motors, and Chrysler were left standing at the end of the decade. In 1929, Chrysler celebrated his success with the construction of the 77-story Chrysler Building on 42nd Street in New York.

Coolidge, Calvin (1872–1933) *politician, U.S. president*

A native of Plymouth Notch, Vermont, Coolidge attended Amherst College and followed a conventional law practice and political career in Massachusetts state government. He was elected governor of Massachusetts in 1919, gaining widespread acclaim during his first year in office by calling out a militia force to put down the Boston police strike. As Harding's vice president, Coolidge kept clear of the graft and corruption scandals that began swamping the administration in 1923 and was reelected by a wide margin in 1924. Coolidge succinctly declared that "The business of America is business," and followed up by practicing a staunchly probusiness presidency, exhorting the public to economize and allowing tax cuts to corporations. Despite his dour and tight-lipped manner, Coolidge rode a crest of economic prosperity that kept his popularity high. He turned down an almost certain reelection in 1928, however, and supported Herbert Hoover, secretary of commerce, as his successor. After Hoover's election, Coolidge retired to Northampton, Massachusetts, to write his autobiography.

Crane, Harold Hart (1899–1932) *poet*

Born in Garrettsville, Ohio, Crane quit a Cleveland high school in 1916 and moved to New York City, where he struggled to support himself as a writer and fought psychological demons surrounding his broken family and his own homosexuality. His first book of poetry, *White Buildings,* appeared in 1926, presenting powerful imagery and wide-ranging, striking metaphors. In *The Bridge* (1930), Crane used the Brooklyn Bridge as a symbol of the vitality of urban life and progress, which he saw on a continuum with a past of powerful mythology and strong religious faith. In 1931, Crane won one of the first Guggenheim fellowships and took a voyage to Mexico, where he completed almost no work and nearly committed suicide by alcohol. On the return trip, on April 27, 1932, he leapt from the deck of a steamer and drowned. Crane had only published two books in his lifetime, yet his poetry gained widespread favor for its originality.

cummings e. e. (Cummings, Edward Estlin) (1894–1962) *experimental poet*

Born in Cambridge, Massachusetts, cummings graduated from Harvard and served as an ambulance driver in France during World War I. His harsh experiences in a French war prison, where he was held for three months on trumped-up charges over allegedly treasonous statements in a letter, inspired his book *The Enormous Room,* which appeared in 1922. His verse, unconscious of traditional grammar, punctuation, syntax, and all other formal conventions, appeared in *Tulips and Chimneys* (1923), *Is 5* (1926), and *95 Poems* (1958). Many critics and readers saw in his works a reflection of the improvisatory explorations of jazz musicians. Cummings also wrote a stage play, *him,* in 1927, and brought out a collection of drawings and paintings entitled *CIOPW* in 1931.

Darrow, Clarence (1857–1938) *defense attorney*

Born in Kinsman, Ohio, Darrow spent most of his professional life in Chicago, where he moved in 1888. He defended labor leader Eugene V. Debs against federal charges arising from the Pullman railroad strike in 1894; from that point on he was well known in Chicago and around the country as an advocate for labor leaders, leftists, socialists, and other relatively unpopular defendants and for his staunch opposition to the death penalty. Darrow's leading boast was that he never saw a client suffer execution, and he followed through on this reputation in his stirring defense of the "thrill killers" Nathan Leopold and Richard Loeb in Chicago in 1924. In the following year, he took on a test case of Tennessee's Butler Act, which made the teaching of evolution a crime. The "Scopes trial," so nicknamed in a reference to the defendant, John Scopes, grew into a nationwide contest between the forces of tradition, represented by prosecuting attorney William Jennings Bryan, and the advocates of pure science and academic freedom from religion, represented by Darrow. Never intending to have his client acquitted of the charge, Darrow used the trial to showcase what he saw as the shallow fanaticism and empty piety of Bryan, one of his chief ideological rivals. After the Scopes trial, he retired to writing and produced *Crime, Its Cause and Treatment* in 1925 and *The Story of My Life* in 1932.

Dawes, Charles Gates (1865–1951) *diplomat, military leader, vice president during the second term of Calvin Coolidge*

Dawes was born in Ohio, where he began his career as a lawyer. A staunch Republican, he made his national reputation with his direction of the presidential campaign of William McKinley in 1896. He rose to the rank of brigadier general of the U.S. Army during World War I; after the war (in 1921) he was named the first director of the newly established U.S. Bureau of the Budget. Dawes's best-remembered accomplishment was the Dawes Plan. Appointed to a commission to study the problem of the bankrupt Germany economy in 1923, Dawes devised a solution to the heavy burden of reparations demanded from Germany by the Treaty of Versailles. The Dawes Plan called for lowered payments from 1924 onward, a stabilization of the inflated German currency, and a reorganization of the debt based on Germany's national income from loans and customs receipts. The plan worked until the end of the decade, when the German economy again crashed and the Dawes Plan was suspended in favor of the Young Plan, which brought about reduced reparations payments. Dawes was appointed ambassador to Great Britain in 1929 and in 1932 joined the Reconstruction Finance Corporation, a Hoover-era agency set up to rescue with public loans failing banks, savings and loans, and other financial institutions.

Debs, Eugene (1855–1926) *socialist leader, presidential candidate*

Born in Terre Haute, Indiana, Debs began working as a railway laborer. His energy and ability eventually landed him a job as city clerk. Not forgetting the harsh conditions suffered by the railway workers, he helped save the Brotherhood of Locomotive Firemen from bankruptcy in 1880 and, in 1893, founded the American Railway Union, the nation's first "industrial" union, open to all workers regardless of position or rank in a single industry. While imprisoned for leading a strike of Pullman workers in 1894, Debs became a socialist. He organized the Social Democratic Party of America in 1898 and became the party's first presidential candidate in 1900. Debs formed the Socialist Party out of a coalition of parties in the next year. Subsequent presidential campaigns in 1904, 1908, and 1912 saw Debs winning an ever-greater number of votes at the head of the socialist ticket. Debs won over his audiences through his speaking skills, not through his writing or theorizing, and his talent for direct communication with the masses made him the most popular socialist leader in the nation's history. But his antiwar position attracted the attention of the authorities and brought about an arrest for an antiwar speech made in Canton, Ohio, in 1918. Sentenced to a long jail term, Debs continued writing and campaigning from the Atlanta penitentiary, where he received almost 1 million votes in 1920 and from which he was pardoned by President Harding in 1921. Debs's book on prison conditions, *Walls and Bars,* was published in 1927 just after his death.

Dempsey, William Harrison "Jack" (1895–1983) *heavyweight boxer*

Born in Manassa, Colorado, Dempsey, after a short but brutal career as a hard-rock miner, began making the rounds of saloon yards in the West, where he earned the reputation as an aggressive and relentless brawler likely as not to do permanent injury to his opponents. In 1919, Dempsey demolished Jess Willard to win the heavyweight title, successfully defending his title against the French fighter Georges Carpentier in 1921 and the Argentinian Luis Angel Firpo in 1926. In the same year, Dempsey lost to Gene Tunney; during a heroic effort to regain the title in 1927, also known as the Battle of the Long Count, he failed to retreat to a neutral corner after a knockdown in the seventh round, giving Tunney critical extra seconds to recover and eventually win the bout. Having won 47 matches by knockouts over a career of 69 professional bouts, Dempsey promptly retired after this loss to become a New York restaurant owner.

Dewey, John (1859–1952) *philosopher, educator*

John Dewey's ideas in teaching and ethics changed many popular concepts of the basic mechanisms of learning. Dewey graduated from the University of Vermont in 1879 and from Johns Hopkins in 1884, after which he taught at the University of Michigan and became a department head in philosophy at the University of Chicago. In 1896 he founded the University Elementary School, also known as the Laboratory School, in Chicago, where he began applying a philosophy of education in which students learn abstract ideas through concrete experience rather than by rote learning. In 1904, he was hired by Columbia University, where he taught in the department of philosophy and later at Teachers College. In 1919, he founded the New School of Social Research in New York. His book *Human Nature and Conduct,* published in 1922, was an investigation of the scientific basis of morals and ethical action. In 1925, he published *Experience and Nature,* a description of his philosophy of aesthestics and an investigation into metaphysics—the search for common traits of physical and mental existence. In 1926, he lectured on social reform at Mexico's national university; in the next year he published *The Public and its Problems.* In 1928 he visited the Soviet Union, where his favorable reports generated a backlash in the United States. The controversy surrounding his later involvement in a mock trial and hearing of Leon Trotsky in Mexico City was a precursor to the nation's second great Red Scare during the 1940s and 1950s.

DuBois, William Edward Burghardt (1868–1963) *leading African-American writer and organizer*

W. E. B. DuBois was born in Great Barrington, Massachusetts, where he was the sole black student to attend the local high school. He attended Fisk University as well as Harvard, where he attained a doctorate in 1895, the first African-American student to do so. His Harvard dissertation, *The Suppression of the African Slave Trade,* was published as his first book in 1896. From 1897 until 1910, he was a professor of history and economics at Atlanta University. In 1897, DuBois also helped to found the American Negro Academy, the first academic organization created by and for African Americans. His essays on the black experience were collected in 1903 in *The Souls of Black Folk,* a volume now regarded as a classic in American literature. In 1905 DuBois helped to found the Niagara Movement, which in 1910 would become the National Association for the Advancement of Colored People (NAACP). As leader of the NAACP, he published *The Crisis,* a magazine outspokenly opposed to the gradualist, accommodative approach to racial equality proposed by Booker T. Washington. DuBois favored agitation, an unyielding demand for equality, and force when and if necessary, as the best road to independence from and equality to the dominant white society. In 1919, he founded the Pan-African Congress for the emancipation of Africans. During the 1920s, he published and promoted many of the writers of the Harlem Renaissance. DuBois left the NAACP in 1948, a time when he also came under criticism and investigation for his actions after World War II, when he was accused of communist sympathies. In 1961, he emigrated to Ghana, where with the collaboration of nationalist leader Kwame Nkrumah he produced the *Encyclopedia Africana.*

Duncan, Isadora (1878–1927) *dancer*

Duncan was born in San Francisco and left home at age 17 to pursue a career in Chicago and then New York. Unable to find an audience for her idiosyncratic style, which was neither classical nor vaudevillian, she left for Europe, where she made a sensation. Dancing barefoot and in long, flowing tunics, she gained widespread approval among European critics and the public. After weathering public scandal over an unconventional private life, she moved to Russia in 1921, where she opened a dancing school in Moscow. She moved back to France after the suicide of her Russian husband and died when she was accidentally strangled by one of her signature long scarves in 1927.

Ederle, Gertrude (1906–) *swimmer*

Born in New York City, Gertrude Ederle is best known for swimming the English Channel on August 6, 1926. Ederle showed astounding swimming ability as a teenager, setting several world records at the age of 15 and reaching the highest ranks of swimming competitions in the early 1920s. She won two bronze medals and a gold medal in the 400-meter relay at the Paris Olympics in 1924. Her 35-mile English Channel crossing, the first ever by a woman, also set a new time mark among all swimmers of 14 hours, 31 minutes. The crossing earned her a ticker-tape parade on her arrival in the

United States. Injuries cut short her competitive career in the 1930s, when she became a swimming instructor.

Einstein, Albert (1879–1955) *physicist*

Born in Ulm, Germany, Einstein published his most important theories of the interrelationship of time, space, and motion while living and working in Europe. He published the special theory of relativity in 1905, and the general theory of relativity in 1916. These two publications made up a foundation of atomic physics, which would suggest, later in the century, the possibilities of atomic weapons as well as power generation by controlled atomic reactions. In 1913 he was appointed director of theoretical physics at the Kaiser Wilhelm Institute in Berlin. By 1921, when he won the Nobel Prize in physics for his theories of relativity and the photoelectric effect, Einstein was a world celebrity. He garnered extensive press coverage everywhere he went, but aside from his scientific theories he was also a committed pacifist and a Zionist, positions which drew fierce criticism and ridicule from the political establishment in Germany. The rise of Adolf Hitler and the German Nazi Party during the 1920s and early 1930s prompted Einstein to emigrate to the United States in 1933, after which his property in Germany was confiscated. He was soon appointed a physics professor at the Institute for Advanced Study in Princeton, New Jersey. Watching and worrying over the development of atomic weaponry in Germany, he warned President Roosevelt of the possibility of atomic weapons in August 1939, an action that eventually led to the establishment of the Manhattan Project and the building of the first atomic weapons by the United States. After the war, Einstein published a theory of the unified field, but rejected the chance outcomes of the new quantum physics, in which traditional mathematic constructions no longer held sway.

Ellington, Edward Kennedy "Duke" (1899–1974) *jazz bandleader, composer*

Born in Washington, D.C., Ellington earned his nickname from his courtly dress and manners, but his musical tastes ran to ragtime and blues, styles which were still held in low regard when he was young. A skilled pianist, he began playing professionally as a teenager, forming his own band, the Washingtonians, that caught attention with the skill of its soloists and the unique, subtle, complex ensemble compositions of its leader. Ellington moved to New York in 1923, where he gathered the city's best musicians into the 12-member

Duke Ellington Orchestra, which had its landmark debut at the Cotton Club in 1927. With arranger Billy Strayhorn, whom he hired in 1939, he composed dozens of jazz masterpieces, including "Take the A Train," "Mood Indigo," "Black and Tan Fantasy," "Sophisticated Lady," and "Satin Doll." The Ellington band took its first national tour in 1931 and was one of the busiest swing orchestras of the 1930s. Over the years, the band would give approximately 20,000 performances. In the 1940s and 1950s, Ellington stretched out into "jazz concertos," tone poems, motion picture soundtracks, an opera, and music for ballet. For his pioneering work in jazz composition he won the U.S. Medal of Freedom in 1969 and the French Legion d'Honneur in 1973.

Fermi, Enrico (1901–1954) *physicist*

Born in Rome, Italy, Fermi, a scientific prodigy, won a scholarship at age 17 to the prestigious Scuola Normale Superiore in Pisa with a paper on sound waves. After earning a doctorate at the University of Pisa in 1922, he moved to Göttingen, Germany, where he studied with physicist Max Born. In 1926 he published a theory of the physicist Wolfgang Pauli's "exclusion principle," which deals with the measurements and characteristics of subatomic particles. In 1927 he was hired as a physics professor at the University of Rome. In the 1930s Fermi worked out the possibilities of controlled atomic reactions, the decay of neutrons, and the creation of new elements through bombardment of other elements by neutrons. In 1938, on being awarded the Nobel Prize in physics for his work on neutron reactions and radioactivity, he emigrated directly from Sweden to the United States, in fear of Fascist reprisals against his family and his wife, who was Jewish. In 1941 Fermi became a professor at the University of Chicago, where, as a leader of the Argonne Project, he designed the first controlled fission reaction, an achievement that led directly to the construction of the first atomic bomb. After the war Fermi oversaw the construction of a pioneering particle accelerator at the University of Chicago. In 1954 he received the first Atomic Energy Commission award, which was renamed the Fermi Award after his death.

Fitzgerald, F. Scott (1896–1940) *novelist, short story writer*

Born in St. Paul, Minnesota, Fitzgerald attended Princeton and enjoyed instant success with his novel of college life, *This Side of Paradise,* in 1920. In the same year, he married Zelda Sayre. The couple moved among a literary echelon, dubbed by Gertrude Stein the "Lost Generation," which also included Ernest Hemingway and which still defines for many the essence of the Jazz Age and the Roaring Twenties. His novel *The Beautiful and the Damned* appeared in 1921, and was followed by *The Great Gatsby,* considered by many to be Fitzgerald's finest work, in 1925. In the 1930s, the Great Depression ended the Fitzgerald's glamorous lifestyle, and Fitzgerald went into a creative slump which reached a low point after he moved to Hollywood to work as a screenwriter. He died of a heart attack in 1940.

Ford, Henry (1863–1947) *industrialist*

Born on a farm in Wayne County, Michigan, Henry Ford found his first stable employment as a mechanic for Westinghouse steam-propelled traction engines. During the 1890s he began assembling internal combustion engines, finally completing a working automobile in June 1896. Backed by William Murphy, a Detroit businessman, Ford founded the Detroit Automobile Company in 1899; after the company failed he turned his attention to racing cars. As the automobile industry developed, Ford earned his greatest early fame not for his products, but for the wages he paid his employees. In 1914, he took the astonishing steps of increasing the wages of his workers to $5 a day and reducing the working day to eight hours. Ford saw his workers as all part of a big family—*his* family, and he carried through by providing housing, recreation, and a very careful watch over their personal lives. Ford's streamlined assembly lines, minutely timed and managed, turned the workers into automatons, decently paid but severely tested by monotony and tyrannical supervision. As an auto producer, Ford succeeded like none other through the early 1920s, when his River Rouge plant turned out about 17 million relatively simple and inexpensive Model T cars. Feeling the competitive heat from Chrysler and General Motors, Ford rolled out a completely new model, the Model A, in 1927, which provided the country with a national media and cultural event.

Frost, Robert (1874–1963) *poet*

Born in San Francisco, Frost moved to New England at the age of 11 after the death of his father. He began writing poetry while in high school and afterwards attended Dartmouth and Harvard without earning degrees. After settling on a New Hampshire farm in

1900, Frost worked as a schoolteacher while trying to get his verses published. At first unsuccessful, he moved to England in 1912, where his first books of poems, *A Boy's Will* (1913) and *North of Boston* (1914) were published. Frost wrote against the symbolist and experimental currents of the time, working in a more traditional lyric vein that stamped him as a literary conservative. His poetry began drawing a large audience in the United States during World War I, especially with the publication of *Mountain Interval,* which includes the classic "The Road Not Taken." After returning to the United States, he settled again in New England. In 1924 he earned the first of four Pulitzer Prizes with his book *New Hampshire,* containing his best-known poem, "Stopping by Woods on a Snowy Evening." Life in rural New England remained the subject of his verses, with tragedy as well as humor expressed in the straightforward and laconic speech of the region.

Garvey, Marcus (1887–1940) *African nationalist*
Born in Saint Ann's Bay, Jamaica, Garvey first worked as a printer's apprentice, then as a printer in the Jamaican capital of Kingston. After traveling through Central and South America, he moved to England in 1912, where the discrimination he witnessed turned him to a deep study and reflection on African history, particularly the story of European colonialism. In 1914, Garvey returned to Jamaica, where he founded the Universal Negro Improvement Association (UNIA), an organization dedicated to "Pan-Africanism" and the founding of an independent black republic on the African continent. Garvey brought the organization to Harlem, where he moved in 1916. His stirring oratory, and the publicity brought to the organization by the *Negro World* newspaper that he founded, quickly grew the UNIA to a membership of several million. Garvey urged total economic and political independence for African Americans, backing up his ideas with the Negro Factories Corporation and the Black Star Line, a shipping concern intended to carry emigrants back to a new African homeland. The Black Star Line quickly failed, however, and in 1922 Garvey was indicted for defrauding investors in the business. He was convicted and sentenced to a term in a federal penitentiary. After serving two years of his sentence, he was deported to Jamaica, while the UNIA died a slow death under less inspired leaders.

Gershwin, George (1898–1937) *musician, composer*
Born in Brooklyn, New York, Gershwin began formal musical training with classical professors, including Henry Cowell and Joseph Schillinger. His first hit song, "Swanee," which was published in 1918, would be popularized by Al Jolson on hundreds of vaudeville stages. Soon after, Gershwin was making a good living by knocking out Tin Pan Alley tunes that he wrote in collaboration with his brother, lyricist Ira Gershwin. The Gershwins wrote their first musical comedy, *La, La, Lucille,* in 1919, and scored a smash hit with *Lady Be Good* in 1924, following up with *Funny Face* in 1927 and *Of Thee I Sing,* the first Pulitzer Prize–winning musical comedy, in 1931. A musician of astounding inventiveness and technique, Gershwin showcased his piano ability at the invitation of bandleader Paul Whiteman, who had heard and admired the composer's opera *135th Street* in 1924. The result was *Rhapsody in Blue,* a "jazz concerto" that debuted in 1924 and brought the popular new musical form to the concert hall stage. The following year he wrote the even more ambitious *Concerto in F.* The *Second Rhapsody* debuted in 1928, and Gershwin's opera *Porgy and Bess,* based on the best-selling novel *Porgy,* by DuBose Heyward, appeared in 1935.

Goddard, Robert (1882–1945) *pioneer rocket scientist*
Goddard was born in Worcester, Massachusetts, where he studied at the Worcester Polytechnic Institute and Clark University. In 1914 Goddard began his career as a physics teacher at Clark; in the meantime he began studying the problems and possibilities of liquid-fueled rocket flight above the earth's atmosphere. During World War I, Goddard created a portable artillery launcher that was later developed into the bazooka. In 1919, the Smithsonian Institution published Goddard's groundbreaking paper, *A Method of Reaching Extreme Altitudes.* In the early 1920s, he began designing fuel tanks and propulsion systems of new rockets to be fueled by gasoline and liquid oxygen, which provided the necessary steady thrust for attaining outerspace flight. On March 16, 1926, in a vacant field in Auburn, Massachusetts, Goddard carried out the first successful launch of a liquid-fueled rocket, which reached an altitude of 41 feet during a flight of 2.5 seconds. In 1929, aviator Charles Lindbergh helped Goddard secure a grant from David Guggenheim to continue his researches. In the 1930s, Goddard moved his workshops and launchpads to the remote deserts of eastern New Mexico, where he worked in purposeful secrecy. During World War II, he was engaged by the U.S. Navy to develop a liquid-propelled aircraft engine, which became an important precursor to the modern jet

engine. In the meantime, Goddard saw many of his ideas adopted by Germany in the design for the V-2 liquid-fueled bomb, an unstoppable weapon that terrorized the people of England.

Grange, Harold Edward "Red" (1903–1991)
football player

Born in Forksville, Pennsylvania, Grange, after a spectacular high school football career in Wheaton, Illinois, played with the University of Illinois team from 1923 until 1925, scoring 31 touchdowns and running for 3,367 yards. His spectacular open field running drew national attention and earned him places each of his three seasons on the All-America team, twice as a halfback and once as a quarterback. After graduation, Grange signed on as a professional with the Chicago Bears, scoring 1,058 points over his 10-year career. The reputation that earned him the nickname of the "Galloping Ghost" in college followed him to the new professional leagues, where he played an important role in establishing the sport. After retiring in 1934, Grange worked as a radio and television announcer.

Griffith, David Lewelyn Wark (D.W.) (1875–1948)
film director

Born in La Grange, Kentucky, D. W. Griffith first appeared in motion pictures as a member of the Biograph acting company in 1907. He directed his first film, *The Adventures of Dollie,* in the next year, and over the next few years directed his own acting company in hundreds of short two-reelers of all genres. Griffith pioneered many techniques that would become Hollywood standards, including closeups, montage, dissolves, flashbacks, and cross-cutting, in which disparate scenes are presented in rapid alteration to build suspense. Working with cameraman Billy Bitzer, Griffith's directing skill and visual imagination made Biograph one of the most respected early movie companies. In 1915, his Civil War epic *The Birth of a Nation* swept the country, drawing packed houses everywhere, but his multistoried historical picture *Intolerance,* released in 1916, proved too complex for the moviegoing masses, and Griffith lost a substantial sum. Griffith's pictures were far ahead of their time, sometimes running several hours, emphasizing grand themes and complex plots. In 1920, Griffith formed United Artists, with Douglas Fairbanks, Mary Pickford, and Charles Chaplin; for this company he would direct *Broken Blossoms* (1919), *Way Down East* (1920), *America* (1924), and *Lady of the Pavements* (1929). The sound era ended his career however, as his only two sound efforts, *Abraham Lincoln* (1930) and *The Struggle* (1931), were box office failures.

Hardin, Lil (1898–1971) *jazz pianist*

A member of the Hot Five and Hot Seven bands, which were founded and led by Louis Armstrong, Hardin moved to Chicago from Memphis in 1918. Her career as a pianist began as a music demonstrator at Jones' Music Store, where she drew large crowds of sheet music customers as well as admiring professional musicians and promoters. After being hired by the New Orleans Creole Jazz Band, she became a citywide sensation. She left to start her own band at the Dreamland Cafe on State Street, after which she joined up with trumpeter Louis Armstrong in Joe "King" Oliver's Creole Jazz Band, which played at Chicago's premier hotspot, the Lincoln Gardens. In 1923, King Oliver's band made a series of historic recordings, the first ever of a black jazz band. Soon afterward Lil Hardin married Louis Armstrong, and both left the band. The remainder of her career was overshadowed by Armstrong's success on radio, in the movies, and on television, but after divorcing Armstrong in 1938 she enjoyed a second career as a swing-band vocalist for Decca Records.

Harding, Warren Gamaliel (1865–1923) *newspaper editor, lawmaker, U.S. president*

Born near Corsica, Ohio, Harding as a boy worked as a typesetter on the *Caledonia Argus,* a local newspaper. After graduating from Ohio Central College, he tried teaching and insurance sales before returning to newspaper work. After being fired from the Marion *Democratic Mirror* for his support of a Republican candidate, Harding bought the rival Marion *Star.* He married Florence DeWolfe in 1891, and with her encouragement and support soon began a political career. Harding was elected a state senator in 1898. He became Ohio's lieutenant governor in 1903; in 1914 he was elected as U.S. senator from Ohio. In 1920, while the Republican party was deadlocked in the effort to choose a presidential candidate, Harding was eagerly promoted by his Ohio campaign manager Harry Daugherty. Harding had a spotty record in the Senate, having introduced no legislation and not bothering to show up for about half of the Senate's roll call votes. Despite the fact that he had no interest in the presidency, no opinions on many issues of national interest, and preferred to remain a senator, he accepted the Republican presidential nomination in August 1920. He then soundly defeated James Cox in November—the first presidential winner to come directly from a term in the U.S. Senate. Harding brought several of his Ohio associates to Washington and awarded them important government posts. But as the scandals surrounding the Ohio Gang began reaching the public, Harding saw his support slipping away. He left on a speaking trip to Canada and Alaska. On returning to San Francisco, he died in his hotel room on August 2, 1923.

Held, John (1889–1958) *highest-paid illustrator of the 1920s*

Held created cartoons, magazine covers, book jackets, comic strips, and prints that captured the scenes and spirit of the Roaring Twenties. After moving to New York from his home in Salt Lake City in 1910, he worked as a freelance illustrator for dozens of publications, including *Life,* the *New Yorker,* and *Vanity Fair.* A typical Held character was a college-age flapper or "sheik," enjoying the decade's new freedoms but caught in a quixotic situation adroitly summarized by a dryly witty caption. Held's best known cartoons and block prints ran in the *New Yorker,* where he enjoyed the patronage of publisher Harold Ross, a Salt Lake City friend. After the 1920s, Held turned to writing and sculpting, finding a depressed market for his Roaring Twenties caricatures; in the atomic age of the 1950s and 1960s, Heldian flappers returned as objects of nostalgia for a happier and more innocent time.

Hemingway, Ernest (1899–1961) *writer*

Born in Oak Park, Illinois, Hemingway, after graduating from Oak Park High School, joined the Kansas City Star as a reporter, but soon volunteered as an ambulance driver on the World War I battlefields of northern Italy. After the war, he wrote for the Toronto *Star,* settling in Paris to work out a new literary style with the encouragement of expatriates Gertrude Stein and Ezra Pound. Hemingway's first books were *Three Stories and Ten Poems* (1923) and *in our time* (1924). He presented a spare, straightforward prose style seemingly stripped of conventional literary sentiment and description, drawing on the cynical despair of a generation stripped of its illusions by the wastefulness of war. The novels *The Sun Also Rises* (1926), *Men Without Women* (1927), and *A Farewell to Arms* (1929) brought Hemingway fame and large sales in the United States, to which he returned in the early 1930s. In his major works of the 1930s, *Death in the Afternoon* (1932) and *Green Hills of Africa* (1932), Hemingway celebrated the raw and dangerous experiences of men working as bullfighters and playing as big-

game hunters. As a writer he sought a voice of authenticity and the impression of direct experience, without which he saw the common secondhand fiction writer as something of an effete phony. Hemingway's approach would influence many of his contemporaries although his own physical and creative decline in the 1950s led to a violent suicide.

Hoover, Herbert Clark (1874–1964) *U.S. president*

Born in West Branch, Iowa, Hoover was the first president born west of the Mississippi River. At the age of 17, Hoover enrolled at Stanford University; after graduating he worked as a mining engineer in Australia and in China, where he served as chief engineer for the Chinese Bureau of Mines. Hoover established his own engineering firm in London in 1908. His skill and knowledge made a success of mining ventures all over the world, and by 1914 he was a wealthy man. On the outbreak of war in 1914, Hoover was appointed head of the Commission for Relief in Belgium. When the United States entered the war, President Wilson appointed Hoover head of the U.S. Food Administration. In this post, Hoover organized food relief for Europe, both during and after the war, and his success made him internationally known. Already considered presidential material, Hoover was asked by President Warren Harding to serve as Secretary of Commerce, a post he held under Harding as well as Harding's successor, Calvin Coolidge. Hoover organized commissions to study child welfare, labor problems, foreign trade, manufacturing, and other issues, and was widely credited with ending the 12-hour workday. In 1928 he was nominated on the first ballot by the Republican Party and, with the help of "Coolidge prosperity," defeated Al Smith, a Democrat, in the election. Seven months after his term began, however, a tremendous stock market crash put a sudden end to the Roaring Twenties and Coolidge prosperity, and Hoover found himself blamed for acting too little and too late to stem the Great Depression. Hoover began several public works programs late in his administration, a move toward government intervention that would be taken up wholeheartedly by Franklin Roosevelt, who defeated Hoover by a large margin in the presidential election of November 1932.

Hoover, John Edgar (1895–1972) *longtime FBI director*

Born in Washington, D.C., Hoover joined the Department of Justice as a "file reviewer" in 1917.

Attorney General A. Mitchell Palmer appointed him special assistant and director of the General Intelligence Division of the Bureau of Investigation in 1919. Given responsibility for tracking the nation's anarchists, socialists, and assorted subversives, as defined by Attorney General A. Mitchell Palmer and later by himself, Hoover created an elaborate filing system of cross-indexed lists of suspects that eventually included 450,000 names. In 1924 Hoover was named head of the Bureau of Investigation, later the Federal Bureau of Investigation (FBI). He would carry his index system forward to cover millions of U.S. citizens suspected of communist sympathies, a system that remained in place at his death. In 1925, Hoover established the Bureau of Investigation's centralized fingerprint file; he would later found a state-of-the-art crime laboratory in 1932 and the FBI academy in 1935.

Hopper, Edward (1882–1967) *painter*
Born in Nyack, New York, Hopper studied with Robert Henri at the New York School of Art and traveled to Europe between 1906 and 1910 to study new painting styles of cubism and surrealism. Instead of taking up these new currents, however, Hopper found inspiration in the more realistic style and subjects of Spanish artist Francisco Goya and the French painter Édouard Manet. Hopper made unblinking realism his hallmark, often utilizing flat, geometric designs suggested by the walls, windows, and corners of the modern urban landscape. After exhibiting at New York's Armory Show in 1913, Hopper struggled for several years while more experimental artists drew attention and eventually the rewards of mainstream status. He held firmly to his own style, depicting the lonely streets, sidewalks, cafes, and storefronts that provided a somber counterpoint to the country's frenetic pace and insistent progress.

Hughes, James Langston (1902–1967) *poet, playwright, columnist, leading figure of the Harlem Renaissance*
Born in Joplin, Missouri, Hughes moved to Lincoln, Illinois, in 1914 after his parents separated, and then to Cleveland, where he finished high school in 1920. His first poem, "The Negro Speaks of Rivers," was published in *The Crisis* in 1921, the year he graduated from high school. Hughes entered Lincoln University in 1926. Upon graduating, he left on an extensive lecture tour during 1931–32; his scathing remarks on the state of black institutions played an important role in future activism among black students throughout the nation.

Hughes was best known as a poet and strongly believed in the power of poetry to protest and improve social conditions for African Americans.

Hurston, Zora Neale (1901–1960) *novelist, short story writer, anthropologist, folklorist*
Born in Eatonville, Florida, Hurston wrote tales and novels drawing on the folklore of the Deep South, of her all-black hometown, and of the Caribbean region. After moving away from Eatonville as a teenager, she worked for a traveling theater troupe that performed works by Gilbert and Sullivan. She quit the troupe when it reached Baltimore, where she enrolled in the Morgan Academy. From 1919 until 1924, she attended Howard University in Washington, D.C., where she first began to write. Her first short story, "John Redding Goes to Sea," appeared in the magazine *Stylus* in 1921. Upon leaving Howard, she won a scholarship to Barnard College in New York, where she studied with Franz Boas, a leading anthropologist, from 1925 until 1928. In New York she grew acquainted with the leading artists and writers of the Harlem Renaissance movement. During this time, she wrote a short story, "Spunk," which appeared in *The New Negro,* and collaborated with Langston Hughes on the periodical *Fire!* She collected her university researches into the folktales and traditions of the South in *Mules and Men,* which was published in 1931 and was the first book of black folklore written by an African American. Hurston's best-known novels date from the 1930s and include *Their Eyes were Watching God* (1937) and *Moses, Man of the Mountain* (1939).

Johnson, James Weldon (1871–1938) *African-American attorney, author, composer, diplomat*
Born in Jacksonville, Florida, Johnson won admission to the Florida bar in 1898, the first African American to do so, but gave up a career as an attorney in 1901 to move to New York City and take up composing with his brother John Rosamond Johnson. Their collaboration resulted in more than 200 songs, including the future anthem "Lift Every Voice and Sing." After supporting Theodore Roosevelt's election in 1904, Johnson was appointed as a consul to Venezuela and then Nicaragua. He wrote *The Autobiography of an Ex-Colored Man,* his best-known work, in 1912. After leaving the foreign service, he moved to Harlem in 1913, becoming a field secretary for the National Association for the Advancement of Colored People (NAACP) in 1916, and then executive secretary of the organization

in 1920. During the 1920s he worked prominently for an end to lynching and for more open and fair voting registration in the south. His book *God's Trombones—Seven Negro Sermons in Verse* was published in 1927. On leaving his post with the NAACP he became professor of literature at Fisk University; during his tenure he wrote *Black Manhattan* in 1930 and *Along This Way,* his autobiography, in 1933.

Jolson, Al (Asa Yoelson) (1886–1950) *vaudeville singer, film star*

Born in Seredzius, Russia, Jolson, after emigrating to the United States and then leaving his Orthodox Jewish home in Washington, D.C. and discarding his given name of Asa Yoelson, succeeded in vaudeville by portraying a black-faced minstrel, a role that he brought to the Warner Brothers studio in 1927 in *The Jazz Singer,* Hollywood's first sound movie. White audiences on Broadway and everywhere else loved his eloquent singing, exaggerated mannerisms, and depiction of black figures nostalgic for a happier and simpler times on the plantations of the Deep South. Jolson made the 1920s' most successful sound recordings and brought his act to the new medium of radio. Several of his hits, including "Toot, Toot, Tootsie," "Swanee," and "California Here I Come," became Jazz Age standards.

Kahn, Albert (1869–1942) *industrial architect*

Kahn created a new and more efficient factory for clients in the automobile, textile, chemical, and food industries. He was born in Germany, the son of a rabbi, and moved to Detroit in 1880. He apprenticed in the architectural firm of Mason and Rice, where he became chief engineer in the 1890s. In 1902, Kahn founded his own firm and soon thereafter won his first big commission, for a group of 10 factories, from Packard Motors. In 1909 Henry Ford hired Kahn to create a single facility in Highland Park, Michigan, in which Ford workers would carry out all stages in the construction of the Model T. The factory, built of a steel frame and reinforced concrete, allowed better light and ventilation for Ford's assembly line workers. Later Kahn built even larger facilities at the River Rouge site, the heart of Ford's manufacturing operations and the country's first modern, integrated industrial plant. In the 1930s, Kahn brought his talents to the Soviet Union, where he played a key role in the forced and frenetic industrialization of Soviet society under Josef Stalin. During World War II, Kahn's firm designed many important military factories, including the Willow Run bomber plant, the Glenn Martin aircraft assembly building, and the Chrysler Tank Arsenal.

Keaton, Buster (1895–1966) *film comedian*

Born in Piqua, Kansas, Keaton was the son of touring vaudeville comedians. He made an early debut on the stage, performing from the age of three with his parents as The Three Keatons. He first appeared on the screen with Fatty Arbuckle in *The Butcher Boy* (1917), and in 1920 was signed by Paramount producer Joseph Schenck to make a series of short films. Over the next several years, beginning with *The Saphead* in 1920, Keaton wrote, directed, and starred in 20 films that brought film comedies to new heights of inventiveness and hilarity. Keaton's stoic and stonefaced character managed to survive frustrations and dangers that would have leveled ordinary, more demonstrative men, providing a satiric counterpoint to the exuberant antics of Douglas Fairbanks Jr. and other, slightly ridiculous, film heroes. Keaton's masterpieces, *The Navigator* (1924), *The General* (1927), and *Steamboat Bill* (1927), have proved to be among the most popular, critically acclaimed, and lasting films of the silent era. In 1928 Keaton was sold by Schenck to Metro-Goldwyn-Mayer, which denied the creative independence granted by Paramount, and his films suffered in quality. His career steadily declined during the early sound era of the 1930s, when physical comedy began to give way to the more sophisticated verbal wit of screwball comedies. Keaton continued to play cameo roles through the 1950s and 1960s and was given an honorary award by the Academy of Motion Picture Arts and Sciences in 1959.

Lardner, Ring (1885–1933) *news columnist, short story writer, playwright*

Born in Niles, Michigan, Ring Lardner gave up engineering for a newspaper career that began in 1905 at the *South Bend Times* and continued in 1919 at the *Chicago Tribune,* when he began a sports column entitled "In the Wake of the News." Finding the truth of professional sports a sound basis for fiction, Lardner began a series of short stories, which he collectively entitled *You Know Me Al,* that used slangy syntax and vocabulary to parody ignorant bumpkins in sports and other walks of life. His clay-footed sports heroes found a substantial audience, allowing Lardner to abandon newspaper work and move exclusively into magazine stories in the early 1920s. He later branched out into theater and songwriting. His short story collections include *Round Up, How to Write Short Stories, The Big*

Town, and *The Love Nest;* his play *June Moon* was written in collaboration with George S. Kaufman and found a loyal Broadway audience in 1929.

Leopold, Nathan (1906–1971) and Richard Loeb (1906–1936) *thrill killers*

Leopold and Loeb gained notoriety for their motiveless slaying of 14-year-old Bobby Franks in Chicago. Leopold was the son of a wealthy box manufacturer who showed brilliance at high school and the University of Michigan, becoming an accomplished linguist as well as an authority on botany and ornithology. Obsessed with Friedrich Nietzsche's theory of the superior intellect and the superman, Leopold acquiesced in his friend Richard Loeb's increasingly violent criminal fantasies, which ultimately resulted in murder. Loeb, the son of a Sears, Roebuck executive, was given a strict upbringing that did not counteract fantasies of a spectacular life of crime. In 1923, at 17, he became the youngest graduate in University of Michigan history, although he was also known on campus as a liar, a heavy drinker, and a thief. He instigated the kidnapping and murder of Bobby Franks in May 1924, which would bring about one of the most sensational murder trials of the century. Although Leopold and Loeb were both convicted, their defense attorney, Clarence Darrow, persuaded the judge to spare them the death penalty with a stirring 12-hour summary of the case against them. Loeb was murdered in prison in 1936; Leopold managed to reform himself, taking part in prison medical testing, educating his fellow inmates, and eventually working as a professor and X-ray technician in Puerto Rico after his release in 1958.

Lewis, John L. (1880–1969) *labor leader*

Born in Lucas, Iowa, Lewis was descended from a long line of Welsh coal miners. He began his own career as a miner after leaving the seventh grade. He moved to Panama, Illinois, in 1906, becoming president of the United Mine Workers (UMW) local, then an American Federation of Labor (AFL) organizer, and later, the national UMW vice president. Lewis attained the presidency of the UMW in 1920, a post he would hold for 40 years. His great physical presence, speaking skills, natural stubbornness, and commitment to the miners' cause brought him national attention and notoriety during the near-constant labor troubles among coal miners of the 1920s. In 1935 he withdrew the UMW from the AFL, forming the Committee of Industrial Organizations to work for the founding of larger industrial unions that would represent workers in entire industries. The committee became the Congress of Industrial Organizations in 1938, with Lewis as its first president. The sit-down strike became Lewis's favored method of stopping auto, steel and other industries, thus forcing employers to accede to his demands for higher wages, shorter hours, and better working conditions for the millions of laborers he represented. Although his actions incurred the wrath of business owners as well as government officials, who saw him as singlehandedly crippling the national economy as well as the war effort during World War II, Lewis maintained enormous respect and favor among industrial workers.

Lewis, Sinclair (1885–1951) *novelist*

Born in Sauk Centre, Minnesota, Lewis was the son of a country doctor. In 1903, he was sent to Yale, where he quickly made his mark in the *Yale Literary Magazine.* After writing several novels that found no publisher, Lewis decided to change his style to satire, succeeding in 1920 with *Main Street,* a tale attacking the smug morals and stuffy manners of a small Midwestern town much like his boyhood home. Lewis considered himself a leader of a new literary vanguard that rejected polite, escapist fiction in favor of naturalistic realism and social criticism. Lewis published his most popular novels during the 1920s: *Main Street, Babbitt* in 1922, and *Elmer Gantry* in 1927. His satires of middle-class values and hypocrisy entertained millions of readers in the hypocritical time of Prohibition. Although he finally won the Pulitzer Prize (for *Arrowsmith* in 1925) that he felt he deserved, the quick-tempered Lewis, feeling slighted for not having received it earlier, refused to accept the award. In 1929, he did accept the Nobel Prize in Literature. He died in Rome in 1951.

Lindbergh, Charles (1902–1974) *aviator, public figure*

Charles Lindbergh's solo flight from New York to Paris in May 1927 became the best-known achievement of the decade. Born in Detroit, Lindbergh moved as a boy to Little Falls, Minnesota, where his father, Charles Lindbergh Sr., served as a state congressman. The younger Lindbergh dropped out of the University of Wisconsin in 1922 to pursue a career as a barnstorming pilot. He joined the U.S. Army Air Corps in 1924 and reached an officer's rank in the next year. In 1926 Lindbergh became one of the nation's first pilots to work a regular airmail route, between St. Louis and Chicago. In quest of the $25,000 Raymond Orteig

Prize for the first transatlantic flight between New York and Paris, he gathered the backing of a small group of St. Louis businessmen, arranged for the construction of a single-engine monoplane from the Ryan Aircraft Company in San Diego, and made preparations for a solo flight—considered an impossible risk in the spring of 1927. The flight in his plane, *The Spirit of St. Louis,* began May 20 and ended 33 hours later at Le Bourget airfield, near Paris. His success and daring turned Lindbergh into an instant international hero; it also earned him a promotion to colonel and a Medal of Honor. In 1929, Lindbergh married Anne Morrow, the daughter of Dwight Morrow, U.S. ambassador to Mexico. Beginning in the fall of 1931, the couple embarked on a series of marathon flights over the Pacific and Atlantic oceans to explore future commercial air routes. Relentless publicity after the kidnapping and murder of their baby son drove the couple to Europe; on the eve of World War II Lindbergh returned to the United States to urge nonintervention in the coming conflict with Germany.

Lynd, Robert (1892–1970) **and Lynd, Helen Merrell** (1896–1982) *sociologists, coauthors*
In 1929 Robert and Helen Merrell Lynd published *Middletown,* a comprehensive, in-depth survey of daily life in the United States. Robert Lynd was born in New Albany, Indiana, graduated from Princeton University, and worked as an editor at *Publishers Weekly,* the publishing house of Charles Scribner's Sons, and *The Freeman Magazine.* After serving during World War I, he moved to New York, where he met Helen Merrell, who was born in La Grange, Illinois and was a graduate of Wellesley College. After their marriage in 1922, Robert Lynd received a divinity degree from Union Theological Seminary, after which the couple worked as missionaries in the western United States. Their experience among struggling communities of miners and oil drillers inspired the Lynds to undertake a series of research projects, which culminated in an exhaustive study of life in the representative small town of Muncie, Indiana, for more than 18 months in 1924 and 1925. The Lynds and their staff conducted interviews and gathered statistics through surveys passed out to every Muncie family, inquiring into work habits, buying habits, leisure habits, child-rearing habits and other aspects of daily life. The resulting book, *Middletown,* was the first large-scale work of sociological research undertaken in the United States, and reached a mass audience through six printings in 1929

alone. Residents of Muncie found the book shallow and insulting, but the materialistic lives depicted in the book inspired outside commentators to further eloquence on the greed and empty culture prevalent in the United States. Robert and Helen Lynd were hailed as founders of modern sociology; Robert Lynd gained a professor's chair at Columbia University while his wife taught at Sarah Lawrence College. Their followup, *Middletown in Transition,* was published in the 1930s.

McPherson, Aimee Semple (1890–1944) *evangelist*
McPherson was born Aimee Elizabeth Kennedy near Ingersoll, Ontario. Soon after marrying Pentecostal missionary Robert Semple in 1908, McPherson traveled to Hong Kong, where her husband died in 1910. After returning to the United States, she married again but left her second husband, Harold McPherson, to take up a career as an evangelist and healer. She inaugurated the enormous Angelus Temple in Los Angeles in 1923, where she gave stirring sermons on the Foursquare Gospel Creed, highlighted by inventive sound and light effects, for the next 20 years. She gained a national audience through boisterous traveling revivals and sermons broadcast over the new medium of radio, and claimed in 1926 to have won 400,000 converts to her newfounded International Church of the Foursquare Gospel. She also founded a Bible school and a magazine. In May 1926, however, she staged her own drowning on the California coast, returning five weeks later with a tale of kidnapping and ransom. When it was revealed the McPherson had been engaging in a very worldly tryst, she was tried for fraud and perjury but acquitted.

Mead, Margaret (1901–1978) *anthropologist*
Born in Philadelphia, Mead attended Barnard College and Columbia University in New York City and, in 1926, became a curator at the New York's American Museum of Natural History, three years before attaining her doctorate from Columbia. In 1925, her interest into primitive societies carried her to the South Pacific region, where she studied family groups, sexual behavior patterns, and child rearing. Her book *Coming of Age in Samoa* was published in 1928, followed by *Growing Up in New Guinea* in 1930 and *Sex and Temperament in Three Primitive Societies* in 1935. Mead found in the practices and norms of these distant, less-developed cultures an antidote to the relentless progressivism, artificial norms, and social alienation that seemed endemic to her native culture. These observations

made her a controversial figure among both academics and the public. After World War II her field of interest grew to include the industrialized nations, described in *Male and Female* (1949), *Soviet Attitudes Toward Authority* (1951), *New Lives for Old* (1956), and *Culture and Commitment* (1970).

Mellon, Andrew (1855–1937) *financier, U.S. Secretary of the Treasury, 1921–32*
After leaving the Western University of Pittsburgh just before graduation, Mellon made his start in the lumber business and later achieved the title of bank president through the appointment of his father, Thomas Mellon. The younger Mellon founded Gulf Oil in 1901, became president of the Mellon National Bank in the next year, and also helped to establish the Aluminum Company of America. A key contributor and adviser to the Republican Party, he played an important role in the Republican-led defeat of U.S. participation in the League of Nations after World War I. He won the appointment as treasury secretary from President Harding for his dependable conservatism, skill, and reputation in the matters of public and private finance. Under his guidance, the administrations of Presidents Harding and Coolidge cut public spending and vetoed congressional bills, among them the Bonus Bill and the McNary-Haugen Act, that would have put new demands on the federal treasury. Mellon also stood for drastic tax reduction for businesses and the wealthy, maintaining that high taxes inhibited new investment and economic growth. Although his plan was strongly opposed by the Democratic Party in Congress, Mellon did manage to reduce estate taxes, end gift taxes, and lower the top rate on personal income taxes by one-half, to 20 percent. Late in the 1920s, he turned to art collecting, amassing an enormous collection of European masterpieces that, after his death, became the foundation of the National Gallery of Art in Washington, D.C.

Mencken, H. L. (Henry Louis) (1880–1956) *journalist, critic*
Born the son of a German cigarmaker in Baltimore, Mencken began his newspaper career with the *Baltimore Morning Herald* in 1899, attaining the editorship of the *Herald* in 1905 but then moving to the *Baltimore Sun* in 1906. In 1914 he founded the journal *Smart Set* with critic George Jean Nathan. The partners folded *Smart Set* in 1923 and, in 1924, founded *The American Mercury,* a journal that would become the most popular and successfully controversial literary monthly of the 1920s and early 1930s. In his columns and articles for the *Mercury,* Mencken wielded a bitter, satiric pen at the absurdities and prejudices of American politicians, business leaders, preachers, moralists, and vulgar middle-class ignoramuses, whom he dubbed the "booboiosie." He reveled in the constant criticism attracted by his opinions and the sometimes daring writing of *Mercury* contributors, at one point having himself willingly arrested on the Boston Common for a short story deemed a danger to public morals. He was a champion of new writers, including Sinclair Lewis and Eugene O'Neill, and also devoted himself to a lifelong study of the English language, as described and praised in *The American Language,* an enormous and thorough work of scholarship that first appeared in 1919 and went through several more editions and supplements. Mencken's articles have been collected into several massive volumes, including *Prejudices* (1919). He told his life story in two autobiographies, *Newspaper Days* (1941) and *Heathen Days* (1943).

Millay, Edna St. Vincent (1892–1950) *poet*
Born in Rockland, Maine, Millay, after leaving Vassar College in 1917, published her first verse collection, *Renascence and Other Poems.* She also wrote *Aria da Capo,* a war drama in verse, for the Provincetown Players in 1919. In the next year her lyric poetry appeared in *A Few Figs from Thistles,* her best-known collection. After *Second April* appeared in 1921, *The Ballad of the Harp-Weaver* won the 1922 Pulitzer Prize for poetry. During 1920s, the straightforward yet novel scenes and emotions depicted in her lyric poetry identified her as a rebel against the stilted Victorian rhymes of the past and as a modern among critics and the public, a reputation enhanced by her life among the literary and bohemian circles of New York's Greenwich Village. Radicalized by the Sacco-Vanzetti case, she then turned to political causes in some of her poetry, and in the view of many readers, lost the freshness and naturalness of her early works. In the 1930s she began working in the sonnet form, bringing out *Fatal Interview,* a cycle of sonnets in 1931, as well as *Collected Sonnets* in 1941.

Mitchell, William "Billy" (1879–1936) *aviator, military adviser*
Billy Mitchell was born in Nice, France, to American parents and grew up in Wisconsin. He enlisted in the U.S. Army at the outbreak of the Spanish-American

War, later rising through the ranks of the army signal corps. During World War I, he learned to fly and became aviation adviser to General John Pershing, head of the American Expeditionary Forces. Mitchell commanded the largest military air group during the war, during which he attained the rank of brigadier general. After the war, Mitchell was named assistant chief of the army air service. Through a series of books and articles, he insisted on the crucial importance of air power in any future conflict and, to demonstrate his belief, arranged a series of spectacular test bombings off the Atlantic coast from 1921 to 1923. Mitchell was tolerated by the military establishment until he began accusing his superior officers and government officials of incompetence and criminal neglect of the development of the nation's military air power. He was court-martialed for insubordination in 1925 and, rather than accept the sentence of a five-year suspension, resigned his commission in the next year. Mitchell continued to call for an independent air force and a unified command for all branches of the service, actions that would finally be taken two years after the end of World War II.

Morrow, Dwight (1873–1931) *banker, diplomat, U.S. senator from New Jersey*
After graduating from Amherst College and Columbia Law School, Morrow joined the firm of Reed, Simpson, Thacher, and Bartlett, which granted him a partnership in 1905. He specialized in corporate finance and banking, and won prominent political appointments in New Jersey, where he served as chairman of the New Jersey Prison Inquiry Commission and the Board of Control, which passed a series of prison reform measures. He joined the banking house of J. P. Morgan in 1914 and earned the Distinguished Service Medal for his work as a civilian aide to General Pershing during the war. In 1927, President Coolidge appointed Morrow ambassador to Mexico, with instructions to straighten out the conflict over oil and sovereignty between the two states. Morrow's ability to listen and sympathize served him well as ambassador, and he quickly gained the trust of the Mexican people and government. During a successful four-year term he steered the two nations away from confrontation and also managed to reconcile the secular Mexican government to the Roman Catholic Church. In 1929, Morrow's daughter Anne married aviator Charles Lindbergh. Morrow was elected to the U.S. Senate in 1930 but his term was cut short by his death in the next year.

Morton, Jelly Roll (Ferdinand Joseph La Menthe) (ca. 1885–1941) *jazz pianist*
Born Ferdinand Joseph La Menthe in New Orleans, Louisiana, Morton was the son of a Creole family. He began his piano career at the age of 10 and later worked in the bordellos of the Storyville district. While drifting through the South and West, Morton worked as a pool shark, professional gambler, pimp, and comedian. He performed for vaudeville and traveling carnivals, working many different forms into his musical repertoire, including Creole, Spanish, blues, and ragtime music. After moving from the west coast to Chicago in 1922, his first jazz records were cut in 1923, in which his first hit, *Wolverine Blues,* made the early fortunes of the Victor recording company. He performed off and on with the New Orleans Rhythm Kings until 1926 and then formed his own small group, the Red Hot Peppers, which made some of the most popular jazz records of the decade. He was one of the first jazz musicians to work out extended compositions, in which individual improvisation was incorporated into careful arrangements expressly designed for the three-minute length of the studio recording. Morton's popularity declined along with the New Orleans and Chicago styles in the 1930s, and by the mid-1930s he was virtually forgotten. A post-mortem revival would bring him recognition as a seminal figure in the development of early jazz.

O'Keeffe, Georgia (1887–1986) *artist*
Born in Sun Prairie, Wisconsin, O'Keeffe studied at the Art Institute of Chicago and at the Art Students League in New York, after which she began a career in commercial art in Chicago and as a teacher in Amarillo and Canyon, Texas. Her first major exhibition, of a series of abstract charcoal drawings, was held in New York in 1916 under the auspices of Alfred Stieglitz, a photographer and art dealer whom she married in 1924. During the 1920s she painted precise and sensuous canvases of flowers as well as the industrial landscapes of New York, leading some critics to place her in league with the urban painters Charles Sheeler and Edward Hopper. In 1929, she moved west to Taos, New Mexico, later moving to remote and unpopulated regions where she applied her unique style to the natural forms of the desert.

O'Neill, Eugene (1888–1953) *playwright*
Eugene O'Neill grew up in a tumultuous family in sight of the Broadway theater district, where his child-

hood gave him sufficient material for a lifetime of playwriting. After being dismissed from Princeton University, O'Neill wandered as a merchant seaman for several years before writing his first play in 1913. Disregarding the commercial conventions of popular theater, O'Neill created dialogue and characters that turned entertainment into drama, and drama into psychological epic. *Beyond the Horizon,* a one-act play produced in 1920, began a productive period that lasted for 15 years and included several landmark plays of the 20th century: *The Emperor Jones* (1920), *Strange Interlude* (1928), *Desire Under the Elms* (1924), and *Mourning Becomes Electra* (1931). Inspired by the classical drama of Greece, O'Neill broke modern conventions by using expressionistic devices such as masks and by experimenting with form and length. He won the Pulitzer Prize in Drama four times and the Nobel Prize in Literature in 1936.

Palmer, A. Mitchell (1872–1936) *U.S. attorney general*
Born into a Quaker family in Moosehead, Pennsylvania, Palmer attended Swarthmore College, graduating with honors at 19. From 1909 to 1915, he served three terms in Congress, and as chairman of the Pennsylvania's Democratic delegation to the 1912 convention, he swung the state and the convention to nominate Woodrow Wilson for president. Offered the post of secretary of war, Palmer declined, accepting instead a judgeship in the U.S. Court of Claims. A steadfast supporter of Wilson and the League of Nations, he was rewarded with appointment to attorney general in 1919. Soon after his home was bombed by an anarchist group in June 1919, he established the General Intelligence Division of the Department of Justice to carry out deportations of undesirables—radicals, anarchists, Bolsheviks, and any immigrants suspected of leftist sympathies. The Palmer Raids continued through January 1920, with more than 4,000 arrests and 600 deportations, but the press and public grew increasingly critical of the arbitrary arrests and detentions. When Palmer predicted a radical coup attempt on May Day 1920, and was proven wrong, his long-held hope for the Democratic nomination for president that summer faded along with his political career.

Parker, Dorothy Rothschild (1893–1967) *poet, critic, short story writer*
Born Dorothy Rothschild in West End, New Jersey, Parker's life had a tragic first act, as she suffered the early death of her mother, the death of her brother Henry aboard the *Titanic* in 1912, and the death of her father in the next year. After leaving the Blessed Sacrament Convent in New York City, Parker joined *Vogue* magazine in 1916 as drama and literary critic, transferring to *Vanity Fair* in 1918, where she worked as the only female drama critic in New York. After she insulted Billie Burke, wife of the influential theatrical producer Florenz Ziegfeld, Parker found herself without a job. However, as an original member of the Algonquin Round Table, Parker was in supportive company, and her articles and short stories found acceptance among publishers who appreciated her dark, sardonic take on current events and society. Her first short story, "Such a Pretty Little Picture," was published in 1922. She contributed to the first issues of the *New Yorker* in 1925, and after returning from a trip to Paris published a volume of poetry, *Enough Rope,* that turned out a commercial and critical success. Her story "Big Blonde" won the prestigious O. Henry Award in 1929, a year that also saw her move to Hollywood and take up screenwriting for Metro-Goldwyn-Mayer. She won an Academy Award for the screenplay of *A Star Is Born* in 1937. Hauled before the House Un-American Activities Committee in 1953, she remained adamantly uncooperative and still suspect in light of her public commitment to socialism and leftist causes that dated from the Sacco-Vanzetti trial of 1927. For this, she was blacklisted.

Pickford, Mary (Gladys Marie Smith) (1893–1979) *film actress*
Born Gladys Marie Smith in Toronto, Canada, Pickford, who began her stage career as a teenager, was mentored by Broadway producer David Belasco beginning in 1907. In 1909 she began appearing in productions by D. W. Griffith, making appearances for the Biograph, Mutoscope, and Majestic studios. Her significant early films include *Madame Butterfly* (1915), *Rebecca of Sunnybrook Farm* (1917) and *Daddy Long Legs* (1919). Her radiant and innocent visage enraptured film audiences, but her nickname of "America's Sweetheart" was belied by a sharp business acumen that rapidly made her one of the best-paid stars in Hollywood. A contract with the Famous Players Company in 1916 netted her a huge salary as well as an independent production company, an arrangement unheard of for Hollywood actors of that time and for long afterward. In 1919, she formed United Artists with D. W. Griffith, Charlie Chaplin, and Douglas

Fairbanks; in the following year she married Fairbanks, thus forming the first superstar couple in Hollywood history. Her credits as producer and actor during the 1920s include *Little Annie Rooney* (1925), *Sparrows* (1926), and *My Best Girl* (1927). She won an Academy Award for best actress in 1929 for *Coquette,* but in the same year, the only film she made with Douglas Fairbanks, *The Taming of the Shrew,* failed at the box office, and Pickford found her audience declining in the early sound era. She retired from the movies in 1933.

Porter, Cole (1893–1964) *popular composer, lyricist*
Born in Peru, Indiana, Porter even as a boy wrote songs. He debuted with "Song of the Birds," which his mother had published in an edition of 100 copies. He followed with a collegiate career at Yale, where he wrote the school anthem "Bulldog Yale," and at Harvard, where he wrote his first musical score for the revue *See America First.* When this show closed quickly on Broadway, he despairingly left for Paris, where he created a spectacular but fictional career in the French Foreign Legion and the French army to raise his profile for newspapers back home. After the war, Porter scrambled for several years, until his first Broadway success with *Paris* in 1928. Audiences enjoyed the show's catchy and sophisticated tunes, which included "Let's Do It," and Porter followed with a series of Broadway triumphs that made the 1930s the most rewarding decade of his life. Porter wrote words, music, and lyrics to *Fifty Million Frenchmen* in 1929, and *Anything Goes* in 1934, and had hit singles with "Night and Day," "Begin the Beguine," "You're the Top," and "What is This Thing Called Love?" Seriously injured and permanently handicapped by a riding accident in 1937, Porter carried on with *Kiss Me Kate* in 1949 and *Can-Can* in 1953.

Post, Emily Price (1872–1960) *author of nationally renowned books on etiquette*
The daughter of a wealthy architect, Bruce Price, Emily Price Post was born in Baltimore and reared in New York City from age five. She attended a well regarded finishing school and enjoyed the privileges of life among the well-to-do. In 1904, she published *The Flight of a Moth,* based on letters she had written home during European voyages. After a divorce from Edwin M. Post, she took up writing to supplement her income, turning out popular novels, stories, essays, and travel memoirs. In 1921 she began a pioneering work

on social etiquette, published the next year as *Etiquette in Society, in Business, in Politics, and at Home.* The book found a wide audience and was immediately accepted as a standard guide to good manners, in an age that saw the proper Victorian foundations being swept away by war, economic turmoil, and shifts in the country's basic social and economic makeup. Post later wrote regular columns for *McCall's* magazine and established the Emily Post Institute to carry on her publishing and business interests.

Pound, Ezra (1885–1972) *poet, critic, editor*
Born in Hailey, Idaho, Ezra Pound determined from an early age to become a poet. He studied at the University of Pennsylvania and at Hamilton College, in New York state. After a short and discouraging attempt to earn his way as a professor and professional poet, Pound emigrated to Europe, where he published his first poetry volume, *A Lume Spento,* in 1908. After a short time in Venice, he moved to London, where he worked as a secretary to Irish poet W. B. Yeats, teacher, and freelance writer for *Poetry* magazine and *The Little Review.* As a poetic scholar, he launched the imagist and vorticist movements; as a literary critic, he edited and sponsored the experimental works of T. S. Eliot, sending Eliot's *The Waste Land* to the United States for publication in *Poetry* magazine in 1915. Pound worked in a decidedly nontraditional style that strove for precise description and emotional complexity and often borrowed from a variety of cultures foreign to the American poetic tradition, including those of Asia and Renaissance Europe. Pound published his collections *Personae* in 1910, *Cathay* in 1915, and *Lustra* in 1916. Inspired by the structure of Walt Whitman's *Leaves of Grass* (ironically, Pound intensely disliked Whitman's actual verse and use of poetic devices), Pound began a sequence of 116 poems under the title of *The Cantos* in 1915, an epic work that would not be completed until 1970. Disgusted with the degraded culture that he saw as a result of advanced capitalism in the United States and western Europe, Pound embraced Mussolini's Fascist Italy in the late 1920s, alienating many of the expatriate writers he had encouraged and fostered in France, England, and Italy. During World War II, he supported the Axis powers in a series of radio broadcasts, an action that brought imprisonment in Italy at the end of World War II and a trial for treason in the United States in 1946. He spent the next 12 years in a prison for the criminally insane and was released in 1958.

Remus, George (1876–1947) *bootlegger*
Born in Germany, Remus emigrated to the United States at age five and passed the Illinois bar exam in 1900. With the passage of the Eighteenth Amendment, Remus gave up his successful law practice in Chicago and moved to Cincinnati, where he began buying distilleries that manufactured legal medicinal alcohol. He then organized a network of operators to steal from his own businesses and sell the goods to distributors, who cut the pure alcohol with water, sugar, and other products and then sold it to the public. In this way Remus served as both originator and middleman and made millions in a short time. He bought a palatial home in Cincinnati and graced it with a $125,000 swimming pool, actions which inspired federal agents to plant a bug in his quarters in the fall of 1920. After being overheard paying off several dozen agents, policemen, and guards, Remus was arrested, fined, and jailed—a total of five times. During one of his terms in the Atlanta federal penitentiary, however, his wife attracted the attention of Franklin Dodge, the federal agent who had arrested her husband. After Remus finished serving his 19-month sentence, he returned to Cincinnati, where he murdered his wife. He was acquitted of this crime on the grounds of temporary insanity and then faded into obscurity.

Robeson, Paul (1898–1976) *football player, actor, singer, activist*
Born in Princeton, New Jersey, to a former slave and Presbyterian minister, Robeson won honors as the first black All-American football player while attending Rutgers University. He attained a law degree from Columbia University in 1923, but had also been playing in amateur theatrical productions in New York. In 1924, Robeson performed in the Broadway production of Eugene O'Neill's play *All God's Chillun Got Wings.* He was cast in the leading role of O'Neill's *The Emperor Jones* in the next year, while simultaneously beginning a singing career as a bass-baritone on the concert stage. He moved to Europe in 1928, where he embraced progressive and socialist causes, and lived for a time in the Soviet Union. His 11 film appearances included a prominent part in *Show Boat* (1936). During World War II, his performance as *Othello* brought lavish critical praise, and the play became the longest-running Shakespearean production in U.S. history. His support for the Soviet cause, however, brought trouble in the 1950s, as the State Department refused him a passport for refusing to disavow his membership in the Communist Party. He published his autobiography, *Here I Stand,* in 1958.

Rogers, William Penn Adair (1879–1935) *actor, writer, comedian*
Born in Oologah, Indian Territory (Oklahoma), Rogers attended the Kemper Military Academy in Boonville, Missouri, but quit school in 1898 to pursue a career as a cowboy. He was hired as a rope-trick artist by a Wild West show in 1902, but found that his quick wit and southern drawl entertained audiences, especially urban and eastern audiences, far more than his skill with a lasso. Rogers first achieved fame in the Ziegfeld Follies of 1916 and remained a Ziegfeld mainstay into the early 1920s. He expanded his humor to cover politics and news events, drawing admiration and laughter from theatergoers as well as senators, cabinet members, and presidents. Rogers began as a newspaper columnist and radio host in the mid-1920s; in a prosperous age he achieved the standing of the highest-paid entertainer in the nation. He died in an airplane crash off Point Barrow, Alaska, in 1935.

Ruth, George Herman "Babe" (1895–1948) *professional baseball player*
Ruth's greatest achievement was reviving the sport of baseball after the Black Sox scandal of 1919. Born in Baltimore in 1895, be began his playing career as a pitcher with Baltimore in the International League. In five years with the Boston Red Sox, he won 88 games and lost 44 as a pitcher; in 1919, as a part-time outfielder, he hit a record 29 home runs. The Red Sox sold Ruth to their rivals, the New York Yankees, in 1920. Ruth ended his pitching career and became a regular outfielder. Over the next 15 years, he helped the Yankees win four World Series. In 1927, he hit 60 home runs, a record that would stand until 1961. By the end of the 1920s, he was the highest-paid player in baseball and the most popular and recognized athlete in the nation. His last playing year was 1935, with the Boston Braves. In the next year, he became the second player, after Ty Cobb, voted to Baseball's Hall of Fame. He died of cancer in 1948.

Sacco, Nicola (1891–1927) **and Bartolomeo Vanzetti** (1888–1927)
Italian immigrants tried, convicted and executed for robbery and murder in Massachusetts
Both men arrived in the United States in 1908, Sacco finding work as a shoemaker and Vanzetti as a peddler.

During World War I, both men joined an Italian anarchist circle and fled to Mexico to escape the draft, actions which made them prominent targets for a Justice Department charged with rooting out foreign radicals in the years following the war. On April 15, 1920, a shoe factory in South Braintree, Massachusetts, was robbed of its $15,000 payroll. The crime left a paymaster and guard dead; three weeks later Sacco and Vanzetti were arrested on a streetcar and charged with participating in the crime. The trial began on May 31, 1921, and despite flimsy ballistics evidence that may have been manufactured by the police, Sacco and Vanzetti were convicted on the grounds of having lied and displayed guilty behavior during their arrest. Judge Webster Thayer pronounced a sentence of execution and later denied all appeals, despite a concerted effort by some writers, editorialists, and prominent jurists to have the sentence overturned and despite a confession in 1925 by Constantine Madeiros, a prison inmate, of having taken part in the crime as part of the Morelli gang of Providence, Rhode Island. Sacco and Vanzetti were executed on August 22, 1927, after the Supreme Court denied their final appeal.

Sanger, Margaret Higgins (1883–1966) *feminist and birth control activist*
Born into a family of 11 children in Corning, New York, as Margaret Higgins, Sanger saw her own mother, Anne Purcell Higgins, die at the age of 50 after a lifetime of unplanned childbirth and financial struggle. After attending nursing school in White Plains, New York, Margaret Higgins married the architect William Sanger. The couple moved to New York City in 1910, where Margaret Sanger worked as a visiting nurse on the Lower East Side. She again witnessed death and illness among poor women caring for large families. Inspired to offer advice and information on birth control, she launched the *Woman Rebel* magazine in 1914 and was promptly indicted for violating the Comstock Act against distributing "obscenity" (i.e., information on sex and birth control, a term she coined) via the mails. Her conviction was dismissed on appeal. In 1916, with her sister Ethel Byrne, she opened the nation's first birth control clinic in Brooklyn. The clinic was closed down after 10 days and Sanger was again indicted, this time for creating a public nuisance. In 1921 Sanger started the American Birth Control League; two years later she organized the Birth Control Clinical Research Bureau, the first clinic to be staffed by doctors. In 1927 she organized the first

World Population Conference in Geneva, Switzerland. She spent many years fighting in court to legalize the distribution of contraceptives and birth control information. In 1941, the American Birth Control League became the Planned Parenthood Federation; in 1953 she became the first president of the International Planned Parenthood Federation.

Smith, Al (1873–1944) *four-time Democratic governor of New York, presidential candidate*
Born into a family of Irish immigrants in New York City, Smith dropped out of school at the age of 13 to take a series of menial jobs to support his family. He was appointed to a clerk's position in 1895, a job that began his long association with the Tammany political machine that controlled the city. In 1904, he was elected state assemblyman and in 1918 won his first term as governor of New York. The energetic Smith saw important labor and housing legislation through a cooperative legislature. In the meantime, his role as social reformer began with a term in the Factory Investigating Commission to study the circumstances of the tragic Triangle Shirtwaist fire that took place in 1911. After a one-term hiatus due to nationwide Republican victories of 1920, Smith was reelected to the governorship in 1922, 1924, and 1926. During his four terms, he sponsored and saw passed important reforms in labor laws, parks administration, housing, and child welfare. He proceeded to the national stage at the 1924 Democratic convention, but his opposition to Prohibition, as well as his urban and Catholic roots, denied him the party's presidential nomination during a bitter, endless combat for delegate votes. Smith won the nomination four years later, the first Catholic to win a major party nomination, but he was defeated by Herbert Hoover in the Republican landslide of 1928. After losing the Democratic nomination to Franklin Roosevelt in 1932, Smith abandoned Democratic politics and reform sentiments to lobby for business. He founded the American Liberty League in 1935 to argue against the New Deal policies formulated by the Roosevelt administration in response to the Great Depression.

Smith, Bessie (1894–1937) *blues singer*
Born in Chattanooga, Tennessee, Bessie Smith remained through much of her short life one of the nation's most popular singers among black audiences. She began her career at 11 by touring with the Rabbit Foot Minstrels through the South. Her first records,

"Gulf Coast Blues" and "Down-Hearted Blues," were made in 1923; she would cut a total of 160 records that were marketed as "race records" and distributed exclusively to black communities. Her deep and expressive voice was a perfect match for the lonely sentiments of the blues. Although she sold several million records, she earned no royalties and only a small fee for her studio work, and when the blues declined in popularity in the late 1920s and early 1930s she found herself poor and forgotten.

Stein, Gertrude (1874–1946) *writer, literary patron*

Born in Allegheny, Pennsylvania, Stein attended Radcliffe College in Boston and Johns Hopkins University in Baltimore, where she dropped her medical studies to take up writing. She moved to Europe in 1903, pioneering a wave of American expatriates who would take up residence in Paris after the end of World War I. She transformed her apartment on the Rue de Fleurus into a literary salon, presided over by her longtime companion Alice B. Toklas and attended by artists and writers including Pablo Picasso, Ernest Hemingway, Sherwood Anderson, and Thornton Wilder. She also began a collection of modern art, in particular cubist works by Picasso and Matisse; displaying these works during salon meetings, she provided a small but encouraging audience for a new generation of artists working in Paris. Her own experimental works, including *Three Lives* (1909) and *The Making of Americans* (1925) found little in the way of popularity or critical understanding, although she gained greater acceptance after publishing her intriguing book *The Autobiography of Alice B. Toklas* (1933) and after World War II, during which she wrote *Paris France* (1940) and *Wars I Have Seen* (1945). Stein also wrote the operatic scores *Four Saints in Three Acts* (1934) and *The Mother of Us All* (1947) with composer Virgil Thomson.

Sunday, William Ashley "Billy" (1862–1935) *professional athlete, evangelist*

Born the son of a Union Army soldier in Ames, Iowa, Sunday played professional baseball in Chicago, Pittsburgh, and Pennsylvania from 1883 until 1891. In 1886, he underwent a religious conversion upon hearing a gospel choir in the streets of Chicago. After his baseball career ended, Sunday took up work with the Young Men's Christian Association in Chicago while working as an aide for Reverend J. Wilbur Chapman. In 1896, he struck out on his own, beginning a sensational career as an evangelist that over the next 20 years

included more than 300 revivals and a total audience estimated at more than 100 million. Sunday's powerful oratory and his use of massive orchestras and choirs brought him national acclaim, and converts by the millions. In 1903 he was ordained as a Presbyterian minister; in the following years he took up the cause of Prohibition, organizing his largest revival ever, in New York City during World War I, to advance the dry cause. He published *Love Stories of the Bible* in 1917 and also began writing a regular newspaper column, "Ma Sunday's Column." During the 1920s Sunday continued his preaching on radio and in the papers, resolutely refusing to abandon the Prohibitionist cause and lending full support to the government's hunt for anarchists, radicals, and undesirable immigrants.

Valentino, Rudolph (Rodolpho d'Antonguolla) (1895–1926) *screen actor*

Born Rodolpho d'Antonguolla in Castellaneta, Italy, Valentino emigrated in 1913 to New York, where he began work as a cafe dancer. He moved to Hollywood in 1917 but found no work other than bit parts until breaking into a starring role in *The Four Horsemen of the Apocalypse* in 1921. His second major film, *The Sheik,* made with director George Melford of Paramount, became a sensational nationwide hit; Valentino's exotic good looks made him the first Hollywood "Latin lover" and the most recognized movie star of the 1920s. During the next five years, Valentino made 30 more films, with his image and fame making him the target of delirious mobs, mostly composed of women, wherever he went. But in the summer of 1926 he suffered a serious ulcer and peritonitis, from which he died in a few days. The funeral and attendant ceremonies were national media events that brought vast, grief-stricken crowds to Los Angeles.

Van Vechten, Carl (1880–1964) *writer, photographer, patron of the Harlem Renaissance*

Born in Cedar Rapids, Iowa, Van Vechten began studies at the University of Chicago in 1899, afterward working as a reporter for the Chicago *American*. In 1906, he moved to New York, where he began work as a music critic for the *New York Times*. He wrote on music, ballet, and opera for the next 15 years, collecting his essays into several volumes. His first book, *Peter Whiffle: His Life and Works,* appeared in 1922. At this time he took a strong interest in emerging African-American writers, who were then gathering in the uptown New York neighborhood of Harlem. Van Vechten's novel *Nigger*

Heaven, although sharply criticized by black writers for what they read as a condescending attitude, brought the Harlem Renaissance to a mainstream white audience, making black writers, musicians, and artists into figures of stylish interest to urban whites, especially in New York. During the 1930s, after being introduced by Miguel Covarrubias for the 35-millimeter camera, Van Vechten began working in still photography, taking portraits of celebrities of the stage and of the Harlem Renaissance as well as landscapes that were widely published and exhibited.

Whiteman, Paul (1891–1967) *bandleader*
Born in Denver, Colorado, Whiteman began his musical career at 16 as a classical violist with the Denver Symphony Orchestra. He became the bandmaster in the U.S. Navy concert band during World War I, and after the war organized a big dance band in California. Whiteman adopted some elements of early jazz into his conventional, "sweet" arrangements, coining the term "symphonic jazz" to describe what he saw as a more serious and noteworthy form of the small-group improvisational style then emerging in New Orleans and Chicago. In early 1924 he engaged composers George Gershwin and Ferde Grofé to create a "jazz concerto," to be part of a long and very formal coming-out ceremony for jazz music in New York's Aeolian Hall. Although the balance of the program came off as pedantic and more than slightly bombastic, Gerhswin's *Rhapsody in Blue* carried the evening. For the rest of the decade, as jazz grew more solo-oriented and formally experimental, Whiteman held to his strict arrangements and his "sweet" style, dating himself among music critics but remaining popular with the public. To further explain and expound on his discovery of jazz during the 1920s, he wrote two books *Jazz* in 1926 and *Records for the Millions* in 1948.

Wilson, Thomas Woodrow (1856–1924) *president of the United States, 1913–1920*
Born in Virginia and the son of a Presbyterian minister, Wilson attended the College of New Jersey, later Princeton University, as well as Johns Hopkins University. Wilson began his teaching career in 1885 at Bryn Mawr College. Five years later he was appointed professor of jurisprudence and political economy at Princeton University. Held in high regard by students as well as peers, Wilson was named president of the university in 1902, but ran into strong opposition from conservative faculty and alumni over proposed reforms

of the university's teaching methods and curriculum. His battles at the university raised his profile throughout the state; as a consequence the Democratic Party of New Jersey nominated Wilson for governor in 1910. Wilson won the election; his subsequent reform of state government made him a darling of liberals and progressives, their agenda then in full strength throughout the Northeast, and a presidential nomination followed in the summer of 1912. Thanks to a split in the Republican Party between the conservative Republican faction supporting William Howard Taft and the Bull Moose faction of Theodore Roosevelt, Wilson gained the presidency in the fall. As president, Wilson lowered tariffs, imposed a federal tax, established the Federal Reserve system, and moved antitrust and child-labor laws through Congress. On the outbreak of World War I, Wilson firmly declared the neutrality of his nation and won reelection in 1916 as a committed noncombatant. However, in 1917, Wilson finally succumbed to public demands for U.S. participation and outrage over Germany's declaration of unrestricted submarine warfare. In April of that year, U.S. troops arrived in France and took to the skies and trenches. In November 1918, the war ended, and Wilson was seem as a heroic figure by Americans at home and by members of the Triple Entente. But his vision of a "just peace" and a League of Nations to maintain it went badly awry at the Versailles peace conference the following year. The allies demanded and received harsh reparations from Germany, and U.S. membership in the League of Nations went down to defeat in the U.S. Congress. Wilson won the Nobel Prize in Peace in 1919 for his efforts, but he felt bitter disappointment at his own failure to convince the U.S. public of the virtues of the League of Nations.

Woodson, Carter (1875–1950) *historian*
Woodson helped establish the field of African-American studies in the United States. The son of sharecroppers and freed slaves, Woodson was born and raised in New Canton, Virginia. He attended Berea College in Kentucky, and then the University of Chicago, after which he worked for several years as a teacher in the Philippines. In 1912, after finishing his thesis at Harvard University, he earned a doctorate in history, the first and only child of former slaves to do so. At Harvard, a casual remark by historian Edward Channing to the effect that American blacks "had no history" sparked in Woodson a fervent desire to establish a new field of African-American studies. In 1915

Woodson established the Association for the Study of Negro Life and History; in the same year he published his first work, *The Education of the Negro Prior to 1861*. Next year he founded the *Journal of Negro History*. In 1919, he was named dean of the liberal arts college at Howard University in Washington, D.C.; in 1920, he began serving as dean at West Virginia State College. In 1921, he established Associated Publishers, Inc., for the purpose of publishing African-American history and letters. To bring African-American history to whites and blacks in the nation's public schools he created Negro History Week in February 1926. His 1922 textbook, *The Negro in Our History,* became a foundation book for African-American studies programs throughout the nation.

Wright, Frank Lloyd (1867–1959) *architect*
Born in Richland Center, Wisconsin, Wright, finding no architecture courses offered at the University of Wisconsin (where he began studies in 1884), took civil engineering instead and applied himself to practical construction projects in the college town of Madison. He joined the Chicago architecture firm of Adler and Sullivan in 1887, where he came under the "form-follows-function" philosophy of architect Louis Sullivan. Wright stated his own firm in 1893, turning to smaller-scale domestic architecture and creating the "Prairie Style," an architectural method that brilliantly reflected natural forms in artificial habitats. Wright helped to develop several architectural innovations in public and private architecture, including the use of precast concrete, glass doors, open floor plans, indirect lighting, air conditioning, and cantilevered construction. After returning from a short exile in Europe, Wright founded Taliesin, a school and workshop at his home near Spring Green, Wisconsin. Through the 1920s, Wright faced continued opposition for his innovations and his startlingly original interior and exterior designs, but he strongly influenced young architects across the country through his writing, teaching, and lecturing.

Ziegfeld, Florenz (1867–1932) *theatrical manager, producer*
Born in Chicago, Ziegfeld first won attention through his musical productions at the Chicago Columbian Exposition of 1893. He then turned to theatrical management, helping to launch the careers of U.S. and European artists including Fanny Brice, W. C. Fields, Eddie Cantor, Billie Burke (Ziegfeld's second wife), and Anna Held, a French star whom he married in 1897 and for whom he produced seven musical shows, including *Miss Innocence* in 1908. Ziegfeld's *Follies of 1907,* one of the first musical revues produced on Broadway, was a glitzy and lavish spectacle of elaborate sets, beautiful chorus girls, and spectacular musical numbers that inaugurated a 20-year run of annual revues, each bigger and brighter, most sold out every night, and many reigning as the season's most popular musical productions. Ziegfeld also produced smaller revues produced at cabarets and dinner theaters, as well as musical comedies, including *Sally* in 1920, *Whoopee* in 1928, Jerome Kern and Oscar Hammerstein's *Show Boat* in 1927, and Noel Coward's *Bitter Sweet* in 1929. As the sound era dawned in Hollywood, Ziegfeld moved to Hollywood to work with producer Samuel Goldwyn on a series of Follies movies. Shortly after his death in 1932, Ziegfeld's life was memorialized in *The Great Ziegfeld* (1936), a nostalgic tribute to the bygone decade of the 1920s and the longest and most lavish film musical of the depression era.

APPENDIX C
Maps, Graphs, and Tables

1. The Presidential Election of 1920
2. The Presidential Election of 1924
3. The Presidential Election of 1928
4. 1930 Census Reapportionment of 435 Seats in the House of Representatives
5. Prohibition on the Eve of the Eighteenth Amendment, 1919
6. Women State Legislators Statistics, 1919–1929
7. Sources of U.S. Immigration, 1891–1920, 1921–1940
8. African-American Migration during the 1920s
9. Persons Lynched in the United States, 1918–1930
10. Degrees Conferred, by Sex, at Institutions of Higher Education, 1918–1930
11. Operating Broadcast Stations (AM)—Radio Sets Produced and Households with Sets, 1921–1930
12. Admissions to Spectator Amusements in Millions of Dollars, 1921–1930
13. Minimum Annual Cost of Living for a Family of Five, 1924
14. Motor Vehicle Sales, 1918–1930
15. Unemployment, 1918–1930
16. Average Weekly Earnings and Hours of Manufacturing Workers, 1919–1930
17. Major Occupation Group of Female Workers, 1920 and 1930
18. Value of Exports and Imports in Millions of Dollars, 1918–1930
19. New Public Construction in Millions of Dollars, 1920–1930
20. Gross National Product in Billions of Dollars, 1918–1930
21. Standard and Poor's Index of Common Stocks, 1918–1930

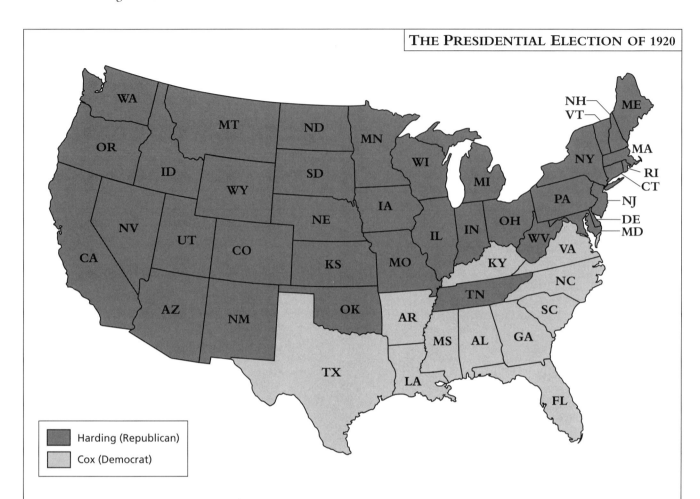

THE PRESIDENTIAL ELECTION OF 1920

Harding (Republican)

Cox (Democrat)

States	Electoral Votes	Harding	Cox	States	Electoral Votes	Harding	Cox
Alabama	12	...	12	Nebraska	8	8	...
Arizona	3	3	...	Nevada	3	3	...
Arkansas	9	...	9	New Hampshire	4	4	...
California	13	13	...	New Jersey	14	14	...
Colorado	6	6	...	New Mexico	3	3	...
Connecticut	7	7	...	New York	45	45	...
Delaware	3	3	...	North Carolina	12	...	12
Florida	6	...	6	North Dakota	5	5	...
Georgia	14	...	14	Ohio	24	24	...
Idaho	4	4	...	Oklahoma	10	10	...
Illinois	29	29	...	Oregon	5	5	...
Indiana	15	15	...	Pennsylvania	38	38	...
Iowa	13	13	...	Rhode Island	5	5	...
Kansas	10	10	...	South Carolina	9	...	9
Kentucky	13	...	13	South Dakota	5	5	...
Louisiana	10	...	10	Tennessee	12	12	...
Maine	6	6	...	Texas	20	...	20
Maryland	8	8	...	Utah	4	4	...
Massachusetts	18	18	...	Vermont	4	4	...
Michigan	15	15	...	Virginia	12	...	12
Minnesota	12	12	...	Washington	7	7	...
Mississippi	10	...	10	West Virginia	8	8	...
Missouri	18	18	...	Wisconsin	13	13	...
Montana	4	4	...	Wyoming	3	3	...
				TOTAL	531	404	127

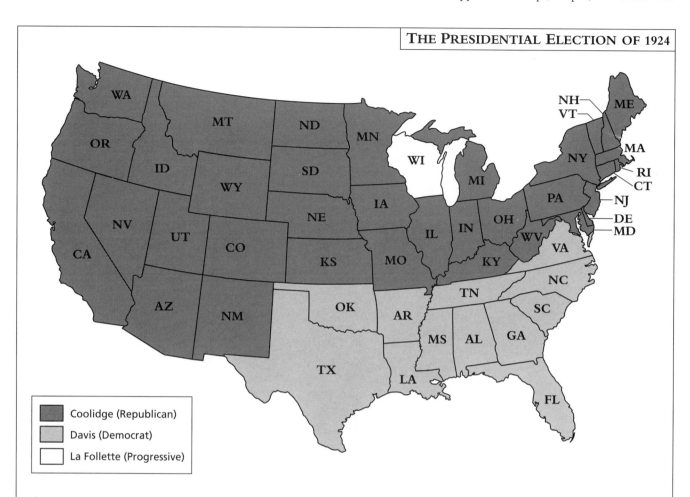

THE PRESIDENTIAL ELECTION OF 1924

Coolidge (Republican)
Davis (Democrat)
La Follette (Progressive)

States	Electoral Votes	Coolidge	Davis	La Follette	States	Electoral Votes	Coolidge	Davis	La Follette
Alabama	12	. . .	12	. . .	Nebraska	8	8	. . .	. . .
Arizona	3	3	. . .	. . .	Nevada	3	3	. . .	. . .
Arkansas	9	. . .	9	. . .	New Hampshire	4	4	. . .	. . .
California	13	13	. . .	. . .	New Jersey	14	14	. . .	. . .
Colorado	6	6	. . .	. . .	New Mexico	3	3	. . .	. . .
Connecticut	7	7	. . .	. . .	New York	45	45	. . .	. . .
Delaware	3	3	. . .	. . .	North Carolina	12	. . .	12	. . .
Florida	6	. . .	6	. . .	North Dakota	5	5	. . .	. . .
Georgia	14	. . .	14	. . .	Ohio	24	24	. . .	. . .
Idaho	4	4	. . .	. . .	Oklahoma	10	. . .	10	. . .
Illinois	29	29	. . .	. . .	Oregon	5	5	. . .	. . .
Indiana	15	15	. . .	. . .	Pennsylvania	38	38	. . .	. . .
Iowa	13	13	. . .	. . .	Rhode Island	5	5	. . .	. . .
Kansas	10	10	. . .	. . .	South Carolina	9	. . .	9	. . .
Kentucky	13	13	. . .	. . .	South Dakota	5	5	. . .	. . .
Louisiana	10	. . .	10	. . .	Tennessee	12	. . .	12	. . .
Maine	6	6	. . .	. . .	Texas	20	. . .	20	. . .
Maryland	8	8	. . .	. . .	Utah	4	4	. . .	. . .
Massachusetts	18	18	. . .	. . .	Vermont	4	4	. . .	. . .
Michigan	15	15	. . .	. . .	Virginia	12	. . .	12	. . .
Minnesota	12	12	. . .	. . .	Washington	7	7	. . .	. . .
Mississippi	10	. . .	10	. . .	West Virginia	8	8	. . .	. . .
Missouri	18	18	. . .	. . .	Wisconsin	13	. . .	. . .	13
Montana	4	4	. . .	. . .	Wyoming	3	3	. . .	. . .
					TOTAL	531	382	136	13

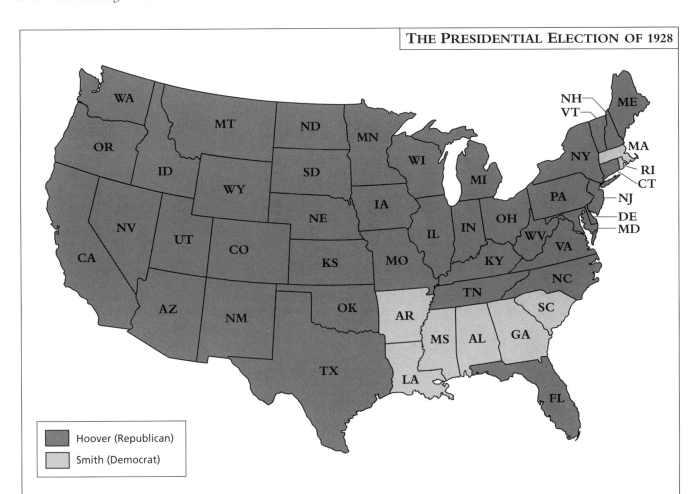

THE PRESIDENTIAL ELECTION OF 1928

Hoover (Republican)

Smith (Democrat)

States	Electoral Votes	Hoover	Smith	States	Electoral Votes	Hoover	Smith
Alabama	12	...	12	Nebraska	8	8	...
Arizona	3	3	...	Nevada	3	3	...
Arkansas	9	...	9	New Hampshire	4	4	...
California	13	13	...	New Jersey	14	14	...
Colorado	6	6	...	New Mexico	3	3	...
Connecticut	7	7	...	New York	45	45	...
Delaware	3	3	...	North Carolina	12	12	...
Florida	6	6	...	North Dakota	5	5	...
Georgia	14	...	14	Ohio	24	24	...
Idaho	4	4	...	Oklahoma	10	10	...
Illinois	29	29	...	Oregon	5	5	...
Indiana	15	15	...	Pennsylvania	38	38	...
Iowa	13	13	...	Rhode Island	5	...	5
Kansas	10	10	...	South Carolina	9	...	9
Kentucky	13	13	...	South Dakota	5	5	...
Louisiana	10	...	10	Tennessee	12	12	...
Maine	6	6	...	Texas	20	20	...
Maryland	8	8	...	Utah	4	4	...
Massachusetts	18	...	18	Vermont	4	4	...
Michigan	15	15	...	Virginia	12	12	...
Minnesota	12	12	...	Washington	7	7	...
Mississippi	10	...	10	West Virginia	8	8	...
Missouri	18	18	...	Wisconsin	13	13	...
Montana	4	4	...	Wyoming	3	3	...
				TOTAL	531	444	87

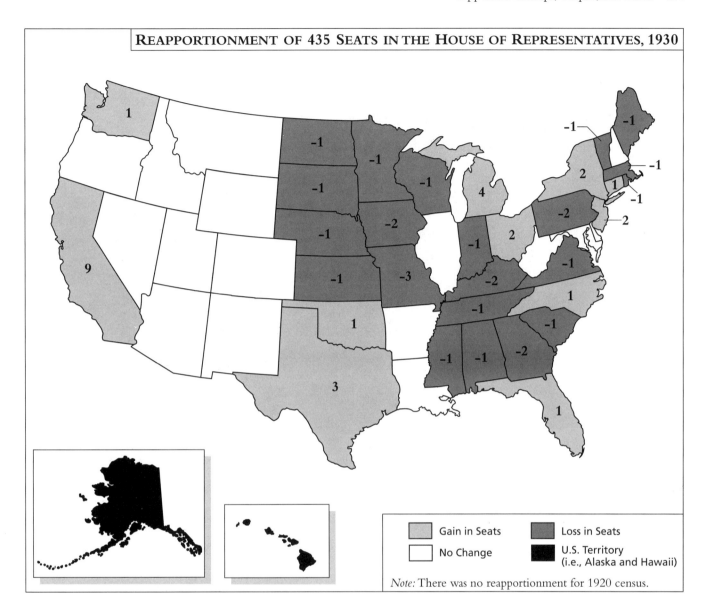

REAPPORTIONMENT OF 435 SEATS IN THE HOUSE OF REPRESENTATIVES, 1930

Gain in Seats

No Change

Loss in Seats

U.S. Territory
(i.e., Alaska and Hawaii)

Note: There was no reapportionment for 1920 census.

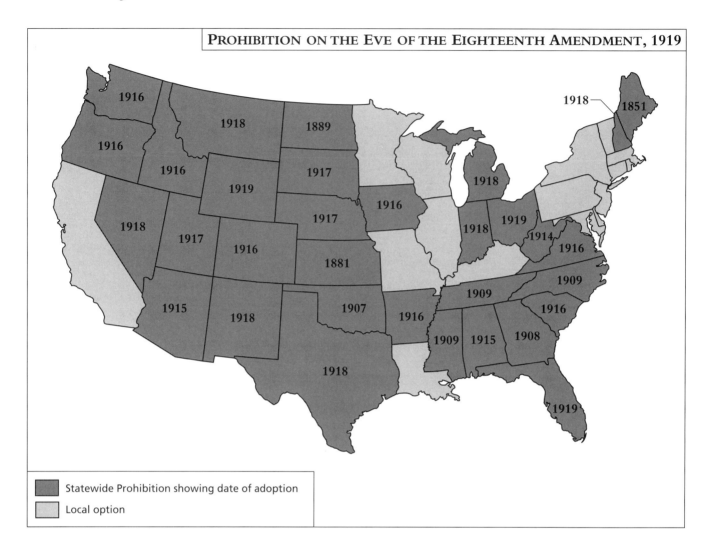

PROHIBITION ON THE EVE OF THE EIGHTEENTH AMENDMENT, 1919

1916
1918
1889
1918   1851
1916
1916
1917
1916
1919
1917
1918
1918   1919
1918
1917
1916
1919
1914
1916
1918
1881
1909
1909
1915
1907
1916
1916
1909   1915   1908
1918
1919

Statewide Prohibition showing date of adoption

Local option

Women State Legislators Statistics, 1919–1929

Year	Senate	House	Democrat	Republican	Independent*	Total Women**	Legislature***	% Women
1919	2	23	12	13	0	25	1314	1.9
1921	5	34	11	27	1	39	3743	1
1923	7	92	37	55	7	99	7045	1.4
1925	10	131	38	99	4	141	7396	1.9
1927	13	115	36	86	6	128	7413	1.7
1929	15	135	42	100	8	150	7557	2

*Independent includes Independents, nonpartisan, and minor parties.

**Total number based on women serving in spring of odd years and does not include those who may have resigned before April or those who were appointed or elected after April. Totals do not include nonvoting delegates in Maine or territorial legislatures.

***Constitutional totals for state legislatures are added as women became eligible to run for state legislature. Forty-eight states included by 1929.

Source: Cox, Elizabeth. *Women State and Territorial Legislators, 1895–1995.* Jefferson, N.C.: McFarland & Co., 1996, p. 327.

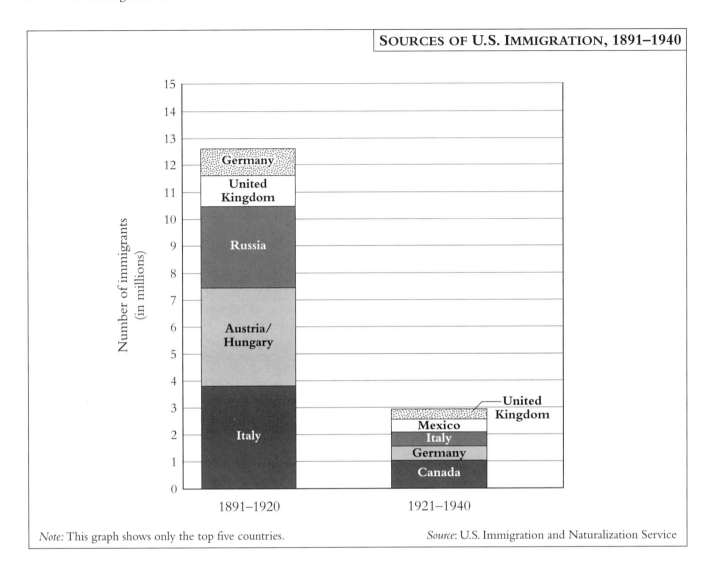

SOURCES OF U.S. IMMIGRATION, 1891–1940

Note: This graph shows only the top five countries.   *Source*: U.S. Immigration and Naturalization Service

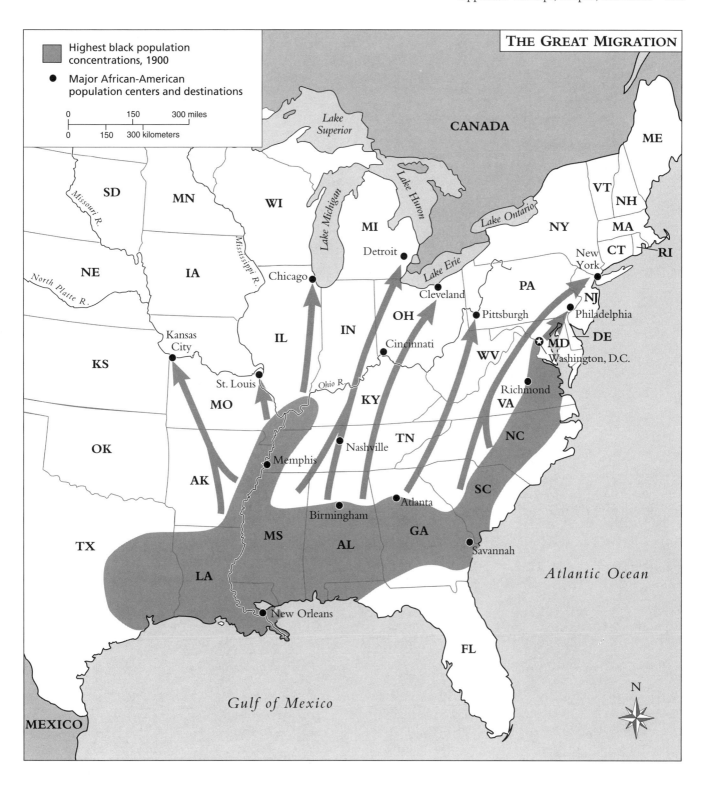

THE GREAT MIGRATION

Highest black population
concentrations, 1900

● Major African-American
population centers and destinations

PEOPLE LYNCHED IN THE UNITED STATES, 1918–1930

Year	Total	White	African American
1918	64	4	60
1919	83	7	76
1920	61	8	53
1921	64	5	59
1922	57	6	51
1923	33	4	29
1924	16	. . .	16
1925	17	. . .	17
1926	30	7	23
1927	16	. . .	16
1928	11	1	10
1929	10	3	7
1930	21	1	20

Source: U.S. Bureau of the Census, *Historical Statistics of the United States,* Washington, D.C.: Superintendent of Documents, U.S. Government Printing Office, 1960, p. 422.

DEGREES CONFERRED, BY SEX, AT INSTITUTIONS OF HIGHER EDUCATION, 1918–1930

School Year Ending	Total, All Degrees	Bachelor's or First Professional		Master's or Second Professional		Doctor's or Equivalent	
		Male	Female	Male	Female	Male	Female
1918	42,041	26,269	12,316	1,806	1,094	491	65
1920	53,516	31,980	16,642	2,985	1,294	522	93
1922	68,488	41,306	20,362	4,304	1,680	708	128
1924	92,097	54,908	27,875	5,515	2,701	939	159
1926	108,407	62,218	35,045	6,202	3,533	1,216	193
1928	124,995	67,659	43,502	7,727	4,660	1,249	198
1930	139,752	73,615	48,869	8,925	6,044	1,946	353

Source: Kurian, George Thomas, *Datapedia of the United States, 1790–2000: America Year by Year,* Lanham, Md.: Berman Press, 1994, pp. 144–145.

OPERATING BROADCAST STATIONS (AM)—RADIO SETS PRODUCED AND HOUSEHOLDS WITH SETS, 1921–1930

Year	Operating Broadcast Stations (AM)	Households with Radio Sets (in thousands)
1921	1*	. . .
1922	30	60
1923	556	466
1924	530	1,250
1925	571	2,750
1926	528	4,500
1927	681	6,750
1928	677	8,000
1929	606	10,250
1930	618	13,750

*First station to receive regular license as of September 15: other stations in operation experimentally.
Note: Figures are as of June 30 for each year.
Source: Kurian, *Datapedia of the United States, 1790–2000,* p. 300.

ADMISSIONS TO SPECTATOR AMUSEMENTS IN MILLIONS OF DOLLARS, 1921–1930

Year	Total	Motion Picture Theaters	Theater Entertainment (Plays, Operas, etc.) of Nonprofit Institutions, except Athletics	Spectator Sports
1921	412	301	81	30
1923	528	336	146	46
1925	588	367	174	47
1927	769	526	195	48
1929	913	720	127	66
1930	892	732	95	65

Source: Kurian, *Datapedia of the United States, 1790–2000,* p. 153.

MINIMUM ANNUAL COST OF LIVING FOR A FAMILY OF FIVE, 1924*

Food $627.08
Clothing
    Husband 87.14
    Wife 105.70
    Boy (12) 73.03
    Girl (6) 41.71
    Boy (2) 31.38
        Total 338.96

Furniture (annual replacement) 60.00
Cleaning supplies 40.13
Rent 300.00
Fuel and light 80.69

Miscellaneous
    Insurance
        Life: $7,500 (straight life) 113.25
        Fire: on $700 (furniture) 1.87
        subtotal 115.12
    Carfare
        Husband 30.00
        All others 20.80
        subtotal 50.80

Help—one day a week (or laundry) 145.60
Maintenance of health 67.00
Amusements 25.00
Newspapers (daily and Sunday) 10.40
Church 15.00
Labor organizations 24.00
Telephone, postage, tobacco, etc. 20.00
One good magazine 1.00

        Total 473.92
        Grand total $1,920.87

*Based on the "Minimum Quantity Budget Necessary to Maintain a Worker's Family of Five in Health and Decency," U.S. Bureau of Labor (*Monthly Labor Review,* Vol. X, No. 6, June, 1920).

Note: Middletown was the pseudonym given to Muncie, Indiana, whose sociologists Robert and Helen Lynd conducted the first detailed, objective examination of an American city. Prices are in all cases Middletown prices in 1924, determined by records kept over a period of weeks by a small group of cooperating Middletown working class housewives and by consultation with retailers.

Source: Lynd, Robert Staughton, and Helen M. Lynd, *Middletown: A Study in Modern American Culture,* New York: Harcourt Brace and Company, 1924, p. 518.

MOTOR VEHICLE SALES, 1918–1930

Year	Number of Passenger Cars	Number of Motor Trucks and Buses*
1918	943.4	227.2
1919	1,651.6	224.7
1920	1,905.5	321.7
1921	1,468.0	148.0
1922	2,274.1	269.9
1923	3,624.7	409.2
1924	3,185.8	416.6
1925	3,735.1	530.6
1926	3,692.3	608.6
1927	2,936.5	464.7
1928	3,775.4	583.3
1929	4,455.1	881.9
1930	2,787.4	575.3

*A substantial portion of the number of trucks and buses consists of chassis only, without bodies.
Note: Number sold includes sales of military vehicles.
Source: Kurian, *Datapedia of the United States, 1790–2000,* p. 267.

AVERAGE WEEKLY EARNINGS AND HOURS OF MANUFACTURING WORKERS, 1919–1930

Year	Average Hourly Earnings	Average Weekly Hours
1919	.47	46.3
1920	.55	47.4
1921	.51	43.1
1922	.48	44.2
1923	.52	45.6
1924	.54	43.7
1925	.54	44.5
1926	.54	45.0
1927	.54	45.0
1928	.56	44.4
1929	.56	44.2
1930	.55	42.1

Source: Kurian, *Datapedia of the United States, 1790–2000,* p. 79.

UNEMPLOYMENT, 1918–1930

Year	Percent of Civilian Labor Force
1918	1.4
1919	1.4
1920	5.2
1921	11.7
1922	6.7
1923	2.4
1924	5.0
1925	3.2
1926	1.8
1927	3.3
1928	4.2
1929	3.2
1930	8.7

Note: Data presented is in thousands of persons 14 years and over.
Source: Kurian, *Datapedia of the United States, 1790–2000,* p. 75.

MAJOR OCCUPATION GROUP OF FEMALE WORKERS, 1920 AND 1930

Major Occupation Group	1930	1920
Total	10,752	8,637
White-collar Workers	4,756	3,353
Professional, Technical, and Kindred Workers	1,482	1,008
Managers, Officials, and Proprietors*	292	191
Clerical and Kindred Workers	2,246	1,614
Salesworkers	736	541
Manual and Service Workers	5,088	4,115
Manual Workers	2,134	2,052
Craftsmen, Foremen, and Kindred Workers	106	105
Operative and Kindred Workers	1,870	1,748
Laborers, Except Farm and Mine	158	199
Service Workers	2,954	2,063
Private Household Workers	1,909	1,360
Service Workers, exc. Private Household	1,045	703
Farmworkers	908	1,169
Farmers and Farm Managers	263	277
Farm Laborers and Foremen	645	892

*Except farm.
Note: Data is in thousands of persons 14 years old and over.
Source: U.S. Bureau of the Census, *Historical Statistics of the United States,* 1960, p. 139.

VALUE OF EXPORTS AND IMPORTS IN MILLIONS OF DOLLARS, 1918–1930

| Year | Merchandise | | Excess of Exports(+) or Imports(-) |
	Total exports and Re-exports	Total General Imports	
1918	6,149	3,031	+3,118
1919	7,920	3,904	+4,016
1920	8,228	5,278	+2,950
1921	4,485	2,509	+1,976
1922	3,832	3,113	+719
1923	4,167	3,792	+375
1924	4,591	3,610	+981
1925	4,910	4,227	+683
1926	4,809	4,431	+378
1927	4,865	4,185	+681
1928	5,128	4,091	+1,037
1929	5,241	4,399	+842
1930	3,843	3,061	+782

Source: Kurian, *Datapedia of the United States, 1790–2000,* p. 356.

NEW PUBLIC CONSTRUCTION IN MILLIONS OF DOLLARS, 1920–1930

Year	Educational Buildings	Military Facilities	Highways, Roads, and Streets	Sewer and Water Systems	Conservation and Development
1920	190	161	656	153	55
1921	274	49	853	178	52
1922	342	25	876	201	48
1923	346	16	805	203	65
1924	353	9	987	263	79
1925	400	8	1,082	278	73
1926	399	11	1,067	285	61
1927	367	12	1,222	312	63
1928	378	15	1,289	300	72
1929	389	19	1,266	253	115
1930	364	29	1,516	343	137

Source: Kurian, *Datapedia of the United States, 1790–2000,* p. 233.

GROSS NATIONAL PRODUCT IN BILLIONS OF DOLLARS, 1918–1930

Year	Current Prices
1918	76.4
1919	84.0
1920	91.5
1921	69.6
1922	74.1
1923	85.1
1924	84.7
1925	93.1
1926	97.0
1927	94.9
1928	97.0
1929	103.1
1930	90.4

Source: Kurian, *Datapedia of the United States, 1790–2000,* p. 89.

STANDARD AND POOR'S INDEX OF THE SHARE PRICES OF COMMON STOCKS, 1918–1930

Year	Total
1918	7.54
1919	8.78
1920	7.98
1921	6.86
1922	8.41
1923	8.57
1924	9.05
1925	11.15
1926	12.59
1927	15.34
1928	19.95
1929	26.02
1930	21.03

Source: U.S. Bureau of the Census, *Historical Statistics of the United States,* p. 1,004.

BIBLIOGRAPHY

BOOKS

Abels, Jules. *In the Time of Silent Cal.* New York: G. P. Putnam's Sons, 1969.

Adams, James Truslow. *Our Business Civilization: Some Aspects of the Culture.* New York: A. & C. Boni, 1929.

Adams, Samuel Hopkins. *The Incredible Era: The Life and Times of Warren Gamaliel Harding.* Boston: Houghton Mifflin, 1939.

Adler, Mortimer, ed. *The Negro in American History, Vol. II: A Taste of Freedom 1854–1927.* New York: Encyclopedia Britannica Educational Corporation, 1969.

Agel, Jerome, ed. *The Words that Make America Great.* New York: Random House, 1997.

Allen, Frederick Lewis. *Only Yesterday.* New York: Harper & Row, Publishers, 1931.

Altman, Billy. *Laughter's Gentle Soul: The Life of Robert Benchley.* New York: W. W. Norton & Co., 1997.

Anthony, Carl Sferrazza, *Florence Harding: The First Lady, The Jazz Age, and the Death of America's Most Scandalous President.* New York: Morrow, 1998.

Asinof, Eliot. *1919: America's Loss of Innocence.* New York: Donald I. Fine, 1990.

Balliett, Whitney. *Jelly Roll, Jabbo & Fats.* New York: Oxford University Press, 1983.

Banks, Ann, ed. *First Person America.* New York: Alfred A. Knopf, 1980.

Baritz, Loren, ed. *The Culture of the Twenties.* New York: Bobbs-Merrill, 1970.

Bartlett, Captain Robert A. *The Log of Bob Bartlett.* New York: G. P. Putnam's Sons, 1928.

Beals, Carlton. *Banana Gold.* Philadelphia: J. B. Lippincott Co., 1932.

Behr, Edward. *Prohibition: Thirteen Years that Changed America.* New York: Arcade Publishing, 1996.

Bemis, Samuel Flagg. *The Latin-American Policy of the United States: An Historical Interpretation.* New York: W. W. Norton & Co., 1943.

Berg, A. Scott. *Lindbergh.* New York: G. P. Putnam's Sons, 1998.

Bergreen, Laurence. *Capone: The Man and the Era.* New York: Simon and Schuster, 1994.

———. *Louis Armstrong: An Extravagant Life.* New York: Broadway Books, 1997.

Berman, Ronald. *The Great Gatsby and Modern Times.* Urbana, Ill.: University of Illinois Press, 1994.

Broun, Heywood. *Collected Edition of Heywood Broun.* Freeport, N.Y.: Books for Libraries Press, 1969.

Bruccoli, Matthew J. *Some Sort of Epic Grandeur: The Life of F. Scott Fitzgerald.* New York: Harcourt Brace Jovanovich, 1981.

Bryan, William Jennings. *Orthodox Christianity Versus Modernism.* New York: Revell, 1923.

Bryn-Jones, David. *Frank B. Kellogg: A Biography.* New York, 1937.

Busch, Francis X. *Prisoners at the Bar.* New York: Bobbs-Merrill, 1952.

Campaign Addresses of Governor Alfred E. Smith. Washington, D.C.: The Democratic National Committee, 1929.

Carroll, Andrew, ed. *Letters of a Nation: A Collection of Extraordinary American Letters.* New York: Kodansha International, 1997.

Carter, Paul Allen. *Another Part of the Twenties.* New York: Columbia University Press, 1977.

Chalmers, David M. *Hooded Americanism: The First Century of the Ku Klux Klan 1865–1965.* Garden City, N.Y.: Doubleday and Company, 1965.

Chaplin, Charlie. *My Autobiography.* New York: Simon and Schuster, 1964.

Chatterton, Wayne. *Alexander Woollcott.* Boston: Twayne Publishers, 1978.

Churchill, Allen. *The Literary Decade: A Panorama of the Writers, Publishers, and Litterateurs of the 1920s.* New York: Prentice-Hall, 1971.

Cleveland, Reginald M. *America Fledges Wings: The History of the Daniel Guggenheim Fund for the Promotion of Aeronautics.* New York: Pitman Publishing Corp., 1942.

Colbert, David. *Eyewitness to America: 500 Years of America in the Words of Those Who Saw It Happen.* New York: Pantheon Books, 1997.

Commager, Henry Steele. *Documents of American History.* New York: Appleton-Century-Crofts, 1958.

Commission of Inquiry, The Interchurch World Movement. *Report on the Steel Strike of 1919.* New York: Harcourt Brace and Howe, 1920.

Correll, Charles, and Freeman Gosden. *All About Amos and Andy.* New York: Rand McNally, 1929.

Cox, Elizabeth. *Women State and Territorial Legislators.* Jefferson, N.C.: McFarland & Co., 1996.

Crawley, Eduardo. *Nicaragua in Perspective.* New York: St. Martin's Press, 1979.

Creighton, Donald. *A History of Canada: Dominion of the North.* Boston: Houghton Mifflin, 1958.

Dahlinger, John Côté. *Ray Dahlinger—The Man I Called Dad.* New York: Bobbs-Merrill, 1978.

Day, Donald, ed. *The Autobiography of Will Rogers.* Boston: Houghton Mifflin, 1949.

De Camp, L. Sprague. *The Great Monkey Trial.* New York: Doubleday & Company, 1968.

Donaldson, Frances, ed. *Yours, Plum: The Letters of P. G. Wodehouse.* New York: James H. Heineman, 1990.

Douglas, George H. *The Early Days of Radio Broadcasting.* Jefferson, N.C.: McFarland & Co., 1987.

Douglas, Susan J. *Listening In: Radio and the American Imagination.* New York: Times Books, 1999.

Downes, Randolph Chandler. *The Rise of Warren Gamaliel Harding 1865–1920.* Columbus: Ohio University Press, 1970.

Dreher, Carl. *Sarnoff: An American Success.* New York: Quadrangle/The New York Times Book Company, Inc., 1977.

Dulles, Foster Rhea. *Twentieth Century America.* Boston: Houghton Mifflin, 1945.

Duncan, Isadora. *My Life.* New York: Boni and Liveright, 1927.

Eisenberg, Dennis, Uri Dan and Eli Landau. *Meyer Lansky: Mogul of the Mob.* New York: Paddington Press, 1979.

Faulkner, Harold U. *From Versailles to the New Deal: A Chronicle of the Harding—Coolidge—Hoover Era.* New Haven: Yale University Press, 1950.

Ferrell, Robert H. *The Presidency of Calvin Coolidge.* Lawrence: University Press of Kansas, 1998.

Fields, Ronald J. *W. C. Fields by Himself: His Intended Autobiography.* Englewood Cliffs, N.J.: Prentice-Hall, 1973.

Fitzgerald, F. Scott. *The Beautiful and Damned.* New York: Charles Scribner's Sons, 1922.

———. *The Great Gatsby.* New York: Charles Scribner's Sons, 1925.

Forbes, B. C., and O. D. Foster. *Automotive Giants of America.* New York: B. C. Forbes Publishing Company, 1926.

Foster, William Z. *The Great Steel Strike and Its Lessons.* New York: B. W. Huebsch, 1920.

Frank, Glenn. *America's Hour of Decision: Crisis Points in National Policy.* New York: Whittlesey House, 1934.

Frankfurter, Marion Denman, and Gardner Jackson, eds. *The Letters of Sacco and Vanzetti.* New York: Viking, 1928.

Furnas, Joseph Chamberlain. *Great Times: An Informal Social History of the United States, 1914–1929.* New York: G. P. Putnam's Sons, 1974.

Gaines, James R. *Wit's End: Days and Nights of the Algonquin Round Table.* New York: Harcourt Brace Jovanovich, 1977.

Garvey, Marcus. *Philosophies and Opinions of Marcus Garvey or Africa for the Africans.* London: Cass, 1967.

Geduld, Harry M. *The Birth of the Talkies: From Edison to Jolson.* Bloomington: Indiana University Press, 1975.

Gelb, Arthur, and Barbara Gelb. *O'Neill.* New York: Harper and Row, 1973.

Gil, Federico. *Latin American–United States Relations.* New York: Harcourt Brace Jovanovich, 1971.

Ginger, Ray. *Six Days or Forever: Tennessee v. John Thomas Scopes.* Boston: Beacon Press, 1958.

Goldsmith, Julia. *Ferber: A Biography.* Garden City, N.Y.: Doubleday, 1978.

Grant, Robert, and Joseph Katz, *The Great Trials of the Twenties: The Watershed Decade in America's Courtrooms.* Rockville Center, N.Y.: Sarpedon, 1998.

Graves, Ralph Henry. *The Triumph of an Idea: The Story of Henry Ford.* Garden City, N.Y.: Doubleday, Doran & Company, Inc., 1934.

"The Great American Ass." New York: Brentano's, 1926.

Harries, Meirion, and Susie Harries. *The Last Days of Innocence: America at War, 1917–1918.* New York: Random House, 1997.

Harriman, Florence Jaffray Hurst. *From Pinafores to Politics.* New York: Henry Holt & Co., 1923.

Haynes, Fred E. *Criminology.* New York: McGraw-Hill, 1935.

Heckscher, August. *Woodrow Wilson.* New York: Charles Scribner's Sons, 1991.

Hemingway, Ernest. *A Moveable Feast.* New York: Scribner, 1964.

———. *In Our Time.* New York: Charles Scribner's Sons, 1925.

Heuvel, Katrina vanden, ed. *The Nation 1865–1990: Selections from the Independent Magazine of Politics and Culture.* New York: Thunder's Mouth Press, 1990.

Hibben, Paxton. *The Peerless Leader: William Jennings Bryan.* New York: Farrar and Reinhart, Inc., 1929.

Hill, Robert A., ed. *The Marcus Garvey and Universal Negro Improvement Association Papers.* Berkeley: University of California Press, 1986.

Hilmes, Michelle. *Radio Voices: American Broadcasting, 1922–1952.* Minneapolis: University of Minnesota Press, 1997.

Hofstadter, Richard, and Michael Wallace. *American Violence: A Documentary History.* New York: Alfred A. Knopf, 1970.

Holden, Anthony. *Behind the Oscar: The Secret History of the Academy Awards.* New York: Simon and Schuster, 1993.

Holem, Bryan, ed. *The Journal of the Century.* New York: Viking Press, 1976.

Hoover, Herbert. *American Individualism.* Garden City, N.Y.: Doubleday, Page and Co., 1922.

———. *America's First Crusade.* New York: Charles Scribner's Sons, 1941.

———. *Memoirs.* New York: Macmillan, 1952.

———. *The New Day: Campaign Speeches of Herbert Hoover.* Stanford, Calif.: Stanford University Press, 1928.

———. *The Ordeal of Woodrow Wilson.* New York: MacGraw-Hill, 1958.

Howe, Frederic. *Confessions of a Reformer.* New York: Charles Scribner's Sons, 1925.

Jablonski, Edward. *Gershwin: A Biography.* New York: Doubleday, 1987.

Jennings, Peter, and Todd Brewster. *The Century.* New York: Doubleday, 1998.

Johnson, Walter, ed. *Selected Letters of William Allen White, 1899–1943.* New York: Holt, 1947.

Joughin, Louis, and Edmund M. Morgan. *The Legacy of Sacco and Vanzetti.* Chicago: Quadrangle Books, 1948.

Klingaman, William K. *1929: The Year of the Great Crash.* New York: Harper and Row, 1989.

Koebel, W. H. *Central America.* London: T. Fisher Unwin, Ltd., 1925.

Krauze, Enrique. *Mexico: Biography of Power: A History of Modern Mexico.* New York: HarperCollins, 1997.

Kuehl, John, and Jackson R. Bryer, eds. *Dear Scott/Dear Max: The Fitzgerald-Perkins Correspondence.* New York: Scribner, 1971.

Kunkel, Thomas. *Genius in Disguise: Harold Ross of The New Yorker.* New York: Random House, 1995.

Kurian, George Thomas. *Datapedia of the United States, 1790–2000: America Year by Year.* Lanham, Md.: Berman Press, 1994.

Lardner, Ring. *Round-Up: The Stories of Ring Lardner.* New York: Charles Scribner's Sons, 1929.

Larson, Edward J. *Summer for the Gods: The Scopes Trial and America's Continuing Debate over Science and Religion.* New York: Basic Books, 1997.

Lawrence, William. *Henry Cabot Lodge.* Boston: Houghton Mifflin, 1925.

Leighton, Isabel, ed. *The Aspirin Age: 1919–1941.* New York: Simon and Schuster, 1949.

Leopold, Nathan. *Life Plus 99 Years.* New York: Popular Library, 1957.

Lewis, Jon E. *The Permanent Book of the 20th Century: Eyewitness Accounts of the Moments that Shaped our Century.* New York: Carroll & Graf, 1994.

Lewis, Tom. *Empire of the Air: The Men Who Made Radio.* New York: HarperCollins, 1991.

Lindbergh, Anne Morrow. *Bring Me a Unicorn.* New York: Harcourt Brace Jovanovich, 1971.

Lindbergh, Charles. *Autobiography of Values.* New York: Harcourt Brace Jovanovich, 1978.

———. *The Spirit of St. Louis.* New York: Scribner, 1953.

Link, Arthur Stanley. *Woodrow Wilson: Revolution, War, and Peace.* Arlington Heights, Ill.: AHM Publishing Corp., 1979.

Lippmann, Walter. *Men of Destiny.* New York: Macmillan, 1927.

———. *Public Persons.* New York: Liveright, 1976.

Locke, Alain. *The New Negro: An Interpretation.* New York, Johnson Reprint Corp., 1968.

Lodge, Henry Cabot. *The Senate and the League of Nations.* New York: Charles Scribner's Sons, 1925.

Longworth, Alice Roosevelt. *Crowded Hours: Reminiscences of Alice Roosevelt Longworth.* New York: Charles Scribner's Sons, 1933.

Loos, Anita. *"Gentlemen Prefer Blondes": The Illuminating Diary of a Professional Lady.* New York: Boni & Liveright, 1925.

Lott, Davis Newton. *The Inaugural Addresses of the American Presidents, from Washington to Kennedy.* New York: Holt, Rinehart, and Winston, 1961.

Lowell, Mary S. *The Sound of Wings: The Life of Amelia Earhart.* New York: St. Martin's Press, 1989.

Lynd, Robert Staughton, and Helen Merrell Lynd. *Middletown: A Study in Modern American Culture.* New York: Harcourt Brace & Company, 1929.

Lyons, Eugene. *David Sarnoff.* New York: Harper and Row, 1966.

MacAdams, William. *Ben Hecht: The Man Behind the Legend.* New York: Charles Scribner's Sons, 1990.

Macdougall, Allen Ross, ed. *Letters of Edna St. Vincent Millay.* New York: Harper & Brothers, 1952.

MacDougall, William C., and Carl Brigham. *A Study of American Intelligence.* Princeton, N.J.: Princeton University Press, 1923.

Marion, Frances. *Off With Their Heads: A Serio-Comic Tale of Hollywood.* New York: Macmillan, 1972.

Martin, John Bartlow, ed. *My Life in Crime: The Autobiography of An American Criminal.* New York: Harper, 1952.

McCoy, Donald. *Calvin Coolidge: The Quiet President.* New York: Macmillan, 1967.

McInnis, Edgar. *Canada: A Political and Social History.* New York: Holt, Rinehart and Winston, 1947.

McKay, Claude. *Home to Harlem.* New York: Harper & Brothers, 1928.

Mellow, James R. *Hemingway: A Life Without Consequences.* Boston: Houghton Mifflin, 1992.

Mencken, H. L. *Letters.* Selected and annotated by Guy J. Forgue. New York: Knopf, 1961.

———. *On Politics: A Carnival of Buncombe.* New York: Vintage Books, 1960.

———. *Prejudices (Fifth Series).* New York: Knopf, 1926.

Merz, Charles. *And Then Came Ford.* Garden City, N.Y.: Doubleday Doran & Company, 1929.

Meyer, Michael C., and William L. Sherman. *The Course of Mexican History.* New York: Oxford University Press, 1979.

Meyers, Jeffrey. *Scott Fitzgerald: A Biography.* New York: HarperCollins, 1994.

Miller, Marc H., ed. *Louis Armstrong: A Cultural Legacy.* Seattle: University of Washington Press, 1994.

Mirsky, Jeannette. *To the North! The Story of Arctic Exploration from Earliest Times to the Present.* New York: Viking Press, 1934.

Mitchell, Wesley Clair. *Recent Economic Changes.* New York: McGraw-Hill, 1929.

Moore, Edmund A. *A Catholic Runs for President: The Campaign of 1928.* New York: Ronald Press Company, 1956.

Mordden, Ethan. *That Jazz! An Idiosyncratic Social History of the American Twenties.* New York: G. P. Putnam's Sons, 1978.

Munro, Dana G. *The United States and the Caribbean Area.* Boston: World Peace Foundation, 1934.

Murray, Robert K. *The Harding Era: Warren G. Harding and His Administration.* Minneapolis: University of Minnesota Press, 1969.

Ness, Eliot. *The Untouchables.* Mattituck, N.Y.: American Reprint Co., 1976.

O'Connor, Richard. *The First Hurrah: A Biography of Alfred E. Smith.* New York: G. P. Putnam's Sons, 1970.

Parrish, Michael E. *Anxious Decades: America in Prosperity and Depression, 1920–1941.* New York: W. W. Norton & Co., 1992.

Patterson, Robert T. *The Great Boom and Panic.* Chicago: Henry Regnery Company, 1965.

Pearson, Lester B. *Mike: The Memoirs of The Right Honorable Lester B. Pearson, Vol. I: 1897–1948.* New York: Quadrangle Books, 1972.

Peterson, H. C. and Gilbert C. Fite. *Opponents of War 1917–1918.* Madison: University of Wisconsin Press, 1957.

Podell, Janet, and Steven Anzovin, eds. *Speeches of the American Presidents.* New York: H. W. Wilson Co., 1988.

Porter, Kirk H., and Donald Bruce Johnson. *National Party Platforms.* Urbana: University of Illinois Press, 1966.

Pringle, Henry F. *Alfred E. Smith: A Critical Study.* New York: Vanguard Press, 1927.

Rasmussen, Knud. *Across Arctic America.* New York: G. P. Putnam's Sons, 1927.

Reynolds, Michael. *Hemingway: The Paris Years.* Cambridge, Mass.: Basil Blackwell, Inc., 1989.

Rich, Doris L. *Amelia Earhart: A Biography.* Washington, D.C.: Smithsonian Institution Press, 1989.

Rickenbacker, Edward V. *Rickenbacker.* Englewood Cliffs, N.J.: Prentice-Hall, 1967.

Rodgers, Marion Elizabeth, ed. *The Impossible H. L. Mencken: A Selection of His Best Newspaper Stories.* New York: Doubleday, 1991.

Rogers, Will. *Will Rogers' Weekly Articles*. Stillwater: Oklahoma State University Press, 1980.

Roosevelt, Elliott. *F.D.R.: His Personal Letters, 1905–1928*. New York: Duell, Sloan and Pearce, 1948.

Ross, Walter Sanford. *The Last Hero: Charles A. Lindbergh*. New York: Harper and Row, 1964.

Russell, Francis. *Tragedy in Dedham: The Story of the Sacco-Vanzetti Case*. New York: McGraw-Hill Book Company, Inc., 1962.

Ruiz, Ramón Eduardo. *Triumphs and Tragedy: A History of the Mexican People*. New York: W. W. Norton & Co., 1992.

Russell, Francis. *President Harding: His Life and Times, 1865–1923*. London: Eyre & Spottiswoode, 1968.

————. *The Shadow of Blooming Grove: Warren G. Harding in His Times*. New York: McGraw-Hill, 1968.

Sann, Paul. *The Lawless Decade*. New York: Bonanza Books, 1957.

Schlesinger Jr., Arthur M. *The Crisis of the Old Order, 1919–1933*. Boston: Houghton Mifflin, 1957.

Schoultz, Lars. *Beneath the United States: A History of U.S. Policy Toward Latin America*. Cambridge, Mass.: Harvard University Press, 1998.

Seldes, Gilbert. *The Years of the Locust: America, 1929–1932*. Boston: Little, Brown, and Company, 1933.

Seroff, Victor Ilyitch. *The Real Isadora*. New York: Dial Press, 1971.

Seymour, Charles. *Woodrow Wilson and the World War: A Chronicle of Our Own Times*. New Haven: Yale University Press, 1921.

Shannon, David A. *Between the Wars: America, 1919–1941*. Boston: Houghton Mifflin, 1979.

Shapiro, Nat, and Nat Hentoff, eds. *Hear Me Talkin' To Ya: The Story of Jazz as Told by the Men Who Made It*. New York: Dover Publications, 1955.

Shipley, Maynard. *The War on Modern Science: A Short History of the Fundamentalist Attacks on Evolution and Modernism*. New York: Knopf, 1927.

Simmons, George. *Target: Arctic*. Philadelphia: Chilton Books, 1965.

Sinclair, Andrew. *The Available Man: The Life Behind the Masks of Warren Gamaliel Harding*. New York: Macmillan, 1965.

Sloat, Warren. *1929: America Before the Crash*. New York: Macmillan, 1979.

Slonimsky, Nicolas. *Lexicon of Musical Invective: Critical Assaults on Composers Since Beethoven's Time*. New York: Coleman-Ross Co., 1965.

Smith, Alfred E. *Progressive Democracy: Addresses and State Papers of Alfred E. Smith.* New York: Harcourt, Brace and Company, 1928.

Smith, Gene. *When the Cheering Stopped: The Last Days of Woodrow Wilson.* New York: Time, Inc., 1966.

Sobel, Robert. *Coolidge: An American Enigma.* Washington, D.C.: Regnery, 1998.

Stevenson, Elizabeth. *Babbitts and Bohemians: From the Great War to the Great Depression.* New Brunswick, N.J.: Transaction Publishers, 1998.

Stoddard, Lothrop. *The Rising Tide of Color Against White World Supremacy.* New York: Charles Scribner's Sons, 1920.

Stone, Irving. *Clarence Darrow: For the Defense.* New York: Doubleday, Doran and Co., 1941.

Stuart, Graham H. *Latin America and the United States.* New York: D. Appleton–Century Company, 1943.

Sullivan, Mark. *Our Times.* New York: Charles Scribner's Sons, 1933. Reprint, New York: Scribner, 1996.

Swanberg, W. A. *Citizen Hearst: A Biography of William Randolph Hearst.* New York: Scribner, 1961.

———. *Dreiser.* New York: Scribner, 1965.

———. *Norman Thomas: The Last Idealist.* New York: Scribner, 1976.

Teresa, Vincent, and Thomas C. Renner. *My Life in the Mafia.* Greenwich, Ct.: Fawcett Books, 1974.

Terkel, Studs. *Hard Times: An Oral History of the Great Depression.* New York: Pantheon Books, 1970.

Thomas, Gordon, and Max Morgan-Witts. *The Day the Bubble Burst.* Garden City, N.Y.: Doubleday, 1979.

Tierney, Kevin. *Darrow: A Biography.* New York: Thomas Y. Crowell, 1979.

Tucker, Mark. *Ellington: The Early Years.* Urbana: University of Illinois Press, 1991.

U.S. Bureau of the Census. *Historical Statistics of the United States.* Washington, D.C.: Superintendent of Documents, U.S. Government Printing Office, 1960.

Wagner, Walter. *You Must Remember This.* New York: G. P. Putnam's Sons, 1975.

Ware, Caroline. *Greenwich Village, 1920–1930: A Comment on American Civilization in the Post-War Years.* Boston: Houghton Mifflin, 1935.

Ware, Susan. *Still Missing: Amelia Earhart and the Search for Modern Feminism.* New York: W. W. Norton & Co., 1993.

Warren, Harris Gaylord. *Herbert Hoover and the Great Depression.* New York: Oxford University Press, 1959.

Weinstein, Edwin A. *Woodrow Wilson: A Medical and Psychological Biography.* Princeton, N.J.: Princeton University Press, 1981.

Wesley, Charles H. *Negro Labor in the United States, 1850–1925: A Study in American Economic History.* New York: Russell & Russell, 1927.

West, Bruce. *Toronto.* Toronto: Doubleday Canada Limited, 1967.

Whitaker, Arthur P. *The Western Hemisphere Idea: Its Rise and Decline.* Ithaca, N.Y.: Cornell University Press, 1954.

White, William. *By-Line: Ernest Hermingway: Selected Articles and Dispatches of Four Decades.* New York: Scribner, 1967.

White, William Allen. *A Puritan in Babylon: The Story of Calvin Coolidge.* New York: Macmillan, 1938.

Wik, Reynold M. *Henry Ford and Grass-roots America.* Ann Arbor: University of Michigan Press, 1972.

Williams, Archibald. *Conquering the Air.* New York: Thomas Nelson and Sons, 1926.

Williams, Martin. *Jazz Masters of New Orleans.* New York: Da Capo Press, 1967.

Wilson, Edmund. *The American Earthquake: A Documentary of the Twenties and Thirties.* Garden City, N.Y.: Doubleday, 1958.

————. *The Twenties: From Notebooks and Diaries of the Period.* Edited with an Introduction by Leon Edel. New York: Farrar, Straus and Giroux, 1975.

Winkelman, Barnie F. *Ten Years of Wall Street.* Philadelphia: John C. Winston Company, 1932.

Wittke, Carl. *A History of Canada.* New York: Alfred A. Knopf, 1928.

Wrenn, John H. *John Dos Passos.* New York: Twayne Publishers, 1961.

Yagoda, Ben. *Will Rogers: A Biography.* New York: Alfred A. Knopf, 1993.

Young, William, and David E. Kaiser. *Postmortem: New Evidence in the Case of Sacco and Vanzetti.* Amherst: University of Massachusetts Press, 1985.

PERIODICALS

"Americana," *The American Mercury,* January 1928, p. 49–51.

"Editorial," *The American Mercury,* February 1927, p. 163.

The American Mercury (editorial from Muscatine *Journal*), March 1928, p. 308.

"Americana," *The American Mercury, (Rev. E. W. Perry),* March 1928, p. 31.

Bagnall, Robert W. "The Spirit of the Ku Klux Klan," *Opportunity,* September 1923, p. 265.

Baldwin, George J. "The Migration: A Southern View," *Opportunity,* June 1924, p. 183.

Barkley, Frederick R. "Jailing Radicals in Detroit," *The Nation,* 1920, p. 136.

Benchley, Robert. "The Making of a Red," *The Nation,* March 15, 1919, pp. 24–25.

Bent, Silas. "Will the Democrats Follow the Whigs?" *Scribner's,* November 1929, p. 473.

Borah, William E. "Neighbors and Friends: A Plea for Justice to Mexico," *The Nation,* April 13, 1927, p. 393.

Bromley, Dorothy Dunbar. "Feminist—New Style," *Harpers,* October 1927, p. 552.

Brooks, George S. "Gas and the Games," *Scribner's,* August 1928, p. 189.

"Calvin Coolidge: Made by a Myth," *The Nation,* August 15, 1923, p. 3.

"Canada's Colossal Smuggling Industry," *The Literary Digest,* May 29, 1926, p. 16.

Caveney, M. J. "New Voices in the Wilderness," *Colliers,* April 1920, p. 18.

Chattanooga Times, April 4, 1925, p. 5.

Clark, Edwin. "A Farewell to Flappers," *The New York Times,* April 19, 1925, p. 9.

Clark, Evans. "The 1918 Socialist Vote," *The Intercollegiate Socialist,* December 1918–January 1919, p. 17.

"Coy Co-Eds," *Time,* October 10, 1927, p. 29.

Daniel, Hawthorne. "Living and Dying on the Installment Plan" *World's Work,* January 1926, p. 329.

Davis, Elmer. "What Can We Do About It? The Candid Misgiving of a Wet," *Harpers,* December 1928, p. 1.

"The Death Penalty," *The Nation,* November 7, 1928, p. 472.

Douglas, W. A. S. "Ku Klux," *The American Mercury,* March 1928, pp. 278–279.

DuBois, W. E. B. "A Lunatic or a Traitor," *The Crisis,* May 1924, p. 8.

———. "Georgia: Invisible Empire State," *The Nation,* January 21, 1925, p. 65.

———. "Returning Soldiers," *The Crisis,* May 1919, p. 14.

"Faith, Brokers, and Panic," *Time,* November 11, 1929, pp. 45–46.

Feld, Rose C. "Interview," *The New York Times,* December 21, 1924, p. 11.

Ford, Henry. "Youth, Industry, and Progress," *Forum,* October 1928, pp. 582–589.

"Ford v. G.M.C.," *Time,* October 19, 1927, p. 32.

Frankfurter, Felix. "The Case of Sacco and Vanzetti," *The Atlantic Monthly,* March 1927, pp. 431–432.

Freeman, James E. "When 'Good Society' Winks," *The Literary Digest,* March 6, 1926, p. 31.

Green, Abel. *Daily Variety,* December 7, 1927, p. 54.

"Hard Boiled," *World's Work,* April 1929, p. 33.

Hartt, Rollin. "Down With Evolution!," *The World's Work,* October 1923, p. 605.

Hughes, Langston. "The Negro Artist and the Racial Mountain," *The Nation,* June 23, 1926, p. 694.

The International Book Review, May 1925, p. 426.

Jackson, Joseph H. "Should Radio Be Used for Advertising?" *Radio Broadcast,* November 1922, p. 76.

James, Edwin L. "Lindbergh Does It! ..." *The New York Times,* May 1, 1927, p. 1.

Johnson, James Weldon. "Race Prejudice and the Negro Artist." *Harper's,* November 1928, p. 769.

Kelly, Fred C. "Logic and the Stock Market," *The American Mercury,* February 1927, p. 148.

Lee, Robert M. "Who is to Be All Highest of World Radio?" *Chicago Tribune,* December 19, 1923, p. 6.

Levitt, Albert. "Anti-Prohibition Hallucinations," *The South Atlantic Quarterly,* January 1926, pp. 10–12.

Lewis, Sinclair. "The Man Who Knew Coolidge," *The American Mercury,* January 1928, p. 3.

"Marines Trapped," *Time,* January 9, 1928, p. 16.

Martin, Edward S. "Our Satisfaction with Mr. Coolidge," *Harper's,* November 1925, pp. 765–766.

McLellan, Howard. "Boys, Gangs, and Crime," *The Review of Reviews,* March 1929, p. 57.

Mencken, H. L. "Obituary of William Jennings Bryan," *The American Mercury,* October 1925, pp. 158–159.

"Mexico Outlawing the Church," *The Literary Digest,* March 6, 1926, p. 31.

Miller, Charles A. "A Capitalist's Confession of Faith," *The Outlook,* January 1920, pp. 15–16.

Miller, Kelly. "Is the American Negro to Remain Black or Become Bleached," *The South Atlantic Quarterly,* July 1926, pp. 240–241.

The Nation, June 15, 1927, p. 655.

The Nation, November 14, 1928, p. 507.

The New Republic, September 7, 1927, p. 57.

New York Daily News, January 19, 1920, p. 1.

"Armistice Signed, End of the War! . . ." *New York Times,* November 11, 1918, p. 1.

"Remick Nips Panic on Stock Exchange," *New York Times,* September 17, 1920, p. 1.

New York Times, January 17, 1924, p. 2.

New York Times, October 18, 1925, p. 8.

"Lindbergh's Own Story of Epochal Flight . . ." *New York Times,* May 23, 1927.

The New York World, October 18, 1925, p. 7.

"The Nicaragua Canal Bobs Up Once More," *The Nation,* April 13, 1927, p. 386.

Noyes, Alexander Dana. "The Course of a Great Stock-Exchange Speculation," *Scribner's,* July 1928, pp. 133–134.

Opportunity, October 1923, p. 290.

"Our Tiff with Mexico Settled," *The Literary Digest,* May 1, 1926, p. 16.

"Our Warning to Nicaragua," *The Literary Digest,* February 13, 1926, p. 12.

Palmer, A. Mitchell. "The Case Against the Reds," *Forum,* February 1920, p. 173.

Pickens, William. "The Emperor of Africa." *Forum,* August 1923, p. 1,790.

"Prohibition—Over the Lake," *Time,* May 23, 1927, p. 10.

"A Radio Church," *The Literary Digest,* May 15, 1926, p. 30.

"Radio Wedding Impressed Listeners," *Radio Broadcasting News,* December 9, 1922, n.p.

Rice, Grantland. "The King Maker," *Collier's,* November 13, 1926, p. 36.

Seldes, Gilbert. *The Dial,* August 1925, p. 162.

Seligmann, Herbert J. "The Conquest of Haiti," *The Nation,* July 10, 1920, p. 35.

Shaw, Albert. "The Progress of the World," *The Review of Reviews,* December 1929, p. 36.

"Shenandoah, Torn From Mast by Gale . . . ," *New York Times,* January 17, 1924, p. 2.

Sherwood, R. E. "Beyond the Talkies—Television," *Scribner's,* July 1929, pp. 7–8.

Shipley, Maynard. "The Fundamentalists' Case," *The American Mercury,* February 1928, p. 228.

Stefansson, Vilhjalmur, "The Airplane and the Arctic: New Pioneers Dispel an Old Myth," *Harper's,* October 1927, p. 599.

Sullivan, Mark. "The Paramount Issues: Prohibition Leaps to the Front," *World's Work,* September 1928, p. 493.

Sunday, Billy. "Historical Fabric of Christ's Life Nothing Without Miracles," *Memphis Commercial Appeal,* February 7, 1925, p. 1.

The Southern Workman, November 1924, pp. 530–536.

Talley, Truman Hughes. "Marcus Garvey—The Negro Moses?" *The World's Work,* December 1920, p. 153.

"Tennessee vs. Truth," *The Nation,* July 8, 1925, p. 58.

Thomas, Norman. "Political Prisoners in the United States," *The Intercollegiate Socialist,* February–March 1919, p. 11.

"Corruption—Oil" *Time,* February 13, 1928, p. 10.

"Radicals—Dynamite," *Time,* May 23, 1927, p. 9.

"World's Series," *Time,* October 17, 1927, p. 36.

Turner, Homer. "Notes of a Prohibition Agent," *The American Mercury,* April 1928, p. 385.

Veblen, Thorstein, "Dementia Praecox," *The Freeman,* June 21, 1922.

The Wall Street Journal, October 4, 1927, p. 1.

"Wall Street Lays an Egg," *Daily Variety,* October 30, 1929, p. 1.

"Wall Street's Crisis," *The Nation,* November 6, 1929, p. 510.

"Wall Street's 'Prosperity Panic,'" *The Literary Digest,* November 9, 1929, p. 5.

White, Walter. "The Causes of the Chicago Race Riot," *The Crisis,* October 1919, p. 293.

———. "Chicago and its Eight Reasons," *The Crisis,* October 1919, p. 296.

Wright, Carol. "The Human Factor," *The Atlantic Monthly,* January 1920, p. 25.

Yust, Walter. *Literary Review,* May 2, 1925, p. 3.

INTERNET SITES

"American Leaders Speak: Recordings from World War I and the 1920 Election, 1918–1920." The American Memory Collection, Library of Congress. Available online. URL: http://memory.loc.gov/ammem/nfhome.html.

"American Life Histories: Manuscripts from the Federal Writers' Project 1936–1940." The American Memory Collection, Library of Congress. Available online. URL: http://memory.loc.gov/ammem/wpaintro/wpahome.html.

INDEX

Page locators in **boldface** indicate main entries. Page locators in *italic* indicate illustrations. Page locators followed by *m* indicate maps.

A

Aberdeen Daily News 248
Abrams v. United States
   291–292
Abyssinian Baptist Church 102
Academy Awards 275
Academy of Motion Picture
   Arts and Sciences 242, 275
Adams, Franklin Pierce 132,
   133
Adams, Sarah Root 178
Addams, Jane 37
Adkins v. Children's Hospital 88
advertising 126
Aeolian Hall 108–111, *113,*
   126
Africa 29
African Americans 97– 111,
   294, **395–396**
African Orthodox Church 101
Agricultural Credits Act 141
Agricultural Marketing Act 276
agriculture
      and tariffs 64
      depression in 97, 249, 251,
         256–257
      postwar 53-54, 249
Aiello brothers 268
air mail service 64, 207–208
Akron, Ohio 112
Alabama 98, 154
Alaska 80, 83, 201–204, 206
Alberta, Canada 182, 184
Alcock, John 13, 209
alcoholism 33
Aldene, New Jersey 125

Alexander, Grover Cleveland
   233
Alexander Woolcott (Wayne
   Chatteron) 146
Alfred E. Smith: A Critical Study
   (Henry E. Pringle) 263
Algonquin Hotel 103, 133
Algonquin Round Table 103,
   133, 147
Alien Land Tax 43
Alien Law of 1918 29
Alien Property Act 258
All About Amos and Andy
   (Charles Correll and Freeman
   Gosden) 145
All God's Chillun Got Wings
   (Eugene O'Neill) 132
Almer Coe & Co. 158
Alsace-Lorraine 2
A Lume Spento (Ezra Pound) 137
Ambassador Billiard Parlor 109
Ambassador Bridge 276
America Before the Crash (Warren
   Sloat) 246
America Between the Wars (David
   Shannon) 21
American Bar Association 196
American Birth Control
   Conference 39
American Birth Control League
   39, 65
"American Bohemians in Paris"
   (Ernest Hemingway) 147
American Civil Liberties Union
   (ACLU) 156, 160, 167, 175,
   343–344
The American Earthquake
   (Edmund Wilson) 247

American Expeditionary Force
   55
American Farm Bureau
   Federation 54
American Federation of Labor
   (AFL) 3, 182
      and Boston police strike
         9, 84
      and immigration 62
      and Samuel Gompers 64,
         112, 141
American Individualism (Herbert
   Hoover) 50
The American Language (H. L.
   Mencken) 132
American League 62, 83,
   232–234
American Legion 13, 15
American Legion Magazine 132,
   211
*American Life Histories:
   Manuscripts from the Federal
   Writers' Project 1836–1940*
   (web site) 48, 119
American Magazine 281
American Mercury 131, 132,
   247
American Railway Union 5
American Reader 20
American Relief Administration
   56
American Society of Equity 54
American Telephone and
   Telegraph (AT&T) 126, 193,
   216
Amherst, Massachusetts 84
Amos and Andy 145
Amundsen, Roald 202, 206

An American Tragedy (Theodore
   Dreiser) 149, 151, 171
anarchism 15, 28, 61
Anarchist Fighters 28
anarchists
      eyewitness testimony
         20–24
      in Canada 182
      and Ku Klux Klan 59
      and labor strife 12
      and Palmer Raids 14, 29,
         58
Anchorage, Alaska 83
Anderson, Benjamin M. 280
Anderson, Marion **362**
Anderson, Mary 42
Anderson, Maxwell 130, 131
Anderson, Regina 102
Anderson, Sherwood 130, 139
Anderson Art Galleries 110
Andree, Salomnon August 203
And Then Came Ford (Charles
   Merz) 247, 261
Angelus Temple 193
Anglo-Japanese Treaty 63
Anheuser-Busch 33
Another Part of the Twenties (Paul
   Allen Carter) 260
Antheil, George 217
Anthony, Susan B. 37
Anthony Amendment *41*
Anti-Evolution League of
   America 154
Anti-Evolution League of
   Minnesota 154, 177
"Anti-Prohibition
   Hallucinations" (Albert
   Levitt) 277

Anti-Saloon League 26, 46, 58
Antonio, Captain 48
Anxious Decades (Michael E. Parrish) 50–51
Aqua Hotel 160
Arbuckle, Minta Durfee 243
Arbuckle, Roscoe "Fatty" 43, 227–228, 242–243, **362**
Arctic (ship) 205
Arctic Circle 201, 202
Arctic region 201–206
Argentina 112, 257
Arizona 190
Arkansas 98, 252, 258
Arlington National Cemetery 63
Armenia 2
Armistice Day 3, 65
Armistice of 1918 1, 16, 28, 53
Armstrong, Edward 124
Armstrong, Louis 88, **362–363**
    in Chicago 107, 115, 119, *121*
Army Reorganization Act 42
Arrowsmith (Sinclair Lewis) 129, 171, 193
Arthur, Jack 242
Asbury, Herbert 132
Asimov, Isaac 41
The Aspirin Age (Isabel Leighton) 89
Atcherson, Lucille 171
Atchison, Kansas 214
atheism 38
Atlanta 58, 59, 60, 101, 229
Atlanta Board of Education 193
Atlanta penitentiary 5, 169
The Atlantic Monthly 132, 170
Aunt Polly's Story of Mankind (Donald Ogden Stewart) 133
Austria 62, 258
auto industry 249–250, **399**
    in Detroit 34
    Dodge Brothers 171
    Ford Motor Company 53, 216, **235–239**
    and stock market 270
    and Taylorism 57
automobiles 25, 40, 64, 251, 254
Automotive Giants of America (B. C. Forbes and O. D. Foster) 246
Ava, Ohio 172
The Available Man (Andrew Sinclair) 70, 91
aviation
    aircraft factories 207
    and Arctic exploration **203–215**

and Department of Commerce 57
distance and time records 240, 275–276
and media *259*
Axel Heiberg Island 205
Azores 209

B

Babbitt (Sinclair Lewis) 129
Babbitts and Bohemians (Elizabeth Stevenson) 45
Bachrach, Benjamin and Walter 159
Backenstahl, Harry 161
Baffin Island 204
Bahamas 34
Bailey v. Drexel Furniture 87
Baker, George F. 273
Baker, Josephine **363**
Baker, Norma Jean 216
Baldwin, Roger Nash 156
The Ballad of the Brown Girl (Countee Cullen) 135
ballet 106
Ballet Mechanique (George Antheil) 217
Baltimore 26, 131
Baltimore *Evening Sun* 88, 131, 161, 166, 265
Baltimore *Morning Herald* 131
Banana Gold (Carlton Beals) 198
Bank for International Settlements 275
Bankers Trust 273
Bankhead, Tallulah 133
bankruptcies 141, 273, 274
banks and banking 249, 256
    postwar depression 54
    and farming 88
    and margin trading 275
    and stock market crash 104, 256, 271, 274, 276
Baptists 154
Bara, Theda 225
Barnard College 135
Barnum, P.T. 133
Barrow, Ed 233
Barrymore, John 216, **363**
Bartók, Béla 109
Barton, Arthur James 46
Barton, Ralph 134
baseball 125, **232–235**
basketball 230
bathtub gin 32, 36
Baylor University 154
Beals, Carlton 189

The Beautiful and Damned (F. Scott Fitzgerald) 90
Behind the Oscar (Anthony Holden) 242
Beiderbecke, Leon "Bix" 107
Belgium 63, 65, 172, 181
Bellanca, Giuseppe 210
Bellevue Hospital 240
Bell Labs 276
Benchley, Robert 132–133, 147, 170, **363**
Benét, Stephen Vincent 134
Benét, William Rose 134
Ben Hecht: The Man Behind the Legend (William MacAdams) 151
Bennett, Arnold 151
Bennett, Floyd 193, 206, 211
Benton Harbor, Michigan 43
Berardelli, Alessandro 167, 168, 169
Berger, Victor 4, 5, 15, **363**
Berkeley Tennis Club 228
Berkman, Alexander 15, 29
Berlin 135
Berlin, Irving 109, 111, **363–364**
Bernhardt, Sarah 134
Bernier, Joseph 202
Bethlehem Steel Company 57
Bethune, Mary McLeod **364**
Beyond the Horizon (Eugene O'Neill) 146
"Beyond the Talkies—Television" (R. E. Sherwood) 262
The Big Money (John Dos Passos) 130
Billings, Montana 8
Birmingham, Alabama 14, 59
birth control **38–39**
Birth Control Clinical Research Bureau 39
Birth of a Nation 28, 225
Bishop, William A. 181
Bixby, Harold 210
Blachen, Bernt 276
Black America 105
Black and Tan Fantasy (Duke Ellington) 108
Blackmer, H. M. 77
Black Sox scandal 43, 138, 232–233
Black Star Line 101
Bladinger, Reddy 83
Blair Company 77
Blake, Eubie 105, 108
Bliss, Tasker H. 17

Bloomsbury Group 136
Bluefields, Nicaragua 188
blues 105
Bly, Nellie 36
Board of Shipping 80
Boas, Franz 135
Bodenheim, Maxwell 151
Boeing 13
Bohr, Niels 88
boll weevil 97
Bologna, Pat 279
Bolsheviks
    fear of 100
    Palmer Raids 30
    Red Scare 62
    in Russia 6, 28, 56, 182
    and strikes 3, 9, 84
Bonfils, Frederick 79
Boni, Albert and Charles 132
Boni and Liveright 132, 134
Bonus Army 140
Bonus Bill 43, 55, 87, 140
Book-of-the-Month Club 193
Bookman, The 132
bootleggers xi, 32–35, 74, 269
Borah, William 8, 189
Boris Godunov 141
Borzoi Books 132
Boston 4, 227
    aviation 207, 214, 215
    and Harding scandals 81
    Palmer Raids 29
    Red Scare 28
    Sacco and Vanzetti trial 168
    See also Boston police strike
Boston Advertiser 247
Boston Harbor 215
Boston Marathon 171, 193
Boston police strike 8–10, 22, 23, 84
Boston Social Club 9
Boston Symphony 216
Boulder Dam 64
Bow, Clara 225, **364**
Bowdoin 20
"Bowling Green" (Christopher Morley) 146
boxing **231–232**
    heavyweight championships 43, 112, 216, 240
    and radio 64, 216
Boxing Age 125
Boyd, Ernest 44
Boyd, Louise **364**
Boyer, Lillian *207*
"Boys, Gangs, and Crime" (Howard McLellan) 278

Bradbury, Ray 42
Bradley, Neil *259*
Braintree, Massachusetts 42
Brando, Marlon 140
Brant Rock, Massachusetts 123
Brehm, Marie C. 140
Briand, Aristide 217
Brink, Mrs. W. W. 66
Brisbane, Arthur 176
British Amateur golf
    championship 229, 230
British Debt Refunding Act 88
British Empire 303–304
British General Post Office 193
British Isles 61
British Open golf championship
    230
broadcasting 128
Broadway (district) 65, 102,
    133, 140, 241
        black theater 102,
        105–106
        and Prohibition 33
        Gershwin musicals
        109–110
Broadway (street) 230
Broken Blossoms (film) 225
Bromwell, Laura 64
Bronx 128
Brooklyn 39, 84, 102
Brooklyn Dodgers 229
Brooklyn Eagle 196
Brooklyn Robins 43
Brooks, Louise **364–365**
Broomfield, Louis 133
Broun, Heywood 132–133,
    170, 179
Brown, Arthur 13, 209
Bruce, Virginia 226
Bryan, Charles W. 86, 140
Bryan, William Jennings xii, 86,
    140, **365**
        death of 171
        and evolution debate 155
        and Prohibition 44
        and Scopes trial 157–158,
        160, **161–167**, 174–176
Bryan-Chamorro Treaty 187
Bucareli Agreements 191
Budget and Accounting Act 55,
    64
Buena Vista, California 75
Buenos Aires 170
Buford (ship) 15, 29
Buick automobiles 251
Bullitt, William C. 8, 17
"Bull Moose" Republicans 30
Bunk (William E. Woodward)
    130–131, 133
Bunting, Frederick 65

Burbank, Luther 193
Bureau of Aeronautics 204
Bureau of Air Commerce 193
Bureau of the Budget 64, 81
Bureau of Foreign and
    Domestic Commerce 57
Bureau of Housing 85
Bureau of Investigation 29, 65,
    74
Bureau of Standards 57
Bureau of Veterans Affairs 65
Burke, Billie 133
Burma 73
Burn, Harry 51
Burns, William J. 65, 74
Burry Port, Wales 215, 258
Bush, Joe *241*
Butler, John Washington 155,
    156, 161
Butler, Nicholas Murray 89
Butte, Montana 42
By-Line: Ernest Hemingway
    (William White) 147
Byng, Lord 184
Byrd, Richard xii
        and Charles Lindbergh
        212
        eyewitness testimony
        218–220
        and long-distance flights
        214–215, 259, 276
        and Orteig Prize 210
        polar expeditions of 193,
        204–206, 208, 259, 276

C

Cabell, James Branch 130–131
The Cabinet of Dr. Caligari 65
Cable Act 87
Caesar, Irving 172
Calgary, Alberta 182
California 8, 83, *247*
        and aviation 215
        chronicle of events 43, 64,
        87, 112, 140, 240, 258
        and Mexican policy 190
        and movie industry 225,
        228
        and Prohibition 35
        and Teapot Dome scandal
        76, 80
Calles, Plutarco Elias 188,
    191–192
Calles-Morrow compromise 192
*Calvin Coolidge: The Quiet
    President* (Donald McCoy)
    22
Cambridge, Massachusetts 141

Camden, Ohio 130
*Campaign Addresses of Governor
    Alfred E. Smith* 264
Canada 38
        and exploration 201–205,
        215
        and immigration 62, 254
        chronicle of events 216,
        240, 275
        eyewitness testimony
        194–195
        politics and economy of
        181–185, 249, 257
        and Prohibition 34, 267,
        269
        and Teapot Dome scandal
        77
"Canada's Colossal Smuggling
    Industry" 194
Canadian Council of
    Agriculture 182
Canadian Expeditionary Force
    181
Canary (airplane) 214
Canton, Ohio 5
Cantos (Ezra Pound) 137
Cape Bridgeman 206
Capitol Curve filling station *239*
Capone, Al 216, 267–269,
    275–278, *281*, **365**
Capone: The Man and the Era
    (Laurence Bergreen) 277–278
Capper-Volstead Act 87
car camping *245*, 250
Cardenas, Lazaro 192
Caribbean 101–102, 113, 185,
    187
Carmanthenshire, Wales 215
Carmichael, Hoagy 119
Carmody, John 81
Carnegie, Andrew 14
Carnegie Hall 109–111, 217
Carpentier, Georges 125, 232
Carranza, Venustiano 190–191
Cart, Hart **367**
Carter, Calvin 187–188
Cartwright, L. M. 162
Carver, George Albert 142
Case, Frank 133
"The Case Against the Reds"
    (A. Mitchell Palmer) 50
"The Case of Sacco and
    Vanzetti" (Felix Frankfurter)
    177
Casper, Wyoming 79
Cass Lake, Minnesota 87
Castle, Vernon and Irene *110*
Cather, Willa 148, **365**
A Catholic Runs for President
    263–264

Catholics 25–26, 59, 252, 254
Catt, Carrie Chapman 36–37,
    366
Caverly, John 159–160
Cedar Rapids, Iowa 134
census 62
Central America (W. H. Koebel)
    19
Central American Court of
    Justice 87
Central American Tribunal 186
Centralia, Washington 15, 83
Central Park 102
The Century 132
Chamberlain, Clarence 211,
    214, 240
Chambers, Emil 65
Chamorro, Emiliano 187–188
Chantier (ship) 206
Chaplin, Charlie 13, 65, 171,
    225–266, **366**
Chappell, George 133
Charleston (dance) 106–107
Charleston, Massachusetts 167
Charleston, South Carolina 99
Charlestown State Prison 240
Chase National Bank 273, 280
Chattanooga 161, 164
Chattanooga *Times* 156, 174
Cherbourg, France 213
Chevrolet, Gaston 42-43
Chevrolet automobiles 237,
    239, 251
Chiang Kai-shek 259
Chicago 5, 37, 54, 55, 85, *121*,
    135, 155, *281*
        chronicle of events 13–14,
        42–43, 88, 132, 140,
        171, 216, 275
        aviation in 207
        and crime xii, 267–268
        and Great Migration
        98–100
        and jazz 104–106
        and Ku Klux Klan 59–60
        and labor trouble 10
        Leopold and Loeb trial
        157–158
        and Palmer raids 29
        and postwar turmoil 4, 6
        and radio 125, 161
        sports in 231–232
"Chicago and its Eight Reasons"
    (Walter F. White) 114
Chicago Commission on Race
    Relations 100
Chicago *Daily News* 108
Chicago *Defender* 98, 108
Chicago *Evening American* 278
Chicago *Tribune* 14, 144, 147

Chicago White Sox 14, 43, 232
child labor 87
Child Labor Amendment 140
Chile 87, 171, 276
China 63, 65, 87, 258–259,
    276
Chinandega province
    (Nicaragua) 188
Chippewa Indians 87
Christensen, Parley P. 42
Chrysler, Walter **366**
Cicero, Illinois 267
Cincinnati 59, 74
Cincinnati Reds 14, 232
Cities Service 255
Citizen Hearst (W. A. Swanberg)
    262
The City of New York (ship) 259
Civic Biology (textbook) 157,
    160, 162–163
Civil Aviation Act 193
Civil War 58, 99, 105, 216
Clarence Darrow: For the Defense
    (Irving Stone) 173
Clark, Barrett 146
Clark, Evans 20
Clark, J. Reuben 259
Clarke, Edward Young 58–59,
    101
Clef Club Symphony Orchestra
    109
Clemenceau, Georges *18*
Cleveland 4, 98, 111, 135, 140,
    275
Cleveland Indians 43
Clifden, Ireland 13, 209
Club Barron's 108
Club 21 33
coal miners 87, 172
coal mining 53, 75, 201–202,
    236, 256
Cobb, Ty 43
Colby, Bainbridge 38
Coli, Francois 210–211
*Collected Edition of Heywood
    Broun* (Heywood Broun) 179
Collier's 143
Collins, Floyd 157
Collins, Lee 122
Colombia 64
Color (Countee Cullen) 135
Colorado 8, 190
Colorado River 64
Color Struck (Zora Neale
    Hurston) 135
Columbia (airplane) 211, 214
Columbia Aircraft Company
    210–211
Columbia Broadcasting System
    (CBS) 108

Columbia University 64, 214
Columbus, Ohio 8, 59, 140
Combs, Earl 235
Coming of Age in Samoa
    (Margaret Mead) 40
Committee on German
    Reparations 275
Commonwealth Edison 1125
communism 28, 30, 135
Communist Labor Party 28
Communist Party 14, 28,
    42–43
Compiègne Forest 13
Concerto for Piano and Orchestra
    (Aaron Copland) 216
Conference for Limitation of
    Armament 65, 87
Conference on Unemployment
    56
Confessions of a Reformer
    (Frederic C. Howe) 24
Congressional Medal of Honor
    206
Congressional Record 91
Congress of the Fourth
    International 135
Connecticut 27, 35, 65
Connecticut Barber
    Commission 65
Connie's Inn 108
"The Conquest of Haiti"
    (Herbert J. Seligman) 195
Conrad, Frank 123–124
Conrad, Joseph 138–139
Conservative Party (Canada)
    183–184
Constitution of 1917 (Mexico)
    188, 199
construction 256, 272, **400**
Continental Trading Company
    77
Contract Air Mail (CAM)
    routes 207
Cook, Frederick 202
Coolidge, Calvin **366–367**
    chronicle of events 42, 43,
        88, 112, 113, 140, 141,
        171, 216, 240, 258
    eyewitness testimony
        93–95
    and Harding
        administration 66
    inaugural address of
        321–324
    as Massachusetts governor
        9–10, 22, 22
    presidency of 83–84, 97,
        102, 186, 188, 191–193,
        196, 204, 214, 249, 256,
        271, 274

    and presidential campaigns
        xi–xii, 86, 252
Coolidge: An American Enigma
    (Robert Sobel) 66, 93
Cooper, Max 248
Copland, Aaron 216
Copper Sun 135
Corning, New York 38
"Corruption—Old Oil" 93
Costa Rica 188
cotton 54, 97
Cotton Club 102, 106, 108, 241
Council of Foreign Relations
    198
"The Course of a Great Stock-
    Exchange Speculation"
    (Alexander Dana Noyes) 266
The Course of Mexican History
    (Michael C. Meyer and
    William L. Sherman) 199
Covenant of the League of
    Nations 181, **285**
Cox, James M. 42
Cox, W. W. 42
"Coy Co-Eds" 52
Cramer, Charles 82, 88
Crane, Hart 134
Crawford, Joan 225
Creole Jazz Band 106
Crerar, T. A. 183
crime 26, 28, 34, **267–269**
Criminology (Fred E. Haynes)
    174
The Crisis (journal) 103
The Crisis of the Old Order
    (Arthur Schlesinger) 17, 93,
    263
Crisis Points in National Policy
    (Glenn Frank) 282
Crissinger, Daniel 73
Cronaca Sovversiva 168
Crosby, Mrs. Fred R. 239
Crowded Hours (Alice Roosevelt
    Longworth) 49, 93
Crowe, Robert E. 159–160
Crowninshield, Frank 132
Cruikshank, Bobby 229
Cruiser Act 275
Cruze, James 228
Cuba 171, 185, 193
cubism 134
Cuesta Ray and Company *250*
Cullen, Countee 102, 135
Cullen, Frederick 102–103, 135
The Culture of the Twenties
    (Loren Baritz) 19, 68
Cumming, Hugh 82
cummings, e. e. 130, 134, **367**
Curtis, Charles *253*, 258
Curtis, Edwin 9

Curtis, Winterton 174
Curtiss planes 112

D

Dakota Territory 201
Damora, Vincenzo 269
dancing *xii*, 39, 84, 106
Dancing in the Dark 128
Daniels, Josephus 76
Darden, James 78–79
Dark Laughter (Sherwood
    Anderson) 130
The Dark Tower 104
Darrow, Clarence xii, **367**
    chronicle of events 141
    eyewitness testimony
        173–176
    and Leopold and Loeb trial
        157–160, 318–321
    and Scopes trial **161–167**
Darrow: A Biography (Kevin
    Tierney) 174–175
Darwin, Charles 153–154, 157,
    161
Darwinism 154
Daugherty, Harry
    as attorney general 73–75
    chronicle of events 87, 140
    and 1920 convention 89
    and Teapot Dome scandal
        78, 80, 82–83
Davenport, Iowa 107
David Sarnoff (Eugene Lyons)
    144
Davis, Harry P. 125
Davis, James J. 19
Davis, John W. 86, 140
Davis, Noel 210–211
Davis Cup 229, 240
Dawes, Charles 55, 112, 140,
    171–172, 240, **367**
Dawes Commission 112
Dawes Plan 112, 140–141, 172,
    275
Dawson 203
The Day the Bubble Burst
    (Gordon Thomas and Max
    Morgan-Witts) 279
Dayton, Tennessee **156–157**,
    160, 164, 166–167, 171
Daytona Beach, Florida 217
Dearborn, Michigan 238
Dear Scott/Dear Max (F. Scott
    Fitzgerald and Maxwell
    Perkins) 147
Death and Taxes (Dorothy
    Parker) 133
"The Death Penalty" 180

Debs, Eugene V. **368**
    chronicle of events 42, 65
    as Socialist candidate 4–5
    on trial 20, 157
    and William Jennings
        Bryan 175
Debussy, Claude 109
Declaration of Rights of the
    Negro Peoples of the World
    294–298
Dedham, Massachusetts 64, 167
Degas, Edgar 64
DeHavilland planes 207
de la Huerta-Lamont
    Agreement 191
Delaware 255
Delmont, Maude 227
Democratic convention of 1896
    155
Democratic convention of 1924
    84–86, 94, 127–128
Democratic convention of 1928
    251
Democratic Party
    chronicle of events 42, 65,
        140, 216, 258–259
    convention of 1924 **84–86**
    convention of 1928
        251–252
    election of 1928 253–254
Dempsey, Jack
    chronicle of events 13, 43,
        112, 216, 240
    career of **231–232, 368**
    versus Georges Carpentier
        125
Denby, Edwin 76
Denby, William 204
Denison House 214–215
Denmark 202, 204, 258
Dennett, Mary Ware 65
Dennison Field 215
Denver 42, 83
Denver Post 79
Department of Commerce
    56–57, 65, 125, 250
Department of Customs and
    Excise (Canada) 184
Department of Justice
    chronicle of events 15, 41,
        65
    during Harding
        administration 73–75, 83
    and Prohibition 31–32
    and Red Scare 29–30
    Sacco and Vanzetti trial
        168–169
Department of Labor 29, 42, 56
Department of State 42, 192,
    205, 259

Department of the Army 80
Department of the Interior 64,
    76–78, 217, 240
Department of the Navy 64,
    77–78, 104, 123, 172, 217
Department of the Treasury 31,
    217
Department of War 13, 81, 172
depression of 1921 **53–56**
    eyewitness testimony **66**
Detroit
    and auto industry 235, 239
    chronicle of events 42, 43,
        171, 275, 276
    crime in 269
    and Palmer Raids 29
    and Prohibition *31*, 34
    and Great Migration 98
"Detroit Motors" (Edmund
    Wilson) 247
Detroit News 142
Detroit Tigers 43
Dewey, John 276, **368**
DeWitt Clinton High School
    157
The Dial 132
Díaz, Adolfo 172, 187–189
Dillon, Read 171
dirigibles 14, 65, 87, 172,
    203–204, 259
Division of Simplified Practice
    250
divorce 26, 39
Documents of American History
    (Henry Steele Commager)
    21, 196
Dodds, Johnny 107, *121*
Dodge Brothers 171
Doheny, Edward 140
Doheny, Edward, Jr. 76, 78, 80,
    140, 190
Dominican Republic 113, 140,
    141, 185–186
Don Juan 216
Doolittle, Hilda (H. D.) 134, 137
Doolittle, James 276
Doran, George H. 130
Dos Passos, John 130, 137, 171
Doubleday 129
Douglas, Aaron 104, 135
Douglass, Frederick 42
"Down with Evolution!"
    (Mordecai Ham) 174
Dreiser (W. A. Swanberg) 149
Dreiser, Theodore 103, 129,
    131, 149, 151, 171
Drinker, Philip 240
drug trafficking 228
DuBois, W. E. B. 101, 103–104,
    134–135, **368–369**

Dugan, Joe 234
Duke, James Buchanan 172
Duke Ellington Orchestra 241
Duke University 172
Duncan, Isadora 51, 240, **369**
Durham, North Carolina 172
Durkee, J. Stanley 99

E

Eagle 203
Earhart, Amelia **214–215,
    223–224,** 258
*The Early Days of Radio
    Broadcasting* (George H.
    Douglas) 142
Eastman, George 259
Eastman, Max 134–135
East Pittsburgh, Pennsylvania
    123
Eatonville, Florida 135
Ederle, Gertrude 216, **369**
Edison, Thomas 275
Edmonton, Alberta 203
education 9, 154, **396**
Eiffel Tower 213
8MK (radio station) 42
Einstein, Albert 13, 64, 170,
    369
El Chipote, Nicaragua 189
election of 1916 27
election of 1918 6
election of 1920 37, **389**
election of 1924 85, 125, 141,
    390
election of 1925 (Canada) 183
election of 1926 216
election of 1928 253–254, 259,
    262–266, 391
Electric Bond and Share 255
Elgar, Edward 111
Eliot, T. S. 136–137
Elk Hills, California 75–76, 78,
    217
Ellesmere Island 204–205
Ellington, Duke 108, 120,
    369–370
Ellington: The Early Years (Mark
    Tucker) 120
Ellis, G. W. 154
Ellis, Havelock 39–40
Ellis Island 29, 62, 85
Elmer, E. P. 215
Elmer Gantry (Sinclair Lewis)
    129
El Paso, Texas 77
El Salvador 188
Emanuel Cohen Center 231
Emergency Immigration Act 62

Emergency Quota Act of 1921
    64, **301–303**
Emergency Tariff Act 55, 64
Emory University 230
"The Emperor of Africa"
    (William Pickens) 116
Empire of the Air (Tom Lewis)
    144
England 39
    and aviation 213
    chronicle of events 13,
        112, 240
    film industry in 225
    and literary scene 134,
        136, 137
    Wimbledon championship
        228
Englewood, New Jersey 276
English Channel 88, 213, 216
The Enormous Room (e. e.
    cummings) 130
Enough Rope (Dorothy Parker)
    133
Erik Dorn (Ben Hecht) 132
Esch-Cummins Transportation
    Act 42
espionage 123
Espionage Act
    chronicle of events 13, 65
    enforcement 5, 23, 65
    passage of 4, 28, 153
    text **285**
Etah, Greenland 205
Europe, James Reese 109, *110*
Evans, Hiram 58, 60
Everest, Wesley 15
Everhart, Mahlon 77
evolution, theory of **153–157,
    162–167,** 171–172, 193
expatriates 132, 136–137,
    145–151
exploration 201–206
exports **400**

F

Fabian, Warner 128
factory labor 97
Fairbanks, Alaska 83, 203
Fairbanks, Douglas 13, 42, 140,
    225–227
"Faith, Bankers, and Panic" 280
Fall, Albert
    chronicle of events 87, 88,
        112, 140
    as secretary of the interior
        73, 91, 199
    and Teapot Dome scandal
        75–79

Famous Players Company 226

A Farewell to Arms (Ernest Hemingway) 139

"A Farewell to Flappers" (Edwin Clark) 149

Faris, Herman P. 140

Farm Board 271

Farmer Labor Party 42

Farmers
  in Canada 182–183
  chronicle of events 64, 87, 141
  and depression of 1921 55
  and politics 86

F.D.R.: His Personal Letters (Roosevelt) 95

Feature Play Company 226

Federal Bureau of Investigation 269, *281*

Federal Farm Relief Board 276

Federal Highways Act of 1916 97

Federal League 232

Federal Power Commission 42

Federal Radio Commission 217

Federal Reserve Bank 275

Federal Reserve Board 256–257, 271–272

Federal War Shipping Board 206

Fédération Aéronautique Internationale (FAI) 214

Felton, Rebecca L. 87

"Feminist—New Style" (Dorothy Dunbar Bromley) 51

Ferber, Edna 133–134, 150, 171

Ferber, Julia 150

Ferber: A Biography (Julia Goldsmith) 150

Ferguson, Miriam "Ma" 171

Fermi, Enrico **370**

Fessenden, Reginald 123–124

Fields, W. C. 143

The Fiery Cross (journal) 60

Fifth Avenue Restaurant 103, 135

Fire!! 135

Firestone, Henry 237

Firpo, Luis Angel 112, 231

First National Bank 273

First Person America (Ann Banks) 48

Fisher, Norman 215

Fisk University 99, 104

Fitzgerald, F. Scott **370**
  career **128–129**, 130, 131, 132
  chronicle of events 171

and Ernest Hemingway 139
  as expatriate **136–138**
  eyewitness testimony **147–148**
  The Great Gatsby xii, 134
  This Side of Paradise 39
  See also specific works

Fitzgerald, Scottie 137

Fitzgerald, Zelda 128, 137–138

Five-Power Treaty 63

Flaming Youth (Warner Fabian) 128

flappers 39–40, 128

Flood Control Act 258

Florence Harding, The Jazz Age, and the Death of America's Most Scandalous President (Carl Sferraza Anthony) 66, 92

Florida 88, 104, 135, 154–155, 171, 216

Fokker aircraft 193, 211, 240, 258

Fonck, René 209

football 41, 64, 125, 230–231

Forbes, Charles
  chronicle of events 65, 88, 113, 171
  as head of Veterans Bureau 74
  Veterans Bureau scandal **80–82**, 91

Ford, Edsel 13, 206, 239, 276

Ford, Henry **370**
  assembly lines of 153
  chronicle of events 13, 14, 171, 258, 259, 275, 276
  eyewitness testimony **245–248**
  and Ford Motor Company **235–239**

Ford, Wallace 226

Ford automobiles 251

Fordlandia 236

Ford Motor Company
  chronicle of events 13, 64, 140, 216, 240, 276
  and depression of 1921 53
  operation of **235–239**

Fordney-McCumber Tariff Act 56, 87

Fordson tractor 237

"Ford v. G. M. C." 246

Forster, E. M. 136

49th Street Theater 133

42nd Parallel (John Dos Passos) 130

Foster, William Z. 10–11, 22, 258

Four Deuces Cafe 267

Four Negro Poets 103

Four-Power Treaty 63, **303–304**

Fourteen Points 1, 7, **284–285**

Fourth Amendment 35

Fox movie studio 216

France
  and Armistice 1–2
  and aviation 208, 210, 211, 213
  chronicle of events 13, 41, 65, 172, 193, 216, 240
  and disarmament 63
  and expatriates 129, 136
  film industry of 225
  and immigration 61, 100, *110*
  tennis championships in 228
  and war veterans 39, 99
  and World War I 181

Franco-Prussian War 2

Frank B. Kellogg: A Biography (David Bryn-James) 199

Frankfurter, Felix 170, 178

Franks, Bobby 140–141, 158–159, 173

Franks, Jacob 159, 173

Franz Joseph Land 203

Free Air 226

The Freeman 132

French Riviera 137

Freud, Sigmund 39–40

Friedrichshafen, Germany 259

Friendship (airplane) **214–215**, 258

From Pinafores to Politics (Florence Jaffray Hurst Harriman) 51

Frost, Robert **370–371**

Frost, Wesley 119

F. Scott Fitzgerald (Jeffrey Meyers) 148

Fuller, Alvan 170, 179

Fuller, Joseph V. 17

Fuller, William "Pop" 228

fundamentalists **153–154**, 156, 161–162, 165

"The Fundamentalists' Case" (Maynard Shipley) 177

Fund for a Devastated France 125

Funny Face (George Gershwin) 240

G

Galileo 163

Galleani, Luigi 168

Four Negro Poets 103

gambling 232, 267–268

"Gangs a la Mode" (Alva Johnston) 277

gangsters 12, 32–34, 267–269

Gardner, Bob 229

Garfield, James R. 75

Garland, Judy 87

Garvey, Marcus 100–102, 117, 294, **371**

Gary, Elbert 10–11

Gary, Indiana 11, 15. 60

"Gas and the Games" (George S. Brooks) 245

Gate City Manufacturing Company 58

Gauthier, Eva 109

Gaynor, Janet 275

Gehrig, Lou 235, *241*

General Accounting Office 64

General Electric 123–124

General Federation of Women's Clubs 107

General Intelligence Division 14, 2

General Motors 237–239, 250, 252

Genesis, Book of 163

Geneva 141, 240

Geneva Convention 171

Gentlemen Prefer Blondes (Anita Loos) 134, 148

George, David Lloyd *18*

George Washington (ship) 1

Georgia 28, 84, 87, 154

"Georgia: Invisible Empire State" (W. E. B. DuBois) 68

German-American Claims Commission 172

German-Americans 26

Germantown, Pennsylvania 57

Germany
  and Armistice 1
  chronicle of events 13, 14, 41, 64, 65, 87–88, 112, 140, 172, 217, 240, 275
  and exploration 202, 214
  film industry in 225
  and immigration 61
  peace agreement of 1921 62–63
  and Treaty of Versailles 2

Gershwin (Edward Jablonski) 120

Gershwin, George **371**
  Aeolian Hall concert **109–111**
  chronicle of events 113, 240, 275
  and Harlem Renaissance 103, 134

Gershwin, Ira 109
Gifford, Walter 216–217
Gilhaus, August 42
Gilman, Lawrence 120
Gitlow, Benjamin 258
Gjoa 202
Glenn, John 64
Globe Theater 172
Goddard, Robert **371–371**
Goldman, Emma 15, 29
The Gold Rush (film) 171
Goldstein, Sam 48
Goldwyn Picture Company 140, 226
golf 117, *226,* 229–230, 250
Gompers, Samuel 9–11, 64, 84, 112, 141
Goodman, Benny 108
Goodman, Freddy 108
Goodman, Harry 108
Goodyear Tire and Rubber Company 112
Gordon, Anna 45
Gordon, Louis 215, 258
Gore, John 161
Gould, Roy 169
Graf Zeppelin 259
Grain Futures Trading Act 65
Grand Ole Opry 172
Grange 54
Grange, Red 230–231, 233, **372**
Grant, Madison 100
Grant, Ulysses S. 130, 133
The Great American Ass (Anonymous) 260
The Great Boom and Panic (Robert T. Patterson) 279–281
Great Britain 86
    and Arctic claims 202
    and aviation 209
    chronicle of events 65, 87, 88, 172, 240
    and disarmament 63
    immigration from 100
    and Latin America 187
    and radio 123
    and Treaty of Versailles 2
    and Prohibition 34
    and World War I 181
Great Depression 56, 104, 140, 251, 274
The Great Gatsby (F. Scott Fitzgerald) 134
    chronicle of events 171
    eyewitness testimony 68, 120, 148, 149
    impact of 138
    gambling in 268

The Great Gatsby and Modern Times (Ronald Berman) 67
The Great God Brown (Eugene O'Neill) 193
Great Migration 103, 105, **114–119,** 395*m*
The Great Monkey Trial (L. Sprague De Camp) 174–176
Great Neck, Long Island 138
Great Northern Railway 5
The Great Steel Strike and its Lessons (William Z. Foster) 22
Great Times (Joseph Chamberlain Furnas) 116
The Great Trials of the Twenties (Katz) 177, 242
Greeks 61
Greely, Adolphus 202
Green, Abel 120
Greenfield Village 238
Greenland 201–206
Greenwich Village 38
Greenwich Village (Caroline Ware) 47
Greenwich Village Theater 193
Green, William 141
Grew, Joseph 17
Griffin, R. L. 76
Griffith, D. W. 13, 58, 225–226, **372**
Grofe, Ferde 109–111
Growing up in New Guinea (Margaret Mead) 40
Guaranty Trust Company 273
Guardia Nacional 187–190
Guatemala 188
Guest, Amy Phipps 214
Guest, Edgar 134
Guest, Frederick 214
Guggenheim Fellowship 135
Guinan, Tex 33
Gulf Coast Investment Company 167
Gulf of Fonseca 186–187
Gulf of Mexico 34, 275
Gulf of Valdez 83

H

Hagen, Walter 240
hairstyles 39
Haiti 185
Halifax, Nova Scotia 215
Hall of Mirrors 2
Hamilton, Arthur 64
Hamilton County, Illinois 60
Hammerstein, Oscar 241
Hammond, Indiana 60, 158–159
Hanson, Ole 3, 4

Happy Rhone's Black and White Club 108
Harbach, Otto 172
Harburg, E.Y. (Yip) 282
Harcourt, Alfred 132
Harcourt Brace 138
"Hard Boiled" 278
Hardin, Lil 107, *121, 122, 372*
Harding, Florence 6, 83
Harding, Warren *8, 228,* **372–373**
    chronicle of events 42, 43, 64, 65, 87, 88, 112, 171
    election of 1920 125
    and Eugene V. Debs 5
    eyewitness testimony 19, 66, 67, **89–92**
    and H. L. Mencken 131
    inaugural address **298–302**
    Latin American policy of 190
    and Palmer Raids 30
    presidency of **54–56,** 62, 63, 186, 249, 274
    and Prohibition 32
    and Teapot Dome scandal **73–84,** 129
Hard Times: An Oral History of the Great Depression (Studs Terkel) 282
Hardwick, Thomas 28
Harlem 102, 106, 108–109, 134, 241
Harlem Renaissance 102–104, 134–136
Harlem Shadows (Claude McKay) 135
Harpers (magazine) 132
Harper's Bazaar (magazine) 134
Harrigan, William 193
Harris Ranch 77
Hart, William S. 225
Harvard Lampoon (magazine) 133
Harvard University 41, 102, 110, 136, 164, 170
Harvey, George 89
Hastings-on-Hudson, New York 38
"Hatrack" (Herbert Asbury) 132
Havana 258
Hawaii 15, 80, 215, 240
Hawkins, John 26
Hawthorne Hotel 267
Hayes, Max S. 42
Hayes, Patrick Joseph 140
Hayes, Roland 102
Haymarket trial 10
Hays, Arthur 162, 164
Hays, Will 227, 228

Hays Code **304**
Hays Office 228
H. D. *See* Doolittle, Hilda
Hear Me Talkin' To Ya (Nat Shapiro and Nat Hentoff) 48, 121, 122
Hearst, William Randolph 262
Hearst newspapers 227
Heart of Darkness (Joseph Conrad) 138
Hecht, Ben 132, 151
Heflin, James 266
Hegenberger, Albert F. 240
Held, John 373
Helsinki 29
Hemingway, Ernest **139, 373**
    eyewitness testimony 20, **149–151**
    in France 136, 137
    and Scribner's 132
    and Sherwood Anderson 130
    See also specific works
Hemingway: A Life Without Consequences (James R. Mellow) 150
Hemingway: The Paris Years (Michael Reynolds) 147
Henderson (ship) 83
Henderson, Fletcher 107, 108
Henry Cabot Lodge (William Lawrence) 16
Henry Ford and Grass-Roots America (Reynold M. Wik) 246, 248
Herbert, Victor 111, 140
Herbert Hoover and the Great Depression (Harris Gaylord Warren) 266
Hergesheimer, Joseph 130
Herrick, James 13
Herrick, Myron 213
Herrin, Illinois 87
Heston, Charlton 112
Hicks, Sue 157, 162
Highland Park, Michigan 236, 238
Hill, Edward Burlingame 110
Hill, James J. 5
Hillman, Morris *231*
Hindemith, Paul 109
Hines, Earl 48, 108
"Historical Fabric of Christ's Life Nothing Without Miracles" (Billy Sunday) 174
A History of Canada (Carl Wittke) 194
Hitchcock, Tommy 138
Hitler, Adolf 112, 136
holding companies 255–256

Holland Tunnel 240
Hollywood 33, 105, 212, 227–228, 275
Holmes, Oliver Wendell 28, 170, 276, **291**
Home to Harlem (Claude McKay) 118
Honduras 87, 171, 186
Hooded Americanism: The First Century of the Ku Klux Klan (David M. Chalmers) 67, 95
Hoop Spur, Arkansas 99
Hoover, Herbert 274, **373–374**
    campaign of 1928 **252–254**
    chronicle of events 13, 65, 217, 258, 259, 275, 276
    as commerce secretary 56, 57, 73, 83, *90*
    eyewitness testimony 92, 260, 271
    presidency of 250, 256–257
    speeches **332–343**
Hoover, J. Edgar 29
Hopkins, Claude 108
Hopper, Edward **374**
Horses and Men 130
Hotel Pennsylvania 13
Hot Five *121*
Houdini, Harry 216
House Judiciary Committee 30
House Ways and Means Committee 55
Houston 251, 252, 258
Howard University 99, 102
Howe, Frederic C. 24
Hoyt, Waite *241*
Hudson automobile company 237
Hudson River 240
Huggins, Miller 233, 244
Hugh Selwyn Mauberly (Ezra Pound) 137
Hughes, Charles Evans
    chronicle of events 112, 193, 258, 259
    eyewitness testimony 195, 196, 199
    postwar diplomacy 62, 63
    and Red Scare 30
    as secretary of state 73, 186
Hughes, Langston 103, 135, **374**
Hughes, Rupert 133
Hull House 85
"The Human Factor" (Carol Wright) 70
Hungary 2
Hunter, George 157, 167

Hurst, Fannie 135
Hurston, Zora Neale 103, 104, 135, **374**
Hutchinson, William 166
Hylan, John F. 262

I

Idaho 8, 136
The Idle Class 65
Illinois 60, 208, 253
    chronicle of events 64, 171
    Leopold and Loeb trial 159
    and Nineteenth Amendment 37
    postwar riots in 100
    and Prohibition 36
imagism 137
I'm Alone 34, 275
Imes, Elmer 135
immigrants **61–62**, 109, 111, 153
    chronicle of events 43, 64, 140, 276
    eyewitness testimony **69–71**
    and film industry 225
    labor shortage 98
    and Prohibition 26
    and Red Scare 28
    and Ku Klux Klan 58
    opposition to 100
    and politics 85, 252, 254
    and Sacco and Vanzetti trial 168, 169
immigration 64, 307–318, **394m**
Immigration Act of 1917 29
Immigration Act of 1924 276, **307–318**
Immigration Quota Law 140
imports **400m**
The Impossible H. L. Mencken (H. L. Mencken) 265
The Inaugural Addresses of the American Presidents (Davis Newton Lott) 19
The Incredible Era (Samuel Hopkins Adams) 91
"In Dead of Night" 71
Indiana 60, 61, 171, 172
Indianapolis 8, 59, 61, 98, 111
Indianapolis 500 auto race 42, 87, 258
Industrial Workers of the World (IWW) 3, 4, 15, 21, 42, 59, 83
inflation 3, 6, 14
Ingenieros, José 195

in our time (Ernest Hemingway) 139
In Our Time (Ernest Hemingway) 20, 139, 150
installment buying 238, 254
Insull, Samuel 256
Intermediate Credit Act 88
Internal Revenue 31
International Church of the Foursquare Gospel 193
International Convention of the Negro Peoples of the World 101
International Peace Bridge 240
"Interview" (Rose C. Feld) 148
In the Time of Silent Cal (Jules Abels) 264
Inventions of the March Hare (T. S. Eliot) 136
Inwood Country Club 229
Iowa 86
Ireland 213, 254
Isle of Pines treaty 171
"Is the American Negro to Remain Black or Become Bleached?" (Kelly Miller) 71
Italians 61, 62
Italy
    chronicle of events 65, 172
    disarmament 63
    and expatriates 137, 138
    and exploration 202
    and immigration 254
    and Versailles treaty conference 2, 6

J

Jackson, Dale 276
Jackson, Ed 60, 61
"Jailing Radicals in Detroit" (Frederick R. Barkley) 49
Jamaica 100, 135
Jane Addams Hull House Band 108
Jannings, Emil 275
Japan
    chronicle of events 65, 87, 140, 240
    and disarmament 63
    Four-Power Treaty **303–304**
    and Latin America 186–187
    and military strategy 75, 78, 203
jazz xi
    chronicle of events 43, 113
    development of **104–111**

eyewitness testimony **119–122**
    and morals 40
    and poetry 136
Jazz Masters of New Orleans (Martin Williams) 122
The Jazz Singer 240
Jefferson, Thomas 201
Jennifer Lorn (Elinor Wylie) 131
Jersey City Journal 200
Jersey City, New Jersey 125, 240
Jews 25, 59, 61
Jim Crow laws 97
Jinotega province (Nicaragua) 189
John Dos Passos (John H. Wrenn) 149
Johns Hopkins University 136, 163
John Simon Guggenheim Foundation 172
Johnson, Andrew 216
Johnson, Charles S. 102, 103, 104
Johnson, Hiram 8, 30
Johnson, James P. 107, 108
Johnson, James Weldon 102, 103, 104, **374–375**
Johnson, John 105
Johnson, Magnus 83
Johnson Act 62
Joliet, Illinois 160
Jolson, Al 109, 228, 240, 259, **375**
Jones Act 36
Jones, Bobby 171, 216, 229–230
Jones, Robert P. 229
Jones, Sam *241*
Jones–White Act 258
Joplin, Missouri 135
Joseph Horne Department Store 125
Joshua, Book of 165
Joyce, James 130, 134, 137
Jozan, Edouard 137
J.P. Morgan and Company 273
Judge's Bill 171
Juilliard, Augustus D. 13
Juneau, Alaska 83, 203
Jung, Carl 40
Jurgen (James Branch Cabell) 130

K

Kahn, Albert **375**
Kansas 35, 36, 37, 227. 258
Kansas City 65, 83, 104, 252

Kansas State College 134
Kaplan, Ernie *231*
Karns, Stella 110
Kasson, Gunnar 171
Katzmann, Frederick 167
Kaufman, George S. 133
The Kawa at the Pole (George Chappell) 133
KDKA 43, 125, 142
Kearns, Jack "Doc" 231
Keaton, Buster **375**
Kellogg, Frank 119, 199
Kellogg-Briand Pact 217, 259, 275–276, **331–332**
Kendrick, John 78, 87
Kennedy, Stetson 48
Kentucky *41*, 157, 236
Kentucky Baptist State Board of Missions 154
Kentucky Club 108
Kern, Jerome 109. 241
Ketchikan, Alaska 83
Keystone Film Company 227
Kimball, James 215
King, B. B. 172
King, Dot 88
King, Martin Luther, Jr. 275
King, William Lyon Mackenzie 82, 183–184, *185*
"The King Makers" (Grantland Rice) 243
King Oliver Creole Jazz Band 107
King's Bay 206
Kinner, Bert 214, 215
Kinner Field 214
Kirby, Rollin *76*
"The Klan's Fight for Americanism" (Hiram Wesley Evans) 68
Knickerbocker Theater 87
Knight, Dysart & Gamble 210
Knights Templar *258*
Knopf, Alfred A. 103, 131, 132, 135
Knoxville 99, 157
Koenig, Mark 234
Kokomo, Indiana 60
"Konklave in Kokomo" (Robert Coughlan) 66
Kramer, John F. 32, 45
Kreisler, Fritz 110
"Ku Klux" (W. A. S. Douglas) 68
Ku Klux Klan xi
    chronicle of events 88, 171, 172
    and Democratic convention of 1924 85–86

eyewitness testimony **66–69**
revival of **58–61**
KYW 125

L

labor
    and automotive industry 237, 239
    in Canada 182, 183, 185
    and depression of 1921 56–57
    during World War I 53
    and election of 1928 254
    eyewitness testimony **20–24**
    laws 85
    postwar labor shortage 98
    postwar turmoil **2–5**, 84
    in New York State 85
    scientific management of 250
    and unemployment 256, **399**
Labrador 204
La Ceriba revolt 171
Lackawanna, New York 216
"Lady Be Good" (George Gershwin) 109
Lady Chatterley's Lover (D. H. Lawrence) 130
Lafayette Hotel 79
Lafayette Theater 105
La Follette, Robert M.
    chronicle of events 87, 140, 141, 171
    election of 1928 254
    and Progressive Party 86
    and Teapot Dome scandal 78, 91
Lake Denmark, New Jersey 216
Lakehurst, New Jersey 259
Lake Michigan 276
Lakota Indians 201
Lamb, L. W. *259*
Lambert, Albert 207, 210
Lambert, Myrtle 207
Lambert, Wooster 210
Lambert Field 207, 208
Lamont, Thomas 93, 273
Landis, Kenesaw Mountain 232, 233
Lansing, Robert 8, 17, 41
Lansky, Meyer 45
Lardner, Ring 133, 228, **375–376**
Larsen, Nella 135–136

Lasky, Jesse 226
The Last Days of Innocence (Meirion and Susie Harries) 20
The Last Hero (Walter Sanford Ross) 200
Latimer, Julian 172, 193
Latin America **185–192**, **195–200**
Latin America and the United States (Graham H. Stuart) 196, 200
The Latin American Policy of the United States (Samuel Flagg Bemis) 195
Laughter's Gentle Soul: The Life of Robert Benchley (Billy Altman) 145
The Lawless Decade (Paul Sann) 178, 278
Lawrence, D. H. 130
Lawrence, William 16
Lazzeri, Tony 234–235
Leacock, Stephen 133
League for Independent Political Action 276
League of Nations 82
    and Canada 181
    chronicle of events 14, 64, 112, 141, 193, 259
    Covenant of **285–291**
    debated by Congress 5–6
    eyewitness testimony **16–20**
    and Latin America 185
    and Woodrow Wilson 1–2
Le Bourget airfield 211, 213
Leeper v. State of Tennessee 162
The Legacy of Sacco and Vanzetti (Louis Joughin and Edmund M. Morgan) 179–180
Legge, Alexander 271
LeJeune, J. A. 79
Leon, Nicaragua 188
Leopold, Nathan 140–141, 158–160, 173, **318–321**, 376
Leopold and Loeb trial **158–160**, 163, **173–174**
Letters of a Nation 179
Letters of Edna St. Vincent Millay 180
Letters of H. L. Mencken (Guy Forgue) 44
The Letters of Sacco and Vanzetti (Marion Denman Frankfurter and Gardner Jackson) 178
Levine, Charles 214, 240
Levitt, Albert 46
Lewis and Clark expedition 201
Lewis, Diocletian 26
Lewis, John L. **376**

Lewis, Nettie 105
Lewis, Sinclair 130, *226*, **376**
    chronicle of events 171, 193
    eyewitness testimony 146
    and *Main Street* 128, 129
    Nobel Prize acceptance speech **344–350**
    See also specific works
Lexicon of Musical Invective (Nicholas Slonimsky) 120
Liberal Party (Canada) 183–185
The Liberator 134
Liberty Bonds 28, 36, 77
Liberty Halls 101
Life Plus 99 Years (Nathan Leopold) 173
Limitation of Naval Armaments Conference 240
Lincoln, Abraham 216
Lincoln, Robert Todd 216
Lincoln automobile 239
Lincoln Memorial 87
Lincoln Park 158
Lincoln Theater 105
Lindbergh, Charles xii, **376–377**
    chronicle of events 217, 241, 276
    eyewitness testimony 200, **220–223**
    in Mexico 192
    New York-to-Paris flight **207–215**
    and Orteig Prize **324**
Lippman, Walter 46, 91
Lisbon 209
Listening In: Radio and the American Imagination (Susan J. Douglas) 143
The Literary Decade (Allen Churchill) 146
Little, Malcolm 171
Little Falls, Minnesota 208
Liveright, Horace 132, 139
"Livery Stable Blues" 110
"Living and Dying on the Installment Plan" (Hawthorne Daniel) 260
Lloyds Bank 136
Locarno Pact 172
Locke, Alain 102–104
Lodge, Henry Cabot 7, 8, 16, 20, 82, 141, 181
Loeb, Richard 140–141, 158–160, 173, **318–321**, 376
Loew, Marcus 226
"Logic and the Stock Market" (Fred C. Kelly) 266
Lolardo, Pasqualino 268

Lombardo, Anthony 268
London 100, 137, 170, 172, 184, 193, 216
London *Daily Mail* 209
London, Meyer 23
Long, Breckenridge 16
Long Island 64, 203, 209, 212, 217, 229
Longview, Texas 99
Loos, Anita 134, 148
Lord Jim (Joseph Conrad) 138
Los Angeles 42, 43, 193, 214, 275
Los Angeles Philharmonic 14
Louis Armstrong: A Cultural Legacy 119
Louis Armstrong: An Extravagant Life (Laurence Bergreen) 115
Louisiana 98
Love, Philip R. 207
Lowden, Frank 100, 253
Lowell, Abbott Lawrence 170
Lowell Commission 179
Lower East Side (New York City) 252
"A Lunatic or a Traitor" (W. E. B. DuBois) 116
Lusitania 172
Lusk, Clayton 23
lynching 59, 65, 97, 99, **396**
Lynd, Robert **377**
Lynd, Helen Merrill **377**

M

MacDonald, Carlyle 213
Macfarlane, Willie 171
Mackenzie, George 205
MacLeish, Archibald 134
MacMillan, Donald 204, 205
Madison Square Garden 101, 127, 239, 251
magazines 25, 40, 129, 138
Maiden, Stewart 229
Main Street (Sinclair Lewis) 128, 129, 132, 146
Maine 25
Maitland, Lester 240
"The Making of a Red" (Robert Benchley) 49
Malone, Dudley Field 163, 164, 167
Mammoth Oil Company 77, 87, 217, 240
Managua, Nicaragua 188
Manassa, Colorado 231
Manchester, Vermont 216
Mandell, Frank 172
Manet, Edouard 64

Manhattan 43, 88, 212, 256
Manhattan Transfer (John Dos Passos) 130, 171
"The Man I Love" (George Gershwin) 109
Manitoba 182
Mann Act 60
Mannington, Howard 74
manufacturing
    and auto industry 236, 237, 239
    automation in 153, 250
    postwar conditions 249, 251, 256, 257
    wages 399
    wartime boom in 53
"The Man Who Knew Coolidge" (Sinclair Lewis) 94
Marconi, Guglielmo 123
Marconi Wireless Signal Telegraph Company 123, 124
The Marcus Garvey and Universal Negro Improvement Association Papers 117, 119
"Marcus Garvey—The Negro Moses?" (Truman Hughes Talley) 114
"Marines Trapped" 197
Marines, U.S. 78–79, 186
Marion Manufacturing Company 276
Marion, North Carolina 276
Marion, Ohio 73
Marks, Percy 128
Marshall, Louis 70
Marshall, Thomas 159
Mason, Charlotte Osgood 104
Massachusetts 7, 212
    chronicle of events 43, 216, 240
    and labor trouble 8–10
    legislature of 84
    and Nineteenth Amendment 37
    and Prohibition 36
    and Sacco and Vanzetti trial 167–170
Massachusetts Supreme Court 10
Massey, Charles Vincent 216
Matagalpa, Nicaragua 188
Mather, Kirtley 164
Matisse, Henri 64, 136
Maurer, James M. 258
Mayer, Louis B. 226
Mayflower (presidential train) 8
Mays, Carl *241*
McAdoo, William 84, 86, 127, 140, 263

McCarl, John Raymond 55
McCoy, Big Bill 34
McCumber, Porter 55
McKay, Claude 103, 134, 135
McKenzie, Fayette 99
McLean, Ned 74, 80
McMunn, Bertha Annie 142
McNamee, Graham 234
McNary-Haugen Bill 112, 216, 258
McPherson, Aimee Semple 193, **377**
M.D. Thatcher Estates Land Company 76
Mead, Margaret 40, **377–378**
meatpacking industries 100
Medeiros, Celestino 169, 170, 177
Meighen, Arthur 182, 184, *185*
Mellon, Andrew 32, 55, 56, 73, **378**
Mellor, Charles 171
Memphis (ship) 214
Men of Destiny (Walter Lippmann) 46
Mencken, H. L. **378**
    and the Algonquin Hotel 133
    career of **131–132**
    eyewitness testimony 44, 146, 149, 175
    and Scopes trial 158, 161, 164, 166
Mendl, Joe 161
Menjou, Adolphe 225
Merchant Marine Act 42, 258
Meredith, Edwin 8
Meridian, Mississippi 167
Merion Cricket Club 229, 230
Merton College 136
Metcalf, Maynard M. 163
Metlakatla, Alaska 83
Metro-Goldwyn-Mayer 140, 226
Metro Picture Company 140, 226
Metropolitan Museum of Art 64
Metropolitan Opera 141
Meusal, Bob 235
Mexican-American War 190
Mexican Constitution of 1917 190
Mexico
    and boll weevil 97
    chronicle of events 14, 88, 193, 216, 241, 275
    eyewitness testimony **198–200**
    and immigration 62
    and oil industry 76

Sacco and Vanzetti in 168
    U.S. relations with **188–192**
Mexico City 112
"Mexico Outlawing the Church" 200
Meyer, Louis 258
Meyer Lansky: Mogul of the Mob (Dennis Eisenberg, Uri Dan, and Eli Landau) 45
Michigan 37
Middleton, J. E. 194
Middletown: A Study in Modern American Culture (Robert S. and Helen Merrill Lynd) 145
Midvale Steel Company 57
Midwest Oil Company 77
"The Migration: A Southern View" (George J. Baldwin) 117
Mike: The Memoirs of the Right Honourable Lester B. Pearson (Lester B. Pearson) 195
Miles, John C. 193
Milhaud, Darius 109
Miljus, Johnny 235
Millay, Edna St. Vincent 131, 132, 134, 170, 180, **378**
Miller, Charles A. 23
Miller, Henry 130
Millet 64
Millikan, Robert 112
Milner, Lucille 156
Milton, George Fort 263
Milwaukee 4, 15, 264
Milwaukee Leader 4
miners 15
mining 75, 239, 251
Minneapolis *127, 231, 258*
Minnesota 30, 83, 209
Minnesota League of Women Voters *52*
Minnewaska 129
Miske, Billy 43
Mississippi 27, 98, 167
Mississippi River 104, 201, 209, 217, 258
Mississippi River Valley 98
Missouri 140, 171
Missouri National Guard 208
Missouri River 201
Mitchell, Abie 105
Mitchell, Charles 273
Mitchell, J. Kearsley 88
Mitchell, William "Billy" 65, 172, 203, 204, **378–379**
Mitchell Field 276
Mobile, Alabama 167
Model A Ford 238–240, 250

Model T Ford 97, 140, 216, 235–238, 240
Moffitt, M. H. 162
Moller, Emil 169
Moncada, José Maria 189, 197
Monroe, James 185
Monroe Doctrine 185, 186, 258, 259
Monroe *Journal* 264
Montana 79, 80, 86
    chronicle of events 112, 140
    and Nineteenth Amendment 37
    and Prohibition 36
    Warren Harding visits 83
Montgomery, Alabama 128
Montgomery Ward 126, 257
Mooney, Tom 4
Moore, Fred 168, 169
Moore, Owen 227
Moran, "Bugs" 268, 269, 275
Morehouse College 99
Morehouse Parish, Louisiana 88
Morelli, Frank 169, 180
Morelli gang 169
Morgan, Howard 163
Morgan, J. P. 10, 28, 86, 192
Morley, Christopher 133
Morrow (publisher) 138
Morrow, Anne Spencer 276
Morrow, Dwight 93, 172, 192, 241, 276, **379**
Morrow, Edwin *41*
Morrow, Mrs. Dwight 200
Mortimer, Elias 80, 81
Morton, Jelly Roll 106, 107, **379**
Moscow 43
"The Most Popular Book of the Month" (Benchley, Robert) 145
Motion Picture Producers and Distributors Association (MPPDA) 227, 228
Motts, Robert T. 105
A Moveable Feast (Ernest Hemingway) 151
movie industry 231
    chronicle of events 212, 216, 259
    eyewitness testimony **242–243**
    growth of **225–228, 397**
    guidelines used in **331**
    Hays Code **304**
    in popular culture 40
    and Prohibition 33, 34
Mullan-Gage Act 85
Mundelein, George 140

Munich, Germany 112
Murphy, Jimmy 87
Murphy, Gerald and Sara 137
Muscle Shoals Bill 258
Muscle Shoals, Tennessee 258
Muse, Clarence 105
Mussolini, Benito 136, 137, 179
"The Mussolini of Highland Park" (Waldemar Kaempffert) 246
My Autobiography (Charles Chaplin) 243
My Life (Isadora Duncan) 120
My Life in Crime (John Bartlow Martin) 279
My Life in the Mafia (Vincent Teresa and Thomas C. Renner) 180
Myers v. United States 216
My Northern Exposure 133

N

Nance, Ethel Ray 102
Narcotics Control Board 87
Nashville 99, 156, 161, 172
Nathan, George Jean 131, 146
Nation, Carrie 26
The Nation (magazine) 132, 189
National Aircraft Board 172
National American Woman Suffrage Association 36–37
National Association for the Advancement of Colored People (NAACP) 99, 100, 103, 114
National Broadcasting Corporation (NBC) 108
National City Bank 271, 273
National Clay Court Championship 229
National Commission 232
National Committee for Organizing Iron and Steel Workers 10, 11
National Convention of the Conference for Progressive Political Action 140
National Geographic Society 204, 205, 206
National Guard 4, 9, 14, 100, 112
National Industrial Conference 11
National League 232, 234
National League of Women Voters 37
National Non-Partisan League 54

National Party Platforms 1840–1964 (Kirk H. Porter and Donald Bruce Johnson) 92
National Progressive Party 183
National Urban League 99, 102
Native Americans 140, 201
naval power 62-63
Navy Club 125
Navy, U.S. 75–76
Neal, John Randolph 157, 160, 167
Near East Relief 58
Nebraska 13, 27, 64, 140, 155, 230
"The Negro Artist and the Racial Mountain" (Langston Hughes) 120
Negro Factories Corporation 101
Negro Labour in the United States, 1850–1925 (Charles H. Wesley) 118
Negro World 101
"Neighbors and Friends: A Plea for Justice to Mexico" (William E. Borah) 200
Nelson, Thomas P. 207
Nest Club, The 108
Netherlands 63, 65, 82, 193, 159
Nevada 8, 36
New Civic Biology 167
The New Day: Campaign Speeches of Herbert Hoover (Herbert Hoover) 264
New Deal 85
New Guinea 40
New Jersey 27, 42
"The New Masses I'd Like" (John Dos Passos) 149
New Mexico 36, 73, 88, 190
New National Policy 182
The New Negro (journal) 102, 117
The New Negro (William Pickens) 104
New Orleans 104, 105, 106, 107, 232
New Orleans Rhythm Kings, 106
"New Voices in the Wilderness" (M. J. Caveney) 142
New York Assembly 30
New York Bar Association 258
New York Board of Health 135
New York Central Railroad 53
New York City 10, 157, 267
    and ACLU 156
    and aviation 206, 207
    banking in 271

    and birth control movement 39
    campaign of 1928 in 264
    and Charles Lindbergh 209, 210, 211, 213, 214
    chronicle of events 13, 15, 41, 42, 43, 64, 65, 112, 140, 141, 171, 172, 193, 216, 217, 240, 259, 275
    and immigration 62
    jazz scene in 104, 105, 107, 108
    and labor troubles 4
    literary scene of 128, 133, 134, 135, 138, 139
    mayoral contest of 1928 262
    and Model A Ford 239
    Palmer Raids in 29
    and Prohibition 31, 32, 33
    and radio 126
    and Red Scare 6, 28
    sports and 231
    and Teapot Dome scandal 77
    trial of Marcus Garvey 101
The New Yorker 132, 133, 171
New York Giants 65, 112, 234
The New York Hat (Anita Loos) 134
New York Herald Tribune 263
New York Industrial Commission 85
New York Public Library 135
New York state
    campaign of Al Smith 252, 254
    and Nineteenth Amendment 37, 38
    and Prohibition 27, 35, 36
New York Stock Exchange 141, 257, 259, 270, 273
New York *Sun* 260
New York Times 103, 134, 213, 246, 274
New York *Tribune* 132
New York *World* 59, 132, 170
New York Yankees
    chronicle of events 41, 65, 112, 240, *241*, 259
    eyewitness testimony **243–245**
    1927 season of **233–235**
New York Zoological Society 100
Newark, New Jersey 125
Newfoundland 13, 209, 212, 213, 258
Newfoundlanders 202
Newman, Paul 171

newspapers *124*
    crime stories in 268, 269
    and Great Migration 98
    and leisure time 138
    and Lindbergh flight 210,
        213
    and radio 125
    spread of 157
    and stock market 255
newsreels 268
Niagara Bible Conference 154
Niagara Falls 275
Nicaragua
    chronicle of events 87,
        171, 172, 193
    eyewitness testimony
        196–197
    and Mexico 192
    U.S. policy and **185–189**
Nicaraguan Assembly 187
"The Nicaraguan Canal Bobs
    Up Once More" 197
Nicaraguan Customs
    Department 188
Nice, France 240
nickelodeons 226
Nietzsche, Friedrich 158, 160
Nigger Heaven (Carl Van Vechten)
    103
nightclubs 99, 104, 106, 275
1919: America's Loss of Innocence
    (Eliot Asinof) 16, 21, 130
Ninth Avenue (Maxwell
    Bodenheim) 151
Nixon v. Herndon 217
No, No, Nanette (play) 172
Nobel Prize 43, 88, 112, 129,
    130, 172
Noblesville, Indiana 60
Nome, Alaska 171, 203
Noonan, Fred 215
Norfolk, Virginia 32, 45
Norge (ship) 206
Normandy 213
Norman Thomas: The Last Idealist
    (W. A. Swanberg) 23
Norris, George 198
Northampton, Massachusetts 9
North Carolina 87
North Carolina Board of
    Education 154
North Clark Street (Chicago)
    269
North Dakota 15, 35, 55
North Pole 193, 202–204, 206,
    208–209, 211
North Side (Chicago) 268, 269
Northwestern University Law
    School 178
Northwest Territories Act 205

Norway 193, 202
Norwegians 202
Nova Scotia 193, 212
Nugent, Richard 135
Nungesser, Charles 210, 211

O

Oak Grove Hotel *127*
Oakland, California 13
Oakley, Annie 87
O'Bannion, Dion 216
Oberholtzer, Madge 60–61
Obregón, Alvaro 88, 191
O'Brine, Forrest 276
Ocotal, Nicaragua 189
Off With Their Heads (Frances
    Marion) 243
Ogontz School 214
Ohio 31, 32, 37, 42, 73, 171, 252
Ohio Gang 74, 75, 84, 93
Ohio Gang Entertainment
    Committee 78
Ohio State University 64
"O Holy Night" 123
Oil
    and automotive industry
        236, 239, 251
    exploration for 201, 202
    and Mexican policy 190,
        191, 192
    and Teapot Dome scandal
        75–77
Oil Producer's Association 190
O'Keeffe, Georgia **379**
Oklahoma 64, 112, 154
Oklahoma Informer 260
Oliver, Joe "King" 107, 108
Olmstead v. United States 35
Olympic Games of 1928 258,
    259
Omaha 6, 8
O'Neal, James 77
135th Street (George Gershwin)
    109
O'Neill (Arthur and Barbara
    Gelb) 146
O'Neill, Eugene 103, 131, 132,
    146, 193, **379–380**
*On Politics: A Carnival of
    Buncombe* (H. L. Mencken)
    50, 91
Ontario 183
open shops 10
Opium Conference 141
Opponents of War (H. C. Peterson
    and Gilbert C. Fite) 23
Opportunity (magazine) 102,
    103, 135

The Ordeal of Woodrow Wilson
    (Herbert Hoover) 17
Oregon 13
Original Dixieland Jazz Band
    106, 110
Orlando, Vittorio *18*
O'Rourke, Willis 278
Orteig, Raymond 209
Orteig Prize 209, 212, **324**
*Orthodox Christianity vs.
    Modernism* (William Jennings
    Bryan) 174
Ory, Kid 107, *121*
Ostfriesland 65
*Our Business Civilization: Some
    Aspects of the Culture* (James
    Truslow Adams) 278
"Our Satisfaction with Mr.
    Coolidge" (Edward S.
    Martin) 93
"Our Tiff with Mexico Settled"
    200
Our Times (Mark Sullivan) 89,
    121
"Our Warning to Nicaragua"
    196
The Outline of History (H. G.
    Wells) 132, 133
The Outline of Man's Knowledge
    133
Overton, Grant 67
Oxford University 102, 136
Oyster Bay, New York 13

P

Pacific Treaty 65
Pacific Ocean 215
Packard 237
Packers and Stockyards Act 65
Paddock, Charlie 64
Palace Hotel 83
Palais Royale 110
Palestine 13
Palm Beach, Florida 80, 269
Palmer, A. Mitchell **380**
    chronicle of events 13, 14,
        42
    eyewitness testimony 20
    and Ned McLean 80
    and Red Scare 6, 28–30
Palmer Raids xi, 14, **29–30,
    49–50, 58**
Panama 64, 185
Panama Canal 187, 189, 203
Pan-American Conference
    258
Pan-American Petroleum and
    Transport Company 76

"The Paramount Issue:
    Prohibition Leaps to the
    Front" (Mark Sullivan) 264
Paramount Pictures 226, 227
Paris
    chronicle of events 13,
        217, 276
    demonstrations in 170
    expatriates in 135, 136,
        137, 139
    and Lindbergh flight 206,
        209, 211, 212, 213
    and Versailles conference
        1, 2, 6
Parker, Charlie 43
Parker, Dorothy 131, 132, 133,
    170, **380**
Parliament of Canada 182, 183
Parmenter, Frederick 167, 169
Parrish, Anne 134
Pasadena, California 193
Passing (Nella Larsen) 135
The Passing of the Great Race
    (Madison Grant) 100
Paulding (ship) 241
Paul Whiteman Orchestra 111,
    113
Payton, Philip 102
Peace of Tipitapa 189
Pearl Harbor, Hawaii 77
Pearson, Lester B. 195
Peary (ship) 205
Peary, Robert 202–203
Peay, Austin 157, 164, 174
*The Peerless Leader: William
    Jennings Bryan* (Paxton
    Hibben) 95
Pegler, Westbrook 228
Pekin Temple of Music 105
Pell, Herbert Claiborne 263
"Penalties of the Sacco-Vanzetti
    Execution" 180
Pennock, Herb 234, *241*
Pennsylvania 14, 28, 37, 136,
    159, 172, 258
Pennsylvania State University
    64
Perelman, S. J. 133
The Perennial Bachelor (Anne
    Parrish) 134
Perkins, Frances 85
Perkins, Maxwell 132, 138, 139,
    147–148
*The Permanent Book of the 20th
    Century* 244
Perry, E. W. 260
Perryville, Maryland 81, 82
Pershing, John "Black Jack"
    126
Peru 80, 87, 171, 276

Peters, Andrew J. 9
Philadelphia
    chronicle of events 88,
        193, 216
    eyewitness testimony 278
    and Frederick Winslow
        Taylor 57
    golf championship in 229
    and Prohibition 35
    and the *Shenandoah* 204
Philippines 65, 113
Phillips, William 216
Phillips County, Arkansas 99
Phillips Exeter Academy 57
Picasso, Pablo 136
Pickens, William 104
Pickford, Mary 13, 42, 225, 26,
    227, **380–381**
Picture Company (Lewis J.
    Selznick) 226
Pike Lake Auto Club *240*
Pinchot, Gifford 78
Pinehurst Gun Club 87
Pinkerton agency 42
Pioneer Oil Company 79
Pipgras, George 234, *241*
Pittsburgh 11, 28, 43, 59, 111,
    125
Pittsburgh Electrical Show 142
Pittsburgh Pirates 234–235, 240
Pittsburgh Sun 125
Pius XI 140
The Plastic Age (Percy Marks)
    128
Platt Amendment 185
Plymouth, Massachusetts 168
Plymouth Notch, Vermont 83,
    88
Pocketful of Poses (Anne Parrish)
    134
Poems (T. S. Eliot) 136
poetry 103, 104, 130, 131,
    134–137
Point Barrow, Alaska 204
poison gas 87
Pole of Inaccessibility 206
Poles 61
Polo Grounds 112
Pomp and Circumstance (Edward
    Elgar) 111
Poor White (Sherwood
    Anderson) 130
Porgy and Bess (George
    Gershwin) 109
Portal, North Dakota 203
Porter, Cole 137, **381**
Portland, Oregon 83
Portsmouth, Virginia 65
Portugal 63, 65
Post, Emily **381**

Post, Louis F. 30
*Postmortem: New Evidence in the
    Case of Sacco and Vanzetti*
    (William Young and David E.
    Kaiser) 177
Potter, Charles 164
Potter, William 273
Pound, Ezra 136–137, 150, **381**
Powell, Adam Clayton 102
Prairie Oil Company 77
The Presidency of Calvin Coolidge
    (Robert H. Ferrell) 197, 199
*President Harding: His Life and
    Times* (Francis Russell) 67, 89
"primitivist" art 103
Princeton, New Jersey 128
Prisoners at the Bar (Francis X.
    Busch) 173
Production Code
    Administration 228
Professional Golfers'Association
    (PGA) tournament 240
Progressive Democracy (Al Smith)
    264
Progressive Farmers and
    Householders Union 99
Progressive Party 86, **304–306**
Progressive Party (Canada)
    183–185
Progressives 30, 78, 140, 141,
    153, 252
"The Progress of the World"
    (Albert Shaw) 281
Prohibition xi, 183
    background of **26–27**
    chronicle of events 13, 14,
        41, 42, 43, 88, 112, 140,
        171, 258, 275, 276
    and crime 267, 268
    debate over **25–26**
    defiance of 106
    enforcement of **30–36,
        388m**
    eyewitness testimony
        44–48, 277–279
    repeal of 269
    and social mores 107, 128
    and politics 84, 85, 156,
        252
    Volstead Act **293–294**
    Wickersham Commission
        report on **350–361**
    and workers 28
Prohibition (Edward Behr) 44
Prohibition Act 15
Prohibition agents *45*
Prohibition Bureau 31, 32, 34,
    217
"Prohibition—Over the Lake"
    194

Prohibition Party 26, 42, 92, 140
Prohibition Reorganization Act
    217
*Prohibition: Thirteen Years that
    Changed America* (Studs
    Terkel) 283
Prosser, Seward 273
prostitutes 33, 39
prostitution 267, 268, 269
Protestants 58, 84, 153, 252
Providence, Rhode Island 169
Provincetown, Massachusetts
    241
Prufrock and Other Observations
    (T. S. Eliot) 136
Public Buildings Act 193
Public Persons (Walter
    Lippmann) 91, 176
Pueblo, Colorado 8, 76, 77
Puerto Cabezas, Nicaragua 188
Puerto Rico 73, 160, 185
Puget Sound 83
Pulitzer Prize 129, 130, 171, 193
Pulitzer Trophy contest 112
Puller, Lewis B. 189
Pullman Palace Car Company 5
Pullman Strike of 1894 157
A Puritan in Babylon (William
    Allen White) 89
Purnell Act 171
Purple Gang 269
Putnam, G. P. 214, 215

Q

Quakers 28, 253
Quebec 183
The Question Mark (airplane) 275
Quicksand (Nella Larsen) 135

R

race films 102
"Race Prejudice and the Negro
    Artist" (James Weldon
    Johnson) 118
Rachmaninoff, Sergei 110
racism 98, 135
radicals 232, 249
"Radicals—Dynamite" 178
radio 25, 213
    advertising xi
    chronicle of events 42, 43,
        64, 112, 217
    as consumer item 238,
        250, 397
    development of 123–128,
        201, 270

    as entertainment medium
        107, 108
    eyewitness testimony
        142–145
    and federal government 57
    and politics xii, 82, 86
    and Scopes trial 161
    and sports 232
    and stock market 255
"A Radio Church" 145
Radio Control Act 216
Radio Corporation of America
    (RCA)
    and broadcasting 125, *143*
    chronicle of events 41, 193
    founding of 124
    patent pool of 125–126
    shares of 254, 257, 270
"Radio Dreams That Can
    Come True" (Stanley Frost)
    143
*Radio Voices: American
    Broadcasting* (Michelle
    Hilmes) 142–143
"Radio Wedding Impressed
    Listeners" 142
Raft, George 268
ragtime 105, 108, 109
Railey, Hilton 214, 215
Railroad Labor Board 42, 64
railroads
    and conservationists 75
    during World War I 2
    and Ford Motor Company
        236
    and Great Migration 97,
        98
    and highway system 239,
        251
    and holding companies 256
    public ownership of 86
    and stock market 270
Rainbow Orchestra 108
Rainey, Ma 105
Rand, Sally 282
Rankin, Jeannette 37
Rantos, Holland 39
Rapid City, South Dakota xi,
    240
Rappé, Virginia 43, 227
Rappelyea, George 156, 157,
    167, 175
Rascoe, Burton 133
Raskob, John J. 252, 254
Raulston, John T. 160–164,
    165–167, 176
Ravel, Maurice 109
Reader's Digest 87
The Real Isadora (Victor Ilyitch
    Seroff) 51

Recent Economic Changes (Wesley Clair Mitchell) 262
Red Scare
 and Al Smith 85
 background and course of **28–30**
 and Eugene V. Debs 5
 eyewitness testimony **48–50**
 immigration and 62
 and labor trouble 4, 6
 and postwar depression 58, 153
Reed, John 43
Reid, Wallace 227
Reilly, E. Mont 73
"Remick Nips Panic on Stock Exchange" (*New York Times*) 50
Remus, George 74, **382**
Report on the Steel Strike of 1919 (Commission of Inquiry) 23
Republican Congressional Committee 55
Republican convention of 1928 252–253
Republican National Committee 13, 228
"Returning Soldiers" (W. E. B. DuBois) 114
Revenue Act 140, 172, 193
Rhapsody in Blue (George Gershwin) 111, 113
Rhea County, Tennessee 160
Rhineland 2
Rhode Island 27, 35, 36
Rice, Goldilocks *xii*
Rice, Grantland 228
Rickard, Tex 232, 243
Rickenbacker, Eddie 16
Rickenbacker (Eddie Rickenbacker) 16
Rickey, Branch 233
"The Right to One's Body" (Margaret Sanger) 51
Riley, William Bell 154, 155, 157, 177
Rio de Janeiro 195
Rio Grande valley 190
riots 6, 14, 22, 87, 99, 115
The Rise of Warren Gamaliel Harding (Randolph Chandler Downes) 19
The Rising Tide of Color Against White World Supremacy (Lothrop Stoddard) 69, 100
Ritz-Carlton Hotel 86
River Rouge plant 140, 238
Rivoli Theater 65
roads 25, 235, 237, 239, 251, **400**

Roberts, A. H. 37
Robertson Aircraft 207–208, 210, *211*
Robertson, Alice 64
Robert T. Meyer v. State of Nebraska 88
Robeson, Paul 102, 103, **382**
Robinson, A. E. 156, 163
Robinson, Bill "Bojangles" 105
Robinson, James T. 258
Robinson, Joseph 252
Robinson, Sugar Ray 42
Robison, James 78, 79
Roche, Patrick 278
Rochester, New York 111, 259
Rock, Joe *xii*
Rockefeller, John D. 28, 172, 206, 273
Rodgers, William 215
Rogers, Charles B. 177
Rogers, Will 20, 95, 133, 140, 192, **382**
Rogers Act 140
Rogers Field 214
Roma 87
Roosevelt, Franklin D. 37, 85, 125, 274
Roosevelt, Theodore
 and Alaska dispute 202
 chronicle of events 13, 42, 141, 259
 eyewitness testimony 16
 Latin American policy of 185
 and Progressive era 36
Roosevelt, Theodore, Jr. 79
Roosevelt (ship) 202
Roosevelt Field 209, 210, 212, 217
Rose Bowl 41, 64
Rosemount, Minnesota *226*
Rose Room 133
Ross, Harold 132, 133
Ross, Nellie Taylor 171
Rothstein, Arnold 45, 138, 268
Round-Up (Ring Lardner) 151
Royal Canadian Mounted Police (RCMP) 22
Rue de Fleurus 136
Ruether, Dutch *241*
Rum Row 34, 35, 36
Runnin' Wild 106
Runyon, Damon 228
Ruppert, Jacob 233–234
Russia
 Arctic exploration and 201, 202
 Bolshevik revolution in 6
 chronicle of events 42, 65
 film industry of 225

food relief in 56
 and Prohibition 28
 and U.S. deportees 29
Russian Civil War 56
Russian Famine Relief Act 65
Russians 61
Ruth, Babe
 as public hero *xii*
 career of **233–235**, 241, 382
 chronicle of events 41, 172
Ryan Aircraft Company 210
Rydal, Pennsylvania 214

S

Saarland 2
Sacasa, Juan Bautista 187, 190
Sacco, Nicola 382–383
 chronicle of events 42, 64, 240
 murder trial of **167–170**
 eyewitness testimony 177–180
Sacco and Vanzetti trial **167–170**, **177–180**, **325–331**
Sacred Wood (T. S. Eliot) 136
St. Cyr, Johnny 121
St. Francis Hotel 227
St. John, Robert 277
St. Louis
 chronicle of events 14, 112, 172, 240
 Gershwin performance in 111
 Harding speech in 82
 and Lindbergh flight 207, 210, 211
 and President Wilson tour 8
 and Veterans Bureau scandal 80
St. Louis Cardinals 233, 234, 259
St. Louis Coliseum 82
St. Louis County Farm Bureau Recreational Institute 240
St. Louis *Post-Dispatch* 210
St. Louis Robins 276
St. Moritz, Switzerland 258
St. Paul 128, 239
St. Raphael 137
St. Valentine's Day massacre *xii*, 269, 275, **277–278**
Salem Methodist Episcopal Church 135
Salgado, Carlos 189
Salinger, J. D. 13
Salon Royale 33

Salt Creek, Wyoming 75
Samoa 40
San Antonio 141
Sanbury, Pennsylvania 64
"Sanctuary" (Nella Larsen) 135
Sanctuary of Our Lady of Victory 216
Sanders, Everett *xi*
San Diego 210-212
Sandino Garcia, Augusto 189–190, 193
San Francisco 43, 64, 83, 88, 140, 227, 231
Sanger, Margaret **38–39**, 65, 383
Sanger, William 38
San Juan Hill 102
San Pedro, California 78
Santa Clara Valley 258
Santa Rosa, California 193
Santo Domingo 141
Sarazen, Gene 229
Sargent, John Singer 171
Sarnoff, David 125, 142, 144
The Saturday Evening Post 83, 129
Savage, Joseph 159
Savoy Ballroom 108
Sawyer, Charles 73, 81–82, 83
Sayville, Long Island 123
Sbarbaro, Joseph 159
Scalise, John 269
Schenck, Joseph 227
Schenck v. United States 13
Schenectady, New York 112
Schick, Jacob 112
Schoenberg, Arnold 109
Schofield, Lemuel B. 278
Schwimmer, Rosika 276
scientific management 56–57, 250, 256
Scopes, John T. *xi*, 156–157, 160-163, 171, 176
Scopes trial 174–177
Scopes Trial Entertainment Committee 160
Scribner's (publisher) 128, 132, 138
Scribner's magazine 132
Seagrave, H. O. D. 217
Searchlight Publishing Company 58–59
Sears, Roebuck 158
Seattle 3–4, 9, 13
Seattle Central Labor Council 3
Seattle Metal Trades Association 3
Seattle Metal Workers Union 3
Seattle Stadium 83
Second Central American Conference 87

"Second Thoughts" (Alexander Woollcott) 146
Sedition Act 28
segregation 101, 102
Seldes, Gilbert 149
Selected Letters of William Allen White (Walter Johnson) 67
Selznick, Lewis J. 226
Semi-Attached (Anne Parrish) 134
"Semi-Symphonic Arrangement of Popular Melodies" (Victor Herbert) 111
The Senate and the League of Nations (Henry Cabot Lodge) 20
Senate Committee on Foreign Affairs 7, 82
Senate Judiciary Committee 30, 31
Senate Public Lands Committee 112
Sennett, Mack 227
Sesquicentennital Exhibition 193
Seward, Alaska 83
Seward River 245
Seward, William Henry 201–202
sex 39–40, 128, 130, 228
Sex and Temperament in Three Primitive Societies (Margaret Mead) 40
The Shadow of Blooming Grove (Francis Russell) 91
Shakespeare, William 227
Shanks, Lew 51
sharecroppers 99
Shaw, George Bernard 170
Shaw, Louis A. 240
Shawkey, Bob 241
Sheffield, James 191, 192, 199
The Sheik (film) 65
Shelton, Harry 163
Shenandoah (dirigible) 172
Sheppard, Morris 27, 32
Sheppard-Towner Act 65
Sherman Anti-Trust Act 42
shoe industry 53
"Should Radio Be Used for Advertising?" (Joseph H. Jackson) 143
Show Boat (Jerome Kern and Oscar Hammerstein) 241
Shuffle Along (Noble Sissle and Eubie Blake) 105
Shuler, George 79, 92
Sikorsky, Igor 209
Silver, Gray 54
Simmons, William Joseph 58–60

Sinclair, Harry 77, 79, 80, 87, 140, 258
Sinco 77
The Singing Fool 259
Sissle, Noble 105
Sister Carrie (Theodore Dreiser) 129
Sitka, Alaska 83
Six Days or Forever (Ray Ginger) 174, 176
Slater and Morrill Shoe Company 167
Slattery, Harry 78
slaves 105
Slavs 61
Sloan, Alfred 237, 250
Smart Set 131
Smith, Al 383
    and campaign of 1924 **84–86**, 127
    chronicle of events 141, 171, 258, 259
    and convention of 1928 252
    and election of 1928 **253–254**
    eyewitness testimony **262–266**
    and Prohibition 36
Smith, Bessie 105, **383–384**
Smith, J. O. 125
Smith, Jess 74, 82
Smith, Milton 159
Smith, T. R. 146
Smith, Willie "The Lion" 108
Smith-Lever Act of 1914 54
Smoot-Hawley Act 56
smuggling 34, 275
Snyder Act 140
So Big (Edna Ferber) 134, 171
Social Democratic Party of America 5
socialism 4, 28, 29, 30, 38, 61
Socialist Labor Party 42
Socialist Party 4, 5, 42, 252, 258
socialists **20–24**, 85, 182
Soldier Field 232
Soldiers Bonus Act 140
Solorzano, Carlos 187
"Someone to Watch Over Me" (George Gershwin) 109
Some Sort of Epic Grandeur (Matthew J. Bruccoli) 149
Son of the Sheik (film) 216
Sorbonne 136
"So This is Venice" 111
The Souls of Black Folk (W. E. B. DuBois) 134
South America 236

Southampton, England 215
South Braintree, Massachusetts 167, 169
Southern Methodist University 154
Southern Publicity Association (SPA) 58
South Pole 259, 276
South Wabash Street 267
Soviet Union 112, 135, 191, 275, 276
Spaatz, Carl 275
Spain 185
Spanish-American War 58, 185, 216
speakeasies 33
Speare, Dorothy 128
Special Claims Convention 112
"The Spirit of the Ku Klux Klan" (Robert W. Bagnall) 68
The Spirit of St. Louis (airplane) 210–213, 217
Spitsbergen 193, 202, 203, 206
sports
    among movie stars 99
    eyewitness testimony 243–245
    journalism 132, 228
    and mass audience 250, **397**
    on the radio 127, 128
    stars and teams **228–235**
    See also individual sports
Springfield, Illinois 211
Springfield, Massachusetts 125
"Spunk" (Zora Neale Hurston) 135
Squantum, Massachusetts 215
Stack, Leo 79
Stackelback, D. F. 79
Stallings, Laurence 130, 133
Stamford, Connecticut 43
Standard Gas and Electric 255
Standard Oil 77, 171, 254
Stardust Road 119
State National Bank of St. Louis 210
State Street 106, 107
Stateville Prison 160
Statue of Liberty 29, 62
Stedman, Seymour 42
steel industry 57, 100, 239, 270
steelworkers 10–11, 88
Steffens, Lincoln 36
Stein, Gertrude 136, 137, 384
Steinmetz, Charles 112
Stephenson, David C. 60–61, 67, 172
Stevens, Harry 184
Stevens, Wallace 134

Stevens Institute of Technology 57
Steward, Eugene 22
Stewart, A. Thomas 160, 162, 165–166, 167
Stewart, Donald Ogden 133
Stewart, Robert 77
Stimson, Henry 188–189, 190, 197, 198, 275, 276
stockbrokers 270
stock market
    eyewitness testimony **266**
    returns of 250
    rise of **254–257**, 269–272, **401**
    speculation in xi, xii, 254
stock market crash of 1929
    chronicle of events 276
    events of **272–274**
    eyewitness testimony **279–282**
    and free market sentiment 56
    and Harlem Renaissance 104
stock pools 270–271
Stockholm 130
Stoddard, Lothrop 100
Stokowski, Leopold 110
Stone Mountain, Georgia 58
Storrow, James J. 9
Storrow Committee 9
The Story of Mankind (Willem van Loon) 133
Storyville 104
Strachey, Lytton 133, 136
Stravinsky, Igor 109
Streett, St. Clair 203
strikebreakers 75, 87
strikes
    among black students 99
    among Boston police **8–10**, 84
    chronicle of events 14, 15, 87, 216, 276
    in coal industry 29
    eyewitness testimony **20–24**
    in postwar years **2–5**, 6
    in railroad industry 75
    in steel industry 9
    in Winnipeg **182–183**
    See also labor; unions
Strike Up the Band (George Gershwin) 275
Stroheim, Erich von 225
Studies in the Psychology of Sex (Havelock Ellis) 40

A Study of Intelligence (William C. MacDougall and Carl Brigham) 70
Stultz, Wilmer 215, 258
stunt fliers 207
submarines 87
suburbia 97, 251
suffrage 13, **36–38**, 41, 42, 51, 52
Sullivan, Henry 88
Summer for the Gods (Edward J. Larson) 174–175
Summer Olympics of 1924 228
"Summertime" (George Gershwin) 109
The Sun Also Rises (Ernest Hemingway) 136, 139
Sunbeam automobiles 217
Sunday, Billy 32, 45, 50, 384
Supreme Court of Mexico 191
surrealism 136
Sutherland, Abby 214
Swanson, Gloria 225
Sweet Little Devil (George Gershwin) 110
Sweetser, Jess 229
Swenson, May 48
Switzerland 171
Swope, Herbert B. 67
Sydney, Nova Scotia 202
The Symbolist Movement in Literature 136
Symons, Arthur 136

T

Tacna-Arica dispute 87, 171, 276
Tacoma, Washington 83
Taft, William Howard 61, 64, 186, 187
Taft administration 75
Tales of the Jazz Age (F. Scott Fitzgerald) 129
Tammany Hall 85
Tammen, Albert 79
Tampa, Florida 98, 244, 250, 262
Tampa Tribune 124
Tapajos River 236
Tar: A Midwest Childhood (Sherwood Anderson) 130
Tariff Commission 56
tariffs 55–56, 64, 182, 258, 271
Tarzan of the Apes 65
taxes
     and Al Capone 269
     in Canada 182, 183
     chronicle of events 65, 172, 276

Coolidge policy and 84
     and Progressive Party 86
     and Revenue Act of 1921 55
Taylor, Frederick Winslow 57
Taylor, William Desmond 227
Teapot Dome scandal
     and Albert Fall 191
     chronicle of events 87, 112, 140, 217, 240, 258
     events of **75–80**
     eyewitness testimony **89–93**
     and oil industry 192
     Senate hearings on 84, **306–307**
telegraphs 123, 270
telephones 255
Telpaneca, Nicaragua 189
Tennessee 37, 43, 155, 156, 171
Tennessee Anti-Evolution Bill (Butler Act) 155–156, 160, 162, 164, 167
Tennessee Department of Education 156
Tennessee Supreme Court 167, 176
Tennessee Textbook Commission 162, 167
Tennessee v. John T. Scopes 171, 172
"Tennessee vs. Truth" 175
tennis 172, 228–229, 240, 250
Tenure of Office Act 216
Ten Years of Wall Street (Barnie F. Winkelman) 282
Teresa, Vincent 180
Terre Haute, Indiana 5
Texas
     boll weevil arrives in 97
     chronicle of events 171, 217
     and Great Migration 98
     Ku Klux Klan in 60
     and Mexico 190
     and Nineteenth Amendment 37
textile industry 53, 276
textiles 251, 256
Thayer, Webster 167, 169–170, 177
The Hague, the Netherlands 87, 193
The Thief of Baghdad (film) 140
35th Division Air Service 208
This Side of Paradise (F. Scott Fitzgerald) 39, 128
Thomas, Norman 21, 23, 252, 258
Thompson, Earl 210

Thompson, John W. 81
Thompson, William "Big Bill" 267, 268
Thompson, William G. 169, 177
Thompson & Black company 80, 81
Thompson & Kelly company 81
Thompson submachine guns 267
Three Hundred Club 33
Three Soldiers (John Dos Passos) 130
Three Stories and Ten Poems (Ernest Hemingway) 139
Three Rivers, New Mexico 76, 77
Three Rivers Ranch 79, 80
Thurman, Wallace 135
Ticknor, F. O. 263–264
Tilden, William "Big Bill" 229, 233
"The Timely Death of President Harding" (Samuel Hopkins Adams) 89
Tin Pan Alley 109
Tipitapa, Nicaragua 189
Toledo Arena 13
Tomb of the Unknown Soldier 65
Toomer, Jean 103
Toronto 194
Toronto (Bruce West) 194, 242
Toronto Star-Weekly 147
The Torrents of Spring (Ernest Hemingway) 139
Torrio, Johnny 267
tourism 247
Tournament of Roses parade 193
track and field 230
Trades and Labour Congress 182
Tragedy in Dedham: The Story of the Sacco-Vanzetti Case (Francis Russell) 178–179
transportaton 183, 249, 251
treaties 113, 171, 193
Treaty of Guadelupe Hidalgo 190
Treaty of Peace and Amity 186, 195
Treaty of Versailles
     chronicle of events 14, 15, 41, 42
     negotiations **1–2**
     debate **5–6**
     eyewitness testimony **16–20**
     reparations fixed by 63

Trepassey, Newfoundland 215
Trinity College 172
The Triumph of an Idea (Ralph Henry Graves) 248
The Triumph of the Egg (Sherwood Anderson) 130
Tropic of Cancer (Henry Miller) 130
Tucker, Louella 102
Tuckerton, New Jersey 123
Tunney, Gene 216, 232, 240
Turner, Homer 47
Turner, Joe 108
Tuskegee 99, 134, 135
Twentieth-Century America 21, 160
Tyler, Elizabeth 58, 59

U

Ulysses (James Joyce) 130
unemployment
     in Canada 183
     in Chicago **281**
     and increasing efficiency 256
     chronicle of events 64
     in Harlem 104
     and Herbert Hoover 56
     rate of 251, 274, **399**
Union of Russian Workers 15, 29
Union Station 82
Unione Siciliano 268
unions
     and black workers 98
     in Boston 8–10
     in Canada 181–183
     chronicle of events 64, 276
     company 75
     and Ford company 237
     and the general public 11
     membership in 12
     postwar organizing **2–5**
     vote among members 254
     See also labor; strikes.
United Artists 226, 228
United Church of Canada 171
United Farmers of Alberta 182
United Farmers of Ontario 182
United Grain Growers 182
United Parcel Service 13
United States Post Office 42
United States Shipping Board 42
United States v. Schwimmer 276
Universal Air Live 275

Universal Negro Improvement Association (UNIA) 100–102, 294
University High School 158
University of Chicago 134, 158, 166–167
University of Illinois 230, 231
University of Michigan 158
University of Tennessee 157
University of Wisconsin 208
The Untouchables (Eliot Ness) 279
U.S.A. (John Dos Passos) 130
U.S. Amateur Open golf championship 229, 230
The U.S. and the Caribbean Area (Dana Munro) 195
U.S. Army 88, 97, 187
U.S. Army Air Service 172, 203, 215
U.S. Army Air Corps 216
U.S. Capitol 65
U.S. Coast Guard 34, 241, 275
U.S. Congress
    chronicle of events 64, 87, 112, 140, 216, 258, 275
    and farm legislation 271
    and Harding administration 55–56
    and Harding scandals 74
    and Prohibition 27, 28, 31
    and *Shenandoah* 204
    and Smith-Lever Act 54
U.S. Constitution 140, 162, 258
    Eighteenth Amendment
        chronicle of events 13, 41, 42
        effect of 267
        enforcement of 30–31
        passage of **25–27**, 35, 388m
        and politics 252
        text **292–293**
    Fifth Amendment 35
    First Amendment 13
    Nineteenth Amendment
        chronicle of events 13, 42, 87
        eyewitness testimony **51–52**
        passage of **36–38**
        text **293**
    Twenty-First Amendment 36
U.S. Customs Service 34
U.S. Foreign Service 140
Usher, Bishop 165
U.S. Lawn Tennis Association 172

U.S. Marines
    at Teapot Dome **78–79**
    chronicle of events 113, 141, 171, 193
    eyewitness testimony 198
    in Latin America 186, 187, 188, 189
U.S. Navy 13, 42, 172, 186, 204, 209
U.S. Open golf championship 171, 216, 229–230
U.S. Reclamation Service 64
U.S. Senate 37, 64, 112, 253
    chronicle of events 13, 15, 87, 88, 140, 171, 193, 216, 275
U.S. Steel 10–11, 14, 88
U.S. Supreme Court
    and Albert Fall 79
    and baseball 233
    chronicle of events 13, 42, 64, 87, 88, 171, 216, 217, 240, 276
    ends debt peonage 97
    and Prohibition 35
    and Sacco and Vanzetti trial 170
    and Scopes trial 167
    See also individual cases.
Utah 8, 82, 83, 190

V

Vahey, George 167, 168
Valentino, Rudolph 65, 216, 225, 384
Valparaiso University 60
Vancouver 13, 83
Vanity Fair 132, 133, 145
Van Loon, Willem 133
Van Vechten, Carl 103, 131, 134, 135, **384–385**
Vanzetti, Bartolomeo **384–385**
    chronicle of events 42, 64, 240
    courtroom speech of **325–331**
    eyewitness testimony **177–180**
    trial of **167–170**
Vásquez, Horacio 186
Vatican 252
vaudeville 106, 107, 109
Veblen, Thorstein 19
The Vegetable (F. Scott Fitzgerald) 129
Veracruz, Mexico 190

Versailles Peace Conference 13, 153
veterans 2, 9, 53, 55, 80, 99, 216
Veterans Bureau 74, 80–82, 84, 88
Veterans Department 171
Victoria, Queen 133
Viking 138
Villa, Pancho 190
Villa America 137
Villa Marie 137
Villard, Oswald Garrison 189
Vimy Ridge 181
Vine-Glo 33, 36
Virginia 35, 59, 65
Virgin Islands 15
Volstead Act
Volstead, Andrew J. 30
    chronicle of events 14, 42, 171, 258
    enforcement of **30–36**
    and gangsterism 267–268
    in New York state 85
    passage of 27
    text of **293–294**
Votaw, Carolyn 80
Votaw, Heber Herbert 73

W

wages 272, 276
Walker, A'Lelia 102, 104
Walker, Jimmy 262
Walker, Madame C. J. 102
Walker, William 186
Wall Street 84, 86, 254, 256, 273, 279
Wall Street Industrial Finance Corporation 131
The Wall Street Journal 78, 279
"Wall Street's Crisis" 280
"Wall Street's Prosperity Panic" 280
Waller, Thomas "Fats" 108
Walsh, Thomas J. 79, 80, 86, 87, 112
Walton, J. C. 112
Wardman Park Hotel 77
Wardner, G. W. 180
Ware, Caroline 47
War Finance Corporation 64
War Food Administration 2, 253
War Industries Board 2
War Industries Labor Board 10
Warner Theater 216
The War on Modern Science (Maynard Shipley) 176
War Prohibition Act 13
War Revenue Act of 1919 87

War Risk Insurance Board 80
Warsaw 170
Wartime Prohibition Law 27
Washington (state) 37, 77, 80
Washington, Booker T. 99
Washington Conference on Central American Affairs 186
Washington Conference on Disarmament 63
Washington, D.C. 6, 8
    Charles Forbes in 81
    chronicle of events 64, 87, 88, 112, 140, 171, 217
    Duke Ellington and 108
    during Harding administration 73, 79
    Ku Klux Klan march on 61
    Lindbergh visits 214
    and Prohibition 26
    Red Scare and 28
    riots in 99
Washington, George 130, 133
Washington Post 74, 80
The Waste Land (T. S. Eliot) 136
Water Power Act 42
Waters, Ethel 102
Watkins, Aaron S. 42
Watson, Thomas 87
WBAY 126
WBZ 125
W. C. Fields by Himself: His Intended Autobiography (W. C. Fields) 143
WDY 125
WEAF 126
The Weary Blues (Langston Hughes) 103, 135
Weatherford, Teddy 108
Wells, H. G. 132, 170
Wells, Ida B. 100
Werner, M. R. 133
West, Dorothy 119
West End, New Jersey 133
West Point 13
West Virginia 42, 86, 140, 154
The Western Hemisphere Idea: Its Rise and Decline (Arthur P. Whitaker) 195
Whitaker, Arthur P.
Western Union 161
Westinghouse 123–124, 125, 126
Wettling, George 121
WGN 161
Whalen, Grover 275
"What Can We Do About It? The Candid Misgivings of a Wet" (Elmer Davis) 277
What Price Glory? (Maxwell Anderson) 130

Wheaton High School 230
Wheaton, Illinois 230
Wheeler, Burton K. 80, 86, 140
Wheeler, Wayne B. 26, 27, 30, 32
"When 'Good' Society Winks" (James E. Freeman) 92
When the Cheering Stopped (Smith) 17
"When You Want 'Em You Can't Get 'Em" (George Gershwin) 109
White, J. Andrew 125
White, Walter 22, 162
White, William Allen 67, 95, 263
White House 54, 60, 79, 88, 127, 276
Whiteman, Paul 108–111, 113, 385
Whitney, Richard 273
"Who is to Be All Highest of World Radio?" (Robert M. Lee) 144
Wichita 8
Wickersham Commission on Prohibition 47, 276, **350–361**
Wiggin, Albert 273
Wigmore, Jon 178
Wilbur, Curtis 204
Wilkerson, James 75
"Will the Democrats Follow the Whigs?" (Silas Bent) 265
Will Rogers: A Biography (Ben Yagoda) 95
Will Rogers; Weekly Articles: The Coolidge Years 1925–1927 (Will Rogers) 20
Willard, Frances E. 26
Willard, Jess 13, 231
William Jennings Bryan University 166
Williams, Al 112
Williams, Bert 105
Williams, William Carlos 134
Willis-Campbell Act 65
Wills, Helen 172, 228, 240
Wills, Harry 232
Wilson, Edith 1, 29
Wilson, Edmund 132, 147
Wilson, William 21, 28, 30
Wilson, Woodrow 84, 86, 186, **385**
  anti-imperialism of 185
  chronicle of events 13, 15, 41, 42, 43, 64, 112

eyewitness testimony **16–20**, 174
  Fourteen Points of **284–285**
  illness of 29
  and immigration 61
  and labor trouble 11
  and League of Nations 181
  and Prohibition 27
  and Red Scare 28
  and suffrage 37
  train campaign of 82
  and Treaty of Versailles 1, 2, **5–8**, 153
  and World War I 155
Wimbledon tennis championship 228–229, 240
Winchester, Tennessee 166
Windsor, Ontario 276
Winesburg, Ohio (Sherwood Anderson) 130
Wings (film) 275
Winnipeg 4, 182–183
Winnipeg General Labour Council 182
Wisconsin (ship) 276
Wisconsin 36, 37, 78, 86, 140, 141, 171
Wit's End: Days and Nights of the Algonquin Round Table (James R. Gaines) 147
WJZ 125, 144
WJZ-WJY 126
WLAG 127
Wodehouse, P. G. 133, 147
women **36–40**, 88, 393, 399
Women's Bureau 42
Women's Christian Temeprance Union (WCTU) 26
Women's Peace Party 37
Wood, Clement 133
Wood, Henry Wise 182
Wood, Leonard 11, 15, 65
Woodford, Helen 244
Woodrow Wilson (August Heckscher) 19
Woodrow Wilson: A Medical and Psychological Biography (Edwin A. Weinstein) 17
Woodrow Wilson and the World War (Charles Seymour) 18
Woodrow Wilson: Revolution, War, and Peace (Arthur Stanley Link) 17

Woodson, Carter **385–386**
Woodward, William E. 130, 133
Woolf, Virginia 136
Woollcott, Alexander 103, 133, 146
Wooster, Stanton 210, 211
workers 272
Workers Party 258
World Court 82, 87, 88, 112, 193, 259
World Series
  and Black Sox scandal 232, 233, 268
  chronicle of events 14, 43, 65, 112, 240, 259
  eyewitness testimony **244**
  President Harding attends *90*
  of 1927 **234–235**
World War I 58, 107, 185, 201
  anarchist opposition to 168
  armistice 1
  and aviation 207, 209
  black migration during 97, 102
  and Canada 181, 204
  and Charles Dawes 55
  chronicle of events 42, 43, 64, 140, 172, 217, 258
  effect on 1920s of xi
  expeditionary forces in 203
  and Herbert Hoover 56, 253
  and immigration 61
  in literature 129, 139
  isolationism caused by 63
  and Jack Dempsey 232
  and Labor 5
  and League of Nations 6
  and movie industry 225
  oil imports during 191
  Prohibition during 25, 26, 27
  and radio 123–124
  and Red Scare 28
  scientific management and 57
  and suffrage 36–37
  and U.S. economy 2–3, 53
  and U.S. politics 75
  veterans of 80
World War Foreign Debt Commission 87

World's Christian Fundamentals Association 157
World's Fair of 1926 216
Wright, Frank Lloyd 386
Wright Aeronautical Corporation 210
Wright-Bellanca aircraft 208–209
Wright-Bellanca company 210
Wright Whirlwind engine 210
Wylie, Elinor 131, 134
Wyoming 171, 190
  chronicle of events 87, 112
  suffrage in 36
  and Teapot Dome 78, 80
  President Wilson's visit to 8

Y

Yankee Stadium 234, 240
Yeats, William Butler 137
yellow-dog contracts 10
Yellowstone Park 83
Youmans, Vincent 172
You Must Remember This (Walter Wagner) 244
Young, Brigham 133
Young, Owen D. 124, 275
Young Plan 140, 275, 276
Yours, Plum (Frances Donaldson) 147
"Youth, Indusry, and Progress" (Henry Ford) 247, 261
Yukon 201, 202
Yukon Gold Rush 201
Yust, Walter 149

Z

Zeilen (ship) 83
Zelaya, José Santos 186
Zevely, J. W. 77, 79
Ziegfeld, Florenz 133, 241, 386
Ziegfeld Follies 88, 140
Zion National Park 83
Zukor, Adolphe 226
Zuppke, Bob 230